18.95

Current Approaches to Down's Syndrome

Edited by

DAVID LANE and BRIAN STRATFORD

CASSELL

Cassell Educational Limited
Artillery House, Artillery Row, London SW1P 1RT

First published 1985
First published in paperback 1987
Reprinted 1988

British Library Cataloguing in Publication Data

Current approaches to Down's Syndrome.
 1. Down's Syndrome
 I. Lane, David   II. Stratford, Brian
 616.85'8842   RC571

ISBN 0 304 31401 3

Typeset by Scribe Design, Gillingham, Kent
printed in Great Britain by Short Run Press Ltd.

Contents

Notes on Contributors

Howard S. Barden is a researcher in the Department of Medical Physics, University of Wisconsin, USA. He was educated at Brown University and the University of Wisconsin, and he taught at the University of Illinois. He is currently researching into the use of non-invasive techniques of single and dual photon absorptiometry, and bone mineral change and osteoporosis in adults.

Tony Booth is a Lecturer in Education at the Open University. He is the author of numerous papers on special education, disability and mental handicap and of *Growing Up in Society*; he also co-edited *The Nature of Special Education* and *Integrating Special Education*. He is currently working on three volumes on 'Curricula for All'. He is particularly interested in ideas about ability in education and the education of the deaf.

Rex Brinkworth MBE is a Senior Lecturer in Psychology and Director of the National Centre for Down's Syndrome at Birmingham Polytechnic. Down's Syndrome has been his concern for twenty-five years and in 1970 he founded the Down's Children's Association.

Susan Buckley is a Senior Lecturer in the Department of Psychology, Portsmouth Polytechnic, and Director of the Portsmouth Down's Syndrome Research Project. She has specialised in working with the mentally handicapped and their families since graduating in psychology at Reading University in 1968. Her main interest has always been in the early development and education of handicapped children.

Janet Carr is a Regional Tutor in the Psychology of Multiple and Mental Handicap at St George's Hospital, London. She was Senior Psychologist at Hilda Lewis House from 1970 to 1978. She has worked in child and adolescent psychology and has carried out longitudinal studies of groups of children with Down's Syndrome and with spina bifida.

Cliff C. Cunningham is a Senior Lecturer at the Hester Adrian Research Centre, University of Manchester, and Director of the Manchester Down's Syndrome Cohort Study, a longitudinal research programme. He has published many articles and papers in academic journals, and books for parents. He is also a regular contributor to television and radio programmes.

Bethan Davies is Consultant Audiological Physician at Charing Cross Hospital and at Paddington Green Children's Hospital, London. Her main professional interests are the assessment of hearing in children who are physically and/or mentally handicapped, whilst her main research interest is the study of auditory function in Down's Syndrome individuals.

Sheila Glenn is a Senior Lecturer in Psychology at Lancashire Polytechnic. After graduating from London University in 1965 she worked at Southampton University, the Open University and the Hester Adrian Research Centre, University of Manchester. She has conducted research into various aspects of mental handicap and has published many journal articles.

Michael Gunn is a Lecturer in Law at the University of Nottingham. He has a particular interest in the law and its relation to mentally handicapped people.

Pat Gunn is a member of the Schonell Educational Research Centre, University of Queensland, Australia, where she is part of a team monitoring the development of Down's Syndrome children from birth. Before her children interested her in the study of child development she was a geophysicist. She later qualified as a remedial teacher and psychologist.

K.A. Hallidie-Smith is Consultant Paediatric Cardiologist and Senior Lecturer at Hammersmith Hospital, London. For many years she has had a close affiliation with the Down's Children's Association and has given lectures in her field to parents and professionals working with Down's children.

Sheila E. Henderson holds a research lectureship in the Department of Child Development and Educational Psychology at the University of London Institute of Education. The main focus of her research is on children with movement problems in ordinary schools. She has also studied more severe motor handicaps, including those found in children with Down's Syndrome and cerebral palsy.

David Lane is Professor of Sociology at the University of Birmingham. Previously he was a Fellow of Emmanuel College, Cambridge and University Lecturer in Sociology and Politics. He has been an office-holder in the Cambridge Society for Mentally Handicapped Children and Adults and has served as Vice-Chairman of the Down's Children's Association; he is currently Secretary of the West Midlands Council for Disabled People.

Gottfried Lemperle is Head of the Department of Plastic and Reconstructive Surgery, St Markus-Hospital, Frankfurt, West Germany, and Associate Professor of Surgery, University of Frankfurt. He has studied in the USA and West Germany and his main scientific interests are cleft-lip and cleft-palate surgery, burn treatment, breast reconstruction, facial palsy and Down's Syndrome.

Roy McConkey is a Senior Research Officer at St Michael's House, Dublin, Eire – an organisation providing a range of services to mentally handicapped people and their families. His research has focused on play, language and parental involvement, and he has published many articles, and books such as *Let Me Play* and *Let's Make Toys*.

Elisabeth A. Millis is Associate Specialist at Paddington Green Children's Hospital, London. The hospital includes a children's developmental assessment unit as a special part of the paediatric ophthalmology department.

John R. Morss is a Lecturer in Psychology at the University of Ulster. He was educated at Sheffield and Edinburgh Universities. He has a long-standing interest in voluntary provision for the mentally handicapped, and he is currently working on a book on the history of ideas in developmental psychology.

Greg Reid is Associate Professor in the Department of Physical Education at McGill University, Canada. His primary concern is in the area of physical activity for special populations; more specifically he is interested in motor learning and performance as well as physical activity programming for mentally handicapped, autistic and physically awkward persons.

Carol Peterson Rolland is Clinical Director of the Developmental Disabilities Center at the Illinois Masonic Medical Center, USA. She directs a multidisciplinary team providing diagnostic and therapy services for children with a wide range of developmental problems. With her colleagues George Smith and Donna Spiker she has conducted a series of studies directed at children with Down's Syndrome.

David Silverman is a Reader in Sociology at Goldsmith's College, University of London. He was the Fulbright Travelling Fellow 1964–65, and the Morris Ginsberg Fellow 1980–81. His books include *The Theory of Organizations* and *Qualitative Methodology and Sociology*; he has also published studies of cleft palates, oncology and CHD clinics. He is currently working on adolescent diabetic care.

Donna Spiker is Deputy Director, Infant Health and Development Program, Stanford University, Centre for the Study of Youth Development. She has held positions in the Department of Psychiatry, University of Chicago; in the Department of Psychology, University of Cincinnati; and in the Department of Pediatrics, Illinois Masonic Medical Center. Dr Spiker is the author of numerous papers on the development of children with Down's Syndrome.

Brian Stratford is at the School of Education, University of Nottingham, where he is responsible for all advanced courses in special education. He is Chairman of the Down's Children's Association Research Council and he is the scientific co-ordinator for the International Down's Syndrome Consortium. He has published many research papers on the development of those with Down's Syndrome, and has travelled widely throughout the world lecturing on the subject. He has also frequently broadcast on radio and television.

Jacek Zaremba is Senior Lecturer in the Department of Genetics at the

Psychoneurological Institute in Warsaw, Poland. He is a specialist in neurology and human genetics and is head of clinical genetics services at the Institute. His main interests are the aetiology of mental retardation, clinical genetics, genetic counselling and prenatal diagnosis.

The editors would also like to express their appreciation for the assistance of Ms Jane Kendrick; Maggie Emsley, the Executive Director of the Down's Children's Association; Dr Barry Richards, former editor of the *Journal of Mental Deficiency Research*; and Alan Macdonald, Secretary of the Down's Children's Association.

Introduction

Down's Syndrome is a condition which has provoked a great deal of scientific inquiry since it was first described as a distinct clinical entity well over a century ago. Over the last twenty years or so, not only has the number of research projects increased but also the range of disciplines involved in Down's Syndrome research has considerably widened. It is not long since research in Down's Syndrome was confined almost entirely to the field of medicine. This is not altogether surprising, since Down's Syndrome still remains one of the unsolved genetic mysteries in the study of human reproduction. Its clinical effects also give rise to a multitude of questions which are firmly based in the domain of medical research. Fundamental to the wellbeing of the individual though these questions might be, human advancement also depends on social and emotional development – on a person's identity and self-awareness and his or her success in co-operating with others.

Just as general health and environmental conditions have improved for all, better health care and an increased life expectancy have brought similar benefits to those with Down's Syndrome. In consequence, interest in areas of development and life possibilities for the Down's person, outside the purely medical, has grown, with the result that an enormous amount is known, with varying degrees of certainty, about every conceivable aspect of Down's Syndrome. But our knowledge of various aspects of this condition is still rudimentary. There has been a tendency in the past to attribute all types of behaviour, attainment and health manifested by people with Down's Syndrome to their genetic condition. But one must take into account, as some of our contributors point out, the environments in which Down's people have been brought up. Many, probably most, of the medical studies in the past have been based on people in institutions, particularly mental hospitals, and such environments have had important effects on the development of Down's people. How the chromosomal anomaly itself influences various types of performance is also little understood. Many studies are at an elementary level of observing correlations, or clusterings, of certain traits manifested by people who have Down's Syndrome.

This knowledge, elementary though it often is, has had the effect of revealing, in sharp contrast, those aspects about which less is understood. Why is it, then, that in spite of much progress we seem to be little further ahead in social improvement and in modifying general public attitudes to those with Down's Syndrome? We can point to examples of good practice here and developments in community care there, but on the whole progress is at best spasmodic, and depends largely on the chance association of like-minded individuals, parents and professionals, who happen to live in a particular area. The more general picture is still one of frustration for the parents trying 'to get something done' for their child, and for the professional being called upon to act in some way, yet not really knowing where to turn for help, advice or information.

There are also a number of reasons why, as more is known, apparently less is communicated. As knowledge about any single aspect increases, further valid investigation requires specialist treatment. Specialists are often very good at communicating the minutiae of results of investigations to other scientists in the same field through their own journals, but neither the language used nor the journals themselves are easily accessible and hence some useful work never becomes known to those whom it is primarily intended to benefit. There is an ever-widening gap between research and practice. Even communication between those allied disciplines involved in the treatment of Down's Syndrome is not easily facilitated. Who tells the teacher that the majority of Down's children have defects in vision and hearing? Who tells the physician that Down's children have a capacity for learning undreamt of in the not too distant past? Who informs the social worker that many Down's people are in fact employable and capable of a fairly independent lifestyle? Disability in general and mental handicap in particular have been the Cinderella areas of most disciplines: ignorance is perpetuated because it is often no one's business to be concerned with the applications of knowledge in the field of Down's Syndrome. The mentally handicapped are unable to articulate their needs and desires and it is often left to individual parents or organisations such as the Down's Children's Association to advocate their cause.

In an effort to assist interdisciplinary communication and mutual understanding, the Down's Children's Association brought together a number of research workers who have made significant contributions to research. The resulting seminar made it clear that a great deal could be gained from collaboration of this kind, even if only at the level of explaining to each other what they had been attempting in their research and where they saw their work heading, and discussing its implications. It was at the same seminar that this book began to take shape. We felt that some of the more practical current approaches to Down's Syndrome should be made more readily available to both parents and practitioners. The objective of this book is not merely to list 'research findings' but to point to the relevance of such study for the wellbeing of those with Down's Syndrome. The book reflects the predominant research role played by medicine. The social and educational aspects are more difficult to study and systematise. But the need here is as great, if not greater, for the parent confronted with the care of the Down's child. Public expectations and awareness of the human potential of Down's people fall far short of the possibilities and seem too often clouded with prejudice. It is hoped that this collection of articles will help create not only an awareness of the problems but a more enlightened set of attitudes and greater public acceptance of people with Down's Syndrome.

David Lane
Brian Stratford

The Social and Historical Context

1 Labels and their Consequences

Tony Booth

INTRODUCTION

The history of our knowledge about Down's Syndrome and our treatment of and attitudes towards people with the condition do not constitute a story of the triumph of science over superstition. Myths and prejudices may be as prevalent today as in the past and, whereas some old ones may be flagging, others have been introduced to take their place.

People with Down's Syndrome are subjected to two sets of prejudices: those concerned with their distinctive appearance and those about their relative incompetence. Theories of racial degeneration have been linked to the perception by some that they look 'Mongolian'. They have been barred from some schools because they 'look handicapped'. They have all been viewed as severely mentally handicapped despite a wide spread of abilities, and, in so far as they have been regarded as mentally handicapped, they have been prey to all the prejudices that attach to that label too. The valuation and devaluation of people because of their appearance and abilities reflect fundamental features of our way of life. Prejudices about talent and beauty are in all of us, they are an integral part of our social structure, and pressure for their removal may provoke deep-seated resistance.

I have attempted in this chapter to uncover and examine past and present prejudices, to assess the consequences they may have for the lives of people with Down's Syndrome, and to look at the possibilities for removing some of them.

THE LABELS WE INHERIT: FROM MONGOLISM TO DOWN'S SYNDROME

I have for some time had my attention directed to the possibility of making a classification of the feeble-minded, by arranging them around various ethnic standards ...I have been able to find among the large numbers of idiots and imbeciles which come under my observation...that a considerable portion can be fairly referred to one of the great divisions of the human family other than the class from which they sprung...A very large number of congenital idiots are typical Mongols. So marked is this, that when placed side by side, it is difficult to believe that the specimens compared are not children of the same parents...It is difficult to realise that he is the child of Europeans; but so frequently are these characters presented, that there can be no doubt that these ethnic features are the result of degeneration...They are, for the most part, instances of degeneracy arising from tuberculosis in the parents...

(Down (1866), pp.212–15)

Dr Down attributed the occurrence of 'Mongolian idiots', albeit with some equivocation, to racial degeneration or atavism:

> Here however we have examples of retrogressive or at all events, of departure from one type and the assumption of the characteristics of another...These examples of the result of degeneracy among mankind appear to me to furnish some arguments in favour of the unity of the human species.
>
> (Down, 1866, pp.216–17)

But, in attributing Down's Syndrome to racial degeneracy, Dr Down conformed to an earlier tradition. In *The Vestiges of the Natural History of Creation* (1844), Robert Chambers elaborated on a view of recapitulation:

> Our brain goes through the various stages of a fish's, a reptile's and a mammifer's brain and finally becomes human. There is more than this, for, after completing the animal transformation, it passes through the characters in which it appears, in the Negro, Malay, American, and Mongolian nations and finally is Caucasian...The leading characters in short of the various races of mankind, are simply representative of particular stages in the development of the highest or Caucasian type. The Negro exhibits permanently the imperfect brain, projecting lower jaw, and slender bent limbs, of a Caucasian child, some considerable time before the period of birth. The aboriginal American represents the same child nearer birth. The Mongolian is an arrested infant newly born. And so forth...In the Caucasian or Indo-European family alone has the primitive organisation been improved upon. The Mongolian, Malay, American, and Negro, comprehending perhaps five-sixths of mankind, are degenerate.
>
> (Chambers, 1844, pp. 306, 307, 309)

A very early reference to Down's Syndrome as 'mongolism' has been attributed to Robert Chambers, when, in the first edition of his book (Chambers, 1844, p.309), though not in later editions, he suggested in justification of his theory of degeneration:'It is found that parents too nearly related tend to produce offspring of the Mongolian type – that is, persons who in maturity still are a kind of children.'

But, whoever should be given credit for drawing people with Down's Syndrome into official 'scientific' discourse and history, it seems likely that midwives and parents of children with Down's Syndrome were aware of their existence as a 'potential' group before either Chambers or Down. (Whether or not this is so is made difficult to trace by the omission from histories of childbirth and midwifery of any consideration of children born with physical impairments, let alone Down's Syndrome (Donnison, 1977; Shorter, 1982).)

The view that people with Down's Syndrome were in some way Mongolian persisted in the 1930s, although it had been challenged by John Down's son Reginald in 1906:

> It would appear that the characteristics which at first sight strikingly suggest Mongolian features and build are accidental and superficial, being constantly associated, as they are, with other features which are in no way characteristic of that race, and if this is the case of reversion it must be reversion to a type even further back than the Mongol stock, from which some ethnologists believe all the various races of men have sprung.
>
> (Langdon-Down, 1906)

Yet, twenty years later, Dr James Kerr alluded to the animal and racial ancestry of people with Down's Syndrome: 'bull-necked and with wrinkled forehead, the joints are all loose, and, as Crookshank notices, the mongol takes after the urang and sits cross-legged like a Buddha...' (Kerr, 1926, p.396). Crookshank, a prolific writer on medicine, psychiatry and philosophy, produced the first edition of *The Mongol in our Midst* in 1924 and a third, rewritten, edition in 1931. In that book, he elaborated and revised Robert Chambers' scheme of development, in which humans pass from the foetal, or 'Negroid', stage through the 'mongoloid', or infant, stage to 'Caucasian' adulthood. He depicted these 'racial divisions' as descended from gorillas, orang-utans and chimpanzees respectively, though at times he appeared to link chimpanzees to a fourth division, 'the semites', leaving Western whites as *sui generis*. He also mixed his degeneration theory with the notion that 'Mongoloids' were *actually* produced by an 'infusion of Mongolian blood'. In view of the serious discussion of and reference made to Crookshank's work within the scientific community, it is worth relating a characteristic story included in his book.

> I brought to a medical gathering, wearing a sailor suit, a nice little boy, born in Stockwell, who appeared to me, although the alleged child of English parents, and not imbecile, to present certain definite mongoloid characteristics. The general feeling of the meeting was indubitably hostile; it was unanimously agreed that no traces of mongolism were present, and I retired discomfited. Later in the day, the little chap's aunt, who had brought him to the meeting, told me that the boy's putative father had quarrelled with his mother, on account of the presence in his house, at the time of conception, of a Japanese lodger, and had felt his suspicions confirmed when the child was born.
>
> (Crookshank, 1931, pp.11–12)

However, many writers gave such views little credence. Gordon *et al.* (1936) argued that 'attempts such as that of Crookshank to attribute the condition to an atavistic reversion to a primitive mongoloid stage in human development do not carry conviction'. Tredgold (1929), in the fifth edition of his book *Mental Deficiency*, doubted whether the theory 'was ever seriously entertained by anyone except its author', but he discussed it carefully enough, and had not abandoned the idea of a hierarchy of races.

> Even if it could be shown that the blood of the Central Asian Mongol was present in the genealogical tree of every case of mongolism (which seems unlikely, even if we agree with Crookshank that there is more of this blood among the European nations than is generally thought), this would not suffice to explain mongolism...the resemblance of these persons to racial Mongols is really a very superficial one...mongolism, whether it occurs in white, yellow or black races is always associated with definite mental deficiency and it certainly cannot be contended that mental deficiency is an essential and constant characteristic of *the racial Mongol or indeed of any early human type*...In short, whilst in mongolism we have a persistence of some of the features of foetal life, which cause these individuals to bear a certain *superficial resemblance to earlier types of mankind*, this persistence cannot be regarded as due to atavism but to an arrest of development which is pathological...
>
> (Tredgold, 1929, pp.216–18, my emphasis)

In view of the direct meaning and connotations of the term 'mongol', it is interesting that its use has persisted for so long. Referring to the switch to the use of the term Down's Syndrome, Clarke and Clarke (1974, p.13) pointed out that: 'In the mid-twentieth century, as world biological science expanded, it became necessary to reject this archaic label in the interest both of scientific precision, and to oppose the perpetuation of an offensive racist label.' Yet, in his major work on Down's Syndrome, David Gibson (1978) subtitled his book 'The Psychology of Mongolism' and wrote a determined defence of the term which owes little to the history of its use: 'The objections...were that it inaccurately allied the condition with one racial group and stigmatised the DS child in the community. The first consideration reflects a kind of condescension that Caucasians often inflict on others. The second concern panders to social prejudice. DS children do, after all, look "Mongolian"...' (Gibson, 1978, p.xi).

Our willingness to say that people with Down's Syndrome 'look Mongolian' does not depend on an objective standard of resemblance, but is a reflection of our attitudes and hence of the priority we give to certain features in determining overall appearance. Thus, in 1911, Sherlock was able to dismiss a resemblance found compelling by David Gibson in 1978. 'Custom has for so long sanctioned the application of the name "Mongolian" to the group of feeble-minded persons . . . even though its suggestion of a resemblance to any of the Chinese types of physiognomy is largely fanciful.' (Sherlock, 1911, p.208).

Brousseau, in 1928, drew attention to the crucial impact that the existence of Down's Syndrome in Japanese and Chinese children might have on our assessment of their features in challenging Crookshank's thesis; though in doing so she unwittingly introduced a new prejudice by overemphasising the difference in the appearance of children with Down's Syndrome from other members of their families: 'This form of mental deficiency is found among the Chinese and the Japanese themselves and the Asiatic children it afflicts do not resemble their normal brothers and sisters. The characteristics of this disorder are pathological and not racial.' (Brousseau, 1928, p.14).

However, an indication of the reluctance of some members of the medical profession to relinquish the 'offensive label' was given during the discussion following the symposium to mark the centenary of Dr John Down's historic paper (Wolstenholme and Porter, 1967) and provocatively entitled *Mongolism*. In his paper, Matsunaga (1967, p.6) from Japan had noted that: 'A superficial resemblance in the appearance of European patients with this abnormality and normal Asiatic peoples has often been alleged, but the clinical features found in typical cases in the Japanese make the patients as markedly different in looks from normal Japanese individuals as European mongoloid patients are from Europeans.'

In the discussion at the end of the symposium, Matsunaga expressed his dissatisfaction with the terms 'mongol, mongolism and mongoloids' and placed responsibility for resolving 'this technical problem' on the 'English-speaking peoples'. However, he received little support from his fellow symposiasts (Wolstenholme and Porter, 1967, pp.88–90):

> I think this is an imagined difficulty. We use many terms containing embalmed errors from the past. The words 'aorta' and 'artery' never arouse in us thoughts of these vessels as air tubes as it was with the ancients; we just use the words as words. And the same applies to the word 'mongolism'. (H. Cummins)

I am surprised that in the United Kingdom the term mongol rather than mongoloid is used: mongoloid is at least a descriptive expression indicating the mongol-like appearance. (C. E. Benda)

I use the term mongol and have taken refuge from the accusation of racial discrimination because the Down's Syndrome type of *mongol* is not spelt with a capital letter whereas the racial type of Mongol is. (L. S. Penrose)

In Holland it is customary for the layman, who can usually recognise patients with Down's Syndrome, to use the Dutch word *mongooltjes* which sounds friendly and is quite innocent. (P. J. Wardenburg)

The members of the symposium went on to discuss the existence in people with Down's Syndrome of tuberosities in the cerebellum which normally disappear before birth and, it is claimed, are similar to those found in mature orang-utans and chimpanzees. The discussion drew on work done in the 1920s which must have owed much of its inspiration to racialist speculation, yet no reinterpretation of it was proposed (Wolstenholme and Porter 1967, pp.90–91). Taken in isolation, the noting of similarities between the brain of a person with Down's Syndrome and that of an orang-utan does not imply prejudice. But persisting without good reason in a search for such similarities and using them to support a case that Down's Syndrome is, by analogy, an 'arrest of development' involving a return to phylogenetic roots, does.

There is little doubt that the use of the term Down's Syndrome has grown in popularity, although there have been suggestions that it should in turn be replaced by the terms trisomy 21 and mosaicism. But 'Down's Syndrome' carries meanings which should not be repressed. It provides an indirect link to the racialist theories of John Langdon Down. It links our understanding of Down's Syndrome to medical practice. It also immortalises a man, part of whose acumen may have involved the appropriation of 'everyday' knowledge into medical discourse. If that seems a wild and unsubstantiated accusation to make about the 1860s, the recent history of the treatment of people with Down's Syndrome suggests that professional knowledge has frequently lagged behind the everyday experience of parents. If this was untrue of the 1860s, then we may need a theory of degeneration to account for its present-day emergence.

THE ABILITIES OF PEOPLE WITH DOWN'S SYNDROME

The rapid fall into disuse of the nick-name 'mongol' in the last ten years and the increasing use of the correct term 'Down's Syndrome' has, I think, reflected the changes in our thinking. It has definitely produced a new image of the condition, which is more in tune with the higher capabilities of persons with Down's Syndrome currently in the community...

I like to think that the changes in terminology in mental handicap have also brought respect and dignity to those members of our society who are mentally handicapped.

(Cunningham, 1982, p.137)

Whereas overall there has been a shift away from overtly racialist interpretations of Down's Syndrome, it is not, however, at all clear that changes in our understanding of the capacities and abilities of people with Down's Syndrome demonstrate the occurrence of steady progress.

Powers of imitation

In 1982, a senior educational psychologist reported on a child with Down's Syndrome whose parents wanted her to attend her local infants school. He had given her an intelligence test (the Binet Intelligence Scale) and found her to be at the 2–3-year level when she was 5 years and 7 months old. He went on to argue:

> In common with all Down's Syndrome children, Sandra is not the type of child who merely through being with normal children can pick up the kinds of learning tasks that they acquire in the normal course of development...She is not able to develop intellectually to a point where she can reason things out for herself...
>
> (A senior educational psychologist (1982)—a personal communication from child's
> parents)

The idea that children with Down's Syndrome cannot learn by imitation or 'spontaneously' is a relatively recent invention and has emerged despite a long-standing opposing stereotype. For example, Dr G. F. Still (1909, p.538) reported that such children are 'quick at mimicry'; Shuttleworth (1900, p.74) had stated that 'the powers possessed by such children of mimicry are often extraordinary'; and in his original description Dr John Down (1866, p.215) reflected similarly on these abilities: 'They have considerable powers of imitation, even bordering on being mimics. They are humorous, and a lively sense of the ridiculous often colours their mimicry. This faculty of imitation may be cultivated to a very great extent, and a practical direction given to the results obtained.'

However, it is possible that the ascription of powers of mimicry to children with Down's Syndrome may have represented a confirmation of a racial stereotype rather than an 'optimistic' assessment of their capacities. A double-edged description of this talent was given by Lapage (1911, p.109) who remarked: 'They have very good powers of mimicry and will imitate animals or sometimes persons very closely...'. Stephen Gould (1981, p.135) argued that a capacity for imitation was 'the trait most frequently cited as typically Mongolian in conventional racist classification of Down's time'. Such views persisted in the 1930s. Lenz (1931), in a chapter discussing the limited intellectual capacities of 'Negroes' and 'Mongols', suggested in terms reminiscent of descriptions of Down's Syndrome: 'In the Mongol, it is above all the hereditary factors tending to promote an aptitude for social life which are well developed; but on the whole he has more capacity for imitation than invention...'

A belief in the lack of imitative abilities of children with Down's Syndrome appears to have been introduced by the application to them of an erroneous generalisation about all children with mental handicaps in some sections of the psychological literature. It is also reinforced by a current in American psychology which separates pupils into different kinds of learners (most notoriously by Jensen, e.g. 1973), with formal, structured, rote methods being advocated for those of limited ability. It was used in almost identical terms to the above report to oppose the wishes of a group of parents of children with Down's Syndrome, whose efforts and achievements in gaining ordinary schooling for their children I was involved in evaluating (Booth and Statham, 1982a). (A colleague reminded me of the fact that when classes for the feeble-minded were set up in the late 19th century they actually segregated pupils away from the drills and rote learning of the ordinary schools!) Will Swann (1983) has recently discussed the shaky foundations of the belief that all children with mental handicaps lack imitative skills or have an 'incidental learning deficit'. In any case, the application of generalisations as the basis for decisions about educational methods and placement of a *particular* child is mistaken in principle. Some children with Down's Syndrome pick up more from other children than others. The extent of their powers can only be discovered by being with them.

Down's Syndrome and severe mental handicap

Assumptions about the abilities of people with Down's Syndrome have varied from period to period, with little regard for evidence. Children with Down's Syndrome may be beginning to emerge now from a general expectation that they are all severely mentally handicapped. Such a limited expectation was certainly supported by James Kerr, who, in 1926 (p. 396), despite noting them as 'imitative', reported that: 'The mental type is low...They are often echolalic, and have defective speech, forming consonants badly; reading and writing are beyond their powers, but most of them like music...the diagnosis of typical mongolism ought to be clear, and when made is hopeless for educational improvement, although the child may seem promising...they never cease to be imbeciles.'

In 1909, Still had presented a contrasting picture:

> The mental condition is usually rather backward than imbecile...These children take considerable interest in their surroundings...quick at mimicry but slow to learn where any process of reasoning is required. At three or four years old they will take an interest in pictures and enjoy scribbling with a pencil, and later some of the highest grade mongols can be taught to read simple words and even to write after a fashion...The mongol at ten years old is like a child of five, but often rather like a precocious than adult one. He may indeed be the *enfant terrible* in the smart things he says, and in his keen observation of people's foibles and peculiarities. I have known a mongol boy at nine years to be quicker in repartee than many normal children, but though the sense of humour is prominent, it is such as one expects in a younger child.
>
> (Still, 1909, pp.537–8)

And, in this regard, Crookshank came out on the side of the optimists:

> Unfortunately most medical men have obstinately refused to recognise the existence of mongoloids who are not imbecile...we should not suppose idiocy or imbecility to be a necessary concomitant or ingredient of 'mongolism'.
>
> (Crookshank, 1931, p.13)

Tredgold (1929) had specified what for a considerable period may have represented a peak of achievement:

> A few are pronounced idiots, the majority belong to the imbecile grade of defect, and a few are merely feeble minded. The imbeciles rarely prove capable of anything beyond the simplest routine outdoor work...the milder grades, on the other hand, learn to read, write and perform simple duties with a considerable amount of intelligence...They take part in ordinary family life, they perform little household duties, and I know some who can manage a weaving machine or perform other kinds of semi-skilled work in quite a creditable manner.
>
> (Tredgold, 1929, p.223)

He had, in fact, upgraded their abilities from his fourth edition of *Mental Deficiency* in 1922, where he regarded 'the clumsy and ill-formed condition of the hands as usually precluding any kind of work requiring dexterity'.

Yet, despite such suggestions, a strand of more pessimistic views has continued, sometimes echoing a phrase introduced by Goddard (1914, p.453), who had maintained that 'It is a remarkable fact that the mentality of mongolian imbeciles is almost always that of a four-year-old child'.

> They are cheerful friendly defectives, usually of medium or low grade...They are stumpy little people...they have little round heads sparsely topped by hair...Few are good enough to benefit from ordinary schooling...Reading and writing are beyond them; speech is often limited to a few words...
>
> (Gibson and French, 1958, pp.35–6)

> Their mean IQ is 28; there is some scatter; the majority will go to a 'special' school for SSN children, but a few will get to an ESN school. They hardly ever learn to read or write...
>
> (Illingworth, 1974, p.107)

The recent views of members of the medical profession that all children with Down's Syndrome are severely mentally handicapped were reflected in the evidence given in the trial of Dr Arthur (*Sunday Times*, 18 October, 1981). What evidence is there for such a view? Rynders *et al.* (1978) examined research into the intellectual and educational attainments of people with Down's Syndrome. They suggested that the overriding problem in learning from such studies is that they are conducted on the assumption that people with Down's Syndrome are all very similar. It is as if the researchers were so deeply convinced that they already knew about the nature of Down's Syndrome that they did not have to pay attention to the details of their data collection. The 105 studies they reviewed with relevant educational information were published between the years 1963 and 1978 and had the following defects.

    (a) Seventy-one did not report on the type of chromosomal defect.
    (b) Sixty-three gave no data on the sex of the people involved.
    (c) Twenty-five gave no indication of whether they lived with their family or in an institution or of the quality of care they received.

These were the largest studies, comprising 79% of the individuals studied. Of the 80 other studies, 74% were of individuals in institutions.

    (d) Forty-six studies grouped data from infancy to adulthood.

On the basis of their analysis of the research findings, Rynders *et al.* argued that the chance of a child with Down's Syndrome being given an IQ figure above 50 was 30–55%. They suggested that doctors should inform new parents of children with Down's Syndrome that:

    (a) there is a definite possibility that their children will not be severely mentally handicapped;
    (b) there is a great variability in their development;
    (c) the limits of the educational capabilities of children with Down's Syndrome are virtually unknown.

Limits to achievement

In an evaluation of the mental development of children with Down's Syndrome, Cunningham found no evidence for the prevalent belief that they deteriorate in relative ability as they get older. He concluded that: 'If they are provided with good health care, emotional security and early education, the majority will fall into moderate or mild categories of retardation' (Cunningham, 1982, p.171). But some people who concede that there may be considerable variation in ability during infancy, nevertheless wish to retain a low upper limit for eventual development in Down's Syndrome.

> Considerations of the qualitative growth aspects of intelligence for DS, in even the brightest, point to a good deal of upward psychometric scatter (based on memory, social habit and speech training) but a persistent failure of any significant growth into Piaget's period of the organisation of concrete operations and beyond. The condition surely has inherent limitations of intellectual growth which are presumably dictated by biogenic events...The influence of nurture is not convincing on the basis of past research.
>
> (Gibson, 1978, pp.32–4)

Gibson is in clear disagreement with the conclusion of Rynders *et al.* in that he attempts to set an upper developmental limit for people with Down's Syndrome (albeit euphemistically) at a mental age of 7 years old (the start of Piaget's stage of concrete operations proper). This would give all adults with Down's Syndrome an IQ less than 50 and place them, in agreement with Penrose (1963, p.206), in a category of severe mental handicap: 'The mental grade varies from idiocy to an upper limit at about the 7-year-old level...so that, in adults, the IQ is below 50.'

Such a view would legitimate the practice of those local education authorities which exclude all children with Down's Syndrome from any form of education other than that provided in ESN(S) schools (schools for children with severe learning difficulties). In support of his view, Gibson (1978) examined possible exceptions to his rule which had been reported in the literature. One of the most instructive of these was written by Butterfield (1961) under the title 'A provocative case of over-achievement in a mongoloid'. This title is thought provoking in itself; it introduces the dubious notion of 'overachievement' and it suggests that such 'overachievement' is or should be 'provocative'. In attempting to understand the power of labels and stereotypes in relation to people with Down's Syndrome, we might need to ask: 'Why are their achievements provocative and who do they provoke?'

Butterfield published case notes about a man born in 1924 who was said to have an IQ of 36 at age 12 and of 28 at age 36. He lived with his mother and, in the later stages of her life, was running their home entirely on his own when in 1955 his mother was in hospital for 6 months. He did all the housework, shopping, paid the bills, supplemented their income by making and selling cards, pens and potholders, and wrote, played the piano and listened to music in his spare time. However, as soon as his mother died, he was 'committed' to the 'state institution for the mentally retarded'.

Some people might find the last event the most 'provocative' in the report. Gibson commented:

> A most obvious interpretation would be for over-training or for some sort of 'idiot-savant' phenomenon. The absence of psychological pressure signs, along with the general life-style of this man tends to discount these explanations. Life success need not, of course, be largely or even significantly rooted in the intellectual process...the alternative is a special abilities hypothesis.
>
> (Gibson, 1978, pp.54–5)

Now, for some people the 'most obvious interpretation' would be that the man was ordinarily capable of looking after himself, his mother and the house. On the face of it, no special explanation may be required. If we do need to account for the low performance of the man on IQ tests, then there are several possibilities. In their study, Rynders *et al.* did not dwell on the validity of IQ assessments for people with Down's Syndrome. Yet, it is simply invalid to use tests designed to measure the capacities of one group to assess another group who may have had different experiences and have a different range of interests and abilities. And, even if tests were used which enable one to make generalisations about the group of people with Down's Syndrome, this does not imply that such statements are true of individuals; that is the clinical or positivist fallacy. Generalisations do not apply to individuals unless what is true in general is also true of *each* individual.

How one interprets information depends on one's assumptions, which may also determine the information which is selected for interpretation. *The World of Nigel Hunt* is a book written about his travels and experiences by a young man with Down's Syndrome, whose parents had been told when he was born that he would be ineducable. (He wanted to concentrate on pop music but his father told him that people would be bored by that!) In the preface to the book, Penrose (Hunt, 1966, p.10) remarked on the achievement: 'His powers of observation are acute and his memory of separate events is extremely good. His manner of thinking, however, is entirely concrete. He is interested in fact, not fancy. He never makes a generalisation.'

One might suppose that intelligence is revealed not simply by a capacity to make generalisations but by an ability to make them when appropriate and refrain from making them when they are inappropriate. The literature about people with Down's Syndrome is littered with inappropriate generalisations.

Gibson (1978, p.56) linked his comment on Hunt's book to a general view of reports of the experiences and achievements of children with Down's Syndrome: 'There is no evidence in *The World of Nigel Hunt* or in any of the "bringing up our mongol" books that the fundamental performance limits of the syndrome have been surmounted or that nurture can influence these performance limits...'

If 'nurture' cannot influence the achievements of people with Down's Syndrome, one might ask why Gibson introduced the notion of 'over-training' to account for the earlier example. In fact, he also says of the Nigel Hunt book: 'An obvious conclusion is that an intensive training regime can produce a much higher functional output than would ordinarily be achieved...' Perhaps a strongly hereditarian position on intellectual capacity coupled with a view about 'fundamental performance limits' has led him into contradiction.

Nigel Hunt's text, however, throws doubt on the views of both Penrose and Gibson. He started his book by describing an illicit trip to London to witness a rehearsal of the Trooping of the Colour:

> At the information office I asked for one single to St James's Park. Then I asked a porteress on the platform to ring my mum and tell her not to worry because I had gone to St James's Park. Then I asked myself and said I had better get out at Victoria.
> I sauntered to the Royal Mews and asked where Buckingham Palace is and the man said 'just keep to the left and you will come to it'. I asked a policeman when the band will be along and he said, 'ten and a half minutes'. So I stood and waited for at least one and a half minutes. I heard a terrific throb and my ears were lifted and with a biff biff bang the band came along, and when they turned the corner up came their oompahs and the miserable trombones and blowed me in the middle of nowhere.
>
> (Hunt, 1966, pp.39–40)

An ability to generalise appropriately is revealed in his use of 'porteress' and in his requests for assistance. A belief in *our* ability to generalise appropriately from our experience is shown by his use of metaphor, which also demonstrates a departure from the 'concrete' into 'fancy'. One of the features of entry into Piaget's stage of concrete operations involves an ability to view things from the point of view of another. He shows that he has accomplished this by attempting to allay his mother's fears, and then reflects on his action ('then I asked myself') and seems to conclude that giving his mother information too soon will spoil his trip. This thinking about thought would appear to be beyond the concrete operational stage. Now, Piaget himself has been accused of rigidity in his application of cognitive stages in development (see Donaldson, 1978). When the actions of children are given a context they demonstrate more complex powers of reasoning than when asked to perform abstract tasks. When we deduce their reasoning from skilled performance in familiar situations (as I have attempted to do from the writing of Nigel Hunt) they perform even better.

Performance and competence depend on context. Allowing this to be true provides a further severe challenge to the notion of 'overachievement', which presumes that performance in only one situation, on the abstract tasks which comprise IQ tests, provides the true indicator of capacity. Such a view indicates, too, a particularly 'unscientific' reaction to evidence which contradicts one's viewpoint. One of the most striking examples of this view was expressed by a psychologist, who in 1979 was involved in assessing children whose parents were attempting to gain ordinary schooling for them. She informed me that the children were 'overcooked mongols'.

THE CLINICAL PERSPECTIVE

> Are there any acceptable alternatives to (the terms) Down's Syndrome and mongolism? One problem is that if we use Down's Syndrome we shall be in difficulties in describing the actual patient...We say: 'the patient had disseminated sclerosis or an intracranial tumour', rather than using the disease-term by itself, but we seem to need to describe some patients by a particular name. I wonder why this is...
>
> (Brain, 1967, p.89)

What we know about Down's Syndrome depends on what we mean by it. Professor Illingworth (1974), one of the paediatricians most widely read in the UK, began his description of the syndrome with the words: 'Mongolism (Down's Syndrome) is a chromosomal abnormality'. Now, few people would want to restrict the term 'Down's Syndrome' solely to refer to facts about chromosomes. Most would also wish it to indicate the physical signs and impairments which might arise from trisomy or mosaicism. Though even in this case there is a danger that all people with Down's Syndrome may be thought to have the impairments possessed by only some of them. But the tendency to talk of Down's Syndrome as if it could define the common physical, intellectual and emotional features of the group of people with trisomy is even more hazardous. Once such 'facts' have been ascertained, they may be reproduced persistently despite contrary evidence, and they may be thought to characterise all people with trisomy without regard to their individual characteristics. The 'clinical' description may become an inaccurate stereotype.

In the above quotation Lord Brain describes a further process in which 'Down's Syndrome' may be used to define a person rather than a condition. The application of a medical label as a name for a person rather than a defect, disease or impairment forms part of what has been called the clinical perspective on handicap (Mercer, 1970; Tim Booth, 1978). A word which might have been used to depict one aspect of a person's body or skills comes to define their whole personality or identity. The reduction of a person to a clinical entity in this way emphasises the similarities between members of the category and may obscure knowledge of their differences. It becomes its own justification for treating people as a separate group and, in promoting a shared biography, amplifies what they have in common. What is seen then as a *typical member* of the group may have been artificially produced as a consequence of labelling. As one mother, whose child with Down's Syndrome attends an ordinary school, observed of a group of 'mentally handicapped' children they had met on a trip to the seaside:

> They came to the beach holding hands, all plodding along with their heads down. They looked as though they'd come straight from an institution. Peter was half a mile away by the sea, having a great time. They didn't do anything, they just sat and stared into space. They didn't communicate at all, whereas Peter had always got something to add to the conversation. Half of them had Down's Syndrome. Why is there such a contrast between Peter and these others?
>
> (Booth and Statham, 1982a, p.25)

The clinical approach to handicap may make it appear that knowledge about certain people as well as decisions about their lives are legitimate areas of professional expertise or are even restricted to certain professional groups. The approach may serve to justify the elevation of medical or other specialists from the role of doctor, adviser or helper to that of custodian. Of course it would be convenient if knowledge about people with Down's Syndrome could reside in the acquisition of a generalised picture or stereotype. But knowledge about the physical and psychological status of any individual has to be acquired through acquaintance with that individual. The adoption of the clinical perspective can create, therefore, an unbridgeable gulf between the knowledge and interests of parents of children with Down's Syndrome and that of the professionals with which they deal. It is strange, then, to find both Booth (1978) and Mercer (1970) conceding its usefulness:

> It is not my purpose to attack the clinical perspective on subnormality...without doubt most of the advances in the care and treatment of mentally handicapped people have been achieved within this tradition.
>
> (Tim Booth, 1978, pp.204, 219)

> For persons who are severely and profoundly retarded and for persons who show clear evidence of organic damage or pathology, the medical model provides a very adequate frame of reference and basis for action. The pathological perspective has proven immensely fruitful in the study of phenyl ketonurea (PKU) of Down's Syndrome and other clearly organic or genetic conditions.
>
> (Mercer, 1970, p.16)

But it can be argued that the persistence of the pathological or clinical perspective is *the* major barrier to the development of appropriate services for people with Down's Syndrome. Seeing the treatment they receive as a consequence of their medical condition obscures the possibilities for change. It may, as Tim Booth also suggests, 'account for the realities of discrimination and prejudice they encounter in terms of the facts of their disability'.

The consequences of the labels

> The new parent pressure groups were politically potent and preached that the mentally handicapped are rejected in the community because stereotypes, medical or social, generate prejudice and prejudice sustains stereotypes. Segregation, justified by labels, was viewed as diagnostically self-fulfilling because deficit is a function of its naming. *Diagnosogenesis* is a genuine phenomenon in some areas of behavioural handicap but *has little force in relation to the severe forms of mental arrest*. The next logical step, following *denial of the problem* was the movement to full integration of the MR into regular classes and regular jobs. It was imagined that the generosity of *the community at large* would guarantee acceptance of *the new citizens* and treat non-acceptance as a product of wilful discrimination.
> That has not happened and clearly the emperor has no clothes. Public attitudes towards the deinstitutionalised and community 'integrated' mentally retarded are still uncertain...There is evidently a need for *both the general public and the mentally retarded in the community* to protect their respective life space and integrity.
>
> (Gibson, 1978, pp.323–4, my emphasis)

By 'diagnosogenesis', Gibson refers to the process of labelling whereby the ascription of deviance or a disorder to a person creates or exacerbates that disorder or deviance. He is willing to recognise that this does happen when people are said to be 'maladjusted' or 'criminal' but not when they are said to be 'mongol' or 'mentally handicapped'. He denies that prejudice in the case of Down's Syndrome can arise because of medical or social stereotypes or that these can contribute towards segregation. But what is the 'next logical step' following the denial of *this* problem? It is to see prejudice and segregation as a *natural* consequence of the condition of Down's Syndrome in exactly the manner depicted by Tim Booth. If people with Down's Syndrome are not accepted within the community, it is because they are not acceptable, not because 'non-acceptance' is a 'product of wilful discrimination'. If they are not part of the general public, it is because they are not part of the general public; they are putative 'new' citizens. If parent pressure groups attribute prejudice and segregation to a different source, then they are denying the reality of their children's handicap. Now, the denial of unwelcome or emotionally disturbing information is a familiar and general problem and clearly not only confined to parents of children with Down's Syndrome. But, even so, a belief that medical or social stereotypes can exacerbate prejudice does not involve a denial of a reality, nor does a pressure towards integration of people with Down's Syndrome or mental handicaps involve a suggestion that their relative incompetence or physical impairments do not exist.

I came across a parallel reaction when I undertook my evaluation study. The psychiatrist in charge of the child development centre which the children had attended asked me if I was going to investigate the 'psychopathology of the parents in not being able to face up to their children's disabilities'. Now, while I am sure that some parents for some periods see their children through a rosy glow or even with a tight-lipped overestimation of their capacities, I have been struck by the times when the 'deviance' in parents has been converted into 'pathology' by professionals. Among the small group of parents I interviewed I could find no evidence that they expected their children to be anything other than limited in their accomplishments, nor did they attribute the *limits* of achievement to prejudice. However, they were particularly keen that their children should have the opportunity of approaching their limits. They lived in an area where at that time children with Down's Syndrome were all assigned to ESN(S) schools irrespective of their ability or the results of their assessments.

Part of Gibson's confusion arises from a misrepresentation and misunderstanding of the labelling process. The 35-year old playing with Lego in the adult training centre is not limited in her performance primarily because of our low expectations. But nor does her 'handicap' reside in her limited performance. Her handicap is a product of attitudes towards her performance and the limits these place on her life and experience. It is important, too, that we do not simply look at the psychological correlates of labelling; the way the grouping of people with disabilities and the words used to describe them reflect and produce our states of mind. For the most profound effects of the way we approach people with Down's Syndrome are to be found in the institutionalised practices or structures, often built in brick or concrete, which are created as a result of our mentality.

ABORTION AND EUTHANASIA

> The ease with which the abortion of Down's Syndrome foetuses is accepted as the best alternative even by people who oppose abortion, may be related to the conventional wisdom or popular misunderstanding of the level of mental retardation or other disabilities associated with this condition.
>
> (Smith, 1981, p.10)

David Smith argues that the abortion of foetuses with Down's Syndrome solely because they have that condition may be due to a 'utilitarian desire to rid society of what are considered useless lives' rather than solely to a 'desire to prevent pain and suffering'. He is concerned that: 'The acceptance of a philosophy of elimination of Down's Syndrome through abortion might represent a backing away from the search for ameliorative measures'.

Despite the fact that the ethical issues may not have been carefully examined prior to its use, the introduction of medical technology creates its own momentum. Wolfensberger (1981) is amongst those who see a current emphasis on the elimination of handicap as dangerously close to the euthanasia policies of Hitler's Germany. His point was emphatically supported by Micheline Mason (1982, p.26), herself born with brittle bones, who argued: 'It is quite normal for some children to be born with disabilities. We are part of normal life...We will not go away. Nor will we stop shouting until the right to choose to live or die is ours, and ours alone.'

Micheline Mason is herself a supporter of a woman's right to choose whether or not to have an abortion. However, she is concerned that that choice should be based on accurate information and be free from pressure:

> Doctors, parents, people in general are notoriously ignorant about disability. Hardly any of my able-bodied friends knew what spina bifida or 'Down's Syndrome' meant. They, like everyone else, were caught up in stereotyped images of helpless vegetables needing 24 hours a day care; slobbering, agonized hopeless lumps of human flesh who ruin everybody else's life as well as their own. In fact, this is hardly ever true. It is people's fears of disability which are the problem!
>
> (Mason, 1982, p.26)

As things are at present, forms of provision and social attitudes as well as the disproportionate burden women shoulder in childcare are all highly pertinent factors in decisions which parents may take following amniocentesis or the birth of a child with a very severe disability. However, it is clear that professional practices can alter the context in which such decisions are reached and that they may supply a false basis for decision, which may also provide an impetus for the introduction and spread of procedures. One psychologist, in a discussion on prevention of disability, advocated that parents of a child with Down's Syndrome should be given an exaggerated version of the difficulties they might face as a deliberate professional policy (Booth and Statham, 1982b, p.193): 'You can make enough certain statements to make parents face the practical issues, like the time, emotional draining and social stigma with which parents will have to contend. Like the educational decisions and conflicts with authority...I think it's the responsibility of professionals to spell out the consequences of having such a child more bluntly than may actually be the case.'

SEGREGATION

Mental handicap hospitals represent the supreme consequence of an inappropriate application of the clinical perspective. In such places, healthy people may live under medical care for life in institutions where with the best will in the world a sense of personal integrity and worth is rarely maintained. This has been made clear in a series of books, reports and enquiries up to the present day (e.g. Oswin,

1978; Ryan and Thomas, 1980) and most revealingly in a series of reports by the Development Team for the Mentally Handicapped leaked to *The Guardian* newspaper on 20th July, 1983. In such circumstances, it is strange to see the virtues of subnormality hospitals implied by influential professionals or academics:

> Mental handicap hospitals are seldom out of the news. Unfortunately, the publicity that they receive is often unfavourable, concentrating on committees of enquiry, legal actions brought against staff, stories of poor conditions, overcrowding and poor staff morale. Rather less attention is paid to the more positive and progressive aspects of the work of the hospitals, the extent to which attitudes and facilities have changed in the past ten years or the enormous difficulties and restrictions under which staff are working. As a result, the general public, as well as families of mentally handicapped people often have a far from accurate picture of the work that their *colleagues* in the hospital service are trying to do.
>
> (Mittler, 1979, p.175, my emphasis)

The attempt to counter criticism of the nature and function of such institutions by the introduction of token changes in regime and method has been described as 'Let them eat programs' by Bogdan *et al.* (1974). Mittler (1979, p.176) himself recognised that the existence of mental subnormality hospitals depended on social anxiety aided by professional opinion committed to eugenic measures to prevent 'national degeneracy'.

Apologias for the existence of mental subnormality hospitals may highlight the dilemmas felt by academics who attempt to balance the conflicting roles of social scientist, member of the helping professions and policy maker with the networks of diplomatic and social contacts that this entails. The dilemmas faced by parents of mentally handicapped children, who live the reality of contemporary institutions, may be greater still. As expressed by one father of a child with a mental handicap: 'We'd all like to see our children die before we do' (Fox, 1974). Yet it is perfectly logical to maintain both that some staff in some mental handicap hospitals manage to overcome the unfavourable contexts and history of their work to provide a decent home for people with mental handicaps and that the resources of all mental handicap hospitals should be redirected towards other forms of care. But, professional or parental dilemmas may lead to an acceptance of the status quo as expressed in a pamphlet on *Residential Care of the Mentally Handicapped* issued by the National Society for Mentally Handicapped Children – '…How a person lives is more important than where a person lives…' (NSMHC, 1973). For such a sentiment may create a conservative struggle to improve essentially stigmatising institutions. Where a person lives is part of the context which determines how they can live.

Now, whereas the way in which past attitudes create and sustain mental handicap hospitals is often clearly recognised and is regularly reinforced by dramatic exposés, the segregation of children in special schools because of their incompetence is questioned more rarely and is often characterised as positive rather than negative discrimination. The emergence of classes for the 'feeble minded' in the 19th century is sometimes portrayed as a self-evident consequence of the fact that ordinary schools could only cope with a limited band of competence and ability. For example, George Thomson writes about Scotland:

The legislation of 1872...brought to light the numbers of children unable to cope with, far less benefit from, compulsory education...extension of the education franchise to encompass compulsorily greater numbers of children, showed up more and more those who were near the borderline of subnormality, a phenomenon which forced on educators the need to diagnose, categorise and provide for their different educational needs...

(Thomson, 1983, p.234)

Children categorised as 'imbeciles' or 'idiots' were excluded from the education system altogether and, while a variety of state provision was gradually made available, they were not included within the education system until 1971 in England and Wales and 1974 in Scotland. In Northern Ireland the date fixed for their inclusion is 1987.

Once one accepts schools as institutions catering for children 'normal' in intellect, physical capacity and bodily appearance, it becomes possible to see the inequities of such a system as residing only in the mistaken allocation of children to the wrong school. The advent of mental testing is sometimes portrayed as a solution to this technical problem:

The separate development of the mental testing industry provided an impetus for more attention to be paid to the mentally handicapped...although it was agreed that subnormals should go to special schools, there were also good grounds for ensuring that less affected children should not. Attendance at a special school inevitably carried a certain stigma which parents were unwilling to incur unless it was clearly in the child's interests.

(Thomson, 1983, p.234)

The educational placement of children with Down's Syndrome is affected by their categorisation in a number of ways. Mistaken views about their abilities, imitative powers and limits to achievement may preclude a realistic assessment of their current achievements and may lead to an uncritical allocation to schools for children with severe learning difficulties. Secondly, prejudices about their appearance may lead to their exclusion from schools anxious to avoid labelling by association (see, for example, Booth, 1982). In recent years, a number of local authorities have responded to pressures to educate children with Down's Syndrome in accordance with their abilities by allocating some of them to schools for children with moderate learning difficulties. However, the stigmatisation of their education primarily occurs as a result of the very existence of a system of segregated special education.

THE POSSIBILITY OF AN INTEGRATED SYSTEM OF EDUCATION

There is no way she could cope in a junior or secondary school however much intensive help were available for her...I therefore do not think that even if she could get intensive help...during her infant years it would make much difference to her overall educational placement. I think it is highly likely that she will require ESN(S) schooling whatever happens, but I suppose there is just the possibility that with a period of intensive help during her infant years she might be appropriately placed at an ESN(M) school, in perhaps two or three years time.

(A senior educational psychologist (September 1982)—personal communication from child's parents referring to Sandra – see p.8 above)

If, as George Thomson suggests, 'attendance at a special school inevitably carries a certain stigma', is there an inevitability about the existence of segregated special education? Both segregation and selection in education rest on the same two beliefs, as I have argued elsewhere (Booth, 1983a): first, that to receive an effective education pupils should be divided into relatively homogeneous groups, and, second, that some of these groups should be educated in distinct buildings. The second of these beliefs cannot be deduced from the first and is itself sustained by the way separated groups of staff and pupils can be given a positive or negative value. If grammar schools are advocated as an educational incentive, then schools for pupils with learning difficulties can be seen as an educational punishment. Since the evaluation of people by ability is such a pervasive feature of our society, such an arrangement of schools can appear both natural and inevitable. The part of such a scheme which has been most frequently and successfully challenged is the creaming off of pupils with high ability at 11+, a practice introduced after 1944 and legitimated itself by intelligence tests. But, the movement to introduce comprehensive secondary education heralded by *Circular 10/65* (DES, 1965) coincided with the period of maximum growth in segregation by ability, disability and behaviour (see Booth, 1981), and evidence for this growth can still be found in the most recently available statistics. This is not true for all groups but is true overall and for groups sent to schools for 'moderate' or 'severe' learning difficulties (ESN(M) and ESN(S) schools).

Examples of the abolition of segregation by low ability in any systematic way remain rare, although sufficient examples of integration of pupils with a wide range of disabilities testify to the possibility of including such children within ordinary schools, irrespective of the severity of their handicap, given the appropriate planning and provision. (For a selected bibliography see Booth and Potts, 1983.) A careful reallocation of resources would enable almost all children currently within schools for those with moderate or severe learning difficulties to attend an ordinary school. In the first instance, most could attend designated schools containing centralised resource bases, though as conditions were created within a greater number of schools to permit the coeducation of children with diverse capacities, talents, as well as backgrounds, the need for centralisation of provision could be reduced.

At present, the lack of a coherent strategy by local education authorities hampers the development of integration. For example, the provision for a single child with Down's Syndrome in an ordinary nursery school with the support of his own welfare assistant is inevitably seen as a special and temporary case. The gradual movement of expertise and provision from a special school to a system of regionalised resource bases can provide permanent and continuing support for a larger number of children. Such a scheme has recently been put into operation in south Oxfordshire, where a school for pupils with severe learning difficulties has placed a class group of children in both the infant and junior departments of a neighbouring primary school and a third group in a nearby comprehensive. Since 1971, the provision for mentally handicapped children aged 3–8 years has been based in infant schools in Bromley. The way in which conflicting policies precluded the extension of this plan is discussed in Booth (1983b). In south Derbyshire, all children with mental handicaps have attended an ordinary primary or secondary school irrespective of the severity of their difficulties. None of these schools can be regarded as educational perfection. Yet, in each case, parents, teachers and pupils are pleased with the system of education.

Knowledge about who *can* be included in ordinary schools cannot actually determine decisions about who *should* attend them. Whether one favours segregation of children by ability or not involves a moral and political choice. And it is this choice which may itself determine the lessons to be derived from an examination of attempts at integration. For, depending on one's assumptions, problems in integration can be viewed as evidence of policy failure or as a challenge to overcome. Sinson and Wetherick (1981, 1982) observed children with Down's Syndrome included singly in ordinary nursery schools and concluded that: 'The benefit to the Down's child of integration into a normal playgroup or nursery at the usual 3-year-old stage is minimal' (Sinson and Wetherick, 1982, p.128). In their earlier paper, they juxtaposed the interests of the child with those of the community and parents in the following way.

> There is no doubt that the parents of the DS children and the local community are benefiting, as ignorance about handicap is dispelled and people realise that the handicapped child is little different to their own child as he is absorbed into the local community. Whether this exercise in integration is worthwhile in the light of the direct benefit to the DS child is, however, questionable...It appears that normal children make heroic but unsuccessful attempts to establish contact with the DS child but eventually give up, with the result that the DS child becomes an isolate in the group – interacting with no-one except the adult helpers.
>
> (Sinson and Wetherick, 1981, p.119)

My own experience with children with Down's Syndrome included in a group of children with learning difficulties in an ordinary school was very different. The other children included them in playground games, for example, in the absence of their own support teacher (Booth and Statham, 1982a). Whereas the group and its base may have been significant in determining the interactions of the children, it also seems possible that different styles of adult support might lead to different forms of interaction with the child. However, Sinson and Wetherick's investigation rests on the assumption that segregation is natural and of positive value and that any departure from it requires a special experimental justification. If, on the other hand, one adopts an integration philosophy, it is the departure from comprehensive nursery, primary and secondary education which requires special justification, and the avoidance of a stigmatised education based on categorisation by ability is seen as of positive value.

CONCLUDING REMARKS – WHAT IS THE HANDICAP OF DOWN'S SYNDROME?

> Peter, a young child with Down's Syndrome, attended a summer playscheme at his local church. He was sent home one day for hitting a small girl but his mother was unable to find out why he had done it. Two weeks later Peter brought up the matter: 'I'll tell you why I hit that girl, I hit her because she said I was handicapped'.
>
> (Personal communication from Peter's parents)

As the other chapters of this book will describe, Down's Syndrome is associated with a number of physical features, some of which amount to physical impairments, though the amount of impairment varies considerably from person to person. As a group, people with Down's Syndrome are relatively incompetent at various tasks when compared with the population as a whole. But, the extent to which their physiognomy, or physical impairment or incompetence is a handicap depends on the way they are treated, the attitudes shown towards them, the provision made for them and the opportunities they are permitted. The way in which stereotyping leads to the treatment of people with Down's Syndrome as a group apart and the negative consequences that may have, have been the major themes of this chapter.

REFERENCES

Bogdan, R., Taylor, S., Degrandpre, B. and Hayes, S. (1974). Let them eat programs: attendant's perspectives and programming on words in state schools. *J. Health & Social Behav.* **15**(2), 142–51.

Booth, Tim (1978). From normal baby to handicapped child: unravelling the idea of subnormality in families of mentally handicapped children. *Sociology* **12**, 203–21.

Booth, T. (1981). Demystifying integration. In Swann, W. (ed.), *The Practice of Special Education*. Oxford: Blackwell.

Booth, T. (1982). Westhall school for children with learning difficulties. In Booth, T. and Statham, J. (eds), *The Nature of Special Education*. London: Croom Helm.

Booth, T. (1983a). Integration and participation in comprehensive schools. *Forum* **25**(2), 40–42.

Booth, T. (1983b). Creating integration policy. In Booth, T. and Potts, P. (eds), *Integrating Special Education*. Oxford: Blackwell.

Booth, T. and Potts, P. (eds) (1983). *Integrating Special Education*. Oxford: Blackwell.

Booth, T. and Statham, J. (1982a). *Parents' Choice: Establishing a Unit for Children With Down's Syndrome in an Ordinary School*. London: Campaign for the Mentally Handicapped.

Booth, T. and Statham, J. (1982b). The prevention business. In Booth, T. and Statham, J. (eds), *The Nature of Special Education*. London: Croom Helm.

Brain, Lord (1967). General discussion. In Wolstenholme, G. E. W. and Porter, R. (eds), *Mongolism*, Ciba Foundation Study Group, No. 25. London: Churchill.

Brousseau, K. (1928). *Mongolism: a Study of the Psychical and Mental Characteristics of Mongoloid Imbeciles*, revised by Brainerd, H. G. London: Baillière Tindall and Cox.

Butterfield, E. C. (1961). A provocative case of over-achievement in a mongoloid. *Am. J. Ment. Defic.* **66**, 444–8.

Chambers, R. (1884). *The Vestiges of the Natural History of Creation*. London: Churchill.

Clarke, A. M. and Clarke, A. D. B. (eds) (1974). *Mental Deficiency*. London: Methuen.

Crookshank, F. G. (1931). *The Mongol in our Midst: a Study of Man and his Three Faces*. London: Kegan Paul, Trench, Trubner.

Cunningham, C. (1982). *Down's Syndrome: an Introduction for Parents*. London: Souvenir Press.

Department of Education and Science (1965). *Circular 10/65*. London: HMSO.

Donaldson, M. (1978). *Children's Minds*. London: Fontana/Collins.

Donnison, J. (1977). *Midwives and Medical Men: a History of Interprofessional Rivalries and Women's Rights*. London: Heinemann.

Down, J. L. H. (1866). Some observations on an ethnic classification of idiots. Cited in Down, J. L. H. (1887). *On Some of the Mental Affections of Childhood and Youth*. London: Churchill.

Fox, M. (1974). *They get this training but they don't really know how you feel.* Horsham: National Fund for Research into Crippling Diseases, Action Research for the Crippled Child.

Gibson, D. (1978). *Down's Syndrome: the Psychology of Mongolism.* Cambridge: Cambridge University Press.

Gibson, J. and French, T. (1958). *Mental Deficiency Nursing.* London: Faber and Faber.

Goddard, H. H. (1914). *Feeble-Mindedness: its Causes and Consequences.* New York: Macmillan.

Gordon, R. G., Harris, N. G. and Rees, J. R. (1936). *An Introduction to Psychological Medicine.* Oxford: Oxford University Press.

Gould, S. J. (1981). *The Mismeasure of Man.* New York: W. W. Norton.

Hunt, N. (1966). *The World of Nigel Hunt: the Diary of a Mongoloid Youth.* The Kennedy-Galton Centre for Mental Retardation Research and Diagnosis, Harperbury Hospital.

Illingworth, R. S. (1974). *The Child at School.* Oxford: Blackwell.

Jensen, A. (1973). *Educability and Group Differences.* London: Methuen.

Kerr, J. (1926). *The Fundamentals of School Health.* London: George Allen & Unwin.

Langdon Down, R. L. (1906). *J. Ment. Sc.* **52,** 188–9.

Lapage, G. P. (1911). *Feeble-Mindedness in Children of School Age.* Manchester: Manchester University Press.

Lenz, F. (1931). Racial psychology. In Baur, E., Fischer, E. and Lenz, F. (eds) (translated 1931), *Human Heredity,* 3rd edn. London: George Allen & Unwin.

Mason, M. (1982). Life: whose right to choose? *Spare Rib* **115,** 26.

Matsunaga, E. (1967). Parental age, live-birth order, and pregnancy-free interval in Down's Syndrome in Japan. In Wolstenholme, G. E. W. and Porter, R. (eds), *Mongolism,* Ciba Foundation Study Group, No. 25. London: Churchill.

Mercer, J. (1970). Sociological perspectives on mild mental retardation. In Haywood, H. C. (ed.), *Sociocultural Aspects of Mental Retardation,* pp. 379–91. Englewood Cliffs: Prentice-Hall.

Mittler, P. (1979). *People Not Patients.* London: Methuen.

National Society for Mentally Handicapped Children (now MENCAP) (1973). *Residential Care of the Mentally Handicapped.* Stamina Paper 3. London: NSMHC.

Oswin, M. (1978). *Children Living in Long Stay Hospitals.* Spastics International Medical Publication Monograph No. 5, 1978.

Penrose, L. S. (1963). *The Biology of Mental Defect.* London: Sidgwick & Jackson.

Ryan, J. and Thomas, F. (1980). *The Politics of Mental Handicap.* Harmondsworth: Penguin.

Rynders, J. E., Spiker, D. and Horrobin, J. M. (1978). Underestimating the educability of Down's Syndrome children: examination of methodological problems in recent literature. *Am. J. Ment. Defic.* **82**(5), 440–48.

Sherlock, E. B. (1911). *The Feeble Minded.* London: Macmillan.

Shorter, E. (1982). *A History of Women's Bodies.* London: Allen Lane.

Shuttleworth, G. E. (1900). *Mentally Deficient Children. Their Treatment and Training.* 2nd edn. London: H. K. Lewis.

Sinson, J. C. and Wetherick, N. E. (1981). The behaviour of children with Down's Syndrome in normal playgroups. *J. Ment. Defic. Res.* **25**(2), 113–20.

Sinson, J. C. and Wetherick, N. E. (1982). Mutual gaze in preschool and normal children. *J. Ment. Defic. Res.* **26**(2), 123–9.

Smith, J. D. (1981). Down's Syndrome, amniocentesis, and abortion: prevention or elimination. *Ment. Retard.* **19**(1), 8–11.

Still, G. F. (1909). *Common Disorders and Diseases of Childhood.* London: Hodder and Stoughton.

Swann, W. (1983). Curriculum principles for integration. In Booth, T. and Potts, P. (eds), *Integrating Special Education.* Oxford: Blackwell.

Thomson, G. O. B. (1983). Legislation and provision for the mentally handicapped child in

Scotland since 1906. *Oxf. Rev. Ed.* **9**(3), 233–40.

Tredgold (1929). *Mental Deficiency.* 5th edn. London: Baillière, Tindall and Cox.

Wolfensberger, W. (1981). The extermination of handicapped people in World War II Germany. *Ment. Retard.* **19**(1), 1–7.

Wolstenholme, G. E. W. and Porter, R. (1967). *Mongolism: in Commemoration of J. L. H. Down.* Ciba Foundation Study Group, No. 25. London: Churchill.

Physical Aspects

2 Recent Medical Research*

Jacek Zaremba

Hundreds of publications on Down's Syndrome appear in medical journals every year. It would not be feasible to consider here all the areas of biology, genetics and medicine to which the study of Down's Syndrome has contributed, since that would require not a chapter but a substantial volume. Instead, a choice has been made to review those subjects of greatest importance and which have recently attracted the attention of medical research workers.

ORIGIN OF THE EXTRA CHROMOSOME IN STANDARD TRISOMY 21

All somatic cells in man and in most other species are diploid, i.e. possess homologous chromosomes arranged in pairs and proliferate through mitotic divisions. The germ cells, however, are haploid, i.e. possess half the number of chromosomes (one of each homologous pair). At fertilisation, the combination of sperm and ovum restores the normal diploid number, a complete haploid set being derived from each parent.

Normal meiosis

Formation of haploid cells is achieved at meiosis, involving first and second meiotic divisions. The processes by which spermatozoa and ova are formed are named spermatogenesis and oogenesis respectively. In the most general terms, meiosis consists of two cell divisions, during each of which the chromosomes divide once (Fig. 2.1). At the beginning of the first meiotic division, the members of each chromosome pair (homologous chromosomes) come to lie side by side and begin to divide longitudinally. The cell divides without the chromosome division being completed, since the centromere remains undivided. The first meiotic division, therefore, reduces the number of chromosomes by half, one member of each homologous pair segregating into a different cell from the other. (The partly divided limbs of each chromosome at this stage are referred to as chromatids.)

*I should like to express my warmest gratitude to Dr B.W. Richards, former Editor of the *Journal of Mental Deficiency Research*, for his help in reading and commenting on the first draft of this chapter. I am also grateful to Dr M. Mikkelsen and to the *Journal of Mental Deficiency Research* for permission to reproduce photographs illustrating the tracing of the extra chromosome 21 (Figs 2.4 and 2.5).

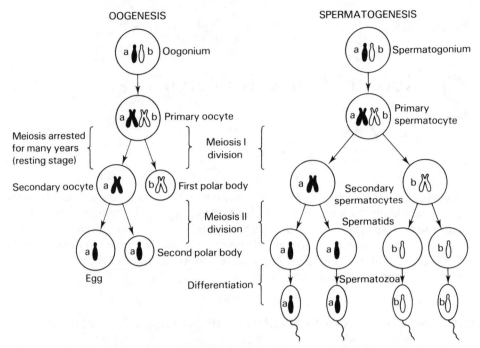

Fig. 2.1 Schematic representation of spermatogenesis and oogenesis. Only one of 23 pairs of chromosomes is shown. Primary oocyte and spermatocyte are diploid – the total number of chromosomes is 46. Following the first meiotic division the number of chromosomes is halved – the cells become haploid. In the case of the primary oocyte, the first meiotic division is arrested for many years (resting stage called dictyotene). Note that four sperm cells are formed from one spermatogonium, whereas only one mature egg is produced from an oogonium; polar bodies are not fertilisable

The second cell division completes the chromosome separation. Oogenesis and spermatogenesis differ in that the division of ova at both first and second meiotic divisions is unequal, producing an oocyte and a polar body. In each case, the polar body degenerates. The end-result of oogenesis is, therefore, a single mature ovum and, of spermatogenesis, four mature spermatozoa.

There is, however, another important distinction between oogenesis and spermatogenesis and this relates to the timing of meiosis in the life of the subject. Oogenesis begins in late foetal life of the female or at about the time of her birth. The process is arrested, however, before the first meiotic division is completed. By or before the end of her foetal life, all the ova that a female is ever going to have are already produced and have reached this (the dictyotene) stage of meiosis. They remain in this state until puberty, and from puberty onwards will ripen at the rate of one a month (or more, since some pregnancies are multiple) until the menopause.

The consequence of this arrangement is that the later in a woman's life that an ovum is fertilised, the longer that ovum has remained, in a sense, 'frozen'. Consequently, the ovum fertilised in a woman of 40 is 20 years older than one fertilised in a woman of 20. But this does not apply to spermatogenesis. Sperm are produced throughout male adult life from puberty onwards. As a result, the spermatozoon of a man of 40 that fertilises an ovum is of recent production, no older than that of a man of 20.

It may be assumed that the retention of the primary oocyte in the resting stage of the first meiotic division for so long is directly connected with what is known as the maternal age effect (see below). The longer the period of the resting stage, it is believed, the higher is the risk of exposure to deleterious factors, which may cause damage to those mechanisms of the cells which control regular separation of chromosomes in a dividing cell. Since there is no equivalent resting stage in the meiotic cycle of spermatogenesis, this might explain the lack of paternal age effect in contrast to the remarkable maternal age effect.

Abnormal meiosis

Most chromosomal aberrations arise as a result of a disturbance in meiotic divisions known as non-disjunction (failure to disjoin), and can occur in male and female alike. Chromosomal trisomy in Down's Syndrome – as a result of non-disjunction – was described in 1959 by Lejeune *et al.* (1959). However, it should be mentioned, perhaps, that 27 years earlier its existence in 'mongolism' had been suggested by Waardenburg (1932). Non-disjunction of chromosomes in meiotic divisions has long been considered as a main source of chromosomal aberrations. It may occur either during the first meiotic division – as a failure of homologous chromosomes to

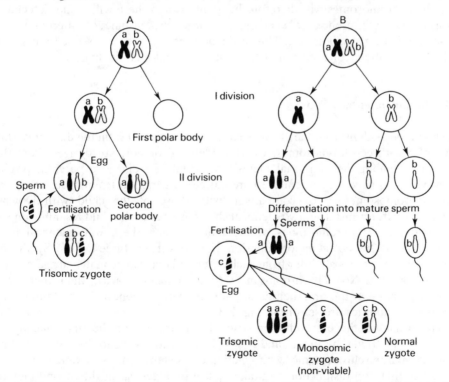

Fig. 2.2 Simplified scheme of non-disjunction of chromosomes 21 in meiotic divisions. (a) Error in the first meiotic division in oogenesis. (b) Error in the second meiotic division in spermatogenesis. As a result of fertilisation in both variants (a and b) trisomic zygotes are formed. Both in oogenesis and in spermatogenesis an error may occur either in the first or in the second meiotic division

separate – or during the second division – as a failure in separation of chromatids. Figure 2.2 shows a simplified scheme with two steps of meiosis in which non-disjunction may occur, leading, after fertilisation, to the production of trisomic zygotes.

Figure 2.2a shows both chromosomes, partly divided, in the developing ovum, neither in the first polar body. (It could, of course, have been the other way round.) The result of the second meiotic division, which occurs normally, is an ovum and a second polar body, in each of which both original No. 21 chromosomes 'a' and 'b' are represented. Should the ovum mature and be fertilised (as illustrated in Fig. 2.2a), there will be trisomy 21, each of the three No. 21 chromosomes being derived from a different original No. 21 chromosome ('a', 'b' and 'c').

In Fig. 2.2b, normal spermatogenesis is shown at the first meiotic division, producing two spermatids each containing one, incompletely divided, chromosome. Non-disjunction occurs at the second meiotic division of the cell on the left, whereas meiosis proceeds normally in the cell on the right. The spermatozoon on the left, if it fertilises a normal ovum, produces a trisomic zygote which, if the chromosome is No. 21, would develop into a subject with Down's Syndrome. It should be noted, however, that the two chromosomes are derived from one of the two original chromosomes 'a' that entered meiosis, by exact duplication of itself. The two chromosomes will therefore be identical and there will be no detectable morphological differences between them. A third chromosome, of different origin, is supplied at fertilisation ('c'). This distinction often makes it possible to diagnose whether meiotic error occurred at the first or second meiotic division.

Meiotic and parental origin

It should be evident from the above account of meiosis and from the diagrams, that two of the three chromosomes, whether identical or not, are derived from the parent in whom the abnormal meiosis occurred. To diagnose parental origin, however, it is necessary to culture parental blood lymphocytes in order to obtain their chromosomes – for comparison with those of the child with Down's Syndrome. If, for instance, two identical chromosomes of the child resemble one of the two No. 21 chromosomes of the mother, then there was maternal non-disjunction at the second meiotic division. If, however, the three Down's Syndrome No. 21 chromosomes all differ from each other and two can be matched against two of the father's No. 21 chromosomes (one matching each), then there was non-disjunction at the first meiotic division of spermatogenesis in the father. The various possibilities are set out in Fig. 2.3.

The origin of the extra chromosome 21 was traced for the first time by de Grouchy (1970) and by Juberg and Jones (1970), who, owing to the presence of an unusual marker chromosome, with deletion of its short arm, were able to provide evidence that non-disjunction had taken place in oogenesis at the second meiotic division.

As a result of the introduction of banding techniques, chromosomes 21 were often found to show polymorphism in such features as the size of the satellites, the

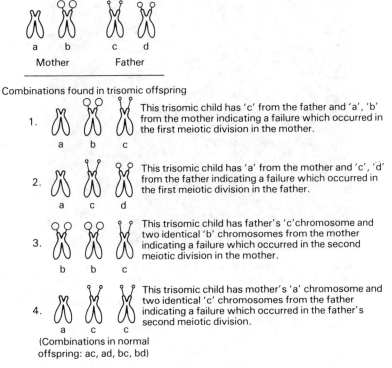

Fig. 2.3 Combinations (1–4) of chromosomes 21 found in the subject with standard trisomy 21. Marker chromosomes help in establishing the origin of the extra chromosome: maternal or paternal. They also make it possible to trace in which meiotic division a failure occurred. In the absence of marker chromosomes the above facts cannot be established, i.e. the family is uninformative.
Examples of marker parental chromosomes:
a, absence of satellites; b, giant satellites; c, small satellites on long stalks; d, well marked satellites of moderate size

stalks of the satellites, and of the centromeric region. Systematic studies using banding techniques were initiated by Licznerski and Lindsten (1972) and subsequently by many other investigators. In a proportion of cases, in which chromosomes 21 are characteristic enough, differential staining (banding) allows for the determination of the parental origin and meiotic origin of the extra chromosome. Fig. 2.3 will help the reader to understand how this may be done (compare it with Fig. 2.2). Three simple rules make it possible to trace the origin of the extra chromosome.

1. If a trisomic individual has three chromosomes all of which differ from one another, then non-disjunction occurred at the first meiotic division.

2. If two chromosomes are identical and the third is different, it occurred at the second meiotic division.

3. Matching chromosomes of a trisomic individual with those of his parents may make it possible (if chromosomes No. 21 show distinguishing features) to establish whether non-disjunction occurred in the mother or in the father.

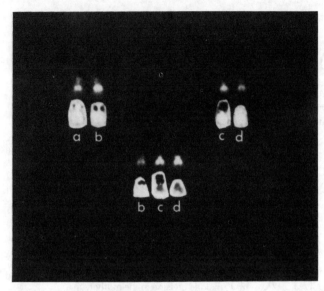

Fig. 2.4 Tracing the extra chromosome 21 in trisomy 21. a and b are chromosomes 21 belonging to the father, and c and d to the mother. The child has b from the father and c and d from the mother, indicating that the failure occurred in the first meiotic division in the mother. Two methods of staining have been used, namely with quinacrine (above) and argentum (below). (Reproduced from Mikkelsen, 1982)

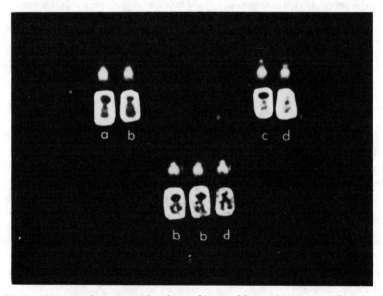

Fig. 2.5 Tracing the extra chromosome in trisomy 21. a and b are chromosomes 21 belonging to the father, and c and d to the mother. The child has two identical chromosomes b,b from the father and chromosome d from the mother, indicating that a failure occurred in the second meiotic division in the father. Methods of staining as in Fig. 2.4. (Reproduced from Mikkelsen, 1982)

Figs 2.4 and 2.5 are photographs obtained by Mikkelsen (1982) from which she traced the non-disjunction of the extra chromosome 21.

Not infrequently, the chromosomes 21 found in a trisomic patient are all so similar (not showing any distinctive features) that their origins cannot be traced. Such cases are considered as uninformative. Mikkelsen collected a substantial number of investigated cases from different laboratories and compiled them together with her own findings. Table 2.1 is a summary of the results drawn from the overall material of fully informative cases. It may be seen that in about 80% of the cases the origin of the extra chromosome was maternal and, in the remaining 20% of the cases, paternal. As regards the tracing of the meiotic division in which

Table 2.1 *Origin of the extra chromosome 21 in Down's Syndrome (regular trisomy) in 344 fully informative cases* (from Mikkelsen, 1982)*

Meiotic failure	Maternal		Paternal		Maternal and paternal	
	Number	%	Number	%	Number	%
Division I	216	62.8	45	13.1	261	75.9
Division II	57	16.6	26	7.5	83	24.1
Overall	273	79.4	71	20.6	344	100.0

*Overall number of cases assembled by Mikkelsen from 12 sources was 641. Of these, 344 (54%) were fully informative (both parental origin and meiotic divisions I and II could be established), 39 (6%) partly informative (only parental origin could be established), and 258 (40%) uninformative.

non-disjunction occurred, it was more frequent in the first meiotic division, particularly in the mothers, less so in the fathers; the proportions of the first to the second division for mothers and for fathers were approximately 4 : 1 and 2 : 1 respectively. Another finding of Mikkelsen was the difference in sex ratio (proportion of males to the total number of cases) dependent on whether non-disjunction was maternal or paternal. If it was maternal, the ratio was 0.55 (indicating relative increase in the number of male trisomics similar to that in the unselected population of patients with Down's Syndrome); if paternal, 0.43. This observation, however, requires confirmation on larger series.

POSSIBLE CAUSES OF NON-DISJUNCTION

Role of maternal age

Investigations of the origin of the extra chromosome have thrown more light on the most intriguing and continually discussed problem of the relative importance of the maternal and paternal age effect in Down's Syndrome. If only the first meiotic division of the female was responsible, then, judging by the data provided in Table 2.1, 63% of the Down's Syndrome cases could be expected to be age dependent, and this is consistent with the assessment of Penrose and Smith (1966). Until recently, in view of the conflicting results of different studies, the problem could not be considered solved, particularly regarding the effect of paternal age. And this in spite of the previously unknown and now well established fact that a substantial proportion of those meiotic errors responsible for trisomy 21 are of paternal origin.

However, paternal origin does not imply paternal age dependence. On the contrary, given the differences in male and female meiosis, paternal non-disjunction may be expected to be free of age dependence.

Factors which may be connected with maternal age may be very different in nature. One of them may be the already mentioned resting stage in the first meiotic division of the oocyte associated perhaps with prolonged exposure to deleterious environmental factors, such as, for instance, radiation. Incidentally, Uchida *et al.* (1968) noticed an increased frequency of Down's Syndrome babies born to mothers exposed to x-ray irradiation. More recently, however, Uchida (1979) reviewed many similar studies. Some of these found significant association between exposure to radiation and increased incidence of chromosomal aberrations; others did not.

The possible role of hormones – another factor, more endogenous in nature, which may be connected with non-disjunction – seems worthy of particular attention. It is a well known fact that, both in spermatogenesis and in oogenesis, hormones exert a controlling influence. A variety of hormones influence oocyte maturation, and oocytes mature one per month in response to hormonal stimulation. There are a few facts which may be related to this.

1. The increased risk of chromosomal aberrations in older women may be connected with less efficient hormonal control as a woman approaches climacterium.

2. There is an increased risk of chromosomal aberrations in teenage girls manifested by a slight increase in Down's Syndrome births in the very youngest maternal age groups (Penrose, 1934; Øster, 1953; Erickson, 1978). This might be connected with not quite mature hormonal control. Higher risk in teenagers, if confirmed, would be in conflict with the possible role of the resting stage in oocyte divisions discussed above.

3. There is some evidence that oral contraceptives containing hormones, such as oestrogen and progesterone, may be associated with an increased incidence of Down's Syndrome in users of the pill.

The importance of maternal age in connection with the production of chromoso-mally abnormal offspring is not in dispute. Some reports, however, appear to indicate that this effect is not due to the age dependence of non-disjunction. Mattei *et al.* (1980), for instance, have pointed out that the relationship between maternal age and the incidence of Down's Syndrome may result from biased ascertainment, i.e. from not taking into account spontaneous abortions of Down's Syndrome embryos, which may be more likely in younger women. Aymé and Lippman-Hand (1982), who studied data from spontaneous abortions, seem to provide evidence that elimination of trisomic embryos does indeed decrease in older women.

On the other hand, a study of spontaneous foetal death following amniocentesis (Hook, 1983) showed that maternal age has little or no association with Down's Syndrome survival following amniocentesis. However, this evidence by itself is not convincing enough because most spontaneous abortions occur in the earlier stages of gestation.

Another interesting observation has been made in the large European series of 52965 amniocenteses performed on mothers aged 35 years or over (Ferguson-

Smith, 1983). Namely, it has been found that the incidence of trisomy 21 at amniocentesis does not appear to rise or even may show some decline over the age of 47 years. This appears to be due to the fact that older mothers become increasingly unable to sustain abnormal pregnancies. Thus, the theory of a defective abortion screen does not seem to be substantiated. On the contrary, it seems that, if a defective abortion screen were the important reason for the maternal age effect, there would not be a so-called age-independent subgroup of Down's Syndrome patients incorporating trisomies due to familial translocations involving chromosome 21. However, no maternal age effect was ever found in transmitted translocation trisomies.

Before definitive conclusions regarding the causes of the maternal age effect are drawn, further studies are necessary: on the origin of the extra chromosomes, on aborted material etc., with consideration of the age of both parents, and in particular on the causes of non-disjunction.

Paternal age at birth

The problem of relative effect of paternal and maternal age was studied simultaneously by Penrose (1933) and Jenkins (1933). Penrose came to the conclusion that only maternal age was of importance, paternal age being 'of no significance'. Jenkins' analysis brought similar results. However, 44 years later, Stene and his associates (Stene *et al.* 1977; Stene and Stene, 1977) were able to demonstrate that a paternal age effect also occurred. They showed a significant increase of Down's Syndrome cases with advancing paternal age for a fixed maternal age. A practical conclusion of these investigations was that men above the age of 55 years have a significantly increased risk of producing children with Down's Syndrome. Later, Stene *et al.* (1981) confirmed their former conclusion on the large number of prenatal diagnoses performed in Germany. Based upon these, they have found an even stronger paternal age effect – significant from 41 years upward.

Table 2.2 *Risk figures for Down's Syndrome at the time of prenatal diagnosis (Stene* et al., *1981)*

Paternal age (years)	Maternal age (years) 35–40	41–46
	Percentage	Percentage
34	0.4	0.8
35–40	0.6	1.2
41–46	1.3	2.8
47	2.0	4.1

Table 2.2 provides percentage risk figures for Down's Syndrome from the study mentioned above. One can see, for instance, that the risk for both parents aged 35–40 is 0.6%. If, however, the father's age is 47 or over (mothers remaining in the same age range), the risk of a child with Down's Syndrome being born is 2%, i.e. more than three times as great.

However, there is still no agreement about the paternal age effect. Erickson (1978), for instance, studied this problem in a group of 4000 cases of Down's

Syndrome and found no independent effect of paternal age. Hook and Cross (1982) investigated a sample 1.5 times larger than that of Stene *et al.* and also found no statistically significant evidence for a paternal age effect independent of maternal age. Ferguson-Smith (1983), on the basis of the analysis of the large European material of amniocentesis, obtained similar results.

Roth *et al.* (1983) also studied paternal age effect in Down's Syndrome. They matched 242 cases of Down's Syndrome and control subjects, taking into account maternal time and place of birth. After adjustment for maternal age, paternal age in both groups was compared and *no* significant differences were found. It seems reasonable, therefore, to agree with Hook and Cross that the figures provided by Stene *et al.* (1981; Table 2.2) should not be treated as empiric risk values for genetic counselling but merely as rates applicable only for the sample from which they were drawn. As Hook and Cross say: 'there are few if any maternal age–paternal age combinations at which consideration of paternal age would appear likely to change a decision to do amniocentesis based solely on maternal age.' Thus, following a few years of doubts, the rightness of the original conclusion of Penrose (1933) and Jenkins (1933) regarding the lack of importance of paternal age was confirmed.

NATURAL SELECTION

There are different ways in which natural selection tends to eliminate weaker, less fit subjects. Elimination does not necessarily involve the death of a given individual – antenatal or postnatal. As far as selection is concerned, it is not a matter of importance whether the affected subject dies sooner or later. Much more important is whether, during their lives, individuals are able to produce offspring, and thereby transmit genetic material responsible for the disease to the following generations. That is why geneticists use the term 'genetic fitness', meaning the ability to reproduce.

The main reason why in Down's Syndrome there is an overwhelming majority of isolated (rather than familial) cases is due to the fact that the condition involves an almost complete reduction of genetic fitness, the fertility of affected subjects being near to zero. Otherwise, the incidence of Down's Syndrome would be much higher, because, if the subject with trisomy 21 were able to produce offspring, the theoretical risk of that offspring being affected would be as high as 1 : 2. Descriptions of 23 such exceptional cases were collected from the literature by Smith and Berg (1976). Without exception they were females: they produced 24 children of whom 9 were also trisomic. (The difference between 9 and 15 may be accounted for by a higher abortion rate of affected cases.)

Another form of selection operates prenatally through spontaneous abortions or foetal death in different stages of gestation. It has been estimated that about 15% of recognised pregnancies end in spontaneous abortion (Warburton and Fraser, 1964), most occurring in the first and in the early second trimesters, i.e. up to the 16th week of gestation. Ninety per cent of abortions occur in the first trimester itself (Boué *et al.*, 1981). According to Werner *et al.* (1971), only 75% of four-week pregnancies terminate in a live birth.

Cytogenetic surveys of early abortuses show that the overall contribution of chromosomal abnormalities among spontaneous abortions is as high as 50–60% (Boué *et al.*, 1975; Hassold *et al.*, 1978). According to Boué *et al.* (1981), trisomy 21 itself accounts for 3% of all abortions.

Trisomy 21 is also a cause of foetal death in the later stages of pregnancy – after the 16th week of gestation. The evidence for this is provided by comparison of its rate of occurrence at amniocentesis and in live births. For instance, in a study based on European data, prenatal rates were about 33% higher than postnatal rates (Ferguson-Smith, 1979). Very similar results were obtained by Hook (1983) by a very interesting direct approach. He managed to obtain from most of North America – through letters sent to 207 centres – information about mothers in whom prenatal diagnosis had shown chromosomal abnormalities but who, for different reasons, declined abortion. Some of the results obtained in this way are presented in Table 2.3. Agreement with the results obtained by using the indirect approach (Ferguson-Smith, 1979) is indeed remarkable.

Table 2.3 *Spontaneous death of foetuses with Down's Syndrome and some other chromosomal abnormalities following prenatal diagnosis (Hook, 1983)*

Chromosomal abnormality	Number of cases	Foetal death		Live births	
		Number	%	Number	%
47, +21/Down's Syndrome	52	17	32.7	35	67.3
47, +18/Edward's Syndrome	21	14	66.7	7	33.3
47, +13/Patau's Syndrome	4	2	50.0	2	50.0
45, X/Turner's Syndrome	11	9	81.8	2	18.2
47, XXX	31	0	0.0	31	100.0
47, XXY/Klinefelter's Syndrome	25	2	8.0	23	92.0
47, XYY	27	2	7.4	25	92.6

Investigations by Boué *et al.* (1981) on tissue cultures established from abortuses with trisomy 21 have shown decreased rate of growth and multiplication of cells. This apparently arises from disturbances in the development of the placenta, which in cases of trisomy 21 reveals growth retardation and hypoplasia. Thus, impairment of the placenta – essential for the development of the embryo and for maintenance of pregnancy – may be a direct cause of spontaneous abortion and foetal death.

It is evident that a very large proportion of conceptuses carrying chromosomal abnormalities are eliminated during pregnancy. Moreover, a substantial number of conceptuses may be eliminated very early, even before pregnancy is recognised. Thus, one should realise that live-born children with chromosomal aberrations constitute only the tip of the iceberg of chromosomally abnormal conceptuses, since chromosomal aberrations, in the overwhelming majority of cases, are not compatible with life.

Trisomy 21 is compatible with life apparently because it involves the smallest autosome in the human karyotype, carrying a relatively small amount of genetic material. In spite of that, as the above data show, a substantial proportion of conceptuses with trisomy 21 – four-fifths according to the estimate of Boué *et al.* (1981) – fail to survive.

ENVIRONMENTAL FACTORS

Richards (1967), in England, estimated the considerable reduction in the number of children with Down's Syndrome born to older mothers and the relative increase in those born to younger mothers which should have resulted from the steady fall of maternal age at the birth of all babies in the general population, over the preceding twenty years. Mikkelsen *et al.* (1976) and a number of other authors have shown the same drop of fertility in mothers over 35 years old. In view of these facts, one could expect a decline of the incidence of Down's Syndrome, and indeed some of the surveys seemed to show such a trend (Collmann and Stoller, 1969; Boylan and O'Brien, 1977). Other studies, however, provided evidence that in spite of a considerable shift in the maternal age distribution to younger maternal ages, the incidence of Down's Syndrome remained unchanged – at least in some areas. This was found by Mikkelsen (1977), Evans *et al.* (1978) and others. Moreover, the data of these authors provided the evidence that in some age-at-birth ranges – particularly that of 35 to 39 years – the incidence of Down's Syndrome is rising. According to Mikkelsen (1977), this could be due to better diagnosis (fewer cases missed – particularly those dying soon after birth – or overlooked) and more efficient treatment of threatened abortion in recent years.

The increase in the incidence of Down's Syndrome has been found to affect mostly younger mothers. Read (1982) came to the conclusion that the cause of this increase must be environmental. But the probable role of many environmental factors, such as x-rays, chemicals and viruses, in causing chromosomal aberrations has not yet been proven in humans. There are, however, indications that hormonal factors may be of importance. A number of studies have shown an increased frequency of chromosomal aberrations in spontaneous abortions of contraceptive pill users (Carr, 1970; Alberman *et al.,* 1976). Lejeune and Prieur (1979) also found an increased incidence of Down's Syndrome among pill users aged 30 to 38 years.

Mikkelsen (1981) quoted the data of Harlop and Davies from Jerusalem in which the incidence of Down's Syndrome in women pill users aged 30 to 38 was significantly higher than in non-users. Read (1982) found that mothers of Down's Syndrome patients had been on contraceptive pills more often than controls. He argues that application of the pills increases the androgen/oestrogen index. Actually, the contraceptive effect of the pill, independently of its composition, is associated with androgenic activity. Such an argument could also help to explain the earlier higher incidence of Down's Syndrome babies among older women since in older women the production of oestrogen is decreased, and the relative effect of androgens increased.

The contraceptive pill may also change the sex ratio in Down's Syndrome patients. As some data have shown (Mikkelsen *et al.,* 1976; Lejeune and Prieur, 1979), there seems to be an excess of females among children with Down's Syndrome born to mothers who use contraceptive pills, whereas in most other unselected series the situation was reversed, i.e. more males than females with Down's Syndrome have been registered. The above data concerning the role of oral contraceptive pills, although intriguing, should be treated with caution, and need to be confirmed by other studies before any positive conclusions are drawn.

PREMATURE AGEING IN DOWN'S SYNDROME

The life span of individuals with Down's Syndrome, although remarkably longer than in the past (Richards and Siddiqui, 1980), still remains much shorter than that of the general population. This is mainly due to the following reasons.

1. High incidence of congenital heart disease – thirty times higher than that of the general population (Park *et al.*, 1977).
2. Immunodeficiency reflected in increased vulnerability to infection and higher risk of malignant diseases. Øster *et al.* (1975), for instance, found a sixty-twofold increase in mortality due to respiratory diseases; Miller (1963) demonstrated a fifteenfold increase in the incidence of leukaemia.
3. High incidence of neurological disorders. According to Øster *et al.* (1975) there is a fivefold increase in mortality due to senility and stroke.

Overall mortality rates for individuals with Down's Syndrome is at present five times greater than in the general population, with a life expectancy of about 35 years. Ages of highest risk in Down's Syndrome are infancy and over 40 years (Forssman and Åkesson, 1965; Deaton, 1973). Of the three categories of diseases given above, the first two are mainly responsible for higher mortality in infancy and childhood, whereas the third is particularly significant over the age of 40 years. Richards and Siddiqui (1980) found that death rates of Down's Syndrome patients and of other mentally retarded patients are virtually the same between age 10 and 30 years. Following the age of 30, however, there is a significant increase of mortality among individuals with Down's Syndrome. This may be mainly due to the premature ageing associated with the condition.

Already in 1876 Fraser and Mitchell had described 'premature senility' in some of their patients with Down's Syndrome. After this, many authors began to report premature ageing, regression and dementia in Down's Syndrome. Some of the earlier reports are those of Bertrand and Koffas (1946), Rollin (1946), Jervis (1948), and more recent ones those of Ropper and Williams (1980), Thase *et al.* (1982), and Miniszek (1983).

In addition to mental regression, a number of authors have described age-dependent deterioration in neurological status (Loesch-Mdzewska, 1968; Wiśniewski *et al.*, 1978) reflected in focal neurological signs, for example, very frequent facial muscle hyperreflexia – commonly seen in senile or presenile dementia and regarded as characteristic of diffuse involvement of the cerebral cortex. As a consequence of ageing, epilepsy may also occur in 1–10% of cases.

Pathology of the brain in Down's Syndrome has been described by many authors. According to Crome and Stern (1972) the brain, in most instances of Down's Syndrome, has a moderately reduced weight and size, with a roundish shape. Frontal lobes, brainstem and cerebellum are particularly reduced in size, although the proportions of the brain (relatively small frontal and middle cerebellar lobes) are similar to those found in a normal human newborn. The development of these structures is closely connected with fine movements of fingers, lips and tongue, which are particularly deficient in Down's Syndrome.

Histological changes associated with precocious ageing become apparent as early as the thirties. In Down's Syndrome they were noticed for the first time by Struwe (1929) and later described by Bertrand and Koffas (1946), Jervis (1948) and many other investigators. These changes are identical with those characteristic of presenile dementia, known as Alzheimer's disease. This disease is a progressive dementia developing usually between the 50th and 60th year of life. Among its clinical signs is a progressive loss of memory, particularly for recent events, psychotic symptoms, disorientation, and confusion; in later stages of the disease focal neurological signs may be present. Not uncommon are aphasia (inability of expression by speech and/or understanding spoken or written language), dysarthria (disturbances of articulation) and apraxia (loss of ability to carry out purposeful movements but with an absence of paralysis). Pathological examination usually reveals symmetrical atrophy of the cortex, most marked in the frontal lobes, and general shrinkage of the brain (Corsellis, 1976). Three main histological lesions present in the grey matter of the brain are: senile plaques, neurofibrillary degeneration and granulovascular degeneration of nerve cells.

In so far as histology of the brain is concerned, Alzheimer's presenile dementia, senile dementia and dementia in Down's Syndrome are indistinguishable. In fact, presenile and senile dementias are now being treated as forms of the same condition (Terry and Davies, 1980). The nature of the pathological process is unknown. There are, however, some interesting theories attempting to find a connection between Down's Syndrome and Alzheimer's disease. Here, three of them are briefly described.

1. Heston and his co-workers (Heston and Mastri, 1977; Heston *et al.*, 1981), studying families affected with Alzheimer's disease, found an excess of Down's Syndrome individuals. Therefore, they suggested that the underlying feature in both these conditions may be basically the same, namely, this may be a disorder of microtubules probably caused by a genetically determined defect of the protein, tubuline. After all, neurofibrillary tangles present in both conditions are composed of the disordered microtubules, which, incidentally, are also the main components of the spindle mechanism involved in separation of chromosomes in meiosis and mitosis. The defect of tubuline might provide an explanation of non-disjunction – the known cause of Down's Syndrome. Interesting as they are, these speculations have not been confirmed experimentally.

2. Another attempt at explanation of the brain lesions in Alzheimer's disease, and possibly in Down's Syndrome, is a putative infection with slow virus. This suggestion is based on an apparent relationship between Alzheimer's disease and Creutzfeld–Jakob disease* (Rice *et al.*, 1980; Masters *et al.*, 1981). The latter has been successfully reproduced in experimental animals (chimpanzees) injected with material obtained from affected patients; genomic integration of the virus in Creutzfeld–Jakob disease has been postulated. Attempts at causing Alzheimer's disease by inoculation of an experimental animal have not as yet proved successful.

---

*Creutzfeld–Jakob disease, or spongiform encephalopathy of viral origin, reveals a mode of transmission resembling autosomal dominant conditions.

However, a viral agent playing a role has not been excluded, and further exploration of such a possibility seems to be worthwhile.

3. The possibility of a defect of neurotransmitters* in both Alzheimer's disease and Down's Syndrome has also been investigated. The synthesis of acetylcholine – a transmitter involved in cholinergic terminals – has been found to be considerably reduced in brains of patients affected with Alzheimer's disease (Davies and Maloney, 1976) and also of those affected with Down's Syndrome (Yates *et al.*, 1980). Cholinergic pathways appear particularly important in 'switching on' and 'tuning' the cerebral cortex.

Other neurotransmitters affecting cortical activity are noradrenaline and serotonin. In Alzheimer's disease their synthesis is reduced in the cerebral cortex but less consistently so than that of acetylcholine (Adolfsson and Gottfries, 1979; Benton *et al.*, 1982).

A deficiency of tetrahydrobiopterin (THB) – a coenzyme playing an important role in the formation of such neurotransmitters as dopamine, noradrenaline and serotonin (Leeming *et al.*, 1981) – has been reported in Alzheimer's disease (Young *et al.*, 1982). There is probably also less THB in the cells of subjects with Down's Syndrome (Aziz *et al.*, 1982). It seems, therefore, that THB may indeed be an important factor in the pathogenesis of dementia in Alzheimer's disease and mental retardation with later developing dementia in Down's Syndrome.

All the above theories, based on more or less documented facts, indicate the trends of investigations aimed at throwing more light on the pathogenesis of Alzheimer's disease and its connection with Down's Syndrome.

Pathological changes characteristic of Alzheimer's disease appear to be present in most cases of Down's Syndrome over the age of 35 years. However, they often appear not to correlate with clinically demonstrable dementia. In the general population, only 14% of people over 65 years of age display moderate to severe dementia (Terry, 1976). In the study of Thase *et al.* (1982), 45% of individuals with Down's Syndrome aged 45 or more had a full-blown syndrome of dementia, as compared to only 5% in age-matched mentally retarded controls. Ropper and Williams (1980) carried out a quantitative analysis of pathological changes in 12 subjects with Down's Syndrome aged 30 to 64 years, and in 8 cases found histological brain changes similar to those reported in the elderly demented people. However, only one of these subjects had demonstrable clinical features of dementia and: 'the severity of neuropathological changes in this case was not greater than in those who were not demented'.

Thus, it appears that there may be some dissociation in Down's Syndrome between dementia and neuropathologic changes. This observation may be partly due to the difficulties of detecting dementia in mentally retarded individuals (the dementia may be masked by mental retardation) and inadequacy of the methods of

---

*There are tiny synaptic gaps between processes of nerve cells. The electric impulses are rapidly transmitted between nerve cells or between nerve and muscle cells by neurotransmitters – chemical messengers crossing the synaptic gaps. A neurotransmitter released by one nerve cell affects permeability of the membrane of the adjacent cell and changes its electrical potential which results in the travelling of an electrical signal.

assessment of their mental performance. As the recent data of Miniszek (1983) indicate, some of the methods available, for instance the Adaptive Behaviour Scale (Fogelman, 1975), may be effective in detecting mental regression in Down's Syndrome. On the other hand, one must avoid being over-enthusiastic in diagnosing dementia in Down's Syndrome because sometimes a reversible pseudodementia, differently caused, may resemble it, such as, for instance, hypothyroidism in the case of a 38-year-old Down's Syndrome patient described by Thase (1982).

PREVENTION

In 1966, Steel and Breg demonstrated that foetal chromosomes can be made available for analysis through the culture of foetal cells present in amniotic fluid. Following this discovery, diagnostic amniocentesis became the most efficient basis for the prevention of Down's Syndrome. Theoretically, it could lead to the complete elimination of most chromosomal aberrations if every pregnancy were to be tested for them. This, however, is impossible for both moral and practical reasons. Some families may wish to have the child – even if it is affected – or on moral grounds are not prepared to accept a so-called therapeutic, or selective, termination in the case of a positive diagnosis. A further barrier is posed by economics. Few countries, if any, could afford the cost of screening all pregnancies with the expensive and time-consuming methods at present available. As a result, the selection of patients for amniocentesis must be based on estimates of the empiric risk of producing offspring with chromosomal aberrations, taking into account the risk of the procedure itself.

Categories of risk

From the point of view of prevention, the most important risk is maternal age-dependent standard trisomy 21. The risk figures based on the incidence of Down's Syndrome at birth by maternal age are given in Table 2.4. These figures, together with the rates at amniocentesis (Table 2.5), may be used for the purpose of genetic counselling. Obviously, the patient should be given the risk figures both at birth and at amniocentesis, and not only of trisomy 21 but of all chromosomal

Table 2.4 *Incidence of Down's Syndrome derived from data from a New York study (Hook and Lindsjö, 1978)*

MA	Incidence	MA	Incidence	MA	Incidence
20	1/1923	30	1/885	40	1/109
21	1/1695	31	1/826	41	1/85
22	1/1538	32	1/725	42	1/67
23	1/1408	33	1/592	43	1/53
24	1/1299	34	1/465	44	1/41
25	1/1205	35	1/365	45	1/32
26	1/1124	36	1/287	46	1/25
27	1/1053	37	1/225	47	1/20
28	1/990	38	1/176	48	1/16
29	1/935	39	1/139	49	1/12

MA = maternal age at birth of child.

Table 2.5 *Number and rates (%) of trisomy 21 and total chromosomal abnormalities in 63 174 pregnancies at amniocentesis carried out because of a maternal age of 35 years and upwards*

Maternal age (years)	European*			American‡			Both samples pooled			All aberrations	%
	Number	DS	%	Number	DS	%	Number	DS	%		
35	4211	15	0.36	4025	11	0.27	8236	26	0.29	111	1.35
36	4883	27	0.55	4030	25	0.62	8913	52	0.58	105	1.18
37	5729	36	0.63	3565	21	0.59	9294	57	0.61	120	1.29
38	6879	52	0.76	2672	31	1.16	9551	83	0.87	150	1.57
39	6383	65	1.02	1994	16	0.80	8377	81	0.97	149	1.78
40	5853	75	1.28	1363	23	1.69	7216	98	1.36	167	2.31
41	3840	53	1.38	888	14	1.58	4728	67	1.42	135	2.85
42	2603	54	2.07	567	12	2.12	3170	66	2.08	119	3.75
43	1576	50	3.17	302	8	2.65	1878	58	3.09	93	4.95
44	836	27	3.23	151	5	3.31	987	32	3.24	48	4.86
45	412	19	4.61	73	7	9.59	485	26	5.36	38	7.83
46	196	14	7.14	18	0	0.00	214	14	6.54	16	7.48
47	62	2	3.23	12	1	8.33	74	3	4.05	5	6.76
48	17	0		7	4	57.14	24	4	16.66	6	25.00
49	13	0		5	1	20.00	18	1	5.55	4	22.22
50	6	0		3	0	0.00	9	0	0.00	0	0.00
Total	43499	489	1.12	19675	179	0.91	63174	668	1.05	1266	2.00

*From Ferguson-Smith (1982).
‡From Schreinemachers *et al.* (1982).
DS = Down's Syndrome.

Table 2.6 *Incidence of Down's Syndrome at amniocentesis as compared to the total chromosomal aberrations at amniocentesis, by maternal age at birth of child. For Down's Syndrome the live-birth rates were assessed indirectly*

Maternal age (years)	Incidence of Down's Syndrome at birth*	Incidence of Down's Syndrome at amniocentesis‡	Total chromosomal aberrations at amniocentesis‡
35	1/500	1/345	1/74
36	1/244	1/172	1/85
37	1/233	1/164	1/78
38	1/164	1/115	1/64
39	1/147	1/103	1/56
40	1/105	1/74	1/43
41	1/101	1/70	1/35
42	1/68	1/48	1/27
43	1/46	1/32	1/20
44	1/44	1/31	1/21
45	1/27	1/19	1/13
≥46	1/22	1/15	1/11

*Rates of Down's Syndrome at birth derived from the rates of amniocentesis (second column) and the data of Hook (1983), according to which foetal death in later stages of gestation (following amniocentesis) occurs in 30% of pregnancies with trisomy 21. They are very close to the rates of Down's Syndrome at birth obtained in large general population studies, as, for instance, those of Hook and Lindsjö (1978); cf Table 2.4.
‡Drawn from data provided in Table 2.5.

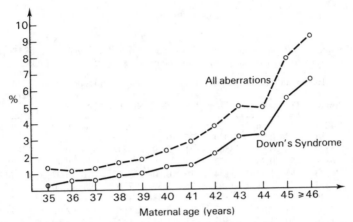

Fig. 2.6 The graphs presenting maternal age-dependent rise in the rates for trisomy 21 and overall chromosomal aberrations (based on the figures in Table 2.5)

aberrations (as provided in Tables 2.5 and 2.6 and Fig. 2.6).The recent data seem to provide convincing support for not treating advanced paternal age alone as an indication for amniocentesis.

Balanced familial translocations involving chromosome 21 constitute a high-risk category for individual parents, although only 3.5–4.8% of the Down's Syndrome cases reveal translocations (Giraud and Mattei, 1975; Yunis, 1977). The risk figures depend upon which of the parents is a carrier: if it is the mother, the risk of transmission is about 10–15%; if the father, 2.5–5% (de Grouchy and Turleau, 1977; Yunis, 1977). Very infrequently, one of the parents carries a t(21q21q), which involves a 100% risk. Obviously, in such a case, amniocentesis is not a solution.

Also constituting high risk are rare instances of parental mosaicism, when one of the parents has two different cell populations, one with trisomy 21 and the other one normal. The risk of a child being trisomic in such a case is not easy to establish. It depends on the proportion of trisomic cells in a mosaic parent, and that is not the same in different tissues. Therefore Yunis (1977) advocates meiotic study of ovary or testes – depending upon which of the parents is a mosaic.

The meiotic study of ovary or testes of the mosaic parent may provide insight into the actual risk involved. According to Mikkelsen (1971), if half of the cells are trisomic, the risk of a trisomic child being born is about 25%. This approach, however, has no practical value since, in every case of detected parental mosaicism, amniocentesis is proposed, independent of the proportion of trisomic cells.

Analysis of dermatoglyphics may help in picking higher risk parents suspected of mosaicism. In this respect, a method of discriminant diagnosis devised by Loesch and Smith (1976) may be particularly useful. According to Loesch (1983) and Rodewald *et al.* (1982), dermatoglyphic features of 21-trisomy mosaicism can sometimes provide additional indication to prenatal diagnosis, particularly in an apparently normal parent who has had a child with Down's Syndrome – even if the results of cytogenetic tests have been negative or doubtful (cases of hidden mosaicism).

Of considerable practical importance is the group of women with normal chromosomes but who have already had a child with standard trisomy 21 – not because of the risk of recurrence (*which is rather low*), but because of the anxiety of the mothers, who in such circumstances often make the issue of amniocentesis a condition, *sine qua non,* of having another baby. In a large European series of 2890 pregnancies tested because of a previous child with a *de novo* chromosomal aberration, the recurrence risk for overall chromosomal aberrations was 1.4% and for trisomy 21 alone (81% of the cases) 0.5% (Stene *et al.,* 1984). In mothers below 30 years, the rates observed were 10–20 times higher than for the mothers of the same age who had not given birth to a chromosomally abnormal child. In most cases, the cause of recurrence of chromosomal aberrations is obscure. This might be an undetected parental mosaicism or perhaps, as some reports suggest, a genetically determined tendency to non-disjunction.

Other risk factors

Some obstetricians treat a history of threatened abortion as a contraindication to amniocentesis. This, however, does not seem to be a proper approach, since bleeding in the first trimester, indicating a threatened abortion, occurs much more frequently in mothers carrying a foetus with trisomy 21 than in those carrying a normal foetus – according to Boué *et al.* (1980), in 26% and 1% respectively.

The risk of complications due to amniocentesis should be pointed out to the patient. Generally it is considered that the procedure is safe, but it is a well established fact that it depends on the experience of the obstetrician carrying out the procedure. For instance, according to Hecht (1982), for a physician who has performed 50 or more procedures the risk is 0.3%, whereas for a physician with less experience the risk is significantly greater. The decision to have an amniocentesis must belong entirely to the patient and to her partner. The role of physicians, independent of their private opinions, is to provide patients with information as comprehensive and up to date as possible and, if indicated, to make amniocentesis available.

Amniocentesis should be performed preferably at the 16th or 17th week of gestation, at the latest at the 20th week. As a routine, it should be preceded by ultrasound studies, which include assessment of the gestational age (based on measurements of the foetus), localisation of the placenta and detection of multiple foetuses. A result of cytogenetic studies is usually available following 10–20 days culture of the foetal cells, i.e. at the 19th–20th week of gestation, but sometimes considerably later.

Difficulties may arise when the foetal karyotype is found to be mosaic, i.e. more than one cell line is found in the amniotic fluid cell culture. In such instances, it must be discovered whether it is a true or pseudomosaicism. The latter is recognised when it arises *in vitro* in a single culture flask. Mosaicism may be considered to be true when it is found in several, independently established cultures. Cases of mosaicism must be interpreted very cautiously. Sometimes, repeated amniocentesis is necessary, and in some particularly dubious cases foetal blood sampling through foetoscopy may be indicated. Even that may leave some doubts since, as we know, abnormal cell lines may be present only in some tissues. Practically, however, by providing additional information, foetal blood sampling may be helpful to the parents in making their final decision regarding selective termination.

First-trimester prenatal diagnosis

The first experimental attempts at foetal tissue sampling in the first trimester were undertaken by Hahnemann and Mohr (1969) as well as by Kullander and Sandahl (1973). More recently, several centres started to develop methods of obtaining chorionic villous material* for diagnostic purposes. In China, sampling of chorionic villi has been done to determine the sex of the foetus (Department of Obstetrics and Gynaecology, Anshan, 1975). Kazy *et al.* (1982) described a safe method of

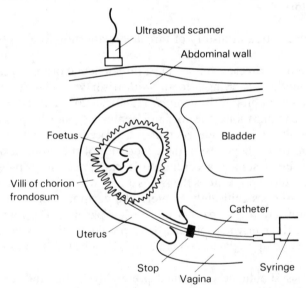

Fig. 2.7 Diagram of the uterus at 9 weeks' gestation, with biopsy catheter introduced into the area from which chorionic villi should be taken. (After Old *et al.*, 1982.) Ultrasound (USG) scanner is additionally shown in order to indicate that the catheter is USG guided

obtaining chorion biopsy specimen for the purpose of foetal sexing and measuring activities of some enzymes. It has also been shown that the same material can be used for obtaining the foetal karyotype (Niazi *et al.*, 1981), for foetal sex determination by means of chromosome-specific DNA probes (Gosden *et al.*, 1982) and for diagnosing haemoglobinopathies with restriction endonuclease analysis of foetal DNA (Williamson *et al.*, 1981; Old *et al.*, 1982).

---

*Chorionic villi are threadlike projections on the external surface of the chorion. The chorion is the external envelope of the fertilised egg, and has a protective and nutritive role. Its external portion (chorion frontalis), from which villi develop, forms the embrionic portion of the placenta.

Most recently, substantial progress has been made by Italian workers who have developed techniques by which the foetal karyotype can be defined within a few hours by chorionic villi sampling (Simoni *et al.*, 1983); they were the first to diagnose trisomy 21 as early as at the 11th week of gestation (Brambati and Simoni, 1983).

Chorionic biopsy in early pregnancy is a newly developed procedure. Several types of approach have been used for transcervical sampling of chorionic villi. In the experience of Simoni *et al.* (1983), the aspiration method with ultrasound-guided catheter, performed between the 8th and 10th weeks of gestation, proved to be the safest and most reliable approach (Fig. 2.7) compared with other methods.

The estimation of the obstetric risk in different methods used remains at present one of the main topics of investigations. An excellent review of this and other problems related to the first-trimester chorion biopsy has recently been given by Rodeck and Morsman (1983).

First-trimester chorionic biopsy is of great advantage in the prevention of genetically determined diseases, and chromosomal abnormalities in particular. It is cheaper and provides much earlier results, and thus in cases of positive diagnosis allows for early termination, which for the patient is much less distressing than late termination following amniocentesis.

REFERENCES

Adolfsson, R. and Gottfries, C.G. (1979). Changes in brain catecholamines in patients with dementia of Alzheimer type. *J. Psych.* **135**, 216–23.

Alberman, E., Creasy, M., Elliott, M. and Spicer, C. (1976). Maternal factors associated with fetal chromosomal anomalies in spontaneous abortions. *Br. J. Obs. & Gyn.* **83**, 621–7.

Aymé, S. and Lippman-Hand, A. (1982). Maternal age effect in aneuploidy: Does altered embryonic selection play a role? *Am. J. Hum. Genet.* **34**, 558–65.

Aziz, A., Blair, J.A., Leeming, R.J. and Sylvester, P.E. (1982). Tetrahydrobiopterin metabolism in Down's syndrome and in non-Down's syndrome mental retardation. *J. Ment. Defic. Res.* **26**, 67–71.

Benton, J.S., Bowen, D.M., Shelley, J.A., Haan, E.A., Davison, A.N., Neary, D., Murphy, R.P. and Snowden, J.S. (1982). Alzheimer disease as a disorder of isodendric core. *Lancet* **1**, 456.

Bertrand, I. and Koffas, D. (1946). Case d'idiotie mongolienne adulte avec nombreuses plaques seniles et concretions calcaires pallidales. *Rev. Neurol.* **78**, 338–45.

Boué, J., Boué, A. and Lazar, P. (1975). Retrospective and prospective epidemiological studies of 1500 karyotyped spontaneous human abortions, *Teratology* **12**, 11–26.

Boué, J., Morer, I. and Vigual, P. (1980). Essai de definition d'un coefficient de risque d'anomalie chromosomique en debut de grossesse. *J. Génét. Hum.* **28**, 149–54.

Boué, J., Deluchat, C., Nicolas, H. and Boué, A. (1981). Prenatal losses of trisomy 21. In Burgio, G.R., Fraccaro, M., Tiepolo, L. and Wolf, U. (eds), *Trisomy 21*, pp. 183–93. Proceedings of an International Symposium, Convento delle Clarisse. Berlin: Springer-Verlag.

Boylan, P. and O'Brien, N. (1977). Down's syndrome. *J. Irish Med. Assoc.* **70**, 122–3.

Brambati, B. and Simoni, G. (1983). Fetal diagnosis of trisomy-21 in first trimester pregnancy. *Lancet* **1**, 583.

Carr, D.H. (1970). Chromosome studies in selected spontaneous abortions: 1. Conception after oral contraceptives. *Can. Med. Assoc. J.* **103**, 343–8.

Collmann, R.D. and Stoller, A. (1969). Shift of childbirth to younger mothers, and its effect on the incidence of mongolism in Victoria, Australia, 1939–1964. *J. Ment. Defic. Res.* **13**, 13–19.

Corsellis, J.A.N. (1976). Ageing and the dementias. In Blackwood, W. and Corsellis, J.A.N. (eds), *Greenfield's Neuropathology*, 3rd edn, pp.796–817. London: Edward Arnold.

Crome, L. and Stern, J. (1972). *Pathology of Mental Retardation*, 2nd edn. Edinburgh, London: Churchill Livingstone.

Davies, P. and Maloney, A.J. (1976). Selective loss of central cholinergic neurones in Alzheimer's disease. *Lancet* **11**, 1403.

Deaton, J.G. (1973). The mortality rate and causes of death among institutionalised mongols in Texas. *J. Ment. Defic. Res.* **17**, 117–22.

Department of Obstetrics and Gynaecology, Anshan (1975). Fetal sex prediction by sex chromatin of chorionic villi cells during early pregnancy. *Chinese Med. J.* **1**, 117–26.

Erickson, J.D. (1978). Down Syndrome, paternal age, maternal age and birth order. *Ann. Hum. Genet. (Lond.)* **41**, 289–98.

Evans, J.A., Hunter, A.G.W. and Hamerton, J.L. (1978). Down syndrome and recent demographic trends in Manitoba. *J. Med. Genet.* **15**, 43–7.

Ferguson-Smith, M.A. (1979). Maternal age specific incidence of chromosome aberrations at amniocentesis in prenatal diagnosis. In Murken, J.D., Stengel-Rutkowski, S. and Schwinger, E. (eds), *Prenatal Diagnosis*, pp. 1–14. Proceedings of the Third European Conference on Prenatal Diagnosis of Genetic Disorders. Stuttgart: Enke.

Ferguson-Smith, M.A. (1982). Collaborative European Study on the maternal age specific incidence of chromosome aberrations at amniocentesis. Cited in Ferguson-Smith, M.A. and Ferguson-Smith, M.E. (1983), *Developments in Human Reproduction and their Eugenic, Ethical Implications*. London: Academic Press.

Ferguson-Smith, M.A. (1983). The impact of fetal chromosome analysis on the birth incidence of chromosome disorders. *Br. Med. Bull.* **39**, 355–64.

Ferguson-Smith, M.A. and Ferguson-Smith, M.E. (eds) (1983). Problems of prenatal diagnosis. In *Developments in Human Reproduction and their Eugenic, Ethical Implications*. London: Academic Press.

Fogelman, C.J., ed. (1975). *AAMD Adaptive Behavior Scale Manual*. Washington DC. American Association of Mental Deficiency.

Forssman, H. and Åkesson, H.O. (1965). Mortality in patients with Down's syndrome, *J. Ment. Defic. Res.* **9**. 146–9.

Fraser, J. and Mitchell, A. (1876). Kalmuc idiocy; report of a case with autopsy; with notes on sixty-two cases. *J. Ment. Sci.* **22**, 161, 169–79.

Giraud, F. and Mattei, J.F. (1975). Aspects épidémiologiques de la trisomie 21. *J. Génét.Hum.* **23**, 1–30.

Gosden, J.R., Mitchell, A.R., Gosden, C.M., Rodeck, C.H. and Morsman, J.M. (1982). Direct vision chorion biopsy and chromosome-specific DNA probe for determination of fetal sex in first trimester prenatal diagnosis. *Lancet* **2**, 1416–9.

Grouchy, J. de (1970). 21p-maternal en double exemplaire chez un trisomique 21. *Ann. Genet. (Paris)* **13**, 52–5.

Grouchy, J. de and Turleau, C. (1977). *Atlas de Maladies Chromosomiques*, Paris: Expansion Scientifique Francaise.

Hahnemann, N. and Mohr, J. (1969). Antenatal fetal diagnosis in genetic disease. *Bull. Eur. Soc. Hum. Genet.* **3**, 47–54.

Hassold, T.J., Matsuyama, A., Newlands, J.M., Matssuura, J.S., Jacobs, P.A., Manuel, B. and Tsuei, J. (1978). A cytogenetic study of spontaneous abortions in Hawaii. *Ann. Hum. Genet.* **41**, 443–54.

Hecht, F. (1982). The physician as a risk factor in midtrimester amniocentesis. *New Engl. J. Med.* **306**, 1553.

Heston, L.L. and Mastri, A.R. (1977). The genetics of Alzheimer's disease. *Arch. Gen. Psych.* **34**, 976–81.

Heston, L.L., Mastri, A.R., Anderson, E. and White, J. (1981). Dementia of the Alzheimer type. *Arch. Gen. Psych.* **38**, 1085–90.

Hook, E.B. (1983). Chromosome abnormalities and spontaneous fetal death following amniocentesis: further data and associations with maternal age. *Hum. Genet.* **35**, 110–16.

Hook, E.B. and Lindsjö, A. (1978). Down's syndrome in live births by a single-year maternal age interval in a Swedish study: comparison with results from a New York study. *Am. J. Hum. Genet.* **30**, 19–27.

Hook, E.B. and Cross, P.K. (1982). Paternal age and Down's syndrome genotypes diagnosed prenatally: no association in New York State data. *Hum. Genet.* **62**, 167–74.

Jenkins, R.L. (1933). Etiology of mongolism. *Am. J. Dis. Childh.* **45**, 506.

Jervis, G.A. (1948). Early senile dementias in mongoloid idiocy. *Am. J. Psych.* **105**, 102–106.

Juberg, R.C. and Jones, B. (1970). The Christchurch chromosome (Gp-) mongolism, erythroleukemia and an inherited Gp- chromosome (Christchurch). *New Engl. J. Med.* **282**, 292–7.

Kazy, Z., Rozovsky, I.S. and Bakharev, V.A. (1982). Chorion biopsy in early pregnancy: a method of early prenatal diagnosis for inherited disorders. *Prenatal Diagnosis* **2**, 39–45.

Kullander, S. and Sandahl, B. (1973). Fetal chromosome analysis after transvisceral placental biopsies during early pregnancy. *Acta Obstet. Gynec. Scand.* **52**, 355–9.

Leeming, R.J., Phesant, A.E. and Blair, J.A. (1981). The role of tetrahydrobiopterin in neurological diseases: a review. *J. Ment. Defic. Res.* **25**, 231–41.

Lejeune, J., Gautier, M. and Turpin, R. (1959). Etudes des chromosomes somatiques de neuf enfants mongoliens, *C.R. Acad. Sci. (Paris)* **248**, 1721–2.

Lejeune, J. and Prieur, M. (1979). Contraceptifs oraux et trisomie 21. Etude rétrospective de sept cent trente cas. *Ann. Genet. (Paris)* **22**, 61–6.

Licznerski, G. and Lindsten, J. (1972). Trisomy 21 in man due to maternal nondisjunction during the first meiotic division. *Hereditas* **70**, 153–4.

Loesch, D.Z. (1983). *Quantitative Dermatoglyphics. Classification, Genetics and Pathology.* Oxford: Oxford University Press.

Loesch, D. and Smith, C.A.B. (1976). Discriminant diagnosis of 21-trisomy mosaicism. *J. Ment. Defic. Res.* **20**, 207–219.

Loesch-Mdzewska, D. (1968) Some aspects of the neurology of Down's syndrome. *J. Ment. Defic. Res.* **12**, 237–46.

Masters, C.L., Gajdusek, D.C. and Gibbs, C.J. (1981). The familial occurrence of Creutzfeldt–Jacob disease and Alzheimer's disease. *Brain* **104**, 535–58.

Mattei, J.F., Aymé, S., Mattei, M.G. and Giraud, F. (1980). Maternal age and origin of non-disjunction in trisomy 21. *J. Med. Genet.* **17**, 368–72.

Mikkelsen, M. (1971). Down's syndrome. Current stage of cytogenetic research. *Humangenetik* **12**, 1–28.

Mikkelsen, M. (1977). Down syndrome: cytogenetical epidemiology. *Hereditas* **86**, 45–50.

Mikkelsen, M. (1981). Epidemiology of trisomy 21: population, peri-, and antenatal data. In Burgio, G.R., Fraccaro, M., Tiepolo, L. and Wof, U. (eds), *Trisomy 21*, pp. 211–26. Proceedings of an International Symposium, Convento delle Clarisse. Berlin: Springer-Verlag.

Mikkelsen, M. (1982). Parental origin of the extra chromosome in Down's syndrome. *J. Ment. Defic. Res.* **26**, 143–51.

Mikkelsen, M., Fischer, G., Stene, J., Stene, E. and Petersen, E. (1976). Incidence study of Down's syndrome in Copenhagen, 1960–1971: with chromosome investigation. *Ann. Hum. Genet.* **40**, 177–82.

Miller, R.W. (1963). Down's syndrome (mongolism), other congenital malformations, and cancers among the sibs of leukemic children. *N. Engl. J. Med.* **268**, 393–401.

Miniszek, N.A. (1983). Development of Alzheimer disease in Down syndrome individuals. *Amer. J. Ment. Defic.* **87**, 377–85.

Niazi, M., Coleman, D.V. and Loeffler, F.E. (1981). Trophoblast sampling in early pregnancy. Culture of rapidly dividing cells from immature placental villi. *Brit. J. Obstet. Gynaec.* **88**, 1081–5.

Old, J.M., Ward, R.H.T., Karagözlu, F., Petron, M., Modell, B. and Weatherall, D.J. (1982). First trimester fetal diagnosis for haemoglobinopathies: 3 cases. *Lancet* **2**, 1414–16.

Øster, J. (1953). *Mongolism.* Copenhagen: Danish Science Press.

Øster, J., Mikkelsen, M. and Nielsen, A. (1975). Mortality and life-table in Down's syndrome. *Acta Ped. Scand.* **64**, 322–6.

Park, S.C., Mathews, R.A., Zuber-Buhler, J.R., Rowe, R.D., Neckes, W.H. and Lennox, C.C. (1977). Down's syndrome with congenital heart malformation. *Am. J. Dis. Childh.* **131**, 29–33.

Penrose, L.S. (1933). The relative effects of paternal and maternal age in mongolism. *J. Genet.* **27**, 219–24.

Penrose, L.S. (1934). A method of separating the relative aetiological effect of birth order maternal age, with special reference to mongolian imbecility. *Ann. Eugenet. Lond.* **6**, 108.

Penrose, L.S. and Smith, G.F. (1966). *Down's Anomaly.* London: Churchill Livingstone.

Read, S.G. (1982). The distribution of Down's syndrome. *J. Ment. Defic. Res.* **26**, 215–27.

Rice, G.P.A., Paty, D.W., Ball, M.J., Tatham, R. and Kertesz, A. (1980). Spongiform encephalopathy of long duration: a family study. *Can. J. Neurol. Sci.* **7**, 171–6.

Richards, B.W. (1967). Mongolism: The effect of trends in age at childbirth on incidence and chromosomal type. *J. Ment. Subnorm.* **13**, 3–13

Richards, B.W. and Siddiqui, A.Q. (1980). Age and mortality trends in residents of an institution for the mentally handicapped. *J.Ment. Defic. Res.* **24**, 99–105.

Rodeck, C.H. and Morsman, J.M. (1983). First-trimester chorion biopsy. *Brit. Med. Bul.* **39**, 338–42.

Rodewald, A., Bär, M., Zankl, M., Zankl, H., Reicke, S. and Zang, K.D. (1982). Dermatoglyphic studies in parents of children with trisomy 21: detection of hidden mosaicism and its role in genetic counselling. In *Progress in Dermatoglyphic Research,* pp. 371–84. New York: Alan R. Liss.

Rollin, H.R. (1946). Personality in mongolism with special reference to the incidence of catatonic psychosis. *Am. J. Ment. Defic.* **51**, 219–37.

Ropper, A.H. and Williams, R.S. (1980). Relationship between plaques, tangles, and dementia in Down syndrome. *Neurology* **30**, 639–44.

Roth, M.P., Feingold, J., Baumgarten, A., Bigel, P. and Stoll, C. (1983). Reexamination of paternal age effect in Down's syndrome. *Hum. Genet.* **63**, 149–52.

Schreinemachers, D.S., Cross, P.K. and Hook, E.B. (1982). Rates of trisomies 21, 18, 13 and other chromosome abnormalities in about 20 000 prenatal studies compared with estimated rates in live births. *Hum. Genet.* **61**, 318–24.

Simoni, G., Brambati, B., Danesino, C., Rosella, F., Terzoli, G.L., Ferrari, M. and Fraccaro, M. (1983). Efficient direct chromosome analyses and enzyme determinations from chorionic villi samples in the first trimester of pregnancy. *Hum. Genet.* **64**, 349–57.

Smith, G.F. and Berg, J.M. (1976). *Down's Anomaly,* 2nd edn. Edinburgh, London, New York: Churchill Livingstone.

Steel, M.W. and Breg, W.R. (1966). Chromosome analysis of human amniotic cells. *Lancet* **1**, 383–5.

Stene, J., Fischer, G., Stene, E., Mikkelsen, M. and Petersen, E. (1977). Paternal age effect in Down's syndrome. *Ann. Hum. Genet.* **40**, 299–308.

Stene, J. and Stene, E. (1977). Statistical methods for detecting a moderate paternal age effect on incidence of disorder when a maternal one is present. *Ann. Hum. Genet.* **40**, 343–53.

Stene, J., Stene, E. and Mikkelsen, M. (1984). Risk for chromosome abnormality at amniocentesis following a child with a non-inherited chromosome aberration. A European Collaborative Study on Prenatal Diagnoses 1981. *Prenat. Diagn.* **4** Spec. No., 81–95.

Stene, J., Stene, E., Stengel-Rutkowski, S. and Murken, J.D. (1981). Paternal age and Down's syndrome. Data from prenatal diagnosis (D.F.G.). *Hum. Genet.* **59**, 119–24.

Struwe, F. (1929). Histopathologische Untersuchungen über Entstehung und Wesen der senilen Plaques. *Zur Gesch. Neurol. Psych.* **122**, 291–307.

Terry, R.D. (1976). Dementia. *Arch. Neurol.* **33**, 1–4.

Terry, R.D. and Davies, P. (1980). Dementia of Alzheimer type. *Annu. Rev. Neurosci.* **3**, 77–95.

Thase, M.E. (1982). Reversible dementia in Down's syndrome. *J. Ment. Defic. Res.* **26**, 111–13.

Thase, M.E., Liss, L., Smeltzer, D. and Maloon, J. (1982). Clinical evaluation of dementia in Down's syndrome: a preliminary report. *J. Ment. Defic. Res.* **26**, 239–44.

Uchida, I.A. (1979). Radiation-induced nondisjunction. *Environ. Health Perspect.* **31**, 13–17.

Uchida, I.A., Holunga, R. and Lawler, C. (1968). Maternal radiation and chromosome aberrations. *Lancet* **2**, 1045–9.

Waardenburg, P.J. (1932). *Das menschliche Auge und seine Erbanlagen.* The Hague: Nijhoff.

Warburton, D. and Fraser, F.C. (1964). Spontaneous abortion risks in man: Data from reproductive histories collected in a medical genetics unit. *Am. J. Hum. Genet.* **16**, 1–2.

Werner, E.E., Bierman, J.M. and French, F.E. (1971). *The Children of Kauai.* Honolulu: University of Hawaii Press.

Williamson, R., Eskdale, J., Coleman, D.V., Niazi, M., Loeffler, F.E. and Modell, B.M. (1981). Direct gene analysis of chorionic villi. A possible technique for first trimester antenatal diagnosis of haemoglobinopathies. *Lancet* **2**, 1125–7.

Wisniewski, K., Howe, J., Williams, D.G. and Wisniewski, H.M. (1978). Precocious aging and dementia in patients with Down's syndrome. *Biol. Psych.* **13**, 619–27.

Yates, C.M., Simpson, J., Maloney, A.F.J., Gordon, A. and Reid, A.H. (1980). Alzheimer-like cholinergic deficiency in Down's syndrome. *Lancet* **2**, 979.

Young, J.H., Kelly, B. and Clayton, B.E. (1982). Reduced levels of biopterin and dihydropteridine reductase in Alzheimer type dementia. *J. Clin. Exp. Gerontol.* **4**, 389–402.

Yunis, J.J. (1977). *New Chromosomal Syndromes.* New York, San Francisco, London: Academic Press.

3 The Heart*

K.A. Hallidie-Smith

INCIDENCE AND MORTALITY OF CARDIAC DEFECTS

The first known reference to heart disease occurring in Down's Syndrome was in 1894 (Garrod 1894), and in 1899 the same author drew attention to its common association with the syndrome (Garrod 1899). It is now accepted that one in two of Down's children are born with a congenital heart defect. Greenwood and Nadas (1976) found a 62% incidence in 369 infants and children admitted to hospital, and Rowe and Uchida (1960) found a 40% incidence in a local survey of a Down's population. The reported incidence is unlikely to be over-estimated as there are probably both late and missed cardiac diagnoses which escape documentation. This high incidence of congenital heart disease in approximately 50% of Down's children contrasts with a reported incidence of 0.7% to 1% of the population as a whole (Richards *et al.*, 1955; Mitchell *et al.*, 1971; Keith *et al.*, 1978).

The most common cardiac defect in the normal population is of isolated ventricular septal defect, which accounts for approximately 28% of all defects in the population as a whole (Keith *et al.*, 1978). A similar incidence (33%) is quoted in Down's syndrome (Rowe and Uchida 1960). However, while the majority of ventricular septal defects in the normal population are of small size and cause no symptoms, the majority of such defects in the Down's infant are large, causing major symptoms and predisposing to pulmonary hypertension. Again, whereas an atrioventricular canal defect is uncommon in the population as a whole, accounting for certainly not more than 2% of all congenital cardiac defects, this complicated and serious malformation is the most common cardiac defect in the Down's child, accounting for some 60% of cardiac findings in an autopsy study (Tandon and Edwards, 1973). It is possible that some of the reported ventricular septal defects and secundum atrial septal defects may represent incomplete forms of the canal, and therefore the true incidence of this complex anomaly may be even higher. Patent ductus arteriosus probably accounts for 5–10% of cardiac defects in Down's Syndrome (Keith *et al.*, 1978) and is a relatively common finding in the normal population, but here again the doctus in Down's Syndrome tends to be large, with early development of pulmonary hypertension. Cyanotic congenital heart disease is referred to in the early literature in Down's Syndrome but it is in fact much less common than in the normal population. Tetralogy of Fallot alone or in combination with atrioventricular canal is the most important cyanotic defect and accounted

*This chapter was submitted in August 1983.

for approximately 14.5% of cardiac defects in the Down's autopsy series of Tandon and Edwards (1973).

The major anatomical defects referred to will be described later, but this brief outline serves to emphasise the high frequency with which very serious cardiac defects occur in Down's children. It is thus perhaps not surprising that congenital heart disease remains the major cause of death in Down's Syndrome, accounting for 30–35% of deaths (Thase, 1982). Chest infections account for approximately the same number of deaths but it is conceivable that a congenital cardiac defect was a contributing factor in some of these patients. Not surprisingly, the mortality from congenital heart disease is highest in the first two years of life. As recently as the last decade, it was believed that only 40–60% of Down's children with congenital heart disease survived beyond the age of 10 years (Fabia and Drolette, 1970; Gallagher and Lowry, 1975; Mulcahy, 1979). The situation is illustrated in Fig. 3.1.

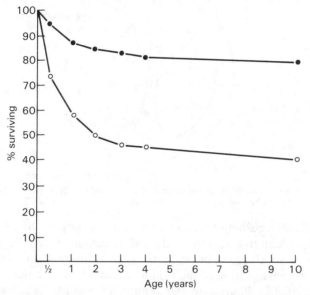

Fig. 3.1 Survival rates for Down's syndrome children with (○) and without (●) congenital heart disease. (From Thase (1982), with acknowledgement)

Many authors have reported a high operative mortality and morbidity in the Down's child undergoing corrective surgery and, as recently as 1977, Kaltick *et al.* found a 30% operative or perioperative mortality and a high incidence of major postoperative complications. Thus, again, the serious nature of cardiac defects in the Down's child and the problems of management are emphasised.

COMMON CARDIAC DEFECTS

The complete form of atrioventricular canal is commonly found in Down's Syndrome (Bharati and Lev, 1973; Tenckhoff and Stamms, 1973). In order to understand the basic anatomy of this complex malformation it is essential to realise that it is a primitive, early developmental fault determined well before the end of the seventh week of foetal life, by which time the heart is structurally complete (Krovetz *et al.*, 1969).

This major defect is primarily due to anomalies in the development of the endocardial cushions in the centre of the heart (Fig. 3.2). These normally grow to divide the atria from the ventricles by fusing with the atrial septum superiorly and the ventricular septum inferiorly. The medial cusp of the tricuspid valve is formed

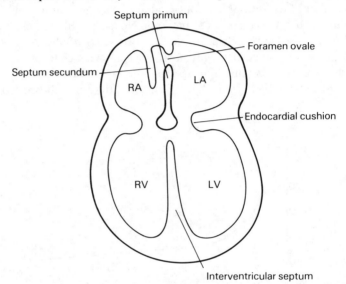

Fig. 3.2 Development of the heart chambers and atrioventricular valves. (RA = right atrium; RV = right ventricle; LA = left atrium; LV = left ventricle)

from the right-sided cushion tissue and the anterior cusp of the mitral valve from the left-sided cushion tissue. If the endocardial cushion tissue fails to fuse with the septum primum, which grows downwards to divide the two atria, then the result is an interatrial communication of the ostium primum type. Similarly, lack of fusion of the endocardial cushions with the ventricular septum results in a ventricular septal defect. At the same time, there is failure of separation of mitral and tricuspid valves. The fused medial leaflet of the tricuspid valve and the anterior leaflet of the mitral valve straddle the defect as a single sheet of tissue, separated from the other valve leaflets. As a result of a complete atrioventricular canal, there is mixing of blood between all chambers of the heart and incompetence of the mitral and tricuspid valves (Fig. 3.3).

The obligatory increase in pulmonary flow determined by this large central defect usually occasions pulmonary hypertension, increase in pulmonary vascular resistance and early pulmonary vascular disease. Partial forms of the atrioventricular canal defect, particularly the ostium primum defect with mitral incompetence due to a cleft mitral valve, are seen far less commonly in Down's Syndrome.

Ostium secundum atrial septal defect is a common form of congenital heart disease in the general population but uncommon as an isolated defect in the Down's child, in whom it is often associated with a canal defect. It results from a

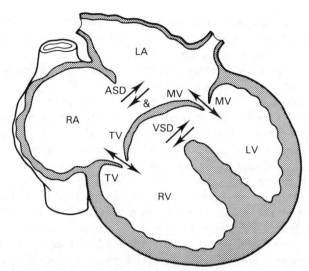

Fig. 3.3 Complete atrioventricular canal showing septal defects and valvar incompetence. (RA = right atrium; RV = right ventricle; LA = left atrium; LV = left ventricle; TV and MV = primitive tricuspid and mitral valve tissue; ASD = atrial septal defect; VSD = ventricular septal defect)

deficiency of the valve or limbus of the fossa ovalis, or foramen ovale, which is an essential foetal posterior ostium in the septum primum, overlapped by the septum secundum, which grows parallel to the septum primum but only partially divides the atria. Isolated secundum atrial septal defects do not normally give rise to symptoms in infancy or childhood. However, the increased pulmonary blood flow in later infancy and childhood may predispose the Down's child to chest infections and possible pulmonary hypertension, although this is by no means invariably the case with this defect.

Isolated patent ductus arteriosus is relatively common in the Down's child, either alone or in combination with other cardiac defects. The isolated ductus is often exceptionally large in diameter, and with such a large communication there may be obligatory pulmonary hypertension and early pulmonary vascular disease.

Again, ventricular septal defect in the Down's child is characteristically large, and, in a personal series of nearly 300 Down's infants and children referred with congenital heart disease, there have been only two patients thought to have small ventricular septal defects, one of which closed spontaneously. It is interesting that approximately 50% of autopsy proven ventricular septal defect in Down's Syndrome proved to be of the atrioventricular canal type, situated immediately below the tricuspid valve (Tandon and Edwards, 1973); the remainder were in the membranous septum.

Large ventricular septal defects permit free transmission of systemic pressure to the right ventricle and pulmonary artery with significant increase in pulmonary blood flow and subsequent increase in pulmonary vascular resistance. These changes may occur in all large intracardiac communications and give rise to failure to thrive, respiratory difficulties, heart failure and proneness to chest infections. Increase in pulmonary vascular resistance initially protects the lungs, and there is improvement in symptoms. Ultimately, however, the pulmonary vascular bed is partially obliterated, and, with increase of the pulmonary vascular resistance to above that of the systemic resistance, the individual becomes constantly cyanosed, due to the mixing of venous and arterial blood.

Tetralogy of Fallot anatomy is that of large ventricular septal defect, pulmonary stenosis and the aortic override of the ventricular septum (Fig. 3.4). There is muscular obstruction of the infundibulum below the pulmonary valve, often associated pulmonary valve stenosis, and underdevelopment of the right ventricular outflow tract. From this brief anatomical outline it is clear that the degree of cyanosis is dependent on the degree of right ventricular outflow tract obstruction and aortic override. Cyanosis depends on venous/arterial mixing through the ventricular septal defect – the flow of venous blood directed to the aorta made possible by overriding of the septum – and the magnitude of the pulmonary blood flow, determined by the degree of right ventricular outflow tract obstruction. In some infants and children, there may be a sudden shut-down of the muscular infundibulum resulting in acute hypoxia (the so-called blue spell). Tetralogy of Fallot is one of the two most common forms of cyanotic congenital heart disease in normal children and is the most common cyanotic congenital defect in Down's Syndrome, but in these children it is often combined with an atrioventricular canal, a combination very rarely seen in the general population. The lungs are protected by pulmonary stenosis in these Down's children, but cyanosis may be extreme because of the additional potential of venous/arterial mixing through the canal.

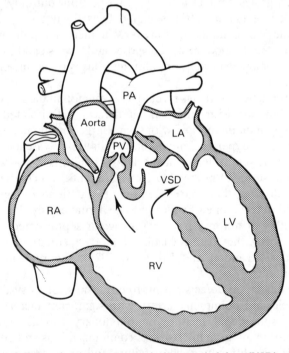

Fig. 3.4 Tetralogy of Fallot showing large ventricular septal defect (VSD), aortic override and pulmonary stenosis. (RA = right atrium; RV = right ventricle; LA = left atrium; LV = left ventricle; PA = pulmonary artery; PV = pulmonary valve)

Pulmonary stenosis, aortic stenosis, and coarctation of the aorta are relatively common in the general population but rarely reported in Down's Syndrome (Keith *et al.*, 1978).

It is interesting to speculate as to why the primitive atrioventricular canal defect is so common in Down's children and so uncommon in the population as a whole. It seems as if the heart in Down's children may always be slightly different from that of the normal child, and studies of normal hearts in Down's Syndrome have shown that there is enlargement of part of the ventricular septum, called the membranous septum (Rosenquist *et al.*, 1975). Rosenquist *et al.* (1975) have demonstrated that the commisure between the anterior and medial leaflets of the tricuspid valve are commonly absent in Down's Syndrome. Very early anatomical development of the Down's heart may be slightly modified in relation to the development of the normal heart, and may predispose to the complete canal defect so commonly seen in these children. The possibility of fundamental differences in the lungs in the Down's child is discussed below in detail, but it is clear that these babies and children have very complicated cardiac defects and early pulmonary hypertension.

PRESENTATION AND DIAGNOSIS OF CARDIAC DEFECTS

One of the difficulties in early recognition of heart disease in infants and children is that so often the sole criterion considered for diagnosis of a heart defect is a heart murmur. This is a complete fallacy in so far as many heart defects are murmur free and, contrarily, heart murmurs can be heard in most normal children. This common misunderstanding is particularly unfavourable to early diagnosis of a heart defect in the Down's baby, in whom the most common heart defect (an atrioventricular canal) is often murmur free, particularly in the young infant. It is not a rare event for a child with Down's Syndrome to present for the first time at a cardiac clinic because of cyanosis. By this time, the child may have established pulmonary vascular disease with reverse of shunt and be murmur free, once again. It is, therefore, particularly important that the earliest signs of heart involvement are thought about by parents, paramedical workers and physicians.

Infants with a large intracardiac defect or ductus, allowing an increase in pulmonary blood flow, will fail to thrive. They breathe rapidly when feeding or crying, do not take their feeds well and fail to gain weight satisfactorily. Sweating and paleness of the skin are important features in heart failure. In complete atrioventricular canal, the baby may appear intermittently cyanosed because of the ease of mixing between the venous and arterial circulations through the large central defect. Later, the child may appear cyanosed because pulmonary vascular resistance has increased to the stage where resistance in the lungs is above that in the systemic circuit, so that there is a constant mixing of venous with systemic blood. While the pulmonary blood flow is still high, there is always enlargement of the heart because of the extra volume load with which it has to cope. This will produce a typical convex deformity of the chest wall, particularly on the left side, and a typical breathing pattern in which there is subcostal recession (Fig. 3.5). In addition to failure to thrive, the muscles of an infant in heart failure are weak and

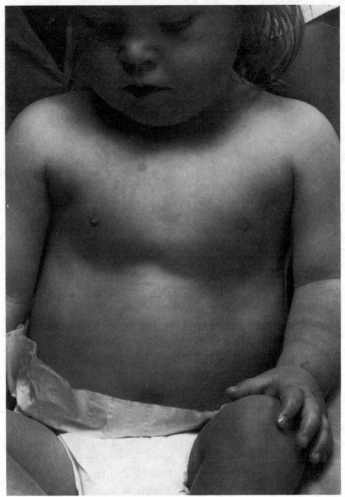

Fig. 3.5 Two-year-old Down's child with complete atrioventricular canal showing typical chest deformity

there is delay in motor development. It is, thus, clear that in the case of a Down's baby a serious heart defect can go unnoticed and accepted as being part of the delay in motor skills and hypotonia expected in Down's Syndrome. Because of the frequency of major cardiac malformations in the syndrome, it is advisable that the baby be thoroughly checked in the newborn period for any abnormal cardiac findings and then re-examined at the six weeks' check-up and subsequently, if symptoms or signs should suggest the possibility. The electrocardiogram of atrioventricular canal is diagnostic from birth and is a very helpful screening investigation, whether or not the chest radiograph appears abnormal at this time.

If there is any doubt about the possibility of a heart defect, referral to a paediatric cardiac centre is justified, and the recent development of two-dimensional ultrasound scanning should make non-invasive structural diagnosis freely available. With the use of this equipment, it is possible to visualise the structure of the heart simply by placing a small-ended transducer on the chest wall (Fig. 3.6). The current trend is to avoid bringing the child into hospital where possible, and to avoid cardiac catheterisation – an invasive procedure involving the introduction of a catheter into the heart through a vein. However, it is sometimes necessary to discover the pulmonary artery pressure and the amount of mixing between arterial and venous circuits. Alternatively, there may be features of the anatomy which can only be solved by angiography, which involves injecting radio-opaque contrast media directly into the heart while recording its circulation using cine angiography. Under these circumstances, full haemodynamic investigation of the child as an in-patient is justified.

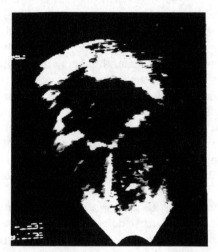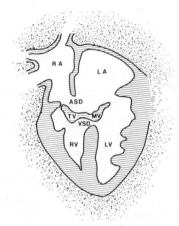

Fig. 3.6 Two-dimensional echocardiogram, showing imaging of complete atrioventricular canal, and illustrative anatomical diagram. (RA = right atrium; RV = right ventricle; LA = left atrium; LV = left ventricle; TV and MV = primitive tricuspid and mitral valve tissue; ASD = atrial septal defect; VSD = ventricular septal defect)

In considering cyanotic congenital heart disease, it is important to remember that the baby may or may not be cyanosed from birth, and shortness of breath may be appreciated before cyanosis becomes obvious. However, the baby should be watched during crying, and cyanosis looked for at these times. The best areas to examine for cyanosis are the tongue, lips and nail-beds. In a dark-skinned child, cyanosis may be very difficult to appreciate, and direct comparison with the mother's nail-beds can be useful. The baby or child is nearly always short of breath on crying or other exercise and the breathing may be of a noisy nature because of acidaemia.

The last-mentioned aspects are apparent in tetralogy of Fallot or atrioventricular canal with tetralogy of Fallot – the most common cyanotic congenital defects in Down's children. The growth can be normal and the chest shape usually remains normal because the heart is not enlarged. There is no subcostal remission because pulmonary blood flow is normal or reduced, and for the same reason these babies and children are not prone to chest infections because of their cardiac defect.

Non-Down's babies and children with severe tetralogy of Fallot are retarded in their physical milestones, and walking may be delayed until 2 years of age or more. Once walking, these children cannot keep up with other children in terms of physical activity but their mental performance is not impaired. Once again, the Down's child with cyanotic congenital heart disease is doubly handicapped and may fall well behind in his expected motor development.

Because less physical achievement is expected of Down's children, they may not seem so unduly physically handicapped and frustrated as a non-Down's child of a comparable age and degree of cyanosis. Blue spells, in which there is a spasmodic shut-down of the right ventricular outflow tract, can occur in tetralogy of Fallot and are a potentially serious portent. Often, such a spell may occur on waking or when first entering a hot bath, or during a febrile illness. The baby or child may scream out and draw up his legs, which may be mistaken for a sign of abdominal pain, though it is in fact due to cardiac pain or angina. The child goes intensely blue, then may go limp, vacant or pale with his eyes rolling up. A generalised convulsion may occur at these times. Such episodes can be fatal, and the child should be referred immediately to hospital. Because of hypoxia, the haemoglobin of the cyanotic child is high, and, because the number of red cells is increased in relation to the volume of serum, the blood can be very sticky. For this reason, such an individual, particularly if deprived of fluids, can suffer a stroke, whether or not related to a blue spell. Although cyanosis does not impair mental function, cerebral damage associated with a severe blue spell could do so and further handicap the already retarded Down's child.

The other group of cyanotic Down's children seen comprises those in whom there is venous/arterial mixing through a large intracardiac defect or ductus because of a high pulmonary vascular resistance. The symptoms are the same as in intrinsic cyanotic congenital heart disease but there may be a history of failure to thrive and symptoms of a large left-to-right shunt in infancy with persisting chest deformity and subcostal recession; signs of pulmonary hypertension will be elicited. Infants with Down's Syndrome are often thought to have increased mottling of the skin and cyanosis of the extremities, which is peripheral and in no way related to the presence or an absence of a cardiac defect. It is believed that their peripheral vasculature may possibly have a different vasomotor regulation to the normal (Benda, 1949). Cyanotic infants and children should have a cardiac diagnosis made to ascertain how they can best be helped, if necessary. Usually, the diagnosis is again made by physical examination, chest radiograph, ECG and two-dimensional scan. However, angiography is indicated if palliative or corrective surgery is contemplated or to clarify anatomical details.

The Down's patient is not usually subject to hypertension, and in fact the Down's population has lower blood pressures than average (Richards and Enver, 1979). It has also been suggested that there is a lower than usual incidence of atheromatous disease (Murdoch *et al.*, 1977).

As with normal infants and children, the index of suspicion of congenital heart disease is extremely important for Down's children. The Down's infant or child often has so many problems that the diagnosis of a heart defect is made later than usual. The late diagnosis may be of no consequence in many cases, but if it is recognised that the child has a major cardiac defect, then the understanding of the child's problems and the planning of management become easier.

THE LUNGS IN DOWN'S SYNDROME

The heart and lungs are interdependent in many primary cardiac or pulmonary disorders. We must, therefore, draw attention to pulmonary anatomy and physiology in Down's children in so far as it may be relevant to the symptoms, natural history and management of their cardiac defects.

Recent work has shown that the Down's child has hypoplastic lungs, regardless of whether or not there is cardiac involvement (Cooney and Thurlbeck, 1982). Although non-Down's children with congenital heart disease may also have hypoplastic lungs, there appear to be specific structural changes unique to Down's Syndrome. There is persistence of the double capillary network in the alveolar wall, which is demonstrated in the normal foetus (Langston and Thurlbeck, 1982), and also a diminished number of alveoli and small alveolar surface area, while the alveolar ductus are enlarged (Cooney and Thurlbeck, 1982). Though impairment of immunological defence mechanisms is considered to be of importance in the Down's child (Rodriguez *et al.*, 1981; Spina *et al.*, 1981), it is also possible that the structural pulmonary changes found in these children predispose them to the respiratory infections to which they are so prone and to which any infant with increased pulmonary blood flow due to large arterial/venous shunts is particularly susceptible. It is also possible that reduction in the cross-section of area of the pulmonary vascular bed may be a predisposing factor towards the early development of pulmonary hypertension and pulmonary vascular disease.

The histological changes which develop in the pulmonary hypertensive lung have been divided in order of severity into six grades (Heath and Edwards, 1958), grades four to six representing irreversible changes, and grades one to three representing reversible changes. The practical implication of these findings is that cardiac surgical intervention has to be carried out before irreversible pulmonary vascular changes occur. In any situation in which there is a large intracardiac or extracardiac communication between systemic and pulmonary circuits, there is obligatory pulmonary hypertension and increased pulmonary vascular resistance, which may ultimately lead to irreversible pulmonary vascular disease. Irreversible pulmonary vascular disease is favoured by a high pulmonary blood flow, a high left atrial pressure, hypoxia from high-altitude living, upper airways obstruction, birth asphyxia and respiratory infections.

There is some controversy as to whether or not Down's infants and children develop pulmonary hypertension and pulmonary vascular disease more readily than their normal peers. The overwhelming weight of clinical opinion (including the author's) is that they do, and this clinical opinion is supported by extensive published work (Soudon *et al.*, 1975; Greenwood and Nadas, 1976; Laursen, 1975; Chi and Krovetz, 1975; Shaher *et al.*, 1972; Rosengart and Isabel-Jones, 1976; Somerville, 1971). However, three careful autopsy studies have failed to differentiate the histological changes in the lungs of Down's and non-Down's children with comparable cardiac defects (Plett *et al.*, 1974; Neufeld *et al.*, 1977; Wilson *et al.*, 1979). Irreversible pulmonary vascular changes were found in complete atrioventricular canal defects in both Down's and non-Down's children as early as 1 year of age and were well advanced by 2 years (Neufeld *et al.*, 1977). However, Chi and Krovetz (1975) carried out cardiac catheterisation on 69 Down's infants and children with major cardiac defects and found that 90% of them had pulmonary hypertension, as opposed to 25% of a control group with comparable cardiac defects, even though the mean age of the Down's children was only 3.2 years, compared with 6.2 years in the normal children. Clearly, the volume of clinical and haemodynamic observation far exceeds that of autopsy documentation, and clinicians would stress the susceptibility of children with Down's Syndrome to pulmonary hypertension, even though it is clear that they have uniquely major cardiac defects.

It is well known that not all non-Down's children born with large ventricular septal defects develop progressive pulmonary vascular disease, and that contributory factors are of the utmost importance in determining the individual's response. Clearly, there are individual hyper-reactors who will develop pulmonary vascular disease if some or all of the factors favouring its development are present (Hallidie-Smith and Goodwin, 1974), and it is conceivable that Down's Syndrome in itself favours this hyper-reaction, just as we know that there are racial susceptibilities. It is also known that pulmonary vasoconstriction, often reversible by pulmonary vasodilators, may be an important factor in some individuals and may exist independently of pulmonary vascular disease or precede its histological development. Pulmonary vasoconstriction, together with the attenuated pulmonary vascular bed due to hypoplastic lungs, may be important factors in Down's Syndrome.

Again, the Down's infant and child is susceptible to hypoxia resulting from chest infections and to upper airways obstruction, which is a well-documented cause of pulmonary hypertension in Down's Syndrome (Rowland *et al.*, 1981), as it is in the population as a whole (Menashe *et al.*, 1965; Levy *et al.*, 1967). In addition to the readily diagnosed upper airways obstruction in the Down's child, many of these children have particularly obstructed breathing at night, and pulmonary hypertension due to sleep apnoea has been convincingly recorded (Loughlin *et al.*, 1981). Once again, though sleep apnoea is also known to be a cause of pulmonary hypertension in normal children (Guilleminault *et al.*, 1976; Felman *et al.*, 1979), the large tonsils, adenoids and tongue, together with Down's physionomy, hypotonia, and subglottic stenosis (Stewart, 1970), favour this clinical complex in Down's Syndrome, and removal of tonsils and adenoids may not always result in the same degree of improvement as has been noted in normal children.

There are no known published studies of the mechanics of breathing in Down's children, but a recent survey has shown that, contrary to generally held belief, there is not an increased incidence of respiratory problems during or after anaesthesia, provided that the possibility of subglottal narrowing is recognised, the airways are kept clear, and over-sedation, which could induce sleep apnoea, is avoided (Kobel *et al.*, 1982). This major review is encouraging in relation to incidental anaesthesia so often required for a Down's child with or without a cardiac defect, as well as more specifically for cardiac catheterisation or cardiac surgery, even though a major cardiac defect must add to the hazards of anaesthesia in any child.

DISCUSSION WITH PARENTS

For many years now, it has been the author's practice to enquire from parents of Down's children their reaction when first told that their child had a cardiac defect. As with parents of normal children, the majority have reported that they were shocked and stunned when they first heard the news. Historically, and to most people, the heart is the central organ of the body, and any potential impairment of its function seems to warn of impending disaster. For the parents of Down's children, as with parents of non-Down's children, the questions asked are very similar: 'Will the child die suddenly?', 'Will he suffer in any way?', 'Will he ever be able to walk or run?', 'Will he ever be able to go to school or play with other children?'.

The parents of Down's children have an additional problem because they already know they have a handicapped child and often they cannot face up to the potential disaster of a second handicap involving the heart. However, interestingly enough, these parents, on the whole, are usually better informed than other parents by the time they are aware that the child has a heart defect. They already know a great deal about the handicapped child and many of them have joined associations which have already made them aware that many children with Down's Syndrome have heart defects and get along quite well. These parents definitely find it much easier to take the cardiac abnormality in their stride. Another group of parents who find it comparatively easy to cope are those who have had particularly good back-up from their doctors and associate workers. Again, there is a group of parents with large families who take the Down's child in their stride and do not find it overwhelmingly distressing when told that the child has an additional problem.

The role of the paediatric cardiologist is to make as accurate a diagnosis as possible on the child by non-invasive means and after this to set aside plenty of time for a full discussion with the parents on all questions raised. It should be possible to set out some sort of plan for infancy and childhood, to outline the quality of life which the child should be expected to enjoy, the place of medical and surgical management, and any modifications of expected life pattern that the cardiac defect may or will impose. It is important that, once the parents understand the nature of the cardiac problem, they are given time to put what questions they wish and are encouraged to express their own opinions and views on basic principles of management, which, in its turn, can be most helpful to the physician concerned. It cannot be overemphasised that a heart defect does not impose further intellectual impairment on the child, and, even if the parents do not raise this question, it should always be brought up, because, even subconsciously, this may be firmly believed. It is a particularly prevalent belief in relation to cyanotic congenital heart disease, and many parents of non-Down's children will expect their child to do better at school if the heart defect is corrected. This is a fallacy, but, of course, the fit child can concentrate on his studies rather better, although his basic IQ will not be changed.

The possible physical handicaps imposed by the child's particular defect must be fully explained with relevance to infancy, childhood and adolescence. In particular, the changing nature of the physiology and adaptation to the anatomy in congenital heart disease should be stressed. For instance, in the case of a young baby with a complete atrioventricular canal, there may be a history of failure to thrive in infancy; a static phase as the pulmonary vascular resistance rises; and a later phase when there is shunt reversal and the child is cyanosed but still able to live a very acceptable life. All these should be explained. It should also be stressed that at all times the objective will be to secure the best possible quality of life for the child and, as professionals, we would plan for him to take his place with other mentally handicapped children at school and in the family unit.

It should be emphasised that regular help will be given to ensure this possibility by means of cardiac follow-up, general advice, medical management and surgical treatment, if indicated. It is always helpful to allude to non-Down's children who are growing up with a similar defect, attending normal school and generally enjoying life. Conversely, if the cardiac defect happens to be a minor one, the parents of the Down's child should be told that this defect will not affect his development, or achievements, in any way. If the infant has a large arteriovenous communication, the parents should be instructed in the more obvious signs of improvement or relapse and in the ideal approach of feeding, which will be small, frequent feeds and early weaning to solids. It may also be helpful to tell them of the importance of keeping the upper airways as clear as possible by positioning the baby and by obtaining ear, nose and throat advice, if necessary.

The parents of cyanotic children with tetralogy of Fallot should always be told of the possibility of blue spells and the action they should take, and they should similarly be told of the general management of such babies and children, emphasising the need for fluid replacement. Parents of a child with established pulmonary vascular disease and reversal of shunt should again be told of the need for always giving the child plenty of fluids, and for letting the child live as equitable and ordered a life as possible. In this way, it has been possible for many non-Down's children to grow up and to take their place as full-time wage earners. By direct comparison, the Down's child should get to know his own levels of activity and be able to have an acceptable way of life within his own family and community.

The rationale of antibiotic prophylaxis for dental work and other surgical procedures should be explained to the parents because of the risks of endocarditis, which is a very serious illness and would occasion considerable suffering to the child and a prolonged period in hospital. Finally, cardiac follow-up visits should be organised in such a way that they are of maximum benefit to parents and child and are not purely routine visits, which would add considerably to the impositions on time already accepted by the parents of a Down's child, who may have multicentre multispecialist visits to undertake.

MANAGEMENT OF THE DOWN'S CHILD WITH A CARDIAC DEFECT

Since there is a 50% chance of a Down's baby having a cardiac defect, the possibility should be considered early and an accurate diagnosis made in order to achieve the most effective management. It is equally important, however, to emphasise that our aims as professionals are to achieve the best quality of life for each Down's child and to realise the full potential of each individual. There is no reason why an already handicapped child should be left with major symptoms from a cardiac defect if he can be helped. Equally, it is unfair to parents to ask them to struggle with the effects of such an additional handicap if it can be avoided, particularly since major symptoms in the early training period may detract considerably from the child's future potential. However, it should be stressed, in relation to cardiac surgery, that Down's children have particularly complicated anatomical and physiological cardiac defects. Moreover, specific cardiac surgery can only be recommended in relation to the results which a particular specialised centre can hope to achieve and at the age when such surgery is ideally indicated, which may be during the first year of life. Thus, the principles of management have to be related to practical possibilities at any particular time, and there is no immediate possibility of substitution of cardiac surgery for medical management in many cases.

Paediatric cardiology and its surgery is a very young specialty, and its fundamentals and areas of development are continuously being modified and developed. As in the normal child, so in the Down's child, the ideal management of a cardiac defect is not necessarily anatomical correction. For instance, nearly 30 years after it became possible to close ventricular septal defects in childhood, we have learnt that, for the most part, the natural history of ventricular septal defect is perfectly acceptable and preferable to surgical closure with its potential short- and long-term problems, even if we have to deal medically with a short period in infancy when the baby fails to thrive and may even be in heart failure. Long-term follow-up studies of normal children who had a large ventricular septal defect with pulmonary hypertension surgically closed after the age of 2 years have shown that the changes due to pulmonary vascular disease may already have been established and can progress (Hallidie-Smith *et al.*, 1977; Hallidie-Smith, unpublished work).

If it is decided not to operate on a Down's child with an atrioventricular canal or large ventricular septal defect, or if the opportunity to operate has already passed and the child has severe established pulmonary hypertension, then we need not necessarily expect a gloomy prognosis for the child. We could, at least, expect the child to grow up and have an acceptable quality of life, just as is possible with non-Down's children under similar circumstances. In fact, the quality of life for a Down's child might be rather better because of their non-athletic aspirations and their satisfaction with non-competitive activities, for the most part. If such children are given good general care, and any intervening illnesses and, particularly, surgical procedures or anaesthetics are treated with meticulous attention to good oxygenation and good fluid balance, then the child should cope with such problems and be able to grow into adult life. It is important, however, that the general routine of day-to-day existence is maintained since individuals with pulmonary hypertension do not easily tolerate sudden changes in their routine. After a period of years the child will obviously become cyanosed or blue in appearance due to deoxygenated blood mixing with the oxygenated blood through the defect. Should the blood become increasingly sticky due to an excess of red blood corpuscles, then small amounts of blood can be removed in order to try to prevent the possible complications of this and also to help the patient feel better and, in many cases, to relieve headaches or other symptoms. There are indications that pulmonary changes established by the age of 1 to 2 years are usually reversible, and, therefore, in general, a case can be made for closing a large defect causing symptoms in a Down's child of a year of age or younger but not for an older asymptomatic child with a similar defect. Again, secundum atrial septal defect remains a controversial area in terms of indication for surgical closure in normal children. These children are usually asymptomatic, and the potential gain would be a very long-term one. Therefore, for Down's children it would be problematical if recommendation for surgical closure of such a defect could be justified.

General management consists of attention to the nutrition of the infant, treatment of intercurrent respiratory infections, and administration of diuretics, digoxin and vasodilators for heart failure. The infant in heart failure, unable to suck, should be fed by a nasogastric tube at frequent intervals and extra calories added. Because upper airways obstruction and sleep apnoea favour the development of hypoxia and pulmonary hypertension, the infant or child should be positioned in such a way that the airways are as little obstructed as possible. This is often in the prone position, with the head turned to the side; there is individual variation, but the sitting position never appears satisfactory. Again, in this regard, expert ear, nose and throat advice should be sought in the management of the child. General support of the cyanotic child is less demanding. Because of the high haematocrit and high viscosity of the blood, the child should be kept well hydrated at all times, and fluid should always be encouraged at times of fever. In the case of blue spells, the parents should be instructed to put the child in the squatting position, and to give him fresh air and comfort him. Urgent medical help should be sought. For a persisting blue spell the child should be given sodium bicarbonate intravenously to counteract the acidity of the blood, and, if necessary, intravenous propranolol can be injected to relieve the right ventricular outflow tract shut-down. Sometimes, maintenance oral propranolol is effective in preventing further attacks, but a shunt procedure or surgical correction is often necessary. More general measures consist of avoiding hot baths and prompt treatment of fevers with salycylates and/or antibiotics because vasodilators decrease the systemic resistance and minimise blood flow.

The Down's child with a minor cardiac defect needs no special management other than prophylactic antibiotics to cover dental extractions and other surgical procedures. A single large dose of amoxycillin is now recommended 1–2 hours before the procedure.

The question of exercise is often raised by the parents of Down's and non-Down's children, paramedical workers and school medical officers. Basically, each child learns his own limits, and this approach is a more effective guideline than any other. However, only very rarely is exercise dangerous for a child with a heart defect, and, if such a situation exists, as in severe aortic stenosis, the treatment is surgical relief. It is rare, then, for a Down's child to have a cardiac defect in which exercise could prove dangerous. The majority of Down's children are not well motivated towards athletic prowess, partly because of hypotonia and reduced muscle strength (Morris *et al.*, 1982), and thus the question of effort tolerance is usually discussed at a lower level than in the general population. When there are major symptoms on exercise, clearly the whole question of possible surgical management has to be considered, but, in general, life can be very tolerable and free of frustration for a cardiac child with some exercise disability, provided his ambitions are not purely of a physical nature. Parents can be very helpful in this regard by encouraging the child in activities which he or she can learn to do well in relation to other children. With regard to the Down's infant, passive stimulation programmes are perfectly safe, but the infant or young child embarking on a more active and vigorous programme should ideally have a cardiological check-up before entering that programme in order to ascertain whether he or she has a major heart defect and whether the programme is suitable or should be modified in any way.

Finally, what results can be expected of cardiac surgery in Down's Syndrome? It was always supposed that Down's Syndrome added to the mortality and morbidity of cardiac surgery (Greenwood and Nadas, 1976), but Katlick *et al.* (1977), although confirming the high overall surgical mortality (38%) in Down's infants and children, did not find any obvious difference in these results and the results of comparable cardiac surgery in non-Down's children. In addition to their severe and complex malformation, pulmonary vascular disease arises early in those Down's children with large arterial/pulmonary shunts. Therefore, in order for corrective surgery to be effective, it has to be carried out in infancy, and, although general results in this age group are improving, we must still accept a mortality of at least 20% for closure of a complete atrioventricular canal in a child of under 2 years of age (Neufeld *et al.*, 1977; Berger *et al.*, 1978; Culpepper *et al.*, 1978; Stewart *et al.*, 1979). Ideally, many of these defects should be closed before the age of 1 year in Down's children, and, even in centres of excellence, we must still expect an overall mortality of 43% for all open-heart surgery carried out under the age of 3 months (Kirklin *et al.*, 1981). Moreover, the repair of a complete atrioventricular canal is one of the most complicated cardiac operations which can be attempted in young infants. It should also be emphasised that the anatomy of the atrioventricular canal can never be entirely elucidated before the heart is opened at surgery, and occasionally the defect is extremely difficult to deal with and could demand the insertion of an artificial valve. In addition, the electrical conducting tissue of the heart can be damaged and the remote but definite possibility of the infant needing a pacemaker must also be borne in mind. Again, the problems of major cardiac surgery are not entirely confined to the operating theatre, and the postoperative course can sometimes be very protracted and full of difficulties, thus posing an enormous strain on both patient and parents. The palliative operation of pulmonary artery banding, to cut down pulmonary blood flow, has been attempted in the atrioventricular canal, but is not a very satisfactory operation because of the large central communication in the heart and the strong possibility of increasing cyanosis and mitral incompetence. It is therefore not recommended for these babies except in isolated instances, but pulmonary artery banding can sometimes be effective for a large ventricular septal defect in a baby under 3 months who is in severe heart failure and unresponsive to medical treatment.

The most generally held current policy regarding surgical treatment for tetralogy of Fallot is to correct the defect fully after the age of 2 years, but under this age to recommend a shunt procedure between a systemic and pulmonary artery to increase the pulmonary blood flow. A second shunt operation on the other side can always be carried out, if necessary. Shunt procedures are generally recommended for Down's children with atrioventricular canal and tetralogy of Fallot because, so far, corrective surgery in this very complex anomaly has carried an unacceptable mortality for total correction.

Both life expectancy and quality of life for the Down's child have improved dramatically over the past 20 years. In 1958, 70% of all Down's children failed to survive the first 10 years and 63% died in the first year (Carter, 1958). From 1960 to 1980, mortality was reduced by 50–60% (Thase, 1982). Although cardiac defects affect prognosis adversely (see Fig. 3.1), it is a strong clinical impression that the situation has improved further since the last available published statistics. The improvement in survival and quality of life of the Down's child born with a cardiac defect is multifactorial. There is now a general realisation that a cardiac defect is common in Down's Syndrome and may be a major one and therefore an important factor in the overall management of the child. We have improved facilities for non-invasive investigation, to which the two-dimensional scan has recently made an outstanding contribution in the understanding of cardiac structure. Current development of pulser Doppler techniques should soon give reliable estimation of shunt through intracardiac defects and ductus. Non-invasive methods of measuring pulmonary and intracardiac pressure are not yet available, but it may be hoped that invasive methods of cardiac diagnosis will be superseded in the foreseeable future. With progressive improvement in the results of cardiac surgery in infancy, we are able to offer this possibility more often, when indicated, to the Down's child. Finally, we have a much more logical attitude towards interdisciplinary co-operation in the management of these challenging children and a much more reasoned and positive approach towards planning the management of their cardiological problems.

REFERENCES

Benda, C.E. (1949). *Mongolism and Cretinism*. New York: Grune and Swallow.

Berger, T.J., Kirklin, J.W., Blackstone, E.H., Pacifico, A.D. and Kouchoukas, N.T. (1978). Primary repair of complete atrioventricular canal in patients less than two years old. *Am. J. Cardiol.* **41**, 906.

Bharati, S. and Lev, M. (1973). The spectrum of common atrioventricular canal. *Circulation* **48**, 416.

Culpepper, W., Kolff, J., Lin, C.Y., Vitrillo, D., Lamberti, J., Arcilla, R.A. and Replogle, R. (1978). Complete common atrioventricular canal in infancy – surgical repair and postoperative hemodynamics. *Circulation* **58**, 550.

Carter, C.O. (1958). A life table for mongols with cause of death. *J. Ment. Def. Res.* **2**, 64.

Chi, T.P.L. and Krovetz, L.J. (1975). The pulmonary vascular bed in children with Down's syndrome. *J. Pediatr.* **86,** 533.

Cooney, T.P. and Thurlbeck, W.M. (1982). Pulmonary hypoplasia in Down's syndrome. *New Engl.J.Med.* **307,** 1170.

Fabia, J. and Drolette, M. (1970). Life tables up to age 10 for mongols with and without congenital heart defect. *J.Ment.Defic.Res.* **14,** 235.

Felman, A.H., Loughlin, G.M., Leftridge, C.A. and Cassisi, N.J. (1979). Upper airways obstruction during sleep in children. *Am.J.Roentgenol.* **133,** 213.

Gallagher, R.P. and Lowry, R.B. (1975). Longevity in Down's syndrome in British Columbia. *J.Ment.Defic.Res.* **19,** 157.

Garrod, A.E. (1894). On the association of cardiac malformations with other congenital defects. *St Bartholomew's Hosp. Rep.* **39,** 53.

Garrod, A.E. (1899). Cases illustrating the association of congenital heart disease with the mongolian form of idiocy. *Trans.Clin.Soc.Lond.* **32,** 6.

Greenwood, R.D. and Nadas, A.S. (1976). The clinical course of cardiac disease in Down's syndrome. *Pediatrics* **58,** 893.

Guilleminault, C., Eldridge, F.L., Simmons, F.B. and Dement, W.C. (1976). Sleep apnea in eight children. *Pediatrics* **58,** 28.

Hallidie-Smith, K.A. and Goodwin, J.F. (1974). The Eisenmenber syndrome. In Yu, P.N. and Goodwin, J.F. (eds), *Progress in Cardiology, Vol.* 3, p.211. Philadelphia: Lea and Febiger.

Hallidie-Smith, K.A., Wilson, R.S.E., Hart, A. and Zeidifard, E. (1977). Functional status of patients with large ventricular septal defect and pulmonary vascular disease 6–16 years after surgical closure of their defect in childhood. *Br.Heart J.* **39,** 1093.

Heath, D. and Edwards, J.E. (1958). The pathology of hypertensive pulmonary vascular disease. *Circulation* **18,** 533.

Katlick, R., Clark, E.B., Neill, C. and Haller, J.A. (1977). Surgical management of congenital heart disease in Down's syndrome. *J.Thorac.Cardiovasc.Surg.* **74,** 206.

Keith, J.D., Rowe, R.D. and Vlad, P. (1978). *Heart Disease in Infancy and Childhood,* 3rd edn. London: Macmillan.

Kirklin, J.K., Blackstone, E.H., Kirklin, J.W., McKay, R., Pacifico, A.D. and Bargeron, L.M. (1981). Intracardiac surgery in infants under age three months: predictors of post-operative in-hospital cardiac death. *Am. J. Cardiol.* **48,** 507.

Kobel, M., Creighton, R.E. and Steward, D.J. (1982). Anaesthetic considerations in Down's syndrome: experience with 100 patients and a review of the literature. *Can.Anaesth.Soc.J.* **29,** 593

Krovetz, L.J., Gessner, I.H. and Schlieber, G.L. (1969). *Handbook of Pediatric Cardiology.* New York: Harper and Row.

Langston, C.L. and Thurlbeck, W.M. (1982). Lung growth and development in late gestation and early post-natal life. *Perspec.Pediatr.Path.* **7,** 203.

Laursen, H.B. (1975). Congenital heart disease in Down's syndrome. *Br.Heart J.* **38,** 32.

Levy, A.M., Tabakin, B.A. and Hanson, J.S. (1967). Hypertrophied adenoids causing pulmonary hypertension and severe congestive heart failure. *New Engl.J.Med.* **277,** 506.

Loughlin, G.M., Wynne, J.W. and Victoria, B.E. (1981). Sleep apnoea as a possible cause of pulmonary hypertension in Down's syndrome. *J.Pediatr.* **98,** 435.

Menashe, V.D., Farrehi, C. and Miller, M. (1965). Hypoventilation and cor pulmonale due to chronic upper airways obstruction. *J.Pediatr.* **67,** 198.

Mitchell, S.C., Korenez, S.B. and Berendes, H.W. (1971). Congenital heart disease in 56,109 births. *Circulation,* **43,** 323.

Morris, A.F., Vaughan, S.E. and Vaccard, P. (1982). Measurements of neuromuscular tone and strength in Down's syndrome children. *J.Ment.Defic.Res.* **26,** 41.

Mulcahy, M.T. (1979). Down's syndrome in Western Australia; mortality and survival. *Clin.Genet.* **16,** 103.

Murdoch, J.C., Rodger, J.C., Rao, S.S., Fletcher, C.D. and Dunnigan, M.G. (1977). Down's syndrome; an atheroma free model? *Br.Med.J.* **ii,** 226.

Neufeld, E.A., Sher, M., Paul, M.H. and Nikaidoh, H. (1977). Pulmonary vascular disease in complete atrioventricular canal. *Am.J.Cardiol.* **39,** 721.

Plett, J.A., Tandon, R. and Muller, J.H. (1974). Hypertensive pulmonary vascular disease. *Arch.Path.* **97,** 187.

Richards, B.W. and Enver, F. (1979). Blood pressure in Down's syndrome. *J.Ment. Defic.Res.* **23,** 123.

Richards, M.R., Merritt, K.K., Samules, M.H. and Lanmann, A.G. (1955). Congenital malformations of the cardiovascular system in a series of 6,053 infants. *Pediatrics* **15,** 12.

Rodriguez de la Nuez, A.L., Sanchez Dominguez, T. and Villa-Alizaga Subira, M.L. (1981). Down's syndrome and immune function. *Am.J.Dis.Child.* **135,** 251.

Rosengart, R.M. and Isabel-Jones, J.B. (1976). Pulmonary vascular involvement in Down's syndrome. *J.Pediatr.* **88,** 161.

Rosenquist, G.C., Sweeney, L.J. and McAllister, H.A. (1975). Relationships of the tricuspid valve to the membranous ventricular septum in Down's syndrome with endocardial cushion defect: study of 28 specimens, 14 with ventricular septal defects. *Am.Heart J.* **90,** 458.

Rowe, R.D. and Uchida, I.H. (1960). Congenital cardiac malformations in mongolism. *Br.Heart J.* **22,** 331.

Rowland, T.W., Nordstrom, L.G., Bearn, M.S. and Burkhardt, H. (1981). Chronic upper airways obstruction and pulmonary hypertension in Down's syndrome. *Am.J.Dis.Child.* **135,** 1050.

Shaher, R.M., Farina, M.A., Porter, I.H. and Bishop, M. (1972). Clinical aspects of congenital heart disease in mongolism. *Am.J.Cardiol.* **29,** 497.

Somerville, J. (1971). Atrioventricular defects. *Mod.Concepts Cardiovasc.Dis.* **40,** 33.

Soudon, P., Stijus, M., Tremoraux-Watticz, M. and Vliers, A. (1975). Precocity of pulmonary vascular obstruction in Down's syndrome. *Eur. J. Cardiol.* **2,** 473.

Spina, C.A., Smith D., Korn, E., Fahey, J.L. and Grossman, H.J. (1981). Altered cellular immune functions in patients with Down's syndrome. *Am.J.Dis.Child.* **135,** 251.

Stewart, D.J. (1970). Congenital abnormalities as a possible factor in the aetiology of post-intubation subglottic stenosis. *Can.Anaes.Soc.J.* **17,** 388.

Stewart, S., Harris, P. and Manning, J. (1979). Complete endocardial cushion defect. Operation technique and result. *J.Thorac.Cardiovasc.Surg.* **78,** 914.

Tandon, R. and Edwards, J.E. (1973). Cardiac malformations associated with Down's syndrome. *Circulation* **47.** 1349.

Tenckhoff, L. and Stamms, J. (1973). Analysis of 35 cases of the complete form of persistent atrioventricular canal. *Circulation* **48,** 416.

Thase, M.E. (1982). Longevity and mortality in Down's syndrome. *J.Ment.Defic.Res.* **26,** 177.

Wilson, S.K., Hutchins, G.M. and Neill, C.A. (1979). Hypertensive pulmonary vascular disease in Down's syndrome. *Pediatrics* **95,** 722.

4 Dentition and Other Aspects of Growth and Development

Howard S. Barden

Chromosomal abnormalities often have profound effects on physical development. Down's Syndrome is the most well known and studied example of the severe growth and developmental abnormalities associated with an extra chromosome. Growth and development of hard tissues in Down's Syndrome are characterised by a generalised retardation in growth and increased variability of measurable characteristics (Barden, 1983). This chapter examines various aspects of growth and development of the dentition (teeth) in Down's Syndrome and compares dental development with other components of skeletal growth and development.

TOOTH SIZE

Tooth size is generally believed to be abnormally small in Down's Syndrome. Early estimates of the percentage of Down's individuals with small teeth (microdontia) ranged from 24% to 53% (Spitzer and Mann, 1950; Levinson et al., 1955; Spitzer and Robinson, 1955; Spitzer and Quilliam, 1958; Spitzer et al., 1961). Many of these studies were based on visual inspections rather than on quantitative measurements.

Cohen and Winer (1965) presented one of the first quantitative demonstrations of the reduction in tooth size in Down's Syndrome. In a study of 13 subjects, all permanent teeth were reported to be smaller than those obtained from a normal control sample. Teeth in the maxillary (upper) arch were generally more affected than corresponding teeth in the mandibular (lower) arch.

Garn and associates (1971) reported that the average reduction in size (crown size) of all permanent teeth was 8.8%, with the reduction in male dentition (8%) somewhat less than that observed in the female dentition (10%). Maxillary second molars, lateral incisors, and canines were the most reduced in size. In general, the most posterior (distal) tooth in a morphological tooth group was reduced to the greatest extent. For example, maxillary first molars in females were reduced 3.7%, compared to a 21.1% reduction for maxillary second molars (Garn et al., 1971). Subsequent studies confirmed the finding of microdontia of the permanent dentition in Down's Syndrome (Cohen et al., 1970; Geciauskas and Cohen, 1970; Jensen et al., 1973; Prahl-Andersen and Oerlemans, 1976; Barden, 1980a).

71

The degree of reduction in tooth size (8.8%) was much less than the 14% to 16% reduction in body size recorded for Down's subjects (Garn *et al.*, 1971). Garn and associates suggested that this difference in magnitude of reduction indicated a smaller overall reduction in dental development than skeletal development. These findings agreed with similar results concerning skeletal maturation and eruption of the dentition in Down's Syndrome (Garn, Stimson and Lewis, 1970; see below).

Although several studies have indicated that tooth size is also reduced in the deciduous (primary) dentition in Down's Syndrome, few studies based this assessment on quantitative determinations. Jensen *et al.* (1973) reported that canines and first molar teeth were reduced from 2.2% to 7.3%.

Barden (1980a) compared deciduous canine and molar measurements of 114 Down's subjects with a large sample of normal subjects and reported that tooth sizes (crown size) of the deciduous canines and first molar teeth were significantly larger than normal. Deciduous first molar teeth were approximately 10% larger in the maxillary dentition and 1–4% larger in the mandibular dentition. Deciduous canines were approximately 4% larger than in the normal sample.

Alexandersen (1969) independently measured nearly two-thirds of the Down's Syndrome dentitions utilised by Barden (1980a) and compared these measurements with those from another sample of normal subjects. Alexandersen's findings of increased tooth size for the first molar and deciduous canine agreed with those of Barden. In addition, Alexandersen obtained a satisfactory sample of deciduous incisor measurements and reported larger than normal tooth sizes for both the central and lateral incisors. Both Barden and Alexandersen reported that the diameter of the deciduous second molar did not significantly differ from normal. More studies of the deciduous dentition in Down's Syndrome are needed to confirm these unexpected results. Larger than normal deciduous teeth may indicate that Down's Syndrome subjects experience a transitory acceleration in growth of developing dental structures during the early period of gestation, when formation of the deciduous dentition occurs (8–18 weeks of gestation). This transitory acceleration would then be followed by the more generally recognised retardation in growth that is apparent in the permanent dentition and in other characteristics of physical development in the syndrome (Barden, 1980a, 1983).

TOOTH MORPHOLOGY

Abnormalities in tooth shape (morphology) are common in Down's Syndrome subjects. Several studies of mentally retarded subjects have noted that morphological abnormalities are especially frequent in those with the syndrome (Spitzer and Mann, 1950; Kraus *et al.*, 1967, 1968). Kraus and associates (1967) reported that individual Down's subjects averaged more than seven abnormal teeth. Retarded subjects with disorders other than Down's Syndrome averaged only 2.5 abnormal teeth. Thirty-four per cent of all teeth examined in Down's subjects exhibited abnormalities of morphology (McMillan and Kashgarian, 1961; Kraus *et al.*, 1967).

Several studies have given detailed descriptions of the many morphological abnormalities present in the dentition in Down's subjects (Kraus *et al.*, 1967, 1968;

Cohen *et al.,* 1970; Shapiro, 1970). For example, deciduous incisors often exhibited underdevelopment of the two lateral mammelons (the three rounded prominences on the cutting edge of an incisor tooth). This deficiency results in a conical or peg-shaped appearance of the tooth. While peg-shaped incisors occurred in 0.5–3.2% of normal subjects (Grahnén, 1956; Das and Das, 1969), Shapiro (1970) reported that 15–40% of Down's subjects exhibited this trait. A second common abnormality was an exaggeration of the talonid (the posterior part, or heel, of a mandibular (lower) molar tooth). Thirty per cent of mandibular first molar teeth in Down's subjects and only 1.5% of this same tooth in control subjects displayed this abnormality.

The location of tooth shape abnormalities differs in Down's subjects, compared to normal subjects, in that dental abnormalities in the upper dentition (33%) were shown to be only slightly more frequent than abnormalities in the lower dentition (29%) (Cohen *et al.,* 1970). In normal subjects, nearly all irregular teeth appeared in the upper dentition. For Down's subjects, the most frequently affected permanent teeth in the upper dentition were second molars (52%), lateral incisors (42%), canines (41%), first molars (40%) and central incisors (35%). The first and second premolars were the least affected teeth (9% and 11%) in the upper dentition, but the most frequently affected teeth in the lower dentition (63% and 48%) (Cohen *et al.,* 1970).

MISSING TEETH

Congenitally missing teeth – a condition known as dental agenesis – occurs among Down's and normal subjects, and reflects the absence of normal tooth development due to hereditary or environmental influences during the early stages of gestation. The reported incidence of dental agenesis varies considerably for both Down's and normal subjects. Differences in reported frequencies of absent teeth reflect the difficulty frequently encountered in determining whether a tooth is congenitally missing, or whether it is merely delayed in eruption, or missing due to trauma or extraction. Errors in diagnosis generally result in overestimates of the incidence of dental agenesis. Radiographs of the dentition and complete, accurate dental histories are necessary to determine accurately whether a tooth is congenitally missing. Because of the relatively high frequency of agenesis of the third molar in normal subjects, this tooth will be excluded from the following discussion.

In general, congenitally missing teeth are relatively uncommon in normal subjects. Reported frequencies of missing teeth range from less than 1% to nearly 9% (Grahnén, 1956). However, agenesis of deciduous teeth occurs considerably less frequently than agenesis of permanent teeth. Barkla (1963) reported that only 2 of 170 normal subjects had congenitally missing deciduous teeth; in each case the lateral incisor was absent. Grahnén and Granath (1961) reported that 0.4% of normal subjects aged 3 to 5 years exhibited missing deciduous teeth.

Congenital absence of permanent teeth has been reported by several researchers. In perhaps the best reported study, Orner (1971) noted that 8% of the normal brothers and sisters of Down's subjects exhibited one or more congenitally missing permanent teeth – most often the mandibular second premolars. Other frequently missing teeth were mandibular central incisors, maxillary second premolars, and mandibular central incisors. Canines and first and second molar teeth were generally not affected in normal subjects.

Dental agenesis of both deciduous and permanent teeth occurs at a much higher frequency among subjects with Down's Syndrome, compared to normal individuals. Barkla (1963) reported that 12% of 122 Down's subjects had one or more congenitally missing deciduous teeth – a tenfold increase over the frequency (1.1%) noted by these investigators for normal subjects. McMillan and Kashgarian (1961) reported that 16.7% of Down's subjects had congenitally missing deciduous teeth, and approximately 50% of Down's subjects were reported to have one or more permanent teeth missing (McMillan and Kashgarian, 1961; Orner, 1971). Among the 174 Down's subjects studied by McMillan and Kashgarian, 35% had congenitally missing deciduous or permanent teeth. Only 6.8% of other institutionalised subjects exhibited this abnormality. Thus, dental agenesis is particularly characteristic of Down's subjects.

The most frequently missing teeth in Down's subjects are lateral incisors. Roche and Barkla (1967) noted that nearly 5% of all deciduous lateral incisors were congenitally missing. McMillan and Kashgarian (1961) reported that 50% of 80 Down's subjects had at least one missing lateral incisor. Brown and Cunningham (1961) found an absence of both maxillary lateral incisors in 43% of 16 Down's subjects aged 8 to 13 years, and Cohen and Winer (1965) reported that 34% of Down's subjects had missing lateral incisors. Orner (1971) reported that the maxillary lateral incisor accounted for 31% of all absent teeth in the permanent dentition. Other teeth with high frequencies of agenesis were mandibular second premolars (26%), maxillary second premolars (18%), mandibular lateral incisors (12%) and mandibular central incisors (7%) (Orner, 1971).

A common finding is that within each morphological tooth group (i.e. incisors, premolars, or molars) the more posterior (distal) tooth is more frequently missing than the more anterior (mesial) tooth. This finding is in general agreement with Butler's (1939) field concept suggesting that a morphogenetic gradient of influence exists over various aspects of tooth development. Within each morphological tooth group, the most distal tooth was predicted to be the least developmentally stable. For example, in Orner's study, the maxillary lateral incisor (distal tooth in upper incisor tooth group) was missing 25% of the time, compared to less than 1% absence for the maxillary central incisor. The maxillary second premolar (distal tooth in the premolar group) was missing 14% of the time, compared to less than 1% for the maxillary first premolar. As in normal subjects, agenesis of the molar and canine teeth was rare in Down's Syndrome. A similar pattern of agenesis was reported for the mandibular dentition (Orner, 1971).

The genetic basis for missing teeth is complex and not well understood (Schulze, 1970; Suarez and Spence, 1974). Missing teeth have been associated with features of normal development (Krogman, 1967), specifically with alterations in size, shape, and timing of developmental events of the remaining teeth, and with reduced body size and increased frequency of prematurity (Garn *et al.*, 1961, 1963, 1964; Keene, 1966; Garn and Lewis, 1970). Third molar agenesis among normal subjects was associated with delayed tooth formation and eruption, especially for the most distal and least developmentally stable tooth within each morphological tooth group. Hypoplastic, or peg-shaped, lateral incisors were particularly common among normal subjects with third molar agenesis. These features were associated with dental agenesis at a substantially increased frequency in Down's subjects.

PERIDONTAL DISEASE AND DENTAL CARIES

Several early investigators of Down's Syndrome reported that peridontal disease was very prevalent among Down's subjects (Brousseau, 1928; Benda, 1949). Peridontal disease has been reported to begin to appear before the age of 5, and by adulthood nearly all Down's individuals were affected (Brown and Cunningham, 1961; Cohen *et al.*, 1961; Miller and Ship, 1977; Saxén and Aula, 1982). The bone loss which accompanies peridontal disease inevitably leads to serious dental problems in Down's individuals. Orner (1976) studied Down's children and their sibs and reported that the prevalence and severity of peridontal disease were three times greater in the former. Marginal gingivitis, alveolar bone loss, and loosening and loss of the lower central incisors were particularly prevalent (Cohen *et al.*, 1961).

Saxén and Aula (1982) compared the incidence of peridontal disease in Down's subjects with an age-matched control population of mentally retarded subjects in the same institution and reported that severe peridontal disease was present in nearly all Down's subjects below the age of 10 years. However, only half of the non-Down's retarded subjects had the disease. Because oral hygiene in both groups was the same, the increased incidence of peridontal disease in Down's Syndrome was attributed to unknown factors related to the chromosomal disorder itself. Decreased resistance to the bacteria that accumulate in the gingival margin may be one contributing factor (Saxén and Aula, 1982).

The incidence of dental caries has frequently been reported as lower in Down's Syndrome (Brown and Cunningham, 1961; Cohen and Winer, 1965). However, Kroll *et al.* (1970) utilised radiographs of the dentition and reported that the incidence of dental caries in Down's Syndrome was not significantly lower than in non-Down's subjects. Twelve per cent of Down's subjects were caries free, compared to 8.3% in the non-Down's group.

TOOTH ERUPTION

Investigations of growth are frequently based on various assessments of an individual's overall developmental maturity. Because individuals develop at different rates, chronological age is often a poor indicator of developmental maturity. Different parts of the body also develop and mature at different rates. Although the developmental sequence of maturational events is generally quite precise among normal individuals, the timing of these events demonstrates a substantial amount of individual variability. Each individual's timetable of development is under considerable genetic control. The timing of the eruption of the dentition is one indicator of the rate of overall maturity of the body.

Reports of dental eruption in Down's Syndrome have generally indicated that eruption is delayed in both deciduous and permanent dentitions. (Spitzer and Robinson, 1955; Spitzer and Quilliam, 1958; Silimbani, 1962; Cohen and Winer, 1965). The deciduous central incisors are the first teeth that erupt in normal subjects – at 6–7 months of age. Oster (1953) reported that initial eruption occurred at or before 6 months of age in only 7% of Down's subjects studied. Brousseau (1928) noted that initiation of eruption of deciduous dentition rarely occurred before the ninth month and was often delayed until after the third or fourth year. However, a carefully controlled study of deciduous eruption noted that the first deciduous tooth erupted between 8.5 and 13.9 months for Down's subjects and between 4.5 and 15.5 months for normal subjects (Roche and Barkla, 1964). The earliest point at which all deciduous teeth had erupted was 30.7 months in Down's subjects and 23.4 months in normal subjects. These differences in time of eruption were significant for all teeth except maxillary first molars and mandibular first and second molars.

Variation in age of eruption was also much greater for Down's subjects than for normal subjects (Spitzer and Robinson, 1955; Roche and Barkla, 1964; Barkla, 1966a, 1966b). Moreover, considerable irregularity in the normally precise sequence of eruption of teeth has also been reported in Down's Syndrome (Brousseau, 1928; Levinson *et al.*, 1955; Roche and Barkla, 1964, 1967).

Lastly, the eruption of the permanent dentition is retarded in Down's Syndrome (Barkla, 1966a; Orner, 1973). Maxillary lateral incisors, canines, and second premolars and mandibular second molars were delayed to the greatest extent (Orner, 1973). Despite this delay, Orner noted that Down's subjects resembled their normal sibs in several general characteristics of eruption, including: earlier eruption of teeth in the mandibular arch; and earlier eruption of each tooth in females compared to males.

SKELETAL MATURATION

Another index of maturity that is frequently used in studies of growth is that of skeletal maturation or bone age (Barden, 1979). Assessment of bone age or rate of skeletal maturation is based upon the finding that many bones progress through a series of precise stages that can be detected with x-rays. These stages include the initial appearance, subsequent morphological changes, and, ultimately, fusion or joining together of primary and secondary centres of bone formation (ossification). As in dentition, the sequential pattern of the initial appearance and subsequent changes leading to maturity generally shows only slight variability among normal individuals. However, the timing of these sequential events varies considerably among individuals and this variation reflects differences in their developmental maturity. Individuals of the same chronological age may differ substantially in their progress toward maturity. Skeletal age assessments are thus very useful in determining maturational age.

Skeletal maturation in Down's Syndrome has been the subject of many investigations and numerous conflicting reports, which have indicated that it is either advanced (Bligh, 1910; Benda, 1939; Caffey and Ross, 1958; Pozsonyi and Zarfas, 1963) or normal (Hefke, 1940; Engler, 1949; Oster, 1953). Methodological problems contributing to these disagreements have been considered elsewhere (Barden, 1983).

Careful studies have concluded that Down's subjects exhibit a general delay in skeletal maturation during at least part of their childhood years. Roche (1967) reported that at all chronological ages, from birth to adulthood, levels of skeletal maturation were below normal mean values. However, retardation in skeletal maturation occurred mainly during the prenatal period and during the first few years of life. From the age of about 3 to 11 years, the mean rate of skeletal maturation was frequently more rapid than normal.

Several others have reported early delays in skeletal maturation, Pozsonyi *et al.* (1964) reporting a delay until 8 years of age. Thereafter, skeletal maturity was often somewhat advanced over the theoretical norm until the termination of growth at about 15 years of age. The greatest delay in bone age was noted for subjects between the ages of 2 weeks and 4 years. Rarick and associates (1964, 1965) conducted longitudinal studies of Down's subjects ranging in age from 7 to 12 years. Each subject was followed for 4 consecutive years. Skeletal age was retarded by nearly 3 years for subjects aged 7 to 9 years. However, by the age of 12 to 14 years these same subjects were only 1 year behind normal. This finding indicated a period of accelerated skeletal maturation. Despite this acceleration, 67% of boys and 72% of girls were significantly below the normal mean for skeletal maturation at each age studied.

Rundle *et al.* (1972) also reported that 8 years of age marked a change in rate of skeletal maturation. They suggested that this point of intersection between a delayed phase and a more rapid phase of growth represented a time of dramatic change in the growth process of Down's subjects – a change that has also been noted for growth in stature (Rarick *et al.*, 1966; Rarick and Seefeldt, 1974); of the tibia (Rarick *et al.*, 1966); and of the small bones of the hand (Chumlea *et al.*, 1979). However, Rundle cautioned that part of the proposed difference in the rate of skeletal maturation between subjects younger than 8 years and those older may have resulted from a factor referred to as age-associated mortality. Because older Down's subjects are, in a sense, survivors of a larger original population of Down's children, they may in some ways be more normal than those that did not survive. Thus, an acceleration toward normality with increasing age might be expected in studies that do not rely totally on longitudinal data. Roche (1967) did not believe that the observed difference between younger and older Down's children could be attributed to age-associated mortality. However, no other explanation for the apparent mid-childhood change in growth in Down's Syndrome has so far been forthcoming.

STATURE

Skeletal growth, like skeletal maturation, is most severely retarded during the early years of childhood in Down's Syndrome, and several cross-sectional studies have proven useful in attempts to characterise the pattern found (Brousseau, 1928; Benda, 1939, 1949; Oster, 1953; Roche, 1965). Roche (1967) has simplified comparisons among these studies by calculating standard deviations from normal values for the measurements reported in each study. Despite obvious differences in the degree of statural reduction, the comparison of the four studies revealed considerable agreement in the pattern of the rate of growth in stature.

Benda's (1949) study may be taken as representative of the pattern of growth revealed by these cross-sectional studies. He reported that between the ages of 2 and 6 years and between 12 years and adulthood, Down's subjects experienced retarded growth. Accelerated growth was observed between birth and 2 years of age and between 6 and 10 years of age. However, at no time during growth was the deviation from normal levels of growth not significant (Roche, 1967). Despite periods of accelerated growth, levels of deviation of stature were greater at adulthood than at birth, an indication that there was a general trend toward increased levels of retardation throughout the postnatal period (Roche, 1965, 1967; Thelander and Pryor, 1966).

Longitudinal studies of growth in Down's Syndrome generally confirm the above findings. A study of subjects from birth to 4 years (Ikeda *et al.*, 1977) confirmed that Down's subjects were retarded in stature at all ages and that a considerable decline in growth rate occurred at approximately 2 years of age. Ikeda and associates concluded that the short stature associated with Down's Syndrome resulted from the severe reduction in growth that occurred during the first few years of life. A study of Down's children from birth to 3 years similarly concluded that much of the deficiency of size in adult Down's subjects could be attributed to deficits in velocity of growth during early childhood (Cronk, 1978).

Longitudinal data for statural growth of Down's subjects aged 6 years and older have been presented by Rarick *et al.* (1966) and Rarick and Seefeldt (1974). These studies are particularly important for their contribution of knowledge concerning growth during the years surrounding puberty. Sixty-eight Down's children aged 5 to 9 years were measured annually for 13 years. At all ages the mean for stature was more than two standard deviations below normal mean levels. However, the rate of growth during the pre-adolescent and adolescent years was not significantly different from normal. Although tibial lengths were well below normal for subjects aged 7 to 18 years, annual increments in growth from age 7 to the time of cessation of bone growth were within normal limits (Rarick *et al.*, 1965).

Growth factors related to sexual maturation and skeletal growth and maturation were associated in Down's Syndrome in a normal manner. The timing of the circumpubertal growth spurt followed the normal pattern for both males and females (Rarick *et al.*, 1966). Between the ages of 10 and 12 years, both normal and Down's females grew more rapidly than males; between the ages of 12 and 14 years, the growth rate of males of both groups exceeded that of females. Down's subjects who experienced early or late onset of fusion of the tibia also experienced the associated early or later development of the signs of puberty. Thus, difference in growth between Down's Syndrome and normal subjects during prepubertal and pubertal years was in the magnitude of growth, not in its form or pattern (Rarick *et al.*, 1975).

Further evidence has been presented that sexual development and maturation in Down's subjects parallel the findings on skeletal growth and maturation noted above. Rundle *et al.* (1959) studied testicular volume and excretion of 17-ketosteroids in Down's males and reported that, although measures were reduced, the overall pubertal spurt was similar to that experienced by normal subjects. Down's females appeared to be somewhat, but not excessively, delayed in age of menarche and pubic hair and breast development (Rundle, 1970). The combined evidence of skeletal maturation and sexual development clearly indicated that the growth processes responsible for the close relationship of puberty and skeletal growth and maturation in normal children (Tanner, 1962) were also present in Down's subjects.

Several studies have indicated that short stature in Down's Syndrome was mainly the result of growth retardation in the long bones of the leg, and a comparison of stature and sitting height (Rarick and Seefeldt, 1974) indicated that retardation in sitting height was not as great as that of stature. Sitting height measurements indicated that growth of the vertebral column was more nearly normal than growth of the long bones of the legs.

Rarick *et al.* (1964) and Roche (1966) have noted greater than normal variability in stature in Down's Syndrome. Cronk and Reed (1981) studied the degree of canalisation of linear growth in Down's and normal subjects and reported that the Down's group exhibited significantly greater than normal variability around the normal growth channel. Results were cautiously interpreted as being evidence for poor canalisation of growth in Down's Syndrome.

VARIABILITY AND AMPLIFIED DEVELOPMENTAL INSTABILITY

Numerous studies of Down's Syndrome have noted that increased variability of traits is one of the prominent characteristics of this syndrome. In the present review, increased variability has been noted for growth in stature (Roche, 1965; Rarick and Seefeldt, 1974), skeletal maturation (Rarick *et al.*, 1964; Roche, 1964, 1967), and various aspects of the dentition (Roche and Barkla, 1964; Barkla, 1966a, 1966b; Shapiro, 1970, 1975). Levinson *et al.* (1955) stated that there is a 'wide range of variability in every single physical and developmental characteristic of mongoloids as well as in the sum total of such characteristics in each individual case' (p. 52). In an excellent review of dental anomalies in Down's Syndrome and in later reports, Shapiro (1970, 1975, 1983) developed the worthwhile concept that many of the growth and developmental abnormalities associated with the syndrome were the result of the negative effect of chromosome imbalance on the stability of developmental pathways.

'Amplified developmental instability' is the term Shapiro has used to describe the effect that the condition of trisomy has on pathways of development in Down's Syndrome (Shapiro, 1975, 1983). Morphologic structures develop along specific developmental pathways or tracts (Waddington, 1942) that represent the outcome of co-adapted genic and chromosomal systems that have evolved because they produced phenotypes that were selected for during the evolutionary history of the species (Shapiro, 1970). Normal phenotypes are believed to be stabilised within certain limits by processes termed 'canalisation' (Waddington, 1942) or 'developmental homeostasis' (Lerner, 1954; Mayr, 1963). Theoretically, pathways of development and growth are buffered so that they are relatively unaffected by either genetic or environmental disturbances. Developmental pathways are believed to differ in their stability in relation to the degree of their canalisation (Bader, 1965; Shapiro, 1970). In other words, some traits may be more influenced by genetic or environmental disturbances than others. These would be the least developmentally stable traits. The chromosomal imbalance caused by the trisomy of the 21st chromosome in Down's Syndrome may upset the evolved genic and chromosomal systems and cause amplified developmental instability (Shapiro, 1975, 1983).

Shapiro (1975) contended that Down's subjects, because of their chromosomal imbalance, should exhibit amplified developmental instability in those traits that have increased variability, and thus reduced developmental stability, in normal subjects. This concept was supported with studies of dental morphology (Shapiro, 1970), palate (Shapiro *et al.,* 1967; Shapiro, 1975), and dermatoglyphics (Shapiro, 1975), which demonstrated an increased phenotypic variability in Down's subjects. Importantly, those traits most variable and theoretically least developmentally stable in normal subjects were disproportionately more variable in Down's subjects than more stable traits. Shapiro (1970) used the principles of Butler's (1939, 1963) morphogenetic field concept to indicate which teeth should exhibit amplified developmental instability. As previously noted, Butler suggested that the most distal tooth within each morphological tooth group would be the least developmentally stable and the most likely to exhibit developmental abnormalities. The present review of dental abnormalities in Down's Syndrome, and the review by Shapiro (1970), generally support the concept of amplified development instability.

Dental asymmetry is another measure of developmental instability. It refers to differences in the size or shape of corresponding teeth within the same dental arch. Thus, differences in size or shape of the right and left maxillary central incisors would be a case of dental asymmetry. Because the genetic contribution to the development of both sides of bilaterally symmetrical traits is assumed to be identical, the magnitude of asymmetry is thought to be a measure of the relative success that developmental homoeostasis has in countering disturbances affecting the development of the structure in question.

Several studies have reported an increase in dental asymmetry in Down's Syndrome (Garn, Cohen and Geciauskas, 1970; Barden, 1980b). Barden's study indicated that dental asymmetry was not only increased, but that the degree of increase for Down's subjects over normal asymmetry values was often greater for the least developmentally stable tooth (distal) within a morphological tooth group. The maxillary lateral incisor, one of the least developmentally stable teeth in normal subjects (Lundstrom, 1960), had one of the largest deviations from normal values of asymmetry in Down's Syndrome. Conversely, the maxillary canine, the most stable tooth in the maxillary dentition (Osborne *et al.,* 1958), had no deviation from normal levels of asymmetry. These findings, then, also give support to the concept of amplified developmental instability in Down's Syndrome.

SUMMARY

Growth and development of hard tissues in Down's Syndrome are generally marked by retardation and increased phenotypic variability. Studies of tooth morphology, tooth size, dental agenesis, and dental asymmetry serve to illustrate the significant amount of abnormal development and increased variability associated with the dentition in the syndrome.

Growth of stature in Down's Syndrome was found to be retarded at birth and continued to be substantially below normal throughout life. The mean rate of statural growth varied with age and appeared to be particularly retarded between the ages of 2 and 6 years. Retardation in skeletal maturation was most evident during the first 6 to 8 years of life. After this initial period of severe retardation, skeletal maturation and rate of statural growth during the pre-adolescent and adolescent years were more nearly normal.

Studies of the dentition indicated that reduction in tooth size and delays in eruption were considerably less than the reported reduction in stature and the delay noted for skeletal maturation. Increased variability in rates of skeletal maturation and ages of dental eruption was also particularly noted. Studies of the dentition supported the concept that many of the growth and development abnormalities associated with Down's Syndrome result from the negative effect that the chromosomal imbalance has on the stability of developmental pathways.

REFERENCES

Alexandersen, V. (1969). The odontological variation of the deciduous and permanent teeth in Down's syndrome. Msc thesis. University of Wisconsin, Madison.

Bader, R.E. (1965). Fluctuating asymmetry in the dentition of the house mouse. *Growth* **29**, 291–300.

Barden, H.S. (1979). Human growth. In Bennett, K.A. (ed.), *Fundamentals of Biological Anthropology*, pp. 420–55. Dubuque: William C. Brown.

Barden, H.S. (1980a). Mesiodistal crown size dimensions of permanent and deciduous teeth in Down Syndrome. *Hum. Biol.* **52**, 247–53.

Barden, H.S. (1980b). Fluctuating dental asymmetry: a measure of developmental instability in Down syndrome. *Am. J. Phys. Anthropol.* **52**, 169–73.

Barden, H.S. (1983). Growth and development of selected hard tissues in Down syndrome. *Hum. Biol.* **55**(3), 539–76.

Barkla, D.H. (1963). Congenital absence and fusion in the deciduous dentition in mongols. *J. Ment. Defic. Res.* **7**, 102–106.

Barkla, D.H. (1966a). Ages of eruption of permanent teeth in mongols. *J. Ment. Defic. Res.* **10**, 190–97.

Barkla, D.H. (1966b). Congenital absence of permanent teeth in mongols. *J. Ment. Defic. Res.* **10**, 198–203.

Benda, C.E. (1939). Studies in mongolism. I Growth and physical development. *Arch. Neurol. Psych.* **41**, 83–96.

Benda, C.E. (1949). *Mongolism and cretinism.* New York: Grune and Stratton.

Bligh, J.M. (1910). Mongolianism. *Liverpool MedicoChir. J.* **30**, 340–46.

Brousseau, K. (1928). *Mongolism. A Study of the Physical and Mental Characteristics of Mongolian Imbeciles.* Baltimore: Williams and Wilkins.

Brown, R.H. and Cunningham, W.M. (1961). Some dental manifestations of mongolism. *Oral Surg.* **14**, 664–76.

Butler, P.M.(1939). Studies of the mammalian dentition. Differentiation of the post-canine dentition. *Proc. Zoo. Soc. (Lond.)* (B) **109**, 1–36.
Butler, P.M. (1963). Tooth morphology and primate evolution. In Brothwell, D.R. (ed.), *Dental Anthropology*, Vol. V, pp. 1–14. Symposia of Society for Study of Human Biology. London: Macmillan.
Caffey, J. and Ross, S. (1958). Pelvic bones in infantile mongoloidism – roentgenographic features. *Am. J. Roentgenol.* **80**, 458–67.
Chumlea, W.C., Malina, R.M., Rarick, G.L. and Seefeldt, V.D. (1979). Growth of short bones of the hand in children with Down's syndrome. *J. Ment. Defic. Res.* **23**, 137–50.
Cohen, M.M., Blitzer, F.J., Arvystas, M.G. and Bonneau, R.H. (1970). Abnormalities of the permanent dentition in trisomy G. *J. Dent. Res.* **49**, 1386–93.
Cohen, M.M. and Winer, R.A. (1965). Dental and facial characteristics in Down's syndrome (mongolism). *J. Dent. Res.* **44** (part 2, suppl.), 197–208.
Cohen, M.M., Winer, R.A., Schwartz, S.I. and Sklar, G. (1961). Oral aspects of mongolism. Part 1. Peridontal disease in mongolism. *Oral Surg.* **14**, 92–107.
Cronk, C.E. (1978). Growth of children with Down syndrome: birth to age 3 years. *Pediatrics* **61**, 564–8.
Cronk, C.E. and Reed, R.B. (1981). Canalization of growth in Down syndrome children three months to six years. *Hum. Biol.* **53**, 382–98.
Das, A.K. and Das, S. (1969). Variability of the permanent maxillary lateral incisors. *J. Ind. Dent. Assoc.* **41**, 89–91.
Engler, M. (1949). *Mongolism*. Bristol: John Wright.
Garn, S.M., Cohen, M.M., Gall, J.C. and Nagy, J. (1971). Relative magnitudes of crown size reduction and body size reduction in 47-trisomy G. *J. Dent. Res.* **50**, 513.
Garn, S.M., Cohen, M.M. and Geciauskas, M.A. (1970). Increased crown-size asymmetry in trisomy G. *J. Dent. Res.* **49**, 465.
Garn, S.M. and Lewis, A.B. (1970). The gradient and the pattern of crown-size reduction in simple hypodontia. *Angle Orthodont.* **40**, 51–7.
Garn, S.M., Lewis, A.B. and Bonne, B. (1961). Third molar polymorphism and the timing of tooth formation. *Nature* **192**, 989.
Garn, S.M., Lewis, A.B. and Kerewisky, R.S. (1963). Third molar agenesis and size reduction of the remaining teeth. *Nature* **200**, 488–9.
Garn, S.M., Lewis, A.B. and Kerewsky, R.S. (1964). Third molar agenesis and variation in size of the remaining teeth. *Nature* **201**, 839.
Garn, S.M., Stimson, C.W. and Lewis, A.B. (1970). Magnitude of dental decay in trisomy G. *J. Dent. Res.* **49**, 640.
Geciauskas, M. and Cohen, M.M. (1970). Mesiodistal crown diameters of permanent teeth in Down's syndrome (mongolism). *Am. J. Ment. Defic.* **72**, 905–917.
Grahnén, H. (1956). Hypodontia in the permanent dentition, clinical and genetical investigation. *Odontol. Rev.* **7**(suppl. to No. 3), 1–100.
Grahnén, H. and Granath, L.E. (1961). Numerical variations in primary dentition and their correlation with the permanent dentition. *Odontol. Rev.* **12**, 348–57.
Hefke, H.W. (1940). Roentgenologic study of anomalies of the hands in one hundred cases of mongolism. *Am. J. Dis. Child.* **60**, 1319–23.
Ikeda, Y., Higurashi, M. and Ishikawa, N. (1977). A longitudinal study on the growth of stature, lower limb and upper limb length in Japanese children with Down syndrome. *J. Ment. Defic. Res.* **21**, 139–51.
Jensen, G.M., Cleall, J.F. and Yip, A.S.G. (1973). Dentoalveolar morphology and developmental changes in Down syndrome (trisomy 21). *Am. J. Orthodontics* **64**, 607–618.
Keene, H.J. (1966). The relationship between maternal age and parity, birth weight and hypodontia in naval recruits. *J. Dent. Child.* **33**, 135–47.
Kraus, B., Clark, G.R. and Oka, S.W. (1968). Mental retardation and abnormalities of the dentition. *Am. J. Ment. Defic.* **72**, 905–917.

Kraus, B.B., Jordan, R.E., Nery, E.B. and Kaplan, S. (1967). Abnormalities of dental morphology in mentally retarded individuals; a preliminary report. *Am. J. Ment. Defic.* **71**, 828–39.

Krogman, W.M. (1967). The role of genetic factors in the human face, jaws, and teeth; a review. *Eugen. Rev.* **59**, 165–92.

Kroll, R.G., Budnick, J. and Kobren, A. (1970). Incidence of dental caries and peridontal disease in Down's syndrome. *N.Y. State Dent. J.* **36**, 151–6.

Lerner, I.M. (1954). *Genetic Homeostasis*. London: Oliver and Boyd.

Levinson, A., Friedman, A. and Stamps, F. (1955). Variability of mongolism. *Pediatrics* **16**, 43–53.

Lundstrom, A. (1960). Asymmetries in the number and size of the teeth and their aetiological significance. *Eur. Orthodontol. Soc. Trans.* **36**, 167–85.

McMillan, R.S. and Kashgarian, M. (1961). Relation of human abnormalities of structure and function to abnormalities of the dentition. II Mongolism. *Am. Dent. Assoc.* **63**, 368–73.

Mayr, E. (1963). *Animal Species and Evolution*. Cambridge, Mass.: Harvard University Press.

Miller, M.F. and Ship, I.I. (1977). Peridontal disease in the institutionalized mongoloid. *J. Oral Med.* **32**, 9.

Orner, G. (1971). Congenitally absent permanent teeth among mongols and their sibs. *J. Ment. Defic. Res.* **15**, 292–302.

Orner, G. (1973). Eruption of permanent teeth in mongoloid children and their sibs. *J. Dent. Res.* **52**, 1202–1206.

Orner, G. (1976). Peridontal disease among children with Down's syndrome and their siblings. *J. Dent. Res.* **55**, 778–82.

Osborne, R.H., Horowitz, S.L. and DeGeorge, F.V. (1958). Genetic variation in tooth dimensions. A twin study of the permanent anterior teeth. *Am. J. Hum. Genet.* **10**, 350–56.

Oster, J. (1953). *Mongolism, A Clinicogeniological Investigation Comparing 526 Mongols Living in Seeland and Neighboring Islands in Denmark*. Copenhagen: Danish Science Press.

Pozsonyi, J., Gibson, D. and Zarfas, D.E. (1964). Skeletal maturation in mongolism (Down's syndrome). *J. Ped.* **64**, 75–8.

Pozsonyi, J. and Zarfas, D.E. (1963). Skeletal age in subjects with mental retardation. *Can. Med. Assoc. J.* **83**, 1038–9.

Prahl-Andersen, B. and Oerlemans, J. (1976). Characteristics of permanent teeth in persons with trisomy G. *J. Dent. Res.* **55**, 633–8.

Rarick, G.L., Rapaport, I.F. and Seefeldt, V. (1964). Bone development in Down's disease. *Am. J. Dis. Childh.* **107**, 7–13.

Rarick, G.L., Rapaport, I.F. and Seefeldt, V. (1965). Age of appearance of ossification centres of the hand and wrist in children with Down's disease. *J. Ment. Defic. Res.* **9**, 24–30.

Rarick, G.L., Rapaport, I.F. and Seefeldt, V. (1966). Long bone growth in Down's syndrome. *Am. J. Dis. Child.* **112**, 566–71.

Rarick, G.L. and Seefeldt, V. (1974). Observations from longitudinal data on growth in stature and sitting height of children with Down's syndrome. *J. Ment. Defic. Res.* **18**, 63–78.

Rarick, G.L., Wainer, H., Thissen, D. and Seefeldt, V. (1975). A double logistic comparison of growth patterns of normal children and children with Down's syndrome. *Ann. Hum. Biol.* **2**, 339–46.

Roche, A.F. (1964). Skeletal maturation rates in mongolism. *Am. J. Roentgenol.* **91**, 979–87.

Roche, A.F. (1965). The stature of mongols. *J. Ment. Defic. Res.* **9**, 131–45.

Roche, A.F. (1966). The cranium in mongolism. *Acta Neurol. Scand.* **42**, 62–78.

Roche, A.F. (1967). Skeletal maturation and elongation in Down's disease (mongolism). *Eugen. Rev.* **59,** 11–21.

Roche, A.F. and Barkla, D.H. (1964). The eruption of deciduous teeth in mongols. *J. Ment. Defic. Res.* **8,** 56–64.

Roche, A.F. and Barkla, D.H. (1967). The development of the dentition in mongols. *Austral. Dent. J.* **12,** 12–16.

Rundle, A.T. (1970). Anthropometry: a ten-year survey of growth and sexual maturation. In Richards, B.W. (ed.), *Mental Subnormality; Modern Trends in Research,* pp. 68–135. London: Pitman Medical.

Rundle, A.T., Donoghue, E., Abbas, K.A. and Krstic, A. (1972). A catch-up phenomenon in skeletal development of children with Down's syndrome. *J. Ment. Defic. res.* **16,** 41–7.

Rundle, A.T., Dutton, E. and Gibson, J. (1959). Endocrinological aspects of mental deficiency. I. Testicular function in mongolism. *J. Ment. Defic. Res.* **3,** 108–115.

Saxén, L. and Aula, S. (1982). Peridontal bone loss in patients with Down's syndrome; a follow-up study. *J. Peridont.* **53,** 158–62.

Schulze, C. (1970). Developmental abnormalities of teeth and jaws. In Gorlin, R.J. and Goldman, H. (eds), *Thoma's Oral Pathology.* St Louis, Miss.: C.V. Mosby.

Shapiro, B.L. (1970). Prenatal dental anomalies in mongolism: comments on the basis and implications of variability. *Ann. N.Y. Acad. Sci.* **171,** 562–77.

Shapiro, B.L. (1975). Amplified developmental instability in Down's syndrome. *Ann. Hum. Genet.* **38,** 429–37.

Shapiro, B.L. (1983). Down syndrome – a disruption of homeostasis. *Am. J. Med. Genet.* **14,** 741–64.

Shapiro, B.L., Gorlin, R.J., Redman, R.S. and Bruhl, H.H. (1967). The palate and Down's syndrome. *New Engl. J. Med.* **276,** 1460–63.

Silimbani, C. (1962). Contribution to the study of dental anomalies in mongolian idiocy. *Panminerva Med.* **4,** 532–45.

Spitzer, R. and Mann, I. (1950). Congenital malformations in the teeth and eyes in mental defectives. *Br. J. Psych.* **96,** 681–709.

Spitzer, R. and Quilliam, R.L. (1958). Observations on congenital anomalies in teeth and skull in two groups of mental defectives (a comparative study). *Br. J. Radiol.* **31,** 596–604.

Spitzer R., Rabinowitch, J.Y. and Wybar, K.C. (1961). A study of the abnormalities of the skull, teeth and lenses in mongolism. *Can. Med. Assoc. J.* **84,** 567–72.

Spitzer, R. and Robinson, M.I. (1955). Radiological changes in teeth and skull in mental defectives. *Br. J. Radiol.* **28,** 117–27.

Suarez, B.K. and Spence, M.A. (1974). The genetics of hypodontia. *J. Dent. Res.* **53,** 781–5.

Tanner, J.M. (1962). *Growth at Adolescence.* Oxford: Blackwell Scientific.

Thelander, H.E. and Pryor, H.B. (1966). Abnormal patterns of growth and development in mongolism – an anthropometric study. *Clin. Ped.* **5,** 493–501.

Waddington, C.H. (1942). The canalization of development and the inheritance of acquired characteristics. *Nature* **150,** 563–5.

5 Hearing Problems

Bethan Davies

INTRODUCTION

Research in recent years has shown the need for all Down's children to have careful audiological evaluation, but the resources to provide such a service are as yet not widely available. Ironically, however, the easily identifiable stigmata of Down's Syndrome sometimes militate against adequate assessment of the needs of the Down's child. A non-Down's child presenting with problems of psychomotor delay, hypotonia, and delayed speech and language development will be seen to require careful assessment to make a medical diagnosis and to organise appropriate services for the child. The Down's child's needs are of course just as great, and yet a detailed assessment may not be carried out because the medical diagnosis is obvious.

There is now a considerable literature on the linguistic and phonological problems of Down's individuals, but it is only in recent years that attention has been turned to their auditory problems. Standard texts known to ENT surgeons and paediatricians often do not yet refer to the hearing problems so common in Down's individuals.

A rigorous search for auditory defects in all children who present with psychomotor delay is clearly essential if such defects are to be treated medically and/or educationally. A child with a severe learning problem and deafness will often have great difficulty in using compensatory strategies which may be used by children of normal intelligence. The possible interaction between auditory deficits and the well-known linguistic difficulties of Down's children remains to be explored in depth. However, it is clear from clinical experience that an improvement in auditory function achieved by surgical intervention or by the use of hearing aids can dramatically improve auditory attention, and can often greatly increase the rate of speech and language progress.

It is important to note the particularly severe synergistic effect of the combination of a visual and hearing problem in Down's children. Even in children of potentially normal intelligence, the combination of moderate undiagnosed vision and hearing impairment, especially if associated with hypotonia, can lead to a misdiagnosis of severe mental retardation. Such children may present with severe language retardation and disturbed behaviour. In a child with a severe learning problem, as may be the case with a Down's child, the additional presence of combined visual and hearing problems, even of moderate degree, may result in the

85

child appearing to be very much more severely retarded than is true. Occasionally such a child, once provided with corrective spectacles, hearing aids and appropriate management, may show quite remarkable improvement in all aspects of development, and especially in his linguistic progress and in his behaviour.

LITERATURE REVIEW

There is an extensive literature on the various aspects of Down's Syndrome, although literature on hearing loss in particular is very limited. In detailed medical overviews of the syndrome, including those of Breg (1977) and Smith and Berg (1976), there is usually very little information about hearing loss. However, a good deal of interest has been shown in the external ears in Down's Syndrome. The characteristically small pinnae lying flat against the head with an angular folded helix and a small ear lobe with stenosed meata have been widely described (see Fig. 5.1), and there are as many references in the literature to the abnormalities of the pinnae as there are to the nature of hearing loss in Down's individuals.

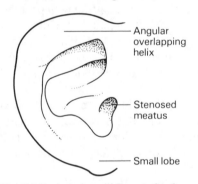

Fig. 5.1 Typical pinna in Down's Syndrome

The early literature on hearing in Down's Syndrome suggested widely disparate figures for the incidence of hearing loss, from as little as 8% to as much as 95%. The early studies of note are those of Rigrodsky *et al.* (1961), McIntire *et al.* (1965), and Glovsky (1966).

Fulton and Lloyd's study (1968) reported a 58% incidence of significant hearing loss, and, among those affected, they reported that 55% had conductive hearing losses, 23% sensorineural hearing losses, and 23% mixed hearing losses.

The first study of auditory function in Down's Syndrome using both pure tone audiometry and tympanometry was carried out by Brooks *et al.* (1972). This was a study of 100 Down's Syndrome individuals varying in age between 12 months and 59 years, who were matched for age and sex with non-Down's individuals. Both populations were in residential care because of mental retardation. To summarise Brooks' findings, he reported that in his Down's Syndrome group only 23% had normal hearing and normal middle ear function, compared with 74% in his control group. If one looked at middle ear function alone, then 60% of the Down's population were abnormal and only 17.5% of the control group.

There was a marked difference in the incidence of sensorineural hearing loss between the two groups, with 21% of the Down's individuals under 20 having a sensorineural hearing loss and 15% of the control group. However, in the individuals aged over 21, 55% of those with Down's Syndrome had a sensorineural hearing loss and only 10% of the controls. Brooks therefore concluded that a sensorineural hearing loss in Down's individuals may well be developing later in life and that the risk of developing such a loss is greater in Down's Syndrome than in retarded individuals without this condition.

Davies and Penniceard (1980) reported a comparison of middle ear function in a group of Down's children compared with normal controls and found 50% of the Down's children had normal tympanograms and 50% abnormal – Jerger type B or C (Jerger, 1970). The comparative figures for normal controls were 96% normal and 4% abnormal. In a further study 3 years later of the members of those Down's groups who were still at school, the tympanometric findings were remarkably consistent: i.e. 55% normal and 45% abnormal. In this case the children were matched with other severely retarded children without Down's Syndrome, and in these 100% of the tympanograms were normal.

So far as hearing levels were concerned, a significant difference was found between the hearing levels of the Down's children and the controls at all frequencies. After 3 years had elapsed there was no significant difference in the thresholds of the Down's children at 250 Hz, 500 Hz and 1 kHz, but there were significant differences at the 5% level at 4 kHz and 8 kHz. There was also a difference at 2 kHz in the expected direction, but the difference was not sufficient to reach statistical significance. It appeared, therefore, that there was evidence of an increasing high-frequency hearing loss in this group of children.

The study also reported on findings in Down's Syndrome children already attending audiology clinics for regular assessment. In a group comprising 73 ears, normal tympanograms were obtained in only 30% and abnormal in 70%. In this group of children, ranging in age from 12 months to 15 years, there was no significant change in the incidence of abnormal tympanograms throughout the age range. The clinic population had a higher incidence of middle ear dysfunction and a higher incidence of significant hearing loss than the school population. This is likely to be due to the fact that many of the clinic children had been specifically referred because of doubt about their auditory function. The commonest audiological findings were of a moderate mixed hearing loss with characteristic sensorineural involvement at 4 kHz and 8 kHz.

Schwartz and Schwartz (1978) reported a study of tympanometry in Down's children and found that 26% of the children had normal tympanograms and 63% abnormal. Balkany, Downs *et al.* (1979) reported a study of children and adults with Down's Syndrome in which 78% of ears showed a significant hearing loss. In 83% of cases, the loss was conductive; in 17%, sensorineural. The tympanograms in the study were classified by Jerger's method. Seventy-six per cent were abnormal and 24% normal.

In a study of a group of Down's and non-Down's retarded individuals, Nolan *et al.* (1980) reported the incidence of hearing loss in the Down's group as 69%, and middle ear dysfunction in 69%. In the non-Down's group, an incidence of hearing loss of 40% and of middle ear dysfunction of 15% was found. This study again confirms that the incidence of hearing impairment and middle ear dysfunction is much higher in Down's Syndrome individuals than in retarded ivdividuals without the syndrome. The English Picture Vocabulary Test (EPVT) was used to investigate receptive vocabulary and no significant correlation was found between the EPVT scores and hearing loss measured by pure tone audiometry in the non-Down's group. However, there was a correlation, significant at the 5% level, between EPVT scores and hearing levels in the Down's group.

Davies and Penniceard (1980) also used the EPVT to look at verbal receptive vocabulary in their Down's and non-Down's groups. They found no significant difference in mean quotient for the two groups, although they did point out that the two groups were not matched for intelligence. However, it is of note that when the EPVT scores on the first test were compared with scores achieved 3 years later by the Down's group, there was a mean change in the recognition quotient of minus 3 – a significant indicator of their very poor language progress.

Cunningham and McArthur (1981) studied 24 Down's Syndrome children, aged 9–32 months, using distraction technique and impedance measurements, and reported that all the children failed the distraction test at screening level and 80–85% were regarded as having a hearing loss of more than 40 dB(A). It is of note that 50% of the sample had passed a routine screening of hearing at a local authority clinic. This would support the generally held view among paediatric audiologists that such children should be routinely assessed in a specialist audiology clinic.

A further study of hearing in adult Down's individuals was carried out by Keiser *et al.* (1981), who reported a 39% incidence of abnormal tympanograms and a high incidence of sensorineural hearing loss, with 23% in the 15–20-year-old age group. This study also identifies the very characteristic loss at 4 kHz and 8 kHz demonstrated by other workers.

Strome (1981) reported an interesting study of Down's Syndrome from an ENT point of view. His finding of an increased incidence of middle ear effusion in those children with stenotic meata is of note, and he also reports a surprising finding that in his series adenoidectomy had little effect on middle ear effusion, breathing problems or rhinorrhoea. He reported a trend towards the disappearance of rhinorrhoea with age, presumably due to anatomical changes, and this finding would be confirmed by most workers in the field. Strome considered that the indications for tonsillectomy in Down's children are very limited, and emphasised the postoperative risks of this operation in these children. In the United Kingdom, there is on the whole considerable conservatism regarding the indications for tonsillectomy in all children, whether or not they suffer from Down's Syndrome.

A considerable degree of agreement therefore exists between different workers looking at auditory problems in Down's individuals – both middle ear function and hearing levels. Unfortunately, information about the actual pathological processes taking place is very limited. The number of temporal bone studies is very small, and there is an urgent need for more studies of this type.

Krmpotic-Nemanic (1970), reporting on a study of the temporal bones in two Down's children, one stillborn baby and one 7-year-old child, noted changes in the whole spiral tract reminiscent of those seen in advanced presbyacusis. Harada and Sando (1981), reporting on temporal bones from seven patients with Down's Syndrome, felt that their findings did not help towards an understanding of the pathology of hearing loss in the syndrome. They did, however, demonstrate that the cochlea was small in many cases, with a reduced number of turns, but they found that the organ of Conti was always well developed. In four cases, they found evidence of middle ear inflammation and they reported that a remnant of mesenchymal tissue obstructing the round window in most of their cases might be significant, although its implications are not yet clear. Igarashi *et al.* (1977) studied four cases of Down's Syndrome, all of whom were babies. They reported significantly shorter cochlear spirals but no significant difference in the widths of the basal coils. There were no other significant inner ear abnormalities. Of the four, three had evidence of middle ear effusions. Balkany, Mischke *et al.* (1979) have reported the presence of abnormalities of the ossicles in some Down's children. This could of course be due to chronic middle ear disease. They also suggest that there may be a higher risk of development of cholesteatoma in Down's children with chronic middle ear disease than in normal children.

It is possible that progressive sensorineural hearing loss in the older Down's child and adult may be secondary to long-standing middle ear disease. One can look here for a parallel with individuals who have repaired cleft palates in whom middle ear effusions are universal and in whom there is an increasing risk of sensorineural hearing loss with age (Bennett *et al.*, 1968; Yules, 1970; Bennett, 1972; Loeb, 1964). Alternatively, the increasing risk of sensorineural hearing loss in Down's individuals with age may be associated with an abnormally rapid ageing process in the cochlea, so that many Down's children are suffering from an apparent presbyacusis early in their life. There is no doubt that the nature of the problem in older children and in young adults with Down's Syndrome is a mixed one, combining a persistent conductive hearing loss with middle ear effusion and a high risk of a sensorineural hearing loss particularly affecting the higher frequencies (4 kHz and 8 kHz). A full understanding of the pathological process which is occurring in these individuals remains to be achieved by further serial audiological studies in Down's individuals and further pathological studies of temporal bones.

THE CLINICAL SITUATION

Audiological assessment

On seeing the Down's child in the clinic with his parents, it is first necessary to take a full history, especially in relation to the frequency of upper respiratory tract infections and any ear, nose and throat problems. The parents' opinions of the child's hearing should also be obtained, together with a history of the child's speech and language development.

Audiological assessment of the Down's child is carried out using standard techniques of paediatric audiology (Fig. 5.2, i-v). The tests used must always be appropriate for the child's mental age at the time of assessment. In a clinic where a large number of Down's children and adults are followed, it is possible to carry out

(i)   **(ii)**

(iii)   **(iv)**

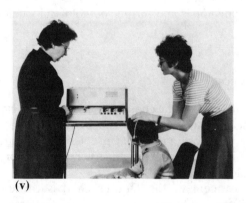

(v)

Fig. 5.2 (i–iv) Stages in testing the hearing of a Down's child. (v) Tympanometry

threshold pure tone audiometry with headphones on a few Down's children at the age of 3–3½ years. In skilled hands, a threshold audiogram can be obtained at a mental age of about 2½ years. However, in the majority of Down's children, a reliable pure tone audiogram will not be obtained until between the ages of 4 and 5 years. Occasionally, in a very severely handicapped older child or adult, techniques usually used only in babies will have to be attempted.

A progressive undiagnosed deafness may produce severe behavioural disorders, especially if the child or adult has poor communication skills. Such patients may be referred for audiological assessment as a last resort because they appear to show psychotic symptoms.

In babies, a distraction test (using the Ewing technique) is usually carried out, and one expects to be able to identify reliable localising responses to sound when the child is at a developmental level of 6–7 months of age, and occasionally a little below this. It is, nevertheless, worthwhile seeing Down's babies before they reach this developmental level, as tympanometry can be carried out and the presence of a middle ear effusion identified. In addition, the nature of the problem can be explained to the parents and they can be helped to understand why it is necessary for their baby to have regular hearing checks. At this point, parents will often ask what will happen if the hearing of the child does deteriorate, and a full understanding of the possibilities in terms of future management is invariably helpful for the parents and ensures their future co-operation.

Several simple techniques and guidelines will make it easier to obtain a hearing assessment. If the child's mental age is around 2 years, attempts should be made to condition the child to sound using speech sounds (e.g. 'go'). Successful approximate thresholds for 'go', and subsequently for the sound 'ss', can then be obtained using play techniques. Later, one can proceed to condition the child to pure tones using a free field audiometer and suitable play material. Once the child is able to co-operate adequately, one can carry out threshold audiometry using headphones. (Some children are unhappy wearing a headset, and for these a single headphone can be used.)

Throughout the testing it is, of course, essential to maintain very close rapport with the child, and the parent(s) need to be close by to provide support if the child becomes anxious. It is essential to have a wide variety of suitable material available for the tests (e.g. stacking beakers, 2.5-cm bricks, large-size wooden pegs) to provide frequent changes of game and maintain the child's interest in the procedure. As in all paediatric audiology, unless the child's interest is sustained and he or she is enjoying the task, reliable results will not be obtained. The testing of Down's children is no different from the testing of other children, except that the procedure takes a little longer and requires a rather greater expenditure of energy by the tester.

Most Down's children thoroughly enjoy the tests, but they may show certain characteristics of response which have to be observed. There may be a delay in response (both in a distraction test and performance), and the timing of signals has therefore to be very carefully controlled. The child has to be encouraged to wait carefully for the signals in pure tone audiometry, but some Down's children become impatient and need a good deal of persuasion. In distraction testing, the length of signal must sometimes be increased for some babies before a response is obtained.

An older Down's child with severe undiagnosed hearing loss may be difficult to test as his auditory attention is usually poor. In these children, the first attempt at pure tone audiometry may be difficult, but often, with adequate control of his or her responses, the child may prove much easier to test on subsequent occasions. It is essential to obtain pure tone levels for air and bone conduction, but it is frequently difficult or impossible to use any masking procedures. Tympanometry requires a suitable impedance bridge and the child should be introduced to the machine in a way which is suitable for his or her mental age. In those children who are unhappy to accept tympanometry, allowing the child to press the buttons of the machine to commence and end the trace will often distract him from his unhappiness at having the small probe in his ear.

A child's thresholds for speech can usually only be explored using toy material (Kendall test or the McCormick test), and ability to perform in these tests will depend not only on auditory acuity but also on linguistic level. Despite the limitations of such tests and their inaccuracy compared with techniques used in older children and adults, they will nevertheless provide useful information on the child's auditory function in relation to speech. Many Down's children now use Makaton signing at school and will respond to the names of the toys, in for example a Kendall test, by signing the appropriate word, instead of pointing to the object. This response is, of course, perfectly acceptable. In older Down's children and adults, word lists can be used (Manchester Junior Words or AB Word Lists), either in free field or through headphones, as one would for normal children. Unfortunately, results may be very difficult to evaluate because of scoring problems caused by phonological errors. Picture identification tests are a useful alternative.

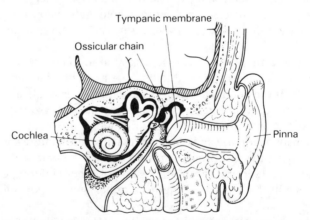

Fig. 5.3 Section of the ear, showing outer earlobe and inner ear

It is rarely necessary to use evoked response techniques (brainstem-evoked responses or electrocochleography) in Down's children. However, for a young child where there is a suspicion of a sensorineural loss and behavioural testing is difficult, such techniques can be used. In young Down's babies behavioural

responses may be difficult to evaluate, but tympanometry provides useful information about middle ear function which is essential in planning future management.

Lastly, the ears should be examined (Figs 5.1 and 5.3). Frequently the pinnae
will be found to be small in dimension, lying flat against the skull and typically with
an angled folded helix and a small ear lobe. Frequently, the meata are stenosed and
occluded with wax and desquamated epithelium. There may be marked nasal
and/or post-nasal obstruction, and it is common to find chronic rhinorrhoea with a
purulent nasal discharge.

Common findings (Figs 5.4–5.7)

Middle ear dysfunction with flat tympanograms and a conductive hearing loss is the
most usual finding in young Down's children. Hearing loss is likely to be between
25 and 50 dB(HL), usually bilateral, and in young children generally of an entirely

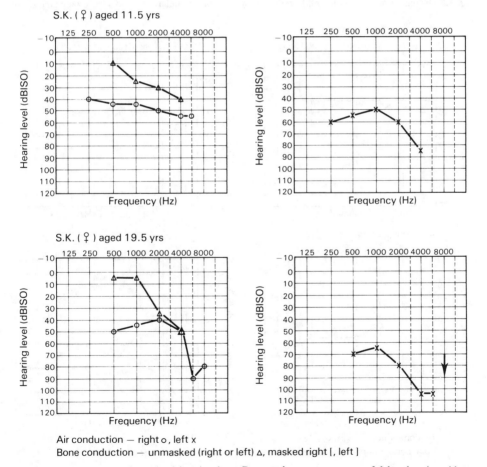

Air conduction — right o, left x
Bone conduction — unmasked (right or left) ∆, masked right [, left]

Fig. 5.4 Typical progressive mixed hearing loss. Repeated surgery unsuccessful but hearing-aid use
successful

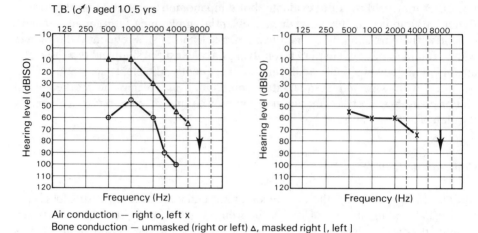

T.B. (♂) aged 10.5 yrs

Air conduction — right o, left x
Bone conduction — unmasked (right or left) Δ, masked right [, left]

Fig. 5.5 Untreated mixed loss in child presenting with disturbed behaviour and severe language delay

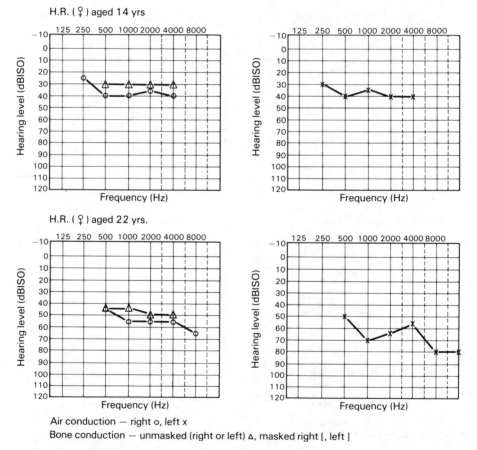

H.R. (♀) aged 14 yrs

H.R. (♀) aged 22 yrs.

Air conduction — right o, left x
Bone conduction — unmasked (right or left) Δ, masked right [, left]

Fig. 5.6 Atypical slowly progressive sensori-neural loss without conductive element. Uses aids successfully

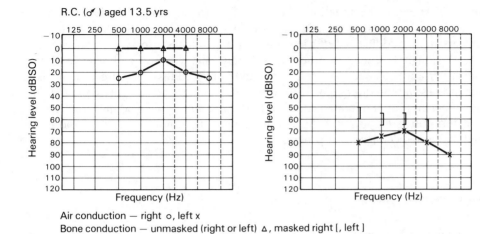

R.C. (♂) aged 13.5 yrs

Air conduction — right o, left x
Bone conduction — unmasked (right or left) ∆, masked right [, left]

Fig. 5.7 Unusual monaural sensori-neural hearing loss in left ear with varying conductive hearing loss in right ear

conductive nature. Severe sensorineural hearing loss is very rarely seen in Down's babies or young Down's children. If the children are reviewed regularly, the tympanograms characteristically remain flat, although the degree of hearing loss may vary from time to time.

This varying hearing loss parallels the well-known natural history of middle ear effusion in normal children. However, the particular characteristic of the condition in Down's children is that the tympanogram rarely returns to normal, even when the child is going through a phase of having relatively good hearing thresholds. As the middle ear disease starts early in life and is so persistent and intractable, it seems likely that this may well have effects on the child's linguistic development. There is a considerable literature on the effects of mild conductive hearing loss in normal children, and in recent years this has become a topic of great interest to audiologists and educationalists alike. The long-term effects of mild to moderate conductive hearing loss in normal children are less well known. A useful review of the literature on this subject has been published by Rapin (1979).

It seems reasonable to extrapolate from work with normal children – in whom the effects of even mild hearing losses on linguistic progress and on educational progress are well known – to the situation of Down's children. They cannot use compensatory mechanisms so effectively as normal children, and a conductive hearing loss of even moderate degree may produce severe problems of auditory attention and, with this, associated delay in linguistic development and delay in progress at school.

In later childhood a high-frequency sensorineural hearing loss frequently develops at 4 kHz and 8 kHz. This may be monaural at first, but then usually affects both ears. There is then a tendency as the years pass for this loss to progress in severity, gradually to affect lower frequencies.

The middle ear effusion characteristically persists in spite of rigorous surgical treatment. In normal individuals, such effusions commonly become much less frequent as childhood progresses, and are relatively unusual after the age of 9 years. This is not the situation in Down's Syndrome, where middle ear effusion frequently persists into adult life. The combination of a conductive hearing loss due to persistent middle ear effusion and a progressive sensorineural hearing loss affecting high frequencies produces a highly characteristic audiometric picture which is frequently seen in adolescents and young adults. The effect of this is to produce a severe auditory handicap, which may well not be recognised in otherwise severely handicapped individuals. The Down's child or young adult whose hearing is deteriorating may show behavioural changes, becoming withdrawn and quiet, and make poor educational progress.

Medical management

It is widely recognised that Down's children are particularly susceptible to frequent upper respiratory tract infections. The characteristic picture of chronic rhinorrhoea with a varying degree of nasal and post-nasal obstruction is very common. Children presenting in this way will very frequently be shown to be suffering from a middle ear effusion with a conductive hearing loss. In spite of a considerable amount of research, it is still not clear why Down's children should have these particular problems. It may well be that the aetiology of their characteristic ENT difficulties is associated with deficiencies in their immune system (Smith and Berg, 1976; Breg 1977), combined with structural abnormalities of the skull (Spitzer *et al.*, 1961), which militate against good middle ear ventilation.

A parallel can be drawn here with children who have a cleft palate, in whom middle ear effusion is virtually universal and in whom the mechanism of failure of middle ear aeration is well understood (Bluestone, 1978). A Down's child who also has a cleft palate is, of course, particularly at risk for severe middle ear problems. Unfortunately, the middle ear effusion tends to persist even after repair of the palate.

The use of decongestants for the management of chronic upper respiratory catarrhal problems with middle ear effusion is a hotly debated topic. Such decongestants are still widely used, although there is as yet no research evidence to show they are effective. In clinical practice there are undoubtedly some children who show some benefit from the use of decongestants, but their use in Down's children tends to be less successful than in normal children. So far as upper respiratory tract infection is concerned, there seems no doubt from clinical experience that some Down's children are much fitter on large doses of Vitamin C, but, again, carefully controlled research in this area is needed. The use of antibiotic treatment for the management of middle ear effusion is hardly relevant in Down's children, where the condition is so chronic and intractable to manage. Most ENT surgeons are not in favour of the use of decongestant nose-drops on a long-term basis.

There is no evidence as yet that there is likely to be an allergic element contributing to the upper respiratory problems of most Down's children, so that this particular avenue of possible treatment remains closed.

Surgical treatment (Figs 5.8 and 5.9)

Those children who have persistent middle ear effusion with a severe conductive hearing loss are frequently subjected to surgery, and this usually takes the form of adenoidectomy with myringotomy and the insertion of grommets. If there is evidence of sinus infection, antral washout at the same time is clearly useful. The immediate results of surgery are usually good, often with a rapid improvement in hearing levels and sometimes a small leap forward in linguistic progress. In the author's practice over the last 10 years, initially many Down's children seen were subjected to this surgery. However, the long-term results were so poor that this line of approach has largely been given up. It is therefore essential that, if the child is to be subjected to surgery, his or her parents are fully in the picture beforehand, i.e. that they are told that any improvement is likely to be temporary and that, although the situation may be controlled for a year or so, the middle ear effusion may recur within a matter of weeks of surgery.

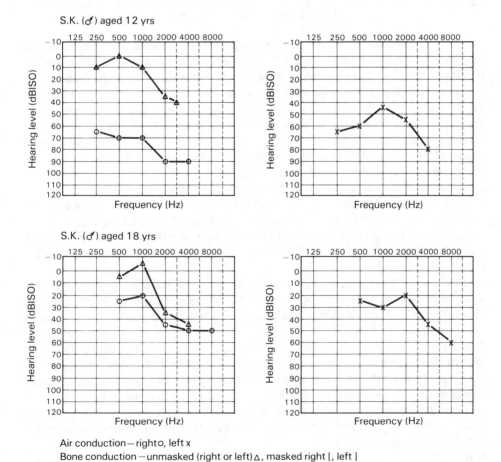

Air conduction — right o, left x
Bone conduction — unmasked (right or left) Δ, masked right [, left]

Fig. 5.8 Typical mixed loss. Results of surgery and hearing-aid use excellent

A.R. (♂) aged 14 yrs

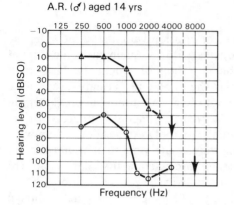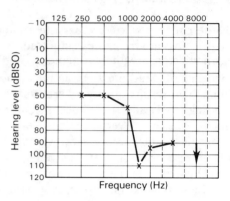

Air conduction — right o , left x
Bone conduction — unmasked (right or left) ∆, masked right [, left]

Fig. 5.9 Late presentation of severe mixed loss. No improvement with surgery or the use of aids. Language levels remain below 2 years

These children may present considerable problems to the surgeon, as the meata may be so severely stenosed that it is impossible to insert grommets. It is of interest that the fluid removed at myringotomy in Down's children is often quite characteristic in nature. In normal children, the viscosity of the middle ear fluid removed at myringotomy is very variable – from a thin serous-like fluid to a thick, highly viscous material, hence the common name of 'glue ear'. In Down's children, the fluid removed is invariably of a highly viscous nature, and can be cartilaginous in quality. However, despite this obvious difference between the middle ear effusion in normal children and Down's children, pathologists have not been able to demonstrate either histological or biochemical differences between the effusions.

In view of the chronicity of the middle ear effusion, if a decision is made to perform a myringotomy, it is useful to insert T-tubes rather than grommets. These are of wider bore than grommets and tend to remain patent for a longer period. They therefore improve the possibilities of maintaining good middle ear aeration for a longer period.

However, both grommets and T-tubes in Down's children often become blocked, and the problem then persists of dealing with a chronic middle ear effusion and its effects on hearing, and making decisions about further anaesthesia for the removal and reinsertion of tubes. Most ENT surgeons are loathe to insert grommets or T-tubes on more than three occasions because of the scarring of the tympanic membranes which may result. If grommets or T-tubes have been inserted, it is important to keep the ears dry, as the introduction of water into the ears certainly seems to predispose to the development of acute middle ear infection.

If middle ear infection with a purulent otorrhoea develops after surgery, this must be rigorously treated with good aural toilet, topical antibiotics, and systemic antibiotics if indicated.

If the Down's child has a mixed hearing loss, it is essential to explain to the parents that surgical intervention will not cure the sensorineural element, and it is important that parents and professionals concerned in the management of the child understand what degree of improvement is likely to occur. It is, of course, essential that for all Down's children who are going to be subjected to myringotomies, careful audiological assessment is carried out beforehand so that both the surgeon and the parents know as precisely as possible what the effects of surgery are likely to be. This principle of course applies to all children being submitted to myringotomies, but unfortunately careful audiological assessment prior to surgery is by no means universal.

There must always be a careful assessment of a Down's child's fitness for anaesthesia, especially if congenital heart disease is present.

Hearing aids

Because of the intractable nature of the middle ear problem and the fact that it is frequently not resolved by surgical intervention, there is an increasing tendency to provide the Down's child with hearing aids as an alternative. In the past there has been a disinclination to use aids in severely retarded children because of alleged difficulties of getting the child to accept the aid. However, with the availability of good post-aural aids in the National Health Service, and particularly since it has been possible to obtain well-fitting ear moulds, the use of hearing aids in Down's children is becoming more and more widely practised. Most practitioners in the field find that Down's children usually accept their aids very well. The first task of the prescriber is, of course, to explain to the parents of the child why this is necessary, because without their enthusiastic support any attempt to fit aids is quite useless.

The main problems in fitting post-aural aids to these children are in finding an aid which is ergonomically suitable (because the pinna is usually so small) and to obtain a well-fitting ear mould. The stenosed meata present considerable problems, but these can usually be overcome by using suitable techniques in taking impressions and a soft material for the construction of the moulds. The choice of aids will, of course, depend on the nature of the hearing loss. Because of the well-known risk of a deteriorating loss, regular assessment of hearing levels (at, say, 6-monthly intervals) is necessary as aids providing higher gain may well be needed as time goes on. For a child to use aids effectively, it is essential that a teacher of the deaf should be involved, and in most cases this will be a peripatetic teacher visiting the child at home and/or at school. The teacher will be responsible for overseeing the use of aids, and it will be his or her task to work with both the parents and the professionals concerned to clarify the implications of the child's hearing loss and teach them how to help the child make the best use of his residual hearing, as well as to improve auditory attention and linguistic progress.

The provision of a support service by teachers of hearing impaired children for those children with severe learning problems is very variable across the United Kingdom, and the amount of time teachers feel able to spend with such children will obviously depend on their own case loads. With an increasing number of Down's children in school provided with hearing aids, there is obviously a need for a regular service from a peripatetic teacher, and it is to be hoped that education authorities will accept the need for such a service to schools.

Schools often have the services of a speech therapist, although the amount of time available to these professionals will vary greatly from school to school. Where a speech therapist is very much involved in organising language programmes within the school, it is of course essential that the teacher of hearing impaired children and the speech therapist work very closely together. Such co-operation is fortunately now the rule rather than the exception.

The frequency with which children and adults are seen will obviously depend on the pressure on local services as well as on the child or adult's individual needs. It is essential that the audiological physician or ENT surgeon concerned works closely with the teachers of hearing impaired children, speech therapists and others who are involved in providing care for these children.

If hearing aids are to be used, there are emotional and practical difficulties for the parents in accepting that the child needs to use such equipment. However, usually the very considerable advantage to the child soon becomes apparent, and, once this occurs, a child's parents are allies with the professionals in trying to maintain the best possible auditory function in their child.

It has to be said, however, that occasionally a child or a young adult will present with a severe hearing loss and the attempt to provide aids fails. This usually occurs in very severely retarded individuals, in whom the indications are that they have had a severe loss which has been unidentified for many years. One may then be faced with the combination of severe mental retardation and a very severe speech and language problem, often associated with behaviour disorder. Even so, protracted attempts to provide amplification with the help of the teacher of hearing impaired children and the speech therapist are well worth while. Where failure occurs, the teacher and/or speech therapist must continue to help all they can, even in the absence of amplification. Strategies to improve auditory attention and the use of visual clues must be tried, but there will, of course, be individual cases where very little improvement can be achieved. Particular difficulties face the severely retarded individual with a previously untreated severe hearing loss who is having to cope with a bilingual situation, for example where there are non-English-speaking parents but English is used by the professionals concerned. For such individuals manual methods of communication, used increasingly in recent years, must be offered.

CONCLUSIONS

There is ample evidence from the small but consistent body of research relating to auditory function in Down's children and adults that all Down's individuals should have careful audiological supervision throughout their lives. Surgery, when indicated, hearing aids and appropriate support services from the professionals concerned should be available to all Down's children. The implications for audiological services are considerable, and it has to be borne in mind that such services are already under very considerable pressure: there is a need for more adequately trained professionals to carry out good audiological assessments on children and adults with severe learning problems; and the training of doctors, teachers and speech therapists needs to be improved so that they can provide a better service for Down's children. Doctors, whether family doctors, paediatricians or ENT surgeons, need to be encouraged to play their part in ensuring that Down's children have as good auditory function as it is possible to provide for them. More research is needed into the auditory problems of Down's individuals, in particular, further studies of post-mortem material to increase understanding of the nature of auditory pathology in Down's Syndrome. Last but not least, the parents of Down's children should be informed about the likelihood of hearing deficits and should be encouraged to ensure that this aspect of their children's development is carefully monitored and appropriate treatment given. Above all, they should be encouraged to refuse any opinion which suggests that 'the child hears well enough for a Down's child'.

REFERENCES

Balkany, T.J., Downs, M.P., Jafek, B.W. and Krajicek, M.J. (1979). Hearing loss in Down's Syndrome. *Clin. Paed.* **18**(2), 116–18.

Balkany, T.J., Mischke, R.E., Downs, M.P. and Jafek, B.W. (1979). Ossicular abnormalities in Down's Syndrome. *Otolaryngol. Head & neck surg.* **87**, 372.

Bennett, M. (1972). The older cleft palate patient. *Laryngoscope* **82**, 1217.

Bennett, M., Ward, R.H. and Tait, C.A. (1968). Otologic and audiologic study of cleft palate children. *Laryngoscope* **78**, 1011–19.

Bluestone, C.D. (1978). Prevalence and pathogenesis of ear disease and hearing loss. In Graham, M.D. (ed.), *Cleft Palate: Middle Ear Disease and Hearing Loss.* Springfield, Ill.: Charles C. Thomas.

Breg, W.R. (1977). Down Syndrome: a review of recent progress in research. *Pathobiol. Ann.* **7**, 257–303.

Brooks, D.N., Wooley, H. and Kanjilal, G.C. (1972). Hearing loss and middle ear disorders in patients with Down's Syndrome. *J. Ment. Defic. Res.* **16**, 21–9.

Cunningham, C. and McArthur, K. (1981). Hearing loss and treatment in young Down's Syndrome children. *Child: care, health and development* **7**, 357–74.

Davies, B. and Penniceard, R.M. (1980). Auditory function and receptive vocabulary in Down's Syndrome children. In Taylor, I.G. and Markides, A. (eds), *Disorders of Auditory Function III.* London: Academic Press.

Fulton, R.T. and Lloyd, L.L. (1968). Hearing impairment in a population of children with Down's Syndrome. *Am. J. Ment. Defic.* **73**, 298.

Glovsky, L. (1966). Audiological assessment of a mongoloid population. *Trng Sch. Bull.* **33**, 27.

Harada, T. and Sando, I. (1981). Temporal bone histopathological findings in Down's Syndrome. *Arch. Otol.* **107**, 96–103.

Igarashi, M., Takahashi, I., Alford, B.R. and Johnson, P.E. (1977). Inner ear morphology in Down's Syndrome. *Acta Otol.* **83**, 175.

Jerger, J. (1970). Clinical experience with impedance audiometry. *Arch. Otol.* **92**, 311–24.

Keiser, H., Montague, J., Wold, D., Maune, S. and Pattison, D. (1981). Hearing loss of Down syndrome adults. *Am. J. Ment. Defic.* **85**(5), 467–72.

Krmpotic-Nemanic, J. (1970). Down's syndrome and presbyacusis. *Lancet* **2**, 670–71.

Loeb, W.J. (1964). Speech, hearing and the cleft palate. *Arch. Otol.* **79**, 20–30.

McIntire, M.S., Menolascino, F.J. and Wiley, J.H. (1965). Mongolism – some clinical aspects. *Am. J. Ment. Defic.* **69,** 794.

Nolan, M., McCartney, E., McArthur, K. and Rowson, V.R. (1980). A study of the hearing and receptive vocabulary of the trainees of an adult training centre. *J. Ment. Defic. Res.* **24,** 271–86.

Rapin, I. (1979). Conductive hearing loss: effect on children's language and scholastic skills – a review of the literature. *Ann. Otol.* **88** (suppl. 60), 3–12.

Rigrodsky, S., Prunty, F. and Glovsky, L. (1961). A study of the incidence, types and association etiologies of hearing loss in an institutionalised mentally retarded population. *Trng Sch. Bull.* **58,** 30.

Schwartz, D.M. and Schwartz, R.H. (1978). Acoustic impedance and otoscopic findings in young children with Down's Syndrome. *Arch. Otol.* **104,** 652–6.

Smith, G.F. and Berg, J.M. (1976). *Down's Anomaly,* 2nd edn. Edinburgh: Churchill Livingstone.

Spitzer, R., Rabinowitch, J.Y. and Wybar, K.C. (1961). A study of the abnormalities of the skull, teeth and lenses in mongolism. *J. Can. Med. Assoc.* **84,** 567–72.

Strome, M. (1981). Down's Syndrome. A modern otorhinolaryngolical perspective. *Laryngoscope* **91**(10), 1581–94.

Yules, R.B. (1970). Hearing in cleft palate patients. *Arch. Otol.* **91,** 319–23.

6 Ocular Findings in Children

Elisabeth A. Millis

REVIEW OF THE LITERATURE

'The eyes are obliquely placed and the internal canthi more than normally distant from one another. The palpebral fissure is very narrow.' This was how Langdon Down (1866) described the ocular features which contributed so much to the characteristic facial appearance of a group of retarded children in his care. Indeed, he commented that the appearance was so typical that a group of unrelated children could be mistaken for siblings.

Down thought that the flat cheekbones and shape of the palpebral apertures suggested that these children looked 'Mongolian', and he used this term to describe the disorder (see Chapter 1). In fact, the apertures are shorter, wider and more tilted than in the true Mongolian, where they are seen to be long, narrow and almond shaped. Despite this disparity, however, Down had succeeded in labelling a particular group of handicapped children, who show a variety of ocular abnormalities. Ormond (1912) remarked that '... almost all have some ocular defect', citing blepharitis, distorted lids, squint, nystagmus and cataract as common problems.

Brushfield (1924) included in his thesis on mongolism a brief review of the ocular features and noted pale-coloured spots on the iris which have continued to be known by his name. These spots are situated at the junction of the middle and outer thirds of the iris and are more easily seen in blue than brown eyes (Fig. 6.1). Indeed, Brooke Williams (1981) could not demonstrate any nodules in the black children he examined. This was almost certainly due to the method of examination employed, as he did not use the slit-lamp microscope. If viewed with sufficient magnification and illumination, the nodules are visible even on the dark-brown iris.

As with many of the features of Down's Syndrome, the spots occur more frequently than in the normal population and are more likely to encircle the iris completely. Donaldson (1961) reported an incidence of 85% as against 24% in normal subjects. The nodules are condensations of the anterior stromal layer of the iris and, in the trisomic patient, are associated with hypoplasia of the iris peripheral to the spots. Lowe (1949) believed this could be related to a hypoplastic iris vasculature.

Brushfield spots have been reported in other syndromes with chromosomal anomalies, and Brooke Williams suggests that they may be an indicator of defective embryogenesis. Donaldson attempted to assess their significance but failed to find a correlation between the spots and either age or IQ.

103

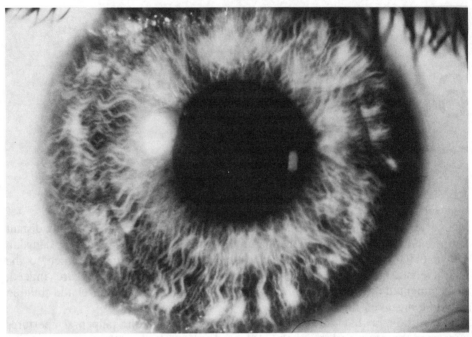

Fig. 6.1 Brushfield spots seen as well-marked, discrete, pale spots on a light-coloured iris

The iris in some reports is referred to as blue, but this probably reflects the racial characteristics of the population examined. Down's Syndrome occurs in all ethnic groups, and eyes can be affected whether blue or brown.

The pupils appear normal but they are abnormally sensitive to atropine (Berg *et al.*, 1959). They show a more rapid dilatation and the reaction is sustained for longer.

In 1963, Allerhand *et al.* examined the composition of the tear fluid and found an overall increase in protein with reduced albumin and an increased globulin content. In particular, they found α-1-globulin in 90% of Down's patients. Normally, this is present only in the first week of life in full-term infants and for up to a month in premature babies.

The most detailed survey of the ocular manifestations of the disease is, in the author's opinion, that undertaken by Lowe (1949). In his well-illustrated account he described all the common features of the disease, with the exception of keratoconus and the more recently described abnormal retinal vessels. In particular, he described four types of cataract, namely, arcuate, sutural, flake and congenital lens opacities. Most investigators since then have based their description on Lowe's classification. He believed the arcuate opacity to be the most characteristic and thought it formed in relation to an abnormal capsulopupillary vessel early in foetal life. Other researchers believed it was a segmental zonular cataract. Because the lens grows throughout life, the site of an opacity will indicate the time in life at which the injury occurred.

Most cataracts are found to be binocular, but are sometimes uniocular. Nearly all studies remark on the presence of more than one type of cataract in any given lens, particularly in older children. They also agree that virtually all these children show some evidence of cataract by the time they are in their 'teens.

Igersheimer (1951) postulated various theories regarding the aetiology of these lens opacities. He believed they could be due to endocrine abnormalities or to intrauterine damage, and agreed with other workers that very young children do not have cataracts. He compared this with other genetic cataracts (e.g. in myotonia dystrophica), which do not appear until several years after birth. These ideas were all conceived before the genetic nature of the disease itself had been discovered.

The incidence of cataract in Down's Syndrome varies. Some investigators only included 'those cataracts which would seem dense enough to cause visual difficulty' (Eissler and Lognecker, 1962), and not all investigators used a slit-lamp to examine the lens, particularly with children. However, the incidence is believed to be of the order of 50%. In all congenital cataracts an incidence of 1–5% in Down's Syndrome has been reported, compared with 0.03% in the general population.

Corneal disease has also been reported in association with trisomy 21. In 1956, MacGirr and Murray reported a case of thyrotoxicosis in Down's Syndrome with a marked exophthalmos and a unilateral marginal corneal ulcer, presumably related to exposure of the cornea. Twelve years later, Schub (1968) examined a similar case in which there were bilateral corneal opacities in the lower corneae. These opacities appeared to be the primary cause of the patient's poor vision.

Several investigators have reported cases of keratoconus (a conical protrusion of the central cornea). It is a degenerative bilateral disease in which there is generalised thinning of the cornea, which, in the acute form of the disease, may lead to rupture of Descemet's membrane causing corneal oedema and scarring. Rados reported two cases in young adults in 1948. Later, Cullen and Butler (1963) examined 143 patients with Down's Syndrome aged 2 to 53 years and found keratoconus in 5.5% of the series. It is a potential cause of blindness due to the severe astigmatism and corneal scarring.

Keratoconus tends to occur around the time of puberty in these children and is often associated with other anomalies, e.g. cataract and glaucoma. The acute form is more common in Down's Syndrome than in any other disorder. The condition is of unknown aetiology but it has been postulated that eye rubbing may be a causative factor due to the liberation of proteolytic enzymes (Pierse and Eustace, 1971). Eye rubbing in such conditions as vernal conjunctivitis and atopic eczema has also been associated with keratoconus.

All series have reported a high incidence of refractive errors (Gardiner, 1967; Fanning, 1971). The results vary depending on the method of testing and the criteria used to define refractive error. Nevertheless, in most series some 30% of the patients examined were found to be myopic, and there was an increased incidence of high myopia, i.e. children with an error greater than –6.00 dioptres.

Fanning found virtually all in his series were hypermetropic, but he used Taits' dynamic retinoscopy to assess the error rather than the more usual static retinoscopy in association with a cycloplegic to prevent the eye from accommodating.

Most authors do not refer to astigmatism, but Gardiner found many of the children in his series were astigmatic.

Strabismus, or squint, is reported by virtually all observers and is commonly convergent. Lowe thought that cataract and myopia were the most important causes of squints. He also found weakness of abduction of the eyes to be a common feature.

Nystagmus was first recorded by Sutherland in 1899. In Lowe's series of 67 patients, only 9 (13%) showed nystagmus and 7 of these had ocular abnormalities, e.g. lens opacities or fundus changes due to high myopia. He therefore felt that these were the most likely causes. Francois *et al.* (1975) found an incidence of 22%. Cataract and myopia were again present in 40% of those with nystagmus; 27% were associated with strabismus; 33% were regarded as 'essential nystagmus'.

The intraocular fluids have not been reported as showing any abnormality, but Williams *et al.* (1973) reported the presence of spoke-like retinal vessels in Down's Syndrome with a higher number of retinal vessels crossing the disc margin. Eighty-eight per cent had 16 or more such vessels, compared with only 16% in the normal population. The vessels were thought to be straighter than normal and to show a spoke-like pattern. No cause for this was suggested.

There have been two reports in the literature of cases of optic nerve hypoplasia in Down's Syndrome. In a paper by Awan (1977), the disc was small and kidney shaped when compared with that on the opposite side.

Trisomy 21 is a neuro-ectodermal disorder, and it is interesting to note that of the nine cases of retinoblastoma associated with mental defect which were reported by Taktikos (1964), one was a 2 year old with Down's Syndrome. He postulated that the underlying genetic change may lead to neoplasia in the neural retinal cells and to changes in the central nervous system.

Finally, in 1961, a study by Butterworth *et al.* found 37 cases of syringoma in 200 Down's Syndrome patients aged 10 to 52 years (6 were between 10 and 14 years old). Syringoma is an epithelioma arising from the sweat and meibomian glands. Butterworth found that it occurred more commonly in females than in males. The incidence in Down's Syndrome was much higher than in other types of mental defect. He reports that, in his series, the lesions were restricted to the area around the eyes, and there appeared to be an increased incidence with increasing age.

THE OCULAR ANOMALIES FOUND IN DOWN'S SYNDROME

The shape of the palpebral apertures and the presence of Brushfield spots have already been described.

Epicanthic folds

These are folds of skin situated on either side of the nose, often overlying the medial canthi (Fig. 6.2). Although usually bilateral, they may be unilateral. When bilateral, they may be more marked on one side than the other. They are common in normal babies but disappear as the nasal bridge and face develop.

In trisomy 21, the bridge of the nose is often very flat, and there are marked epicanthic folds in all cases in babies. It was probably the presence of these folds

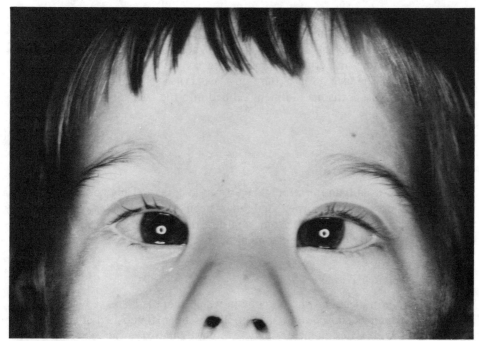

Fig. 6.2 Facial appearance in an infant showing convergent squint, epicanthic folds and watering (epiphora)

which caused Langdon Down to conclude that the eyes were set further apart than in the normal subject. The folds are more marked and persist for much longer in these children than in normal children. They do, however, eventually disappear, usually as the child enters teenage.

Epicanthic folds can give rise to an apparent squint, either when the folds themselves are asymmetrical or, more commonly, because the child appears to squint when he looks to one side. The reason for this is that the eye moving towards the nose tucks behind the fold of skin, thus giving the impression of overturning. An apparent squint can be differentiated from a true squint by observing corneal reflections and by the cover test.

Blepharitis

In this condition, the eyelids become red and irritable, and characteristically dry flakes appear on the lashes. Blepharitis is due to a chronic staphylococcal infection of the lash follicles, and occurs frequently in Down's Syndrome. The abnormal skin found in the disorder is particularly susceptible to infection.

The condition causes irritation resulting in eye rubbing, and this may then lead to distortion of the lids, which may turn in (entropion) or out (ectropion). Ectropion results in a stagnant pool of tear fluid collecting behind the lid, which causes further infection. The irritation may possibly be aggravated by the abnormal tear fluid previously discussed.

Rubbing the irritating lids also results in distortion of the lashes (trichiasis), and ingrowing lashes may rub on the cornea causing further problems. There is no need to treat the condition in the quiescent state but lid toilet is most important. Lids should be kept clean and crusts removed from the lashes using warm water and cotton wool. In the event of a flare-up, lash crusts should be removed and neomycin and hydrocortisone ointment rubbed into the lash roots.

Corneal disease

Corneal opacities

These are scars, usually in the stromal layers of the cornea. They occur most often in the lower part of the cornea and have been reported in association with thyrotoxicosis. They may result from exposure due to any cause and also from infection, particularly during the neonatal period.

Keratoconus (conical cornea)

This is a condition of unknown aetiology in which there is increased curvature of the cornea, which becomes cone shaped. It has been found in both acute and chronic forms and causes an increasingly severe astigmatism, which reduces vision. In the acute form, there is a sudden cone formation with considerable thinning of and damage to the cornea. The endothelium becomes decompensated, and the stroma becomes waterlogged (corneal oedema). Damage to Descemet's membrane in the cornea results in permanent scarring.

There is little difficulty in recognising the acute form, which causes pain and distress to the patient and may result in blindness. It is more difficult to identify the chronic form, but suspicions are aroused when an increasing astigmatism is found in one of these patients. The diagnosis can be confirmed on slit-lamp biomicroscopy and by measuring the corneal curvature (keratometry). The acute form will require hospital admission, sedation and a pad and bandage. Steroid eye-drops have also been given. In some of these patients it is virtually impossible to maintain the pad in place, but the cone may resolve spontaneously.

Cataract

Cataracts are found in many Down's Syndrome patients by the time they are teenagers. Most authors quote an incidence of 50%, and it is common for these children to show more than one type of cataract in any one lens.

Flake opacities

The most common form of cataract is the dot or flake opacity (Fig. 6.3). These small opacities have an oil-drop appearance and may be variously coloured blue, brown, grey or white. They occur initially in the lens periphery and may be sparsely

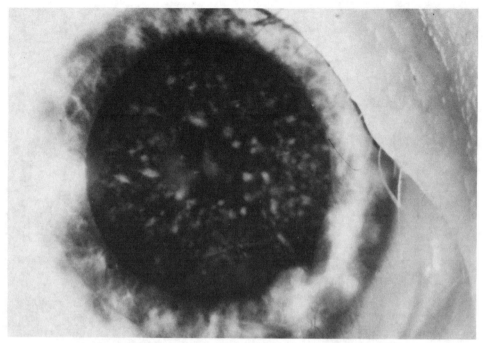

Fig. 6.3 Multiple flake opacities seen in the lens of a 9-year-old boy

distributed. For this reason, they may easily be overlooked unless the slit-lamp is used in conjunction with a dilated pupil. They increase in number and density over the years and are most readily seen in older teenagers and adults. However, because of their small size and peripheral distribution they are not thought to affect vision until later in life, when large numbers may be present and encroach on the visual axis.

Sutural opacities

Sutural opacities appear to develop within the foetal sutures some time after the sutures are laid down and to increase slowly with age. They form in the anterior Y suture (Fig. 6.4) and the posterior, inverted Y suture of the foetal nucleus, deep within the lens. They are usually linear but may be feathery and occur even in quite young children. Moreover, since they are often very delicate, they are best seen using the slit-lamp microscope. The anterior suture is more often affected than the posterior, and the condition is generally bilateral, although one eye may be affected before the other.

Arcuate opacities

Lowe described these as forming in the foetal nucleus, where they are seen as a small, white arc situated deeply in the lens as they arch round the equator of the nucleus. They are probably a sectoral form of zonular cataract rather than a separate entity and are not common.

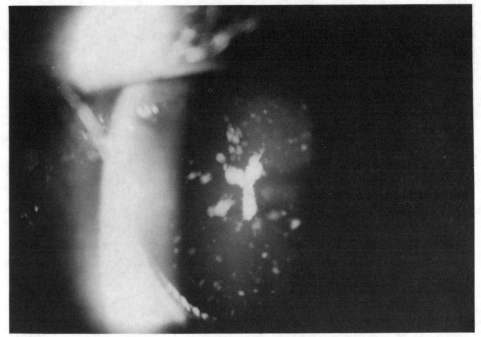

Fig. 6.4 Sutural and flake opacities seen in the lens of a 10-year-old girl

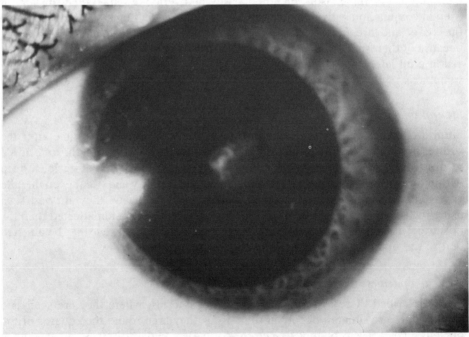

Fig. 6.5 Posterior polar lens opacities in a 13-year-old girl. There are a few peripheral flake opacities also present

Congenital cataracts

These cataracts are present at birth and include disc-shaped, nuclear and posterior polar cataracts (Fig. 6.5). They may be associated with trisomy 21 or due to an unrelated cause. They are the same types as congenital cataracts found in the normal population, and some are very similar to those found in myotonic dystrophy.

Depending on their size and density, they may interfere seriously with the development of vision, and therefore these cataracts, unlike the other varieties, may require early surgical removal.

Cataract extraction involves the removal of the lens from the eye and therefore after surgery the child will need spectacles in order to see clearly. Some surgeons have successfully fitted these babies with contact lenses but it is too early at the present time to be certain how the children will tolerate the lenses as they grow up. Small children will permit their regular removal and insertion but older children may resist these procedures. More importantly, there is a greater risk of ocular infection because of their blepharitis and associated eye rubbing. The latter may also result in damaged lenses causing problems.

If surgical removal of the cataract is not advised or has to be delayed, perhaps because of the child's general health, some help to vision may be given by dilating the pupil so that the child can obtain some vision round the centrally placed cataract. Spectacles can be given to correct any refractive error.

Refractive errors

These consist of short sight (myopia), long sight (hypermetropia) and astigmatism. The last condition occurs when the curvatures of the cornea and/or the lens are not equal in the vertical and horizontal meridians. Normal refraction is called 'emmetropic'.

In all young children and in the majority of handicapped children of all ages, it is necessary to test for a refractive error using cycloplegic eye-drops. These dilate the pupils and temporarily paralyse the focusing. Drops in use today have a much shorter duration of action, and vision may be blurred for close work for less than 24 hours, although this is subject to some individual variation.

The patient's refractive error is measured by a technique called retinoscopy – an objective method of accurately estimating refractive error. From the results obtained, the strength of spectacle lens required can be calculated.

Myopia

Children with myopia have reduced distance vision but can usually read unaided by holding the book close. Indeed, the parents may first suspect the condition when the child peers closely at objects. Some children with Down's Syndrome show a very considerable degree of myopia. Myopia is corrected with spectacles having concave lenses. The image, which had previously been focused in front of the retina, can then be brought to a focus on the retina.

Hypermetropia (hyperopia)

Despite the high incidence of myopia, the majority of Down's children are long sighted (hypermetropic). Hypermetropia requires convex lenses to correct it, but many manage very well without a spectacle correction (this is true for those with low refractive errors). Small amounts of hypermetropia affect vision less than the corresponding amount of myopia. The majority of these children read books with relatively large print, and their distance vision is not greatly affected by the small error. They may not, therefore, be keen to wear spectacles as they notice relatively little improvement.

Astigmatism

Astigmatism causes a problem as there is a distortion of the image both close to and at a distance, so that there may be no point from which a clear image can be focused on the retina. Astigmatic correcting lenses are more powerful in one meridian than the other.

Amblyopia

The more common term for this is a 'lazy eye'. It is frequently associated with squint (see later). However, it can occur when the refractive error in one eye differs markedly from that in the other (anisometropic amblyopia). All three types of refractive error are potential causes of amblyopia.

The treatment of amblyopia is to prescribe spectacles of the required strength and to patch (occlude) the better eye. If possible, a full spectacle correction is ordered, but occasionally the difference between the two eyes is such that it would not be practical to make spectacles with such differing lenses. In these cases the affected eye may have to be undercorrected.

The attempted correction of anisometropic amblyopia is unrewarding in the adult patient and in most children after the age of 10. The longer the amblyopic eye is left untreated, the less likely will there be a return to normal vision. It is therefore important to start treatment as early as possible.

SPECTACLES FOR DOWN'S CHILDREN

Spectacles should be provided whenever they appear clinically necessary. Most patients will wear their spectacles happily. For those who are less willing, it may be possible for the teacher at school to persuade them to wear them in class. Alternatively, at home, co-operation is often more easily obtained if spectacles are put on to watch a favourite television programme. The period of wear can then be gradually increased. When treatment for amblyopia is being carried out with spectacles and occlusion it is important that they should be worn for the prescribed period each day.

Fitting spectacles for these children is not easy. They tend to have broad heads with broad, flat nasal bridges and small, soft, low-set ears. All these factors pose problems for the optician. Spectacle frames need to have a narrow, conventional bridge and often fit better if the nose pads are reduced and splayed back. A round eye shape is preferred (Fig. 6.6) so that the central part of the lens is less affected if the spectacle frame is bent. Short sides are needed by many Down's children, and these are often better with curl ends, particularly in young children. For very small children it is possible to obtain tie-on frames in either metal or plastic.

Fig. 6.6 Spectacle frame to suit most children with Down's Syndrome. The pads are splayed back and the eye frame is rounded

An accurate fit is important as, particularly when strong lenses are needed, the distance between the eye and the lens affects the effective power of the lens. The stronger the lens, the thicker it will be, and the weight of the resulting lens must be considered. Careful choice of eye size, good fitting and care in lens manufacture can help to reduce these problems. Plastic lenses will help to reduce weight and are less likely to shatter. It is best to order two pairs of spectacles for each child. Breakages are frequent, and even minor ones mean that a good deal of time is spent repairing the spectacles. Repeated interruptions in wear prevent effective treatment.

SQUINT

This condition exists when the visual axes of the eyes are out of alignment and the axis of only one eye is directed at the object (see Fig. 6.2). A point source of light (e.g. from a pen torch) will be seen to be reflected asymmetrically from the corneas (corneal reflection test – see Fig. 6.2). The eyes may turn inward (convergent squint) or outwards (divergent squint). The incidence of squint in Down's Syndrome is much higher than in the normal population, but only convergent squints have been reported.

A simple assessment of the degree of squint can be made from the position of the corneal reflections. The test is carried out on the undilated pupil with the eye in the primary position. If the corneal reflection is at the pupillary edge of the iris, the deviation is about 10 – 15°; if halfway between the pupil margin and the outer edge of the iris, 25°; and a reflex at the outer edge of the iris indicates a 35–40° turn. This is the simplest and least accurate assessment. The presence of squint is confirmed using the cover test. A latent squint is demonstrated using the alternate cover test.

The orthoptist will also measure the deviation using the prism cover test. This is very accurate but unsuitable for large angles of deviation. The patient is required to fixate a light while the test is carried out for near and distance.

These three tests are those most commonly used for assessing squint in children with Down's Syndrome.

Treatment of squint

The treatment of squint can take three forms: correction of the refractive error with spectacles, and occlusion where necessary; and, in some cases, surgery.

Correction of refractive error

Spectacles are given to those children with a significant refractive error. The aim is to provide a clear image in each eye, and this may act as a stimulus to the child to straighten the eye. This is particularly so in the case of accommodative squint – that is, the squint is linked to accommodation and appears mostly when fixating near objects. In particular, a hypermetropic refractive correction will aid convergent and accommodative squints. Myopic corrections will help divergent squints.

Occlusion

In a small child, when one eye turns constantly, the eye becomes lazy (amblyopic) and the vision in that eye deteriorates. The longer the condition remains untreated, the worse the vision will become, and the less likely that it can be returned to normal.

In order to improve vision, the eye with good vision is covered for at least part of each day with an adhesive patch. While the eye is covered the patient is employed in some visual task (e.g. drawing), which stimulates the visual pathway in the squinting eye. Gradually, the vision in this eye may improve, and occlusion is continued until no further improvement is obtained. As the acuity improves, so some straightening of the eye may be seen. During this time, the child is examined, often at monthly intervals.

Surgery

If spectacles and occlusion, where necessary, fail to straighten the eye, then surgical correction must be considered. This involves realigning the muscles of the eye so that the balance of the eye movements is restored. Usually, surgery is performed on one or two muscles of the affected eye or sometimes on one muscle of each eye.

Surgery is performed for one of two reasons:

(a) to improve vision and gain binocular function;
(b) to improve the cosmetic appearance.

In the first case, surgery is performed fairly early, as the surgeon believes that straightening the eye will lead to the patient being able to use the two eyes together normally. In the case of cosmetic surgery, there is less urgency, and correction can be undertaken at any time. Indeed, where the eye is convergent and the vision very poor, there will be a tendency for the eye to diverge over the years and the turn will gradually reduce. To operate early under these circumstances may risk the eye turning out at a later date.

Where the child has a manifest, constant, convergent squint and little or no refractive error, it is unlikely that spectacles will correct the deviation. In such cases early surgery is advised. Whenever surgery is to be performed, whether for squint or cataract, the general health of the child must be taken into consideration. The indications for surgery are the same as for the non-Down's population, given that the child's general health is satisfactory. No special precautions are necessary other than a sympathetic attitude of staff, who should understand the nature of a Down's Syndrome child.

NYSTAGMUS

The word nystagmus is derived from the Greek and means 'to nod'. It describes the constant, involuntary movements seen in some of these children, likened to a 'wobbling' of the eyes.

Nystagmus is classified into (a) congenital, and (b) acquired. The majority of those seen by the author involving Down's Syndrome are congenital in origin.

The movements of the eyes are rapid and may be of very small amplitude, so that the condition is often difficult to recognise unless a special search is made for it. The movements are generally of the pendular type and most frequently horizontal. Typically, with congenital nystagmus, the movement increases on fixation and reduces on converging the eyes. This accounts for the fact that near vision is less affected than distance vision in these children.

Some children adopt a head tilt, as there may be a particular position of gaze in which the eye movements are reduced to a minimum, and vision is best at this point. For this reason, it is unwise to insist on correction of this head posture.

The majority of affected children show manifest nystagmus but some have a latent form of the condition. In these cases, nystagmus is only demonstrable when one or other eye is covered. This can cause problems when testing visual acuity. Occlusion of either eye results in nystagmus occurring in the uncovered eye and a consequent reduction in visual acuity. These children are better tested by blurring the occluded eye, e.g. with a lens of very high power, or by recording vision with both eyes open as well as with each eye separately.

Nystagmus may also be more easily observed when the fundus is viewed through an ophthalmoscope. Very fine movements are easily seen, as the fundal features move rapidly in the observer's field of vision.

THE SIGNIFICANCE OF THE OCULAR FINDINGS

These may be divided into two groups:

(a) diagnostic;
(b) therapeutic.

Diagnostic features

These involve the ocular anomalies which do not affect vision and include those featured in the classical descriptions of the early investigators. They are present at birth and make the Down's baby readily identifiable, in the majority of cases. In a few children, the features are present but less marked. This is particularly true of epicanthic folds and the presence of a broad nasal bridge.

The smooth, even curve of the eyelids is common to all groups of patients and is a more reliable diagnostic feature together with the characteristically sloping, short palpebral apertures and other non-ocular features, e.g. low-set ears, single palmar crease.

Brushfield spots are likely to be missed on the dark-brown iris unless a specific search is made for them, and the presence of well-marked spots in a blue iris does not confirm the diagnosis.

The presence of these features does not appear to influence the vision in these children. Finding a number of these features in any one patient should alert the observer to the possibility of diagnosing Down's Syndrome but is not pathognomonic.

Therapeutic features

These are the ocular anomalies for which some treatment is available and which may affect vision.

Corneal opacities will only reduce vision significantly if they are permanent scars situated on the visual axis. Superficial epithelial lesions usually cause only temporary scar formation, which ultimately resolves with no deleterious effects.

The chronic form of keratoconus causes a gradually increasing astigmatism, which can be minimised with spectacles. The acute form may be treated as already described, and the final effect on vision will depend on the site of the cone and residual scarring. Active treatment will minimise the damage done to the cornea and may prevent the eye becoming blind. Ophthalmological advice should therefore be sought early.

Cataracts have been assumed not to interfere greatly with vision in the majority of these children. This is because many exhibit only a few sparse flakes within the lens until well into their teens. However, a few children show considerable numbers of flakes at a relatively early age, and the author believes that in these cases some interference with vision is inevitable.

It is common in the lenses of these children to find two or three types of cataract, and the presence of multiple types of cataract is of considerable diagnostic significance. Indeed, in the author's opinion it is the most characteristic feature of the lens in Down's Syndrome, particularly in the adolescent. However, because of the size and delicate nature of many of these cataracts in the child, they are easily missed unless the lens is examined with the slit-lamp biomicroscope through the dilated pupil.

Strabismus will result in amblyopia if it is constant. Careful observation of alternating squints is required to ensure that they do not become constant and result in reduced vision. No true squint will cure itself, and, if a squint is suspected, the child should be seen by an ophthalmologist. Referral should occur when the squint is first noted, as the earlier treatment is commenced the better the result is likely to be. In this respect it is important to consider the history given by the mother. She may remark that the squint is intermittent, present only when looking closely at things or when tired. It is the practice of the author and colleagues to accept the mother's statement as factual, even if the child is not squinting at the time of examination. Any refractive error is corrected with spectacles, and the child is kept under orthoptic observation. Children for whom there is a family history of squint are also not discharged until it is unlikely that strabismus will develop, say after 5 years of age.

SUMMARY

Damage to the eyes, to a greater or lesser extent, is a feature of all children with Down's Syndrome. Generally, both eyes are affected equally, although changes may occur in one earlier than in the other. In the past, the assessment and active treatment of Down's children have often been dismissed as practically impossible or not worthwhile. Modern methods have, however, made the task easier, and treatment is becoming more readily available.

Spectacles

Many Down's children benefit from wearing spectacles. These may be used to correct refractive error, to help treatment in cases of squint, or to aid vision after cataract extraction. They may even be ordered for babies if the refractive error is such that, if uncorrected, the vision is likely to be seriously affected.

Surgery

Surgery is required only for a minority of these children. It may be necessary to remove dense congenital lens opacities in order to obtain vision and encourage the visual development of the eye. In these cases, cataract extraction is undertaken as early as possible.

The surgical realignment of the eye by operation on one or more of the extraocular muscles may be indicated where spectacles and occlusion have proved insufficient to correct a squint. Squint surgery may also be performed when the child is older to improve his or her general appearance.

Supervision and management

It is important that any child who is suspected of having an ocular problem should be seen by an ophthalmologist. Advice should be sought early, as those conditions which can affect vision do not resolve spontaneously, and the earlier treatment is started the better the result is likely to be. It is the author's opinion that all Down's babies should be seen for a routine ophthalmic assessment within the first year of life. For those children with no immediate problem, a follow-up visit for a preschool assessment is made. At this visit, the parents can be advised if findings suggest that vision may cause problems at school.

Follow-up visits are also made for those children whose parents notice a squint, even if it is not present at the time of examination. Any refractive error is corrected and the child is kept under observation. Similarly, children for whom there is a family history of squint are not discharged until it is unlikely that strabismus will develop, say after 5 years. Those children who have alternating squints should be seen regularly to ensure the squint does not become constant and result in reduced vision.

Further routine visits should be arranged as the children get older to monitor visual acuity, refractive error and cataract. In addition, in the secondary school age group, the possibility of keratoconus must be kept in mind. Because cataracts are believed to increase with increasing age, and vision may deteriorate, it is important that these children should not be lost to follow-up, and the purpose of visits should be explained to parents so that they do not feel that time is being wasted.

ACKNOWLEDGEMENT

Photographs reproduced by kind permission of the Audiovisual Department, Western Ophthalmic Hospital, London.

REFERENCES

Allerhand, J., Karlitz, S., Isenberg, D. and Pembharkkul Sand Ramos, A. (1963). The lacrimal proteins in Down Syndrome. *J. Paediat.* **62**, 235–8.
Awan, K.J. (1977). Uncommon ocular changes in Down's Syndrome. *J. Paediat. Ophthal.* **19**, 14(4), 215–16.
Berg, J., Brandon, M. and Kirman, B. (1959). Atropine in Mongolism. *Lancet* **2.**
Brooke Williams, R.D. (1981). Brushfield spots and Wolfflin nodules in the iris: an appraisal in handicapped children. *Dev. Med. Child Neurol.* **23**, 646–50.

Brushfield, T. (1924). Mongolism. *Br. J. Child. Dis.* **XXI**, 241–58.

Butterworth, T., Strean, L. and Beerman, H. (1961). Syringoma in Mongolism. *Arch. of Dermatol.* **90**, 483–7.

Cullen, J.F. and Butler, H.G. (1963). Mongolism (Down's Syndrome) and keratoconus. *Br. J. Ophthal.* **47**, 321.

Donaldson, D. (1961). The significance of spotting of the iris in Mongoloids. *Am. Med. Assoc. Arch. Ophthal.* **65**, 26.

Down, J. Langdon H. (1866). Observations on an ethnic classification of idiots. *Clinical Lectures & Reports by the Medical & Surgical Staff of the London Hospital* **3**, 259.

Eissler, R. and Lognecker, P. (1962). The common eye findings in Mongolism. *Am. J. Ophthal.* **54**(3), 398–406.

Fanning, G.S. (1971). Vision in children with Down's Syndrome. *Austral. J. Optom.* **54**, 74–82.

Francois, J., Berger, R. and Saraux, H. (1975). *Chromosomal Aberrations in Ophthalmology.* Assen/Amsterdam: Van Gorcum.

Gardiner, P. (1967). Visual defects in Down's and other mentally handicapped children. *Br. J. Ophthal.* **57**, 469–74.

Igersheimer, J. (1951). The relationship of lenticular changes to Mongolism. *Trans. Am. Ophthal. Soc.* **49**, 595–624.

Lowe, R.F. (1949). The eyes in Mongolism. *Br. J. Ophthal.* **33**(3), 131–174.

MacGirr, E.M. and Murray, I.P. (1956). Thyrotoxicosis in a Mongol. *J. Clin. Endocr.* **16**, 160–63.

Ormond, A.W. (1912). Notes on the ophthalmic condition of 42 mongolian imbeciles. *Trans. Ophthal. Soc. U.K.* **32,** 69–76.

Pierse, D. and Eustace, P. (1971). Acute keratoconus in Mongols. *Br. J. Ophthal.* **55**, 50–54.

Rados, A. (1948). Conical cornea and Mongolism. *Arch. Ophthal. (Chicago)* **40**(4), 454.

Schub, M. (1968). Corneal opacities in Down's Syndrome with thyrotoxicosis. *Arch. Ophthal. (Chicago)* **80**, 618–21.

Sutherland, G.A. (1899). Mongolian imbecility in infants. *Practitioner* **63,** 632

Taktikos, A. (1964). Association of retinoblastoma with mental defect and other pathological manifestations. *Br. J. Ophthal.* **48**, 495.

Williams, E.J., McCormick, A. and Tischler, B. (1973). Retinal vessels in Down's Syndrome. *Arch. Ophthal.* **89**, 269–71.

7 Nutritional Treatment for Children

Carol Peterson Rolland and Donna Spiker

The medical profession and the general public are becoming increasingly interested in the effects of nutrition on behaviour and intelligence, and the association of good health with the use of nutritional supplements such as vitamins and minerals. In 1981, a study was published in the USA (Harrell *et al.*, 1981) suggesting that nutritional supplements could substantially improve the intellectual functioning of mentally retarded children. Sixteen mentally retarded children, given supplements over an 8-month period, showed IQ gains of 10–25 points. Of the group, three of four children with Down's Syndrome showed the greatest improvement – an average increase of 16 IQ points over the period of supplementation.

The report caused great interest in the scientific community and in the lay media. Our centre in Chicago and centres elsewhere began to receive requests for information about the use of the vitamin supplements. Although Harrell and her colleagues had titled their report 'preliminary' and called for further research, the findings as reported were so positive and extraordinary that parents, on their own initiative, began using the vitamin supplement for their retarded children. Since the effect of the treatment and its safety were not proven, additional research with this vitamin supplement was needed.

In 1981, a clinical trial was conducted in Chicago to determine the efficacy of this particular vitamin/mineral supplement, especially on the intellectual growth of children with Down's Syndrome (Smith *et al.*, 1983, 1984). This chapter will focus on the Chicago study in detail, not only presenting the results but offering the study as a methodological model for conducting clinical trials.

RATIONALE FOR NUTRITIONAL TREATMENTS

Children with Down's Syndrome have long been the focus for experimental nutritional studies. For example, Turkel's U series (Turkel, 1975), which contains 50 different substances, including vitamins, minerals and enzymes, was designed to stimulate the metabolism of children with Down's Syndrome and has been used for many years. Unfortunately, reported improvements have not been supported with appropriate data and have not stood up to scientific test. Bumbalo *et al.* (1964) carried out a 12-month, double-blind clinical trial using the Turkel protocol, with 24 Down's children, aged 3 months to 11 years, and found no significant difference between the treatment and placebo groups. Similar nutritional studies in Europe and Japan have not demonstrated positive results (Pueschel, 1981).

Nutritional treatment, which often includes administration of large doses of vitamins and minerals, has been labelled 'orthomolecular' by Pauling (1968). Orthomolecular therapy may be defined as 'the treatment of mental disorders by the provision of the optimum molecular environment for the mind, especially the optimum concentrations of substances normally present in the human body'. One of the best examples of the importance of diet for adequate mental functioning comes from studies showing that protein deficiency and calorie depletion as seen in chronic malnutrition can result in mental retardation, which may be lessened by providing a proper diet and environmental stimulation (Denhoff and Feldman, 1981). Genetic conditions requiring dietary management are also known, such as phenylketonuria, which is effectively treated in children by providing a diet low in the amino acid, phenylalanine. There are also cases of mental retardation caused by biochemical abnormalities that are improved through the administration of individual vitamins, e.g. thiamine-responsive, maple syrup urine disease (Scriver *et al.*, 1970) and methylmalonic acidemia (Rosenberg *et al.*, 1968).

Appropriate nutritional treatment for children with Down's Syndrome has proved problematic, but there is good rationale for pursuing this type of research. Various metabolic and biochemical abnormalities have been identified in Down's patients. Palmer and Ekvall (1978) reviewed reports on abnormalities in protein, carbohydrate, fat and vitamin metabolism, as well as in mineral, electrolyte and enzyme levels in Down's Syndrome. The authors concluded that certain biochemical parameters are altered in Down's Syndrome, but these changes appear to be quantitative rather than qualitative, not highly specific, and extremely difficult to interpret. The possibility of improving either the mental or physical condition of Down's children through a nutritional treatment programme remains a goal for further research.

Harrell and her colleagues based their recent work on the 'genetotrophic' theory (Williams 1956) that 'mental retardations are diseases in which the genetic pattern of the afflicted individual requires an augmented supply of one or more nutrients such that, when these nutrients are supplied, the disease is ameliorated' (Harrell *et al.*, 1981). The particular supplement used for the research was not chosen on the basis of the individual needs of the children, but because it was thought to be a broad-based, generous, limited risk supplement. The nutrients were to work together, in some as yet unspecified way, to promote normal metabolism. However, there was no suggestion that this particular supplement was best for fostering mental and physical development. Thus, the dramatic outcome of the Harrell study was difficult to explain and warranted further investigation.

Major methodological flaws in the design and procedure of the Harrell study prevented definitive conclusions regarding the effectiveness of this particular supplement. The groups were small (5 in the treatment group and 11 in the control group) and poorly matched on such variables as age and sex, which are known to influence IQ test scores (Clements *et al.*, 1976; Morgan, 1979). The assessment procedures were not standardised. Because it is known that different intelligence tests yield different intelligence quotients, they should not be directly compared, as was done in the Harrell procedure (Sattler, 1982). Lastly, after the initial 4-month period, all the children were put on supplements. Parents and investigators could no longer be considered 'blind' to the group's assignment. Only the initial findings clearly met the requirement for a double-blind study.

THE CHICAGO STUDY

In order to evaluate the effects of nutritional supplements on the intellectual functioning of Down's children, it was necessary to design a careful study. Major decisions had to be made about the procedures of the study. It was decided that all children would be given the same intelligence test, since different tests yield somewhat different results. It was also important that the two groups (supplement and placebo) matched on significant factors known to influence test performance. Thus, it was essential that the two groups be divided into comparable cross-matched pairs of children at the beginning of the study. It was also necessary to monitor the intake of the supplements carefully – to make sure that the participants were indeed ingesting the pills. Absolutely crucial to evaluating this question was the requirement that the examiners and the parents of the children be 'blind' about the group of the children. This eliminated bias in the data collection. It also minimised the possibility that parents would treat their own child differently if they had knowledge about the child's group. In addition, data were collected on other observations about the social, motor, and personality characteristics of the children as assessed by parents, teachers and psychologists. These data help to describe the sample. They also provide valuable information about children with Down's Syndrome *per se*.

Method

Sample

Home-reared children with Down's Syndrome between the ages of 7 and 15 years were recruited through parent groups and schools throughout the greater Chicago, Illinois, area. This age group was selected for study for three major reasons: (1) it would be possible to use the same IQ test for all the children (that is, the Wechsler Scales – either the preschool or the school-age version); (2) the reliability of test results is significantly greater for this age range than for infants and preschool children; and (3) the dosage of supplement had been used with this age range with no reported adverse effects. (It was suspected that reduced dosage levels would be needed with younger children.) The contents of the supplement are presented in Table 7.1. These vitamins and minerals are the same product from the same pharmaceutical company as used in the Harrell study.

Following the completion of the initial testing, summary data were sent to a 'blind' co-investigator (Dr Danta Cicchetti), who assigned the two groups, supplement versus placebo. The two groups were formed by matching pairs of children on five criteria: chronological age, sex, initial level of intellectual functioning, the socioeconomic status of their family, and the nature of the child's educational programme.

Table 7.1 *Daily doses of supplementary vitamins and minerals (12 tablets)*

Vitamin A palmitate	15 000 iu*
Vitamin D (cholecalciferol)	300 iu
Thiamin mononitrate	300 mg
Riboflavin	200 mg
Niacinamide	750 mg
Calcium pantothenate	450 mg
Pyridoxine hydrochloride	350 mg
Cobalamin	1 000 µg
Folic acid	400 µg
Vitamin C (ascorbic acid)	1 500 mg
Vitamin E (d-α-tocopheryl succinate)	600 iu
Magnesium (oxide)	300 mg
Calcium (carbonate)	400 mg
Zinc (oxide)	30 mg
Manganese (gluconate)	3 mg
Copper (gluconate)	1.75 mg
Iron (ferrous fumarate)	7.5 mg
Calcium phosphate (CaHPO$_4$)	37.5 mg
Iodide (KI)	0.15 mg
Biotin	300 mcg

*Vitamin A reduced to 5000 units for months 5–8

The final sample consisted of 56 children who were 6½–15½ years of age at the first testing period. Sixty-four children were initially tested. The 8 children not included in these analyses were excluded for the following reasons: 2 families moved out of the Chicago area; 3 children were too low functioning to be given the Wechsler Scales (they were examined separately with the Bayley Scales of Infant Development); 2 children were unable to swallow the pills; and 1 family decided to withdraw after initial testing, on the advice of the child's physician.

The two matched groups of children were very comparable on all of our variables, after the initial testing period. Each group consisted of 28 children – 20 males and 8 females. Table 7.2 shows the mean chronological ages for each group. It also shows the mean developmental age for performance on the Peabody Picture Vocabulary Test – Revised (Dunn, 1981) at initial testing for each group. This age was used in the matching for intellectual level. These ages were correlated positively with scores on the Wechsler Scales (Wechsler, 1967, 1974). As can be seen, the developmental ages were mostly between 3 and 6 years.

The two groups were also comparable on other matching variables, socioeconomic status – which is known to influence intellectual development (Clements *et al.*, 1978) – and school placement. Five levels of family socioeconomic status, based on education and occupation, were represented (Hollingshead, 1975). The families ranged from level 1, which represented professional status, to level 5, which included unskilled and/or less educated families. The sample was middle to lower-middle class, on average.

The two groups were matched according to the nature of the child's school programme, since this variable could possibly affect test performance. Two characteristics of school programmes were considered: educable versus trainable programme and integrated versus segregated settings. In the US, educable-type programmes in special education tend to place more emphasis on the kinds of

Table 7.2 *Description of subjects according to treatment group*

Criterion	Vitamin/mineral (n = 28)	Placebo (n = 28)
Chronological age		
(in years–months)		
Mean	11–4	11–0
S.D.	2–11	2–7
Cognitive level[1]		
(Age equivalent in years–months)		
Mean	4–6	4–4
S.D.	1–8	1–5
Socioeconomic status[2]		
(scores = 1–5)		
Number of subjects		
1	8	5
2	12	11
3	4	9
4	3	2
5	1	1
Mean score	2.2	2.4
Level of school programme		
Number of subjects (%)		
Educable	8 (29)	10 (36)
Trainable	20 (71)	18 (64)
Type of school		
Number of subjects (%)		
Segregated	13 (46)	12 (43)
Integrated	15 (54)	16 (57)

[1]Based on Peabody Picture Vocabulary Test—Revised (Form L) (12).
[2]Based on Hollingshead's Four-Factor Index of Social Status (16).

academic material included in IQ tests than do the trainable type. Care was taken to assure that the results would not be grossly confounded by this environmental factor. About one-third of the children were in educable programmes and two-thirds were in trainable programmes. Also, it was determined whether the child's classroom was in a completely segregated special education school building or integrated and housed in a school building with regular, normal classrooms. The groups were comparable on both of these school characteristics, with slightly more of each group being in integrated settings.

Karyotypes revealed that the majority of the children (90%) had the standard trisomy for Down's Syndrome; 8% had translocation, and 2% were mosaic form.

Overview of the study design

When parents called to inquire about the study, a brief interview was carried out to gather information about the health, sensory (hearing, vision), developmental and school programme characteristics of the child. Prior to the beginning of initial testing, parents were oriented about the study, the participation requirements were explained, and informed consent was obtained. All parents agreed to cease giving their children regular vitamin/mineral supplements for the course of the study.

The overall design called for testing each child on a battery of standard tests to evaluate intelligence and motor skills. Social skills and personality characteristics were rated by parents and teachers. Behavioural observations during the test sessions were collected from the psychologists who performed the testing. Each child received a physical examination, including weight and height measurements and a blood test. Children were then matched for either the supplement or the placebo group. Parents gave the children 12 pills or capsules daily for a 4-month period, keeping a daily record of intake and health or behavioural changes. A typical weekly diet record was also collected early in the study. After this time, the intelligence and physical examinations were repeated. Parents were interviewed about their observations of the children. The children then received another 4 months' supply of pills. Testing and parent interviews were repeated for a third time after that period. At the 4- and 8-month testings, hair samples were taken for measurement of mineral absorption.

A group of 13 psychologists gave the standard tests to the children. All were 'blind' about the children's groups. Each test session for each child was done by a different psychologist, to reduce test bias. In addition, psychologists were randomly assigned children to assure that the individual psychologists tested an equal number of children from each group.

All of these design features were carefully considered for two reasons: to make sure that the two groups were comparable after the initial testing, and to make sure that random errors would be equal for the two groups.

Standard measures used

All the children were given one of the Wechsler Scale of intelligence tests, either the school-age version or the preschool/primary version. Each of these tests consists of 12 subtests measuring different abilities. Six of these are verbal subtests and six, performance, or non-verbal. For each child, a range of information may be obtained. This includes an overall, or full scale, IQ, a verbal IQ, a performance IQ, and an age-equivalent for each of the 12 individual subtests.

At the initial testing, the school-age Wechsler Intelligence Scale for Children – Revised was attempted with each child. If the child failed to achieve a raw score on at least four of each type of subtest, we then gave that child the Wechsler Preschool and Primary Scale of Intelligence test. This ensured that we had a reasonable measure of each ability for each child. Again the two groups were comparable in that, within each group, 14 children received the WISC-R and 14 children received the WPPSI.

All the children were also given the Peabody Picture Vocabulary Test – Revised at each time period. This is a measure of receptive vocabulary, which correlates highly with other global IQ measures. To minimise retest effects, form L was used at baseline and eighth-month periods, and form M was used at the fourth-month testing.

Two other tests were given at the baseline and eighth-month periods. One was the Beery Developmental Test of Visual–Motor Integration (Beery, 1982). This is a form-copying test measuring visual–motor skill. Overall gross and fine motor skills were evaluated with the Bruininks–Oseretsky Test of Motor Proficiency – Short Form (Bruininks, 1978). This test consists of 14 items tapping gross motor balance, agility and strength, as well as fine motor accuracy, speed and co-ordination. These tests were included to see if specific motor behaviours might be affected by the nutritional supplements. They could also help in interpreting intelligence test results if group differences were found.

Results

Full-scale, verbal and performance IQs were computed. These are shown for the two groups in tables 7.3, 7.4 and 7.5. All of the IQ scores are based on calculations derived from the mean age-equivalents for the individual subtests, using the $IQ = MA/CA \times 100$ described by Wechsler in the test manuals. This was done because the standard norms tables for the Wechsler Preschool and Primary Scale of Intelligence could not be used, since our children were older than the sample norm; scale scores to derive IQ scores could not be obtained in the standard manner. For raw scores below the norm tables, age-equivalents for individual subtests were extrapolated.

Table 7.3 shows the overall IQ scores for the two groups. The mean IQ scores are equivalent for the two groups at all three time periods. There were no significant

Table 7.3 *IQ scores—full scale**

Group	Baseline			4 months			8 months		
	$\bar{x}$	S.D.	Range	$\bar{x}$	S.D.	Range	$\bar{x}$	S.D.	Range
Supplement	45.0	10.6	27.5–69.7	44.6	9.9	26.2–65.5	43.9	10.5	26.8–65.9
Placebo	46.2	10.1	30.3–75.7	45.7	10.6	31.4–76.2	45.0	9.4	32.8–68.2

*Based on $n = 28$ for each group; 14 children in each group received the WISC-R, 14 received the WPPSI.

Table 7.4 *IQ scores—verbal**

Group	Baseline			4 months			8 months		
	$\bar{x}$	S.D.	Range	$\bar{x}$	S.D.	Range	$\bar{x}$	S.D.	Range
Supplement	43.2	11.5	25.7–70.7	42.4	10.8	23.3–65.3	41.6	11.7	24.1–67.7
Placebo	44.8	11.5	25.3–77.3	42.5	11.4	24.6–73.0	42.8	11.6	27.2–69.3

*Based on $n = 28$ for each group; 14 children in each group received the WISC-R, 14 received the WPPSI.

Table 7.5 *IQ scores—performance scale**

Group	Baseline			4 months			8 months		
	$\bar{x}$	S.D.	Range	$\bar{x}$	S.D.	Range	$\bar{x}$	S.D.	Range
Supplement	46.8	10.0	27.6–68.6	46.8	9.8	26.6–60.8	46.2	8.4	29.6–64.1
Placebo	47.9	9.2	33.1–74.0	48.9	10.4	33.5–79.4	47.2	8.2	33.2–67.1

*Based on $n = 28$ for each group; 14 children in each group received the WISC-R, 14 received the WPPSI.

differences between the groups, and there were no changes in scores over time for either group. The range of scores was also comparable for the two groups, both within and across time periods. Tables 7.4 and 7.5 show the same pattern of non-significant change for both verbal IQ and performance IQ scores. Table 7.4 shows results for verbal IQ scores. Table 7.5 shows the performance IQ scores. Here again, the range of scores was comparable. As might be expected, perform-ance (non-verbal) IQ scores were higher than verbal IQ scores by about 4 to 6 points, on average, for both groups.

This same pattern of non-significant group mean differences was also obtained for the other tests given. Table 7.6 shows average age-equivalents in months for the Peabody Picture Vocabulary Test. Note that the two groups are equivalent at the initial testing, with average age-equivalents of about 4½ years. There is a slight improvement, on average, after 4 months (but this occurs for both groups) and the mean changes are not different by group. Some of this improvement is probably due to the fact that Form M of this test yields slightly higher scores than Form L.

Table 7.7 shows mean age-equivalents in months for the fine motor form-copying test. Here again, there are no group differences. Note that the average levels for both groups at all times were almost at a 5-year level. Finally, Table 7.8 shows mean group scores for the motor test. The numbers shown are total numbers of

Table 7.6 *Peabody Picture Vocabulary Test–Revised Scores*. Age equivalent (in months)*

	Baseline		4 months		8 months	
Group	$\bar{x}$	S.D.	$\bar{x}$	S.D.	$\bar{x}$	S.D.
Supplement	53.9	19.8	60.9	20.8	57.3	20.8
Placebo	52.1	16.6	56.7	17.6	55.8	16.0

*Form L was given at baseline and 8 months. Form M was given at 4 months.

Table 7.7 *Developmental test of visual–motor integration (VMI). Age equivalent (in months)*

	Baseline			8 months		
Group	$\bar{x}$	S.D.	Range	$\bar{x}$	S.D.	Range
Supplement	56.0	9.6	36–72	58.5	11.1	38–82
Placebo	58.3	11.2	38–88	58.7	10.6	38–82

Table 7.8 *Bruininks–Oseretsky test of motor proficiency scores*

	Baseline		8 months	
	Total point score			
Group	$\bar{x}$	S.D.	$\bar{x}$	S.D.
Supplement	18.6	10.4	23.8	10.9
Placebo	17.0	8.9	23.1	8.8
	Gross motor point score			
Group	$\bar{x}$	S.D.	$\bar{x}$	S.D.
Supplement	8.8	6.5	10.2	6.7
Placebo	8.6	5.6	9.5	5.9
	Fine motor point score			
Group	$\bar{x}$	S.D.	$\bar{x}$	S.D.
Supplement	7.7	4.4	10.4	4.4
Placebo	6.4	3.6	10.4	4.6

points for the entire short form of the test. Although we did not specifically match the two groups on this measure at the initial test period, it is obvious that the groups were comparable. It is also apparent that both groups showed a comparable amount of improvement with no difference between the two groups.

All of these group analyses clearly show that there were no significant improvements on intellectual or motor functioning for a group of school-aged children with Down's Syndrome who took large doses of nutritional supplements for 8 months. An additional way to examine the data is to calculate the average amount of change in scores over the three time periods. We looked at each child's IQ score to see if it increased or decreased over the course of the study. These data are shown in Table 7.9. As can be seen, for both groups, for all time periods, the average change in IQ scores was negligible. In fact, these results indicate that the scores were relatively stable over this period of time. It is likely that the slight changes that did occur can be accounted for entirely by error factors. For the majority of children, IQ scores for the three time periods were within 5 points of each other, which is what would be expected by chance over time.

Table 7.9 *Mean changes in IQ scores*

IQ by group	0–4 months	4–8 months	0–8 months
Full IQ			
Supplement	−0.4	−0.7	−1.1
Placebo	−0.2	−1.0	−1.4
Verbal IQ			
Supplement	−0.8	−0.75	−1.6
Placebo	−1.6	−0.3	−2.2
Performance IQ			
Supplement	0	−0.7	−0.7
Placebo	+1.2	−1.7	−0.6

Nine children (16%) of the total sample had changes (either increases or decreases) in IQ scores of between 5.3 and 8.7 over the 8-month period, with no child showing a change in IQ score of 9 or more points. In the vitamin/mineral group, 5 children showed the following full-scale IQ point changes from baseline to 8 months: +8.7, +7.5, −7.1, −8.6, and −6.5. In the placebo group, 4 children showed the following full-scale IQ point changes from the baseline to 8 months: −7.5, −7.2, −5.8, and −5.3.

The initial daily dose of vitamin A was 15 000 units in the nutritional supplement, and this dosage was used for the first 4 months of the study until the 4-month psychological testing was completed. For the second 4 months of the study (months 5 through 8), the vitamin A daily dose was reduced to 5000 units to prevent any toxic reactions to the vitamin. Psychological tests, comparing the two 4-month periods of time in which the different dosages of vitamin A were used, show no significant differences in test scores during these periods.

In the study by Harrell *et al.* (1981), thyroid medication was used intermittently and was given to both the nutritional supplement and the placebo groups and, therefore, thyroid medication did not influence their final results. In the present study, no thyroid medication was used. All the children in the study had normal thyroid function as demonstrated by a battery of thyroid tests that were done at the start of the study and repeated at 4 and 8 months after the study was begun. In the Chicago study and the study by Harrell *et al.*, the issue is whether or not megadoses of vitamins and minerals affect intelligence; it has nothing to do with the attributes of thyroid medication under similar circumstances.

Conclusions

The results of the Chicago study demonstrated that the use of this combination of nutritional supplements in school-aged children with Down's Syndrome, over an 8-month period of time, did not lead to improvements in intellectual test performance. Changes in IQ scores were negligible and could be accounted for by test–retest and error factors. Subsequent to the initial publication of these findings (Smith *et al.*, 1983), other investigators utilising double-blind procedures published failures to replicate the findings of Harrell *et al.* (1981), both with children (Bennett *et al.*, 1983; Weathers, 1983) and with adults (Ellis and Tomporowski, 1983). Thus, careful investigation of this topic disclosed no basis for providing megadoses of vitamins and minerals to children with Down's Syndrome. While current knowledge suggests nutritional treatment with megavitamins plays no role in amelioration of the mental deficiency seen in Down's Syndrome, the good health of these children depends on adequate nutritional management. Specific nutritional difficulties have been reported, including a tendency for obesity in later childhood, dental problems and the development of some specific vitamin deficiencies. Thus, comprehensive paediatric care, including dental care, is recommended. (See Palmer and Ekvall (1978) for a detailed nutritional protocol for Down's children.)

Basic research into metabolic and biochemical abnormalities in Down's Syndrome should be encouraged. These studies may lead to medical or nutritional treatments which ameliorate the physical and intellectual deficits associated with this syndrome. Each hypothesis must be subjected to careful clinical study before instituting treatments which may at the least lead to disappointment and dashed expectations, and at the worst to harm for those children we are so anxious to help.

Although the children in the Chicago study did not respond differentially to the vitamin/mineral supplement, wide variation in their abilities was found. Investigation of home, school and community factors, which are related to this variation, need further research. Such studies would offer to families of children with Down's Syndrome the knowledge they need for providing optimal environments for their children's development and intellectual functioning.

ACKNOWLEDGEMENTS

The authors would like to thank the children and parents whose generous and faithful co-operation made the Chicago study possible. We are also indebted to the other members of the research team, most notably our principal investigator, George F. Smith MD, and to Pat Smith for her editorial and administrative assistance.

REFERENCES

Beery, K.E. (1982). *Revised Administration, Scoring, and Teaching Manual for the Developmental Test of Visual–Motor Integration*, Chicago: Follett.

Bennett, F.C., McClelland, S., Kriegsmann, Andrus, L.B. and Sells, C. (1983). Vitamin and mineral supplementation in Down syndrome. *Pediatrics* **72**(5), 707–713.

Bruininks, R.H. (1978). *Bruininks–Oseretsky Test of Motor Proficiency: Examiners' Manual.* Circle Pines, Minnesota: American Guidance Service.

Bumbalo, T.S., Morelewicz, H.V. and Berens, D.L. (1964). Treatment of Down syndrome with the 'U' series of drugs. *J. Am. Med. Assoc.* **187**, 125.

Clements, P.R., Bates M.V. and Hafer, M. (1976). Variability within Down's syndrome (Trisomy # 21): Empirically observed sex differences in IQ. *Ment. Retard.* **14**, 30–31.

Clements, P.R., Hafer, M. and Pollock, J.L. (1978). Parental education and rate of intellectual development of Down's syndrome (Trisomy # 21) children. *Res. & Retard.* **5**, 15–19.

Denhoff, E. and Feldman, S.A. (1981). *Developmental Disabilities, Management through Diet and Medication.* New York and Basel: Marcel Dekker.

Dunn, L.M. (1981). *Peabody Picture Vocabulary Test (Revised): Manual for Forms L and M.* Circle Pines, Minnesota: American Guidance Service.

Ellis, N.R. and Tomporowski, P.D. (1983). Vitamin/mineral supplements and intelligence of institutionalized mentally retarded adults. *Am. J. Ment. Defic.* **88**(2), 211–214.

Harrell, H.F., Capp, R.H., Davis, D.R., Peerless, J. and Ravitz, L.R. (1981). Can nutritional supplements help mentally retarded children? An exploratory study. *Proc. Natl. Acad. Sci. USA* **78**, 574–8.

Hollingshead, A.B. (1975). *Four Factor Index of Social Status.* Unpublished manuscript, Yale University.

Morgan, S.B. (1979). Development and distribution of intellectual and adaptive skills in Down syndrome children: Implications for early intervention. *Ment. Retard.* **15**, 247–9.

Palmer, S. and Ekvall, S. (eds) (1978). *Pediatric Nutrition in Developmental Disabilities.* Springfield, Ill.: Charles C. Thomas.

Pauling, L. (1968). Orthomolecular psychiatry. *Science* **160**, 265.

Pueschel, S. (1981). Treatment approaches. In De la Cruz, F. and Gerald, P., *Trisomy 21.* Baltimore: University Park Press.

Rosenberg, L.E., Lilljequist, A.C. and Hsia, Y.E. (1968). Methylmalonic aciduria: Metabolic block localization and Vitamin B12 dependency. *Science* **162**, 805–807.

Sattler, J.M. (1982). *Assessment of Children's Intelligence and Special Abilities*, 2nd edn. Boston: Allyn and Bacon.

Scriver, C.R., Mackenzie, S., Clow, C.L. and Delvin, E. (1970). Thiamine-responsive maple syrup urine disease. *Lancet* **i**, 310–13.

Smith, G.F., Spiker, D., Peterson, C. Cicchetti, D. and Justice, P. (1983). Failure of vitamin/mineral supplementation in Down syndrome. *Lancet* **ii**, 8340–41.

Smith, G.F., Spiker, D., Peterson, C., Cicchetti, D. and Justice, P. (1984). Use of megadoses of vitamins with mineral in Down Syndrome. *J. Ped.* **105**(2), August.

Turkel, H. (1975). Medical amelioration of Down syndrome incorporating the orthomolecular approach. *J. Orthomol. Psych.* **4**, 102–115.

Weathers, C. (1983). Effects of nutritional supplementation on IQ and other variables associated with Down syndrome. *Am. J. Ment. Defic.* **88**(2), 214–17.

Wechsler, D. (1967). *Manual for the Wechsler Preschool and Primary Scale of Intelligence.* New York: The Psychological Corporation.

Wechsler, D. (1974). *Manual for the Wechsler Intelligence Scale of Intelligence for Children – Revised.* New York: The Psychological Corporation.

Williams, R.J. (1956). *Biochemical Individuality: The Basis for the Genetotropic Concept.* Austin: University of Texas.

8 Plastic Surgery

Gottfried Lemperle

Parents in general are proud of their children and try to make them as presentable as possible, sending them to the hairdresser to get a good haircut and buying them nice clothes. Eventually, parents may send a child to the plastic surgeon if he or she has protruding ears which result in the child being teased. Appearance is much easier to correct than deficiencies in schoolwork or in sports.

The child with Down's Syndrome may not notice his or her different appearance and is, in general, happy with it. It is the parents who are disturbed by the differences between their Down's child and others and who often approach the plastic surgeon to ask for corrective treatment. Also the increased life expectation of people with Down's Syndrome has led to new challenges, such as training for a job, social integration and sexual maturation. All this increases the importance of improving appearance. There are, however, other areas, besides appearance, where the plastic surgeon can help – notably in the functional improvement of the tongue and therefore speech.

The clinical entity of Down's Syndrome comprises a number of characteristic traits in the face and extremities, which are listed below.

1. Mongoloid folds (epicanthus).
2. Oblique lid axis.
3. Unilateral squinting (strabismus).
4. Saddle nose.
5. Flat jaw bones (dish face).
6. Large hypotonic tongue (macroglossia).
7. Hypotonic lower lip (cheilosis).
8. Receding chin (microgenia).
9. Double chin.
10. Protruding ears (cockleshell ears).

In addition to a congenital mental handicap of varying degrees, these children present a thickset stature, pasty skin, generalised muscular hypotonia with unilateral strabismus, hyperextensibility of the joints, the well-known simian crease, and a so-called sandal gap (i.e. a gap between the first and second toes). Not infrequently, they also suffer from a congenital heart defect (see Chapter 3).

DOWN'S SYNDROME AND PLASTIC SURGERY

At the meeting of the Latin American Society of Plastic Surgery in Quito in 1967, Otermin Aguirre (1968 from Argentina presented the first 10 cases of Down's Syndrome after surgical correction. In the same year, Höhler (1977) from Frankfurt operated on a girl by augmenting her hypoplastic nose and receding chin with polyethylene implants (Figs 8.1 and 8.2). As a result the girl looked much less abnormal and underwent noticeable developmental changes (Fig. 8.3). Later, Lemperle and Radu (1980) started a larger series of operations on children with Down's Syndrome, followed by Olbrisch (1982, 1983), Regenbrecht (1981), Wexler and Peled (1983), Rozner (1983), and many others. From August 1977 to

Table 8.1 *Operations in children with Down's Syndrome (1977–1982)*

Total	186
Questionnaires	158
Answers	119 (75%)
Tongue reductions	107 (90%)
Nasal implants	51 (32%)
Mongoloid folds	25 (16%)
Lid axis	21 (14%)
Other corrections	35 (22%)

December 1982, a total of 187 children with Down's Syndrome were operated on in Frankfurt (Table 8.1). A further 250 children were treated in Munich, mainly for tongue reductions. Their ages ranged from 2 to 22 years, with a peak between 4 and 8 years.

FUNCTIONAL CORRECTIONS MADE

Hypotonia of the tongue

The tongue is the mediator between our thoughts, wishes, responses and the world around us. Consequently, the tongue occupies quite a large area in our sensory and motor brain cortex. Apart from mental retardation, the late speech development of children with Down's Syndrome may also be caused by the ease with which they become fatigued as well as the well-known hypotonia of their muscles. As with patients with muscular dystrophy, the body may try to overcome diminished function by hyperplasia. The large tongue of patients with Down's Syndrome does not form a concave dish with its upper border connecting with the upper molars, but lies like a convex loaf of bread in the oral cavity (Fig. 8.4). Castillo-Morales et al (1982) developed a palatal device, a plate with a central knob of 8 cm in diameter and 3 mm in height (Fig. 8.5). The child is forced to move its tongue constantly in an attempt to get rid of the knob.

The palatal plate is worn 24 hours a day, except during meals, for at least 1 year. It can be applied to infants from the second month of life up to puberty. It is fitted every 3 months by the orthodontist and corrected, when necessary, by enlarging or repositioning the knob.

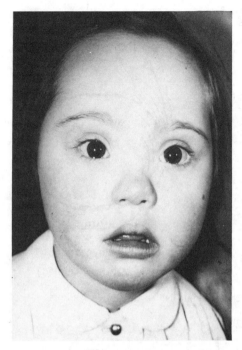

Fig. 8.1 A 5-year-old girl with typical features of Down's Syndrome

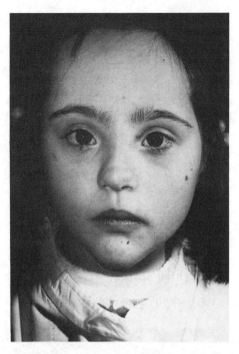

Fig. 8.2 Same girl as in Fig. 8.1 after augmenting the saddle nose and receding chin with polyethylene implants

Fig. 8.3 The same girl as in Figs 8.1 and 8.2 aged 18 years old, 2 years after exchange of implants

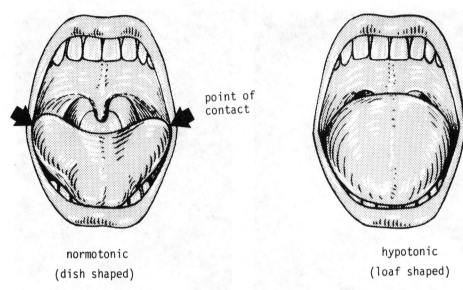

point of
contact

normotonic   hypotonic
(dish shaped)   (loaf shaped)

Fig. 8.4 The shape of the tongue in a normal child and in a child with Down's Syndrome

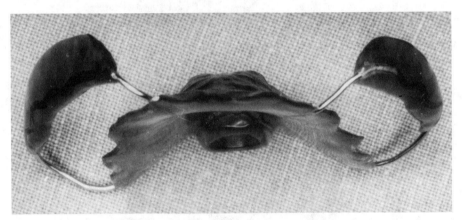

Fig. 8.5 The disturbing knob of the palatal device of Castillo-Morales

Macroglossia

In most of the patients reported on, the protruding tongue was reduced by means of a large rhomboid excision of the tip. In patients who have a broad-based tongue, the wedge-shaped excision must extend dorsally, up to a distance of approximately 1 cm from the papillae. Care must be taken that at least 3 cm of the frenulum remains, so the tip of the tongue does not become too round. Later, the patient should be able to reach the entire prolabium with the tip of the tongue to prevent saliva from crusting (Fig. 8.6). The tongue is initially greatly swollen, and will assume its final, smaller, size only after 4 to 6 weeks.

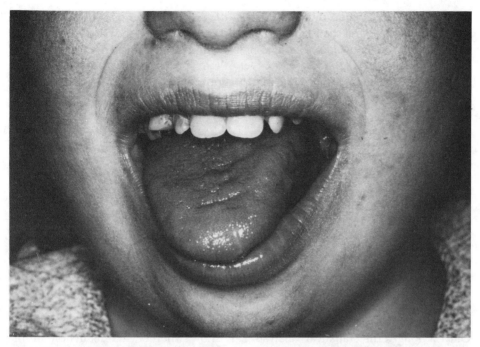

Fig. 8.6 Result of tongue reduction with inverted and running resorbable sutures

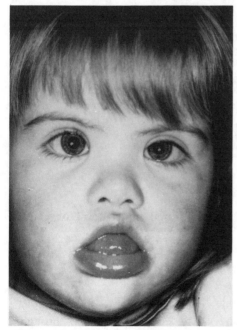

Fig. 8.7 A 3-year-old girl with antimongoloid folds and open mouth

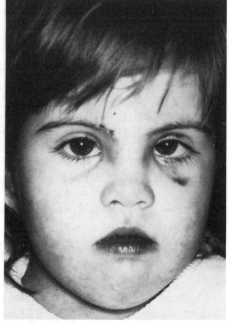

Fig. 8.8 Disappearance of epicanthus 6 days after nose augmentation and closure of the mouth after tongue reduction

The success of tongue reduction is best illustrated by the fact that most of the children suddenly kept their mouths closed (Fig. 8.8). It was the open, moist mouth with the protruding oversized tongue that was the most striking overt sign of their mental deficiency (Fig. 8.7). Moreover, their speech, which before had been slurred and inarticulate, became much more intelligible due to the enlarged intraoral resonance box, which, in turn, led to improved communication skills (Table 8.2).

Table 8.2 *Parental views of the effect of tongue reduction (total = 107)*

Parents' views	Number (%)
Speech improved	73 (68)
Speech unchanged	22 (20)
Speech worse	7 (7)
No answer	5 (5)

It is often asked whether these children may not suffer from an impaired sense of taste, due to the excision of the proglossis. The answer is that the sensations for sweet and salty taste extend relatively far toward the side of the tongue, and none of the patients has so far indicated any loss of taste. Moreover, for most of these children, a slight reduction in their predilection for food should only be welcomed. Only a long-term statistical analysis can show whether the reduction in the incidence of nasopharyngeal infections (also reported by many parents) can be related to the tongue reduction.

Strabismus

One-third of all children in our series had an obvious unilateral strabismus (squint). Since squinting is a rather disturbing feature in communication with any child, we put pressure on parents to seek operative treatment by an ophthalmic surgeon. Ophthalmologists, however, still tend to view the chances of surgical repair of a squint with great reservation (see Chapter 6).

AESTHETIC IMPROVEMENT

The following aesthetic corrections can be performed under local or general anaesthesia in one operation.

Saddle nose

The hypoplastic and frequently sunken bridge of the nose is raised by means of a straight silicone implant (Fig. 8.9) which is inserted into the nose through a vestibular incision. The medical trade supplies different sizes and shapes of silicone implants, which can be cut down further to fit the individual patient's nose. At the beginning we had some problems finding the right size of implant (Table 8.3).

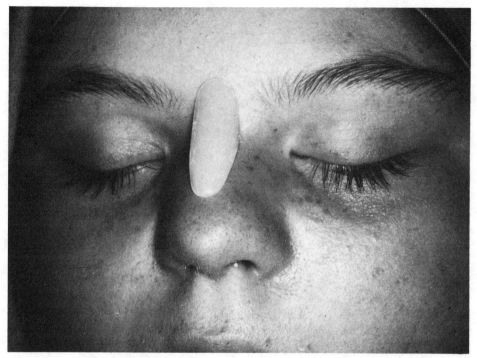

Fig. 8.9 Silicone implant for nasal augmentation

Table 8.3 *The effect of nasal implants (total = 51)*

	Number (%)
Improvement	40 (78)
Too big	7 (14)
Removed	4 (8)

Epicanthus

The epicanthal fold is often very conspicuous (Fig. 8.10), and in most cases is reduced by raising the bridge of the nose. This means that an additional Z-plasty (Fig 8.11) above the inner canthus becomes necessary only if the epicanthus is very pronounced or if a nasal implant would greatly impair the profile.

Lid axis

So far, the oblique lid axis has been corrected in 21 children in this study (Table 8.4), by lowering the raised lateral canthus (Figs 8.12, 8.13 and 8.14). Since a proper lateral canthal ligament was rarely found during surgery, a triangular segment was raised from the upper portion of the orbicular muscle and sutured to the periosteum of the outer lower orbital angle.

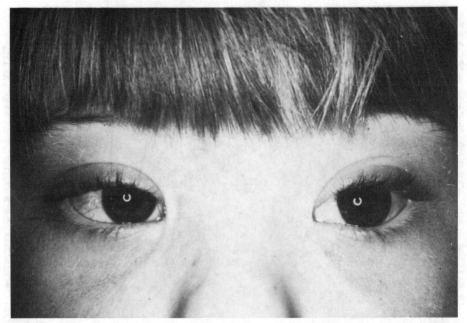

Fig. 8.10 Typical epicanthal fold in a 5-year-old boy

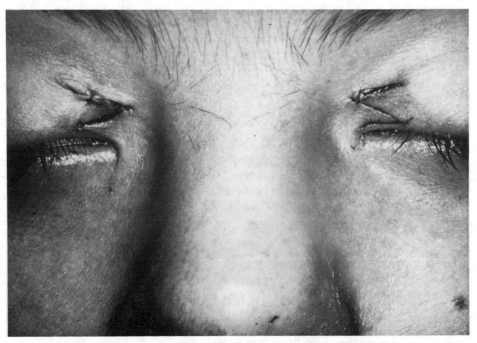

Fig. 8.11 The same boy as in Fig. 8.10 after nasal implant and Z-plasty

DELIVERY ADDRESS
Will Podmore
The British School Of Osteopathy
Avon House, 275-287 Borough
High Street,
LONDON

SE1 1JE,
UNITED KINGDOM

Bookbarn International Ltd
Unit 1 Hallatrow Business Park, Wells
Road, Hallatrow,
Bristol
Somerset, BS39 6EX,
UNITED KINGDOM

Packing Slip / Invoice
Price: £2.81
Standard

Order Date:	20/04/2017		Shipped:	20/04/2017

BBI Order Number: 528422

Customer Contact: Will Podmore

Website Order ID: 204-6564955-9021903

SKU InvID	Locators	Item Information
1866300 9028669	C63-14-06 211514 White PAP ExLib - Y U:G	**Current Approaches to Downs Syndrome** Lane, D. & Stratford, Brian Ex Library.

If you wish to contact us regarding this order, please email us via Amazon quoting your order number.

amzuk

Thanks for shopping with us

www.bookbarninternational.com

528422

BOOKBARN
I N T E R N A T I O N A L

Millions of Books | Thousands of Topics | One Bookbarn

Dear Customer,

Thank You For placing this Order!

In doing so you've helped us grow as an independent bookseller.

We hope you're happy with your purchase, and we'd love it if you could tell us how we did. Rating us online takes just a few seconds on the website you used to place your order.

Giving us a negative rating can be very damaging so please, if we have not met your expectations, contact our Customer Care Team who will work to assist you as quickly as possible.

Our small and committed team provides a fast response to ensure you are fully satisfied. We look forward to hearing from you soon!

Kind regards,

The Bookbarn International Team

We'd love to see photos of you with your books! Follow us on Instagram
@bookbarn_international to carry on the conversation.

UK +44 (0)1761 451 777
bookbarn@bookbarninternational.com

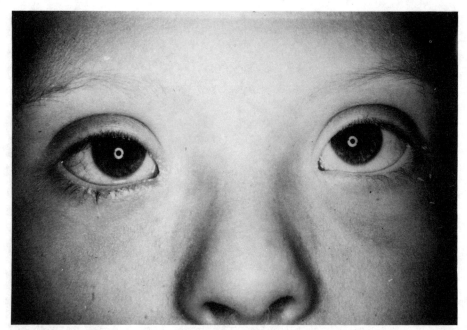

Fig. 8.12 Oblique lid axis

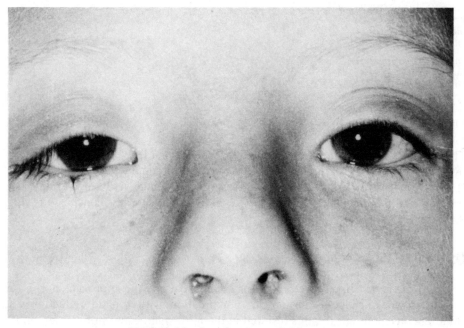

Fig. 8.13 After lowering the canthal ligament

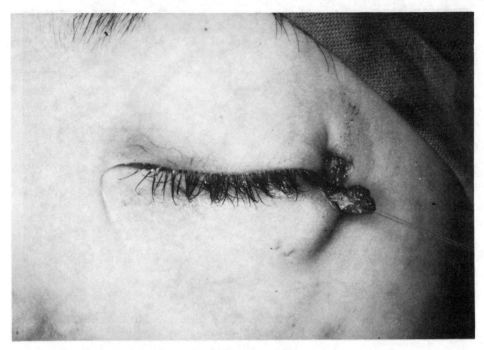

Fig. 8.14 Fixation of the lateral canthal ligament to the orbital rim

Table 8.4 *Effects of plastic surgery on the epicanthic fold and oblique lid axis*

	Number (%)
Epicanthic fold ($n = 25$)	
Inconspicuous	22 (88)
Still obvious	3 (12)
Oblique lid axis ($n = 21$)	
Improved	20 (95)
Unchanged	1 (5)

Microgenia

The easiest way to augment the small chin, which is made even more pronounced by the protrusion of the teeth, is also by means of a commercial silicone implant (Fig. 8.15). It is inserted through an incision in the labiogingival fold. Frequently, this will also help to make the fleshy neck and double chin less conspicuous (Figs 8.16 and 8.17).

Hypotonia of the lower lip

The hanging lower lip required repair in 23 children, and the approach chosen was a sagittal wedge-shaped excision. In combination with tongue reduction and simultaneous mentoplasty, this resulted in the most significant improvement in the children's appearance.

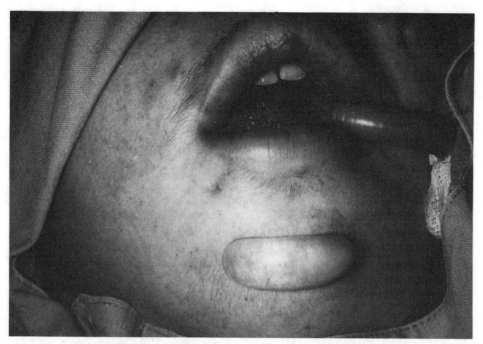

Fig. 8.15 Chin implant, inserted through the labial mucosa

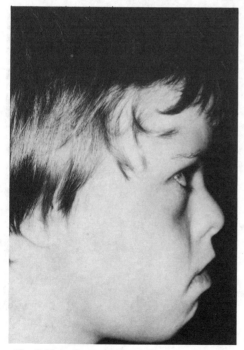

Fig. 8.16 An 8-year-old boy with a receding chin

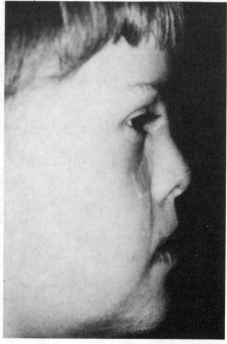

Fig. 8.17 The same boy as in Fig. 8.16, 4 days after improvement of his profile with chin and nasal implants. (He might need malar implants too.)

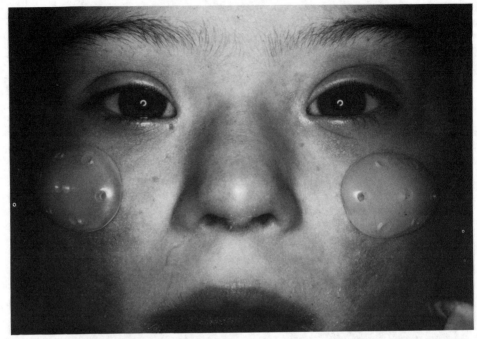

Fig. 8.18 In children with 'dish face', malar implants are inserted through a lower lid incision

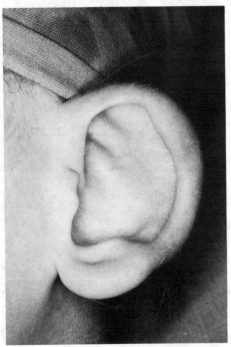

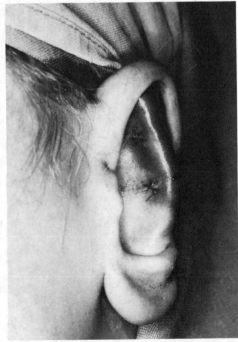

Fig. 8.19 'Cockleshell' ear

Fig. 8.20 Correction of 'cockleshell' ear, according to Stenström

Hypoplasia of the malar bones

Most children with Down's Syndrome have rather flat jaw bones (see Fig. 8.16). In selected cases, augmentation with commercial silicone implants (Fig. 8.18) improved facial appearance.

Protruding ears

One-quarter of our children had protruding ears. Since most of these children have a rather broad face, these ears are even more conspicuous and tend to make the child look less intelligent. They can be corrected by one of the many methods in plastic surgery (Figs 8.19 and 8.20).

COMPLICATIONS

So far, there have been eight complications in the form of dislocations or infections as a result of the plastic implants (see Table 8.3). However, parents were warned that the nose or chin implants inserted in early childhood might have to be replaced by larger ones after puberty. In 12 children, a suture dehiscence occurred at the tip of the tongue between the third and the sixth postoperative days, which required secondary suturing. The cause was a severance of the wound edges by the sharp resorbable sutures and a continuous compulsive mastication by the children concerned.

TIMING

We consider the pre-school age (between 4 and 6 years) to be the most favourable time for the above-mentioned surgical repairs. The children will then be less conspicuous, even in kindergarten, and will suffer less from taunts from their schoolmates. It is only at this stage that the speech-related effect of tongue reduction can be assessed properly. Exceptions to this age rule are, of course, cases of extreme macroglossia, which, for functional reasons, should be repaired at the age of 2, i.e. before assessment of speech. There is, however, no upper age limit if these simple repairs promise significant improvement.

The surgical interventions for saddle nose, epicanthus, lid axis and microgenia in children should be performed under general anaesthesia. They normally require no more than 30 minutes. Hospitalisation of 2 to 6 days is recommended. However, hospitalisation can be dispensed with, e.g. in the case of a close mother–child bond.

DISCUSSION

Most Down's children have enlarged adenoids and tonsils resulting in narrowing of the lower pharynx and of the superior laryngeal aperture. In addition, the nasal airways are often obstructed by chronic infection, hyperplastic conchae, a thick nasal septum or small nostril openings. The gaping mouth and protrusion of the tongue seen in many of these patients relate to the need to provide an airway. Removal of obstructions may help many of them to close their mouth and may perhaps favourably influence jaw development.

On the other hand, macroglossia is a main symptom, and the reduction of the tongue to a normal size is thought to have its benefits for throat infection rate, drooling, appearance (Figs 8.21 and 8.22), as well as social integration in the eyes of the parents (see Table 8.2). Children with Down's Syndrome who have a lesser degree of mental deficiency are themselves aware of the changes brought about by surgery. This is borne out by the fact that they often ask why and where they have been operated on. After surgery, they tell other children and adults about their operation. One 10-year-old girl told us, after three surgical repairs, 'Now I am perfectly normal'. It is hoped that this child, at least, has gained an enhanced self-concept which, in turn, will lead to a greater degree of outward communication. That accomplishment will enable her to find better acceptance and less prejudice from the world around her. The surgical procedures outlined are so simple and risk free for the patient that we feel that they should be offered to all parents.

It would certainly be premature to speculate about the effect of plastic facial surgery on the mental development of these children. With a 10% exception, their highly critical and committed parents have been satisfied and gratified by the results achieved (Table 8.5). They report that other people keep saying how much better the children look and how well they suddenly articulate. Fortunately, a person's appearance is not dependent solely on the size of the tongue or the shape

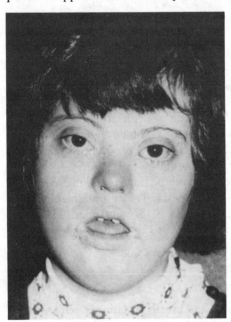

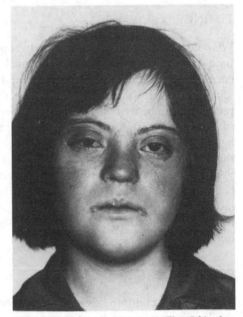

Fig. 8.21 A 16-year-old girl with Down's Syndrome

Fig. 8.22 The same girl as in Fig. 8.21 after correction of the lid axis, nasal augmentation and tongue reduction

Table 8.5 *Parents' answers to the question: Would you send your child again for this operation? (total = 119)*

	Number (%)
Without reservations yes	93 (78)
With reservations yes	12 (10)
Don't know	7 (6)
*No	7 (6)

*All 7 children had complications with their tongues.

of the nose; it is made up of a mass of features including posture, behaviour and self-confidence.

SUMMARY

These six minor corrections to the faces of children with Down's Syndrome can clearly improve their facial expressions. Reduction of macroglossia may facilitate articulation and phonation. Augmentation of the bridge of the nose effaces the epicanthus. The lid axis, the hypotonic lower lip, and microgenia can be repaired. However, while the parents have been satisfied with the results of surgery, a positive effect on social behaviour and mental development of the children has not yet been proven.

REFERENCES

Caronni, E.P. (1985). Surgical correction of some defects in Down's syndrome. In: Caronni, E.P. (ed.), *Craniofacial Surgery*, pp. 211–14. Boston/Toronto: Little Brown and Co.

Castillo-Morales, R., Crotti, E. and Limbrock, G. (1982). Orofaziale Regulation beim Down-Syndrom durch Gaumenplatte. *Sozialpädiatrie* **4**, 10–17.

Höhler, H. (1977). Changes in facial expression as a result of plastic surgery in mongoloid children. *Aesth. Plast. Surg.* **1**, 245–50.

Lemperle, G. and Radu, D. (1980). Facial plastic surgery in children with Down's syndrome. *Plast. Reconstr. Surg.* **66**, 337–42.

Lemperle, G. and Nievergelt, J. (1983). Plastisch-chirurgische Korrekturen im Gesicht von Kinder mit Down-Syndrom. *Plastische Chirurgie bei Menschen mit Down Syndrom, Lebenshilfe Marburg* **9**, 19–32.

Olbrisch, R.R. (1982). Plastic surgical management of children with Down's syndrome: indications and results. *Br. J. Plast. Surg.* **35**, 195–200.

Olbrisch, R.R. (1983). Plastic surgery in 250 children with Down's syndrome: indications and results. In *Transactions of the Eighth International Congress of Plastic Reconstructive Surgery, Montreal*, pp. 702–703.

Otermin Aguirre, J.A. (1968). Mongolism and plastic surgery. *Bol. y Trab. Acad. Argent. Circ. Buenos Aires* **29**, 1.

Rand, Y., Mintsker, Y. and Feuerstein, R. (1984). *Reconstructive Plastic Surgery in Down's Syndrome Children and Adults: Parent's Evaluations – follow up data.* Jerusalem: Hadassah–Wizo–Canada Research Institute.

Regenbrecht, I. (1981). Operative Korrectur der Trisomie 21. *Allg. Arzt.* **3**, 333–4.

Rozner, L. (1983). Facial plastic surgery for Down's Syndrome. *Lancet* **ii**, 1320–23.

Wexler, M.R. and Peled, I. (1983). Plastic surgery in Down's syndrome. *Down's Syndrome* **6**, 7.

Educational Aspects

9 Learning and Knowing: the Education of Down's Syndrome Children

Brian Stratford

Until recent times too many professionals shared the view, regarding the educability of Down's children, of an experienced and prominent physician who wrote: 'You show me just one mongoloid that has an educable IQ. I have never seen one' (Restak, 1975). Fortunately, more professionals are becoming aware of the potential of Down's Syndrome children and consequently not only do they tend to be less gloomy in their predictions, but also their advice is less likely to be based on such a narrow observation. Unfortunately, at the same time there are too many of those still around who are unduly pessimistic about developmental potential and future employability. The majority of parents interviewed in a study by Springer and Steele (1980) had been given a fairly negative picture by their physicians, and although the greater number of these parents indicated that they had not just passively accepted the depressing clinical picture given them, we must not assume from this that such early counselling is totally without effect. If parents are told by a representative of a respected profession that their child will never walk, talk or learn in any reasonable way, then they might be less inclined to encourage such developments. Early counselling of parents should ideally emphasise the positive factors in reaching goals and producing attainments. The most important basic element is a warm, loving and stimulating home environment (Centerwell and Centerwell, 1960; Brinkworth, 1975).

INTELLIGENCE TESTING AND ASSESSMENT

Although the level of attainments which might be reached varies considerably in Down's Syndrome, information can be presented to parents in such a way as to be encouraging and optimistic, but without leading to unrealistic expectations. New parents of Down's children are particularly vulnerable and often expect far worse than is the case. To be realistic, Down's children should be viewed as children with certain limitations but who, given the right kind of special education, could reach a stage of development which would enable them to have a semi-independent existence and to enjoy a reasonable life-style within their limitations, contributing, too, to the development of those around them (Aronson and Fallstrom, 1977). Do we in fact ask for any more from our 'normal' children? The real problem is that

149

Down's children are identified, categorised and isolated on the grounds of their pathological condition, obvious in their appearance, rather than on intelligence levels. It is no good pointing to those Down's children who can read, write, calculate and so on – the myth persists. I have no wish to go on defending the place of IQ in educability, and, furthermore, intelligence levels of Down's children have been well covered in another chapter. It should, however, be repeated that the measurement of individual human intelligence is at best a crude process and becomes even less reliable as an indicator of potential when applied to handicapped children. Indeed, tests can only work on the assumption that, given the combination of a competent psychologist, a well standardised individual test and a child free from sensory and emotional handicaps, who has enjoyed the modest degree of acculturisation assumed by the test, a reasonable approximation to a true measure of innate potential will emerge.

There cannot be many still around who believe that intelligence tests directly measure inborn qualities. Most would agree with the Canadian psychologist Hebb (1972), who described an innate intelligence varying from one person to another and setting some sort of limit to the speed and complexity of intellectual operations of which an individual would be capable. This inborn intelligence, corresponding to some property of the central nervous system, is described as Intelligence A and, from conception onwards, is acted upon by the environment. The quality of stimulation received during infancy is critical in determining how much of the original Intelligence A will be available for mental operations. By the end of infancy, there will be in evidence a general level of intellectual functioning which is known as Intelligence B. This is a kind of amalgam of the original genetic endowment – Intelligence A – and the environmental forces which have been in operation. It is this Intelligence B – present mental efficiency – which we attempt to measure by intelligence tests. Actual scores obtained will be approximations to the true value of Intelligence B, and for report purposes or remedial action will always require a certain amount of interpretation in accordance with the kind of test used and other information available about the child.

It is understandable that a great deal of work has gone into the development of programmes for the pre-school Down's child as the quenching of potentiality will seldom be so severe as during the critical years of infancy. However, the suggestion that if, for some reason, advantage has been missed and the early years have been deprived of specific stimulating programmes, then some permanent damage has been done and it is too late to do anything about it, is not only a dangerous nonsense, but is also untrue and misleading. Intelligence B itself will tend to fluctuate during school years and after, in response to the quality of intellectual stimulation afforded by the school and home. For this reason alone it is a pity that there is less attention given by researchers to development at school and almost none to the post-school years. So much encouragement can be drawn from studies demonstrating positive gains as a result of educational intervention in the pre-school years. Pueschel and Rynders (1983) have written an extensive review of such projects. Rynders (1983), however, draws attention to the paucity of studies promoting academic achievement for older children. He suggests that a spurious logic might be operating which would be reinforced through expectation fulfilment:

how can we expect Down's children to learn, understand or make achievements in a scholastic sense when they are severely mentally handicapped? After all they were officially regarded as quite ineducable in Britain until 1971. Some researchers have refused to accept this pessimistic view and have shown that children with Down's Syndrome, given good and appropriate teaching, can learn relatively sophisticated academic skills. Rynders cites one or two of these studies, but one is of particular interest because it explodes another of those myths which seem to accrue to Down's Syndrome. Dalton *et al.* (1973) demonstrate ability in mathematics commonly believed to be outside the range of achievement possibilities for Down's children. The study examined the effectiveness of a token economy system in promoting mathematics achievement. Subjects were 13 Down's children whose ages ranged from 6 to 14 years and whose IQs ranged from 30 to 64. They were assigned at random to a token or no-token group. During the course of the 8-week study, baseline conduct scores (e.g. disruptive noise, aggression, task-relevant behaviour) were taken daily on the children in both groups using a behaviour rating scale. Academic scores (e.g. sentence repetition, counting objects, counting of events in time, pointing to specified numerical symbols) were obtained at both the beginning and the end of the 8 weeks, and again 1 year later. Instructional items were drawn from the DISTAR programme (Englemann and Carmine, 1969).

Children in the token group earned poker chips (on a partial reinforcement schedule) accompanied by praise (on a continuous reinforcement schedule) from the teacher for correct answers. At the end of each day, chips were exchanged for treats. Children in the no-token group had identical treatment except they received no token or treats, though they did receive praise following correct answers. At the end of the programme the *conduct* scores of the two groups were not significantly different. However, every child in the token group made gains in *arithmetic* achievement, while only three in the no-token group made gains in arithmetic.

There were methodological flaws in this experiment but the study is encouraging. Very few studies are perfect; human behaviour is difficult to control; human nature is even more difficult to manipulate. This study does, however, suggest that perhaps we have been too ready to avoid extending the concept of number with Down's children. Admittedly, it may well be a specific weakness more common in Down's children than in others, but this only suggests that more attention needs to be given to teaching methods and forms of encouragement which lead to success. It is likely that poor short-term memory accounts for difficulties in many aspects of learning; this will be particularly evident in number work.

SIMILARITIES AND INDIVIDUAL DIFFERENCES

There are a number of other widely held beliefs about Down's Syndrome which probably owe more to hearsay than to fact. People who are only slightly acquainted with the condition can be relied on to offer the information that 'they are fond of music'. Fraser and Mitchell first made a reference to Down's Syndrome individuals having 'a marked sense of rhythm' in 1876, and this has been repeated so often since that it has become 'common knowledge'. Yet recent experimental work

(Stratford and Ching, 1983) has shown that there is no detectable difference in rhythmic ability between Down's children and mental-age-matched normal children. Actually, neither group has anything like 'a marked sense of rhythm'. Any difference seems to lie in other mentally handicapped children being significantly worse, and here may lie the basis of the fiction. A comparison can be drawn with Langdon Down's description of his 'mongols' as accomplished mimics. It may be true, but research results suggest that Down's children are only similar to normal learners in this respect; they use imitation as part of the learning process (Coggins and Morrison, 1981). It may only be noticeable because learning is a slower process for the Down's child and consequently this kind of imitative behaviour persists longer.

A sympathetic, but misplaced, viewpoint, which is happily passing, is the notion that all Down's children are the same. Individual differences are as common in Down's children as they are in normal children. As Eden (1976) points out: ...there is a popular impression that all mongols are affectionate, exuberant, happy, biddable and musical. It is probably safer to say that mongols are individuals like the rest of us and are not obliged to be any of these things.' Even researchers are not immune from this sentiment. Rynders *et al.* (1978), in their call for more research focusing on individuals aimed at detecting these individual differences, expressed the view that: '...many researchers apparently think of the condition as unitary and invariable and have little regard for the possibility of individual differences in traits and abilities.'

Parents have their individual differences too. Though it is never actually stated, there is often an implied acknowledgement that parents of Down's children also belong to some identifiable group. If this were not so, there would have been no research attempting to examine such 'groups'; yet there are a number of studies of this kind. A study of learning behaviour in Down's children by Fraser and Sadovnik (1976) claimed that parents who themselves had high IQs had Down's children with higher IQs. Bennett *et al.* (1979), however, found no such trend, and they further demonstrated that any IQ variance depended more on the quality of the child's educational experience. Carr gives a full account of these experiments in this volume (p.178). Bennett and his associates criticised the earlier study on the grounds that Fraser and Sadovnik did not take into account the well documented evidence of decreasing IQ scores with increasing age among Down's children, but even this evidence has come under attack from Connolly (1978), who suggested that the observed decreases may be due either to test items which are inappropriate for Down's children or to poor educational opportunities; sometimes perhaps both. There is, as Carr points out, conflicting evidence on the topic of the influence of parental intelligence; what is undeniable is the influence of good and appropriate teaching.

Dealing with individual differences, Gillham (1981) draws attention to the fact that, even when differences are likely to be due to genetic factors, as in Down's Syndrome, they are still capable of environmental modification. The differences Gillham speaks of, however, are group differences such as those which Down's children exhibit when compared with 'normal' children. It is largely this collective difference which draws our attention to similarities within the Down's group.

Individual differences within groups, whether Down's children or non-handicapped children, are as much a consequence of environmental conditions as they are of the original genetic endowment. Good teaching and a favourable environment can be far more influential in promoting cognitive development than the IQ of either the parent or the child. Of course, the reverse is true also, and this will inevitably widen the differences. To regard all Down's children as possessing identical rates of growth and development and similar temperaments and personalities is to deny them both the opportunity of benefiting from their individual learning strengths and the help they may need in specific weaknesses.

THE STUDY OF LEARNING BEHAVIOUR

Psychologists have often been criticised for examining the minutiae of human behaviour, and nowhere is this more true than in the study of learning behaviour. It is, however, necessary to understand how Down's children learn; what kind of errors they make; what kind of strategies they employ in their learning. At the same time as making allowances for individual differences already stressed, there are many similarities which are peculiar to Down's Syndrome and which cannot be ignored, as Share and Veale (1974) and authors of other chapters in this volume have made clear. The following experiments illustrate some of the distinctive characteristics in problem-solving strategies employed by many Down's children.

Visual perception

Other chapters have dealt with specific learning skills: reading, writing, language, motor skills etc. The studies to be considered in detail here apply to the principles of learning in the field of visual perception. It would be an exaggeration to say that proper development in visual perception will ensure speedy development in all areas of learning and knowing, but it would be true to say that adequate development in visual perception is basic to making sense of the world and therefore being able to respond to it, and without this, any sort of learning will be seriously impeded.

It has been established that even by the age of 6 months, Down's infants are showing different preferences in their attention to visual stimuli than those shown by normal children (Miranda and Fantz, 1973, 1974). Down's infants fix their attention on single aspects of an image, where normal infants sample more widely. Anwar (1983) gives a full account of this scanning problem. Down's infants also show a distinct preference for simple stimuli and avoid complex patterns, and this kind of behaviour tends to continue into later childhood. Consequently, errors in reproduction of visually perceived forms are more likely to arise from attention deficits than from perceptual inaccuracies (House and Zeaman, 1959, 1960). Attention appears to be directed either to irrelevant aspects of a presentation or only to parts of it. As a result, only a limited amount of information is processed. This frequently causes reproduction errors which can easily be interpreted as having resulted from some disorder in the perceptual system and gives support to those who see Down's children as virtually ineducable. Goldstein and Scheerer (1941), Strauss and Lehtinen (1947), and Strauss and Kephart (1955) contributed to a theory which claimed that distorted images, resulting from some form of brain damage, lead attempts at reproduction to reflect this distorted registration. Later experimental work cast doubts on this theory (O'Connor, 1958; Bortner and Birch, 1960, 1962; Ball and Wilsoncroft, 1966; Stratford, 1980a).

Difficulties arise when the choices in discrimination tasks become more numerous and/or more complex, for then attention can become distracted from one element to another. This is an aspect of behaviour which will be taken up later.

A great deal can be learned about mentally handicapped children's interpretation of visually perceived stimuli from an examination of their performances on very simple tasks requiring the manipulation of one dimension only. Through a careful inspection of the errors which arise, one can then look for an indication of the strategies employed. A small-scale study on these lines was conducted by Stratford (1979a) who presented a simple task to Down's children requiring them to arrange three single-coloured cards of different sizes in all six permutations. The three cards were openly displayed, and the subjects were invited to copy the array using an identical set. This resulted in a significant number of 'reversals' when the cards were arranged in a monotonic order (i.e. ranging from small to large or vice-versa). As only a small number of subjects had been examined and such findings are often the genesis of rumour, the results were regarded with caution. A larger scale study was mounted involving 349 subjects distributed as shown in Table 9.1 (Stratford and Alban Metcalfe, 1982).

Table 9.1 *Characteristics of an experimental population (MA range 2.5–7.0). From Stratford and Metcalfe (1982). Reproduced with permission.*

Subjects	*n*	CA range	Mean CA	SD	Mean MA	SD
Down's Syndrome	118	5.6–17.5	10.6	3.92	4.9	1.36
Non-Down's Syndrome	108	5.9–17.1	11.2	5.1	4.6	1.42
Normal	123	3.6–8.0	5.0	1.36	4.8	1.21

MA = mental age; CA = chronological age; SD = standard deviation.

After an interval of more than 2 hours, the experiment was repeated. This time, however, the subjects were required to reproduce the arrangement from memory after each display had been observed and then concealed. The reason for this, and for the memory variable being introduced to all visual perception tasks described here, is the well documented evidence that young children have poorer visual recall than auditory recall. Down's children have been reported to have specific problems with visual processing skills even when compared with other mentally handicapped children of the same IQ or MA (Bilovsky and Share, 1965; Evans, 1973; Pendleton, 1973; McDade and Adler 1980). However, Anwar (1983) has presented evidence to suggest that Down's children are better at dealing with visually presented material than in auditory skills, though her experiments conducted with Hermelin (Anwar and Hermelin, 1982) certainly indicated difficulties encountered by Down's children in reproducing drawings. The degree of difficulty was related to the method of presenting the task – a general problem when designing experimental work with Down's children.

Although relatively few children achieved correct results in all six trials, especially in both tasks, it was equally true that only in a few cases were there any indications of purely random selections (Table 9.2). For each group of subjects, the

Table 9.2 *Numbers and percentages of monotonic 1.2.3. or 3.2.1. responses. From Stratford and Metcalfe (1982). Reproduced with permission.*

	Matching		Memory	
	Number	%	Number	%
(i) Reversals of orders 1.2.3. and 3.2.1.				
Down's Syndrome	56	23.73	94	39.83
Non-Down's Syndrome	28	12.96	31	14.35
Normal	6	2.44	12	4.88
(ii) Subjects reversing both orders 1.2.3. and 3.2.1.				
Down's Syndrome	10	4.23	23	9.74
Non-Down's Syndrome	4	1.85	4	1.85
Normal	0	0.00	4	1.65
(iii) Orders 1.2.3. and 3.2.1. imposed when stimulus model was neither of those. Number of times this occurred and percentages.				
Down's Syndrome	32	6.78	73	15.46
Non-Down's Syndrome	9	2.08	15	3.47
Normal	6	1.22	10	2.00

average performance, especially in the exposed matching task, was better than that expected by chance, suggesting deliberate or 'non-random' behaviour. There is, however, less to be learned from an examination of correct results than from an examination of errors. There may be a great number of explanations as to how children produce correct results, but their strategies become more obvious from a careful consideration of the nature of their errors.

Overall differences between handicapped and normal subjects in the memory task deserve comment in the light of observations on memory deficits briefly referred to earlier. Significant, if low, positive correlations were detected between mental age and results in the memory task among all three groups, whereas overall differences between normal and handicapped subjects are evident. A key to understanding differences both between groups and between experiments may lie in a superior ability of normal children to make sense (i.e. give meaning) to a stimulus, as the result of perceiving it as a *gestalt*, and doing so without distortion as opposed either to making 'sense' of a stimulus, but with perceptual distortion, or to perceiving only single cues, rather than a *gestalt* (with or without distortion). In terms of information theory, a *gestalt* and a single cue carry the same number of 'bits' of information. Thus, mentally handicapped and normal subjects may remember the same 'bits' of information, while differing in the nature of that information (Stratford and Alban Metcalfe, 1981).

Such an explanation is consistent with the significantly higher level of performance of non-handicapped children on the memory task and may also have explanatory value in relation to the findings for the performance of the Down's children in the memory task. The most striking feature of the results presented in

Table 9.2 is the disproportionately high level of monotonic responses given by Down's children. This tendency towards monotonic responses appears equally common under matching conditions and may be interpreted in terms of what has been described as 'attraction to good form' (see below). A significantly higher proportion of Down's than non-Down's or normal children tended to impose a monotonic 'stepped' structure, whatever the stimulus, and they did so even when (as under matching conditions) the stimulus was in view throughout the operation. Such responses show ability to form *gestalten* in that the three cards appeared to be processed in a manner meaningful to one another, but it also shows perceptual distortion. Thus, the results presented in Table 9.2(i) may better be regarded as evidence of imposition of 'good form' than of perceptual distortion resulting in reversal. This imposition of 'good form' can also be observed in normal children. It was observations of this kind which moved us to look for further confirmation of the theory (Stratford, 1979b).

Wholes and parts

Wertheimer (1960) offered some explanations as to how children perceive visual form. He observed that under experimental conditions visual patterns and dimly seen forms tend to be perceived as symmetrical, or meaningful, even when displays presented were not so. The Gestalt School would maintain that there exists a natural tendency to organise, or re-organise, what is perceived into configurations which satisfy a basic need for 'goodness of fit' or 'good form'. In other words, perception is characterised by the law of totality. It is expressed in terms of 'wholes' rather than of individual elements which make up the totality. It would seem possible, therefore, to conclude that the discrimination of pattern (or a 'pattern' composed of a number of parts) would precede discrimination of single shapes. A characteristic of mentally handicapped children is their tendency to attend more to details within the form than to its total configuration. O'Connor and Hermelin (1962) summarised this characteristic: 'In perceptual activities the act of comparing is a constant component. It seems likely that subnormals persist in fixating isolated aspects of a display.'

An apparently attractive picture, for example, which might appeal to a teacher or parent as a useful teaching aid could in fact contain too much information, be too confusing and lead to the very opposite of the educational intention. Even what might be thought of as single cues, animals for example, can often be seen by the Down's child in components of the whole. I observed one Down's child in such an activity. 'Show me another one like this,' I said, pointing to a horse. The child pointed to a camel. This was another animal with four legs. Likewise a donkey was identified as a rabbit; the child focused on the long ears. Down's children are frequently most helpful in *finding* some answer to a question even if it is not the correct one; however, the answer will generally be based on some kind of logic.

In order to test out the theory that Down's children had a pull to symmetrical forms and that this was one influence in their strategy for organising visually presented material, a number of two-inch square plastic pieces were obtained, five to be given to the subject, and five for the tester to present a design for reproduction. Seventy-five subjects were drawn from the groups already described, 25 subjects from each group, matched for mental age. Three displays were presented separately, one symmetrical, one asymmetrical and one inviting reversal (Fig. 9.1).

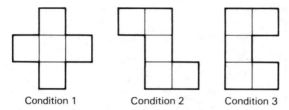

Condition 1   Condition 2   Condition 3

Fig. 9.1 Displays. From Stratford (1979b). Reproduced with permission.

The results shown in Table 9.3 were quite startling. Only 5 of the Down's children correctly matched the symmetrical display (condition 1), but 17 imposed a symmetrical error. Certainly, the symmetrical stimulus had evoked a symmetrical response, even when there was no correspondence.

Table 9.3 *Results of a test to find the number of symmetrical-type errors made. From Stratford (1979b). Reproduced with permission.*

Subjects	Conditions	Matching task		Memory task		Total symmetrical-type errors	
		Errors	Symmetrical-type errors	Errors	Symmetrical-type errors	Matching	Memory
Down's	1	18	17	20	18		
Syndrome	2	24	17	23	20		
(n = 25)	3	9	6	6	4	40	42
Normal	1	11	8	13	8		
(n = 25)	2	17	9	13	7		
	3	5	2	5	2	19	17
Non-Down's	1	16	11	16	10		
subnormal	2	24	13	21	15		
(n = 25)	3	9	5	6	5	29	30

More mistakes were made in condition 2 (the asymmetrical display), but the mistakes again were symmetrical. Very few mistakes were made in condition 3. Errors were divided into those which were symmetrical and those which were asymmetrical, whether or not they corresponded to one of the displays in the experiment. The Down's group and other handicapped children had a numerically greater tendency to produce symmetrical models, particularly in the memory task. It was interesting to see that all groups were attracted to symmetry, though by no means equally. The real difference was in the *extent* to which each group was attracted to symmetry and away from asymmetry. The profiles shown in Fig. 9.2 help to make this clear.

Following the Gestalt School, then, there appears to be a strong attraction to symmetry in all of us from the very early stages in our development. Some of this is retained throughout life. Why, for example, do we, if given a couple of vases and a clock to arrange on the mantlepiece (unless we are consciously striving for effect), place the clock in the middle? In this respect, Down's children are no different from the rest of us. It just so happens that it takes them longer to grow out of the very early stage of needing to make most things adhere to this kind of 'good form'.

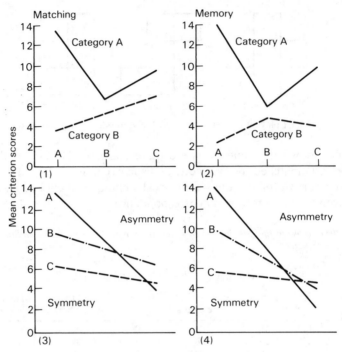

Fig. 9.2 Groups and categories: attraction to symmetry. Category A, symmetry; Category B, asymmetry; A, Down's Syndrome; B, non-Down's Syndrome; C, controls. From Stratford (1980b). Reproduced with permission.

Coupled with this aspect of retardation in the developmental process is the parallel one of poor ability to transfer learning from one discrete element to another which involves similar principles, as well as to generalise information. Thus, Down's children find it very difficult to profit from incidental learning. What most of us pick up as part of our maturational process, Down's children need to be actively taught. Research studies from many aspects of the educational process have reached this conclusion (e.g. Brassell and Dunst, 1978; Mittler, 1979, 1982; Morss, 1983).

Attention

Another study related to the way Down's children attend to tasks involving attention to visual cues was carried out by Stratford (1980b). This was an experiment based on work by Cunningham (1974), who had suggested that mentally handicapped children shifted their attention from one dimension to another. In a series of matching tasks, he had used a set of cards with patterns increasing in complexity and a second set with designs increasing towards reality (e.g. from a triangle to a ship). It appeared that, as complexity or reality increased, correct responses diminished, even though more cues were available.

Stratford's experiment tested the hypothesis that Down's children have a tendency to shift their attention from one dimension to another and consequently become confused when a task demands attention to more than one dimension. Thirty-four subjects were selected from those normal and Down's children who had successfully completed the three ranging size cards experiment described earlier. In this way it could be assumed that all the subjects (17 in each group) were competent in handling one dimension of the task. The experimental conditions were similar, subjects having to match three cards, first from an exposed display and then the same from memory. The first set of cards tested subjects on increasing pattern complexity and the second set tested the same again but with an added size dimension (Figs 9.3 and 9.4). (N.B. All the subjects had been successful at matching size alone.)

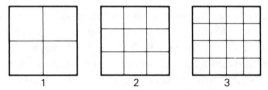

Fig. 9.3 Two sets of three cards with increasing pattern complexity. From Stratford (1980b). Reproduced with permission.

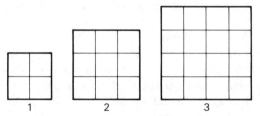

Fig. 9.4 Cards increasing in both size and complexity of pattern. From Stratford (1980b). Reproduced with permission.

Both normal and Down's children were weaker in pattern discrimination, but the results showed quite clearly that, whereas the normal children improved their performance on the weaker dimension with the additional cues from the variations in sizes, the Down's children deteriorated even further. It was obvious that attention was being switched from one dimension to the other with a consequent loss of confidence in both. Fig. 9.5 gives a clear illustration of this tendency.

There are important implications for teachers in the results of this experiment and in a follow-up study which gave further confirmation that while Down's children might seem to be good at sorting shapes and matching colours, they are not so good at organising both together (Stratford and Mills, 1984). It is commonplace for teachers to add a second dimension, if only using capital letters

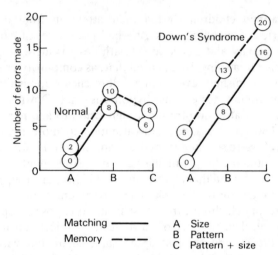

Fig. 9.5 An indication of how Down's children make errors in pattern and size combined, while normal children make fewer. From Stratford (1980b). Reproduced with permission.

and/or coloured chalk to draw attention to an important point. Teachers also know that, proceeding from the known to the unknown, it is generally effective to capitalise on an area of competence which children have already acquired to incorporate new material where difficulties are being encountered. Experimental results from normal children showed that teachers are right to assume this principle into their classroom work, but results from the Down's children indicate that such approaches will not work for them. A great deal of practice in understanding and manipulating more than one dimension is called for in the teaching of Down's children.

It is interesting to note, especially in view of convincing evidence that females perform better on IQ tests than males (Carr, 1970, 1975; Clements *et al.*, 1976; Connolly, 1978; Carr and Hewett, 1982), that in none of these experiments concerned with tasks related to visual perception was there any significant sex difference. Neither was there a strong relationship with IQ or MA, except as might be expected in the tasks involving memory.

There can be little doubt that attention plays an important part in learning, whether it is the ability to make appropriate shifts in the *direction* of attention or the capacity to concentrate and sustain attention to a task. Most studies of attention have centred around the latter, and more often on the aspect we might call 'vigilance', i.e. sustained attention to an event, requiring the subject to detect changes over long periods of time, as might be expected in the attention given to radar screens.

Although more work of this kind has been conducted with normal children and adults, similar techniques have also been applied to studies of vigilance in handicapped populations (Frankmann and Adams, 1962; Gibson, 1969; Miezejeski, 1974; Zekulin *et al.*, 1974; Goldberg and Konstantereas, 1981; Swanson, 1981). These studies have been mainly concerned with reaction time and confirm what might be expected, that handicapped subjects have significantly slower reaction times and cannot concentrate for long without a dramatic decline in accuracy.

Teachers might say that a child is paying attention when he is looking at, listening to, or interacting with a task in front of him. They might also say that background noise and other external stimulation will cause attention to be disrupted in such a way that the task performance will deteriorate or break down. They would add that this is particularly true of mentally handicapped children. Although there is a good deal of common ground, when speaking about attention, teachers and researchers are not always talking about the same thing. The essential difference between the nature of attention deficit examined in the laboratory and the application of attention expected by teachers in the classroom lies in the control of the stimulus. Usually in laboratory experiments, the technique is to require the subject to respond to a stimulus controlled by the experimenter, a flashing light for example, or a reaction to a display as described earlier, while in the classroom, attention is normally self-initiated and controlled by the subject, *after* a task has been presented by the teacher. Here, rate, accuracy and time are all in the hands of the child. There have been few studies which have attempted to relate the variety of laboratory attention measures directly to the performance of the child in the classroom, and fewer still have addressed themselves to the behaviour of mentally handicapped children. Lunzer and Stratford (1984) set out to examine Down's children along with normal and other handicapped children under normal class-room conditions in a self-paced task of moderate difficulty (actually recognising, selecting and deleting in an act of comparing geometric shapes). The experiment was then repeated to the accompaniment of a tape recording of highly distracting sounds.

The most salient feature of the results was that all three groups showed very different trends. Both handicapped groups increased in errors over the 9-minute period of the test, while the younger normal children showed a slight reduction in errors. All groups differed in rate: the normal group maintained a steady rate of work; the Down's group *increased* in rate, but at the expense of accuracy; the non-Down's handicapped slowed down their rate over the time, yet their error rate went up most of all. Despite the difference in task, the findings with respect to the distractor effect were generally in accord with those of previous researchers (e.g. Turnure and Zigler, 1964; Zekulin *et al.*, 1974; Swanson, 1981). The presence of the audial distractor led to improvement in every aspect of the performance. In view of certain parallel findings of Turnure (1970), it is likely that this was associated with enhanced arousal. If so, it is important to note that the effect was present in both handicapped groups as well as in the normal group, and, if anything, was more pronounced in the former. However, it does seem clear that mentally handicapped children fail to capitalise on learning occasions when these encounters are under their own control; therefore over time their cognitive development is slower, or even 'different' if one accepts the reasoning of Morss (1983) and his account in Chapter 13.

The choice of task in the enquiry described above was determined in large part by teachers' own concerns: most teachers believe that learning difficulty is strongly associated with disturbance in attentional capacity as displayed in, say, getting on with written classwork. Both time and distraction are likely to be relevant features. Nevertheless, we found that the distractor effect was paradoxically facilitating – provided that the task is of moderate difficulty and the distractor uses a different modality from that required in the task. For example, certain kinds of music might facilitate a sorting task – or even written work – but would be less than helpful in a simultaneous listening task.

We asked ourselves, as did the teachers, why this marked difference in the performance of the two handicapped groups. Suppose there is a real decrement in functional capacity due to the accumulation of some inhibitory product or process in the nervous system. How then can we account for the fact that the non-Down's group slows up while the Down's group speeds up, yet their loss in accuracy is even greater? Could it be that there are two quite different mechanisms, one which operates for Down's and another for other forms of mental handicap? What makes this unlikely is that, whereas the Down's group is homogeneous in aetiology, the non-Down's group is heterogeneous. An alternative possibility is that both groups suffer from one and the same defect, which will make for reduced rate and increased error, but this is compensated in the Down's group by an opposing trend: a sort of mounting excitement acting as positive feedback. Such a tendency is not out of character.

It must be stated that, although it was the teachers who alerted us to its importance, the evidence is that teachers cannot make a useful assessment by informal observation of behaviour: in all three groups, teachers' ratings correlated well with mental-age-dependent measures (i.e. rate and error), but not with stability of performance (change in rate and change in error).

CONCLUSIONS

Some time has been spent in describing these experiments here, not because they are *so* intrinsically important in themselves, but to demonstrate the importance of looking beyond the obvious or what might be thought of as 'common sense' deductions. What is apparently good common sense reasoning may just sometimes be false. This is a point made by Henderson (p.202), though in a different context. After all, at one time it was a matter for 'common sense' to assume that Down's children were quite incapable of learning. We do need to look for reasons why Down's children behave in the way they do in their learning strategies. To know more about this aspect of development will inevitably influence our own teaching strategies, whether we be parent or teacher. It would, perhaps, be useful to design the approach to teaching specific programmes to combat weaknesses (real or implied) in the style or manner as one might design a scientific experiment, as meticulously observed and equally well recorded, so that results can then be measured, or otherwise evaluated, and compared in order that real achievements can be sorted out from the hopeful or spurious, where there has been no effective gain or change. In the latter case, a different approach will need to be made. It is always more difficult to say that it is one's teaching which may be at fault rather than the child's inability to learn. Particularly with the move towards integration, it is essential for teachers who are more accustomed to children learning in particular ways, making similar kinds of mistakes, reaching goals through well trodden paths, to understand that some children may do things quite differently. Down's children frequently proceed quite logically, but it is a kind of logic which often leads them to fundamental errors.

It is to be hoped that the trend towards integration will continue. It is a long time coming; but to be successful, real integration depends more on changing attitudes than on legislation. Teachers need to be well prepared so that they can meet this challenge with professional confidence. The Court Committee recognised that 'special expertise' was required to serve the developmental needs of mentally handicapped children. They saw too that the needs of these children go beyond medical care, and Professor Court drew attention to the fact that, like all other children, they have social, personal and emotional needs which are all too often neglected. Down's children do need specialist help, but a timely reminder from the Court Report (1976) was echoed in many of the recommendations in the later Warnock Report (1978): 'Mentally handicapped children have more in common with other children because of their childhood than they do with mentally handicapped adults because of their common disability.'

Eventually, however, Down's children do grow up and, though valiant efforts are being made by well disposed and able individuals, we have not yet scratched the surface of educational needs in the post-school years. Perhaps we are too confined in our concept of education, too much tied to the calendar; chronological age is only one measure of development. It is a long time since it was recognised that 13 was too young for normal children to be leaving school. It is also freely acknowledged that the 'abnormally' clever need educational provision well into adulthood. It is therefore of major importance that it is now accepted that the education of Down's and other mentally handicapped children should also continue beyond the present school-leaving age. Many now continue to stay at school until age 19, and it is becoming more frequently the case that educational provision is made in the adult training centres. At times progress in this way seems slow, but the precedent has been established.

Finally, in our search for deeper understanding of cognitive development and learning principles, we must not lose sight of the whole child. The chapters in this book each deal with some specific aspect of the growing Down's child, but the essential business for a civilised society is to put these together into an integrated whole so that we may see this child as part of our richer biological inheritance. If we can manage to do this, it may help us to recognise the part Down's children play in our own development. Thomas Weihs (1967) once spoke of this as 'the two-way process'. A vivid illustration of this principle was recorded by McNally (1979) when he described how thought, feeling and action coalesce in one moment of triumph in an encounter with a Down's child in a test session. He was testing 5-year-old Pippa on the Stanford–Binet Intelligence Scale; she had achieved some success in a visual discrimination task but needed to identify one more shape to pass this sub-test at the 4-year-old level. The shape was not one of the simpler ones, it was an irregular polygon, and a trapezium and parallelogram were tempting distractors. McNally takes up the story: 'Pippa surveyed the large card time and time again, periodically referring to the small card in her hand on which was the shape she had to match. Again her hand hovered over the correct area, another glance at my expressionless face. Hadn't I given the test more than a thousand times? I knew how to be objective. Further surveys, more hesitancies – and then – "Oh you good girl." My objectivity was annihilated. Pippa, stretched to the very limit of her discriminative ability, shrieked out her joy. She had done it, really truly done it. I remember another testing session when a 10-year-old boy explained in 14-year-old terms how reputation was what other people thought of you, but character was what you really were. There was much reciprocal pleasure in assessing such talent, but Pippa's modest, hard won success brought reciprocal joy and it was a privilege to be part of it.'

REFERENCES

Anwar, F. (1983). The role of sensory modality for the reproduction of shape by the severely retarded. *Br. J. Develop. Psychol.* **1**, 317.

Anwar, F. and Hermelin, B. (1982). An analysis of drawing skills in mental handicap. *Aust. & N.Z. J. Develop. Disab.* **8**, 147.

Aronson, M. and Fallstrom, K. (1977). Immediate and long-term effects of developmental training in children with Down's Syndrome. *Develop. Med. Child Neurol.* **10**, 489.

Ball, T.S. and Wilsoncroft, W.E. (1966). Perceptual-motor deficits and the phi phenomenon. *Am. J. Ment. Defic.* **71**, 797.

Bennett, F.C., Sells, C.J. and Brand, C. (1979). Influences on measured intelligence in Down's Syndrome. *Am. J. Dis. Childh.* **133**, 700.

Bilovsky, D. and Share, J. (1965). The ITPA and Down's Syndrome: An exploratory study. *Am. J. Ment. Defic.* **70**, 78.

Bortner, M. and Birch, H.G. (1960). Perceptual and perceptual–motor dissociation in brain damaged patients. *J. Nerv. & Ment. Dis.* **130**, 49.

Bortner, M. and Birch, H.G. (1962). Perceptual and perceptual–motor dissociation in cerebral palsied children. *J. Nerv. & Ment. Dis.* **134**, 103.

Brassell, W. and Dunst, C.J. (1978). Fostering the object construct: large scale intervention with handicapped children. *Am. J. Ment. Defic.* **82**, 523.

Brinkworth, R. (1975). The unfinished child: Early treatment and training of the infant with Down's Syndrome. *Roy. Soc. Health* **2**, 73.

Carr, J. (1970). Mental and motor development in young mongol children. *J. Ment. Defic. Res.* **14**, 205.

Carr, J. (1975). *Young Children with Down's Syndrome*. London: Butterworth.

Carr, J. and Hewett, S. (1982). Children with Down's Syndrome growing up: a preliminary report. *Assoc. Child Psych. & Psychol. News* **10**.

Centerwell, S. and Centerwell, W. (1960). A study of children with mongolism reared in the home compared to three reared away from home. *Paediatrics* **25**, 678.

Clements, P.R., Bates, M.V. and Hafer, M. (1976). Variability within Down's Syndrome (Trisomy 21) empirically observed sex differences in IQ. *Ment. Retard.* **14**, 30.

Coggins, T.E. and Morrison, J.A. (1981). Spontaneous imitations of Down's Syndrome children: a lexical analysis. *J. Speech & Hearing Res.* **24**, 303.

Connolly, J. (1978). Intelligence levels in Down's Syndrome children. *Am. J. Ment. Defic.* **83**, 193.

Court Report: Child Health Services (1976). *Fit for the Future*. Commd. 6684. Vol. l.l. Vol. 2 (Append). London: HMSO.

Cunningham, C.C. (1974). *Visual Discrimination in the Mentally Handicapped*. Manchester: Hester Adrian Research Centre, University of Manchester.

Dalton, A., Rubino, C. and Hislop, M. (1973). Cited in Rynders, J.E. (1983). *Valuable Pottery from Ordinary Clay: new insights concerning the achievements and achievement potential of persons with Down's Syndrome*. Paper presented at the Second International Down's Syndrome Convention, Mexico City, Mexico.

Eden, D.J. (1976). *Mental Handicap – An Introduction*. London: George Allen & Unwin.

Englemann, S. and Carmine, D. (1969). *DISTAR: Arithmetic I: An Instructional System*. Chicago: Science Research Associates.

Evans, S. (1973). *A study of selected aural-oral skills of children with various chromosomal abnormalities*. MSc thesis, University of Tennessee.

Frankmann, J.P. and Adams, J.A. (1962). Theories of vigilance. *Psychol. Bull.* **59**, 257.

Fraser, F.C. and Sadovnik, A.D. (1976). Correlation of IQ in subjects with Down's Syndrome and their patients and sibs. *J. Ment. Defic. Res.* **20**, 179.

Fraser, J. and Mitchell, A. (1876). Kalmuck idiocy – reported case with autopsy, with notes on 62 cases by A. Mitchell. *J. Ment. Sci.* **22**, 161.

Gibson, E.J. (1969). *Principles of Perceptual Learning and Development*. New York: Appleton Century Crofts.

Gillham, W.E.C. (1981). Individual differences. In Howarth, C.I. and Gillham, W.E.C. (eds), *The Structure of Psychology*. London: George Allen & Unwin.

Goldberg, J.O. and Konstantereas, M.M. (1981). Vigilance in hyperactive and normal children on a self-paced operant task. *J. Child Psychol. & Psych.* **21**, 77.

Goldstein, K. and Scheerer, M. (1941). Abstract and concrete behaviour: an experimental study with special tests. *Psychol. Mono.* **53**(2).

Hebb, D.O. (1972). *A Textbook of Psychology*, 3rd edn. Philadelphia: Saunders.

House, B.J. and Zeaman, D. (1959). Positive discrimination and reversals in low grade retardates. *Trng. Sch. Bull.* **56**, 62.

House, B.J. and Zeaman, D. (1960). Visual discrimination learning and intelligence in defectives of low mental age. *Am. J. Ment. Defic.* **65**, 51.

Lunzer, E.A. and Stratford, B. (1984). Deficits in attention in young children, with specific reference to Down's Syndrome and other mentally handicapped children. *Early Child Development and Care.* **17**, 131–54.

McDade, H.L. and Adler, S. (1980). Down's Syndrome and short-term memory impairment: A storage or retrieval deficit? *Am. J. Ment. Defic.* **84**, 561.

McNally, J. (1979). Care, concern and compassion. In Stratford, B. (ed.), *Teaching Children with Severe Learning Difficulties*. Tunbridge Wells: Costello Educational.

Miezejeski, C.M. (1974). Effect of white noise on the reaction time of mentally retarded subjects. *Am. J. Ment. Defic.* **79**, 39.

Miranda, S.B. and Fantz, R.L. (1973). Visual preferences of Down's Syndrome and normal infants. *Child Dev.* **44**, 555.

Miranda, S.B. and Fantz, R.L. (1974). Recognition and memory in Down's Syndrome and normal infants. *Child Dev.* **45**, 651.

Mittler, P. (1979). In Stratford, B. (ed.), *Teaching Children with Severe Learning Difficulties*, Tunbridge Wells: Costello Educational.

Mittler, P. (1982). *People Not Patients*. London: Methuen.

Morss, J.R. (1983). Cognitive development in the Down's Syndrome infant: Slow or different? *Br. J. Ed. Psychol.* **53**, 40–47.

O'Connor, N. (1958). Learning and mental defect. In Clarke, A.D.B. and Clarke, A.M. (eds), *Mental Deficiency: The Changing Outlook*. London: Methuen.

O'Connor, N. and Hermelin, B. (1962). *Speech and Thought in Severe Subnormality*. Oxford: Pergamon Press.

Pendleton, H. (1973). *A Study of selected oral language and visual perceptual skills of children with chromosomal abnormalities*. Master's thesis, University of Tennessee.

Pueschel, S. and Rynders, J.E. (1983). *Down's Syndrome: Advances in Biomedicine and the Behavioral Sciences*. Cambridge, MA: The Ware Press.

Restak, R. (1975). Cited in Rynders, J.E., Spiker, D. and Horrobin, J.M. (1978). Underestimating the educability of Down's Syndrome children: examination of methodological problems in recent literature. *Am. J. Ment. Defic.* **82**(5), 440–48.

Rynders, J.E. (1983). *Valuable Pottery from Ordinary Clay: new insights concerning the achievements and achievement potential of persons with Down's Syndrome*. Paper presented at the Second International Down's Syndrome Convention, Mexico City, Mexico.

Rynders, J.E., Spiker, D. and Horrobin, J.M. (1978). Underestimating the educability of Down's Syndrome children: examination of methodological problems in recent literature. *Am. J. Ment. Defic.* **82**(5), 440–48.

Share, J.B. and Veale, A.M.O. (1974). *Developmental Landmarks for Children with Down's Syndrome.* Dunedin, N.Z.: University of Otago Press.

Springer, A. and Steele, M.W. (1980). Effects of physician's early parental counselling on rearing of Down's Syndrome children. *Am. J. Ment. Defic.* **85**, 1.

Stratford, B. (1979a). Discrimination of size, form and order in mongol and other mentally handicapped children. *J. Ment. Defic. Res.* **23**, 44.

Stratford, B. (1979b). Attraction to 'good form' in Down's Syndrome. *J. Ment. Defic. Res.* **23**, 243.

Stratford, B. (1980a). Perception and perceptual–motor processes in children with Down's Syndrome. *J. Psychol.* **104**, 139.

Stratford, B. (1980b). Preferences in attention to visual cues in Down's Syndrome and normal children. *J. Ment. Defic. Res.* **24**, 57.

Stratford, B. and Alban Metcalfe, J. (1981). Position cues in discrimination behaviour of normal, Down's Syndrome and other mentally handicapped children. *J. Ment. Defic. Res.* **25**, 89.

Stratford, B. and Alban Metcalfe, J. (1982). Recognition, reproduction and recall in children with Down's Syndrome. *Aust. & N.Z. J. Devel. Disab.* **8**, 125–32.

Stratford, B. and Ching, Y.Y.E. (1983). Rhythm and time in the perception of Down's Syndrome children. *J. Ment. Defic. Res.* **27**, 23.

Stratford, B. and Mills, K. (1984). Discrimination of colour in Down's Syndrome children. *Aust. & N.Z. J. Devel. Disab.* **10**, 151–55.

Strauss, A.A. and Kephart, N.C. (1955). *Psycho-pathology and the Brain Injured Child. Vol. II Progress in Theory and Clinic.* New York: Grune and Stratton.

Strauss, A.A. and Lehtinen, L.E. (1947). *Psycho-pathology and the Brain Injured Child.* New York: Grune and Stratton.

Swanson, L. (1981). Vigilance deficit in learning disabled children: a signal detection analysis. *J. Child Psychol. & Psych.* **22**, 393.

Turnure, J.E. (1970). Children's reactions to distractors in a learning situation. *Dev. Psychol.* **2**, 115.

Turnure, J. and Zigler, E. (1964). Outer-directedness in the problem solving of normal and retarded children. *J. Abnor. & Soc. Psychol.* **69**, 427.

Warnock Report (1978). *Special Educational Needs.* Report of the Committee of Inquiry into the Education of Handicapped Children and Young People. London: HMSO.

Weihs, T.J. (1967). *In Need of Special Care* (published public lecture). Leeds: University of Leeds and Trinity and All Saints College.

Wertheimer, M. (1960). *Productive Thinking.* London: Tavistock.

Zekulin, X.Y., Gibson, D., Mosley, J.L. and Brown, R.I. (1974). Auditory–motor channeling in Down's Syndrome subjects. *Am. J. Ment. Defic.* **78**, 571.

10 The Development of Intelligence

Janet Carr

CROSS-SECTIONAL AND LONGITUDINAL STUDIES

Early reports based on anecdotal evidence put forward the view that most 'mongols' could be classified as 'idiots' with IQs below 25, while others regarded the majority as 'imbeciles' with IQs between 25 and 49 (Tredgold, 1908; Shuttleworth, 1909). Subsequently, reports have been based on intelligence testing and have in the main consisted of cross-sectional studies. Pototzky and Grigg (1942), testing 21 institutionalised Down's individuals with ages ranging from 7.10 to 47 years, found a mean overall IQ of 46. Wallin (1949) gave an average Binet IQ for 26 clinic cases of 36.2 (CA 4.1–14.4) and felt that Pototzky and Grigg's results were aberrant, suggesting that some of their cases may have been misdiagnosed on the basis of minimum stigmata, that they were 'mongoloids rather than frank mongolians'. Dunsdon et al. (1960) deliberately sought for high-grade cases, selecting for study only those who had been placed in primary, ESN (ESN(M) in later terminology) or private schools 4 years earlier. They estimated that the proportion attaining IQs of over 45, out of the whole group of 390 children originally tested, would have been about 6–7%.

Most of the early studies (Øster, 1953; Loeffler and Smith, 1964) found a tendency to lower IQs with increasing age. Loeffler and Smith studied children living at home and found mean DQs on the Cattell Infant Intelligence Scale (CIIS), which fell sharply from 65 during the first year to 46 at 2½, and Stanford Binet IQs that levelled out at 43 between 3 and 9 years. Dividing the children into those under 3 and those between 3 and 9 years, none of the younger but 9% of the older group had quotients under 35; the proportion scoring over 50 fell by more than half, from 70% in the younger to 29% in the older group, with 23% in the younger and none in the older group scoring over 70; while those scoring between 25 and 49 doubled, from 30% in the younger to 62% in the older group. No details are given as to the composition of this cross-sectional sample, but these results are generally in line with those of later studies.

In an early series of studies using the Gesell scales, the development of a group of 16–24 infants was shown to decline from a mean DQ of 71 in the first year, to 63, 55 and 47 in the second, third and fourth years respectively (Share et al., 1961; Koch et al., 1963). It was nevertheless emphasised that MA continued to increase. The children developed new skills, albeit at a slower rate than that found in normal children, as they grew older.

167

In one of the first longitudinal studies, Dameron (1963) gave the California First Year Mental Scale at 3-month intervals to 12 infants between the ages of 3 and 18 months and found ratio DQs that declined gradually from 94 to 46. The same group of children was followed up at an average age of about 28 months, and gained mean DQs of 37.3, range 17.2–37.13 (Stedman and Eichorn, 1964), and of 29.8, range 54–71, at a mean of 61 months (Bayley *et al.*, 1966). The means of 10 matched home-reared children were 52.1 at 28 months and 40.4 at 61 months. At this point, although both Dameron, and Stedman and Eichorn comment that the environment at Sonoma State Hospital where the children were living was 'richer' than would be found at most institutions, some further enrichment was introduced in the form of 5 hours a day of structured group activities and an average of 15 minutes per day of individual instruction for each child (Bayley *et al.*, 1966). At an average 13 months later, the mean DQ of the institution group was 36.3, that of the home-reared 42.5, and the significant difference previously seen between the scores of the two groups had disappeared.

Centerwall and Centerwall (1960) studied two groups of 32 children, one group placed in foster homes in the neonatal period, and the other brought up in their own homes until the age of at least 2½. All the children were then admitted to a mental deficiency hospital, where they were tested, and then retested at an average age of 7 years. The mean IQ of the home-reared group was 43 on the first occasion and 23 on the second, that of the placement group 34 and 16 respectively. In addition, the home-reared group was taller, better nourished and walked earlier. The authors noted that the homes into which the placement children went in the neonatal period were mostly small and of not more than 12 children. The same point was made by Shipe and Shotwell (1965), who studied 42 'mongols' who had been patients in a state hospital for 3 years or more: 25 had been reared in their own homes until after 2 years, and 17 placed in small private institutions at or soon after birth. The home-reared were superior in both IQ (on the Stanford or Kuhlman–Binet Tests) and in Vineland SQ, though the gap between the two groups had narrowed from the previous study (Shotwell and Shipe, 1964).

In a cross-sectional study of home-reared children aged between 4 and 17 years old, Cornwell and Birch (1969) found Stanford Binet IQs that fell from about 54 at 4 years to 44.6 at 11, and to about 32 at 17. (However, after the age of 11 numbers at each age refer to either one or three subjects, so that the means from 11 to 17 years are of dubious value.) They comment on the small increase of mean basal ages – maximum 2.6 years – although the maximum mean terminal age increased by 5 years, and feel that these results were brought about at the lower level by 'limitations in language and numerical skills' and at the upper level by 'inability to develop concept formation and the relationship of concepts among objects'. When mental age was plotted against chronological age, the slope of best fit was 30°.

Melyn and White (1973) presented developmental data (some collected retro-spectively) on 612 children from birth to age 16. Psychological test data were available from 565, gathered from the CIIS, Merrill Palmer, Leiter, all forms of the Stanford Binet and the WISC. 'Most' children were tested on a longitudinal basis, but numbers varied from 76 tested at an average of about 5 years to 4 at 13.5 years, and the data are probably better regarded as cross-sectional. Mean DQ/IQs declined steadily from an unusually low figure of 58 at a mean of 6 months (though the absence of any data on the scatter of age of the children tested makes it difficult to assess the significance of this) to 38 at 13.5 years. A similar pattern was presented by Connolly (1978) from the scores of children tested apparently cross-sectionally between the ages of 6 months and 18 years. (Again, as numbers of children tested over the age of 10 ranged between one and four, these latter figures are of doubtful value.) Scores were based mainly on the 1960 revision of the Stanford Binet, with 10% tested on the WISC or CIIS, and declined regularly from 64 at 6 months to 40 at 7 years, thereafter showing some fluctuation until 10 years, when the mean score was 45. In another, presumed cross-sectional, study, Clements *et al.* (1976) presented IQs for children in 2-year age groups and found a similar decline, from 59 at 3–5 years to 29 at 11–13 years. Similar results were reported by Morgan (1979), also from a cross-sectional study, of 217 home-reared children, ages ranging from 3 months to 15 years. Mean IQs (*sic*) ranged from 73 at below 1 year to 33.4 between 9 and 11, and 26.8 between 11 and 15 years. (This group contained only 13 children.) The author pointed out that there was a 'shift from relatively high to relatively low functioning with increased age', and that the range of scores narrowed from 69 IQ points at ages 1–3 to 27 IQ points at 9–11 years.

A longitudinal study of a population sample of children concerned all the children born within a defined geographical area during one year (Carr, 1970, 1975; Carr and Hewett, 1982). Fifty-four children surviving to 6 weeks old were included, 45 brought up at home and 9 in various foster homes and institutions. At 4 years, 45 children and, at 11, 44 were still in the study. The children were tested on the Bayley Scales, gaining mean ratio DQs that rose from 70 at 6 weeks to 77 at 6 months and then declined steadily to 46 for the home-reared and 35 for the boarded-out children at 4 years old. At 11 years old, mean scores on the Merrill–Palmer Scale for the two groups were 37 and 36 respectively. On this test, then, the significant difference between the groups found at the earlier ages had disappeared, perhaps because the Merrill–Palmer Scale contains relatively few verbal items. There were marked differences in scores on the Reynell Language Scales: in comprehension, the home-reared and boarded-out groups had mean scores of 34.2 and 25.7 respectively, while in expressive language the difference was even greater, the mean scores being 35.6 and 21.2 respectively. At 11, 84% of the children had IQs falling within the severely mentally handicapped range, with 5% (two girls) having IQs in the ESN(M) range of 55 and 57, and 11% (four boys and one girl) having IQs below 20.

The studies discussed so far have shown that intelligence or developmental quotients of Down's children decline as the children mature, although there are variations in the mean levels and in the rate of decline reported. One study that reports data that are at variance with this finding is that of Kostrzewski (1974). Results are given for 165, apparently home-based, people ranging in age from 7 months to 24 years at first examination and 1 year 4 months to 31 years at the final examination. A total of 625 test scores were obtained, giving an average of nearly four per individual. All were tested at least twice, and 19.3% between 6 and 12 times. Numbers tested vary from 6 at a mean CA of 10 months (and 7 between 18 and 31 years) to 69 at a mean of 7.5 years. Tests used were the CIIS, Stanford Binet 1937 Form L, and the WISC and Wechsler–Bellevue. Remarkably, IQs were almost identical at the first and last ages (37.0 at a mean of 10 months, 37.3 at a mean of 20.6 years) and, between these, ranged from a maximum of 42.6 at 2½ to a minimum of 32.7 at 16.9 years. The author states that examination of IQ changes of individuals showed that over the average interval of 4 years between first and last tests no significant change occurred in almost 74% of the group, a significant decline in 8%, and a significant improvement in 18%, although no details are given as to whether the ages of these three groups differed.

Apart from the lack of decline in mean scores with increasing age, the outstanding feature of this study was the very low scores gained by the younger members. The mean quotient of 37 at 10 months old was between 21 and 38 points lower than those of children tested at comparable ages in other studies. Why these young children had scores that were so very much lower than those of children in all other published studies is a matter for speculation – possibly the CIIS translated badly into Polish or was poorly standardised in translation. At the other end of the age range, the scores at 11 and 13 years are comparable with those found in other studies.

GROWTH CURVES

A number of authors have explored ways of arriving at expressions of IQ in Down's Syndrome which, allowing for the observed changes with age, would provide estimates that would be equivalent from one age to another. Zeaman and House (1962) proposed the formula $MA = \log CA$, and later Silverstein (1966) employed the formula: MA estimate $= 20.87 \log CA - 5.77$, where MA estimate and CA are in months and the logarithm is to the base 10. Then MQ (Mongoloid Quotient) may be found by the formula:

$$MQ = 100 \times \frac{MA}{MA \text{ est.}}$$

Using this approach to the test scores of 101 institutionalised patients who had been tested twice, with a mean interval between tests of 7.2 years, mean MQs were 100.3 and 99.4 respectively, whereas conventional IQs were 30.6 and 26.5. A further study (Demaine and Silverstein, 1978) showed that curves fitted to data from 189 institutionalised Down's people and from a matched group of people from other diagnostic categories were similar in showing a strong linear trend from 4 to 16 years, after which the curves tended to level off. They also showed that the curve for the Down's group was below that for the non-Down's group.

Meindl *et al.* (1983) presented growth curves derived from scores on non-institutionalised children between the ages of 1 and 16 years and compared these with curves derived from Zeaman and House (1962) and Silverstein (1966). The authors stated that 'the curve for the non-institutionalised children begins lower than those for those who were institutionalised, and ascends to a higher level by age

16 years'. However, since the 'beginning' of the curve for the institutionalised children was an extrapolation of dubious validity of the original curves, and since the 'higher level' of the non-institutionalised children was based on the scores of a total of only 28 children dispersed through the age groups from 11 to 16 years, little confidence can be placed in this comparison, as the authors themselves point out.

In general, the usefulness of this approach is questionable, and figures derived from it have little advantage over raw data, where these are derived from adequate numbers of subjects and especially those based on longitudinal studies. From such data it should be possible to obtain a more reliable picture of age-related IQ changes in people with Down's Syndrome. The studies discussed have been concerned with the developmental rates of home- and out-of-home reared children. Table 10.1 shows the mean IQs reported by different workers for these two groups, the tests used and total numbers tested, and, in those studies in which numbers tested at different ages varied, the numbers tested on each occasion are given in bold type. For the sake of simplicity, IQs containing figures after a decimal point have been rounded to the nearest whole number.

Fig. 10.1 is derived from Table 10.1 and presents the mid-point scores at each age. The mid-point of a range of 10 DQ/IQ points has been taken; where results from individual studies are outside this range, these have been indicated on the

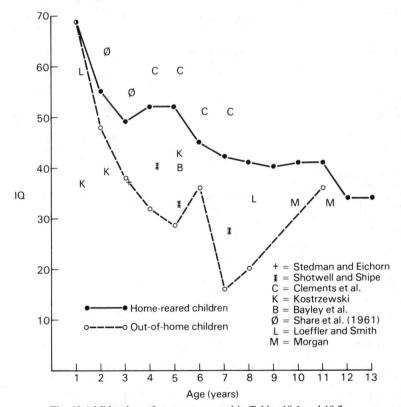

Fig. 10.1 Mid-points of scores presented in Tables 10.1 and 10.2

Table 10.1 *Mean IQs over time*

Study	n	Tests	Age (years) 1	2	3
Home-reared children					
Share et al. (1961)	16	Ges	71	63	55
Koch et al. (1963)	23	Ges	71	60	53
Share et al. (1961)	45	Ges	68	58	51
*Loeffler and Smith (1964)	81	CIIS, SB	**10** 59	**12** 50	**5** 42
Stedman and Eichorn (1964)	10	Bay			52.1
Bayley et al. (1966)	10	Bay			
Shotwell and Shipe (1964)	25	KB, SB/L		53	
Shipe and Shotwell (1965)	25	KB, SB/L			
Cornwell and Birch (1969)	44	SB			
*Dicks-Mireaux (1972)	21	Ges	72 70 75 70	58	
Melyn and White (1973)	612	SB, WISC, MP, CIIS, L	**70** 58	**75** 58	**75** 54
Kostrzewski (1974)	625	CIIS, SB/L, WISC, W	**6** 37	**22** 39	**25** 43
Carr (1975)	40	Bay	**25 34 38 40** 70 77 67 62	**40** 56	**39** 48
Carr and Hewett (1982)	38	Bay, MP			
Clements et al. (1976)	194	SBL-M			
*Connolly (1978)	180	SB, WISC CIIS	**11** 64	**17** 50	**26** 52
Ludlow and Allen (1979) A	72	Gr	**25** 80	**43** 70	**68** 63
Ludlow and Allen (1979) B	62	Gr	**9** 69	**28** 61	**52** 53
Morgan (1979)	217	SB, CIIS	**39** 73	**38** 58	
Ramsay and Piper (1980)	27	Gr Bay	**6 10 11 8** 81 75 69 58 80 64 53 51		
Out-of-home children					
Centerwall and Centerwall (1960)	32‡ 32	SB/L, KB			43 34
Dameron (1963)	10	Calif	**6 11 10 6 6 5** 94 71 66 59 52 46		
Stedman and Eichorn (1964)	10	Bay			37
Bayley et al. (1966)	10	Bay, SB			
Shotwell and Shipe (1964)	17	KB, SB		41	
Shipe and Shotwell (1965)					
Carr (1975)	9	Bay	6 w 6 m 10 m 15 m **4 8 8 7** 71 80 56 50	**7** 45	**6** 37
Carr and Hewett (1982)		MP			
Ludlow and Allen (1979) C	24	Gr	**6** 68	**12** 45	**22** 42

*IQs calculated by J. Carr
‡Brought up at home until 2.5 years
Tests
Bay: Bayley Scales of Infant Development.
Calif: California First Year Scale.

CIIS: Cattell Infant Intelligence Scale.
Ges: Gesell Scale.
Gr: Griffiths Mental Development Scale.
KB: Kuhlmann Binet.
L: Leiter International Performance Scale.

Age (years)

4	5	6	7	8	9	10	11	12	13	14	15	16	17	18
45														
46	49													
6	**7**	**7**	**4**	**2**	**3**									
53	46	39	44	34	40									
	40		42											
40	33													
			27											
5	**3**	**3**	**6**	**3**	**7**	**2**	**5**	**1**			**3**	**1**	**1**	**3**
54	57	49*	42	44	41	37	45	45			35	31	37	32
73	**76**	**76**	**66**	**36**	**34**	**28**	**15**	**9**	**6**	**4**				
54	49	48	45	44	45	43	41	37	34	38				
37	**42**	**41**	**46**	**69**	**62**	**61**	**50**	**36**	**35**	**33**	**24**	**14**	**11**	**7**
42	42	42	39	36	36	37	38	38	38	38	37	36	33	37
39														
46							**38**								
							37							
34		**71**		**39**		**29**		**21**						
59		51		46		43		29						
17	**32**	**21**	**10**	**16**	**10**	**10**	**3**	**4**	**1**	**1**		**4**	**1**	**2**
46	49	43	40	45	38	45	34	50	49	50		46	20	30
72	**71**	**67**	**59**	**47**	**40**	**28**								
58	56	54	53	52	51	49								
59	62	58	51	50	45	44								
49	44	43	44	43	43	43								
48		**43**		**22**		**14**	←		**13**	→				
46		41		38		33			27					
			23											
			16											
	30	36												
29	27													
				20										
6														
35						**6**								
						36								
24	**22**	**22**	**21**	**23**	**20**	**17**								
41	38	35	32	29	27	25								

MP: Merrill Palmer Scale.
SB: Stanford Binet.
WISC: Weschler Intelligence Scale for Children.

W: Weschler–Bellevue Scale.

w, weeks; m, months.

figure. (Discrepant scores based on small numbers, of four subjects or fewer, are ignored.)

Fig. 10.1 is not intended to suggest average scores for people with Down's Syndrome, but rather to call attention to the consistency of the findings of differences between the scores of home- and out-of-home reared children. It is worth noting, however, that in no case did a mean score for non-home-reared children exceed the mid-point score for the home-reared.

It is now widely accepted that institutions are not appropriate places in which to bring up children, retarded or non-retarded, with Down's Syndrome or with other forms of mental handicap. Children's wards in long-stay institutions are closed or closing, and parents are encouraged to keep their children at home, or foster homes approximating as near as possible to normal family homes are sought. Some of the impetus for this has come from studies showing that handicapped children make better progress if brought up at home, and yet doubts have been expressed as to the validity of this observation. Birch and Belmont (1961) put forward the view that the differences found between home- and institution-reared children could be more parsimoniously explained not by differences in the rearing environments but by selective factors determining which children should be fostered; that, in the study under discussion (Centerwall and Centerwall, 1960), 'the data presented quite strongly support (the) inference that the foster placement group was in fact initially significantly more defective than were the home-reared infants'. In a later paper, a more moderate view, that the relative rôle of environmental and genetic factors is as yet undecided, is expressed (Cornwell and Birch, 1969). Gibson (1978, pp. 93–5) also feels that no conclusions can be drawn from the 'home versus hospital studies' because the 'institutions' involved have almost always been large and poorly staffed, while the homes have been middle class with the families working closely with research institutes. He also points out that the initial comparability of the samples, especially in neuro-maturation, has not been established, and that 'the reasons parents choose early institutionalisation are complex but not accidental with regard to the clinical and psychological status of the handicapped offspring'; that long-term studies are missing; and that tests designed for normal children within family environments may be inappropriate for institutionalised children.

Some of these points cannot be held against all the studies which have reported advantage to home-reared children. For example, in Carr's study the placements of the boarded-out children were generally favourable, and the families of the home children were equally divided between middle and working class. That parents may be more likely to institutionalise the more retarded children could certainly apply to older children, but it is very difficult to credit that it could apply to those children institutionalised in the neonatal period (Shotwell and Shipe, 1964; Carr, 1970, 1975) or within the first 4½ months (Dameron, 1963; Stedman and Eichorn, 1964). Since professionals do not now recommend that infants be removed from their homes, this would require that the parents themselves, never having seen a Down's Syndrome baby before, should be able to recognise that one was more neuro-maturationally retarded than another and to dispatch him to an institution. This requires a suspension of disbelief that is far from parsimonious, and, where early institutionalised children are concerned, can probably be discounted.

Gibson points to Carr's study as evidence in support of his contention that those in the boarded-out group were constitutionally inferior because, although DIQs at 6 weeks and 6 months were almost identical, motor scores were different from the outset. In fact, mean motor age was slightly higher for the boarded-out children at 6 weeks (when only four of these children were seen), and by 6 months the mean motor quotients were within 0.16 points of each other; so the evidence here too is tenuous. It would be extremely difficult to demonstrate convincingly that children institutionalised early were constitutionally identical to those reared at home, if only because early tests, of both mental and motor abilities, correlate poorly with later tests. Such evidence as we have, however, offers little support to the 'constitutional inferiority' hypothesis. The alternative hypothesis, that the difference between home- and institution-reared children is due to environmental influence, not only accounts more simply for the facts but is also in accord with the effects on these children of environmental enrichment (Bayley *et al.*, 1966). Although Down's babies are unlikely to be subjected in the future to institutional upbringing, this debate is relevant to the current concern with early stimulation and so is still of importance.

DECLINE IN IQ WITH INCREASING AGE

Almost all studies, of children who have participated in early intervention programmes as well as those, in de Coriat's phrase, of 'spontaneous evolution', have documented a progressive decline in scores, from below but near normal in the early months to scores within the ESN range by school age. Much discussion centres round the question: what causes the decline? Some writers have suggested that it is due to a deterioration process in cerebral function which begins at or soon after birth (Griffiths, reported in Kirman, 1969; Dicks-Mireaux, 1972). Bilovsky and Share (1965) felt that the decline was brought about by the 'increased psycholinguistic demands of later tests', a view shared by others (Melyn and White, 1973). In most studies, however, the most rapid decline takes place before 3 years (when tests contain numerous non-verbal items), and continues more slowly after that, when tests become more verbally loaded. Furthermore, data supplied by Piper and Pless (1980) showed that scores on all the Griffiths' subscales declined sharply over the 6-month period of their study, apart from a lesser decline in those on the hand–eye scale. Gibson (1978, pp. 30–34), in a penetrating discussion, suggests that several factors may contribute to the decline. Specific neuromotor and sensory disabilities may emerge only as the infant grows older; the Down's Syndrome child appears to have greater difficulty in 'bridging the gap' between sensory–motor and cognitive performance than has the non-handicapped child. Moreover the decline may be a function of both 'progressive central nervous system arrest (and a secondary) growing deficiency of the sensory and expressive periphery'. He warns against facile acceptance of the cerebral deterioration hypothesis, but states that 'the condition surely has inherent limitations of intellectual growth that are presumably dictated by biogenic events'. The reasons for the decline, then, are still not clear, and, more importantly, it is not clear what remediation methods might be effective in combating it. Early intervention has succeeded in raising the level of children's IQs, but has not markedly affected the rate of decline of scores (see p.181). This task awaits the interventionists of tomorrow.

CORRELATIONS BETWEEN SCORES AT DIFFERENT AGES

Of the studies reporting correlations, Koch *et al.* (1963) gave figures of 0.77 or more for correlations between MA scores obtained between the first and fourth year. Bayley *et al.* (1966) reported significant correlations of 0.70 or greater, for both the home- and hospital-reared children, between scores at 5 and 6 years, but only for the hospital-reared children's scores between 2.5 and 6 years. For neither group were their scores between 2½ and 5 years significantly correlated.

Carr (1975) found insignificant correlations between scores at 6 weeks and at all subsequent ages up to 4 years, but from 10 months correlations were of 0.62 or more and, from 15 months, 0.72 or more. These correlations were generally higher than those for the controls, supporting other findings that infant tests are more efficient predictors of the later ability of retarded than of non-retarded children (Knobloch and Pasamanick, 1960). In the same study, correlations between motor ages for the Down's children were generally over 0.62 after 10 months, while same-age correlations of mental and motor ages were over 0.72 after 6 months, reflecting the close relationship between the physical and mental development of these children (none of the correlations for the controls between DIQs and DMQs reached that level).

VARIABILITY OF SCORES

Most studies present mean scores of groups of subjects, these usually showing a quite regular decline in IQ over age. These mean scores mask fluctuations in individual scores, which can be considerable. Kostrzewski (1974) presented curves of MA scores that in individuals are quite erratic. Laveck and Brehm (1978) stated that the stability of IQ in the six children they studied was variable, although they did not give figures. Carr (1975) found that 'small gains and losses of score occurred between every adjacent pair of ages, but large variations (of 20 or more DIQ points) were in the downward direction in every case except between 10 and 15 months'. At this time, the scores of five children rose, by between 1 and 45 points, while those of four children dropped by between 20 and 35 points.

These results could not be explained by variation in test conditions, and it was suggested that the pattern of development of Down's children might be different from that of normal children, that they might remain longer on 'plateaux' of achievements, which could produce the fluctuation of scores described. Other writers, too, have had the impression that such plateaux occur (Gibson, 1978, p.

49), while Cunningham (1979, p. 191) stresses that these should be regarded not as times of no development but as times of consolidation of behaviours.

SEX DIFFERENCES

Two early studies reported sex differences and in each case found that the scores of females tended to be higher than those of males (Brousseau and Brainerd, 1928; Wallin, 1949). Analysis of Pototzky and Grigg's (1942) figures shows that for 10 males and 10 females (omitting the 8-year-old female), mean CA for each was 22 years, and mean IQ for the males was 44.2 and for the females 50.4. Subsequent studies have generally borne out these findings. In Carr's studies (Carr, 1970, 1975; Carr and Hewett, 1982), mean scores of the girls were consistently above those of the boys, and this trend over time was significant (at < 0.025 level) when the 11-year-olds' scores were included (mean girls' IQ = 55; mean boys' IQ = 45). Inspection of the top and bottom quarter of the scores at each age shows that almost two-thirds in the bottom quarter (65%) were of boys' scores, while almost the same proportion in the upper quarter (63%) were of girls' scores. So, in this study, the superiority of the girls' mean scores seems to be due to a combination of a preponderance of high-scoring girls and of low-scoring boys. Clements *et al.* (1976), claiming that 'no-one has as yet investigated the relationship of genetic sex to IQ', also found IQs of females to be higher than those of males, the trend being significant at < 0.025. Connolly (1978) found mean female IQs to be higher at almost all ages from 1 to 18 years (although, since from age 6 onwards his groups contained three or fewer girls, these later figures must be treated with caution), and overall means of 41.7 for males and 49.9 for females (no indication is given as to whether this difference is significant). A re-analysis of Cornwell and Birch's (1969) figures shows that, of 18 males and females with mean CAs of 8.7 and 8.4, IQs were 42.4 and 47.4 respectively. Melyn and White (1973) do not give data on IQ by sex, but on four developmental measures (sitting, standing, walking and saying first word), girls were more advanced than were boys. Finally, Ramsay and Piper (1980), in a study of young children, found no significant sex differences.

This last study excepted, all those which have looked at sex differences have found girls' mean scores to be higher than those of boys. Various explanations have been suggested for this: that the presence of the XX sex chromosomes 'may tend to reduce the severity of measured mental retardation within ... Down's Syndrome children' (Clements *et al.*, 1976); that parents may interact differently with their Down's Syndrome children according to sex (Connolly, 1978) – an interesting suggestion which might repay further study, although this would be beset by the difficulty of teasing out the interactional effect of child's intelligence and parental response. A plausible explanation concerns selective mortality (Gibson, 1978; Connolly, 1978). Mortality in the early years is higher for females than for males (Fabia and Drolette, 1970; Scully, 1973) and it may be that the more retarded girls are more vulnerable than the boys. This would fit the observed pattern of greater numbers of severely retarded boys than girls, but would not explain the preponderance of high-scoring girls. However, since this latter finding is reported from only one study population (Carr, 1975; Carr and Hewett, 1982), it may be due to chance factors.

FAMILY VARIABLES

In non-handicapped populations, the intelligence of the children is commonly found to be positively related to parental factors such as social class (Hindley, 1962) and parental IQ and educational level (Vernon, 1979). Some studies have looked at similar relationships between Down's children and their families.

Fraser and Sadovnik (1976) tested 25 institutionalised and 23 home-reared Down's subjects, and as many parents and sibs as were willing to co-operate – 19 and 21 mothers, 12 and 14 fathers, and 29 and 26 sibs of institutionalised and home-reared subjects respectively. All subjects were over the age of 5 years, but otherwise no ages are reported. Correlations between scores of mothers, fathers and sibs and scores of home-reared subjects were, respectively, 0.42, 0.50 and 0.59; equivalent correlations with the scores of institutionalised subjects were respectively 0.69, 0.29 and 0.20, only the first of these being significant. The figures for the home-reared children are similar to those (of around 0.5) found in studies of non-handicapped children and their parents and sibs (Vernon, 1979, p. 164). The authors focus on these results and conclude that Down's children of high-ability parents are likely, if they are raised at home, to have greater intellectual potential than those 'who have parents of comparable socio-economic class with low IQs' (although no data are given to show that social class was equated for high and low IQ parents). The findings concerning the institutionalised group are puzzling, especially, perhaps, that which shows the correlation between mothers and their institutionalised children to be the highest of all those reported in this paper, and far higher than the correlations of 0.28 and 0.33 reported between natural mothers and their (non-handicapped) adopted-away children (Horn, 1983; Scarr and Weinberg, 1983). Correlations between scores of fathers and sibs with those of the institutionalised children are insignificant, the latter being lower than the median correlation of 0.47 reported for sibs reared apart (Vernon, 1979). The authors do not discuss these conflicting findings and it is difficult to account for them.

Golden and Pashayan (1976) studied 34 home-reared children who had been tested at between 3½ and 16 years of age and obtained questionnaire data on the educational level of 34 mothers and 31 fathers. The parents were placed into four groups according to whether they had reached postgraduate, college, high school or grammar school levels of education, and the means of their children's IQs were calculated as 50.0, 51.0, 50.6 and 34.6 respectively. The authors claim that these results demonstrate a trend, which they patently do not. Results for the first three groups are extremely similar; there are only six children in the last group, one of whom is given a score of 0 as 'untestably low'. If, as seems likely, this meaningless score of 0 has been included in the mean score, the mean score of the remaining five children is 41.6 – still lower than in the other groups but, especially with such small numbers involved, certainly not constituting a 'trend'. With other figures in this paper gone awry (the 11 group 1 children are compared with one mother and nine fathers – not even one parent apiece), the paper should perhaps be treated with caution.

By contrast, Bennett *et al.* (1979) studied two groups, a younger group of children aged from 1 to 5 years tested on the Bayley and an older group of children aged 4 to 13 years tested on the Binet. Each child's score was related to a graph of mean scores plotted over age, derived from Melyn and White's (1973) data, and so was reported in terms of points above or below the mean for the child's chronological age. When these scores were averaged according to parents' years of education, no significant trend could be discerned, whether the younger, the older or both groups combined were concerned. This applied particularly to the mothers, children with mothers in the lowest education group showing the best performance for age, although in the younger group of children those with high-education fathers had the highest scores. The authors point out that this is a relatively isolated finding and conclude that 'highly educated parents can have severely retarded children with Down's Syndrome just as poorly educated parents can have children with Down's Syndrome with mild involvement'.

In general agreement with this are the findings from Carr (1975), which showed scores for working-class Down's Syndrome children to be slightly but insignificantly above those for the middle-class children (and this remained true at 11 years), although in the controls the middle-class children's scores were significantly higher than those for the working-class children.

The findings from these studies, then, are inconsistent, two tending to show that parental factors are positively related to the intelligence of their children, and two suggesting that they are not. The measures used to correlate with the children's IQs (parental IQ, educational level and social class) are not identical, and this may have contributed to the conflicting results, although these measures are highly correlated in general populations and two studies with conflicting results used similar measures of parental education (Golden and Pashayan, 1976; Bennett *et al.*, 1979). The most impressive results are those of Fraser and Sadovnik (1976), showing that in home-reared children correlations with their parents' and sibs' IQs were of the same order as similar correlations carried out on the scores of normal sibs and their parents. Gibson (1978) stated uncompromisingly: 'It is reasonable to conclude that intelligence for DS is not dependent, even in part, on hereditable competency in the parents', and it would be interesting if the results of Fraser and Sadovnik could be replicated. In the meantime, it would probably be unwise (and patronising) to suggest that 'in cases where the parents' education is limited a more vigorous program be considered and where possible implemented for their child at an early age' (Golden and Pashayan, 1976).

THE EFFECT OF EARLY INTERVENTION

The earliest study of the effect of intensive early stimulation is that by de Coriat *et al.* (1967) who drew up a programme of stimulation for mothers to apply under the guidance of a trained teacher.

Later studies have looked at the effects of stimulation and training given in out-of-home situations. Two concerned institutionalised children: one the study already described by Bayley *et al.* (1966), the other by Aronson and Fällström (1977). In this latter study two matched groups of eight children, one of whom received an hour's training twice a week, were tested five times over a period of 2.5 years. At the end of the 18-month training period the experimental group had gained 10.5 months of MA compared with 3.5 for the controls. Follow-up a year later showed that although the experimental group was still slightly ahead, the differences were not now significant. The authors comment that 'while early training is effective for mentally retarded children it must be a continuous process to achieve long-term benefit'.

In other studies, mother and baby attended a clinic where the baby was put through a programme of educational and remedial activities while the mother looked on, and she was then encouraged to continue with similar activities at home. Connolly and Russell (1976) offered parents training for half a day a week over 10 weeks, followed by home visits, and parents were 'urged' to continue the programme at home. Motor milestones were compared with those reported by Fishler *et al.* (1964), showing the Early Intervention (EI) children achieving the milestones earlier. Twenty of the original 40 children were followed up at between 3.2 and 6.3 years of age (Connolly *et al.*, 1980). Results from these children were compared with those from 53 children from the Fishler *et al.* (1964) study, closely matched for chronological age and parental educational level. Although the programme was terminated at 3 years, there was still a significant difference in test results at a mean CA of 4½.

A large study in Kent concerned children in one geographical area (maximum number 72) whose mothers attended a developmental clinic twice a week for between 2 and 8 years (Ludlow and Allen, 1979). The children were engaged in nursery-type activities, and the mothers encouraged to attend the groups 'so that the stimulus given two days a week (might) be continued at home seven days a week'. The developmental progress of these children, measured on the Griffiths and Stanford Binet scales, was compared with that of children from a different geographical area (maximum number 79) who did not have access to similar clinics.

Table 10.2 *Mean annual changes in Griffiths Scale IQs and mean annual IQ differences: stimulated and non-stimulated children. (From Ludlow and Allen, 1979.)*

Year	Changes in IQs		
	Stimulated children	Non-stimulated children	Difference in IQ
0–1	–	–	10.4
1–2	−9.8	−8.4	9.0
2–3	−7.3	−7.9	9.6
3–4	−4.9	−4.3	9.0
4–5	−1.3	−4.4	11.1
5–6	−2.3	−1.0	10.8
6–7	−0.9	+0.4	9.5
7–8	−1.4	−1.2	9.3
8–9	−1.2	+0.5	7.6
9–10	−1.8	−0.5	6.3
Total IQ loss	−30.9	−26.8	−4.1

Results showed once again that the experimental group was consistently ahead of the controls. Changes in scores for each group on the Griffiths Scale, and the differences between their scores at each age, have been calculated from the published data and are given in Table 10.2. The authors suggest that the rate of decline is more rapid after the third year in the controls; in fact, the graph of the two sets of scores is almost parallel (and Group B made two small increases in mean scores, which did not occur in Group A) until the gap between them narrows towards the end of the period (Fig. 10.2).

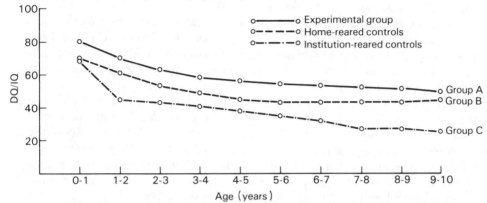

Fig. 10.2 Graph of DQ/IQs (from Ludlow and Allen, 1979). Reproduced with permission.

The mean overall drop in scores is 30.9 for the experimental and 26.8 for the home control children. This suggests that the extra stimulation the children received gave them an initial advantage which they largely retained until after the eighth year (after which it diminished to about two-thirds of its original level), but that it was not able to affect the rate of decline of scores. At the end of the study, just over a quarter of the experimental group were attending normal primary or ESN(M) schools, compared with about 5% of the home controls. This difference was highly significant, and was held to provide independent evidence of the effectiveness of the intervention (Ludlow, 1980), although it is possible that other factors, such as a more ready acceptance of the children into non-ESN(S) schools in that part of Kent, may have had some effect.

An alternative intervention strategy is for families to be visited at home, the parents given advice about what and how the children should be taught, and for all the teaching to be carried out by the parents. This was the pattern adopted by one of the first and most influential workers (Brinkworth, 1973). In another study (Hanson and Schwarz, 1978) the families of 12 infants were visited weekly or bi-weekly for a mean of 2 years and were given step-by-step educational programmes to follow. The programmes were strenuous but by the end of the study parents were assessing their children independently, establishing goals and writing teaching programmes. Results were assessed in terms of developmental milestones and compared with those reported by Share and his colleagues (Share, 1975) and with norms for non-handicapped infants. The experimental children attained the milestones at a slightly older age than the norms but consistently earlier than Share's controls did.

Cunningham (1982), as part of an important series of studies of intervention with Down's children, studied a group of 32 infants whose families were given advice on ways of stimulating their babies from 6 weeks old, and another group of 13 whose families came into the programme when the child was 6–12 months old. Compared with the data given in Carr's (1970) study, the scores of the group receiving intervention from birth showed the least decline, while the scores of the delayed-treatment group were similar to those of Carr's home-reared group up to the age of 1 year, after which they caught up with the early-treated group. (See Chapter 17 for Cunningham's description of some of his work.)

One study employed a different approach, the intervention being carried out by group training (Bidder *et al.*, 1975). Mothers of eight Down's children had 12 sessions of group training in behaviour modification techniques and counselling over a period of 6 months, and were given aims for training their children at home. A comparison group of eight mothers of children matched for sex and for chronological and mental age received no extra training. Mean chronological age at the outset was 23.8 months for the experimental group and 24.5 for the controls: mean mental ages were 16.6 and 14.8 months respectively. Thus, the experimental children were initially somewhat more advanced than the controls. Results on the Griffiths Scale showed significant gains for the children in the experimental group, of 6.56 months on the language and 7 months on the performance scale, compared with the control group's 2.56 and 4.37 months respectively.

Finally, one study, in contrast to the others reported, found no significant differences between children who did or did not receive early training. Piper and Pless (1980) instituted a programme of centre-based, biweekly, one-hour sessions of stimulation for the children and teaching for the parents, who were also given written instructions to carry out at home. Thirty-seven children, referred between July and December, constituted the experimental group, and 21, referred between March and June, the control group. The children were tested at the outset and at the end of the 6 months on the Griffiths Scale. An unusual feature of this study was that all the testing was carried out by a specially appointed psychologist 'who was kept unaware of the group status of the subjects and of the basic design of the study'. Following the 6 months' intervention, the scores of both groups had declined somewhat; on four out of the six Griffiths scales, scores of the experimental group had declined more than those of the controls, although none of the differences was significant.

This study has been criticised by Bricker *et al.* (1981) on the grounds that the 6-month intervention period was very short, that the Griffiths Scale may have been an insufficiently sensitive instrument, and that the authors did not assess how far the parents actually implemented the programmes at home. However, these criticisms apply equally to the study by Bidder *et al.* (1975) which showed significant advantages in the experimental group. Bricker *et al.* do not discuss the question of independence of assessors. Piper and Pless state explicitly that assessments were done blind, whereas this was clearly not the case in some studies (Brinkworth, 1973; Cunningham, 1982; Hanson and Schwarz, 1978; Ludlow and Allen, 1979), whilst in others no information on this point is given.

The current emphasis on early intervention, the proliferation of programmes to offer stimulation to the children and guidance and encouragement to the parents, is a major development for those concerned with children with Down's Syndrome and their families. The published studies generate enthusiasm and much may be hoped for in the future. However, there is still a need for some caution. Most of the published studies are methodologically less than satisfactory, and long-term follow-up studies, to see whether initial advantages are maintained, are lacking. The evidence from longitudinal studies (Ludlow and Allen, 1979; Cunningham, 1982) suggests that the average IQ increase for stimulated children is of the order of 10 points, and that scores decline over age in these children at a similar rate as (albeit on a higher level than) do the scores of non-stimulated children. At present, there is no evidence to show what are the effects of early stimulation of these children on their lives as adults, although this will undoubtedly be forthcoming in the future.

Cunningham (1982) states that 'we are better to err on the side of optimism since expectation is the force behind change', and this is a cogent argument. Nevertheless, it is important that the benefits to be expected from the intervention programmes be firmly established. Parents can find the programmes make heavy demands on them (Fulwood, 1981). If they are to be encouraged to commit themselves to these pressures, it should be in the confidence that it will confer benefits that parents can see as worthwhile for their children.

CONCLUSIONS

Studies of the intelligence of people with Down's Syndrome go back over more than 40 years, during which time attitudes and practices in relation to mentally handicapped people have changed considerably. Over this time, the main emphasis of the investigations has altered, from the simple measurement of intelligence over wide age ranges, to examination of the effects of home or institution rearing, to the current emphasis on the effects and effectiveness of early stimulation programmes. The published studies vary widely as to the populations studied, the tests used, and the numbers tested, while the results from early intervention studies suggest that estimates of expected IQ level gained from earlier work may now be out of date. Consequently, it is difficult to arrive at hard and fast conclusions. Tentatively, however, we may say that people with Down's Syndrome are virtually always mentally handicapped to some degree; that by school age the majority have been found to fall within the severely handicapped range, with a minority (about 10%) falling within either the profoundly handicapped or the ESN(M) range. Females are generally found to have higher mean IQ levels than males, but there are many individual exceptions. Evidence regarding the effects of social class and parental educational level is conflicting.

The most important recent development has been the growth of early intervention programmes. These have not yet overcome their methodological problems, especially those of selected samples, and lack of independent assessments and of long-term follow-up. Despite this, in view of the near-unanimity of positive outcome, the likelihood is that the programmes *are* conferring real benefit to the children in raising their overall IQ levels, at least in the short term, although it has not been unequivocally established that they also prevent the usual IQ decline. It is undoubtedly true, too, that for many parents the programmes offer hope, and the opportunity to give their children practical help. For some parents, however, the involvement required is too much, and it is important that these parents should feel able to opt out of the programmes if they wish. For the sake of both groups of parents, and for the children themselves, we need further, more firmly based, long-term research to show clearly the effects of early intervention on the abilities and the lives of Down's people.

REFERENCES

Aronson, M. and Fällström, K. (1977). Immediate and long term effects of developmental training in children with Down's Syndrome. *Dev. Med. Child Neurol.* **19**, 489–94.

Bayley, N., Rhodes, L. and Gooch, B. (1966). A comparison of the growth and development of institutionalized and home-reared mongoloids. A follow-up study. *Calif. Ment. Health Res. Digest* **4** (3), 104–5.

Bennett, F.C., Sells, C.J. and Brand, C. (1979). Influences on measured intelligence in Down's syndrome. *Am. J. Dis. Child.* **133**, 700–703.

Bidder, R.T., Bryant, G. and Gray, O.P. (1975). Benefits to Down's syndrome children through training their mothers. *Arch. Dis. Childh.* **50**, 383–6.

Bilovsky, D. and Share, J. (1965). The ITPA and Down's syndrome: an exploratory study. *Am. J. Ment. Defic.* **70**, 78–82.

Birch, H.G. and Belmont, L. (1961). The problem of comparing home-rearing versus foster home rearing in defective children. *Pediatrics* **28**, 956–61.

Bricker, D., Carlson, L. and Schwarz, R. (1981). A discussion of early intervention for infants with Down Syndrome. *Pediatrics* **67**, 45–6.

Brinkworth, R. (1973). The unfinished child. Effects of early home training on the mongol infant. In Clarke, A.D.B., *Mental Retardation and Behavioural Research*. London: Churchill Livingstone.

Brousseau, K. and Brainerd, H.G. (1928). *Mongolism: a Study of the Physical and Mental Characteristics of Mongolian Imbeciles*. London: Baillière, Tindall and Cox.

Carr, J. (1970). Mental and motor development in young mongol children. *J. Ment. Defic. Res.* **14** (3), 205–20.

Carr, J. (1975). *Young Children with Down's Syndrome*. London: Butterworth.

Carr, J. and Hewett, S. (1982). Children with Down's syndrome growing up: a preliminary report. *Assoc. Child Psychol. & Psych. News* **Spring**, 10–43.

Centerwall, S.A. and Centerwall, W.R. (1960). A study of children with mongolism reared in the home compared to those reared away from home. *Pediatrics* **25**, 678–85.

Clements, P.R., Bates, M.V. and Hafer, M. (1976). Variability within Down's syndrome (Trisomy-21): empirically observed sex differences in IQs. *Ment. Retard.* **14** (1), 30–31.

Connolly, B., Morgan, S., Russell, F. and Richardson, B. (1980). Early intervention with Down syndrome children: follow-up report. *Phys. Ther.* **60** (11), 1405–8.

Connolly, B. and Russell, F. (1976). Interdisciplinary early intervention program. *Phys. Ther.* **56** (2), 155–8.

Connolly, J.A. (1978). Intelligence levels of Down's syndrome children. *Am. J. Ment. Defic.* **83** (2), 193–6.

Coriat, L.F. de, Theslenco, L. and Waksman, J. (1967). The effects of psycho-motor stimulation on the IQ of young children with trisomy-21. In Richards, B. (ed.), *Proceedings of the First Congress of the International Association for the Scientific Study of Mental Deficiency*, pp. 377–85. Reigate: Michael Jackson.

Cornwell, A.C. and Birch, H.G. (1969). Psychological and social development in home-reared children with Down's syndrome (mongolism). *Am. J. Ment. Defic.* **75** (3), 341–50.

Cunningham, C.C. (1979). Early stimulation of the mentally handicapped child. In Craft, M. (ed.), *Tredgold's Mental Retardation*, 12th edn. London; Baillière Tindall.

Cunningham, C.C. (1982). Psychological and educational aspects of handicap. In Cockburn, F. and Gitzelman, R. (eds), *Inborn Errors of Metabolism*. Lancaster: MTP Press.

Dameron, L.E. (1963). Development of intelligence of infants with mongolism. *Child Dev.* **34**, 733–8.

Demaine, G.C. and Silverstein, A.B. (1978). MA changes in institutionalized Down's syndrome persons: a semi-longitudinal approach. *Am. J. Ment. Defic.* **82** (5), 429–32.

Dicks-Mireaux, M.J. (1972). Mental development of infants with Down's syndrome. *Am. J. Ment. Defic.* **77** (1), 26–32.

Donoghue, E. (1975). Some physical measurements on 40 pairs of patients with Down's disease and undiagnosed mentally retarded controls matched for age, sex and IQ. In Kirman, B. and Bicknell, J. (eds), *Mental Handicap*, p.134. London: Churchill Livingstone.

Dunsdon, M.I., Carter, C.O. and Huntley, R.M.C. (1960). Upper end of range of intelligence in mongolism. *Lancet* **i**, 565–8.

Fabia, J. and Drolette, M. (1970). Malformations and leukaemia in children with Down's syndrome. *Pediatrics* **45**, 60–70.

Fishler, K., Share, J. and Koch, R. (1964). Adaptation of Gesell developmental scales for evaluation of development in children with Down's syndrome. *Am. J. Ment. Defic.* **68**, 642–6.

Fraser, F.C. and Sadovnik, A.D. (1976). Correlation of IQ in subjects with Down syndrome and their parents and sibs. *J. Ment. Defic. Res.* **20**, 179–82.

Fulwood, D. (1981). Mum or supermum? *Austral. Citizen Ltd* **August**, 241–7.

Gibson, D. (1978). *Down's Syndrome: the Psychology of Mongolism*. Cambridge: Cambridge University Press.

Golden, W. and Pashayan, H.M. (1976). The effect of parental education on the eventual mental development of non-institutionalized children with Down syndrome. *J. Ped.* **89** (4), 603–5.

Hanson, M.J. and Schwarz, R.H. (1978). Results of a longitudinal intervention program for Down's syndrome infants and their families. *Ed. & Train. Ment. Ret.* **13** (4), 403–7.

Hindley, C.B. (1962). Social class influences on the development of ability in the first five years. In *Proceedings of the XIV International Congress of Applied Psychology, Vol. 3, Child and Education*, pp.29–41. Copenhagen: Munksgaard.

Horn, J.M. (1983). The Texas Adoption Project: adopted children and their intellectual resemblance to biological and adoptive parents. *Child Dev.* **54**, 268–75.

Kirman, B.H. (1969). Down's syndrome. In Wortis, J. (ed.), *Mental Retardation*. New York: Grune and Stratton.

Knobloch, H. and Pasamanick, B. (1960). An evaluation of the consistency and predictive value of the 40-week Gesell developmental schedule. *Psych. Res. Rep.* **13**, 10–41.

Koch, R., Share, J., Webb, A. and Graliker, B.V. (1963). The predictability of Gesell developmental scales in mongolism. *J. Ped.* **62**, 93–7.

Kostrzewski, J. (1974). The dynamics of intellectual development in individuals with complete and incomplete trisomy of chromosome Group G, in the karyotype. *Pol. Psychol. Bull.* **5** (3), 153–8.

LaVeck, B. and Brehm, S.S. (1978). Individual variability among children with Down's syndrome. *Ment. Retard.* **16** (2), 135–7.

Lejeune, J., Gautier, M. and Turpin, R. (1959). Les chromosomes humains en culture de tissus. *C. R. Acad. Sci.* **248**, 602.

Loeffler, F. and Smith, G.F. (1964). Unpublished observations.

Ludlow, J.R. and Allen, L.M. (1979). The effect of early intervention and pre-school stimulus on the development of the Down's syndrome child. *J. Ment. Defic. Res.* **23**, 29–44.

Ludlow, A.R. (1980). Early intervention in Down's syndrome (letter). *Br. Med. J.* **281**, 1143.

Meindl, J.L., Yater, A.C., Lamp, R.E. and Barclay, A.G. (1983). Mental growth of non-institutionalized and institutionalized children with Down's syndrome. *Br. J. Ment. Subnorm.* **29** (1), 50–56.

Melyn, M.A. and White, D.T. (1973). Mental and developmental milestones of non-institutionalised Down's syndrome children. *Pediatrics* **52** (4), 542–5.

Morgan, S.B. (1979). Adaptive skills in Down's syndrome children: implications for early intervention. *Ment. Retard.* **17** (5), 247–9.

Øster, J. (1953). *Mongolism.* Copenhagen: Danish Science Press.

Piper, M.C. and Pless, I.B. (1980). Early intervention for infants with Down syndrome: a controlled trial. *Pediatrics* **65** (3), 463–8.

Pototzky, C. and Grigg, A.E. (1942). A revision of the prognosis in mongolism. *Am. J. Orthopsych.* **12**, 503–10.

Ramsay, M. and Piper, M.C. (1980). A comparison of two developmental scales in evaluating infants with Down syndrome. *Early Hum. Dev.* **4** (1), 89–95.

Scarr, S. and Weinberg, R.A. (1983). The Minnesota Adoption Studies: genetic differences and malleability. *Child Dev.* **54**, 260–67.

Scully, C. (1973). Down's syndrome. *Br. J. Hosp. Med.* **10**, 89–98.

Share, J.B. (1975). Developmental progress in Down's syndrome. In Koch, R. and de la Cruz, F.F. (eds), *Down's Syndrome (Mongolism): Research, Prevention and Management.* New York: Bruner/Mazel.

Share, J., Webb, A. and Koch, R. (1961). A preliminary investigation of the early developmental status of mongoloid infants. *Am. J. Ment. Defic.* **66**, 238–41.

Shipe, D. and Shotwell, A.M. (1965). Effect of out-of-home care on mongoloid children: a continuation study. *Am. J. Ment. Defic.* **69**, 649–52.

Shotwell, A.M. and Shipe, D. (1964). Effect of out-of-home care on the intellectual and social development of mongoloid children. *Am. J. Ment. Defic.* **68**, 693–9.

Shuttleworth, G.E. (1909). Mongolian imbecility. *Br. Med. J.* **2**, 661–5.

Silverstein, A.B. (1966). Mental growth in mongolism. *Child Dev.* **37** (3), 725–9.

Stedman, D.J. and Eichorn, D.H. (1964). A comparison of the growth and development of institutionalized and home-reared mongoloids during infancy and early childhood. *Am. J. Ment. Defic.* **69**, 391–401.

Tredgold, A.F. (1908). *Mental Deficiency (Amentia).* London: Baillière, Tindall and Cox.

Vernon, P.E. (1979). *Intelligence: Heredity and Environment.* California: W.H. Freeman.

Wallin, J.E.W. (1944). Mongolism among school children. *Am. J. Orthopsych.* **14**, 104–12.

Zeaman, D. and House, B.J. (1962). Mongoloid MA is proportional to log CA. *Child Dev.* **33**, 481–8.

11 Motor Skill Development

Sheila E. Henderson

The study of motor development in the mentally handicapped has followed a similar pattern to that evident in the study of normal development. The goal of early work was largely descriptive, documenting, in terms of *what* and *when*, the differences between retarded and normal individuals. Recently, the more theoretical question of *how* the mentally retarded differ from normal has received at least as much attention. These two approaches have tended to be characterised by different methodologies. Attempts to identify the processes underlying the performance of skilled movements have been almost exclusively experimental, whereas questions of what and when have been addressed more globally using clinical and psychometric approaches. Both types of approach have contributed to our understanding of how Down's Syndrome individuals differ from their normal peers, and in what follows I will attempt to review what we have learned from each.

The first section presents the descriptive approach, commencing with attempts to specify the neurodevelopmental foundations of motor ability, then continuing with a chronicle of the acquisition of basic skills such as walking, reaching and grasping. (More complex skills are dealt with by Reid in Chapter 12.) The section concludes with a brief discussion of whether motor competence in Down's Syndrome children can be accelerated by early intervention. In the second section, attention shifts to characterising the processes underlying motor control. Curiously, this characterisation focuses for the most part on momentary 'snapshots' of performance rather than on the developing nature of the skill. In an attempt to impose some shape on a discussion of many, diverse experiments, studies in which no time constraints were imposed upon performance are considered first, and then experiments in which speed or timing is of the essence. The chapter ends with a brief concluding section.

NEURODEVELOPMENTAL FOUNDATIONS OF MOTOR ABILITY

Even in the absence of clear neuromuscular abnormality, such as spasticity, mental retardation is often associated with considerable delay in motor development. While this may not be surprising at an intuitive level, the reasons for it are not well understood. One possibility is that the delayed acquisition of motor milestones is directly related to the intellectual deficit, and is part of a general disposition reflected in lack of motivation and diminished exploratory behaviour. An alternative is that the aberrant motor development is a consequence of impairment of the neuromotor system, even though a precise identification of that impairment has not yet been made.

In the first few months of life, the aberrant motor behaviour of the Down's child is characterised by two main features – muscular hypotonia and an abnormal timetable of emergence and dissolution of reflexes. Although it is impossible to separate these two components completely, in that muscular hypotonia has a profound effect on the emergence of several of the reflexes and automatic movement patterns (Cowie, 1970), it is possible to discuss hypotonia separately to some extent.

The hypotonic (or 'floppy') infant is relatively easy to describe at a clinical level (see, for example, Dubowitz, 1980). What is much more difficult is the objective measurement of either the state of the muscular system or the other clinical features almost invariably present. At a basic descriptive level, the hypotonic infant has been likened to a rag doll. Dubowitz (1980) points out that this is a very apt comparison, as the movement of a rag doll mimics many of the clinical features used in the diagnosis of the syndrome as a whole. These are: (1) increase in the range of movement of the joints; (2) diminished resistance of the joints to passive movements; and (3) unusual postures such as the frog-like position of the legs adopted in the supine position. In addition to its presence in Down's Syndrome infants, muscular hypotonia is associated with a variety of other conditions. In his excellent review of the topic, Dubowitz presents a guide to the differential diagnosis and classification of its causes. For example, he lists the many loci at which damage can occur, including the higher level components of the central nervous system, such as the cortex, basal ganglia and cerebellum, the anterior horn cells, the nerve fibres, the neuromuscular junctions, the muscles themselves and the tendon and supportive tissues. In Down's Syndrome individuals, the fault is believed to be of central origin, but the exact mechanism whereby the chromosomal abnormality causes hypotonia seems to be unknown (Crome *et al.*, 1966; Cowie, 1970; Dubowitz, 1980).

As may be obvious from the description above, hypotonia in an infant is best assessed by taking a number of measures together and producing a composite score. In her study of Down's Syndrome infants, Cowie (1970) based her score on four components: resistance to passive movement, palpation of muscle mass, observation of various postures, and flexibility around the joints. As Cowie points out, this system has shortcomings. Not only is it completely subjective but, more important, the tone of all parts of the body is represented in one rating. These criticisms apart, the results were absolutely clear. First, not a single baby in the sample showed normal muscle tone. (Excellent photographs of babies showing extreme hypotonia are presented in the book.) This finding replicated that of McIntire and Dutch (1964), who found hypotonia present in all but 2 of a sample of 86 Down's infants. Second, there was a distinct reduction in severity over time, in that the preponderance of children in the first 2 weeks of life showed extreme hypotonia, whereas at 10 months most showed only moderate amounts.

Given Cowie's finding that muscle tone seems to improve in the first year of life, it is important to ask what happens as the child matures, acquires some basic skills and is, therefore, afforded more opportunity to use his muscles in physical activity.

In his discussion of hypotonic infants in general, Dubowitz (1980) notes that 'although there may be a tendency for tone to improve as motor ability improves, even after the child is able to stand and walk tone is often still diminished and there also appears to be laxity of joint ligaments.' However, he presents no empirical evidence in support of this view. As far as Down's children specifically are concerned, there seem to be few studies which contain relevant data, and in those that do, the data are often very imprecise. For example, Loesch-Mdzewska (1968) noted that in some of her 123 subjects aged between 3 and 62 years, hypotonia remained present. Morris *et al.* (1982) provide data on a group of children aged between 4 and 17 years old, but the presentation of their results is frustrating in that they neither give raw data nor do they analyse the effect of age. What they did show, however, was that, overall, Down's children scored significantly below their normal peers on two measures of muscle tone.

In summary, the situation in infancy is quite clear: almost without exception, Down's children suffer hypotonia which may affect their early motor development. As they grow older, however, the picture is less clear, and the extent to which existing lack of muscle tone affects the performance of motor skills once they have been acquired has not been studied.

The other feature of early motor development which is noticeably different in the Down's infant is the emergence and dissolution of reflexes and automatic patterns of movement. The notion that a complex hierarchy of reflexes and automatic movement patterns forms the foundation upon which normal voluntary control and posture are built is not new (Magnus, 1926; Sherrington, 1961), and the idea has received substantial empirical support in the last 20 years (Easton, 1972, 1978). Although the normal newborn infant is equipped with the potential to acquire highly sophisticated skills, his motor behaviour in the neonatal period consists largely of reflexive or automatic reactions to stimuli and spontaneous, apparently random movements. Adaptive control emerges generally as maturation of the central nervous system proceeds.

By far the most comprehensive study of the emergence and dissolution of these behaviours in Down's infants is that of Cowie (1970). Her results document a clearly aberrant course of development. Sixty-seven infants were observed on five occasions between birth and 2 years of age. In addition to observation of muscle tone (discussed above), eight reflexes were examined; all proved to be abnormal in some way. The early reflexes, such as the Moro response, the palmar and plantar grasp reflexes and the automatic stepping response, showed delayed dissolution, and the traction response, patellar jerk and posture in ventral suspension were abnormal, both in terms of degree of response and time scale. Two of Cowie's conclusions are of interest here: (1) that marked hypotonia was an essential part of the syndrome and was related to poor position in ventral suspension, a weak patellar jerk, poor traction response and, in the early weeks, a partial or absent Moro reaction; and (2) the pattern of relationships between the variables became progressively more definitive and clear cut as time went on. Unfortunately, there are no studies which directly explore the relationship between these abnormal patterns of movement and the patterns of movement the Down's Syndrome child employs in performing later skills. Lydic and Steele (1979) provide some evidence which suggests that young Down's children exhibit odd patterns of movement. For example, many sit up from a prone position by spreading their legs apart into a full-split position, then pushing up with their hands or even head. However, whether these patterns evolve as a result of the abnormalities of tone or reflex development we have just discussed remains an open question.

In addition to the behavioural features described above, in the case of Down's Syndrome children there exists some indirect evidence of damage to the neuro-motor system. The brain, brainstem and cerebellum are all lighter in weight in Down's subjects, particularly the last two (Jebsen *et al.*, 1961; Crome *et al.*, 1966). From neurophysiological studies we also know that the cerebellum and brainstem are intimately involved in the control of movement. It has been suggested, for example, that the cerebellum is the seat of the mechanism which compares the commands to the muscles and the feedback from them (Evarts, 1973; Allen and Tsukahara, 1974), and that it has a particular role to play in the execution of fast ballistic movements (Kornhuber, 1974). However, as far as Down's individuals are concerned, too many authors simply refer to the smallness of the cerebellum as if that in itself constituted a satisfying functional explanation of motor deficiencies.

What do these various findings contribute to our understanding of motor control in Down's Syndrome? First, let us consider the implications of the anatomical findings. The weight of brain tissue is no more transparently related to the efficiency of motor function than it is to intellectual function. The weight of a neural structure is as difficult to interpret as it is simple to measure, and far from providing us with an insight into the process disturbance underlying poor performance, it actually offers an even more undifferentiated view than does behaviour itself.

Whether hypotonia is a factor in later motor dysfunction remains in doubt. It is clear that at least in some individuals it never disappears and might therefore influence specific aspects of control directly. For example, Morris *et al.* (1982) obtained a significant correlation between degree of hypotonia and strength. A much more fundamental consequence of hypotonia is suggested, however, by Davis and Kelso's study (1982). They suggest that the motor system of the Down's individual is slow to respond to changes in load (i.e. the force exerted on a joint or muscle group), and oscillates more on arrival at a new position as the change in load is adjusted to. Whether this difficulty could be attributed to hypotonia is a question of considerable interest.

As far as the abnormal pattern of reflex development is concerned, there is a strong possibility that the effects last much longer than has yet been established. If, as Easton (1972) suggests, the patterns of movement in the reflexes form the basis of the fundamental movement patterns observed in later life, then the consequences of delayed onset or persistence are bound to be far reaching. Not only might a particular milestone be achieved later than expected, but the possibility also arises that the actual pattern of movement adopted might be different from normal. Although we do not yet understand how the reflexes are incorporated into the mature motor system, or even if they are, we do know that they remain present throughout life at some level. In cases of adult neurological disease, for example, the primitive reflexes sometimes reappear. Important to note, also, is the point made by Hogg (1982) that central nervous system anomalies, although present at birth, may not manifest themselves until the stage at which they have their effect is reached. An added complication (which is outside the bounds of this discussion) is the change which may take place much later in the life of the Down's individual as a result of the progression of an Alzheimer-like disease process.

THE ACQUISITION OF BASIC SKILLS

As children grow older they gradually acquire a broader repertoire of motor skills. For the most part, the development of these skills is sufficiently predictable to permit what Laszlo and Bairstow (1985) describe as 'a sketch of a collective child', providing estimates of the chronological age at which particular motor characteristics generally appear. As far as normal children are concerned, there is no shortage of these 'what happens when' accounts of motor development. For example, the study of infant development is dominated by the now classic works of Shirley (1931), Bayley (1935) and Gesell (1941). These authors provided us with exceptionally detailed descriptions of the early development of skills such as reaching, grasping, sitting and walking. Although less cohesive, accounts of the course of motor development in the older child also exist (e.g. Cratty and Martin, 1969; Keogh, 1973; Rarick and Dobbins, 1975; Gallahue, 1982).

Before discussing particular issues, it might be useful to consider how the domain of motor behaviour has been mapped and conceptualised. During the earliest stages of development, primary interaction with the environment is through the medium of movement. To be able to interact efficiently with the environment, infants must master three types of movement. First, they must establish and maintain the relationship of the body to the force of gravity in order to obtain an upright sitting or standing posture. Second, they must acquire basic locomotor skills in order to move through the environment, and, third, develop the rudimentary abilities of reaching, grasping and releasing in order that meaningful contact with objects can be established (see Gallahue (1982) for a review).

Without these skills to form the building blocks for the more complex skills which develop later in life, the normal pattern of development may be considerably disrupted. If we pause to consider the extent to which skilled movement is essential for every-day living, then the overlap between motor and other aspects of behaviour becomes evident. Consider, for example, the requirements of independent living: going to the toilet, dressing and eating all require considerable degrees of both gross and fine motor control. The way we move influences considerably the success of social interactions. Speech, our primary means of communication, requires the co-ordination of an amazingly complex sequence of movements for it to be clear and understandable. We could go on documenting instances of the importance of skilled movement in many different domains of behaviour, but suffice it to say that skilled movement subserves much of our cognitive and social interaction with the environment. The extent to which there is overlap between apparently different domains of behaviour is evident in the contents of the various tests which are used to assess cognitive and social behaviour. Early tests of infant 'intelligence', for example, are almost entirely motor in content (e.g. Bayley, 1935, 1969; Gesell and Armatruda, 1941), and a considerable level of 'motor' skill is necessary to pass tests purporting to assess 'social' competence. In this section we will find that this fact is both a help and a hindrance.

Turning now to the literature on Down's Syndrome, we are faced with an awkward situation. On the one hand, there is a dearth of studies which deal *directly* with motor development. On the other, there is in fact no lack of data; they are just not easily accessible. The problem is that most studies were done for other reasons. They were concerned with the question of whether early developmental test results predicted later IQ, whether there was a difference between children brought up at home and in an institution, the relationship between number of physical stigmata and IQ, and so on. Thus, a good deal of the evidence students of motor development might seek is concealed in global reports of IQ, DQ (development quotient) or SQ (social quotient). However, as mentioned above, we know from the content of the tests that many of the items require motor skill for their completion, and hence a lower DQ or IQ furnishes presumptive evidence of a motor lag, if not direct evidence. Even when separate motor quotients are given, these too are often a result of compounding quite radically different aspects of motor performance, such as manipulative skills and gross locomotor skills. Although informative to a limited extent, such data do not help us to understand the nature of the deficit and become particularly vexatious when one tries to analyse the underlying processes which might account for them. Fortunately, there are one or two recent studies which acknowledge these problems and provide us with more informative data (Cunningham, 1979; Hogg and Moss, 1983b).

Despite the difficulties of access to data, three points which characterise the motor development of individuals with Down's Syndrome emerge consistently throughout the literature. The first is that at most stages they function less well than their normal peers. Second (a point which is of considerable practical importance) is that there are enormous individual differences within the syndrome. The third and least well understood fact is that Down's Syndrome individuals seem to fall further and further behind their normal peers (in terms of both motor and intellectual development) as they get older.

There is little dispute about the fact that *on average* Down's Syndrome infants are less competent on tests of motor performance than their normal peers. Evidence of this is present in many studies which discuss progress in terms of overall developmental quotients (Share *et al.*, 1961, 1964; Dameron, 1963; Cornwell and Birch, 1969) or, slightly more specifically, in terms of a separate motor quotient (Fishler *et al*, 1964; Carr, 1970, 1975; Dicks-Mireaux, 1972). Examination of the average age at which certain skills develop reveals a slight tendency towards earlier attainment as studies become more recent (i.e. Down's infants nowadays are more competent), but there is no evidence so far that they can be made to catch up with their normal peers. Taking Cunningham's work as representative of recent work in this area, Table 11.1 shows current estimates of what can be expected of the Down's Syndrome child in various areas of motor performance (Cunningham, 1982). As Cunningham points out, the recent tendency towards earlier attainment may have a variety of causes. Health care and dietary

Table 11.1 *Developmental milestones for children with Down's Syndrome. Adapted from Cunningham (1982). Reproduced with permission.*

	Children with Down's Syndrome		'Normal' children	
	Average age (months)	Range (months)	Average age (months)	Range (months)
Gross motor activities				
Holds head steady and balanced	5	3–9	3	1–4
Rolls over	8	4–12	5	2–10
Sits without support for 1 min or more	9	6–16	7	5–9
Pulls to stand using furniture	15	8–26	8	7–12
Walks with support	16	6–30	10	7–12
Stands alone	18	12–38	11	9–16
Walks alone	19	13–48	12	9–17
Walks up stairs with help	30	20–48	17	12–24
Walks down stairs with help	36	24–60+	17	13–24
Runs	Around 4 years		–	
Jumps on the spot	4–5 years		–	
Fine motor activities				
Follows objects with eyes, in circle	3	1.5–6	1.5	1–3
Grasps dangling ring	6	4–11	4	2–6
Passes objects from hand to hand	8	6–12	5.5	4–8
Pulls string to attain toy	11.5	7–17	7	5–10
Finds objects hidden under cloth	13	9–21	8	6–12
Puts 3 or more objects into cup or box	19	12–34	12	9–18
Builds a tower of two-inch cubes	20	14–32	14	10–19
Completes a simple three-shape jigsaw	33	20–48	22	16–30+
Copies a circle	48	36–60+	30	24–40
Matches shapes/colours	4–5 years			
Plays games with simple rules	4–5 years			
Personal/social/self-help activities				
Smiles when touched and talked to	2	1.5–4	1	1–2
Smiles spontaneously	3	2–6	2	1.5–5
Recognises mother/father	3.5	3–6	2	1–5
Takes solids well	8	5–18	7	4–12
Feeds self with biscuit	10	6–14	5	4–10
Plays pat-a-cake, peep-bo games	11	9–16	8	5–13
Drinks from cup	20	12–30	12	9–17
Uses spoon or fork	20	12–36	13	8–20
Undresses	38	24–60+	30	20–40
Feeds self fully	30	20–48	24	18–36
Urine control during day	36	18–50+	24	14–36
Bowel control	36	20–60+	24	16–48
Dresses self partially (not buttons/laces)	4–5 years			
Uses toilet or potty without help	4–5 years			

(often too small to get up on to a toilet, unless a special step is available)

control have improved and early intervention programmes have become more common. Also, changes in social policy and attitude to the handicapped, in general, have led to increased expectations of such children.

Although authors of earlier studies made some perspicacious remarks about the problems associated with using global measures of performance (Dameron, 1963; Carr, 1970), it is only recently that detailed analyses of performance on individual test items have come to be presented, enabling the specific observation of the strengths and weakness of the Down's Syndrome infant (Cunningham, 1979; Carr, 1970; Hogg and Moss, 1983b). For example, by performing the kinds of analyses he did, Cunningham (1979) was able to show that the order of difficulty of the component test items was not the same for the Down's infant as for a normal child; that particular items presented much more difficulty than would be expected given levels of performance on other skills; that Down's infants often spent longer at one stage before progressing to the next in certain areas. It is only this kind of analysis that will enable us to understand fully the exact nature of the motor difficulties experienced by the Down's child and perhaps in future to design more specific intervention programmes.

As far as the older child is concerned, the picture is rather similar to that reviewed for the Down's infant. There is a considerable amount of indirect evidence that, like all mentally retarded individuals, Down's persons lag behind their normal peers (Rarick, 1973; Bruininks, 1974; and Reid, Chapter 12 in this volume). What is important to note is that most Down's children eventually learn many of the basic skills a normal child learns, even if their performance lacks grace and facility. They walk, run, climb and ride bicycles; most learn to dress, go to the toilet and eat tidily. However, more demanding motor skills are often very difficult for them to learn. There are many reasons for this, but one contributing factor may well be that the level of competence they have reached on the component skills is such that it does not permit further refinement or flexibility. For example, although the Down's child walks, he often does so on a broad base, signalling, perhaps, a less well developed sense of balance. Another problem is that more complex tasks often demand fast perceptual and cognitive judgements. Thus, even if the motor system is in principle capable of producing an appropriate response, the co-ordination of planning and execution upon which fluency depends may be lacking. We will return to these issues later.

What of the variability within the syndrome? Intuitively, one might expect Down's individuals to form a more homogeneous group than normals in ability. However, this is not so. In fact, the opposite seems to be true. For example, whereas a normal child walks between 9 and 17 months, for Down's children the range is 13–48 months, or more (see Table 11.1). While some have speculated about the origin of this variability, few studies have attacked the question directly. As Gibson (1978) points out, the origins of developmental differences are likely to include the variable effects of karyotype, secondary organic processes, physical nurture, health status, stimulation level, sex, and the morphological factors peculiar to the syndrome. An important implication of this variability is, of course, that summary landmarks cannot be used indiscriminately to counsel parents or plan educational management regimes.

The third and final point to be considered in our description of motor skill development in Down's children is the question of why they seem to fall further and further behind their peers as they grow older. As this issue has been considered in other chapters, it will be dealt with only very briefly here. What has been suggested is that the Down's child does not progress with age in the same way as a normal child. If one simply looks at the IQ scores given in various studies, the average Down's baby seems to score around 70 in the first few months of life, then the scores drop quickly thereafter (Share *et al*, 1964; Carr, 1970; Cunningham, 1979). This does not mean, of course, that the child with Down's Syndrome makes no progress. It is now clear that, at least in part, the apparent decline is artefactual and results from faults in both the tests and the method used to calculate IQ. For example, the Down's infant may gain higher scores in the first few months of life because the test items used are very crudely scored and are insensitive to the kinds of deficits that we have discussed above. Even when these artefactual problems are accounted for, however, it does seem that the progress of the Down's child is not just one of 'slowed down normality'. It would seem that there are times when the infant manifests no apparent progress and others when development is rapid and many new skills emerge (Cunningham, 1979).

In describing these 'phases' it is, of course, almost impossible to separate motor development from other components. Sometimes, the development of new skills awaits the development of a specific motor skill, such as the ability to sit or stand. At other times, new skills result from the crossing of some other hurdle concerned with language or social development. Although various explanations have been proposed to account for this pattern of development, no satisfactory account as yet exists (see Cunningham and Mittler (1981) for a discussion).

EARLY INTERVENTION: IS IT EFFECTIVE?

Although (as Carr points out, p.174 above), it is now widely accepted that institutions are not appropriate places in which to bring up children, retarded or normal, studies which compare the development of children reared in different environments remain informative in that they draw attention to the importance of environmental influences on development. They, therefore, contribute to the current debate about how much change can be affected by systematic intervention. Carr has reviewed the studies which demonstrate that the Down's child, like any other, develops more slowly when brought up in an institution (Centerwall and Centerwall, 1960; Shotwell and Shipe, 1964; Shipe and Shotwell, 1965; Carr, 1970, 1975). Not surprisingly, the effects on motor development tend to parallel those on intellectual and social development. Children brought up in institutions start to walk later, have poorer manipulative skills, and develop self-help skills which require motor competence later than they otherwise would. The fact that this need not necessarily be so, however, is hinted at by Stedman and Eichorn (1964). The institutionalised children in their group were brought up in what the authors described as an enriched environment, where, for example, the opportunity for play with large toys was provided and social interaction with peers and caretakers was encouraged. There were still differences between these and the home-reared controls, but they were much smaller than in other studies. Stedman and Eichorn's discussion of their study is exemplary in that they try to deal with specific aspects of institutional care rather than with 'presence in an institution' as a single variable.

This approach is taken much further by Francis (1971). Not only does she examine specific aspects of the care given to home-reared and institutionalised children, but she also provides more detailed information on certain aspects of motor behaviour than has previously been available. Four groups of children were involved, Down's children brought up at home and in an institution, and normal children similarly reared. All of the observed behaviours involved movement, ranging from diffuse undirected movements of the limbs to more sophisticated skilled movements involving object manipulation and locomotion. The results can be summarised in two parts. First, there were differences between the Down's Syndrome and normal children regardless of whether they were institutionalised or not. At all developmental levels, the normal children were more alert and active than those with Down's Syndrome. This showed up in the early stages as more frequent movement of the limbs, later in more active exploration of objects, and finally in more locomotion. The second important conclusion Francis reached was that the Down's child was *more* affected by institutional rearing than the normal child. For both normal and Down's children, the institutions provided fewer toys, more physical restraint, and less social contact, but these seemed to affect the Down's children more than their normal peers.

Out of the studies which showed that the Down's child was negatively affected by an unstimulating environment grew the idea that enrichment might ameliorate the retardation to some extent. Again, some of these studies have been reviewed by Carr in Chapter 10 (Bidder *et al.*, 1975; Connolly and Russell, 1976; Aronson and Fällström, 1977; Piper and Pless, 1980; Cunningham *et al.*, 1982). On the whole, these studies are positive, concluding, in particular, that early intervention reduces the decline in development observed in Down's infants (de Coriat *et al.*, 1967; Ludlow and Allen, 1967; Connolly and Russell, 1976; Cunningham *et al.*, 1982). However, as Carr points out, 'there is still a need for some caution. Most of the published studies are methodologically less than satisfactory and long-term follow-up studies, to see whether initial advantages are maintained, are lacking.'

In addition to Carr's note of caution, a number of other issues are raised by the studies which mention motor development specifically. First, there is the question of the age at which intervention is more effective. In a study by Bidder *et al.* (1975), early intervention appeared to have little or no effect on motor development. These authors investigated the effects of the mothers of Down's infants working systematically with their children for a period of 6 months. In contrast to a control group, the intervention group made significantly more progress on the speech and performance scale of the Griffiths Test but not on the locomotor, eye–hand or personal social scales. In their discussion of the failure to obtain improvement in motor performance, Bidder *et al.* considered the possibility that there is a predetermined limitation in this area which is not present in other areas of development at this stage. Were this to be established, it would certainly go some way towards accounting for the differences between their study and that of Aronson and Fällström (1977), who reported differences on all six subscales of the Griffiths Test between a treated and untreated group. As Aronson and Fällström's subjects were slightly older than those of Bidder *et al.*, one might argue that they had matured to a point where intervention became effective whereas Bidder's had not. However, one would need many more data before such a conclusion could be drawn. Furthermore, such a view is not consistent with that presented by Connolly and Russell (1976) or by Cunningham (1983), who presented some evidence suggesting that children who did not begin to participate in an intervention programme until they were 6 months of age exhibited greater delays in most areas than children who began earlier.

Another extremely important issue is the extent to which specific intervention generalises to other situations or settings (for a review of this issue, see Stokes and Baer, 1977). There are at least three studies which address this question, all in slightly different ways (Harris, 1981; Hogg, 1981; Saltzberg and Villani, 1983). All three draw attention to the fact that automatic transfer to apparently related skills, new situations and settings should never be assumed. For example, Harris (1981) showed that specific facilitation of righting reactions and enhancement of normal patterns of movement were effective in improving these aspects of motor functioning but did not transfer to the sorts of motor behaviours tested on the Bayley Scales. Saltzberg and Villani (1983) showed that certain aspects of speech and language behaviour only generalised to new settings if parents were instructed to use the training procedures in more than one setting. In the third study (Hogg, 1981), three children with Down's Syndrome were taught a fine motor task. Although the children learned the task satisfactorily and generalised their skill to other material in the teaching setting, evidence of spontaneous generalisation during free play was very slight. In addition to the practical implications of this type of study, it also raises all kinds of interesting theoretical questions. For example, what is it we learn when we acquire a motor skill? How do we define the point at which a skill is developed well enough to be used flexibly in a variety of different circumstances? What is the relationship between the cognitive, social and motor development?

The question of whether early intervention is effective as far as motor development is concerned does not at present permit a clear answer. Despite the general air of optimism that pervades the literature, much work remains to be done before we can confidently specify effective intervention programmes.

THE PROCESSES UNDERLYING MOTOR CONTROL

Despite the fact that there is an impressive number of experimental studies which have attempted to specify the processes which might be deficient in the control of movement in Down's individuals, it is difficult to impose any order upon this part of the review. Beginning from Bernstein's (1967) definition of a motor skill as a 'solution to a movement problem constrained by spatial, temporal and force requirements', I began by examining the kinds of tasks which have been employed and the extent to which spatial, temporal and force requirements have been manipulated. Whereas both spatial and temporal demands have been varied frequently, the control of force has received little attention. Somewhat arbitrarily, I chose the time dimension as my means of grouping the studies. Broadly speaking, two categories of task can be identified. In the first, no time constraints are placed on the subject, whereas in the second, several kinds of constraints are imposed. The relevant studies will be considered under these two headings.

Motor control without temporal constraints

Consider a task such as reaching for and grasping an object, drawing a triangle or pointing to a target. Actions such as these with predetermined goals require precise perceptual information about the environment and the disposition of the body. How can we shape the investigation of impaired performance in such simple tasks? The approach adopted here is to construct a framework in which the processes that underpin performance are specified in as general and theoretically neutral terms as possible. We can then pose for each process in turn the question of whether a defect in that processing stage can give a satisfactory account of the impairment. Such a framework is set out in Fig. 11.1.

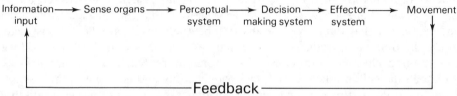

Fig. 11.1 A simple information processing model: cycle of information from reception of sensory information to movement

This model allows us to consider a number of distinct possibilities that are not mutually exclusive. First, the sensory systems involved may be defective. This could mean either that the receptor cells located in the muscles, joints, skin, eyes and ears malfunction, or that the messages received from the receptors are not efficiently transmitted to the brain. Second, the sensory systems may be intact but the strategies adopted for extracting the available information may be inadequate. This might mean, for example, that although a subject could 'see' perfectly well, the way he moved his eyes across a stimulus resulted in poor analysis of what was there to be seen. A third possibility is that failure is due to a deficit in pattern recognition. What is meant by such a deficit might best be illustrated by describing the now famous studies of chess players, which showed that skilled players perceived and remembered much more information about a briefly viewed position on a chess board than unskilled players. Their knowledge of the game allowed them to analyse the visual scene in a way that was not possible for the unskilled individual. Thus, we are referring here to knowledge which accumulates with experience and influences directly the way sensory information is processed.

Continuing the analysis of the possible defects which result in the inability to draw a triangle, it might be that none of the above processes are defective. The deficit might be in the 'output' component of the system. In the same way as a perceptual deficit may result from a purely sensory defect, the motor deficit may have its origin in the muscles, joints etc. Cerebral palsied children, for example, often have no trouble recognising triangles yet may be unable even to draw a line on a piece of paper. Alternatively, the locus of the deficit may be in the mechanism which translates the perceptual information into movement. This process of translation from perceptual input to motor output is frequently labelled 'motor programming' or 'planning'. Put more generally, the problem might be that the

Down's child's spatial representation of the world is not very precisely 'mapped on' to the neuromotor system, and so, although precise movements are *physically* possible, there is no means whereby they can be planned. Another way of putting this is that the motor system of the Down's child never becomes very accurately calibrated with respect to the spatial world. Finally, we must contemplate the possibility that more than one of these hypothetical deficits exists. Furthermore, the extent to which any one contributes to an observed behavioural problem may be dependent on the demands of the task.

The first possibility to be considered is that purely sensory deficits exist which then affect all other aspects of performance. Apart from the presence of squints in many Down's children (Cowie, 1970), at a purely physical level there seems to be no evidence which might lead us to believe that the receptors should not function normally. Nevertheless, when the efficiency of the auditory and visual sensory processes is tested, a proportion of Down's individuals have less than perfect acuity (Clausen, 1968). However, these defects can be corrected in the same way as they are in normal subjects, and there is very little evidence to support the idea that such defects could be responsible for failure on more complex tasks. As far as the tactile and proprioceptive senses are concerned, the available data are difficult to interpret. On close examination, nearly all the studies purporting to examine proprioceptive sensitivity are flawed in one way or another. For example, sometimes the task demands are complex and require operations such as ranking a number of stimuli by weight (Knights *et al.*, 1967). One then wonders whether the difficulty resides in the conceptual aspects of the task rather than in perceptual discrimination itself. Clausen (1968) was responsible for the only clear test of tactile sensitivity. Measuring two-point threshold, he found that all of his retarded subjects had higher thresholds than their normal counterparts but that the Down's and other retarded individuals did not differ from each other.

Thus, it seems unlikely that purely sensory defects underlie perceptual–motor problems experienced by Down's individuals. Although we cannot exclude the possibility of a proprioceptive deficit with certainty, visual and auditory defects can probably be discounted, and tactile loss, if it does affect performance, probably does so in only a very limited range of tasks and would not account for systematic differences between groups of retarded people.

The possibility that crucial differences reside, not in sensory discrimination, but instead in the activity directed towards the extraction of sensory information from the world has received a great deal of attention (Gordon, 1944; O'Connor and Hermelin, 1961; Belmont, 1971; Komiya 1981, 1982; and Stratford 1979, 1980 and Chapter 9 in this volume). Typically, these studies measure recognition performance by requiring some different judgements about pairs of shapes or objects presented in different ways. Comparisons of conditions in which the shapes have been haptically explored with those in which they have been inspected visually have commonly led to the conclusion that Down's individuals are particularly weak in tactile/proprioceptive perception. This view seems to have become so entrenched that Lewis and Bryant (1982) claim: 'This (the tactual deficit) is probably the most reliable perceptual anomaly ever demonstrated with any kind of mental subnormality'. However, I think this proposition requires some clarification.

First, it is important to start with the words used. As Anwar (1983a) points out, much confusion is caused by lack of consistency in terminology. The terms 'stereognostic', 'haptic', 'tactile', 'tactual', 'proprioceptive' and 'kinaesthetic' are used freely and often interchangeably without regard for the information available in the task being described. The most precise term to describe the information which is usually available in experiments of this type is 'haptic'. Haptic exploration may yield tactile information about texture and pressure, kinaesthetic or proprioceptive information about the location of the joints, muscles, etc, and also a central record of the plan of the movement. This last source of information is often labelled the 'efference copy'. Even though experience may bind these processes into an apparent composite 'feel' of the object, it is important to realise that underlying this is a set of anatomically distinct and functionally separable receptor systems. Condensing these into one, often inappropriate term, is therefore not only inaccurate but also unhelpful when we come to try to understand failure. Although this objection might seem like quibbling over terms, it has been shown quite clearly that the distinctions which can be made regarding the various kinds of sensory information available are also 'psychologically' real in terms of the efficiency with which this information is used (see Schmidt (1982) for a review). For example, in the literature on memory for movements, one of the firmest findings is that proprioceptive information presented passively is much less easy to remember than the same information obtained through active movement (Jones, 1974; Schmidt, 1982).

Yet, if we examine in detail the various studies which have tackled this general question of comparing performance in one modality with that in another, we find that, with the exception of Anwar's studies (1981) of pointing accuracy, none clearly distinguished purely tactile information from proprioceptive, or proprioceptive information derived passively from that which involves active movement yielding an efference copy of the movements made.

A number of other difficulties deserve mention. In all the studies which compare visual with haptic discrimination, the visual stimulus is presented statically whereas the haptic information is derived dynamically. At first sight, this may seem to present no problem as this is how such information is obtained in the real world. Haptic perception involves the sampling of aspects of features of the object and integrating these over time into a mental model of the shapes. However, this process necessarily makes complex and interesting demands on perceptual working memory. While some theorists of visual pattern recognition have assumed that visual recognition is constructed out of successive samples (fixations?) of the visual display, on the face of it vision makes less demand on working memory since the information present in the static display remains simultaneously available. Now, whether one calls a difficulty with this temporally extended process of constructing a spatial model 'haptic' or not is to some extent a matter of taste. Certainly, natural haptic perception seems intrinsically to require these conceptual processes in a way that vision does not. On the other hand, it is possible to conceive of simplified haptic matching tasks which are free of these conceptual demands, and which would, therefore, provide a cleaner test of the modality specific hypothesis.

The notion of consistency is the point we must now take up with regard to the haptic component of the tasks. In handling a shape or object which one cannot see there are a whole range of things one can do to try to work out what it is, dependent to some extent on the size of the object, its complexity, and so on. These range from simply holding a small shape without moving it to having to turn it, feel round it, select a particularly salient feature, etc. None of the authors who use haptic tasks actually describes what the subjects did with the shapes they were trying to recognise (O'Connor and Hermelin, 1961; Komiya, 1981, 1982; Lewis and Bryant, 1982). Yet, Davidson *et al.* (1980) have shown quite clearly that accuracy on shape-matching tasks of this kind was related to the way the shape was handled. They make the further point that both stimulus complexity and mental age affect the style of haptic search adopted by a child, and note informally that their Down's children seemed different from the other mentally handicapped children. The fact that the way the non-visual information is obtained may be crucial is also suggested in a study by Anwar (1983b), who found that her Down's subjects were *better* at drawing a shape after it had been presented proprioceptively than visually. This finding might seem inconsistent with the findings of the authors we have just quoted, who propose that the haptic channel is in some way deficient. However, if we examine what Anwar actually did, we see that she physically guided the child's finger round the shape. Thus, she imposed an order on the extraction of non-visual information which was not present in the visual condition. Therefore, when the child's attention was drawn to that source of information and organised for him, it became manageable.

Before leaving the question of modality specific deficits, it might be useful to consider in detail one study (Lewis and Bryant, 1982) which investigates visual and haptic perception in very young Down's infants. Lewis and Bryant (1982) state as their general concern the relationship between hand and eye and the role the hand plays in learning about objects. As mentioned above, they start from the view that the 'tactual' deficit in Down's adults has been clearly demonstrated, and they set out to investigate whether the same deficit is evident in Down's babies. The design of the experiments was ingenious. There were two conditions, visual–visual matching and haptic–visual matching. In the visual–visual condition, the baby was shown two objects: one was then made to bleep while the other remained silent. The two objects were then placed in front of the child and the experimenter noted which one she reached for. In the haptic–visual condition, a noisy object was placed in the baby's hand without it being visible: then the two objects were placed on the table as before. Reaching for the noisy object was obviously taken as recognition of it. The older normal babies had no difficulty with either task, whereas 7 of the 16 younger ones failed to reach for a shape previously placed in their hands. The younger Down's children did not show any systematic preferences, so little can be said about them. The older group performed quite accurately in the visual–visual matching tasks but failed in both tasks when the first stimulus was presented in the hand. Although there were individual differences within the Down's group, it does seem that, even at this early age, Down's children have some difficulty with non-visual information. As Lewis and Bryant point out, this experiment does not allow us to decide whether the deficit is located exclusively in the haptic channel or whether it involves the establishment of a relationship between visual and non-visual information. Furthermore, as they present no data on the motor competence of their subjects or on how they handled the objects placed in their hands, the question of how the haptic information was dealt with is not answered. One might ask, for example, were the Down's infants seeking haptic information systematically but not receiving it, or was the strategy they adopted to obtain it so unsystematic that what was available was simply not integrated into a usable schema or image?

In a second experiment, Lewis and Bryant complicate the picture even further by showing that there were differences not only in the amount of time Down's and normal children spent touching objects but also in the amount of time they spent looking at them. Although they seemed to realise that objects were touchable, the extent to which they actively exercised their visual and exploratory skills seemed to be limited. In summarising the findings of their two experiments, Lewis and Bryant indirectly reject the hypothesis that a specific deficit limited to the processing of haptic information is present in the Down's child and draw attention to the differences in visual behaviour as well as haptic. It seems to me that one might even appeal to the third of the hypothesised perceptual (or cognitive) deficits outlined above (p.198) – that of a pattern recognition problem. Whereas, in the normal child, knowledge of the visual properties of objects may 'suggest' a strategy for obtaining non-visual information, in the Down's child it may not.

We have attempted to evaluate one line of enquiry which explores the possibility that one of the deficiencies which contributes to poor motor competence in Down's Syndrome individuals is poor extraction of sensory information, particularly non-visual. So far, I do not think that we have any evidence of a deficiency in any one channel. What I think these experiments demonstrate is that under certain conditions Down's subjects have difficulty deciphering sensory information which is available to them. As there are so many methodological difficulties with the studies we have reviewed, as well as theoretical problems, it is not yet possible to conclude that this is modality specific. But we must pay more attention in future to the strategies adopted by the subjects in performing tasks of the kind discussed here.

Before moving to studies which consider the interaction between perceptual input and motor output at various levels, it might be helpful to move to the last box in our hypothetical model and examine one of the first studies to tell us something about the efficiency with which the mature Down's individual can exert control over his musculature (Davis and Kelso, 1982). As mentioned above (p.189), we know that at least some Down's individuals always exhibit a measurable amount of hypotonia. We also noted that the implications of this fact for performance were not at all clear. Davis and Kelso's (1982) study seems to represent a fruitful approach to this question. It is also the first study, to my knowledge, which examines in detail the control of force or effort in Down's individuals. For two reasons I will not attempt to summarise the theoretical underpinning of this study. First, the mass spring theory of motor control is complex and impossible to deal with in a few sentences (see Kelso *et al.* (1980) for a review). Second, it is not strictly necessary to understand the theory in order to discuss the results. Davis and Kelso presented two experiments involving Down's subjects and a control group of normal young adults. In the first experiment, the subject's task was to hold his finger in position against a resistance. He was instructed *not* to interfere with the movement of his finger if the resistance (or load on the finger) changed. The results showed that the quantitative changes in the angle of the joints were identical for the two groups. However, there were two interesting qualitative differences between the Down's and normal subjects. First, the Down's subjects took longer to reach the new angle expected as a result of the change in load, and second, the Down's subjects were less able to maintain steadiness after reaching the new position. In the second experiment, the task was identical except that the subjects were told to tense their muscles and try to maintain their original position when the resistance changed. Although the Down's subjects were to some extent able to increase the stiffness of their muscles in response to the changes in resistance, they did so less precisely. Overall, Davis and Kelso drew two conclusions: (i) that the gross movement *organisation* in Down's and normal individuals was similar, and (ii) that the groups differed in their ability to respond accurately to changes in resistance and to hold a position once attained.

There are two comments we might make about these results. The first concerns the organisation of the movements made by the Down's subjects. In this case, and in other studies we will come to (e.g. Hogg and Moss, 1983b), the patterns of movement adopted were similar, yet at other times we noted patterns of movement that were different (e.g. Lydic and Steele, 1979). This conflict raises an important question which we will return to later, but what we must be clear about is the level at which we are describing patterns of movement. For example, the pattern of movement around a single joint might be the same, whereas a sequence of movement, such as that involved in throwing, might be different. The second point concerns the implications of the delay in timing and the oscillation about the target point. It seems unlikely that these differences have no influence on more complex tasks. The question then becomes what kind of tasks might be affected? Are movements requiring frequent changes in direction or fast precise movements more likely than slow movements?

Having examined the studies which take as their focus the role of either perceptual or motor deficits in an overall perceptuo–motor deficiency, we now turn to those which attempt to examine the integration of the two. Two very different levels of analysis are represented. First, I will examine studies of postural control (Butterworth and Cicchetti, 1978; Shumway-Cook and Woollacott, 1984), where the integration of perceptual input and motor output takes place at what might best be described as an automatic level. In other words, motor responses are made which are not easily controlled voluntarily by the subject, if they can be at all. At a completely different level, we will then examine the voluntary efforts of Down's children to perform motor tasks which require matching movement sequences to quite precise spatial demands.

We will begin with two experiments concerned with how postural control develops. In the first (Butterworth and Cicchetti 1978), the infant's task was an apparently simple one – to sit or stand upright. In order to maintain balance in upright positions such as sitting or standing, two things must be possible. First, the muscles have to be able to respond in the correct sequence, producing the appropriate spatial and temporal pattern of contraction, and, second, the movements must be made in response to accurately perceived visual, vestibular and somatosensory stimulation. The question Butterworth and Cicchetti asked was 'What is the role of vision in the development of upright posture?' In 1975, Lee and Lishman demonstrated that normal infants use visual information to monitor their posture when they learn to stand. This was done by manipulating the available visual cues in such a way that the pattern of visual stimulation was identical to that which occurs when one is falling over. This was achieved by having the infant sit or stand on a stable floor inside a 'moveable' room. The room could be moved backwards and forwards in the plane parallel to the infant's line of vision. In this situation, even though the internal receptors specify stability, infants who have just learned to stand or sit are apparently completely unable to ignore misleading visual information. Consequently, they try to accommodate for the apparent loss of balance, with the result that they fall over. Lee and Aronson (1974) argue that, in this situation, vision operates as a proprioceptive sense in that it *directly* specifies information about balance (see Gibson (1966) for a review of these thorny conceptual issues). As infants gain experience of sitting or standing they become less influenced by the discrepant visual information. They then seem to 'know' that the visual information is misleading and may well laugh at the trick.

Following the experiments of Lee and his colleagues, Butterworth and his collaborators (Butterworth and Hicks, 1977; Butterworth and Cicchetti, 1978) explored the possibility that different amounts and different kinds of motor experience might affect the development of this aspect of perceptuo–motor control. They undertook a comparison of Down's and normal infants of approximately 3 years of age. The infants were matched on the amount of time which had elapsed since they learned to sit or stand, and so were of very different chronological ages. The reactions of the two groups were quite different. The Down's infants who had recently learned to sit were much less responsive to the movement of the room than the normal controls, whereas those who had just learned to stand unsupported were much more so. Since it was not the case that the seated babies failed to perceive the movement of the room, it seems that they differed in the way they responded to it in the two positions. Butterworth and Cicchetti discuss a number of alternative explanations of their findings before concluding that 'whatever the origin of the proprioceptive function of vision, the theory which seems best able to account for the results is that postural control depends on congruence between mechanical–vestibular and visual indices of postural stability.' They further argue that the stability of the posture is related to the amount of discrepancy tolerated by the system. In a relatively unstable posture, for example, a very small discrepancy between visual and mechanical proprioception will produce compensatory movements. Hence, standing is on average more influenced by the surroundings than sitting. This, in turn, suggests that the function of visual proprioception may be to calibrate the internal system against the stable surround. As the child gains control over his internal system he becomes more and more independent of visual cues so that eventually he can override the effects of the discrepant visual input.

As far as the implications of these findings for later motor skill development are concerned, Butterworth and Cicchetti make two suggestions which seem intuitively very appealing. First, they suggest that the sequence of postures preceding standing forms part of a hierarchy of motor systems, such that later postures grow out of and are dependent upon the development of earlier ones. Thus, failure to calibrate earlier postures might be expected to add an increment to the acquisition of later postures. With respect to the Down's infants, they suggest that the mechanical –vestibular component of the postural control system is 'damped down' and, therefore, requires a higher level of stimulation before a discrepancy can be detected between internal and external sources of perceptual information. They also suggest that in the Down's infant the sitting position was not adequately calibrated, which then resulted in the excessive responses which were evident in the standing position.

Second, they propose that failure to gain complete control of sitting may impede the development of fine motor skills, such as reaching and tool using, in which the trunk is taken as a stable frame of reference allowing attention to be confined to the hand. They then speculate that since fine motor skills of this kind are often taken as precursors of cognitive activity, failure to acquire autonomous control over the postural subsystem may suggest an ontogenetic link between early motor and subsequent intellectual retardation.

This line of enquiry has recently been extended much further in the work of Shumway-Cook and Woollacott (1984) who also studied the organisation of the postural control system. They showed that, in comparison to normal children, Down's children showed deficits which were still present at the age of 6. Their postural responses were not only slower but also more poorly organised than normal. As a result, they were much less capable of compensating for perceptual discrepancies which the experiments produced. They swayed more, and more often fell over than their normal counterparts. Though not as general as Butterworth and Cicchetti in their conclusions, Shumway-Cook and Woollacott also believe that these deficits may underly the functional perceptuo–motor problems that we observe in the day-to-day activity of the Down's individual.

The last possibility we will explore in this section is that poor perceptuo–motor performance in Down's persons results from a failure to develop and produce motor programmes. The concept of a motor programme (or plan) has been formulated in a variety of different ways, but at this point I will focus on the interpretation of Hogg and Moss (1983b). What Hogg and Moss describe as motor programming is the integration of a set of previously independent but well learned individual movements into a sequence. Once consolidated, the sequence of movements can then be adapted easily to meet the environmental constraints of the task. Before describing the experiment, it might be useful to consider one or two issues which this interpretation raises. First, it is important to note that they are concerned with voluntary behaviour, or conscious attempts to deal with the environment, not the automatic sequences of movement described by Shumway-Cook and Woollacott (1984) in their study of postural control. Second, there is the question of how the unit of movement in a sequence (or sub-routine) might be defined and how it develops. We have touched upon this question earlier in our discussion of reflexes and their role in later development. For example, does the grasp reflex form the foundation of the mature grip we see at a later stage? Finally, there is the question of how we define integration. We often describe skilled movement as fluent, smooth or rhythmical, but these things are difficult to measure. So far our best measure of this characteristic is to look at various aspects of the temporal organisation of the movement.

Although Hogg and Moss have performed a series of studies on the development of manipulative skills in Down's and other handicapped children (Hogg and Moss, 1983a,b), I will describe here only one study. I have chosen this one as an example of how research in this field should be conducted in the future. The main point to note about its methodology is that they were so careful in their consideration of intervening variables that they could be more confident than usual about their interpretation of the main findings. As many others have done, Hogg and Moss obtained two groups of subjects matched on mental age, one Down's, one normal. However, what these authors did which others have omitted to do was to perform a detailed analysis of the profiles of scores obtained by the two groups on the matching test (Bayley Scale). An interesting finding was revealed. Although the groups were matched on overall scores, they arrived at the same totals in a completely different way. The Down's subjects failed more of the motor items and fewer of the language items, which meant that there was already a difference between the two groups of infants before the experimental study of their performance began. Another factor which Hogg and Moss considered necessary to take account of was the size of the child's hand. Although anatomical differences between Down's and normal children are well documented, few studies ever mention their possible effects on motor performance. This particular experiment involved handling wooden rods, and no differences were in fact apparent, but, as Davidson *et al.* (1980) mentioned in passing, the small hands and short fingers of the Down's subjects seemed to affect performance in a task involving haptic search.

Turning now to the primary question of planning and executing a sequence of movements, the children's task was a simple one – to place different sized wooden rods in appropriately sized holes. As only one rod and one hole were presented simultaneously, the task did not involve working out which rod fitted into which hole. All that was required was that a sequence of movements be planned to meet the spatial constraints of a task which increased progressively in difficulty as the rods and holes became smaller. Although the infant was not aware of a time factor, two aspects of the time taken to complete the task were measured: (1) the time from when the child actually grasped the rod to when it was brought into contact with the plate in which the hole was located, and (2) the time between touching the plate and successfully inserting the rod. In addition, a description of the grip used to hold each rod was recorded.

The results of the study were extremely interesting. With respect to prehension, the two groups of children did not differ either in their use of digital grips or in the use of bimanual co-ordination. Following Connolly's (1973) suggestion that grips represent the sub-routines within manipulative strategies, Hogg and Moss conclude that Down's children had, at least at this stage, developed the necessary sub-routine to the same degree as normal children of the same mental age. Thus, the general organisation of their movement seemed normal.

When the timing measures were considered, however, the picture was quite different. The Down's infants were slower both at picking up the rods and at inserting them in the holes. Thus, despite having the necessary movements available, they found it more difficult both to select a response which met the spatial constraints placed upon them and to make the appropriate movement once it had been selected.

Taking the movement pattern and timing results together, Hogg and Moss concluded that the manipulative difficulties experienced by Down's children are due, not to a failure to develop 'specific behaviours of a given topography (grips) but in organising them as efficiently as their non-handicapped peers'. Specified in this way, they feel that their view is quite compatible with other authors' notions of a motor programming or planning deficit (e.g. Frith and Frith, 1974).

The picture that emerges from what we have learned so far is not a neat and tidy one. We can begin by rejecting the notion that a specific deficit located in any one of the hypothetical 'boxes', as proposed, can account for the problems we have described. Rather, there seem to be a number of deficiencies which probably affect different aspects of performance at different times. For example, as far as the uptake of perceptual information is concerned, the Down's person does seem to have difficulty, but the most parsimonious interpretation of existing findings is that this is not modality specific but depends on the mode of presentation, the kind of response to be made, etc. Slowness is one of the most pervasive characteristics of the syndrome and occurs at a number of different levels. This must surely influence performance in a number of tasks, especially those which we will discuss in the next section. Another characteristic which seems to emerge is that the movement of Down's persons lacks precision. Although the patterns of movement are generally organised in the same way as in normal individuals, it would seem that it is more difficult or takes longer to refine movement to meet precise spatial demands. Whether this is the result of an intrinsic restriction in the 'motor' part of the system or is the outcome of inadequate perceptual and cognitive decision processes is as yet unclear. It is probable that a number of deficits contribute to the overall functional problem.

Motor control with temporal constraints

The experiments discussed in this section differ from those considered so far in that the tasks involved are not self-paced. Instead, the subject is asked to respond to a stimulus as quickly as possible (reaction time), to make as many movements as possible in a given time (tapping), or to follow a target which is moving at a predetermined speed (tracking). Each of these tasks will be considered in order.

Reaction time tasks

Perhaps the most consistent finding in the literature on mental retardation is that mentally handicapped individuals perform more slowly than their normal peers. (For detailed reviews of the issues involved, see Baumeister and Kellas, 1968, and Brewer and Smith, 1981.) Furthermore, although there are some contradictory findings, the bulk of the evidence seems to suggest that Down's individuals perform even more slowly than other retarded subjects of the same mental age. As the focus of this book is on the performance of Down's individuals specifically, this chapter will concentrate on this latter difference rather than on the more general question of why retardation tends to imply slowness.

Before proceeding to analyse the available data on this topic, it might be useful to state briefly the rationale which lies behind the use of reaction time tasks and to describe more recent approaches to the measurement of ever more detailed components of the total response (see Schmidt, 1982). Response time measures are common in research on skills for several reasons, but by far the most important is that they are seen as measures of the time taken to complete mental activities, such as stimulus processing, decision making and planning a motor response. By manipulating the complexity of the stimulus (e.g. four lights instead of one), or the difficulty of the response (a 1-inch button instead of a 3-inch plate), changes in the speed of response can be measured and inferences made about the relative contribution of the processes involved. As far as individuals who are believed to be deficient in some way are concerned, the question then becomes, can the stage at which the deficiency occurs be located? Since the first studies on reaction time were published in the mid-nineteenth century, the inferences derived from response time measures have become more and more sophisticated. For example, early studies did not differentiate between the time to initiate a movement (the decision time) and the time taken to execute the movement (movement time). More recent studies not only differentiate between decision time and movement time but also divide the decision time component itself into a number of sub-components. One way of doing this involves the electrical activity which takes place in the musculature of the limb to be moved (EMG). During a substantial part of the decision time, the EMG is silent, indicating that a command to move the finger, say, has not yet reached the musculature. Later in the interval, the muscle is activated but no movement occurs for several milliseconds, then the movement begins. The interval from the signal to the first change in EMG is termed 'pre-motor RT' and is thought to be taken up by central processing, and the interval between the first change in EMG and the actual movement of the finger is termed 'motor RT' and represents processes associated with the musculature itself. 'Movement time' is the remaining component of the overall reaction time, i.e. the time between the physical response actually beginning and ending. A diagrammatic representation of these various stages is shown in Fig. 11.2.

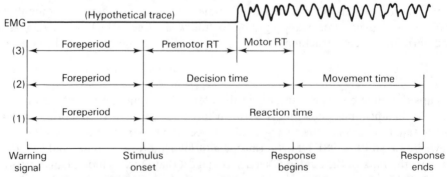

Fig. 11.2 Functionally significant measures which can be extracted from reaction time tasks

Berkson (1960a,b,c) was one of the first authors to report systematic differences in reaction time between Down's and other mentally retarded subjects. Using a series of tasks of increasing difficulty, he found that the Down's subjects were not only slower generally but also fell more and more behind as the task became more complex. The basic finding of an RT disadvantage for the Down's group has been replicated in some studies (Hermelin, 1964; Hermelin and Venables, 1964; Belmont, 1971). Others (Astrup *et al.*, 1967; Knights *et al.*, 1965) have found non-significant tendencies in the same direction. Especially in the early studies, the kinds of explanations we find for the slowness of response in Down's parallel closely those we have encountered in the first part of this section. Sensory deficits (e.g. Hermelin and Venables, 1964), motor execution deficits (Berkson, 1960a,b,c; O'Connor and Berkson, 1963), and some combination of these (Belmont, 1971) have all been implicated. As Davis *et al.* (1984) point out, however, many of these studies involved very small samples of subjects, and the conclusions reached were based on shaky ground.

There are two recent studies which attempt a more detailed analysis of reaction time in Down's subjects (Saqi, 1981; Davis *et al.*, 1985). In the first, Saqi (1981) separates decision time from movement time and, in the second (Davis *et al.*, 1984), all of the component processes outlined in Fig. 11.2 were measured. Saqi reported two experiments on Down's and matched retarded controls. The first involved a simple reaction time task to a visual stimulus, the second a choice reaction time task also involving visual stimuli. No differences at all were found on the movement time component of the response, indicating that once the Down's subjects had actually begun to move they were just as fast as the controls. However, there was a difference in the decision time component of the response.

The most detailed study of reaction time in Down's subjects is that of Davis *et al.* (1984). These authors compared the performance of Down's, other retarded and normal subjects. Normal subjects were faster on all four measures outlined in Fig. 11.2. The differences between the Down's and the other retarded subjects were extremely interesting. The data on movement time were consistent with those of Saqi (1981) in that *no* differences emerged on movement time, confirming once again that, once a movement has begun, it can be executed at a similar speed by both groups, albeit much more slowly than by their normal peers. As far as the decision time component was concerned, the results supported the view that Down's subjects are slower than other retarded individuals. When Davis *et al.* examined the pre-motor and motor components of the reaction time separately, they found in both that the differences between the two retarded groups were significant. If, as they suggest, the pre-motor and motor components of RT are independent of each other and can be influenced by different factors, then experiments must be planned to replicate and extend these findings. By so doing, we will begin to accumulate information which specifies more exactly the origin of the slowness in Down's subjects.

Tapping tasks

Here, as in most other performance tests, the differences between mentally retarded subjects taken as a group and their normal peers are clear, but that between Down's and other retarded subjects is less so. Three studies present reasonably comprehensive data on speed of tapping in Down's subjects. Two claim to find no difference between Down's and other subnormal groups (Clausen, 1968; Seyfort and Spreen, 1979), whereas the third (Frith and Frith, 1974) reports a highly significant one, with Down's subjects being worse. Methodological differences are a constant source of frustration when trying to compare the results of such studies. For example, it is questionable whether one can compare studies which require the subject to alternate between two targets (Clausen, 1968; Seyfort and Spreen, 1979) with those which involve only one (Frith and Frith, 1974). Taking the two-plate tapping studies together, we find an unreconcilable difference. When Down's subjects were compared with a matched group of other retarded subjects in Clausen's study (Clausen, 1968), tapping speed was almost identical for the two groups. Seyfort and Spreen (1979), on the other hand, reported no differences in overall speed but this was only at the expense of not meeting the task requirements. As the Down's subjects made many more repetitions on the same plate (errors), it seems reasonable to assume that if they had been compelled to alternate they would have been slower. This outcome would then be consistent with the findings of Frith and Frith (1974), who showed not only that their Down's subjects made fewer taps per unit time, but also that their speed was positively correlated with variability. In other words, the faster a subject tapped, the more irregular he was likely to be.

As Frith and Frith (1974) discuss the slowness on this task alongside failure to improve on a pursuit rotor task, they consider the deficit to be of central origin and postulate a deficit in the ability to plan a sequence of movements in advance. However, one observation that is frequently made when watching Down's subjects try to move fast is that they tend to substitute an increase in pressure for an increase in speed. It is difficult to see how this observation can be aligned with the notion of an inability to plan sequences ahead. It may be necessary, therefore, to consider the possibility of a peripheral deficit co-occurring with a central planning deficit. For example, if the motor system is slow to respond to changes in load and oscillates more on arrival in a new position, as Davis and Kelso suggested, then it may be intrinsically difficult for the Down's subject to make rapid changes in direction of movement.

Tracking tasks

Tracking tasks differ from the others we have examined in a number of ways. First, they involve continuous movement as opposed to discrete movements which have a clear beginning and end. Second, the temporal constraints they place on the subject are different from those involved in the other tasks. The subject is neither free to move at his own pace nor is he instructed to perform as quickly as possible (i.e. it is timing rather than absolute speed that matters). Such tasks allow us to examine aspects of motor control which cannot be explored in any of the other activities we have considered. As with reaction time, there is an enormous literature on tracking performance in normal individuals, but here we will consider only those experiments in which Down's subjects have been compared with their normal and retarded peers and explore what they have contributed to our knowledge of Down's Syndrome. The focus will be on two experiments closely linked to each other in rationale (Frith and Frith, 1974; and Henderson *et al.*, 1981).

In the first experiment (Frith and Frith, 1974), the subject was required to follow a target with his finger for two 3-minute sessions with a rest between sessions. The target moved on a predictable course and at constant speed. When normal adults perform this task they improve relatively little during the first session, then, after a brief rest period, find the task much easier and perform much better. Frith (1973) has shown that in the second session, when the subjects have learned the task, they do not simply follow the target but *anticipate* its movements. In Frith and Frith's study (1974), normal 6 year olds improved significantly in the second session. In contrast, most of the Down's group failed to improve at all. This finding has recently been replicated by Hogg and Moss (1983a). When Frith and Frith considered these results and those of the same children performing a tapping task (reported above), they concluded that Down's individuals are deficient in evolving motor programmes necessary for fast predictive movement.

This notion was then explored further by Henderson *et al.* (1981). Henderson *et al.* employed a tracking task in which the subject had to try to follow a regular wave-like (sinusoidal) track for 5 minutes. Although the subjects were matched on their ability to follow a stationary track, the Down's subjects had much greater difficulty with the moving target than the other retarded subjects. Now, with the stationary target there was no need to plan ahead because the track was always present, there were no time constraints, and the subject could use a strategy of continuously monitoring progress while moving. A similar strategy used with a moving target, however, is ineffective in that one is always lagging behind the target rather than keeping up with it. To perform adequately, it is essential to learn something about the movement of the target and plan a matching sequence of responses in advance. In our experiment, there was evidence that the subjects had learned something about the shape of the track since they could draw it on a stationary piece of paper after they had performed the task for the requisite 5 minutes. However, what they could not do was represent it on a moving piece of blank paper as the tracking situation required. The computation involved in combining the spatial and temporal dimensions of the task was clearly too difficult for them. Whether they would have improved significantly on any of these tasks with more practice, of course, remains unclear, but what we can conclude from these studies is that Down's subjects find it more difficult than other retarded individuals to perform a continuous sequence of movement when constraints on timing are imposed externally.

Taken together, the results of the studies which have attempted to alter the pace at which the Down's person naturally moves, suggest that this creates considerable problems for them. Not only do they have difficulty producing fast movements in absolute terms, but also they seem to find it difficult to match the tempo of their own movements to an externally imposed tempo. Although the idea of a deficit in motor programming or planning in advance is an appealing one, it does not seem to account adequately for the general picture of slowness which seems to pervade every level of motor control. What is possibly required is an explanation which takes account of the delays inherent at the neuromotor level as well as those imposed by the deficiencies in the cognitive processes involved in complex motor skill performance.

CONCLUSION

'The study of Down's Syndrome has been a fractionated business, each discipline pressing exclusive views about mechanisms and management.' This is how Gibson (1978) begins his book on Down's Syndrome in general, but it might equally well be a description of the literature concerned with motor skill development. In this chapter, we have considered motor performance under three separate headings, each representing a different level of analysis. Although it proved convenient to do so in terms of examining studies which were similar both in methodology and in level of interpretation, we are now faced with the question of whether we can successfully put Humpty Dumpty together again.

Before considering the question of whether such an enterprise is either possible or sensible, I will attempt to extract one or two clear conclusions. As Hogg (1982) points out, it is now well established that delays in motor development and competence accompany the cognitive and language deficit observable in mentally handicapped people. This point is not under debate, and intervention to facilitate motor skill learning in the retarded child or adult is commonplace. What is less clear, however, is whether Down's individuals differ from other mentally retarded individuals of similar mental age. In this review, we have considered many studies which compare Down's persons with their normal counterparts, and most, if not all of those, which compare them with other mentally retarded persons. Despite the fact that this literature seems to contain more than its fair share of poorly designed and inadequately analysed studies, I think there is now enough evidence to support the proposition that Down's individuals are indeed different and may require different kinds of intervention from that most suitable for subjects who are otherwise retarded. In this review I have tried to indicate the most informative studies and those which signal the way research might best develop in the future by devoting most attention to them. However, there is one line of enquiry which is not well represented in even the best of the studies mentioned, and that is the question of how motor skills are learned by Down's individuals. With very few exceptions, the focus is on performance as opposed to learning, a state of affairs which requires urgent attention.

As far as the practical implications of the differences between Down's and other retarded individuals are concerned, not very much can be said at present. One possibility is that such differences as do exist are of more concern to physiotherapists, who are more likely to deal with early development, than to physical education teachers, whose role may be to build on what has already been achieved. Another point, of course, is that recent work on intervention places considerable stress on the need to individualise programmes of education or therapy. As many authors have noted, there are large individual differences within the Down's population, and it is possible that in practice these might outweigh the differences between aetiologically defined subgroups. What does seem to be clear from studies of children with motor deficits in general is that early intervention is beneficial, although there is no consensus on what kind of intervention is best.

Finally, we return to the question of whether we can find a coherent explanation of the different kinds of deviations from normal which we have described. In my view, the answer is no, not yet. What we can do positively is reject the notion that a single deficit might underly all the behavioural manifestations of motor delay and incompetence which we observe in Down's individuals. What is required is a theory which takes account of the complex interaction between abnormalities in the neuromotor organisation of movement and the deficits in perceptual and cognitive functioning which cause a variety of different problems in executing motor acts. Although we have made considerable progress in understanding specific components of this system, we are a long way from understanding the exact nature of the interaction, and in particular how this changes with age. To avoid ending on a negative note, it might be useful to point out that this problem is not peculiar to the study of Down's Syndrome. The field of motor development in general does not yet have a well articulated theory awaiting critical test. It is, therefore, little wonder that we cannot fully explain the motor problems of Down's individuals.

ACKNOWLEDGEMENTS

I am grateful to Phillip Bairstow, Uta Frith, Jack Keogh, Neil O'Connor, David Sudgen and in particular to Leslie Henderson for helpful comments on various drafts of this paper. I would also like to thank Anna Brett and Shirley Cotton, who typed the manuscript, and Peter Jobbins for preparing the figures.

Two aspects of motor control are not discussed in this chapter. The first (dealt with by Reid in Chapter 12) concerns the effect of factors such as anthropometric differences, physical defects, heart conditions and respiratory problems on performance. Although relatively little is known about the interaction between such varied factors and motor development, it seems to be the case that their effect is indirect or secondary in the sense that they place restrictions on *maximum* performance but do not influence directly the acquisition of skill (Malina and Rarick, 1973). The second (dealt with by Gunn in Chapter 14) is speech production. All too frequently, the fact that the efficient execution of oral communication requires a very precise degree of *motor* control is forgotten. It is important to remember, therefore, that some of the issues raised in this chapter are relevant to the discussion of speech and the converse.

REFERENCES

Allen, G.I. and Tsukahara, N. (1974). Cerebro-cerebellar communication systems. *Physiol. Rev.* **54**, 957–1006.

Anwar, F. (1981). Visual–motor target localisation in normal and subnormal development. *Br. J. Psychol.* **72**, 43–57.

Anwar, F. (1983a). Vision and kinaesthesis in motor movements. In Hogg, J. and Mittler, P.J. (eds), *Advances in Mental Handicap Research*, Vol. 2. London: John Wiley.

Anwar, F. (1983b). The role of sensory modality for the reproduction of shape by the severely retarded. *Br. J. Dev. Psychol.* **1**, 317–27.

Aronson, M. and Fällström, K. (1977). Immediate and long term effects of developmental training in children with Down's Syndrome. *Dev. Med. Child Neur.* **19**, 489–94.

Astrup, C., Sersen, E.A. and Wortis, J. (1967). Further psychophysiological studies of retarded, neurotic, psychotic and normal children. In Wortis, J. (ed.), *Recent Advances in Biological Psychiatry*, Vol. 9. New York: Plenum Press.

Baumeister, A.A. and Kellas, G. (1968). Reaction time and mental retardation. In Ellis, N.R. (ed.), *International Review of Research in Mental Retardation*. New York: Academic Press.

Bayley, N. (1935). The development of motor abilities during the first three years. *Mono. Soc. Res. Child Dev.* **1**, 1–26.

Bayley, N. (1969). *Manual for the Bayley Scales of Infant Development*. New York: Psychological Corporation.

Belmont, J.M. (1971). Medical behavioral research in retardation. In Ellis, N.R. (ed.), *International Review of Research in Mental Retardation*. New York: Academic Press.

Berkson, G. (1960a). An analysis of reaction time in normal and mentally deficient young men: duration threshold experiment. *J. Ment. Defic. Res.* **4**, 51–8.

Berkson, G. (1960b). An analysis of reaction time in normal and mentally deficient young men: variation of complexity in reaction time tasks. *J. Ment. Defic. Res.* **4**, 59–67.

Berkson, G. (1960c). An analysis of reaction time in normal and mentally deficient young men: variation of stimulus and of response complexity. *J. Ment. Defic. Res.* **4**, 69–77.

Bernstein, N. (1967). *The Co-ordination and Regulation of Movements*. New York: Pergamon.

Bidder, R.T., Bryant, G. and Gray, O.P. (1975). Benefits to Down's Syndrome children through training their mothers. *Arch. Dis. Childh.* **50**, 383–6.

Brewer, N. and Smith, G.A. (1981). Cognitive processes for monitoring and regulating speed and accuracy of responding in mental retardation. A methodology. *Am. J. Ment. Defic.* **87**, 211–22.

Bruininks, R.H. (1974). Physical and motor development of retarded persons. In Ellis, N.R. (ed.), *International Review of Research in Mental Retardation*. New York: Academic Press.

Butterworth, G. and Cicchetti, D. (1978). Visual calibration of posture in normal and motor retarded Down's Syndrome infants. *Perception* **7**, 513–25.

Butterworth, G. and Hicks, L. (1977). Visual proprioception and postural stability in infancy. A developmental study. *Perception* **6**, 255–62.

Carr, J. (1970). Mental and motor development in young mongol children. *J. Ment. Defic. Res.* **14**, 205–220.

Carr, J. (1975). *Young Children with Down's Syndrome*. London: Butterworth.

Centerwall, S.W. and Centerwall, W.R. (1960). A study of children with mongolism reared in the home compared to those reared away from home. *Pediatrics* **25**, 678–85.

Clausen, J. (1968). Behavioral characteristics of Down's Syndrome subjects. *Am. J. Ment. Defic.* **73**, 118–126.

Connolly, B. and Russell, F. (1976). Interdisciplinary early intervention program. *Phys. Ther.* **56**, 155–8.

Connolly, K. (1973). Factors influencing the learning of manual skills in young children. In Hinde, R.A. and Stevenson-Hinde, J. (eds), *Constraints on Learning*. London: Academic Press.

Coriat, L.F. de, Theslenco, L. and Wakman, J. (1967). The effect of psychomotor stimulation on the IQ of young children with trisomy-21. In Richards, B. (ed.), *Proceedings of the First Congress of the International Association for the Scientific Study of Mental Deficiency*, pp. 377–85. Reigate: Michael Jackson.

Cornwell, A.C. and Birch, H.G. (1969). Psychological and social development in home reared children with Down's Syndrome (mongolism). *Am. J. Ment. Defic.* **74**, 341–50.

Cowie, V.A. (1970). *A Study of the Early Development of Mongols*. Oxford: Pergamon.

Cratty, B.J. and Martin, M. (1969). *Perceptual Motor Efficiency in Children*. Philadelphia: Lea and Febiger.

Crome, I., Cowie, V. and Slater, E. (1966). Statistical note on cerebellar and brain stem weight in mongolism. *J. Ment. Defic. Res.* **10**, 1969–72.

Cunningham, C.C. (1979). Aspects of early development in Down's Syndrome infants. PhD Thesis. University of Manchester.

Cunningham, C.C. (1982). *Down's Syndrome: An Introduction for Parents*. London: Souvenir Press.

Cunningham, C.C. (1983). Early support and intervention: The Hester Adrian Research Centre Infant Project. In Mittler, P. and McConacine, H. (eds), *Parents, Professionals and Mentally Handicapped People: Approaches to Partnership*. London: Croom Helm.

Cunningham, C.C., Aumonier, M.E. and Sloper, P. (1982). Health visitor services for families with a Down's Syndrome infant. *Child: Care, Health and Development* **8**, 311–26.

Cunningham, C.C. and Mittler, P. (1981). Maturation, development and mental handicap. In Connolly, K. and Prechtl, H.V. (eds), *Maturation and Development: Biological and Psychological Perspectives*. London: Heinemann Medical.

Dameron, L.E. (1963). Development of intelligence of infants with mongolism. *Child Dev.* **34**, 733–8.

Davidson, P.W., Pine, R., Wileskettenmann, M. and Appelle, S. (1980). Haptic–visual shape matching by mentally retarded children: explanatory activity and complexity effects. *Am. J. Ment. Defic.* **84**, 526–33.

Davis, W.E. and Kelso, J.A.S. (1982). Analysis of 'invariant characteristics' in motor control of Down's Syndrome and normal subjects. *J. Motor Behav.* **14**, 194–212.

Davis, W.E., Ward, T. and Sparrow, W.A. (1985). Fractionated reaction times in Down's Syndrome and other mentally handicapped adults. Submitted for publication.

Dicks-Mireaux, M.J. (1972). Mental development of infants with Down's Syndrome. *Am. J. Ment. Defic.* **77**, 26–32.

Dubowitz, V. (1980). *The Floppy Infant*, 2nd edn. Clinics in Developmental Medicine No. 76. Spastics International Publications. London: Heinemann.

Easton, T.A. (1972). On the normal use of reflexes. *Am. Sci.* **60**, 591–9.

Easton, T.A. (1978). Co-ordinative structures – The basis for a motor program. In Landers, D.M. and Christina, R.W. (eds), *Psychology of Motor Behavior and Sport*. Champaign, Ill: Human Kinetics.

Evarts, E.V. (1973). Brain mechanism in movement. *Sci. Am.* **229**, 96–103.

Fishler, K., Share, J. and Koch, R. (1964). Adaptation of Gesell developmental scales for evaluation of development in children with Down's Sydrome. *Am. J. Ment. Defic.* **68**, 642–6.

Francis, S.H. (1971). The effects of own-home and institution rearing on the behavioural development of normal and mongol children. *J. Child Psychol. Psych.* **12**, 173–90.

Frith, C.D. (1973). Learning rhythmic hand movements. *Quart. J. Exp. Psychol.* **25**, 253–9.

Frith, V. and Frith, C.D. (1974). Specific motor disabilities in Down's Syndrome. *J. Child Psychol. & Psych.* **15**, 293–301.

Gallahue, D.L. (1982). *Understanding Motor Development in Children.* New York: Wiley.

Gesell, A. (1941). *The First Five Years of Life.* London: Methuen.

Gesell, A. and Armatruda, C.S. (1941). *Developmental Diagnosis. Normal and Abnormal Child Development.* New York: Hoeber.

Gibson, D. (1978). *Down's Syndrome: The Psychology of Mongolism.* Cambridge: Cambridge University Press.

Gibson, J.J. (1966). *The Senses Considered as Perceptual Systems.* Boston: Houghton Mifflin.

Gordon, A.M. (1944). Some aspects of sensory discrimination in mongolism. *Am. J. Ment. Defic.* **49**, 55.

Harris, S. (1981). Effects of neurodevelopmental therapy on motor performance of infants with Down's Syndrome. *Dev. Med. & Child Neurol.* **23**, 477–83.

Henderson, S.E., Morris, J. and Frith, U. (1981). The motor deficit in Down's Syndrome children: A problem of timing? *J. Child Psychol. & Psych.* **22**, 233–45.

Hermelin, B. (1964). Effects of variation in the warning signal on reaction time of severe subnormals. *Quart. J. Exp. Psychol.* **16**, 241–9.

Hermelin, B. and Venables, P. (1964). Reaction time and alpha blocking in normal and subnormal subjects. *J. Exp. Psychol.* **67**, 365–72.

Hogg, J. (1981). Learning, using and generalising manipulative skills in a preschool classroom by non-handicapped and Down's Syndrome children. *Educ. Psychol.* **1**, 319–39.

Hogg, J. (1982). Motor development and performance of severely mentally handicapped people. *Dev. Med. Child Neurol.* **24**, 188–92.

Hogg, J. and Moss, S.C. (1983a). *The Development of Skilled Motor Sequences in Down's Syndrome Children.* Final Report to the Joseph Rowntree Memorial Trust.

Hogg, J. and Moss, S.C. (1983b). Prehensile development in Down's Syndrome and non-handicapped preschool children. *Br. J. Dev. Psychol.* **1**, 189–204.

Jebsen, R.H., Johnson, E.W., Knobloch, H. and Grant, D.K. (1961). Differential diagnosis of infantile hypotonia. *Am. J. Dis. Child.* **101**, 8–17.

Jones, B. (1974). Role of central monitoring of efference in short term memory for movement. *J. Exp. Psychol.* **103**, 522–9.

Kelso, J.A.S., Holt, K.G., Kugler, P.N. and Turvey, M.T. (1980). On the concept of co-ordinative structures in dissipative structures: Empirical lines of convergence. In Stelmach, G.E. and Requin, J. (eds), *Tutorials in Motor Behaviour.* Amsterdam: North Holland.

Keogh, J. (1973). Development in fundamental motor tasks. In Corbin, C.B. (ed.), *A Text Book of Motor Development.* Dubuque, Iowa: Brown.

Knights, R.M., Atkinson, B.R. and Hyman, J.A. (1967). Tactual discrimination and motor skills in mongoloid and non-mongoloid retardates and normal children. *Am. J. Ment. Defic.* **71**, 894–900.

Knights, R.M., Hyman, J.A. and Wozny, M.A. (1965). Psychomotor abilities of familial brain-injured and mongoloid retarded children. *Am. J. Ment. Defic.* **70**, 454–7.

Komiya, M. (1981). An experimental study of tactual and visual discrimination in children with Down's Syndrome. *Jap. J. Special Educ.* **19**, 17–18.

Komiya, M. (1982). An experimental study of tactual and visual discrimination in children with Down's Syndrome – The variety of discrimination responses effected by different kind of stimulus presentation. *Jap. J. Special Educ.* **19**, 2.

Kornhuber, H.H. (1974). *Cerebral cortex, cerebellum and basal ganglia: An introduction to their motor functions.* In Schmitt, F.O. (ed.), *The Neurosciences III*, Cambridge: MIT Press.

Laszlo, J.I. and Bairstow, P.J. (1985). *Perceptual–Motor Behaviour: Development and Therapy.* London: Holt Saunders.

Lee, D.N. and Aronson, G. (1974). Visual proprioceptive control of standing in human infants. *Perception & Psychophysics* **15**, 529–32.

Lee, D.N. and Lishman, J.R. (1975). Visual proprioceptive control of stance. *J. Hum. Movement Stud.* **1**, 87–95.

Lewis, V.A. and Bryant, P.E. (1982). Touch and vision in normal and Down's Syndrome babies. *Perception* **11**, 691–701.

Loesch-Mdzewska, D. (1968). Some aspects of the neurology of Down's Syndrome. *J. Ment. Defic. Res.* **12**, 237–46.

Ludlow, J.R. and Allen, L.M. (1979). The effect of early intervention and preschool stimulus on the development of the Down's Syndrome child. *J. Ment. Defic. Res.* **23**, 29–44.

Lydic, J.S. and Steele, C. (1979). Assessment of the quality of sitting and gait patterns in children with Down's Syndrome. *Phys. Ther.* **59**, 1489–94.

McIntire, M.S. and Dutch, S.J. (1964). Mongolism and generalised hypotonia. *Am. J. Ment. Defic.* **68**, 669–70.

Magnus, R. (1926). Physiology of posture. *Lancet* **2**, 531–6; 585–8.

Malina, R.M. and Rarick, G.L. (1973). Growth, physique and motor performance. In Rarick, G.L. (ed.), *Physical Activities: Human Growth and Development.* New York: Academic Press.

Molnar, G.E. (1978). Analysis of motor disorder in retarded infants and young children. *Am. J. Ment. Defic.* **83**, 213–22.

Morris, A.F., Vaughan, S.E. and Vaccaro, P. (1982). Measurement of neuromusculer tone and strength in Down's Syndrome children. *J. Ment. Defic. Res.* **26**, 41–6.

O'Connor, N. and Berkson, G. (1963). Eye movements in normals and defectives. *Am. J. Ment. Defic.* **68**, 85–90.

O'Connor, N. and Hermelin, B. (1961). Visual and sterognostic shape recognition in normal children and mongol and non-mongol imbeciles. *J. Ment. Defic. Res.* **5**, 63–6.

Piper, M.C. and Pless, I.B. (1980). Early intervention for infants with Down's Syndrome: A controlled trial. *Pediatrics* **65**, 463–8.

Rarick, G.L. (1973). Motor performance of mentally retarded children. In Rarick, G.L. (ed.), *Physical Activity, Human Growth and Development.* New York: Academic Press.

Rarick, G.L. and Dobbins, D.A. (1975). Basic components in the motor performance of children six to nine years of age. *Med. & Sci. in Sports* **7**, 105–110.

Saltzberg, C.L. and Villani, T.V. (1983). Speech training by parents of Down's Syndrome toddlers: Generalisation across settings and institutional contexts. *Am. J. Ment. Defic.* **87**, 403–413.

Saqi, S.M. (1981). Reaction times and movement times of Down's Syndrome children. Unpublished MSc Thesis. Institute of Education, University of London.

Schmidt, R.A. (1982). *Motor Control and Learning.* Champaign, Illinois: Human Kinetics.

Seyfort, B. and Spreen, O. (1979). Two-plated tapping performance by Down's Syndrome and non-Down's Syndrome retardates. *J. Child Psychol. & Psych.* **20**, 351–5.

Share, J., Koch, R., Webb, A. and Graliker, B. (1964). The longitudinal development of infants and young children with Down's Syndrome (mongolism). *Am. J. Ment. Defic.* **68**, 685–92.

Share, J., Webb, A. and Koch, R. (1961). A preliminary investigation of the early developmental status of mongoloid infants. *Am. J. Ment. Defic.* **66**, 238–41.

Sherrington, C. (1961). *The Integrative Action of the Nervous System.* New Haven: Yale University Press.

Shipe, D. and Shotwell, A.M. (1965). The effect of out-of-home care on mongoloid children: A continuation study. *Am. J. Ment. Defic.* **69**, 649–52.

Shirley, M. (1931). *The First Two Years: A Study of Twenty-Five Babies.* Minneapolis: University of Minnesota Press.

Shotwell, A.M. and Shipe, D. (1964). The effect of out-of-home care on the intellectual and social development of mongoloid children. *Am. J. Ment. Defic.* **68**, 693–9.

Shumway-Cook, A. and Woollacott, M.H. (1984). *Dynamics of Postural Control in the Child with Down's Syndrome.* In Press.

Stedman, D.J. and Eichorn, D.H. (1964). A comparison of the growth and development of institutionalised and home-reared mongoloids during infancy and childhood. *Am. J. Ment. Defic.* **69**, 391–40.

Stokes, T.F. and Baer, D.M. (1977). An implicit technology of generalisation. *J. Appl. Behav. Anal.* **10**, 349–67.

12 Physical Activity Programming

Greg Reid

Down's Syndrome children, adolescents and adults should become acquainted with, and practised in, a wide range of leisure activities from arts and crafts, to music, social recreation and physical pursuits. This chapter concentrates on the last-mentioned.

Regular physical exercise of sufficient duration and intensity can help maintain or promote a healthy body. Those who are physically fit have a reduced tendency to contract minor illness, have sufficient energy to carry out employment and recreational tasks, and can perform more work with less time needed to recover. Coleman *et al.* (1976) have shown that the mentally retarded often have insufficient stamina to carry out many vocational tasks. The need for physical exercise is almost self-evident. Furthermore, exercise plays an important role in weight control, a common problem in Down's Syndrome.

Another benefit derived from physical activity programmes is the learning of new motor activities. Swimming, cycling and gymnastics can be enjoyable avenues for improving physical fitness as well as providing opportunities for social interaction. However, it is imperative that the mentally handicapped be exposed to programmes which actually improve their state of motor functioning; it is not sufficient simply to ensure that they go to the swimming pool or sports field once a week. They must be taught in such a manner that there is an increase in their physical skills repertoire. Only with this attitude will the individual with Down's Syndrome acquire the motor skills necessary for independent action, for it is the ability to carry out a motor task independently and efficiently that enables the participant to grow socially or emotionally through the physical milieu.

PHYSICAL PERFORMANCE OF DOWN'S SYNDROME YOUNGSTERS

For the purposes of the present chapter, physical performance includes both motor performance and physical fitness. Motor performance refers to abilities such as balance, agility, ball throwing and catching, whereas physical fitness involves measures of strength, power, muscular endurance, flexibility and cardiorespiratory endurance.

Clinical evidence, practical experience and comparative physical performance data for retarded and non-retarded youngsters (Rarick *et al.*, 1976) indicate that individuals with Down's Syndrome lag behind non-retarded persons of comparable chronological age in terms of motor performance and physical fitness. The more

219

interesting, as well as more theoretically and practically important question, is whether persons suffering from Down's Syndrome perform less well than their retarded peers of similar chronological and mental age. If such differences exist, then a strong argument for differential programming might be advanced.

There is some evidence that Down's Syndrome individuals perform less well than other retarded persons in terms of reaction time (Berkson, 1960), attainment of motor milestones during infancy (Carr, 1970), tapping and rotary pursuit tasks (Frith and Frith, 1974) and wave-tracking tasks (Henderson, Morris and Frith, 1981). The reason(s) for this lack of proficiency is the focus of considerable contemporary investigation. But the question remains whether the difficulties exhibited by Down's Syndrome subjects in such laboratory tasks manifest themselves on large-muscle, gross-motor performance tasks.

Somewhat surprisingly, there are very few data on the comparison between Down's Syndrome and non-Down's Syndrome retarded children, adolescents and adults, with regard to gross motor performance. As Henderson, Morris and Ray (1981) pointed out, despite frequent reference to motor awkwardness of Down's Syndrome children, it is more common for authors to describe observations than to study the issue itself.

Investigations of the motor performance of Down's individuals have typically used the Cratty Gross Motor Test (Cratty, 1969) – a six-component device which purports to measure body perception, gross agility, balance, locomotor agility, ball throwing and ball tracking. Cratty (1974) concluded that subjects with Down's Syndrome were generally inferior to other mentally retarded subjects on the test battery. In particular, he noted difficulties with balance and visual tracking.

LeBlanc *et al.* (1977) studied the often cited balance problems in Down's Syndrome. Balance and locomotor agility items from the Cratty Gross Motor Test were administered to 25 children with Down's Syndrome and 25 non-Down's retarded children with comparable IQs and chronological ages. There was no significant difference between the groups on the balance item, while the Down's children were superior to their retarded peers on the measure of locomotor agility.

The complete Cratty battery was used by Henderson, Morris and Ray (1981) to study the motor performance of 18 Down's and 18 other retarded children matched on chronological and mental age. When the data were subjected to statistical analysis, the groups were not differentiated by total scores, and only results from the first level of gross agility and locomotor agility tests indicated that the Down's subjects were inferior to their matched peers. The latter finding is at odds with that of LeBlanc *et al.*, who demonstrated Down's Syndrome superiority in locomotor agility.

Henderson *et al.* noted that their findings and Cratty's were also inconsistent. They claimed that only ball throwing, ball tracking and gross agility tasks resulted in significantly poorer performance on the part of the Down's individuals in the Cratty study. Thus, the only overlap from a statistical perspective is that both studies differentiated between Down's and non-Down's subjects on gross agility – a speed item in the battery.

The three studies cited (Cratty, 1969, 1974; Henderson *et al.*, 1981; LeBlanc *et al.*, 1977) provide a rather cloudy picture of the motor performance in Down's Syndrome. From a strictly statistical viewpoint, the data across the three studies are not conducive to an interpretation of motor performance inferiority by Down's subjects above and beyond that demonstrated by non-Down's but equally mentally handicapped persons. Thus, there is minimal support for differential programming in Down's Syndrome. On the other hand, the authors (with the exception of LeBlanc *et al.*) clearly discuss their findings, statistical results notwithstanding, from the perspective of difficulties inherent and unique to Down's Syndrome. Two of the papers, for example, comment on the balance difficulties demonstrated by Down's subjects (Cratty, 1974; Henderson *et al.*, 1981). Henderson *et al.* postulated that balance problems were apparent in the gross and locomotor agility test items, which depend in part upon balance proficiency. Their suggestion that more dynamic movement sequences, such as the locomotor agility task involving a large balance contribution, may impede Down's subjects more than non-Down's retarded subjects deserves further investigation. However, from the static balance findings in the three studies, persons with Down's Syndrome do not appear to differ in their ability to maintain equilibrium when compared to non-Down's retarded individuals.

Several avenues of potential research suggest themselves from the present discussion. First, a test battery of gross-motor activities which would be composed of more dynamic and open movements than those in the Cratty test (indeed, movements that approximate to 'real' play and game skills) could be developed. Given the difficulties subjects with Down's Syndrome seem to have with reaction time, developmental milestones and tracking (Berkson, 1960; Carr, 1970; Henderson, Morris and Frith, 1981), and given abundant clinical statements of their awkwardness, one would expect to demonstrate that the Down's youngsters are less co-ordinated than the non-Down's retarded groups. Secondly, a more vivid developmental picture is needed. While the retarded in general have been described as deficient in motor skills when compared to the non-retarded, their pattern of change with age is consistently noted as being similar to that of the non-retarded (Francis and Rarick, 1959; Rarick *et al.*, 1970). There are no clear data in this regard on motor performance in Down's Syndrome; indeed, investigators have often 'lumped' together an age range of 7 or even 10 years in their discussions. Inasmuch as a decline in both mental age and motor quotient in the first years of life has been identified with Down's Syndrome (Carr, 1970), and there is evidence of an irregular pattern of development on some items on the Cratty test (Cratty, 1974), a clearer developmental picture would be desirable. Thirdly, gender differences and similarities should be explored. Only Henderson, Morris and Ray (1981) analysed their data with this variable, although no male–female differences were shown. Finally, physical activity programmers might benefit from a qualitative description of the motor patterns of Down's and non-Down's retarded peers, previous work having restricted itself to quantitative measures of how many, how fast and how far.

A variety of test items and batteries has been used in an attempt to portray the physical fitness of persons with Down's Syndrome. Common test items to measure the components of physical fitness are outlined in Table 12.1. While there are many more sophisticated means to assess fitness, they are often expensive and impractical for schools, clubs and centres.

Down's individuals are unusually short in stature with disproportionately short

Table 12.1 *Common test items for evaluating the fitness of mentally retarded persons*

Fitness component	Definition	Test item*	Source
Muscular strength	Force in maximum single muscular contraction	Grip strength via dynamomenter	Clausen (1968)
Muscular endurance	Ability of muscles to contract many times	Flexed arm hang;	Canada Fitness Award (1983)
		sit-ups	Johnson and Londeree (1976)
Cardiorespiratory endurance	Ability to supply oxygen to tissues for a prolonged period	300 yard (274 m) run–walk;	Johnson and Londeree (1976)
		600–2000 m run–walk depending upon age	Canada Fitness Award (1983)
Flexibility	Range of motion about a joint	Sit and reach apparatus	Johnson and Londeree (1976)
Body composition	Percentage of fat and fat-free body mass	Skinfold calipers	
Power/speed	Work or performance per unit of time	Standing long jump;	Johnson and Londeree (1976)
		50-yard (46 m) dash	Canada Fitness Award (1983)

*There are other items in fitness batteries, such as shuttle runs and softball throws, but it is not clear what components or combination of components they are measuring.

limbs (Mosier *et al.*, 1965; Thelander and Pryor, 1966). Their muscles are flaccid and they are often described as extremely flexible. Given these unique physical characteristics, it might be expected that their levels of physical fitness would not be similar to those of their chronological and mental age peers. No published studies appear to exist, however, using a comprehensive physical fitness battery in comparing intellectually matched Down's and non-Down's subjects. Thus, the research discussed below must be evaluated in that light. While comparisons with non-Down's moderately retarded groups are common, the lack of control for intellectual ability provides little information with regard to the unique fitness parameters of Down's persons.

Oseland (1980), Wang and Eichstaedt (1980) and Londeree and Johnson (1974) have evaluated the physical fitness of hundreds of moderately mentally handicapped non-Down's and Down's children. The test items included the flexed arm hang, sit-ups, shuttle run,* standing long jump, 50-yard (46 m) dash, softball throw and endurance runs. While fitness performance generally increased over age (Oseland, 1980), no consistent differences were found between the sub-group with Down's Syndrome and the remaining subjects. Wang and Eichstaedt (1980) felt that Down's subjects could be placed and taught in physical fitness activities alongside moderately retarded individuals.

The Canada Fitness Award Program has recently been adapted for the moderately mentally retarded with a cross-Canada sample (Findlay, 1981). This test

---

*This test involves running 30 yards (27 m) from the starting line to pick up a small block, returning and placing the block at the starting line and then returning once again to pick up a second block and return it. The 30-yard (27 m) distance is thus traversed four times.

battery includes: flexed arm hang, shuttle run, sit-ups, long jump, 50-m run and an endurance run of 600m (7–9 year olds), 1200m (for 10–12 year olds) or 2000m (for 13 year olds and older). Data comparing Down's with moderately retarded youngsters have not yet been published. However, the standards for receiving one of four awards (Excellent, Gold, Silver, Bronze) have recently been released (Canada Fitness Award, 1983). The standards are provided for each age (6 through 12) and both genders. On all items, except the endurance run, separate standards are provided for Down's and non-Down's youngsters. The researchers presumably felt that the two groups differed sufficiently to warrant a different set of standards. In approximately 83% of the flexed arm standards, 78% of the shuttle run standards, 88% of the sit-up standards, 86% of the long jump standards and 80% of the 50-m run standards, the Down's subject can reach a given level (e.g. Gold) with a score inferior to that of the non-Down's performer. This would suggest that the Down's group suffers particularly in fitness when compared to moderately retarded groups.

Seefeldt (1966, as cited in Sherrill, 1981) reported that 88% of his Down's sample had hyperextensible joints. Laffoon (1968) compared Down's, non-Down's and non-retarded subjects on several tests of extent flexibility. Generally the results favoured the Down's youngsters over the other two groups. Thus, research data appear to support the observation that Down's Syndrome is associated with remarkable flexibility.

Measures of strength and body composition have not commonly been used with Down's subjects. In one study, Clausen (1968) did not differentiate between Down's and non-Down's subjects on grip strength measures. Body composition appears not to have been assessed with Down's Syndrome. However, given the finding that the estimated body fat (measured via the skinfold technique) of moderately retarded adults far exceeds that of non-retarded adults (Reid and Montgomery, 1983), and the corpulent nature of so many Down's subjects, one would expect that their percentage of body fat would exceed acceptable health standards.

In summary, individuals with Down's Syndrome suffer from poor levels of physical fitness and are in need of regular exercise to increase their strength and stamina and to keep their weight in check. Also, their proficiency in many motor tasks is sufficiently low to justify remedial programmes designed to augment their often clumsy performance. It remains a theoretically interesting point, however, whether Down's persons are particularly deficient in motor performance and physical fitness when compared to retarded individuals of similar age and mental competence.

ASSESSMENT FOR PHYSICAL ACTIVITY

Assessment is an essential process for physical activity programming. The ultimate goal of assessment is to allow programmers to make intelligent and informed decisions about the individuals they serve (Salvia and Ysseldyke, 1978). Decisions based on assessment to be made by physical activity programmers include the following.

1. Placement. Given the skills* of this individual and the prerequisite skills of programme A, is there a high probability that the individual will be successful in programme A?

2. Programme planning. If the Down's participants possess abilities *a* to *p*, how will I borrow from previous programmes to adapt to their learning styles?

3. Programme evaluation. Was the programme effective in meeting the objectives established?

4. Individual progress evaluation. John has not succeeded in previous physical activity programmes but in this swimming programme he has progressed from a reluctant participant to a swimmer of one width of the pool.

5. Personnel evaluation. Were the instructors and support staff effective?

6. Procurement of funding. Excuse me, Mr Administrator, but our assessment of the clients suggests that to maximise improvement we need this list of equipment and two additional volunteers next time we run the programme (Cratty, 1980, p. 30; Salvia and Ysseldyke, 1978, Chapter 2; Wade and Davis, 1982).

Assessment is much more than testing. A test is usually designed to yield a score as a result of the individual reacting to a series of tasks or questions which are chosen to elicit certain types of behaviour. A task might be the 50-m dash. This yields a score in seconds, which is purportedly an indication of speed or power. According to Salvia and Ysseldyke (1978, Chapter 1), assessment is a multifaceted process which might include testing but is also: (1) a consideration of performance of tasks in a variety of contexts; (2) an understanding of the meaning of a performance in relation to the total functioning of the person; (3) a knowledge that performance on a task is influenced by task demands as well as by the history and characteristics which the individual brings to the task; and (4) an evaluation of performance which might be based in part on parent and teacher observations. Therefore, the time in the 50-m dash is considered by the physical activity programmers to be an invalid estimate of Susan's speed because she has just recovered from a lengthy illness or is particularly shy in a new environment and simply does not try until she gets to know you. Thus, 'assessment is the process of understanding the performance of students in their current ecology' (Salvia and Ysseldyke, 1978, p. 4).

There are a number of tests that might be used as part of the assessment of Down's individuals in physical activity programmes. They are usually one of two types, norm-referenced or criterion-referenced. Most people are familiar with the more common norm-referenced test, as we have been exposed to these throughout our school years. Its goal is to discriminate amongst individuals. The usual maths exam or fitness tests which we have taken would never be considered worthwhile if everyone received the same score. It would be called too easy (if we all got 100), or too difficult (if we all got zero). Rather, variability of scores is desirable.

---

*In the present context 'skills' include those of a physical, social/emotional, intellectual and self-help nature.

Norm-referenced tests usually involve interpretation of an individual's score relative to those of others. Indeed, norm-referenced tests often have published norms or averages for the complete test and/or individual test items. Thus, Philip's score of 17 is below the average of 35, or possibly at the 20th percentile for boys of the same age.

Norm-referenced tests are broad based. That is, they tend to measure rather large areas of behaviour such as physical fitness, gross-motor performance, visual–motor skills, etc. While some of the sub-tests might be as 'specific' as hand–eye co-ordination, the resulting numerical score usually masks how individuals throw and catch, whether they are capable of catching when the ball is not thrown directly at them (an important skill on a real playground or gymnasium), how fast they react to a throw, etc.

Finally, many norm-referenced tests are diagnostic or process oriented. In some cases, they might attempt to diagnose neurological dysfunction or school readiness – a far cry from the skills usually directly tested. More commonly, norm-referenced tests of a physical nature tend to view motor skills as general rather than specific. That is, there are underlying motor abilities which are common and transferable from one skill to another. Thus, an individual's score on one skill should be predictive of his or her score on a second skill which relies on similar underlying abilities (Wade and Davis, 1982). Balance is an ability which is important in many specific skills and is therefore found in most norm-referenced tests of motor proficiency.

Norm-referenced tests have often been used with Down's individuals. In the motor performance area, the Cratty Six Category Gross-Motor Test is an example. In the physical fitness area, the Adapted Canada Fitness Test for the Trainable Mentally Retarded (Findlay, 1981) and the Motor Fitness Testing Manual for the Moderately Mentally Retarded (Johnson and Londeree, 1976) have been used with people with Down's Syndrome.

Norm-referenced testing has been criticised on several grounds.

1. The information given to the teacher is seldom specific enough to be a meaningful point of departure of instruction, since the tests are usually so broad based.

2. Such tests are often not related to curricula, and therefore provide minimal information for programme planning.

3. Since they are broad based, they may be insensitive to real but small improvement.

4. The tests may be too difficult for handicapped students; after all, a score of zero tells us very little.

5. Norm-referenced motor-proficiency tests are often based on the questionable assumption of general motor abilities. (Motor skill specificity has received appreciably more support (Kerr, 1982).) Thus, a single test of balance is likely to be measuring balance on that single test rather than a more comprehensive ability.

Criterion-referenced testing is a more recently developed alternative and yields measurements which are interpretable in terms of performance standards (Glaser and Nitko, 1971), often in the context of an existing curriculum. Whereas a

Table 12.2 *Scoring for a criterion-referenced test of the overarm throw: arm action component (Mosher and Schutz, 1983)*

Arm action
  1. No evidence of overarm throwing pattern.
  2. Slight retraction of arm with the throwing hand initiating forward movement from a position even with or very slightly behind the ear; elbow well flexed.
  3. Preparatory phase shows evidence of greater retraction of throwing arm, i.e. 'wind-up' evident where ball is cocked well behind the body, rather close to the head. Ball is 'pushed' toward target area as a result of horizontally adducting the arm until the elbow is approximately in front of the shoulder before the forearm is extended.
  4. Forearm flung forward in 'whipping', rather than 'pushing', fashion; forearm close to full extension at time of release.
  5. As in 4 above, with the addition of 'forearm lag'; the forearm and ball appear to lag, i.e. to remain almost stationary behind the body as the shoulders move toward front facing.

norm-referenced score for an individual is compared to those of others of similar age and gender (i.e. norms), the criterion-referenced score indicates in quite precise performance terms what the individual can do. The criterion for success is the performance standard. An example (Table 12.2) is the scoring for one component of an overhand throwing test (Mosher and Schutz, 1983). A score from 1 to 5 is possible in each of three components: foot placement, body rotation, and arm action. A score of 4 on the arm action indicates that the forearm is flung forward in a whipping action and is close to full extension when the ball is released. The score of 4 is meaningless as a norm or average performance but is a very meaningful description of an individual's skill.

While all students in a class are not likely to receive identical scores, it is not the purpose of a criterion-referenced test to discriminate between individuals. Rather, such tests aim to describe the capabilities of the individuals according to some performance standard or criteria. It is possible for everyone to be successful.

Finally, criterion-referenced tests are often directly related to curricula. Consequently, they view motor skills as specific entities and tend, therefore, to be more narrowly based than norm-referenced tests. The I CAN curriculum produced at the University of Michigan (Wessel, 1983) and the PREP Play Program, a product of the University of Alberta, are examples of criterion-referenced measurement as part of curricula. Identified steps to accomplish a task are listed (Table 12.3) and each step has clear criteria to measure successful completion. If an individual is capable of step 2 but not step 3, the teacher knows that activities designed to develop competencies of step 3 are the order of the day. Testing and teaching therefore become intricately interwoven. While norm-referenced tests are typically administered at the beginning and end of a programme, criterion-referenced testing

Table 12.3 *Six skill levels for the front crawl* (Wessel, 1983). Reproduced with permission.*

1. To perform the arm action with assistance
2. To perform the arm action without assistance
3. To perform the front crawl without assistance
4. To perform the front crawl with periodic breathing
5. To perform the front crawl with rhythmic breathing
6. To perform a functional crawl

*From I CAN. It should be noted that behavioural objectives accompany each level.

Table 12.4 *Physical performance tests for the mentally retarded**

Name of test	Criterion (C) or norm (N) referenced	Physical fitness (PF) or motor performance (MP)	Source
Motor Fitness Testing Manual for the Moderately Mentally Retarded	N	PF & MP	Johnson and Londeree (1976)
Special Fitness Test Manual for Mildly Mentally Retarded Persons (1968)	N	PF	AAPHERD Washington, DC
Canada Fitness Award Manual Adapted for Use by Trainable Mentally Handicapped Youth	N & C	PF	Fitness and Amateur Sport Government of Canada Ottawa (1983)
I CAN: Health and Fitness	C	PF	Hubbard Publishing Co.
I CAN: Body Management	C	MP	P.O. Box 104
I CAN: Fundamental Skills	C	MP	Northbrook, Illinois USA 60062
Project ACTIVE	N	PF & MP	Ocean Township School Dist. Dow Avenue Oakhurst, New Jersey, USA 07755
Cratty 6 Category Gross Motor Test	N	MP	Cratty (1969)
Scale of Intra-Gross Motor Assessment	C	MP	Ohio State University
Bruininks–Oseretsky Test of Motor Proficiency	N	MP	American Guidance Service Inc. Circle Pines, Minnesota USA 55014
PREP Play Program	C	MP (play skills)	Watkinson and Wall (1979)

*Tests which have been designed for, or extensively used with, the mentally retarded.

is a cumulative process linked to teaching and will occur throughout a programme. Tables 12.2 and 12.3 also highlight another characteristic of criterion-referenced testing, i.e. they are usually detailed. Unlike the broad base of a norm-referenced test, the criterion-referenced test deals with a smaller sample of behaviour but yields much more teacher-relevant information. For example, the overhand throwing test (see Table 12.2) provides the instructor with detailed information on how the individual is throwing, not just the fact (common with norm-referenced tests) that the throw, however accomplished, managed to propel the ball 20 m.

Criterion-referenced testing is thus an attractive alternative, avoiding the problems which confront norm-referenced testing. Physical activity programmers dealing with individuals with Down's Syndrome have a considerable number of tests from which to choose. These tests (Table 12.4) have been developed for, or used successfully with, the mentally handicapped, and one's choice depends first and foremost on the purpose of the assessment.* If the purpose is to compare groups of Down's persons with matched peers, then norm-referenced testing is appropriate. Some of the decisions in programme planning or placement might be aided by norm-referenced scores. However, the bulk of the intelligent and

---

*Questions of validity, reliability, tester expertise required, etc., are obviously important but are beyond the scope of this chapter.

informed decisions programmers are requested to make with regard to establishing objectives of the programme are likely to be more effectively made with the help of criterion-referenced testing.

PROGRAMMING

Physical activity programming is clearly a multidimensional process. It involves issues as diverse as selecting appropriate content, establishing desirable partici-pant–instructor ratios, choice of equipment, use and training of volunteers, obtaining facilities and raising funds. While these and other components of programming are imperative for a successful enterprise, the focus of this portion of the chapter will be on selecting content (including contraindications), broad models for presenting the content, and examples of four programmes designed for the mentally handicapped in the physical domain. A later section of the chapter will deal with a specific dimension of programming termed individual instruction.

Selection of content

Physical activity programmers must select activities from a wide range of physical pursuits from hiking to canoeing, from basketball to gymnastics. A number of factors should be considered in arriving at a decision.

1. *Age.* Activities appropriate to the age of the participants are important. Too often there is a tendency for programmers to select activities which are designed for much younger people, arguing that the older Down's individual lacks the skills necessary for age-appropriate activities. Seeing a young adult playing a game such as ring-around-the-rosy simply reinforces the overly dependent, 'eternally a child', poorly skilled notion of the mentally handicapped – an unfortunately common belief for most people uninformed about mental retardation. Choosing age-appropriate activities for profoundly and severely retarded persons can be difficult, for their genuine interests may be very childlike. However, most people with Down's Syndrome are indeed capable of age-appropriate activities which for the adult might include swimming, bowling, skiing, gymnastics and skating.

2. *Functionally appropriate.* Physical activity programmers should select activi-ties which have a high probability of occurring in the lifestyle of the individual (Brown *et al.*, 1979). For younger children, walking on balance beams can be enjoyable and challenging. Youngsters will often place themselves in the precarious position of balancing along the curbs of pavements etc, and balance beam walks may approximate a skill that is functional. However, some movement specialists seem too enthusiastic about the beam and ask their charges to walk backward with blindfolds! While this might be appropriate as a 'challenge' stunt from time to time in the programme, it is inappropriate as a typical part of the programme content.

For older participants in particular, activities which occur as part of the national culture and/or local geography should be highlighted. It is these that the Down's individual will be able to use in a family setting or community centre. For example, a group in Western Canada has actively promoted curling for the mentally handicapped because it is a sport that is popular in the local area. And adults may play soccer in clubs or swim at local centres but seldom are they involved in highly specialised activities such as throwing the discus. Activity selection for adults with Down's Syndrome should reflect these realities.

3. *Physical and intellectual activities.* Groups of Down's people are not as physically fit or as motor-proficient as their non-retarded peers. There is a tendency, therefore, for physical activity programmers to underestimate their potential skills. However, a realistic match of the demands of the activity and the potential of the individual (physically and intellectually) is necessary in programme selection. Otherwise, both instructor and participant are doomed to experience more failure than success.

4. *Participant interest.* Participants, particularly adults, ought to be consulted about their physical-activity preferences. This should raise motivational levels and provide new insights into functional activities for potential programming.

5. *Life skills prerequisites.* Programmers should be aware of the life skills needed to participate in certain physical activities. For example, a participant in a swimming programme must be able to change into a bathing suit, dry off and get dressed. Programmers may need to provide helpers for such tasks (see 7 below).

6. *Social/emotional prerequisites.* Some degree of appropriate social/emotional functioning is necessary in most physical activities. Team activities, for example, require concepts of sharing, working towards a common goal, waiting for one's turn, etc. Do the participants have the requisite social/emotional characteristics for the planned activity?

7. *Available support systems.* Volunteers are an example of a support system. For example, in a hiking and camping programme, which involves certain high-risk skills, a low ratio of participants to instructors is necessary for the success of the programme.

Contraindications in activity selection

Some restrictions on physical activity will be necessary for certain individuals. While the participant's doctor can best guide the programme leaders, certain contraindications are relatively common.

1. Many Down's individuals will suffer from congenital heart problems, which may, but certainly will not always, result in some physical activity restrictions. A physician must be consulted with regard to specific limitations of individuals.

2. Sherrill (1981, p. 445) has suggested that almost 90% of children with Down's Syndrome have umbilical hernias. While the condition is usually self-corrective, she indicated that straight-leg lifts and holds are not appropriate.

3. Swimming is certainly not a contraindication, but incomplete drying afterwards is a definite problem. Down's individuals are susceptible to respiratory infections, and it is therefore mandatory that the body, and particularly the head, is carefully dried after swimming or showering.

4. Approximately 10% of persons with Down's Syndrome may have a condition known as atlanto axial subluxation, a malalignment of the first two cervical vertebrae. With gross hyperextension or flexion of the neck, the spinal cord becomes vulnerable to serious injury, which can result in permanent paralysis. An x-ray is required by a physician knowledgeable about the condition in order to detect its presence in a particular individual. The Special Olympics Inc. (Shriver, 1983) has established a policy of avoiding the following activities for people with atlanto axial subluxation: gymnastics, diving, butterfly stroke in swimming, diving start in swimming, high jump, pentathlon, soccer, and any specific exercise which places pressure on the head and neck muscles. It is advisable, therefore, that Down's participants be screened via the x-ray procedure prior to engaging in physical activities which might result in traumatic injury. For additional information see Cooke (1984).

Approaches to physical activity programming

There are three basic approaches to physical activity programming for mentally handicapped persons. These include the objective data-based approach, the process/ability approach, and the developmental movement approach. While instructors may use a combination of approaches or emphasise one over the other for certain activities or age groups, the following discussion will, somewhat artificially, describe them in isolation. As Groves (1979) has noted, no system holds all the answers.

Objective data-based instruction

Proponents of objective data-based instruction advocate instruction in the specific skills with which the individual is having difficulty but which nonetheless represent important and functional behaviours. This approach to programming is usually accomplished through task analyses, criterion-referenced measurement, behavioural objectives and formative evaluation.

Task analysis is a systematic description of the components of a task, with the components usually arranged in a hierarchy of difficulty. For example, in a given dance, the following movements might be required: skipping, sliding and walking in a circle. The analysis could go further since skipping is composed of a hop and a step with feet alternating. It is possible that a particular child is having difficulty with the dance because of an inability to skip, specifically a problem with hopping on the right leg. By analysing a task and identifying specific skills and deficits, the teacher knows exactly where to initiate instruction.

Table 12.5 contains additional examples of task analyses. It is important to note that the components of a task are highly specific; one does not usually find reference to general terms such as 'balance' or 'strength'. While there are many different approaches to task analysis (Reid, 1976), it is important to consult with experts and read the literature thoroughly to conduct a meaningful analysis of a task. Furthermore, task sequences will vary in length according to the extent of the analysis needed. Generally, a task will be broken down further if an individual is having particular difficulty.

Table 12.5 *Examples of task analysis*

A. *To catch a ball*
  1. Visually track the ball
  2. Have hands and arms in preparatory position
  3. Adjust position of body (forward, backward, sideways) if necessary
  4. Contact with hands
  5. Flex elbows to absorb shock
B. *To place head under water in a pool*
  1. Walk onto poolside
  2. Sit on poolside, feet in water
  3. Stand in the shallow end of pool holding on to the side
  4. Stand in the shallow end of pool
  5. Put face into water while holding on to the side
  6. Put face into water
  7. Place head under water while holding on to the side
  8. Place head under water

Following a task analysis, behavioural objectives are established for each step in the hierarchy. A behavioural objective is one that specifies the behaviour to be demonstrated, the conditions under which the behaviour will occur, and the criterion for success (Mager, 1975). Table 12.6 includes several behavioural objectives.

The result of the analysis and the objectives is a criterion-referenced test. (This is the approach which physical activity specialists have used, although it varies somewhat from strict application of the theory of criterion-referenced measurement.) If the instruction enables the Down's individual to accomplish a new component of a task, or the complete task itself, the success is recorded, and the person is now capable of attempting the next behavioural objective. This continual recording of progress throughout instruction is called 'formative evaluation'.

Champions of the objective data-based approach to programming argue that it demonstrates programme effectiveness by objective means. Also, when specific objectives are not being met, there is clear evidence of lack of learning which should signal a modification of individual instruction, a change of task sequences, or a move to a totally new task at which success can be achieved. The instructors can therefore be held accountable for what they are doing and any failure is a fault of the system of instruction rather than an indication of something inherently wrong with the individual per se.

Table 12.6 *Example of behavioural objectives (from tasks identified in Table 12.5)*

1. The participant will catch an 8-inch (20-cm) diameter playground ball thrown at chest height from an instructor standing 10 feet (3 m) from the participant, and be successful 4 out of 5 times.
2. The participant will get into the shallow end of the swimming pool, stand and hold on to the side of the pool. The participant will then lean forward to place the head into the water so that the mouth, nose and eyes are under water. This will be accomplished when verbally requested by an instructor standing on the poolside.
3. The participant will stand in the shallow end of the water and bend the knees so that the head is completely submerged. This will be accomplished when verbally requested by an instructor standing on the poolside.

Process/ability instruction

Advocates of this approach presuppose that general motor abilities form the foundation of many specific skills and can be identified and remedied. Testing is usually norm-referenced and conducted before and after the programme. Usually the logic is that poor performance with, for example, a catching task, is indicative of a hand–eye co-ordination problem. The programme consists of exposing the children to a host of ball-related activities in the hope of alleviating the hand–eye problems. The effectiveness of the programme is typically determined by a comparison of pre-test and post-test norm-referenced scores.

The difficulties with this approach have already been mentioned in the previous discussion of norm-referenced testing. Austin (1978) was particularly critical of this type of instruction and described it as 'as effective as trying to repair a defective leaking faucet by classifying it as a plumbing defect and then working randomly on selected plumbing items. One might or might not happen to include the leaking faucet in the items selected.' Particularly damaging to the approach are research data from the motor learning literature, which suggest that motor skills are highly specific and that training in the presumed underlying abilities is not likely to result in any meaningful gains on the specific skills (Magill, 1980; Kerr, 1982).

Before dismissing the process/ability approach altogether, however, it should be noted that retarded youngsters have no doubt learned something with this regime. Indeed, many of the so-called ability activities could be considered functionally important skills in their own right. However, other activities, as noted previously, probably do not represent skills that have a high probability of being required in the behavioural repertoire of the individual. While acquisition of new skills may have occurred with this instructional approach, they were seldom recorded and possibly not reflected in the norm-referenced test at the end of the programme.

Developmental movement approach

Sherborne (1979) has argued that too many physical activity programmes for the retarded place total emphasis on developing physical skills to the detriment of attention or self-awareness of the body. She suggests that a balanced programme should include developmental movement and physical skills training.

The purpose of developmental movement is to teach body and movement awareness, and it is particularly suitable for younger children. Sherborne has listed the following areas of programme content for developmental movement.

1. *Awareness of the ground*. Activities such as rolling and lying on the ground are suggested as vehicles to help the child become aware of his or her trunk, hips and shoulders, as such parts are felt against the ground. These activities are also the beginning of weight transfer – jumping, falling and spinning movements make up part of this phase.

2. *Awareness of the centre of the body*. Curled rolls, making oneself into a knot, sliding along the floor and rolling over people are included here.

3. *Locomotion.* Experiences in pulling oneself along while on the stomach, pushing the body forward and backward while lying on the back, and wriggling, slithering and crawling in different directions are important here.

4. *Awareness of knees.* Activities of slapping the knees, walking with bent knees, letting the knees 'melt', purportedly develop awareness of the control which comes from the knee joints.

5. *Awareness of hips.* The hips are important because they also support weight. Sliding along the floor on the hips, lifting and lowering the hips from the prone or supine position, and making 'bridges' for others to crawl under should develop this aspect of awareness.

6. *Awareness of other body parts.* Hands, feet, elbows and shoulders must not be forgotten as they contact each other and the floor, and, in turn, are the focus of additional movement experiences.

7. *Stability.* Partner work is advocated here, as activities which vary the base of support are enjoyed with a colleague, who at times aids, and other times challenges, the individual's stability.

8. *Quality of movement.* Activities which promote a sense of gentleness and lightness are proposed. Sherborne suggests that Down's youngsters are particularly adept in light and delicate movements.

There appears to be no formal testing in the developmental movement approach, which relies for assessment on the skilful eyes of the teacher. Empirical demonstrations of the efficacy of developmental movement are therefore not readily available. It is also assumed that the physical skills programme of aquatics, ball games, dance and gymnastics will be enhanced if the participant is well grounded in developmental movement. This assertion may seem self-evident, but it remains to be verified by controlled research with the mentally handicapped. Finally, developmental movement purportedly helps the youngster socially, emotionally and intellectually. However, it behoves the advocates of this approach to clarify and demonstrate how and to what extent it will benefit the mentally handicapped in these areas.

Examples of physical activity programmes

I CAN

This is an objective-based programme developed at Michigan State University by Dr Janet Wessel and associates. It has been extensively field tested with mentally handicapped performers, including those with Down's Syndrome, as well as with individuals with other disabilities. As outlined in Table 12.7, the programme content is divided into three sections (pre-primary, primary and sport–leisure), with 28, 73, and 79 performance objectives respectively. Each performance objective represents a functional skill which is task analysed into various skill levels. The behavioural objectives written for each skill level result in a criterion-referenced test for each programme objective. For each skill level there is extensive documentation of teacher cues, class organisation, equipment and activities.

Table 12.7 *I CAN curriculum*

Pre-primary	Primary	Sport–Leisure	
Body management	Body management	Backyard/neighbourhood activities	
Body control	Body control	Badminton	Roller skating
	Body awareness	Croquet	Tetherball
		Horseshoes	
Fundamental skills			
Locomotor	Fundamental skills		
Object control	Locomotor and rhythm	Outdoor activities	
	Object control	Backpacking	Hiking
		Camping	Cross-country
Health/fitness			skiing
Physical fitness	Health/fitness		
	Physical fitness	Dance and individual sports	
Play participation	Postural	Bowling	Gymnastics
		Folk dance	Track and field
	Aquatics		
Play equipment	Basic skills	Team sports	
	Swimming	Basketball	Softball
		Kickball	Volleyball

It should be noted that the I CAN programme represents a broad-based curriculum, from play skills at the pre-primary level to outdoor pursuits, such as backpacking, in the sport–leisure section. The programme is published by Hubbard (PO Box 104, Northbrook, Illinois 60062, USA).

PREP play program

This programme was designed and validated at the University of Alberta by Doctors Jane Watkinson and Ted Wall. The programme has run for almost 10 years, with approximately half of the participants suffering from Down's Syndrome. The goal of the PREP programme is to teach play skills to young moderately mentally retarded children. The contents of the programme are included in Table 12.8.

Like I CAN, the PREP programme is based on criterion-referenced assessment of the play skills noted in Table 12.8, and includes instructional sequences developed from a task analysis, valuable teaching suggestions and activities. A particular strength of the PREP instructional model is detailed analysis of instructor behaviour via the response-prompting continuum and the teaching episode. These will be described in the following section on individual instruction. The *PREP Program Book* is available from the Canadian Association of Health, Physical Education and Recreation (CAHPER Publications, 333 River Road, Ottawa (Vanier), Ontario, Canada).

Special Olympics

The Special Olympics is a competitive sports programme which originated in the USA and has grown to involve over 40 countries. It is sponsored by the Joseph P.

Table 12.8 *PREP play program (from Watkinson and Wall, 1979). Reproduced with permission.*

Skills for locomotion	Skills for large play equipment	Skills for small play equipment	Skills for play vehicles
Running	Ascending an	Throwing	Riding a scooter
Ascending stairs	inclined bench on	Kicking	(sitting)
Descending stairs	stomach	Catching	Riding a scooter
Jumping down	Ascending an	Bouncing	down an incline
Jumping over	inclined bench on	Hitting with a	(sitting)
Hopping on one foot	hands and knees	baseball bat	Tummy riding on a
Forward roll	Walking up an	Striking with a	scooter
Backward roll	inclined bench	hockey stick	Tummy riding down
	Jumping on a	Stopping a puck	an incline on a
	trampoline	with a hockey stick	scooter
	Seat drop on a	Passing a puck with	Pulling a wagon
	trampoline	a hockey stick	Riding a wagon
	Swivel hips on	Jumping a rope	Riding a tricycle
	trampoline	turned by two	Riding the back of a
	Sliding down a slide	people	tricycle
	Climbing on a box		
	Swinging on a rope		
	Swinging on a bar		
	Swinging on a swing		
	Hanging from knees		
	on a horizontal		
	ladder		
	Rolling around a bar		
	Ascending a ladder		
	Descending a ladder		

Kennedy, Jr Foundation in Washington, DC. Thousands of athletes with Down's Syndrome have been involved since its inception in 1969. There are local, regional, national and international competitions.

The programme material available is quite extensive: there are booklets on Special Olympics rules and training programmes, as well as individual booklets for each sport. The newest editions of the sport booklets include teaching points and task-analysed teaching sequences. Materials are available from Special Olympics Inc. (Joseph P. Kennedy Jr Foundation, 1701 K Street NW, Suite 205, Washington, DC 20006, USA).

Project ACTIVE

Project ACTIVE (All Children Totally Involved Exercising) was produced by Dr T. Vodola for a school district in New Jersey, USA. There are several volumes in the programme (Table 12.9). Both the low physical vitality and the motor ability volumes may be particularly beneficial to those working with the mentally retarded. The programme has a norm-referenced testing, process/ability focus. It is available from the Township of Ocean School District (Dow Avenue, Oakhurst, New Jersey, USA, 07755).

Table 12.9 *Project ACTIVE*

Low motor ability
Low physical vitality
Postural abnormalities
Nutritional deficiencies
Auditory/visually handicapped
Motor disabilities/limitations
Breathing problems

INDIVIDUAL INSTRUCTION

Participants with Down's Syndrome, like everyone else, benefit occasionally from individual instruction. Such instruction may only last for 10 or 20 seconds, if the person is in a group, or for up to 30 minutes if a programme provides or necessitates a 1 : 1 participant–instructor ratio. The goal of individual instruction is to provide the person with new skills which can be performed independently.

Watkinson and Wall (1979) described individual instruction from the perspective of the teaching episode and the response-prompting continuum. A teaching episode is the period of teacher–pupil interaction which has three phases: a pre-response, response, and post-response phase. The pre-response phase may include a verbal prompt ('Look at me') to gain attention, a demonstration of the desired action, or even physically placing the participant's body in the position required to initiate the response. Following the response, the teacher can reinforce ('Good jumping, Bill') and/or provide information feedback ('Land on two feet next time'). Some research has suggested that a peer might be an effective model or demonstration for certain tasks (Feltz, 1980).

A variety of prompts can be used in all phases of the teaching episode. Watkinson and Wall (1979) have coined the term 'response-prompting continuum' to denote the gradation of prompts available (Table 12.10). In both pre- and post-response phases, the participant's independence increases with a decrease in the use of physical, visual and verbal prompts (in that order). The result is independent performance by the participants.

The teaching episode and the response-prompting continuum represent a systematic approach to individual instruction. It is not completely novel, since teachers have used some of the suggestions for many years and the notion of prompting for a correct response is common in special education circles. However it is a system which is easily learned by assistants and volunteers and has been effectively employed to teach play skills to the moderately retarded (Watkinson *et al.*, 1979). We (Goldberg and Reid, 1981) have also used the response-prompting continuum as a fundamental aspect of a cross-country skiing package for the moderately retarded.

The procedures to individualise instruction discussed thus far are designed primarily to impart new skills. In the area of physical fitness, the issue may not be one of teaching new movements per se, but rather of motivating the participant to do the movement many times. As a result, the sit-up can be taught via prompts etc.,

Table 12.10 *Response-prompting continuum (Adapted from Watkinson and Wall, 1979). Reproduced with permission.*

Participant's independence increases

Physical prompts
  Complete manipulation—participant's body is moved through the complete desired response
  Manipulative prompting—physical assistance provided at beginning *or* middle *or* end of response
  Minimal guidance—physical contact to signal what body part to move

Visual prompts
  Complete skill demonstration—teacher or another child demonstrates complete response
  Partial skill demonstration—teacher or another child demonstrates one component of response
  Gestural prompting—a gesture which indicates which response is required

Verbal prompts
  Skill cues—action words which describe a component of a response, e.g. 'Bend your knees'
  Skill mands—commands or questions, e.g. 'Jump down'
  Action cues—words of motivation rather than description of a response, e.g. 'One, two, three, go'

No prompt
  Initiation with environmental goal—teacher places an object in environment to encourage response by participant
  Imitative initiation—child responds after seeing another child perform
  Initiation in free play—child responds in appropriate free play without peer demonstration

Teacher assistance decreases

but the gain in muscular endurance of the abdominal muscles is not realised unless the Down's individual can be enticed into repeating the exercise as often as possible. Some of the following suggestions are described under individual instruction because they may provide such individual motivation to perform physical fitness exercises over an extended period of time.

The mentally handicapped, including those with Down's Syndrome, enjoy seeing their progress on fitness tasks which are scored by number or time. Sit-ups, time for a run, and weights lifted are examples. Thus, by regularly recording and individually charting performance during the programme, improvement can be visually represented. Fig. 12.1 represents this technique with a Down's adult during a programme at McGill University.

Verbal encouragement from an instructor who runs and performs the specific exercise with the individual is also beneficial. The need for verbal encouragement should be self-evident: the instructor's participation seems to aid the individual in persevering, particularly in cardiovascular activities such as jogging. Since individuals with Down's Syndrome tend to be rather slow moving, cajoling by the participating instructor may be necessary.

Exercise to a background of popular music is also a powerful motivator. Indeed, simply dancing to popular music when performed with sufficient intensity and duration can be a means of promoting cardiovascular fitness (as aerobics enthusiasts demonstrate). It is commonly observed that Down's individuals enjoy music, although this may not result from inherently greater sensitivity to music (Peters

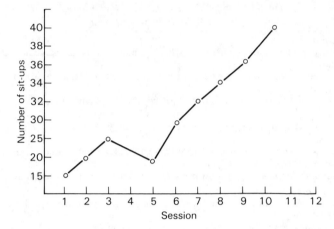

Fig. 12.1 Charting progress can be an effective motivator

1969). However, upbeat music, known to the participants, is likely to enhance their energy output in the form of physical exercise.

Techniques of behaviour modification can also be used to entice Down's participants to become actively involved in exercise programmes. Linford and Duthie (1970) have provided one such example. They used food reinforcers and verbal praise to teach Down's children a chain of three exercises: a shuttle run, which increased in distance from 20 to 160 yards (18 to 146 m); an agility run involving climbing up and through an inclined ladder; and a strength unit of lifting a 10 lb (4.5 kg) ball and dropping it through a chute. As a consequence, once the activities were learned, the children were able to sustain their effort as they completed the chain or circuit on subsequent days. Behaviour modification techniques might therefore be considered to promote motivation of physical exercise.

SUMMARY

Individuals with Down's Syndrome can be characterised by physical features, stature and structure. Yet the available evidence does not overwhelmingly suggest these are manifested in unique deficits of motor performance or physical fitness. Compared to matched retarded peers, their physical performances are remarkably similar, but compared to the non-retarded it is clear that vigorous programming is necessary to upgrade their physical skills, broaden their leisure options, and promote their physical fitness.

Physical activity programmers are urged to select age- and functionally appropri-ate tasks within the capabilities of the Down's participants. As skills in such tasks are achieved, meaningful integration into community-based programmes, as well as physical recreation in the family unit will become possible. The objective-data-based approach to programming, with criterion-referenced measurement, seems most appropriate for the development of physical skills. Certainly, contemporary curriculum models (e.g. I CAN, PREP Play Program and Special Olympics Inc. packages) have used this approach with success with individuals with Down's Syndrome.

The integration of Down's youngsters is, and will continue to be, an issue for physical activity programmers. Careful evaluation of the effects of individual instances of integration will be necessary, especially from the social and emotional perspectives.

While the physical performance section of this chapter was descriptive by intention, research projects exist which are attempting to ascertain the underlying mechanism of motor control in Down's subjects (see Chapter 11). It is hoped that this research and other studies which have explored the use of cognitive strategies to enhance motor performance (e.g. Reid, 1980) will suggest new directions of teaching physical skills to Down's subjects.

Finally, the Down's Syndrome population is enjoying a longer life expectancy. With this change must come new thinking in physical activity programming to meet the challenges of the older Down's participant.

REFERENCES

Austin, P. (1978). A model for adapted physical education. *CAHPER J.* **44**, 6–13.

Berkson, G. (1960). An analysis of reaction time in normal and mentally defective young men I, II and III. *J. Ment. Defic. Res.* **4**, 51–77.

Brown, L., Branston, M.B., Hamre-Nietupski, S., Pumpian, I., Certo, N. and Gruenewald, L. (1979). A strategy for developing chronological-age-appropriate and functional curricular content for severely handicapped adolescents and young adults. *J. Special Ed.* **13**, 81–90.

Canada Fitness Award (1983). Adapted for use by trainable mentally handicapped youth. Fitness and Amateur Sport, Canada.

Carr, J. (1970). Mental and motor development in young mongol children. *J. Ment. Defic. Res.* **14**, 205–220.

Clausen, J. (1968). Behavioral characteristics of Down's Syndrome in subjects. *Am. J. Ment. Defic.* **73**, 118–26.

Coleman, E., Ayoub, M.M. and Friedrich, D. (1976). Assessment of physical work capacity of institutionalised mentally retarded males. *Am. J. Ment. Defic.* **80**, 629–35.

Cooke, R.E. (1984). Atlantoaxial instability in individuals with Down's Syndrome. *Adapted Physical Activity Quarterly* **1**, 194–6.

Cratty, B.J. (1969). *Perceptual–Motor-Behavior and Educational Processes*. Springfield, Ill.: Charles C Thomas.

Cratty, B.J. (1974). *Motor Activity and the Education of Retardates*, 2nd edn. Philadelphia: Lea & Febiger.

Cratty, B.J. (1980). *Adapted Physical Education for Handicapped Children and Youth*. Denver: Love Publishing.

Feltz, D.L. (1980). Teaching a high-avoidance task to a retarded child through participant modeling. *Ed. & Train. Ment. Ret.* **15**, 152–5.

Findlay, H. (1981). Adaptations to the Canada Fitness Award for Special Populations: A report from phases 1 and 2. *CAHPER J.* **48** (1), 5–12.

Francis, R.J. and Rarick, G.L. (1959). Motor characteristics of the mentally retarded. *Am. J. Ment. Defic.* **63**, 792–811.

Frith, U. and Frith, C.D. (1974). Specific motor disabilities in Down's Syndrome. *J. Child Psychol. & Psych.* **15**, 293–301.

Glaser, R. and Nitko, A.J. (1971). Measurement in learning and instruction. In Thorndike, R.L. (ed.), *Educational Measurement* 2nd edn. Washington: American Council on Education.

Goldberg, C. and Reid, G. (1981). Teaching cross country skiing to retarded adolescents. In Skrotzky, K., Caron, F., Jankowski, L.W. and Reid, G. (eds), *Recherches Actuelles en Activité Physique Adaptée*. Université de Montréal.

Groves, L. (1979). *Physical Education for Special Needs*. Cambridge: Cambridge University Press.

Henderson, S.E., Morris, J. and Frith, U. (1981). The motor deficit in Down's Syndrome Children: A problem of timing? *J. Child Psychol. & Psych.* **22**, 233–45.

Henderson, S.E., Morris, J. and Ray, S. (1981). Performance of Down's Syndrome and other retarded children on the Cratty Gross Motor Test. *Am. J. Ment. Defic.* **85**, 416–24.

Johnson, L. and Londeree, B. (1976). *Motor Fitness Testing Manual for the Moderately Mentally Retarded*. Washington, DC: American Alliance for Health, Physical Education and Recreation.

Kerr, R. (1982). *Psychomotor Learning*. Philadelphia: Saunders.

Laffoon, W.L. (1968). A comparison of flexibility in mongoloid, other mentally retarded and normal children. Masters Thesis, Hendrix College. Summary in *Annotated Research Bibliography in Physical Education, Recreation and Psychomotor Function of Mentally Retarded Persons*. Washington, DC: AAHPER, 1975.

LeBlanc, D., French, R. and Shultz, B. (1977). Static and dynamic balance skills of trainable children with Down's Syndrome. *Perceptual and Motor Skills* **45**, 641–2.

Linford, A.G. and Duthie, J.H. (1970). The use of operant technology to induce sustained exertion in young, trainable Down's Syndrome children. In Kenyon, G.S. (ed.), *Contemporary Psychology of Sports*. Chicago: The Athletic Institute.

Londeree, B.R. and Johnson, L.E. (1974). Motor fitness of TMR vs EMR and normal children. *Med. Sci. in Sports* **6**, 247–52.

Mager, R.F. (1975). *Preparing Instructional Objectives*, 2nd edn. Belmond, California: Fearon.

Magill, R.A. (1980). *Motor Learning: Concepts and Applications*. Dubuque, Iowa: Wm. C. Brown.

Mosher, R.E. and Schutz, R.W. (1983). The development of a test of overarm throwing: An application of generalizability theory. *Can. J. Appl. Sport Sci.* **8**, 1–8.

Mosier, H.D., Grossman, H.J. and Dingman, H.F. (1965). Physical growth in mental defectives. *Pediatrics* **36**, 465–519.

Oseland, D.J. (1980). Physical fitness comparisons between Down's Syndrome students and moderately mentally impaired students. Unpublished MS Thesis, Illinois State University.

Peters, M.L. (1969). Music sensitivity: A comparison of mongoloid and normal children. *J. Leisure Res.* **1**, 289–95.

Rarick, G.L., Dobbins, D.A. and Broadhead, G. (1976). *The Motor Domain and its Correlates in Educationally Handicapped Children*. Englewood Cliffs, NJ: Prentice Hall.

Rarick, G.L., Widdop, J. and Broadhead, G. (1970). The physical fitness and motor performance of educable mentally retarded children. *Exceptional Children* **38**, 509–519.

Reid, G. (1976). Task analysis and the specification of short term objectives. Unpublished manuscript.

Reid, G. (1980). The effects of memory strategy instruction in short term memory of the mentally retarded. *J. Motor Behav.* **12**, 221–7.

Reid, G. and Montgomery, D.L. (1983). The effects of a physical fitness program on absenteeism from workshops by mentally retarded adults. Final Report to Fitness Canada.

Salvia, J. and Ysseldyke, J.E. (1978). *Assessment in Special and Remedial Education.* Boston: Houghton-Mifflin.

Sherborne, V. (1979). Movement and physical education. In Upton, G. (ed.), *Physical and Creative Activities for the Mentally Handicapped.* London: Cambridge University Press.

Sherrill, C. (1981). *Adapted Physical Education and Recreation*, 2nd edn. Dubuque, Iowa: W.C. Brown.

Shriver, E.K. (1983). Memo to Chapter/National Directors and Board Presidents. *Special Olympics Inc.*

Thelander, H.E. and Pryor, H.B. (1966). Abnormal patterns of growth and development in mongolism. *Clin. Ped.* **5**, 493–501.

Wade, M.G. and Davis, W. (1982). Motor skill development in young children: Current views of assessment and programming. *Cur. Top. Early Childh. Ed.* **4**, 55–70.

Wang, P. and Eichstaedt, C.B. (1980). *A Study of Physical Fitness Levels of Mentally Handicapped Children and Adolescents in Illinois.* Normal, Ill.: Illinois State University.

Watkinson, E.J. and Wall, A.E., (1979). *The PREP Play Program.* Edmonton, Alberta: Department of Physical Education, University of Alberta.

Watkinson, E.J., Wall, A.E., Shatz, D.M. and Castle, C. (1979). Final Report of the PREP Program field test project. Edmonton, Alberta: University of Alberta.

Wessel, J.A. (1983). Quality programming in physical education and recreation for all handicapped persons. In Eason, R.L., Smith, T.L. and Caron, F. (eds), *Adapted Physical Activity: From Theory to Application.* Champaign, Illinois: Human Kinetic.

13 Early Cognitive Development: Difference or Delay?

John R. Morss

INTRODUCTION

Every approach to education or intervention involves assumptions concerning the nature of the target population. These assumptions constitute a 'theory' of whichever special group is concerned. In the case of mental handicap, there are two broad kinds of theory available: the mentally handicapped person is held either to be basically *different* from the non-handicapped, or to be basically similar but developmentally delayed. In general, those who work with the adult mentally handicapped have agreed that the 'difference' assumption is more useful.

Now, it might be thought that if a 'difference' theory is valid for adulthood, then it must also be valid for childhood. However, it is a more commonly held view that the mentally handicapped child is not different, but merely delayed in development.* Clearly, there is a problem here: the theory of 'slow development' in childhood is not compatible with a 'difference' view of the adult. Further, the idea of slow development is unsatisfactory from a conceptual point of view (see Morss (1979) for a full discussion). But more important, perhaps, 'slow development' is unhelpful in the context of intervention. If taken at face value, it would imply that parents and educators merely *wait* for the child – not a very positive recommendation. There would, therefore, seem to be a need to look more carefully at what a 'difference' theory might mean for the Down's infant and young child.

Having rejected the concept of 'slow development', it might seem strange that this chapter is concerned with developmental change. But it is in the area of development that the question of difference *versus* delay is most important, and the two concepts most difficult to disentangle. It has often been assumed that delay is the only possible description for development in the mentally handicapped child. If the difference approach is to be taken seriously, however, this assumption must be re-examined. Certainly, the infant and child with Down's Syndrome can be expected to achieve 'milestones' in various areas of development later than the

---

*It is sometimes argued that the 'slow development' position does not apply to the 'organically impaired' such as Down's persons (Weisz *et al.*, 1982). However, 'slow development' is commonly held to apply to Down's Syndrome in children (e.g. Illingworth, 1980), and the specific extension of the theory to include this population has recently been urged (Cicchetti and Pogge-Hesse, 1982).

normal child (Carr, 1975). Summarising this pattern as 'slow development' explains nothing, however, unless one very specific view of development is adopted – that an individual's course of development is totally predetermined. If any role is granted to learning and experience, then 'slow development' cannot be considered meaningful.

Early studies of mental development in the Down's infant (e.g. Dicks-Mireaux, 1972) sometimes suggested that the course of development (in terms of mental age) was indeed predetermined. But findings on the results of intervention (e.g. Cunningham, 1979), as well as theoretical advances within psychology, have now shown that this view is no longer tenable. The course of development must be seen in terms of complex and changing interactions between the child and his environment, and such a conceptualisation makes it possible to investigate the nature and impact of handicaps in development.

The strongest tradition within developmental research on Down's infants has been broadly psychometric (see Chapter 10) but, despite its undoubted importance, this approach does have certain limitations. It tends to assume that a child's developmental status can meaningfully be expressed by a value on a single dimension. The most important alternative to the psychometric approach is that derived from the work of Jean Piaget. Piaget's theoretical position is extremely complex, and a vast amount of subsequent research has extended and refined his approach. Several aspects of the Piagetian approach should be emphasised. First, attention is not restricted to achievements; failures are of equal (if not greater) interest. Taken together, successes and errors are used to derive a broad picture of the response strategies currently available to the child. Second, an attempt is made to investigate developmental progression in related tasks. For this reason, tasks are specifically designed to test precise strategies and to look for specific kinds of error. In many ways, Piaget has presented an alternative method of conceptualising and investigating intelligence in childhood. Rather than looking for global comparisons with respect to a unitary scale of mental age, attention is focused on the growth of intelligent *action*. This is referred to as the cognitive–developmental approach.

Piaget's account of cognitive development in the child's early years is expressed in terms of 'sensorimotor intelligence'. This refers to the intelligent and purposive co-ordination of perception and action. For the normal child, the period of sensorimotor intelligence roughly corresponds with infancy (0–2 years). Piaget (1953) described general changes in sensorimotor intelligence in terms of six stages, conventionally referred to as Stages I–VI. Stage VI is the culmination of infancy and prepares for the emergence of the representational abilities of childhood (including language). Piaget (1955) further presented an account of development in specific areas of behaviour, according to the six stages. This latter account has been used by Uzgiris and Hunt (1975) to construct a set of scales for the assessment of sensorimotor intelligence.

Piaget gave prominence to one type of task, and much recent research has concentrated on this area. Quite simply, the tasks involve hiding an attractive toy and challenging the infant to retrieve it. Variation lies in the manner in which concealment is carried out. Piaget showed that the infant's growing understanding of the behaviour of physical objects could be traced by the successively more complex versions of the hiding task. Further, the kinds of error made by infants prior to achievement seemed to be consistent with their current successes on lower levels of the task. Piaget's explanation for development in this area is in terms of 'object permanence'. Without necessarily accepting Piaget's explanatory position, this term is useful for reference to these tasks.

Object permanence development is held to be central to infant cognitive development. Numerous suggestions have been made concerning relationships between object permanence and other areas of development, such as communicative and language development. For example, it has been argued that a certain level of object permanence is necessary for the emergence of language (Kahn, 1976; Moore and Meltzoff, 1978). Certainly, object permanence is a key area in sensorimotor development and hence is part of the foundation for subsequent cognitive development.

Little direct evidence is available on the nature of cognitive development in the Down's infant and young child. Some information can be derived from studies in which assessment of cognitive status was incorporated in a broader design. In general, however, assumptions have been made about Down's infants on the basis of research with heterogeneous groups of mentally handicapped children of varying degrees of handicap. This research, moreover, has rarely studied the longitudinal development of cognitive skills, typically giving single cross-sectional assessments only. Further, it has usually studied handicapped groups in isolation, without providing direct comparison with the non-handicapped. At best, comparison has been with the norms of standardisation samples. It should also be noted that several investigators (e.g. Woodward, 1979; Cicchetti and Pogge-Hesse, 1982; Weisz *et al.*, 1982) interpret their findings in terms of *similarities* between the mentally handicapped and the normal child. However, 'similarity' usually means that no differences have been observed – a finding which cannot provide strong evidence for any claim. For this reason, this article will concentrate on positive findings (or suggestions) of differences. Broadly descriptive accounts will be employed, and findings relating to the training of cognitive–developmental performance will be discussed in a later section.

Woodward (e.g. 1959, and summarised in 1979) categorised the behaviour of profoundly handicapped children (27% of whom had Down's Syndrome) into Piaget's six sensorimotor stages. (The early study of Inhelder (1968), Piaget's close collaborator, was concerned with later stages of cognitive development (especially conservation tasks) and with subjects of vastly differing age and aetiology (see Weisz *et al.*, 1982).) Woodward's studies have often been taken as providing strong evidence for straightforward 'slow development'. However, although stage congruence (agreement on stage placement) was 87% between object permanence and general sensorimotor intelligence, it was only 43% between 'problem solving' and 'circular reactions' (a measure based on object manipulation and hand movements). Woodward's (1959) strongest finding was an agreement between the order of difficulty of tasks across subjects and the stage reference of the tasks. However, it should be stressed that although some of the subjects were tested on several sessions, no longitudinal data were obtained. It also should be noted that Woodward has recently (1979) expressed reservations on the validity of categorising profoundly handicapped children or adolescents into sensorimotor stages.

Using the Uzgiris and Hunt (1975) instrument, it has been shown that the performance of the profoundly handicapped across the seven scales does not show the even profile observed in the normal infant (Gregory, 1973; MacPherson and Butterworth, 1981). Specifically, the area of imitation is observed to be depressed more than the other areas of sensorimotor intelligence. The independence of vocal imitation has been demonstrated with less severely handicapped children (Dunst *et al.*, 1981). Low intercorrelation between scores on the different scales has been observed in a number of studies. Kahn (1976) found that 90% of scale intercorrelations were below 0.7* for a group of severely and profoundly handicapped subjects of whom one-third were affected by Down's Syndrome. Rogers (1977) found levels of agreement on stage placement to vary between 10% and 58% (for severely and profoundly handicapped subjects of whom 10% were Down's). Dunst *et al.* (1981) describe scale interrelationships for a sample of 143 retarded infants, 20% of them Down's. Intercorrelations across scales were all low, means ranging from 0.28 to 0.41 for three different age groups. Mean stage congruence across scales was also low, varying from 28% to 40%. Dunst has recently carried out a similar study on interscale relationships in Down's Syndrome alone (Dunst and Rheingrover, 1983). By contrast, very high levels of agreement for scores on the different scales have been observed for normal infants. Uzgiris and Hunt (1975) reported intercorrelations averaging 0.87 and ranging from 0.80 to 0.93.

The finer analysis of performance on specific scales of the Uzgiris–Hunt instrument has also yielded differences with similar populations of children. Ordinality of items in a scale – the extent to which items rank consistently in order of difficulty across subjects – has been found to be low. Silverstein *et al.*, (1975), using the Uzgiris–Hunt and the similar Corman–Escalona scales, found that indices of consistency for all scales were well below the levels of around 0.9 found by Uzgiris and Hunt (1975) in a standardisation sample of normal infants. The sample of severely and profoundly handicapped children included those with Down's Syndrome as one of the most common subgroups. A similar finding was reported by the same authors in a subsequent study (Silverstein *et al.*, 1982).

The studies so far discussed have been basically cross-sectional. Wohlheuter and Sindberg (1975) observed object permanence development over a period of up to 1 year in a group of retarded children (of whom an undisclosed number were affected by Down's Syndrome). It was found that, of the children not reaching Stage VI on object permanence, only one-third demonstrated the steady progress associated with the normal infant's development. Another one-third demonstrated little progress over the period, and the remaining one-third showed extensive variability in performance. Further, frequent 'skipping' of stages was observed, a phenomenon not predicted for the normal infant. Finally, some evidence is available concerning structural aspects of sensorimotor intelligence specifically in Down's infants. Dunst *et al.* (1982) investigated structural relationships in performance on the Uzgiris–Hunt scales for a group of 48 Down's infants. Although not compared directly, evidence was presented to suggest that the nature of 'clustering' among

---

*Correlation measures the agreement between two scales with respect to the scores of individuals. Perfect positive correlation is equal to 1.0. A value of 0.7 indicates that less than half the variance on one scale is predicted by scores on the other scale (variance given by the square of the coefficient).

scales differed from that observed in normal infants. In another paper, Dunst and Rheingrover (1983) presented further information on relationships between scales. Correlations across scales are very low, with mean correlations of 0.23 and 0.29 for home-based and centre-based testing respectively. Stage congruence is again low, with means of 34% and 33% respectively. Overall, the authors comment that, in comparison with findings on normal infants, Down's infants demonstrate more variability with respect to stages of development.

These studies offer suggestive evidence that important differences might be anticipated in the fine detail of cognitive development in the Down's infant. Such differences might include poor consistency across different areas of sensorimotor development and a lower degree of hierarchical ordinality within scales. In general, cognitive structure and development might be expected to be less highly organised than is the case for the normal infant. The bulk of the evidence, at least in the form of suggestive findings from mentally handicapped children in general, points this way.

It should be noted that the performance of older Down's children has also been found to be less well organised than that of matched normal children (for example, on tests of perceptual judgement: see Stratford and Alban Metcalfe, 1983). Neither with infants nor with children is it being argued that fundamentally different *processes* are at work in Down's Syndrome. It is in the organisation, the structure of these processes – both in competence and in performance – that differences lie.

Descriptive studies have been limited in their usefulness by a number of factors. These include the use of 'single-shot' cross-sectional rather than longitudinal design, the absence of direct comparison with normal infants, and a lack of fine detail in the analysis of performance (typically restricted to scale scores). Further, the heterogeneity of samples is a limitation for the purposes of the student of Down's Syndrome. The study reported below attempted to overcome some of these limitations.

LONGITUDINAL STUDY OF OBJECT PERMANENCE DEVELOPMENT

The aim of the first set of studies was to follow, in detail, the course of object permanence development in a group of Down's infants and to make comparison with that of normal infants. (For a more technical account, see Morss, 1983.) Parents of Down's infants were invited to make regular visits to the laboratory, on which occasions a small group of tasks would be presented to the infant. Sessions would be recorded on video, and then transcribed in detail on to permanent records. Such records would include (as far as possible) the exact response of the infant to each trial (where a trial is the single concealment of an object). This detailed level of recording would be essential for subsequent comparison with equally detailed results for normal infants. It should be noted that a much more summary form of recording is more usual, even in cognitive–developmental research. A similar procedure was carried out with normal infants, except that, for practical reasons, data were yielded by a larger number of subjects over a shorter period of time.

The Down's group consisted of eight infants (six girls, two boys) aged from 12 to 22 months at the start of the study. The behavioural criterion used to select the eight subjects was that the infant should be capable of picking up a small object from a table-top. This criterion was necessary in order that results on the tasks could be meaningful. Hence, more severely handicapped infants were excluded from the study.

Normal infants were selected from a pool of infants whose parents had volunteered their participation in research studies. The group consisted of 26 infants (12 girls, 14 boys) selected for age such that at the start of the study a pair of infants represented each month of age from 9 to 21 months inclusive. No attempt was made to carry out extensive matching between the groups. What was of interest was performance on an identical set of tasks. Indeed, the procedure of matching mentally handicapped with normal children is extremely problematical. The assumption that it can be carried out with precision relies on the validity of mental age-type assessments.

Tasks involved the use of small, attractive toys and two kinds of occluder – white cardboard screens and white cardboard cups. Three kinds of task were employed. In describing them, emphasis will be placed on both the successful and erroneous strategies normally observed. In the first kind of task, an object was hidden on two successive occasions in one location (e.g. behind one of two screens) and the infant challenged to retrieve it. On a third trial, the object was hidden in a different location (behind the other screen). Success consists of retrieval of the object on all three occasions. It has been observed that the younger infant may, after successfully retrieving the object on the first two trials, erroneously search at this same location on the third trial. This is known as a 'place error' and cannot be attributed merely to memory processes. It seems to indicate a conviction on the infant's part that this location is where the object is to be found.

In the second kind of task, the object was concealed in one of two containers and the two containers transposed – thus, the object's location being changed. Success consists of direct search in the correct container. The characteristic error associated with failure consists of searching in the wrong container – that is, searching in the place where the object was seen to be concealed. It should be noted that such a strategy is *successful* for the previous task. This kind of relationship between what is successful at one level, but unsuccessful at another, is central to the Piagetian approach. Further, it should be stressed that this error is not just a single mistake; it may persist over a series of trials, with the object moving in alternate directions. It is therefore appropriate to describe such behaviour in terms of strategies of response.

In the third kind of task, an object was concealed in a cup and the cup was moved to a position behind one of two screens. The cup was then moved back to its original position, but leaving the object behind. The infant's task was first to carry out a search of the cup and to work out, having noted the object's absence, its new location. Success therefore involves what might be described as a kind of 'deduction'. The infant who has yet to achieve success should not be able to comprehend the object's absence from the cup. Considerable surprise may be shown, and no search to the screens should be carried out.

The three kinds of task were presented to each infant in each session. Initial analysis considered overall success or failure for a task within a session. More detailed analysis considered the kinds of errors observed for both groups. As might have been expected, the carrying out of this kind of research was found to be much more difficult with the Down's than with the normal infants. With occasional exceptions, it was not usually difficult to engage the attention of the normal infant sufficiently to encourage the infant to carry out a search. Further, such attention and motivation could usually be sustained over a number of trials of the same task. With the Down's infants (again with exceptions), attention was generally harder to gain and sustain. Many more trials had to be re-presented due to inattention on the part of the infant. Even in such general aspects of performance, then, clear differences could be observed between the two groups.

With respect to performance on the tasks, a first comparison was made between the ages of first achievement for each task. For all tasks, first achievement (age at which success was first recorded) was delayed, to a significant degree, in the Down's infants. Such a result would have been predicted from the known findings on delayed achievement in other areas of development. The overall sequence of achievement was not dissimilar between the two groups, but nothing conclusive can be stated on this point due to the small numbers involved and the relatively narrow range of tasks studied (Piaget's sensorimotor Stages IV–VI). Next, attention was focused on a less familiar aspect of achievement. It was decided to look at the extent to which success, once achieved, was repeated in subsequent sessions. For the Down's infants, success on a task in one session was repeated in the following session on an average 61% of occasions. That is, a successful achievement was reproduced in the next testing occasion only a little over half the time.

This finding has a number of implications. It suggests that a single, initial success on a task should not necessarily be given too much weight, or at least that it should be regarded with caution. At the same time, it should be noted that any single testing session can be expected to 'miss' certain of the infant's achievements (whatever status such achievements are given). The task of assessing the Down's infant is clearly a difficult one. In more theoretical terms, the finding suggests that achievements may not be well consolidated or integrated into the infant's response system. Clearly, any account of cognitive development in the Down's infant which considers first success only must be potentially misleading.

It might be expected that the normal infant should demonstrate perfect reliability. In fact, the value obtained for the normal infants was only 77%. This value, however, is significantly better than that for the Down's infant, and a definite difference has therefore emerged. (Uzgiris and Hunt (1975) found that stability of performance on all items of all seven scales averaged 78% over a period of 48 hours for their sample of normal infants.) In a sense, the normal infant is more like the 'ideal' (or 'textbook') infant than is the Down's infant. First success can, to a large extent, be taken as an index of solid achievement in the normal infant. As in other contexts, then (e.g. in IQ testing), the normal infant is 'easier' to assess.

Analysis was then carried out on errors for the various types of task. In general, a comparison was made between the two groups in terms of the proportions of errors which were of the 'characteristic' or predicted nature for the task. It should be stressed that comparison was not in terms of total numbers of errors, but in the relative frequency of those types observed. For the 'place error' tasks, the characteristic error consists of perseveration of search at the initial location following two correct retrievals there. Such perseveration should be indicated as 'strong' by a lack of self-initiated correction. The relative frequencies of such a strong error were 34% for the Down's infants, and 38% for the normal infants.

Although in the predicted direction, this difference is not statistically significant. It should be noted that the figure for normal infants is low for what is held to be a 'characteristic' error (similar levels have been noted by other workers) and a 'floor' effect might therefore have been operating. One important difference was that normal infants demonstrated a clear developmental progression within their error types, from an uncorrected error (no further search) to a spontaneously corrected error. These infants were clearly approaching success in a systematic manner. No such progression was observed in the Down's infants; the likelihood of correction remained constant over time.

For the 'switching' tasks, the characteristic error consists of the *consistent* search at the initial (pre-transposition) location. Here, this was defined as such a search on two successive trials, which must be in alternate directions (object starts left, then right, or vice versa). Relative frequencies were 30% for the Down's infants and 51% for the normal infants. Here, then, a clear difference emerged. If failing a task, the normal infant was more likely to commit the consistent, systematic error than was the Down's infant. This finding fits in with the observations on the 'place error' tasks. As noted above, the consistent error on the 'switching' task is an accompaniment of systematic success on the 'place error' task – searching at the place where an object was seen last. Errors on the part of the Down's infant were more likely to be *transitory* side preferences. These could not be accounted for by any observable handedness factors. Most important, consistent sequences of errors were not observed for the Down's infants. Although the minimal criterion was two successive errors, normal infants were observed carrying out up to four such erroneous searches, on alternating sides.

For the 'deduction' tasks, the characteristic error consists of 'stilling' following initial search of the (empty) cup. The requirement of such a search is important since it is the infant's response to the object's unexpected absence that is of interest. Average proportions for the characteristic error were 26% for the Down's infants and 58% for the normal infants. For the latter, initial search of the cup was often accompanied by signs of surprise and, following stilling, by a 'global search' of the immediate environment (e.g. under or behind the table). Such responses were rarely seen in the Down's infants, who were more likely to search at the incorrect screen or to play with the empty cup.

In general, then, results of error analysis supported the earlier findings. The Down's infants were less likely than the normal infants to conform to predicted patterns. Normal infants were more likely to manifest the kinds of error appropriate to their current cognitive–developmental status. Such errors may be considered in some sense conducive to subsequent developmental progress. They may be thought of as hypotheses which, having been successful in the past, are being 'tested out' on new tasks. The kinds of error observed in the Down's infant could not be described in this way. Such differences suggest that the whole process of cognitive development is less well organised in the Down's infant. The poor reliability of achievement would support this view.

Another apparent difference observed gives further support. For any task, various criteria might be chosen for a 'pass' (e.g. two or four consecutive successful trials; see Morss (1983) for the criteria used here). In general, the use of different 'levels' of success made little difference to classification of the normal infants. Once the infant had registered the lower level of success, the higher (more stringent) level could generally be assumed. Down's infants appeared more likely to demonstrate a delay between the achievement of lower and higher levels of success on a task. Again, the simple procedure of taking the first achievement of one level of success on a task is clearly inadequate. The choice of a lower level might in some sense overestimate the infant's status, while waiting for a higher level might in some sense underestimate it. In neither case could a normal and a Down's infant be said to be matched on the basis of a single achievement.

It was argued above that the poor reliability of success must represent an important characteristic of the developmental process in the Down's infant. It could be suggested, alternatively, that such instability of achievement might represent a more general feature of performance not specifically related to cognitive development. To test this, it was decided to make a brief study of the young Down's child who, at some 2 years or so older than the infant sample, might be expected to have thoroughly mastered the tasks appropriate to infancy. If the instability were a general feature of performance, then it should still be observed. Four Down's children, aged 3½–5 years, participated (none having been part of the previous study). The standard tasks were presented, and re-testing was carried out 1 week later. Almost perfect success on the tasks was observed on both sessions. Clearly, the poor reliability observed in the infant is an aspect of the acquisition phase of the task. It would be predicted that if tasks had been presented which were more appropriate to the young children's current status, then poor reliability would again have been observed. This feature might therefore be seen as a characteristic of the 'leading edge' of the child's cognitive development.

In drawing general implications from the findings, it should first be emphasised that the results discussed are for the Down's group as a whole. Considerable variation was observed within the group, but the overall trend was clear. Initial success in the Down's infant was less likely to indicate secure achievement, and the kinds of errors observed were less likely to be of the kind associated with systematic progress. The whole fabric of cognitive development therefore appears to differ from that of normal children. As suggested by various studies with mentally handicapped children in general, cognitive structure and development in the Down's infant appears to be less highly organised than is the case with the normal infant.* One important implication of this difference should now be discussed.

---

*Further research in this area is currently being undertaken by J. Wishart at the University of Edinburgh. Wishart is studying cognitive competence and performance in Down's infants of under 3 years, and is including developmentally earlier tasks than those used in the present study.

The accurate assessment of cognitive status in the Down's infant is a difficult procedure. A single testing session could not be expected to yield a valid picture. It could well include successes on items which the infant might subsequently fail, and it might yield failure on items which the infant had previously passed. These problems should be borne in mind in any use of clinical scales. It is, indeed, difficult to know how to *describe* the status of the Down's infant at any one time. The normal infant may be described in terms of 'stages', that is in terms of broad systems of response leading to consistent types of successes and errors, but the assumptions underlying the concept of stage do not seem to be valid in the case of the Down's infant.

A further point relating to assessment touches on the link between object permanence and language. At least one Down's infant was using appropriate single words during task performance before achieving success on the final (Stage VI) steps. This observation is consistent with the findings of Greenwald and Leonard (1979). Language use would thus not seem to require the complete conquest of object permanence, and it would certainly be a mistake to use such tasks as a test of 'readiness' for language. The relevant relationships between early cognitive development and the emergence of language still have to be defined. These relationships are clearly very complex in the Down's child, and the research message here must be one of caution.

Finally, the possible role of motivational factors should be mentioned. It could be suggested that the differences observed might be due to poor motivation on behalf of the Down's infants. Motivational factors could not, however, suffice to explain the findings. The kinds of errors in the 'deduction' task often consisted of search at the incorrect screen where the normal infant's error is cessation of search. More generally, motivation cannot be isolated from cognitive structure. This point is nicely made by Bower (1982, p. 254), who, in his summary of the present results, suggests that 'the simplest way to understand these fluctuations (in cognitive acquisition) is to assume normal cognitive rules, invested with less than normal confidence'.

ENHANCEMENT OF COGNITIVE–DEVELOPMENTAL PERFORMANCE

The kinds of differences described above suggest that the central problem of the Down's infant might relate to the *learning* processes involved in cognitive development, where his or her progress might be described as laborious. That is to say, the process by which cognitive skills are acquired may be less efficient than in the normal infant. There is a limit to what can be learned from merely following the 'spontaneous' course of development, and much more may often be learned from controlled attempts to induce change. Indeed, it might be argued that a focus on the capacity for change rather than on 'baseline' status should be the general policy for mental handicap research (Borkowski and Cavanaugh, 1979).

Most attempts to enhance the performance of mentally handicapped children have been based, even if loosely, on behaviour modification techniques, which are designed to work *directly* on desirable behaviour, and to shape behaviour towards selected goals. Procedures include prompting of the infant's response and involve especial attention to the extrinsic rewarding of correct responses. Training may involve the breaking down of tasks into component steps, and the gradation of versions of a task (e.g. employing various degrees of partial hiding of an object). Reference should be made to Cunningham (1979) for the clear description of a typical programme.

Some success has been reported using such direct approaches. Robinson (1974) demonstrated successful training of a version of the 'place error' task (successive concealment in different wells) by the use of a fading technique (successively closing the well covers). Immediate reinforcement was given for correct responses. Brassell and Dunst (1976, 1978) demonstrated the short-term effectiveness of direct training on object permanence tasks with a group of severely mentally handicapped children. However, no greater effect was found for a procedure involving small, systematic steps as compared with the straightforward practice of tasks. Further, a later post-test demonstrated no long-term effects of training in comparison with a control group. Kahn (1977) showed that intensive direct training of object permanence tasks led to marked improvement in performance in four severely handicapped children as compared to a control group. Training involved fading techniques and immediate reinforcement. Henry (1977) reported successful training of object permanence and imitation in a large sample of mentally retarded infants. Generalisation of training was also observed, with improvements on Uzgiris–Hunt scales for areas not directly trained. Kaiser (1978), however, failed to demonstrate the effectiveness of 'systematic instruction' on object permanence with a small sample of Down's infants. Procedures included reinforcement for successive approximations, cueing, fading, prompting and correction of errors.

The above studies all involved the direct training of task performance. Another study by the author, reported here, employed one kind of direct approach, and demonstrates some of the problems that all direct training may encounter. The study involved one subject only (a subject from the longitudinal study), but is presented because it illustrates some important limitations of direct training. The study was designed to improve the infant's performance on the 'switching' task, the standard version of which involves two cardboard cups. It has been shown that the use of *transparent* cups creates (at least initially) similar difficulties for the infant (see Bower, 1982). It was therefore intended to present the 'switching' task with transparent cups, for one direction of movement only, until perfect response was achieved for this direction. Testing would be carried out on both directions of transposition with the standard, opaque cups, and, it was posited, would constitute a valid presentation of the task.

Initial response to the left–right transposition of the transparent cup consisted of spontaneously corrected errors. For seven training trials, some degree of physical constraint was imposed to discourage the infant from picking up the left-hand cup. Finally, for three training trials without constraint, the correct response was made on the left–right transposition. The standard cups were then introduced, with testing being carried out alternately left–right and right–left. On all trials, initial response was to the right-hand cup, with errors being corrected. Finally, the object was concealed on two trials beneath the left-hand cup, with no transposition being carried out. On both occasions, response was made to the right-hand cup and then corrected.

Clearly, what training achieved was the creation of a strong preference for the infant's right. Performance on the standard version of the task was not improved. A substitution of preference took place as a result of the training programme. There would seem to be considerable drawbacks to the intensive training of a single response even (or especially) if such training is successful. In this case, the 'overlearned' response was wrongly applied to a much simpler task, a highly undesirable result. There is, clearly, considerable short-term plasticity in response, but inducing progressive change is by no means as easy. It should be noted here that Robinson (1974) showed that normally erroneous search strategies could be trained if reinforcement contingencies were appropriately controlled.

Even when successful, little is learned about the Down's infant from these direct procedures. Indirect methods, which avoid the training of specific responses, offer the possibility of yielding greater insight into the learning processes available to the Down's infant. Further, it would seem more satisfactory if training could leave the final step to the child himself. In this way, intervention works with the child as an active partner rather than as a passive recipient of training. The attempt reported next therefore employed an indirect training method.

To some extent, the simple left–right structure of the 'switching' task might have been especially vulnerable to the operation of side preferences (whether spontaneous or brought about by manipulation). It was therefore decided to employ the more complex 'deduction' task in the next attempt at an enhancement technique. Further, it was decided to devise a different kind of training method. The relative complexity of the 'deduction' task suggested that certain more simple but related tasks might be devised and that training could involve such simpler tasks. Ideally, these simpler tasks would already be within the infant's repertoire. In that case, the programme would involve practice on these tasks and testing on the standard version of the task.

Two simpler tasks ('steps') were devised. In the first, the cup was moved, with the object in it, to a position behind the screen but was then returned without leaving the object behind. In the second, the cup, with the object still in it, was left behind the screen. In both cases the infant was required to retrieve the object. It should be noted that both steps involve the object's being found in the cup, which might be thought to increase the infant's general expectation for this. In addition, the second should encourage attention to the trajectory of the cup. Both features would seem to be relevant to success in the standard task.

In the design of the training procedure, it was necessary to include trials of both the training steps and the standard task. As with the first attempt, however, it was important that training of the solution of the standard task did not take place. The answer was for both training steps to be presented with respect to the same side (e.g. the left-hand screen), and for a single trial of the standard task to be presented with respect to the *other* side (in this case, the right-hand screen). The two training steps could therefore be presented next on this new (right) side, and a second trial of the standard task then presented on the left. In this way, a sequence of trials could be presented which would include a valid set of trials of the standard task, separated by pairs of training steps.

Four Down's infants took part in an investigation of this programme. (For a more technical account, see Morss, 1984.) All had been subjects in the earlier longitudinal study, but had shown no success (or no recent success) in the 'deduction' task. Mean age was 25 months. The standard task was presented first, up to a maximum of four trials. The training sequence was then presented. All infants failed the pre-test. All succeeded in the training steps without special training being required. Three of the four infants passed at least two consecutive trials of the standard task within the sequence. These infants therefore reached the usual criterion of success in this task. The standard task, without intervening steps, was finally presented to two only of the infants (due to fatigue and inattention). Both had passed the task trials in the sequence. One passed the post-test. It should be stressed, however, that it was performance within the sequence that was the focus of interest.

Three of the four infants had demonstrated that, with the problem presented in a certain way, they could successfully solve the 'deduction' task. What seemed to have happened was that experience of the training steps – both, apparently, within their capabilities – made it possible for the solution of the 'deduction' task to be constructed. Clearly the close proximity of the training and the testing trials must be credited with an essential role here. Enhancement of performance was achieved by manipulation of the form of presentation, not by direct training.

Nine normal infants were presented with the same training sequence as the Down's infants. Seven, like the Down's infants, did not require training in the steps, but only one of these passed the trials of the standard task within the sequence. The restructuring of the task would not, therefore, seem to make it easier, or the single trials within the sequence invalid. For the normal infant, failure on the task is not readily overcome by the restructuring of task presentation. In a sense, failure, like success, is more 'solid' in the normal infant. Again, the Piagetian model of cognitive development – in which the infant at one stage is not readily moveable to a higher stage – seems much more appropriate to the normal than to the Down's infant.

To some extent, in that they were more able to take advantage of the restructuring, the Down's infants could be said to be superior to the normal infants. At the same time, the Down's infants would not have been in this situation if their developmental progress had not already been adversely affected. It is clearly not possible to make a global comparison between the two. This emphasises the misleading nature of a mental age-matching procedure, which would claim that the Down's infant is equivalent to the normal younger infant of a certain age. A matching procedure which attempts to 'control' for chronological age is fraught with problems.

It is now possible to discuss the results for the Down's infants in more detail. What seems to have occurred is that skills already in the infants' repertoire were harnessed in such a way that success on this task could be constructed. At the same time, the achievement was of a very limited kind. Only two of the infants were presented with a post-test of the standard task, and only one of these registered a pass. This does not suggest that permanent achievement of the task is likely to be attained through this procedure. Indeed, results of the earlier study make it clear that single successes must not be given too much weight. What was demonstrated by the Down's infants' success here was that they were, in some sense, capable of passing the task prior to 'spontaneous' achievement. Questions might therefore be asked about why such achievement had not yet been attained. The answers must involve the nature of the learning process in the Down's infant. One aspect of this might be that competence does not crystallise out into performance as readily as in the normal infant. The Down's infant seems especially sensitive to the presentation structure of tasks. And this conclusion is consistent with the need for 'structured' approaches to teaching generally acknowledged for the school-age and older Down's child. In many ways, the systematic nature of the *normal* infant's approach to cognitive development consists of the infant imposing order on his environment. The Down's infant seems much less well equipped to structure his own learning environment in this way, and, in general, therefore, seems to require the deliberate structuring of this environment by the parent or educator.

DISCUSSION

The general conclusion is that the cognitive development of the Down's infant must be thought of as different, in important respects, from that in the normal infant. Differences have been emphasised here since previous studies have focused almost exclusively on similarities in the nature of development. Attention must, however, be devoted to both similarities *and* differences if an accurate picture is to be arrived at. With respect to similarities, it should be stressed that many aspects of developmental change must be the same for both Down's and normal infants. Similar achievements are required, and many gross features of development towards such achievements will apply equally to both populations. In general, then, the order of emergence of 'milestones' or 'stages' may be expected to be similar (but *not* necessarily identical) in the Down's infant. Similarity at this level of analysis does not preclude differences in the underlying structure and processes of development. The model being presented here might therefore be termed a 'developmental difference' theory (Morss, 1979).

The 'developmental difference' theory proposes that, in the mentally handicapped, there are important differences in the processes underlying developmental change, which give rise to inefficiency in developmental progress. Outcomes include the late emergence of critical achievements as well as more fine-grained effects. Differences are therefore expressed within development and cannot be comprehended except within a developmental context. In opposition to what is usually termed the 'developmental' theory, this approach argues that 'slow development' cannot be considered as explanatory but must itself be considered a phenomenon in need of explanation. Moreover, in opposition to the orthodox 'difference' theory, this approach focuses attention on developmental processes and accepts that many similarities must hold at a molar level of developmental analysis. This model is consistent with an epigenetic, differentiation approach to development (Bower, 1979), and the differences proposed might be conceptualised in terms of quite high-level rules for controlling behaviour.

The conclusion that early cognitive development in the Down's infant must be considered as different, in certain respects, is consistent with the findings and indications summarised in the introductory section. It is also consistent with other developmental findings on Down's infants. Differences have been observed with respect to (for example) the intensity of affective expression (Cicchetti and Sroufe, 1976; Emde *et al.*, 1978; Freudenberg *et al.*, 1978), the strength of attachment behaviour (Serafica and Cicchetti, 1976), the nature of mother–infant interaction (Jones, 1977), and the development of symbolic play (Hill and McCune-Nicolich, 1981). Such differences go beyond the late emergence of developmental 'milestones'. At the same time, they are differences of degree rather than absolute deficits. The impact of such differences must be established within a developmental framework. The concept of 'developmental difference' might therefore be seen as of general relevance to the early years of the Down's child.

The research reported in this chapter has shown that there are theoretical, as well as pragmatic, limitations to purely descriptive studies of Down's children. Accounts of the 'natural' or 'spontaneous' course of development can yield only approximate indications of underlying processes. Manipulative research offers the possibility of getting closer to these processes. In parallel, more attention should be directed to relevant aspects of learning in the Down's child. Learning research with the mentally handicapped has tended to focus on the limited area of conditioning processes, but kinds of learning with greater relevance for the acquisition of developmental skills should be investigated. Several of the differences identified in the current research could be formulated in terms of learning. Problems of inadequate response strategies, and of the inadequate consolidation or maintenance of acquired skills, are of general concern to students of mental handicap (see Borkowski and Cavanaugh, 1979). Research should attempt some cross-fertilisation between the findings of developmental investigation and the study of strategic functioning in the mentally handicapped. The role of instruction is, for example, a central concern of the latter.

Care has been taken in this chapter to separate research aims from intervention aims. Research is directed towards the long-term improvement of our understanding of the nature of the handicap associated with Down's Syndrome. It has been argued above that manipulation – e.g. training or acceleration – is an especially important research tool with the mentally handicapped child, and clearly such an approach also yields information directly relevant to the design of intervention techniques.

To conclude this chapter, general implications for intervention will be summarised, and the difficulty of accurately assessing cognitive functioning in the Down's child should be re-emphasised. Categorisation into a well-defined 'stage' is hazardous, and single achievements can carry little weight as indicators of more general levels of development. To this extent, the kind of detailed behavioural assessment included in Portage-type schemes would seem essential. At the same time, it should not be assumed that training must inevitably consist of the reinforcement of specific responses. Whatever learning competence is available to the child should be exploited to the maximum. Although not discussed in this chapter, such exploitation would also involve the optimising of motivational characteristics of the learning situation.

More generally, intervention cannot hope to be successful without a precise picture of the differences presented by the child with Down's Syndrome. The statement that the child is 'developing slowly' is at best unhelpful and at worst seriously misleading. It suggests an inevitable and predetermined developmental outcome. If, instead, the child's problems are due (albeit cumulatively) to ongoing factors – limitations, for example, on the extent to which the child can learn spontaneously from his environment – then intervention becomes possible. The Down's child, it appears, is less able than his non-handicapped peer to generate his own learning environment. His developmental progress requires more support. The aim of research should be to establish the precise nature of the support required, and the conditions under which such support may be minimised.

ACKNOWLEDGEMENTS

The research reported here received financial support from the Medical Research Council (UK) (Grant No. G972/186/N). I would like to express my grateful thanks to the parents and children who participated in the studies. I am especially grateful for the help and encouragement of the Down's Children's Association (West of Scotland) – now the Scottish Down's Syndrome Association – and Aid for Down's Babies, Edinburgh. This chapter is dedicated to the memory of A.L.M. and of A.L.

REFERENCES

Borkowski, J. and Cavanaugh, J. (1979). Maintenance and generalization of skills and strategies by the retarded. In Ellis, N. (ed.), *Handbook of Mental Deficiency. Psychological Theory and Research*, 2nd edn. Hillsdale, NJ: L. Erlbaum.

Bower, T.G.R. (1979). *Human Development*. San Francisco: W.H. Freeman.

Bower, T.G.R. (1982). *Development in Infancy*, 2nd edn. San Francisco: W.H. Freeman.

Brassell, W. and Dunst, C.J. (1976). Comparison of two procedures for fostering the development of the object construct. *Am. J. Ment. Defic.* **80**, 523–8.

Brassell, W. and Dunst, C.J. (1978). Fostering the object construct: large-scale intervention with handicapped infants. *Am. J. Ment. Defic.* **82**, 507–510.

Carr, J. (1975). *Young Children with Down's Syndrome*. London: Butterworth.

Cicchetti, D. and Pogge-Hesse, P. (1982). Possible contributions of the study of organically retarded persons to developmental theory. In Zigler, E. and Balla, D. (eds), *Mental Retardation: The Developmental-Difference Controversy*. Hillsdale, NJ: L. Erlbaum.

Cicchetti, D. and Sroufe, L.A. (1976). The relationship between affective and cognitive development in Down Syndrome infants. *Child Dev.* **47**, 920–29.

Cunningham, C. (1979). Early stimulation of the severely handicapped child. In Craft, M. (ed.), *Tredgold's Mental Retardation*, 12th edn. London: Baillière Tindall.

Dicks-Mireaux (1972). Mental development of infants with Down's Syndrome. *Am. J. Ment. Defic.* **77**, 26–32.

Dunst, C., Brassell, W. and Rheingrover, R. (1981). Structural and organisational features of sensorimotor intelligence among retarded infants and toddlers. *Br. J. Educ. Psychol.* **51**, 133–43.

Dunst, C., Gallagher, J. and Vance, S. (1982). *Developmental Characteristics of Sensorimotor Intelligence Among Mentally Retarded Infants: Preliminary Findings.* Paper presented to Gatlinburg Conference on Research in Mental Retardation, Gatlinburg, Tennessee, USA.

Dunst, C. and Rheingrover, R. (1983). Structural characteristics of sensorimotor development among Down's Syndrome infants. *J. Ment. Defic. Res.* **27**, 11–22.

Emde, R., Katz, E. and Thorpe, J. (1978). Emotional expression in infancy: II Early deviations in Down's Syndrome. In Lewis, M. and Rosenblum, L. (eds), *The Development of Affect.* New York: Plenum Press.

Freudenberg, R., Driscoll, J. and Stern, G. (1978). Reactions of adult humans to cries of normal and abnormal infants. *Inf. Beh. & Dev.* **1**, 224–7.

Greenwald, C. and Leonard, L. (1979). Communicative and sensorimotor development of Down's Syndrome children. *Am. J. Ment. Defic.* **84**, 296–303.

Gregory, O. (1973). *The Use of Piagetian Assessment Techniques in the Assessment of Profoundly Retarded Children.* Paper presented to Third International Congress of I.A.S.S.M.D., The Hague.

Henry, J. (1977). The effects of parent assessment and parent training of preschool mentally retarded children on Piagetian tasks of object permanence and imitation. Unpublished Dissertation, Temple University, USA.

Hill, P. and McCune-Nicolich, L. (1981). Pretend play and patterns of cognition in Down's Syndrome children. *Child Dev.* **52**, 611–17.

Illingworth, R. (1980). *Development of the Infant and Young Child: Abnormal and Normal,* 7th edn. London: Churchill Livingstone.

Inhelder, B. (1968). *The Diagnosis of Reasoning in the Mentally Retarded.* New York: John Day. (Originally published 1943.)

Jones, O. (1977). Mother–child interaction with pre-linguistic Down's Syndrome and normal infants. In Schaffer, H.R. (ed.), *Studies in Mother–Infant Interaction.* London: Academic Press.

Kahn, J. (1976). Utility of the Uzgiris and Hunt scales of sensorimotor development with severely and profoundly retarded children. *Am. J. Ment. Defic.* **80**, 663–5.

Kahn, J. (1977). Piaget's theory of cognitive development and its relationship to severely and profoundly retarded children. In Mittler, P. (ed.), *Research to Practice in Mental Retardation,* Vol II. Baltimore: University Park Press.

Kaiser, C. (1978). Acceleration of object concept development in Down's Syndrome children aged one through three: A study in infant learning. Unpublished PhD Thesis, University of Washington, USA.

MacPherson, F. and Butterworth, G. (1981). *Application of a Piagetian Infant Development Scale to the Assessment of Profoundly Mentally Handicapped Children.* Paper presented to Annual Conference, Brit. Psychol. Soc. (Developmental Psychology Section), Manchester.

Moore, M.K. and Meltzoff, A. (1978). Object permanence, imitation and language development in infancy. In Minifie, F. and Lloyd, L. (eds), *Communicative and Cognitive Abilities – Early Behavioral Assessment.* Baltimore: University Park Press.

Morss, J.R. (1979). A comparative study of the cognitive development of the infant with Down's Syndrome and the normal infant. Unpublished PhD Thesis, University of Edinburgh.

Morss, J.R. (1983). Cognitive development in the Down's Syndrome infant: Slow or different? *Br. J. Educ. Psychol.* **53**, 40–47.

Morss, J.R. (1984). Enhancement of object-permanence performance in the Down's Syndrome infant. *Child: Care, Health and Development* **10**, 39–47.

Piaget, J. (1953). *The Origin of Intelligence in the Child.* London: Routledge and Kegan Paul. (First published 1936.)

Piaget, J. (1955). *The Construction of Reality in the Child.* London: Routledge and Kegan Paul. (First published 1937.)

Robinson, C. (1974). Error patterns in Level 4 and Level 5 object permanence training. *Am. J. Ment. Defic.* **78**, 389–96.

Rogers, S. (1977). Characteristics of the cognitive development of profoundly retarded children. *Child Dev.* **48**, 837–43.

Serafica, F. and Cicchetti, D. (1976). Down's Syndrome children in a strange situation: Attachment and exploratory behaviors. *Merrill-Palmer Quarterly* **22**, 137–50.

Silverstein, A., Brownlee, L., Hubbell, M. and McLain, R. (1975). Comparison of two sets of Piagetian scales with severely and profoundly retarded children. *Am. J. Ment. Defic.* **80**, 292–7.

Silverstein, A., Pearson, L., Keller, M. and McLain, R. (1982). A test of the similar sequence hypothesis. *Am. J. Ment. Defic.* **86**, 551–3.

Stratford, B. and Alban Metcalfe, J. (1983). *Development of Size Judgement Ability among Down Syndrome and Normal Children.* Paper presented to Seventh Biennial Meetings, International Society for the Study of Behavioural Development, University of Munich, FRG. Published on microfilm: ERIC ED 238 949.

Uzgiris, I. and Hunt, J. McV. (1975). *Assessment in Infancy: Ordinal Scales of Psychological Development.* Urbana: University of Illinois Press.

Weisz, J., Yeates, J. and Zigler, E. (1982). Piagetian evidence and the developmental–difference controversy. In Zigler, E. and Balla, D. (eds), *Mental Retardation: The Developmental–Difference Controversy.* Hillsdale, NJ: L. Erlbaum.

Wohlheuter, M. and Sindberg, R. (1975). Longitudinal development of object permanence in mentally retarded children. *Am. J. Ment. Defic.* **79**, 513–18.

Woodward, M. (1959). The behaviour of idiots interpreted by Piaget's theory of sensorimotor development. *Br. J. Educ. Psychol.* **29**, 60–71.

Woodward, M. (1979). Piaget's theory and the study of mental retardation. In Ellis, N. (ed.), *Handbook of Mental Deficiency. Psychological Theory and Research,* 2nd edn. Hillsdale, NJ: L. Erlbaum.

14 Speech and Language

Pat Gunn

'Because of my tongue, it's usually thick. It's very hard for my speech to come through clearly...sometimes it's stuck and I can mumble. People don't understand me.' explained David, the Down's Syndrome teenager in the 'Man Alive' television programme (Canadian Broadcasting Commission, 1979). David's description coincides with that by Langdon Down, a hundred years earlier, who reported 'thick and indistinct' speech as characteristic of the syndrome. Yet it would be premature to conclude from this that an accurate description of Down's Syndrome speech has been available for more than a century. It seems rather that agreement is restricted to 'the clinically obvious' (Gibson, 1978), and there is still some confusion about the characteristics and correlates of both speech and language for Down's Syndrome.

Part of this uncertainty is caused by the wide variability in the syndrome, part by limitations of some early studies, and part by the state of flux in our present knowledge of how language develops. Syndrome variability is reflected in cognitive development (LaVeck and Brehm, 1978; Rynders, 1982), in motor development, and in the extent and type of secondary impairment (Gibson, 1978). Moreover, like others, Down's children and adults are subject to a range of environmental opportunities, and interactions with these opportunities are influenced by diverse motivational and temperamental attributes (Gunn *et al.*, 1981; Bridges and Cicchetti, 1982).

If the current trend to regard language as developing within an interactive context is accepted, these many sources of variance imply that the course of language development will not follow the same immutable path for all with Down's Syndrome. To some extent this is reflected in the wide range of ages commonly reported for speech milestones, for example the first word from 6 to 84 months and the first sentence from 17 to 132 months (Melyn and White, 1973). Similarly, language attainments are reported as varying from mutism (Buddenhagen, 1971) to a proficient writing level (Seagoe, 1965).

At present, the factors which have contributed most to these reports of variability have not been identified. Rynders (1982) has criticised the inadequacies of past research concerning the lack of information about karyotyping, sex, residence and the basis for subject selection. In the light of such basic deficiencies, it may seem extravagant to suggest that other subject characteristics such as hearing status, thyroid function, vocal anatomy and additional organic impairment are also relevant to language and speech research. Given that most syndrome-specific

260

studies are limited by small sample size, the results would be more informative if the effect of these relevant subject characteristics could be controlled.

One longitudinal study of Down's Syndrome, which included biomedical data, has reported that muscle tone was a 'powerful' predictor of language development at 36 months (Reed *et al.*, 1980). Since there is now greater knowledge of the specific health care needs for the syndrome, it is hoped that variability introduced by such factors as hypotonia are at a minimum in the more recent research studies reviewed in this chapter.

COMMUNICATION DURING INFANCY

Considerable interest has recently been shown in the pre-speech period as the precursor to spoken language. This interest is fostered by the recognition that language is a system for coding a communication and that language development takes place in a social context. With this perspective, speech is seen primarily as a vocal–motor method of expressing a language. The child's first words are not necessarily the child's first attempts to express the language and they are not the first acts of communication.

Since the most salient and regular communications for the baby and toddler are likely to be with mother, many studies have focused on mother–child interaction. It has been suggested that these interactions expose the child to the speech of the culture, to the conversational conventions for turn-taking and pausing, and to the meaning and function of certain acts, objects and events (Stern, 1977). Although some research has argued that the rudiments of intentional behaviour are reflected in early infant communications (Trevarthen, 1977), other studies have attributed the apparent turn-taking role to the mother's skill in monitoring her infant's behaviour (Schaffer, 1977; Hayes, 1978; Kaye and Fogel, 1980). Mothers watch their babies almost continuously during a one-to-one interaction so that the probability of eye-to-eye contact is enhanced and their skill in filling in the gaps between the infant's vocalisations creates the impression of conversation. Moreover, according to Bruner (1975), a mother's response to her infant's signals (looking, vocalising, smiling, etc.) invests these behaviours with purpose. They are treated as intentional requests for action or information, and it is presumed to be within this context that the child learns to communicate intentionally and to 'crack the linguistic code'.

Certain differences have been observed between mother–infant interactions in which the infant has Down's Syndrome and those in which the infant is not developmentally delayed. The Down's baby is reported to be delayed in vocalisation, eye contact, and smiling (Emde and Brown, 1978; Berger and Cunningham, 1981), with emotional expression dampened in intensity (Cytryn, 1975; Cicchetti and Sroufe, 1976; Emde *et al.*, 1978; Sorce and Emde, 1982).

It has also been suggested that the vocal exchanges during mother–infant interaction show less turn-taking for Down's Syndrome dyads. There are more occasions when the partners vocalise together (Jones, 1977; Berger and Cunningham, 1983). An alternating pattern in vocalisation was seen by these researchers as a forerunner to conversation, but co-vocalisation is important too, since it often occurs at times of high mutual involvement (Stern, 1977; Thoman, 1981).

In addition to vocalising behaviour, looking patterns are also significant for communicative interactions (Gunn *et al.*, 1979). Although very young infants selectively attend to faces, by about 6 months of age they normally show increased interest in objects and events in the wider environment. It is believed that this interest leads to comment by the mother and to the development of the child's verbal reference and looking referential skills. Berger and Cunningham (1981) have reported delays in the onset of eye contact, and a number of studies have reported that Down's babies show less referential looking (Jones, 1977; Dunst, 1979; Gunn *et al.*, 1982). At 6 months of age, the control group in the Gunn *et al.* study were looking around the room for 74% of the interaction time. By contrast, the Down's children at both 6 months and 9 months of age spent almost 50% of the time looking at their mothers' faces. This difference could not be attributed to differences in the mothers' behaviours. It may, however, be related to the finding from studies which suggest that Down's infants fixate longer and show less response to novelty, because of a slow development of competing responses (Miranda and Fantz, 1974), a deficit in the arousal system (Cicchetti and Sroufe, 1976), or an impaired ability to habituate to a stimulus (Barnet *et al.*, 1971; Cohen, 1981).

Similarly, Krakow and Kopp (1982) reported different patterns of visual attention for older Down's infants (mean development age = 17 months), with less time spent in social activity than normally developing children of the same mental age.

It is also pertinent to relate these early interactions to affective development. Not only do the interactions play an important role in the development of the child's communication skills, but they also contribute to the development of attachment (Emde and Brown, 1978; Stone and Chesney, 1978). In spite of the differences which have been reported for interactions involving Down's babies, research studies have suggested that most Down's infants proceed through the normal stages of attachment but at a slower rate (Blacher and Meyers, 1983). One implication is that mothers adapt their expectations and methods of interaction to the child's mode of functioning. For instance, a mother may work harder to find the level of stimulation which will make the baby smile. The smile is rewarding and the interaction continues so that it is enjoyable for both participants.

MATERNAL LANGUAGE

A similar adaptation has been reported from research which has been concerned with the characteristics of a mother's speech to her child. Mothers appear to match their speech to the capabilities of the child, and many different aspects are modified. Even to children who are developing with no known delay, sentences are shorter, syntax is simple, intonation is marked, and there is much repetition (Broen, 1972; Snow, 1977; Cross, 1978).

These interactions, however, are not usually intended as language development lessons. Newport *et al.* (1977) concluded that they were intended to control the child's behaviour 'right now', while Snow (1977) suggested that the mother's intention was to maintain a 'conversation'. Nevertheless, the mother's language does seem to be related to some aspects of the child's language development. On a coarse scale, 'more language input from adults is related to more and better language in children' (Bates *et al.*, 1982). On a more precise scale, directive or intrusive aspects of a mother's language seem to influence the child's first words (Nelson, 1973) and, later, aspects of her questioning seem to influence the child's acquisition of syntactic elements (Newport *et al.*, 1977). The child, however, plays an active role in this process. Newport *et al.* suggested that children pay selective attention to certain parts of the language input (for example, initial words and items which are clearly co-ordinated with what is being pointed to or looked at). At the same time, these authors suggested, learning depends 'on what the children are disposed to notice in that environment, on their strategies of listening and on the hypotheses they are prepared to entertain'.

Most research in maternal language has been directed to children who are not delayed in development, but there are a few studies of Down's children. Buium *et al.* (1974) compared Down's children of 2 years chronological age (CA) with non-retarded children of the same age. Certain features of maternal language were found to be different for the two groups of children: the Down's children were exposed to shorter, frequent utterances with more incomplete and imperative sentences. Rondal (1977), however, criticised the chronological age matching and demonstrated that when normally developing children (20–32 months of age) were matched with Down's children (3–12 years of age) according to their mean length of utterance (MLU), there were no significant differences in maternal speech. Confirmation of this result was obtained in two similar studies of younger Down's children, mean CA = 20 months (Cook and Culp, 1981) and mean CA = 38 months (O'Kelly-Collard, 1978).

Another investigation which suggested that mothers adapt their language to the linguistic capabilities of their Down's children was undertaken by Petersen and Sherrod (1982). This study found significant differences between the language addressed by mothers to high MLU children and that to low MLU children. On the other hand, maternal MLU for 9-month-old Down's infants was found by Buckhalt *et al.* (1978) to be the same as that reported by Buium *et al.* for 24-month-old children. Buckhalt *et al.* proposed that maternal speech does not increase in complexity during this 9 to 24 month period. It was inferred that a certain level of child language competence is required before such an increase can take place. A longitudinal study of one Down's boy from 3 to 17 months of age (Gunn *et al.*, 1980), however, suggested that MLU may be an unsuitable characteristic for measuring the changes in a mother's speech to her young baby. The mother of the child in this study did appear to adapt her speech to the developmental level of her child. This adaptation was not reflected so much in maternal MLU as in characteristics such as 'reference to objects' and 'testing–teaching' strategies. Both these characteristics may have important implications for the child's language and conceptual development.

PRE-SPEECH VOCALISATION AND GESTURE

A further area of research which has been concerned with the sequence of development from pre-speech to speech has concentrated on the nature of the infant's vocalisations. In the past, it has been assumed that these vocalisations are not related to the sounds of the adult system (Lennenberg, 1964). More recently, however, some elements of infant vocalisation which seem to be related to the phonology of speech have been outlined (Carter, 1979; Stark, 1979), and observations suggest that the sound patterns of the pre-speech period may have some significance for later speech development.

Very few descriptions of these patterns for Down's infants are available. When Dodd (1972) compared the babbling patterns of ten normally developing infants with ten Down's infants, she measured frequency, length of utterances, and the variety of vowels and consonants. There were no significant differences between the groups on these measures.

Smith and Oller (1981) suggested an extension of this study and they recorded the vocalisation of 19 infants (9 Down's) on a longitudinal basis. They found that the onset of reduplicated babbling, age trends for place of consonant articulation, and age changes in vowel quality were substantially the same for both normally developing and Down's infants. The mean onset of reduplication was 8.4 months for Down's, 7.9 months for the control group; the shift in consonant production from velar to alveolar was approximately 6 months for both groups; there were few back vowels, and high vowels tended to be less frequent than mid or low vowels for both groups of children. These authors noted, like Dodd, that motor skill deficits had not caused a significant delay or alteration to the babbling patterns. They suggested, however, that a more extensive phonetic analysis and an analysis of the functional use of those vocalisations would be valuable. Halliday (1975) described a number of different functions in the pre-speech vocalisations of his son, but no similar analysis is available for a Down's child.

The meaning and function of the child's pre-speech acts and gestures, however, have been investigated to determine if these reflect a continuity from the pre-speech period to the first word. Greenwald and Leonard (1979) compared the communicative development of 15 Down's children (CA 10–26 months; IQ 37–79) with that of 20 other children at the same sensorimotor stage of development (CA 7–13 months; IQ 97–144). Communicative development was measured in terms of looking, reaching, pointing, showing, or vocalising acts, and the children were at either Stage 4 or Stage 5 of sensorimotor development. It was found that the Down's children used more gestures and fewer vocalisations than the other group, but that the level of communication for each group was associated with sensorimotor stage. A later study confirmed the specific delay in spoken language (Mahoney *et al.*, 1981).

FIRST WORDS

The age at which the first word is spoken reflects marked individual differences, even in children who are developing normally. There are also differences in the type of words first acquired by individual children. These differences have been described in terms of categories which either 'refer' to objects or 'express' social knowledge (Nelson, 1973), or in terms of 'code-oriented' versus 'message-oriented' speech styles (Dore, 1975). The distinction is between children who tend to use their first words to refer to objects ('car', 'ball') and those who tend to use words for social interaction ('no', 'bye-bye'). Nelson proposed that these different categories arose from an interaction between the child's mode of functioning and the mother's language style and responsiveness. A similar analysis for Down's children has not been reported but it may be expected that they too show individual styles in using their first words.

With the acquisition of more words, it is the similarities in expressions which become notable. With single word utterances and two-word combinations, children 'talk about objects; the fact that objects exist, disappear, and recur; they talk about actions; the fact that persons move and act on objects; and they talk about locations...' (Bloom *et al.*, 1981). The correspondence with sensorimotor intelligence and the child's own activities is accentuated by this description and reflects the focus of many studies which have been concerned with the relationship between these early expressions and sensorimotor development. A handful of these studies has been concerned with Down's children.

Palermo-Piastra (1981) reported that four Down's children progressed in language skills through Stages 4 to 6 of the sensorimotor period with a variety of semantic categories being expressed at Stage 6. Coggins (1979) found that the two-word utterances of four Down's children (CA 3:10–6:3 years) expressed essentially the same basic relationships reported for normal language development: 'Down's children talk about immediate space and practical action in much the same way as do children developing language normally.' Similarly, Michaelis (1977) reported that the action relationships appeared in the language of a 6-year-old Down's girl. There were, however, fewer relationships and fewer morphemes than expected for her MLU level (MLU = 3.47). Broffman (1981) also reported a delay in morpheme development (-s, -ed, -ing, etc.), but the position of the morphemes in an utterance followed normal rules.

There has also been some consideration of the role of imitation in acquiring new words and the combinations which embody basic semantic relationships. Bloom *et al.* (1974) argued that children selectively imitate and that this imitation helps the child to learn either new words or new grammatical constructions. They provided evidence of a development shift from imitative to spontaneous use of words and constructions.

Coggins and Morrison (1981) investigated the unprompted imitations of four Down's children (CA 3:10–6:3 years; MLU 1.22–2.06). They reported that these children imitated different words from those they used in spontaneous speech. It was suggested that this evidence of selective imitation indicates that Down's children are similar to children whose language is developing normally. It was proposed that they, too, imitate utterances which are not yet stabilised in spontaneous speech but which they are in the process of learning. Since the study was not longitudinal, the hypothesis that a significant proportion of the imitations would occur later in spontaneous speech was not tested.

Another approach to the characteristics of spontaneous imitation was under-taken by Rondal (1980). He compared a group of Down's children with a group of non-retarded children who were matched on three MLU levels (1.00–1.50, 1.75–2.25, and 2.50–3.00 morphemes). There were significant differences in the frequency and type of imitation at different language levels, but the majority of comparisons showed no difference between the Down's children and their matched counterparts.

SENTENCE DEVELOPMENT

During the early stages of language acquisition, the child's understanding of language and the interpretation of the child's speech depend heavily upon the supporting context. Children with limited comprehension skills need context, movement and gesture to support the speech addressed to them (Chapman, 1981). Similarly, an observer needs the help of context clues to decipher the meaning of the child's words. Does 'kick' refer to the child, a picture, a moth, turtles on TV, or a ball (Bowerman, 1976)?

The next stage in the sequence of language development is characterised by a decreased reliance on context and by the mastery of the rules which govern sentence construction. The mastery of these rules by Down's children has been investigated by analysing their spontaneous speech and by measuring their performance on structured tasks.

Andrews and Andrews (1977) investigated the spontaneous language of 39 Down's children (CA 5:8–17:9 years; IQ 31–60) during the school day. They reported that, with increasing age, the proportion of utterances which were grammatical sentences also increased. A decrease in the actual number of spontaneous utterances was observed for the older children but this probably reflected school practice rather than child ability. At 5–7 years of age, there were more one-word utterances than sentences; by 11–13 years, more grammatical sentences than either one- or two-word utterances were recorded. A similar rise in language expression with age has also been reported by Evans (1976, 1977) for an age range from 8 to 31 years and by Smith and Phillips (1981) for children at ESN schools (CA 7:0–13:0 years).

Other research studies have compared the spontaneous language of Down's children with that of normally developing children of equivalent mental age. Wiegel-Crump (1981) reported that the Down's children in her study (CA 6:0–12:7 years; MA 2:0–6:11 years) used lower level syntax with limited variety in their syntactic structures. Layton and Sharifi (1978) found that their Down's group (CA 7:4–12:2 years; MA 3:2–5:9 years) used qualitatively similar structures to a comparison group (CA 2:10–5:4 years; MA 3:6–4:11 years), but the Down's children were less consistent. They seemed not to have fully stabilised some of the structures in their spontaneous speech. Ryan (1975) noted that the Down's children in her study were similar in performance to handicapped children of comparable CA and MA (CA 5:0–9:0 years; MA 2:6–3:6 years) but they had a better noun vocabulary and used less complex grammar than normally developing children of the same mental age.

Sentence imitation tasks have been used by a number of researchers to determine mastery of grammatical rules. Semmel and Dolley (1971) reported that the errors made by Down's children (CA 6:0–14:0 years; IQ 22–62) reflected the complexity of the grammar. Declarative sentences were imitated correctly but errors were made on sentences with optional transformations (e.g. passives or negatives). Gordon and Panagos (1976) compared a low mental age Down's group (CA 6:8–19:0 years; MA 3:2–3:11 years) with a high mental age Down's group (CA 10:4–17:1 years; MA 4:0–4:11 years). They, too, found that the number of errors reflected grammatical complexity. In addition, there was evidence of continuity from one level of development to the next, with a gain in grammatical response. Rondal *et al.* (1981) compared Down's children (CA 5:2–12:7 years; IQ 40–49) with other children of corresponding chronological age and IQ. Again, the errors on the sentence imitation task reflected the complexity of the grammar. The Down's children, however, obtained lower scores than the comparison group and showed more echolalia in their responses. Rogers (1975) also reported lower results on the Reynell expressive language scale when he compared Down's children (CA 4:5–16:1 years; MA 1:8–7:8 years) with a group of children with comparable chronological and mental ages.

Chipman (1981) assessed knowledge of grammatical rules by means of a task in which the children had to act out the meaning of sentences with toys. He reported that comprehension of the passive voice and understanding of sentences linked by a personal pronoun showed the same pattern of difficulty as had been recorded for normal language development. The Down's children and adolescents, however, were more variable in their responses.

Taken overall, this research suggests that Down's children progress from one-word utterances to sentences which obey adult rules for grammar. The syntax appears to be less complex than is usual for the same level of development. There is a more limited repertoire of grammatical structures and there is some inconsistency during periods in which the structures are not fully stabilised. Echolalia was measured as an additional characteristic only by Rondal *et al.* (1981). As yet, the echolalic responses of Down's children, in a natural setting, have not been classified, so it is not known whether they serve a variety of functions (Prizant and Duchan, 1981).

Although most Down's Syndrome language research has been directed towards children or adolescents, there are a few reports which have been concerned with the language of Down's adults. These have suggested that, although spoken language may be restricted, even the severely retarded may be competent in some aspects of communication. For example, nine Down's men who had been institutionalised for periods from 29 to 49 years, and whose language varied from unintelligible one-word utterances to complete sentences, were found to be communicating successfully during their daily routines (Price-Williams and Sabsay, 1979). Leudar *et al.* (1981) also found that Down's adults in a training centre were capable of communicating appropriately with both acquaintances and strangers. Although some did not reply to questions, half the trainees responded to every question they were asked during conversation with others. Although they spoke less than their conversational partner and the topics of conversation were limited, these Down's adults obeyed the rules of conversation.

In summary, the studies from the pre-speech period to adulthood suggest that communication may be delayed in Down's people in terms of the onset of vocalisation, the number of morphemes in early utterances and the complexity of later sentences. When these vocalisations, morphemes and sentences are analysed, however, they are found to be the products of rule-generated behaviour, and these rules appear to be similar to those followed in normal language development and do not reflect unique, bizarre or random processes.

While most differences from normal development appear to be merely delays in the sequence, there are a few qualitative differences which may be the result of a longer period at the one cognitive level. As Bodine (1974) pointed out, although a Down's Syndrome 5-year-old may have acquired 'no more of the model language than a normal toddler', the Down's child has been a participant in communicative sequences for much longer. Consequently, 'the range of topics he converses on is much greater than that of the normal toddler. A normal twenty-month-old does not itemize what he ate for his last several meals or insist on reciting all the television shows he has ever seen, as Tommy does.' The use of generalised utterances which may be heard by the listener as no more than inarticulate grunts was seen by Bodine to be the strategy used by these children to fill in the gaps caused by their delayed articulatory and linguistic skills. The use of miming and demonstration is another common strategy used to fill in gaps in an animated conversation, as I have seen, for example, when the fun of using the citizen band radio in father's truck is being described.

Another result of the longer experience with communication is that, on some tests, Down's language shows a higher association with chronological age than with mental age. For instance, Greenwald and Leonard (1979) reported the use of words by older Down's children (CA 31–54 months) who were still only at a pre-symbolic stage of sensorimotor development. Similarly, it has been suggested that noun vocabularies are in advance of syntax because the long exposure to language (Ryan, 1975) or to 'sterile naming exercises' (Mittler and Berry, 1977) has meant that single words, though not their sequences, have been mastered.

A longer period at the one level also seems to be characteristic of adult Down's language. It seems that this is usually at a concrete level and that there are limitations on abstract development (Cornwell, 1974).

DISORDERS OF SPEECH PRODUCTION

Even if a speaker understands and produces sentences which are acceptable grammatical constructions, the message will be interpreted most easily if the speech is fluent and clear. Unfortunately, it seems that many Down's people do not speak either fluently or clearly, and there are a number of speech disorders which have been commonly reported for the syndrome. To some extent these can be explained by reference to the physical system which produces the final speech product.

The sound heard by a listener originates with air forced from the lungs past the vocal cords in the larynx of the speaker. As this air passes through the vocal cords, its frequency of vibration is determined by the action of laryngeal muscles in changing the stretch and shape of the vocal cords.

After passing from the larynx and through the pharynx, the vibrating air passes through the cavities of the mouth or nose. Different movements of the lips, the tongue and the palate then influence the articulation of the sound, while the shape of the mouth, the nasal cavities, the pharynx and the chest act as resonators which affect the quality of the sound.

A number of anomalies in these systems are common in Down's Syndrome. Frequent respiratory infections and hypertonia influence the initial volume of air expelled by the lungs, the fundamental frequency of vibration of the vocal cords, and the movements of the mouth, tongue and lips. In addition, defects of these latter structures make articulation difficult. A protruding thick tongue, a high arched palate, a shorter than normal or a forward-protruding jaw, and teeth defects are some of the attributes which need to be considered in this context. The nasality of the voice is determined by the balance between the oral and nasal cavities, and this too is influenced by respiratory infection and structural defects.

In addition to the actual production systems, voice characteristics are influenced by the speaker's ability to monitor the final speech product so that any corrections or adjustments can be made. If hearing is impaired, errors in articulation and syntax, abnormal intonation or loudness are likely to remain uncorrected. The consistent reports of hearing loss in the Down's population (see Chapter 5) suggest that this is a factor which should not be forgotten in any consideration of Down's Syndrome speech.

To some extent, the effect of these factors on voice quality is confirmed in research reports. The voice has been perceived as hoarse (Bergendal, 1976), breathy (Montague and Hollien, 1973; Wold and Montague, 1979), and as being more hypernasal (Kline and Hutchinson, 1980). It may also be expected that the fundamental frequency of the vocal cords would be lowered by hypertonia of the laryngeal muscles. If the hypertonia decreases with age, this effect should be at its maximum during early childhood. Some evidence for this hypothesis comes from the finding that the low pitch of the pain cry of Down's infants is one of the characteristics which differentiate that cry from the norm (Lind *et al.*, 1970). Listener judgements of the speaking voices of Down's children have also suggested low pitch as a characteristic (Strazulla, 1953; Montague *et al.*, 1978).

Acoustic analysis, however, has failed to confirm these reports. Instead, Montague *et al.* (1974) found no difference in speaking fundamental frequency (SFF) between Down's and other children near 10 years of age, while higher SFF has been reported for children aged 5–6 years (Weinberg and Zlatin, 1970) and for adults (Moran and Gilbert, 1978). Weinberg and Zlatin suggested that the literature reflects a decrease over the decades in normal child SFF and that such a decrease in their matched group has contributed to the apparently high SFF for the Down's children in their study. Montague *et al.*, on the other hand, speculated that improved health care (for respiratory and thyroid problems) may have changed the SFF for Down's Syndrome.

The small numbers at the youngest ages, the large range or no data for IQ in many reports, the almost tantalising limitation on data for hearing and vocal pathology, and the great age range in the adult studies are all factors which influence the interpretation of this research. It seems probable that some of the contradictory results between studies are due to individual differences related to age, mental development and degree of auditory or physical impairment. Even those attributes consistently associated with Down's Syndrome are not universal characteristics for the syndrome, and some of them (for example, hypotonia, tongue protrusion and respiratory infection) decrease with age or treatment. It would seem that a better definition of these relevant characteristics is required for the subjects in speech disorder studies. It is also true that studies which focus on one attribute of voice quality (SFF or nasality) fail to capture the complexity of the voice as it is perceived by a listener. As Moran and Gilbert (1982) have indicated, a listener's judgement of voice quality depends on the interactions between various acoustic properties and listener perceptions.

In addition to examining voice quality, other studies of Down's Syndrome speech have been concerned with the incidence of stuttering (Preus, 1972) and with articulation errors. Although structural defects and hypotonia increase the possibility of articulation error, several studies have suggested that these anomalies are not the major cause of Down's Syndrome speech defects (Lennenberg *et al.*, 1962; Dodd, 1975, 1976). Dodd found that her subjects were capable of correct articulation as long as they were allowed to repeat the words without delay.

Dodd suggested that the echoic programme for immediate reproduction was different from the central motor programmes used to generate and to control spontaneous speech. She extended the Frith and Frith (1974) conclusion, that there is a specific deficit in Down's Syndrome for tasks requiring predetermined motor sequences, to include speech and language among these tasks. However, Seyfort (1978) investigated this proposal by comparing 18 Down's males with a non-Down's group matched for age and IQ. Her data supported the Frith and Frith hypothesis of a specific motor deficit for Down's Syndrome, but this was not reflected in the speech and language comparisons.

Some of the effects of central control factors, however, are found in the work of Farmer and Brayton (1979), who reported that some Down's adults in their study were unintelligible and not fluent in conversation but capable of articulating single words without error. When the speech of these adults was analysed, the timing for vowels was found to be too short and a cause of unintelligibility.

A number of recent studies have also investigated the articulation errors in the speech of Down's children. This research has suggested that these errors are often the result of rule-governed processes of simplification. As such, these rules are similar to those used by children who are not developmentally delayed but are at a transitional stage in speech development (Bodine, 1974; Dodd, 1976; Stoel-Gammon, 1980; Bleile, 1982).

INTERVENTION

Although these research results confirm that correct articulation of single words does not guarantee an intelligible flow of conversation, it would be remiss not to provide conditions for people with Down's Syndrome which promote good voice quality and articulation. Appropriate measures should be taken to remedy respiratory and thyroid problems, hypotonia and hearing impairment. Some orthodontic work, palate repair and removal of tonsils and adenoids may also be desirable (Ardran *et al.*, 1972).

Further steps suggested by the speech disorder research include some analysis of the rules governing articulation errors, as this may be useful in determining which phonemic groups can be taught most efficiently. As more of these analyses become available, some common strategies may be clarified. Other steps to improve articulation are suggested by Dodd (1975), whose study indicated that accurate articulation of new words is fostered by immediate imitation and that a visual prompt may help reproduction after delay. To improve the intelligibility of conversation or a sequence of words, a slowing down of speech is required so that vowel timing approaches intelligible rates (Farmer and Brayton, 1979). Informal observations suggest that teaching a child to read words is one method which helps some children to slow down.

Perhaps the most important implications of the research studies, however, are not so much concerned with the quality of speech as with the quality of the language. Normally developing children learn to use their language in a continuing interaction with the world around them. This interaction starts at birth and continues through the lifespan.

Bricker and Carlson (1981) summarised the research which has most implication for language intervention as suggesting: (1) a continuity between pre-linguistic communication and language; (2) a relationship between language development, cognition and affect; and (3) an important role for context and feedback.

The continuity between pre-linguistic and linguistic communication, the importance of affect, context and feedback, all suggest that interactions with the parents or primary care-givers are important from birth. These interactions should be part of the intervention efforts.

Bricker and Carlson's second point – the relationship between cognition, language and affect – describes a complex association, the precise form of which has yet to be determined. It is acknowledged, however, that children play an active role in developing their own language, and that what children 'talk about with their first word(s) bear(s) out the relationship between early conceptual attainments and their linguistic realization' (Schiefelbusch and McCormick, 1981). In reviewing research into the structure of the early word combinations, Cromer (1981) also stressed this active role and suggested that, to the child, the language system is 'a conceptual puzzle' to be solved.

In addition, Cromer drew attention to the need to investigate specific cognitive or processing deficits since these have consequences for choosing the most appropriate language programme. There have been several attempts to delineate distinctive deficits for Down's Syndrome which have implications for language development, for example ITPA profiles with motor encoding (use of gestures) superior to auditory–vocal abilities (Kirk and Kirk, 1971; Rohr and Burr, 1978); a left ear advantage for dichotic processing of verbal stimuli (Sommers and Starkey, 1977; Hartley, 1981); limitations in memory for auditory information (McDade and Adler, 1980; Marcell and Armstrong, 1982).

Other deficits which seem to impinge on language development are those relating to the attention patterns and referential looking of young Down's children (Jones, 1977; Gunn *et al.*, 1982; Krakow and Kopp, 1982). These appear to be connected with the processing which Newport *et al.* (1977) attributed to children in extracting syntactic elements from their mothers' language, i.e. selective attention to appropriate cues, listening, and noting the referent with which the input language is co-ordinated. It is also relevant to note the similarity between these processes and what is commonly called on-task, or pre-verbal, behaviours. It would seem that instruction which develops these behaviours may need to be included in an intervention programme which is designed specifically for Down's Syndrome. Rynders *et al.* (1979) have similarly commented on the possibility that 'young Down's Syndrome children will require careful, sensitive task introduction and structuring in order to engage successfully in instruction delivered verbally'.

Studies of the evoked potentials of Down's children and adults have also given results which suggest processing deficiencies. These studies have indicated a difficulty in inhibiting the response to repetitive stimulation (Barnet *et al.*, 1971; Furutsuka, 1977–8; Schafer and Peeke, 1982). Under normal circumstances, a response to repetition is dampened down and the brain is then more responsive to a new stimulus. A failure to inhibit the response to repetition may mean that the brain keeps processing a signal which contains no new information (perhaps even just background noise). It seems plausible to suggest a relationship between selective attention and these evoked potential measurements. Some supporting results have been reported by Zekulin *et al.* (1974), who demonstrated that Down's children seemed to be distracted from a pegboard task more easily than other children by a continuous monotonous background noise. Again, this could be interpreted as a difficulty in inhibiting a response to a repetitive sound. (The intensity of the sound was roughly equivalent to that of a vacuum cleaner.) It also suggests that some of the programmes for children with specific learning disabilities could be tapped for appropriate exercises in auditory figure-ground perception, and for structuring the learning environment (for example headphones, study carrels) to decrease distractions.

It is also pertinent to note here that difficulties specific to the syndrome may be compounded by other conditions which foster communicative failure, for example hearing impairment or dysarthria (Fraser, 1981). The best language programme will not be one designed specifically for Down's Syndrome but one which is specific for the individual Down's person.

Other individual differences which influence learning include emotional factors. These are reflected in Glovsky's (1972) description of the Down's child 'who during times of stress at the cottage or in school, walks about the grounds with his fingers in front of his ears, a symbolic shutting out of communicating world'. Glovsky went on to warn that it is 'difficult and meaningless to attempt a language evaluation of this child without a complete understanding of the total environment'.

An evaluation of the total environment was also urged by Mahoney (1975), who contrasted the natural language-learning environment with contrived programmes which reward children for producing a correct word or syntactic structure. He suggested that in the natural situation, 'children are reinforced for their ability to communicate rather than their ability to use appropriate linguistic structure', whereas some programmes encourage children 'to use language to procure candy rather than to interact socially'. Mittler and Berry (1977) emphasised that there are many everyday opportunities which can be used to promote language interaction. Most infant stimulation programmes would regard feeding, dressing and bathing routines as such opportunities. A checklist of parent strategies for encouraging the child to communicate has been devised by Cairns and Pieterse (1983) as part of their Teach Early Language for Living (TELL) programme. These strategies are appropriate for both the pre-verbal period and later.

Some programmes (including TELL) have also used natural situations to develop the child's language beyond the one-word stage. One example is the programme designed by Cheseldine and McConkey (1979), who asked the question 'What would happen if mothers (and fathers) raised their expectations and adapted their speech in an attempt to help their Down Syndrome child to progress to the next level of language development?' They found that parents could effectively modify their own language and teach their child to develop two-word utterances. Some did not need explicit training but only general advice on using play as the teaching medium.

MacDonald *et al.* (1974) have also reported a successful programme for Down's pre-schoolers who were speaking primarily only single words. Again, the parents implemented the programme at home. In this case, however, the parents were trained to teach the child to use two-word combinations in imitation, in conversation, and during play.

The simultaneous training in natural usage as well as in imitation sets this programme apart from other structured programmes which rely on imitation training. Some of these have found that new words or combinations elicited in imitation do not generalise to contexts away from the specific programme (e.g. Taylor *et al.*, 1976). This lack of generalisation supports Mahoney's criticism that such methods distort language acquisition by neglecting the interpersonal aspects of language interaction. The structured behavioural training programmes appear to be most successful with the child who is mute or echolalic and who has minimal social or self-help skills. The training starts with verbal imitation at a concrete level before progressing to more abstract concepts of space and time. There is, however, no general agreement on the optimal programme: 'We really don't know what program should come first, to be followed by what sequence' (Devany *et al.*, 1981).

In comparison with programmes for younger children, very little has been reported about language programmes for Down's teenagers and adults. Glovsky (1972) is one exception. However, the basic principles for successful language intervention would seem to hold for all age groups. Interpersonal factors, conceptual understanding, context and feedback must all be considered in addition to current linguistic ability (Mahoney, 1975; Bricker and Carlson, 1981).

Most people, those with Down's Syndrome included, probably find more pleasure in communicating with a person who is trusted and gives supportive feedback. It is probably also true that most people would prefer to have something to talk about rather than a set of stereotyped questions to answer. The knowledge and interests gained from past experiences usually form the substance of natural conversations. It seems reasonable to suggest that this (with its implications for appropriate experiences) should apply to those with Down's Syndrome too.

As far as the most efficient sequence of interventions is concerned, however, there is no one precise definition. Instead, there is an acknowledged 'need to test different paths' (Brinker and Bricker, 1980). The nature of these paths and their final destination will depend not only on the knowledge, skills and enthusiasm of the guide, but also on the guide's sensitivity to the Down's person's needs and interests.

NON-SPEECH SYSTEMS

For a few children, the acquisition of speech is so delayed that their opportunities for learning through communication with others become severely restricted. They are also likely to become frustrated and unhappy because of the difficulty in expressing their thoughts and needs.

For this reason, it is important to recognise that speech is only one mode of expressing the language; writing, signing and using communication boards are others. A failure to speak and be understood may reflect a total communication problem or it may reflect a deficit in the speech mode only. The implications of interpersonal communication for emotional and conceptual development are so great that it seems to be unwise to ignore the possibility that another mode or combination of modes may be successful when speech alone is failing.

One common concern is that an introduction of signing or another non-speech technique will delay the development of speech and language. For this reason, these techniques are often not introduced until speech and language programmes have clearly failed. There is some evidence, however, which suggests that non-speech techniques do not impede speech development if they are presented concurrently with spoken language (Schaeffer, 1980; Weller, 1981). It is hoped that if a combined method were successful at an early age, the emotional complications of communication failure could be avoided. At the present time, however, there is no intervention sequence which 'has been empirically validated as the efficient road to language' (Brinker and Bricker, 1980). This conclusion referred to spoken language programmes, and the validation of an intervention which includes non-speech techniques is a greater challenge for the future.

However, it would seem to be logical to claim that many principles for programme intervention remain unchanged whether speech, non-speech, or a combination of these is used as the system for expressing language. First, it must be recognised that the choice of system must be related to the needs of the individual person. And these needs will vary according to developmental level and impairment.

The second requirement is to recognise that the main function of a language intervention programme is not to build up a corpus of words, signs or symbols, but to teach the person how to communicate with these tools. Consequently, the total environment including interpersonal factors, must be considered if the programme is to be effective.

SUMMARY

There are three propositions which have been avoided in this chapter: 'critical period', 'Language Acquisition Device' (LAD), and 'arrested development' (Chomsky, 1959; Lennenberg, 1967; McNeill, 1966; Burr and Rohr, 1978). This has been a conscious decision because of their negative connotations for Down's Syndrome development. The case for a critical or sensitive period for language development has not been proved, and the only benefit accruing to Down's children from such a concept has been the increased attention to early stimulation. It can otherwise be a dangerous notion if it diverts us from the acknowledgement that 'continuous efforts during the whole period of development are crucial' (Kraft, 1980). Similarly, an LAD, even in its weakest form, can be used to excuse non- (or weak) intervention if it encourages the assumption that the effect of this 'device' (or thing that solves the conceptual puzzle) is more influential than conscious human efforts. The notion of 'arrested development' is even more harmful since it fosters the belief that, come adolescence, intervention is of no avail.

It is ironic that high-school teachers post Bullock (1975) recognise that their students are still not proficient in all the forms and functions of language. There is an acknowledged need to develop the language proficiency of these high-school teenagers, yet it is rarely recognised that Down's adolescents and adults, whether they be at school, training centre, or institution, may also benefit from continued language instruction. As Evans (1974) commented in summarising his research findings on Down's language, there is a 'need for education efforts to continue – even to be intensified, rather than terminated' when the Down's child has left school. Furthermore, it must be conceded that there is no age at which communicative competence ceases to be important. Gains in knowledge and self-respect are of value throughout the life-span.

REFERENCES

Andrews, R.J. and Andrews, J.G. (1977). A study of the spontaneous oral language of Down's Syndrome children. *Exceptional Child* **24**(2), 86–94.

Ardran, G.M., Harker, P. and Kemp, F.H. (1972). Tongue size in Down's syndrome. *J. Ment. Defic. Res.* **16**(3), 160–66.

Barnet, A.B., Ohlrich, E.S. and Shanks, B.L. (1971). EEG evoked responses to repetitive auditory stimulation in normal and Down's syndrome infants. *Dev. Med. & Child Neurol.* **13**, 321–9.

Bates, E., Bretherton, I., Beeghly-Smith, M. and McNew, S. (1982). Social bases of language development: A reassessment. In Lipsitt, L.P. and Spiker, C.C. (eds), *Advances in Child Development and Behavior* **16**, 7–75. New York: Academic Press.

Bergendal, B. (1976). Language and voice in mongoloid children. In Loebell, E. (ed.), *Proceedings of 16th International Congress of Logopedics and Phoniatrics, Interlaken, Switzerland*, pp. 28–32. New York: Karger.

Berger, J. and Cunningham, C.C. (1981). The development of eye contact between mothers and normal versus Down's syndrome infants. *Dev. Psychol.* **17**(5), 678–89.

Berger, J. and Cunningham, C.C. (1983). The development of early vocal behaviors and interactions in Down's syndrome and non-handicapped infant–mother pairs. *Dev. Psychol.* **19**(3), 322–31.

Blacher, J. and Meyers, C.E. (1983). A review of attachment formation and disorder of handicapped children. *Am. J. Ment. Defic.* **87**(4), 359–71.

Bleile, K. (1982). Consonant ordering in Down's syndrome phonology. *J. Commun. Dis.* **15**, 275–85.

Bloom, L., Hood, L. and Lightbown, P. (1974). Imitation in language development: If, when, and why. *Cogn. Psychol.* **6**, 380–420.

Bloom, L., Lifter, K. and Broughton, J. (1981). What children say and what they know: Exploring the relations between product and process in the development of early words and early concepts. In Stark, R.E. (ed.), *Language Behavior in Infancy and Early Childhood*, pp. 301–322. New York, Amsterdam, Oxford: Elsevier/North Holland.

Bodine, A.A. (1974). A phonological analysis of the speech of two mongoloid (Down's syndrome) boys. *Anthro. Ling.* **16**, 21–4.

Bowerman, M. (1976). Semantic factors in the acquisition of rules for word use and sentence construction. In Morehead, D.M. and Morehead, A.E. (eds), *Normal and Deficient Child Language*. Baltimore: University Park Press.

Bricker, D.D. and Carlson, L. (1981). Issues in early language intervention. In Schiefelbusch, R.L. and Bricker, D.D. (eds), *Early Language: Acquisition and Intervention*, pp. 477–516. Baltimore: University Park Press.

Bridges, F.A. and Cicchetti, D. (1982). Mothers' ratings of the temperament characteristics of Down syndrome infants. *Dev. Psychol.* **18**, 238–44.

Brinker, R.P. and Bricker, D. (1980). Teaching a first language: Building complex structures from simpler components. In Hogg, J. and Mittler, P. (eds), *Advances in Mental Handicap Research*, Vol. 1, pp. 197–223. New York: John Wiley.

Broen, P.A. (1972). The verbal environment of the language learning child. *Am. Speech & Hearing Assoc. Mono.* **17**.

Broffman, S.B. (1981). The development of positional patterns in the early multimorphemic utterances of five Down's and two normal children: A descriptive comparison. Unpublished Ph.D. dissertation, New York University.

Bruner, J. (1975). The ontogenesis of speech acts. *J. Child Lang.* **2**, 1–19.

Buckhalt, J.A., Rutherford, R.B. and Goldberg, K.E. (1978). Verbal and non-verbal interaction of mothers with their Down's syndrome and nonretarded infants. *Am. J. Ment. Defic.* **82**, 337–43.

Buddenhagen, R.G. (1971). *Establishing Vocal Verbalizations in Mute Mongoloid Children.* Champaign, Illinois: Research Press Company.

Buium, N., Rynders, J. and Turnure, J. (1974). Early maternal linguistic environment of normal and Down's syndrome language-learning children. *Am. J. Ment. Defic.* **79**(1), 52–8.

Bullock, A. (1975). *A Language for Life: Report of the Committee of Inquiry Appointed by the Secretary of State for Education and Science*, pp. 141–61. London: HMSO.

Burr, D.B. and Rohr, A. (1978). Patterns of psycholinguistic development in the severely mentally retarded: A hypothesis. *Social Biol.* **25**(1), 15–22.

Cairns, S. and Pieterse, M. (1983). *T.E.L.L. A Communication Program*, pp. 285–91. Sydney: Macquarie University.

Canadian Broadcasting Commission (1979). *David.* Man Alive television series. Toronto.

Carter, A.L. (1979). Pre-speech meaning relations: An outline of one infant's sensorimotor morpheme development. In Fletcher, P. and Garman, M. (eds), *Language Acquisition: Studies in First Language Development*, pp. 71–92. Cambridge: Cambridge University Press.

Chapman, R.S. (1981). Cognitive development and language comprehension in 10- to 21-month-olds. In Stark, R.E. (ed.), *Language Behavior in Infancy and Early Childhood*, pp. 359–91. New York, Amsterdam, Oxford: Elsevier/North-Holland.

Cheseldine, S. and McConkey, R. (1979). Parental speech to young Down's syndrome children: An intervention study. *Am. J. Ment. Defic.* **83**(6), 612–20.

Chipman, H.H. (1981). Understanding language retardation: A developmental perspective. In Mittler, P. (ed.), *Frontiers of Knowledge in Mental Retardation*, Vol. 1, pp. 181–9. Baltimore: University Park Press.

Chomsky, N. (1959). A review of B.F. Skinner's *Verbal Behavior. Language* **35**, 26–58.

Cicchetti, D. and Sroufe, A. (1976). The relationship between affective and cognitive development in Down's syndrome infants. *Child Dev.* **47**(4), 920–29.

Coggins, T.E. (1979). Relational meaning encoded in the two-word utterances of stage 1 Down's syndrome children. *J. Speech & Hearing Res.* **22**(1), 166–78.

Coggins, T.E. and Morrison, J.A. (1981). Spontaneous imitations of Down's syndrome children: A lexical analysis. *J. Speech & Hearing Res.* **24**(2), 303–308.

Cohen, L.B. (1981). Examination of rehabilitation as a measure of aberrant infant development. In Friedman, S. and Sigman, M. (eds), *Pre-term and Post-term Births: Relevance to Optimal Psychological Development*, pp. 241–53. New York: Academic Press.

Cook, A.S. and Culp, R.E. (1981). Mutual play of mothers with their Down's syndrome and normal infants. *Int. J. Rehab. Res.* **4**(3), 542–4.

Cornwell, A.C. (1974). Development of language, abstractions, and numerical concept formation in Down's syndrome children. *Am. J. Ment. Defic.* **79**(2), 179–90.

Cromer, R.F. (1981). Reconceptualizing language acquisition and cognitive development. In Schiefelbusch, R.L. and Bricker, D.D. (eds), *Early Language: Acquisition and Intervention*, pp. 51–137. Baltimore: University Park Press.

Cross, T.G. (1978). Mother's speech and its association with rate of linguistic development in young children. In Waterson, W. and Snow, C. (eds), *The Development of Communication*, pp. 199–216. New York: John Wiley.

Cytryn, L. (1975). Studies of behavior in children with Down's syndrome. In Anthony, E.J. (ed.), *Explorations of Child Psychiatry*, pp. 271–85. New York and London: Plenum Press.

Devany, J.M., Ricover, R. and Lovaas, O.I. (1981). Teaching speech to nonverbal children. In Kauffman, J.M. and Hallahan, D.M. (eds), *Handbook of Special Education*, pp. 512–30. Englewood Cliffs, N.J.: Prentice-Hall.

Dodd, B.J. (1972). Comparison of babbling patterns in normal and Down syndrome infants. *J. Ment. Defic. Res.* **16**, 35–40.

Dodd, B. (1975). Recognition and reproduction of words by Down's syndrome and non-Down's syndrome retarded children. *Am. J. Ment. Defic.* **80**(3), 306–311.

Dodd, B. (1976). A comparison of the phonological systems of mental age matched, normal, severely subnormal and Down's syndrome children. *Br. J. Dis. Commun.* **11**, 27–42.

Dore, J. (1975). Holophrases, speech acts and language universals. *J. Child Lang.* **2**, 21–40.

Down, J.L.H. (1866). Observations on an ethnic classification of idiots. *Rep. Lond. Hosp.* **3**, 259–62.

Dunst, C.J. (1979). Cognitive–social aspects of communicative exchanges between mothers and their Down's syndrome infants and mothers and their nonretarded infants. Unpublished PhD dissertation, George Peabody College for Teachers.

Emde, R.N. and Brown, C. (1978). Adaptation to the birth of a Down's syndrome infant. Grieving and maternal attachment. *J. Am. Acad. Child Psych.* **17**, 299–323.

Emde, R.N., Katz, E.L. and Thorpe, J.K. (1978). Emotional expression in infancy: II. Early deviations in Down's syndrome. In Lewis, M. and Rosenblum, L.A. (eds), *The Development of Affect*, pp. 351–60. New York: Plenum Press.

Evans, D. (1974). Language development in mongols. *Spec. Ed. Forward Trends* **1**(4), 23–5.

Evans, D. (1976). Language development in Down's syndrome retardates: A factorial study. *Cont. Ed. Psychol.* **1**, 319–28.

Evans, D. (1977). The development of language abilities in mongols: A correlational study. *J. Ment. Defic. Res.* **21**, 103–117.

Farmer, A. and Brayton, E.R. (1979). Speech characteristics of fluent and dysfluent Down's syndrome adults. *Fol. Phon.* **31**, 284–90.

Fraser, W. (1981). Clinical presentations of retarded language. In Fraser, W.I. and Grieve, R. (eds), *Communicating with Normal and Retarded Children*, pp. 84–110. Bristol: John Wright.

Frith, V. and Frith, C.D. (1974). Specific motor disabilities in Down's syndrome. *J. Child Psychol. & Psych.* **15**, 293–301.

Furutsuka, T. (1977–78). The characteristics of the information processing mechanism of the Down's syndrome patients: Why are they good at mimicking? In *Annual Report, 1977–1978*, pp. 45–50. Research and Clinical Centre for Child Development, Hokkaido University.

Gibson, D. (1978). *Down's Syndrome: The Psychology of Mongolism*, pp. 19–34, 233–60. Cambridge: Cambridge University Press.

Glovsky, L. (1972). A communication program for children with Down's syndrome. *Train. School Bull.* **69**(1), 5–9.

Gordon, W.L. and Panagos, J.M. (1976). Developmental transformational capacity of children with Down's syndrome. *Perceptual Motor Skills* **43**(3), 967–73.

Greenwald, C.A. and Leonard, L.B. (1979). Communicative and sensorimotor development of Down's syndrome children. *Am. J. Ment. Defic.* **84**(3), 296–303.

Gunn, P., Berry, P. and Andrews, R. (1979). Vocalization and looking behaviour of Down's syndrome infants. *Br. J. Psychol.* **70**, 259–63.

Gunn, P., Berry, P. and Andrews, R.J. (1981). The temperament of Down's syndrome infants: A research note. *J. Child Psychol. & Psych.* **22**, 189–94.

Gunn, P., Berry, P. and Andrews, R.J. (1982). Looking behavior of Down syndrome infants. *Am. J. Ment. Defic.* **87**(3), 344–7.

Gunn, P., Clark, D. and Berry, P. (1980). Maternal speech during play with a Down's syndrome infant. *Ment. Retard.* **18**, 15–18.

Halliday, M.A.K. (1975). *Learning How to Mean – Explorations in the Development of Language*, pp. 18–119. London: Edward Arnold.

Hartley, X.Y. (1981). Lateralization of speech stimuli in young Down's syndrome children. *Cortex* **17**(2), 241–8.

Hayes, A. (1978). Mother–infant interactions – Coincidental conversations? *Socioling. Newsletter* **9**, 37–8.

Jones, O.H.M. (1977). Mother–child communication with pre-linguistic Down's syndrome and normal infants. In Schaffer, H.R. (ed.), *Studies in Mother–Infant Interaction*, pp. 379–401. London, New York, San Francisco: Academic Press.

Kaye, K. and Fogel, A. (1980). The temporal structure of face-to-face communication between mothers and infants. *Dev. Psychol.* **16**, 454–64.

Kirk, S.A. and Kirk, W.D. (1971). *Psycholinguistic Learning Disabilities: Diagnosis and Remediation*, pp. 31–2. Urbana: University of Illinois Press.

Kline, L.S. and Hutchinson, J.M. (1980). Acoustic and perceptual evaluation of hypernasality of mentally retarded persons. *Am. J. Ment. Defic.* **85**(2), 153–60.

Kraft, M. (1980). Some developmental neurobiological conditions seen in relation to the early habilitation of handicapped children. In Marckmann, L. (ed.), *Auditory Training of Hearing Impaired Pre-school Children*, pp. 59–68. Stockholm: The Almqvist and Wiksell Periodical Co.

Krakow, J. and Kopp, C. (1982). Sustained attention in young Down syndrome children. *Top. Early Childh. Spec. Ed.* **2**, 32–42.

LaVeck, B. and Brehm, S.S. (1978). Individual variability among children with Down's syndrome. *Ment. Retard.* **16**(2), 135–7.

Layton, T.L. and Sharifi, H. (1978). Meaning and structure of Down's syndrome and nonretarded children's spontaneous speech. *Am. J. Ment. Defic.* **83**(5), 439–45.

Lennenberg, E.H. (1964). Speech as a motor skill with special reference to nonphasic disorders. *Soc. Res. Child Dev. Mono.* **29**, 115–27.

Lennenberg, E.H. (1967). *Biological Foundations of Language*. New York: Wiley.

Lennenberg, E.H., Nichols, I.A. and Rosenberger, E.F. (1962). Primitive stages of language development in mongolism. In *Disorders of Communication*, Vol. 47, pp.

119–37. Association for Research in Nervous and Mental Disease: Research Publications 42.

Leudar, I., Fraser, W.I. and Jeeves, M.A. (1981). Social familiarity and communication in Down syndrome. *J. Ment. Defic. Res.* **25**, 133–42.

Lind, J., Vuorenkoski, V., Rosberg, G., Partanen, T.J. and Wasz-Höckert, O. (1970). Spectographic analysis of vocal response to pain stimuli in infants with Down's syndrome. *Dev. Med. Child Neurol.* **12**(4), 478–86.

McDade, H.L. and Adler, S. (1980). Down syndrome and short-term memory impairments: A storage or retrieval deficit? *Am. J. Ment. Defic.* **84**(6), 561–7.

MacDonald, J.D., Blott, J.P., Gordon, K., Spiegel, B. and Hartmann, M. (1974). An experimental parent-assisted treatment program for preschool language-delayed children. *J. Speech & Hearing Dis.* **39**(4), 395–415.

McNeill, D. (1966). The creation of language by children. In Lyons, J. and Wales, R.J. (eds), *Psycholinguistics Papers.* pp. 99–115. Edinburgh: Edinburgh University Press.

Mahoney, G.J. (1975). Ethological approach to delayed language acquisition. *Am. J. Ment. Defic.* **80**(2), 139–48.

Mahoney, G., Glover, A. and Finger, I. (1981). Relationship between language and sensorimotor development of Down syndrome and nonretarded children. *Am. J. Ment. Defic.* **86**(2), 21–7.

Marcell, M.M. and Armstrong, V. (1982). Auditory and visual sequential memory of Down syndrome and nonretarded children. *Am. J. Ment. Defic.* **87**(1), 86–95.

Melyn, M.A. and White, D.T. (1973). Mental and developmental milestones of noninstitutionalised Down's syndrome children. *Pediatrics* **52**(4), 542–5.

Michaelis, C.T. (1977). The language of a Down's syndrome child. PhD dissertation. Michigan University.

Miranda, S.B. and Fantz, R.L. (1974). Recognition memory in Down's syndrome and normal infants. *Child Dev.* **45**, 651–60.

Mittler, P. and Berry, P. (1977). Demanding language. In Mittler, P. (ed.), *Research to Practice in Mental Retardation*, Vol. 2, pp. 245–51. Baltimore: University Park Press.

Montague, J.C., Brown, W.S. and Hollien, H. (1974). Vocal fundamental frequency characteristics of institutionalised Down's syndrome children. *Am. J. Ment. Defic.* **78**(4), 414–18.

Montague, J.C. and Hollien, H. (1973). Perceived voice quality disorders in Down's syndrome children. *J. Commun. Dis.* **6**, 76–87.

Montague, J.C., Hollien, H., Hollien, P.A. and Wold, D.C. (1978). Perceived pitch and fundamental frequency comparisons of institutionalised Down's syndrome children. *Fol. Phon.* **30**, 245–56.

Moran, M.J. and Gilbert, H.R. (1978). Speaking fundamental frequency characteristics of institutionalised adults with Down's syndrome. *Am. J. Ment. Defic.* **83**(3), 248–52.

Moran, M.J. and Gilbert, H.R. (1982). Selected acoustic characteristics and listener judgments of the voice of Down syndrome adults. *Am. J. Ment. Defic.* **86**(5), 553–6.

Nelson, K. (1973). Structure and strategy in learning to talk. *Mono. Soc. Res. Child Dev.* **38**(1–2), 1–135.

Newport, E.L., Gleitman, H. and Gleitman, L.R. (1977). Mother, I'd rather do it myself: Some effects and non-effects of maternal speech style. In Ferguson, C. and Snow, C. (eds), *Talking to Children*, pp. 109–149. London and New York: Cambridge University Press.

O'Kelly-Collard, M. (1978). Maternal linguistic environment of Down's syndrome children. *Aust. J. Ment. Retard.* **5**(4), 121–6.

Palermo-Piastra, E.A. (1981). A longitudinal study of Down's syndrome children's language during sensorimotor Stages IV through VI. PhD dissertation. Michigan University.

Petersen, G.A. and Sherrod, K.B. (1982). Relationship of maternal language to language development and language delay of children. *Am. J. Ment. Defic.* **86**(4), 391–8.

Preus, A. (1972). Stuttering in Down's syndrome. *Scand. J. Ed. Res.* **16**, 89–104.

Price-Williams, D. and Sabsay, S. (1979). Communicative competence among severely retarded persons. *Semiotica* **26**, 35–63.

Prizant, B.M. and Duchan, J.F. (1981). The functions of immediate echolalia in autistic children. *J. Speech & Hearing Dis.* **46**(1), 241–9.

Reed, R.B., Pueschel, S.M., Schnell, R.R. and Cronk, C.E. (1980). Interrelationships of biological, environmental and competency variables in young children with Down syndrome. *Appl. Res. Ment. Retard.* **1**, 161–74.

Rogers, M.G.H. (1975). A study of language skills in severely subnormal children. *Child: Care, Health and Development* **1**, 113–26.

Rohr, A. and Burr, D.B. (1978). Etiological differences in patterns of psycholinguistic development of children of IQ 30 to 60. *Am. J. Ment. Defic.* **82**(6), 549–53.

Rondal, J.A. (1977). Maternal speech in normal and Down's syndrome children. In Mittler, P. (ed.), *Research to Practice in Mental Retardation.* Vol. 2: *Education and training*, pp. 239–43. Baltimore: University Park Press.

Rondal, J.A. (1980). Verbal imitation by Down syndrome and nonretarded children. *Am. J. Ment. Defic.* **85**(3), 318–21.

Rondal, J.A., Lambert, J.L. and Sohier, C. (1981). Elicited verbal and nonverbal imitation in Down's syndrome and other mentally retarded children: A replication and extension of Berry. *Lang. & Speech* **24**(3), 245–54.

Ryan, J. (1975). Mental subnormality and language development. In Lennenberg, E.H. and Lennenberg, E. (eds.), *Foundations of Language Development*, pp. 269–78. New York: Academic Press.

Rynders, J.E. (1982). *Research on Improving the Social Adaptation of Children with Down Syndrome.* Paper presented at the Sixth World Congress of the International Association for the Scientific Study of Mental Deficiency, Toronto.

Rynders, J.E., Behlen, K.L. and Horrobin, J.M. (1979). Performance characteristics of preschool Down's syndrome children receiving augmented or repetitive verbal instruction. *Am. J. Ment. Def.* **84**(1), 67–73.

Schaeffer, B. (1980). Spontaneous language through signed speech. In Schiefelbusch, R.L. (ed.), *Nonspeech Language and Communication: Analysis and Intervention*, pp. 421–46. Baltimore: University Park Press.

Schafer, E.W. and Peeke, H.V. (1982). Down syndrome individuals fail to habituate cortical evoked potentials. *Am. J. Ment. Defic.* **87**(3), 332–7.

Schaffer, H.R. (1977). Early interactive development. In Schaffer, H.R. (ed.), *Studies in Mother–Infant Interaction*, pp. 3–16. London: Academic Press.

Schiefelbusch, R.L. and McCormick, L. (1981). Language and speech disorders. In Kauffman, J.M. and Hallahan, D.P. (eds), *Handbook of Special Education*, pp. 108–139. Englewood Cliffs, N.J.: Prentice-Hall.

Seagoe, M.V. (1965). Verbal development in a mongoloid. *Exceptional Children* **31**, 269–73.

Semmel, M.I. and Dolley, D.G. (1971). Comprehension and imitation of sentences by Down's syndrome children as a function of transformational complexity. *Am. J. Ment. Defic.* **75**(6). 739–45.

Seyfort, B.M.A. (1978). An investigation of syndrome specific language impairment in Down's anomaly. Unpublished PhD dissertation. University of Victoria, Canada.

Smith, B.L. and Oller, D.K. (1981). A comparative study of pre-meaningful vocalizations produced by normally developing and Down's syndrome infants. *J. Speech & Hearing Dis.* **46**(1), 46–51.

Smith, B. and Phillips, C.J. (1981). Age-related progress among children with severe learning difficulties. *Dev. Med. & Child Neurol.* **23**, 465–76.

Snow, C.E. (1977). The development of conversations between mothers and babies. *J. Child Lang.* **4**, 1–22.

Sommers, R.K. and Starkey, K.L. (1977). Dichotic verbal processing in Down's syndrome children having qualitatively different speech and language skills. *Am. J. Ment. Defic.* **82**(1), 44–53.

Sorce, J.F. and Emde, R.N. (1982). The meaning of infant emotional expressions: Regularities in caregiving responses in normal and Down's syndrome infants. *J. Child Psychol. & Psych.* **23**(2), 145–58.

Stark, R.E. (1979). Prespeech segmental feature development. In Fletcher, P. and Garman, M. (eds), *Language Acquisition: Studies in First Language Development*, pp. 14–32. Cambridge: Cambridge University Press.

Stern, D. (1977). *The First Relationship: Infant and Mother*, pp. 14–15. London: Fontana/ Open Books.

Stoel-Gammon, C. (1980). Phonological analysis of four Down's syndrome children. *Appl. Psycholing.* **1**, 31–48.

Stone, N.W. and Chesney, B.H. (1978). Attachment behaviors in handicapped infants. *Ment. Retard.* **16**(1), 8–12.

Strazulla, M. (1953). Speech problems of the mongoloid child. *Quart. Rev. Ped.* **8**, 268–72.

Taylor, J., Berry, P. and Conn, P. (1976). A study of language learning through imitation. In Berry, P. (ed.), *Language and Communication in the Mentally Handicapped*, pp. 114–28. London: Edward Arnold.

Thoman, E.B. (1981). Affective communication as the prelude and context for language learning. In Schiefelbusch, R.L. and Bricker, D.D. (eds), *Early Language: Acquisition and Intervention*, pp. 181–200. Baltimore: University Park Press.

Trevarthen, C. (1977). Descriptive analyses of infant communicative behavior. In Schaffer, H.R. (ed.), *Studies in Mother–Infant Interaction*, pp. 227–70. New York: Academic Press.

Weinberg, B. and Zlatin, M. (1970). Speaking fundamental frequency characteristics of five- and six-year-old children with mongolism. *J. Speech & Hearing Res.* **13**, 418–25.

Weller, E.L. (1981). A comparison of oral and signed-english communication training with Down syndrome children in a parent-assisted language intervention program. Unpublished PhD dissertation. University of California, Los Angeles.

Wiegel-Crump, C.A. (1981). The development of grammar in Down's syndrome children between the mental ages of 2-0 and 6-11 years. *Ed. & Train. Ment. Ret.* **16**, 24–30.

Wold, D.C. and Montague, J.C. (1979). Preliminary perceived voice deviations and hearing disorders of adults with Down's syndrome. *Perceptual and Motor Skills* **49**, 564.

Zekulin, X.Y., Gibson, D., Mosley, J.L. and Brown, R.I. (1974). Auditory–motor channeling in Down's syndrome subjects. *Am. J. Ment. Defic.* **78**(5), 571–7.

15 Play

Roy McConkey

In days gone by, when some children were known as *handicapped*, much money was spent on so-called *programs* for them. These were designed by State-employed staff – some calling themselves *therapists*, while others preferred strange titles like *psychologist*. As many as six different people could be involved in planning programs for one child. Money was plentiful in those days.

Strangely enough, all these programs would focus on what children could *not* do, rather than on their capabilities and what they enjoyed doing. The emphasis was always on learning new skills, chosen, not by the child, but by the designer of the program.

There was a widespread belief that such programs were a success. If children failed to learn, this was explained by lack of personnel or insufficient time or due to the severity of the child's handicap.

The demise of programs was hastened by several factors. Programs for training workskills became unnecessary as unemployment soared and the advance in micro-electronic aids made other remedial programs redundant. But the biggest blow came when our educators discovered the power of self-initiated learning and as a society we started to value people's feelings and the importance of relationships rather than prizing abilities. It took some time to re-orientate the old style programmers but most can now manage to play happily with children.

(From *The Follies of Yesteryear* by O.I. Remember, published by Longmemories, London, 2084.)

Play, unlike some other childhood topics, engenders a poetic response. Advocates wax lyrical about it:

Play is life. It is instinctive. It is voluntary. It is spontaneous. It is natural. It is exploratory. It is communication. It is expression. It combines action and thought. It gives satisfaction and a feeling of achievement.
(*Declaration of the Child's Right to Play*, International Playground Association, 1977.)

Of course, much the same could be said of bowel control. The fact that it is not, is surely revealing. Could it be that everyone is so convinced of its value that rhetoric becomes unnecessary?

The attitude of professional workers to play is quite paradoxical. Of all the advice they give to parents, surely the most common must be 'Play with your child'.

The preparation of this chapter was supported by St Michael's House Research Fund. My ideas on play have been shaped by my co-researchers – Sally Cheseldine, Finola Gallagher, Simon Hewson, Heather Martin, John McEvoy and Jodie Walsh – but a special thank you must go to Dorothy Jeffree, who believed in the value of play long before any of us.

Yet professionals would consider it positively insulting to hear their work described as play. This is especially so in the realm of handicap. Here, the emphasis is on enabling people with disabilities to look after themselves, live independently and earn a living – that is serious business. Moreover, the attitudes our society has to disability – sympathy, sadness, regret – are the opposite of what it associates with play. Indeed, Kay Mogford (1977, p. 173) rightly concluded that there was a 'pervasive belief that the mentally handicapped did not play and only indulged in repetitive and stereotyped behaviour'.

Questions about play

The aim of this chapter is to summarise what is known about the play of Down's children or, more generally, that of children who are developmentally delayed, mentally handicapped or intellectually impaired. There are five basic questions which need to be answered.

1. What is their play like: who do they play with and what do they play at?
2. What differences are there between the play of the child who is handicapped and that of a non-handicapped child?
3. Can we identify any reasons for the variations among mentally handicapped children in their play patterns? Are they due to age, mental ability, sex – or what?
4. What is known about the way parents play with their children and of their attitudes towards play?
5. How can we nurture the play of mentally handicapped children?

The chapter is divided into six sections, five devoted to answering the above questions within the confines of currently available research data, and a final one summarising the value of play and issues which we need to face in the future. And, because play never ends but merely changes its name to leisure or sport, the review also includes relevant studies with adults who are mentally handicapped. Summary information about research published up to April 1984 is contained in Tables 15.1–15.5 of the Appendix to this chapter.

PLAY AND LEISURE PATTERNS

Play partners

A basic question is with whom does a Down's infant play? Figure 15.1 gives the answer for 100 families in Dublin, Ireland, with children aged 5 years and under (Walsh and McConkey, 1983). In fact, a similar pattern was found with other age-matched mentally handicapped infants except they had fewer opportunities for daily play sessions with siblings (64% as opposed to 82% of Down's infants). Moreover, the number of different daily playmates was significantly higher for the Down's infants.

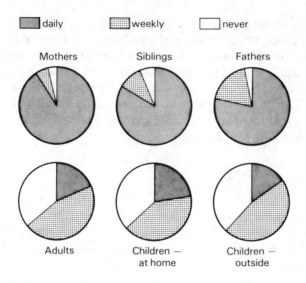

Fig. 15.1 Play comparisons of Down's Syndrome infants (from Walsh and McConkey, 1983)

There were no differences between boys and girls, and the same pattern emerged irrespective of mothers' age. However, there was a tendency for younger fathers – 35 years and under – to play only occasionally or not at all with their children, whereas older fathers – over 35 years – were inclined to play regularly.

However, the most striking feature is the dearth of play opportunities with people outside of the family. Play with other adults was more likely to be found in families in lower socioeconomic groups; 37% of infants had regular play opportunities of this type compared with only 15% of professional and skilled families. The chance to play regularly with other children was uniformly lacking for three out of four Down's children.

Other surveys have discovered that this pattern continues into adulthood. Cheseldine and Jeffree (1981) found that only one in four mentally handicapped adolescents in Greater Manchester ever went to visit a friend or had a friend visit them; McConkey *et al.* (1981), in a Dublin survey of mentally handicapped adults living in the community, found that only two in five had a friend, and Reiter and Levi's (1981) study in Israel found that under one-third of the moderately and mildly retarded adults met friends at least weekly, compared to over four in five of young Israeli adults.

Play activities

We have amazingly little information regarding mentally handicapped children's choice of play activities in natural surroundings. Available data suggest that their play is retarded, but, as Fig. 15.2 illustrates, this is more apparent with 'other' mentally handicapped children than it is with Down's infants (McConkey and

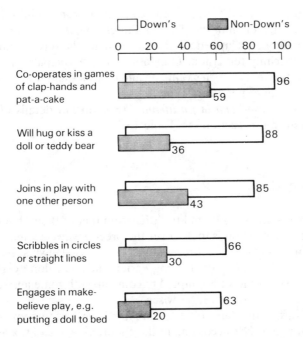

Fig. 15.2 The percentage of children reported to be capable of certain play skills (from McConkey and Jeffree, 1975)

Jeffree, 1975). These play skills are normally shown by 2 year olds, yet all the handicapped children were aged between 3 and 5 years. Richardson's (1979) data for Scottish children are very similar.

McEvoy and McConkey (1983), in a sample of 67 families living in Dublin, asked mothers to recall their children's 'typical' activities when playing alone or with other members of the family – mothers, fathers, siblings.

There was a striking variation in play activities with different playmates. For example, pretend play tended to occur more frequently with siblings or mothers; fathers rarely engaged in this type of play. Rather they tended to go for gross-motor activities, and this was also the most popular among siblings. As might be expected, the majority of exploratory play behaviours occurred when the children were alone, and the frequency of fine motor activities was also highest at this time. Passive pastimes were most frequently associated with mothers, who in general covered a wider and more varied span of activities with the children than did other members of the family.

Overall, the most frequently reported actions were of a gross-motor nature or passive pastimes such as watching television. The latter were more frequently reported for the 6–15 age group than for the younger children. Only a minority engaged in the more cognitive or social play activities such as symbolic play, conceptual play, books, etc.

Unfortunately, we do not have comparable data for non-handicapped infants so it is not possible at this point to claim that these findings are atypical. However, we shall return to this point in the next section.

Once again, the childhood pattern seems to carry over into adulthood. Studies in England, Ireland, Israel and the United States found that the most popular pastimes of mentally handicapped adolescents and adults were listening to records or the radio or watching television. Only a minority participated in sports, youth clubs or community events – such as cinema and dances – and few were said to have hobbies such as reading, needlecraft, etc.

The habits of childhood can last a lifetime. (For further details of the research studies mentioned in this section see Table 15.1.)

PLAY COMPARISONS

The play of Down's infants is bound to differ from that of their able-bodied peers. The more intriguing question is to discover the precise ways in which it varies. This means comparing the play of representative groups of Down's and able-bodied infants. However, the truism of it being easier said than done certainly applies here. To date, 12 studies have attempted to come up with some answers (see Table 15.2) but we are, I fear, only a little wiser.

Here are the difficulties our noble researchers have had to contend with.

We know that play varies according to the children's age and sex as well as their social and educational backgrounds. Hence, before we can ascribe differences to the children's syndrome we have to ensure that the groups are matched on all other relevant variables. These are sometimes confounded. For example, in one study, retarded children were in institutional care while the non-handicapped youngsters lived at home with their parents.

The standard way of coping with the effects of multi-variables is by having *large* representative samples so that the variability is randomised. None of the studies listed in Table 15.2 can claim to have done this.

Most researchers have been tempted to match their groups not on age but rather on the children's mental abilities. The intention is laudable, namely to determine if there are any specific differences in the play of mentally handicapped children once you have allowed for their overall developmental delay. However, this strategy is fraught with even more difficulties. We have no accurate measure of general development, and certainly existing tests of intelligence – the most frequently used measures thus far – are not adequate for making comparisons of play.

Moreover, a consequence of matching on developmental age is that the differences in the children's life experiences are deliberately widened – the mentally handicapped children are chronologically older – and this introduces another confounding variable. Baumeister's (1967) solution – to have two samples each of normal and atypical children cross-matched on chronological and developmental age – is ideal but impractical given the need for large representative samples.

These, then, are the difficulties, but looking on the positive side some information is preferable to none. So what can we glean from the 12 studies carried out to date? Remember, *these are very tentative conclusions.*

Exploration

Three studies suggest that Down's children are less likely to manipulate and explore objects even when an attempt is made to equate their developmental progress (Serafica and Cicchetti, 1976; Switzky *et al.*, 1979; Bradley-Johnson *et al.*, 1981).

Play activities

Phemister *et al.* (1978) found no differences between the proportion of time which mentally handicapped children and normal 1 year olds played with toys when they were observed *at home*, but those who were studied in day centres, schools and hospital wards spent significantly less time in attentive play and in interactions with adults. Instead, they had higher levels of self-stimulation and inactivity. This study is a reminder that situation is yet another variable which influences the play of mentally handicapped children; a point illustrated even more clearly in the famous Brookland's experiment (Tizard, 1964).

Four further studies (Horne and Philleo, 1942; Tilton and Ottinger, 1964; Hulme and Lunzer, 1966; Weiner and Weiner, 1974) tried to determine whether mentally handicapped children's preferences for play activities differ from those of their able-bodied peers, and their conclusions were contradictory. The diversity of methodologies they used – and some were very questionable – makes it impossible to reconcile these discrepancies, and it is safest to conclude that there are no differences when the children are of comparable developmental status.

Representational play

In general, no differences have been found in the pretend play of developmentally matched Down's and normal children (Jeffree and McConkey, 1976; Riguet and Taylor, 1981; Casby and Ruder, 1983). Riguet and Taylor's study also included a group of autistic children who were found to play and imitate less than the normal and Down's children, who were generally comparable in their play patterns, but with one exception. Down's children produced significantly fewer different substitute symbolic uses for the objects, which the investigators ascribe to 'their tendency to elaborate the same idea repeatedly throughout a play period' (p.447). This echoes a speculation of Hulme and Lunzer's that, 'subnormal children are more content to repeat familiar routines with the different materials available, while normal children of similar mental age would be more apt to vary their use of materials' (p. 118). However, Casby and Ruder did *not* find this effect under test-like conditions.

Energetic play

Finally, only one study has sought to explore differences in children's gross motor play. Linford *et al.* (1971) found that Down's children moved much less often than normal and younger children (they tended to remain in the free space rather than interacting with the equipment provided), and they also showed marked differences in their preferences for equipment. The non-Down's children preferred climbing in and out of large wooden boxes, going on the rocking boat, and using bricks and planks, whereas the Down's children preferred the open tunnel and the high tressel (climbing frame). The investigators made no mention of possible balancing and co-ordination problems with the Down's children that could explain their avoidance of some activities (see Chapter 11 in this volume).

In summary, the strategy of comparing the play of mentally handicapped and normal children has not been particularly productive. The real fault lies not with the answers but with the naivety of the question. By definition, Down's children are different. The concept of eliminating the difference by matching on crude variables such as chronological age or mental abilities can be seen in retrospect as naive in the extreme. A more fruitful approach is to focus resources on mentally handicapped children so as to identify the influences on their play.

INFLUENCES ON PLAY

Why is it that mentally handicapped children differ in their play, even though they are of the same age and they are given the same toys? What is it that causes the same child to vary his or her play? These and similar questions will be addressed in this section and details of research studies are given in Table 15.3.

By far the most popular topic in play research with mentally handicapped children has been the relationship between the children's developmental level or mental abilities and the complexity and/or maturity of their play. The answer invariably seems to be 0.59! Let me explain. Cunningham and colleagues (1984), with a sample of 52 Down's children, found a correlation of 0.59 between scores on a test of symbolic play (Lowe and Costello, 1976) and the children's MA derived from the Bayley or Stanford Binet tests as appropriate. Odom's (1981) correlation, using a more general type of play scale and developmental scores from the Denver Test, was also 0.59. Riguet and Taylor (1981) found that the correlation for 10 Down's children on rating scale scores and results from the Peabody Picture Vocabulary Test was – yes, that's right – a correlation of 0.59. Not to be outdone, Dorothy Jeffree and McConkey (1976) managed to produce exactly this correlation for one measure of imaginative play and developmental age scores from the Griffith's Test, but given the small number of subjects it was not statistically significant. (But two other measures reflecting better the quality of children's play were correlated significantly.) Motti and colleagues (1983) also reported significant correlations between symbolic play ratings and Bayley Mental Scale scores, and once again it was 0.59. And, finally, Hill and McCune-Nicolich (1981), the sixth and final study of this type, managed to find a correlation of 0.59 but it was between the infants' chronological age and Bayley Test Mental Scale scores. The correlation between play measures and mental age was even higher – 0.75 – whereas that with the chronological age was only 0.44. In fact, when chronological age scores were partialled out, the correlation between MA and play was 0.66.

The common correlation of 0.59 is patently a coincidence, but we can confidently conclude from these six studies that with mentally handicapped children there is a relationship – albeit an imperfect one – between their level of play and their overall developmental progress. In short, play does not merely change with the passage of time but rather with the children's acquisition of new skills and abilities – though which is the chicken and which is the egg is a topic for future research.

The establishment of this general truism has opened several avenues of more detailed research.

Play and development

First, are there any correspondences between particular play behaviours and aspects of development? McConkey and Martin (1984a) found that children's exploratory and relational play was correlated significantly with Bayley *motor* scale scores at 12 months but not at 18 or 24 months of age, whereas the converse pattern held with *mental* scale scores, the correlation becoming significant only at 24 months when children had begun to pretend.

However, the main thrust of research in this area for various theoretical reasons has been the possible link between symbolic play and language acquisition (McCune-Nicolich, 1981). Casby and Ruder (1983) reported a strong relationship between symbolic play scores and measures of expressive language obtained from natural observations. This was true for mentally retarded and normal children. Other studies suggest an even closer correspondence between measures of pretending and children's verbal comprehension than with their expressive language. Cunningham *et al.* (1984), with 29 Down's children, reported a significant correlation of 0.60 between verbal comprehension (Reynell Tests) and play, whereas that for expressive language was non-significant at 0.30. (In both instances, the effects of CA were partialled out.) In a smaller scale study with 10 mentally handicapped children, I found a similar pattern of correlations.

Wing *et al.* (1977), in a 'population' study with 108 children showing language and developmental delays, found that *all* the children who were rated as having symbolic play had verbal and non-verbal comprehension ages of 24 months or above – suggesting a close correspondence between symbolic and linguistic competence.

Play sequences

Another approach to the relationship between play and development is to ascertain whether or not mentally handicapped children follow the same developmental sequence in their play with objects as do normal infants.

Cunningham *et al.* (1984), in an item analysis of the Lowe and Costello Symbolic Play Test, found an almost identical order of difficulty for Down's children to that reported for ordinary infants (rho = 0.95), and Whittaker (1980) found a comparable developmental order with older, hospitalised, profoundly retarded children.

But, Hill and McCune-Nicolich (1981) had to adapt the developmental sequences in pretend play hypothesised for normal infants (Nicolich, 1977) in order to obtain a scale which fitted the data obtained from Down's infants in their cross-sectional study. In particular, they merged single pretend acts into one category, even though ordinary infants invariably begin to pretend at their own activities (self-pretending) rather than with a doll or another person. With Down's infants either can come first. This suggested difference is further confirmed by the results of a longitudinal study with 10 Down's infants followed throughout their second year of life by McConkey and Martin (1985) and McConkey (1985). It was found that the order in which infants acquired new exploratory and relational play actions was similar to that reported for ordinary infants, albeit at a later age. However, the onset of self-pretend acts was particularly delayed, and had a low frequency of occurrence, certainly by comparison with data obtained by Rosenblatt (1977) (see Fig. 15.3).

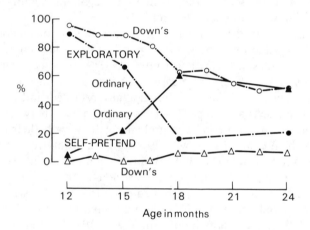

Fig. 15.3 Percentage of exploratory and self-pretend actions in the play of Down's Syndrome and ordinary infants (from McConkey and Martin, 1985, and Rosenblatt, 1977)

It is hard to find an adequate explanation for these findings. It may be that a re-appraisal of the play categories used in past studies with normal infants would credit them with fewer self-pretend acts. Hence Down's infants may not be very different after all. Alternatively, it could be that the lack of self-pretend acts is symptomatic of a specific deficit with Down's infants, the argument being that they are less inclined in their play to use affective reactions to signal pretence, e.g. smiling, adding noises, etc. Limited support for this hypothesis comes from a study by Motti *et al.* (1983). They report that Down's children with high ratings for symbolic play also scored higher on ratings of enthusiasm and positive affect in play. More significantly, past records showed that as infants they had smiled, laughed and cried more often in tests of affective reactions (see later). Further study of the relationship between affect and ability in children's play is required.

Adults' effect on play

McConkey and Martin (1985) reported that Down's infants showed higher levels of pretend actions when their mothers were playing with them rather than merely watching, although the overall frequency of play actions was similar in both situations. They attribute this effect to the mothers' spontaneously modelling appropriate play for the children.

Previous investigators have included modelling as an experimental condition. Jeffree and McConkey (1976) reported that it was effective at increasing the frequency and duration of imaginative play acts for both mentally handicapped and normal children, but that it did not affect either the number of different pretend acts the children performed or the 'elaborateness' of their actions. Moreover, with the Down's children, the effects of modelling did not carry over when the experimenter reverted to being an observer, whereas this did happen with the normal infants. Riguet and Taylor (1981) reported exactly the same results with Down's and autistic children. Again, modelling had an immediate rather than a carry-over effect.

However, in both these studies the adults' modelling lasted for 5 minutes at the most. If these children are 'slow learners', then they could well benefit from longer periods of modelling.

Toys and play

Not surprisingly, toys also elicit different play actions with mentally handicapped children. McConkey and Martin (1985) found more exploratory play actions when children were given a selection of toys rather than a single ring-stacking toy. With the latter there was a higher incidence of relational or combinatorial actions.

Flavell and Cannon (1977), in a study with severely retarded female adults, found that they had marked preferences for certain toys and showed it by the length of time they played with each. In fact, when the ten most popular toys were made available, the amount of play was twice as high as that when the ten least popular were available. The moral is obvious: if children like toys, they are inclined to play with them. Interestingly, this study also showed that more expensive toys were not necessarily the most popular, and that predictions made by care staff about the clients' preferences for toys were often quite wrong.

Unfortunately, few studies have gone on to identify further what it is about toys that appeals to children. A notable exception, though, is the work of Thomas *et al.* (1981), who found that even profoundly mentally handicapped children were enticed into playing with a specially designed novel toy which lit up and emitted sound as they manipulated it. In a follow-up study they showed that the mere addition of lights, sound or bright colours to a toy did not generally attract children to it. Rather, it is the effect the children produce with the toy that sustains their play. Another outcome of Jeffree and McConkey's (1976) study suggests that realistic-looking pretend toys elicit more pretend acts than less structured junk material such as cardboard boxes and pieces of wood. Exactly the same effect occurs with normal infants, and it is thought to be a reflection of their capacity to represent reality.

Hence, children's failure to play can be as much a reflection of the toys made available to them as of any inherent disability on their part.

Sex differences

Although this is a favourite theme in play research with children, it has received scant attention in the context of mental handicap. Only van der Kooij (1978) has reported detailed comparisons of boys' and girls' play and found no differences in their style of play but predictable variation in their toy preferences. Girls chose dolls, dolls' houses and Lego, whereas boys opted for model trees, bridges, cars and soldiers.

Similarly, Cunningham *et al.* (1984) found no differences between the pretend play of boys and girls, but they did discover differences in the correlations with language measures. These they attributed to Down's girls acquiring expressive language skills earlier than boys.

Social play

It has been more convenient for researchers to study one child playing with a set of toys than to measure the interactions among a group of children or even between one child and an adult. Hence, this section on social play will be much shorter than the preceding.

Again, the dominant concern has been a link between social play and cognitive development. Cicchetti and Sroufe (1976) attempted to find out what made Down's infants laugh. They found a close association between scores on an index of affective reactions and mental scales scores from the Bayley Test (rho = 0.89). Moreover, the Down's infants laughed to a group of stimulus items in the same order as did a previous sample of normal infants, although the process was delayed by several months. Mothers' tactile efforts (blowing on baby's hair, vigorous bouncing on knees, tickling under chin) and auditory games (such as varying tone and level of voice) were more likely to elicit smiling and laughter than were more social games (peek-a-boo, sticking out tongue for baby to grasp) or visual efforts (such as funny walks, pretend to drink from baby's bottle – the things mothers are asked to do in the cause of science!). But one other feature marked out the Down's infant. He or she was much more likely to smile, whereas normal infants of similar developmental abilities tended to laugh. Cicchetti and Sroufe attributed this to slower processing ability, i.e. the children fail to react to the incongruity which in normal children produces a tension that either laughing or crying releases. Indeed, Serafica and Cicchetti (1976) found that Down's infants were much less likely to cry when their mothers left them and, equally, on her return, the normal infants were more inclined to approach her and vocalise than were Down's infants. Overall, then, the data do suggest that Down's infants have lower levels of reactivity. One implication is that Down's babies need more time to express a reaction – a point to take up in Berger and Cunningham's research discussed in the next section.

Reactions to other children were the focus of Crawley and Chan's (1982) study. They observed small groups of mentally handicapped children aged 4.5–9 years in an outdoor playground for about 45 minutes, over a 4-week period. They found that teacher approaches decreased with age, as did the proportion of time the children were unoccupied. By contrast, solitary or parallel play increased as a function of age and mental abilities, but peer interaction only increased with older mildly and not moderately retarded children. However, Crawley and Chan drew attention to the low frequency of peer interaction even among the less handicapped children – a finding reminiscent of data presented on p. 284.

The biggest compliment that can be paid to the researchers included in this section is that their efforts have raised more questions than answers. Would the outcomes be similar with a wider age and /or ability range of children? Do the same influences affect play patterns in unstudied areas such as gross-motor play, team games and creative activities? And we are left speculating on the influence of other untested variables – the effect of settings (such as home, playgroups, neighbour-hood) or of people, or the influence that familiarity or novelty has on children's play repertoires.

So where have we got to in our research? Churchill's words seem most appropriate – we are but approaching 'the end of the beginning'.

PARENTS' PLAY

It is remarkable that so few studies have concerned themselves with parents' play, given the exhortation of many professionals. (See Table 15.4 in the Appendix for details of studies.) Moreover, all but one have focused on mothers.

Mothers' reactions to play

In a survey with 67 mothers of moderately and severely mentally handicapped children, McEvoy and McConkey (1983) found that all but one agreed that 'play is very important for children'. Moreover, 9 out of 10 felt that 'mothers should make time to play with their child', and 8 out of 10 asserted, 'I make sure my child has something to play with when I'm busy'.

However, when it came to the child's play, over three-quarters felt that it was repetitive; nearly half were of the opinion that their child got bored easily when they played together, and 4 out of 10 felt their child was more playful when left alone. Two-thirds were in favour of the child playing outside with other children or exploring in the neighbourhood, but against this, 8 out of 10 felt that it was too dangerous to let their child play out of doors.

On a specially designed inventory to tap mothers' reactions to various interac-tions they had with the child, mothers' 'enthusiasm' (i.e. 'I have fun with the child', 'a relaxing situation for me', 'we do this often', etc) was highest in the play context and lowest when they were shopping with the child. Likewise, Richardson (1979), in his Mother Tolerance Scale, found that playing received the second highest number of positive responses after cuddling and loving. The events least liked by mothers were feeding and changing nappies.

Thus, overall, mothers view play as an opportunity for positive and enjoyable interactions with their handicapped child. We await data on fathers' interactions.

Are they any different in this respect than parents of ordinary children? Jeffree and Cashdan (1971) rated parents' responses in an interview according to the amount of stimulation given to the children, i.e. language, involvement in adult activities, outings, play materials available, etc., and found no overall difference between the two groups of mothers, although the range of scores was much wider for mothers of handicapped children than for mothers with young non-handicapped children – a finding that is not too surprising given the wider age range of handicapped children.

Wulbert *et al.* (1975) also found no difference between mothers of normal and Down's infants using the Caldwell Inventory of Home Stimulation – a mixture of interview-cum-observational items, for which a rating can be obtained in six different areas. However, later studies by Bradley and Caldwell (1977) and Piper and Ramsay (1980) found significant relationships between three areas of the home environment and declines in the children's developmental quotients: in particular, poor organisation of the physical and temporal environment, fewer provisions of appropriate play materials, and less maternal involvement with the child. Similar data are reported for non-retarded infants (Elardo *et al.*, 1975).

Observing parents at play

In a study by Cook and Culp (1981), in which mothers were directly observed playing with a standard set of toys, no differences were found between the two sets of mothers in the number of toys they offered their children or in the way the children played with the toys – the groups having been matched developmentally. Again, though, Cook and Culp allude to the variation between mothers within both groups.

By contrast, studies concerned with face-to-face interactions between mothers and their Down's children suggest that there could well be differences between these mothers' reactions and those of normal childen's mothers. Berger and Cunningham (1983), in a longitudinal study of infants from 1 to 6 months of age, found that after 3 months mothers with Down's babies talked more often and that the turn-taking was impaired, i.e. there were more interruptions of each others' turns. This 'excessive maternal activity' they attributed to mothers' anxiety about the child's development and to a desire 'to produce responses in order to prove to oneself and others that he (the child) is not too handicapped' (p. 59).

Whether or not this interpretation is accurate, it could be applied also to mothers of older children because their behaviour is very similar. For example, Eheart (1982) studied mothers with 4-year-old mentally handicapped children. She found they initiated twice as many interactions and used over three times the number of directives as did mothers of ordinary children, who, instead, were much more inclined to centre their interactions around toys and activities chosen by the child.

A study by Stoneman *et al.* (1983) confirmed these results and found that this style of interaction held also for fathers, although to a lesser degree. The investigators concluded that parents of handicapped children tended to be the 'managers and teachers' of the play session, whereas parents with non-handicapped children were 'playmates'.

Crawley and Spiker (1983) questioned whether this parental directiveness was necessarily a bad thing. They devised comprehensive and reliable rating schemes of mothers' and children's behaviour during free play. An analysis of the resulting relationships on these scales suggested that: (a) mothers can be both directive and yet sensitive to their children – indeed, over half the mothers in the study were rated highly sensitive; (b) mothers were more directive when their children showed little interest in play – thus, this is an adaptive response from mothers; and (c) those mothers who combined directiveness and sensitivity in a way which stimulated the child (e.g. elaborating on the child's play) tended to have more competent children.

But a striking feature of all these studies is the wide, inter-parent variation, even with children of comparable ages and abilities. Having a handicapped child is therefore insufficient reason for assuming that these adults form a homogeneous group. We need to respect their individuality by studying it more often.

Changes in mothers' style

To date, only one study has attempted to trace changes in the way parents play with their children. McConkey and Martin (1983) observed the mothers of 10 Down's infants with two sets of toys – a ring-stacking toy and a collection of doll–play materials – at periodic intervals over the course of a year. They found that: (a) mothers' actions varied with the toys: they were twice as active with the ring-stacking and focused more on getting the child to produce specific responses, usually placing rings on to the stack, whereas they tolerated more open-ended play with the other set of toys; and (b) there were significant changes in the mothers' play acts over the year: they changed the type of prompts used with the ring-stacking toys and the models given with the pretend objects. Mothers appeared to anticipate and support their child's play until such times as the child was playing appropriately. Then the mothers withdrew their help. This effect is reminiscent of the parental scaffolding described by Bruner (1972) with normal infants. Interestingly, it emerged in a group discussion with the mothers at the end of the year that all felt they were still playing with their child in much the same way as they had at the beginning of the study.

The balance sheet of lessons learned is somewhat easier to draw up for this section. The small number of investigations may be a blessing for the reviewer, but in reality it is a disgrace. When so much of young children's play is family and parent centred, it is surprising that most researchers have chosen to focus exclusively on the child. Little wonder that the resulting photographs have blurred and undeveloped edges.

The few studies using a wider-angled lens show that not only do parents play with their handicapped children, but they make extra efforts – for better or worse – to help their child along. But, even more significant, parents enjoy themselves and their children when they are playing. Long may we continue to advise them to play with their children.

FACILITATING PLAY

So far, questions about the who, what, when and where of play have been covered, but two remain – why and how? I have chosen to answer them in the context of attempts to facilitate the play of mentally handicapped children.

Why bother?

More articles dealing with play have been published in the 1980s than in all the previous years put together. The dearth of studies prior to 1975 speaks volumes regarding commonly held values of play. It was seen as purposeless: mentally handicapped children were no better or no worse for playing. Moreover, there were more pressing priorities of adult concern, for instance self-care skills, behavioural disturbance, good quality out-of-home care.

The late 1970s saw a change of heart. First, as this volume documents, much progress had been made in these priority areas. Researchers could afford to spread their wings. Second, there was an upsurge of interest in home-based services. Third, increased interest in the play of normal children led developmental psychologists to appreciate more the value of play in the acquisition and mastery of new skills. And, fourth, and most recent of all, play is now seen as a reflection of the quality of life; it is important in its own right.

How?

In what way, by what means, and to what extent can we develop children's play? Researchers, wisely enough, began with the common-sense approach of trying out what people thought would work, first using the structured teaching derived from behavioural psychology and which had been successfully applied in other aspects of development such as self-care training; second, the provision of specially designed toys and equipment to elicit more purposeful play; and third, seeing the effect of adults modelling play for the children. Table 15.5 in the Appendix gives details of studies in this area.

Structured teaching

To date, five studies (all American) have explored the feasibility of this approach, the chief proponent of which is Wehman (1978). In a study with three severely retarded institutionalised women, he and his co-workers (Wehman *et al.*, 1976) induced much higher levels of interaction with toys by making social reinforcement contingent on the women's response to the toys. Smaller increases in peer interactions were also noted, as was a decrease in self-stimulatory finger flicking and body rocking.

Similarly, Knapczyk and Yoppi (1975) and Strain (1975) were able to develop and maintain co-operative and competitive social play in mentally retarded children through a combination of special praise and token rewards.

More recently, Schleien *et al.* (1981) and Anderson *et al.* (1983) have designed and evaluated leisure training programmes for mentally handicapped adults. That of Schleien *et al.* was a comprehensive programme that included the teaching of new games, counselling on leisure skills, and a points system of rewards for engaging in 'high-quality' leisure behaviour. The six residents living in the group home when the programme was implemented all showed a transformation of their leisure activities from passive pursuits, like watching television, to active participation with others in a range of leisure pastimes. Anderson's programme was more ambitious but less successful. It involved 60 residents of a large state facility for mentally retarded persons, ranging in age from 23 to 66 years with a mean length of institutionalisation of 24 years. After 9 weeks, there was no change in the frequency of residents' social contacts, although there was a slight increase in their duration. Obviously 9 weeks is too short a time in which to counteract 24 years of institutionalisation.

These studies all suggest that play and leisure behaviours can be increased given sustained effort on the part of the 'trainers'.

Toys

Commercially available toys are not always the most suitable for, or indeed the preferred toys of, handicapped children. However, available research suggests that specially designed or easily modified toys can successfully elicit play behaviours from even the most severely retarded child.

The case study described by Hewson *et al.* (1980) showed how a ring-stacking toy, with built-in lights and sounds that came on when the child interacted with it, could trigger major advances in the child's ability to play appropriately with it and other toys. Similarly, Richardson *et al.* (1981) found that a range of play materials designed for multiply handicapped children prompted more developmentally productive kinds of manipulative play than did a selection of comparable conventional toys.

McConkey (1980) illustrated how toys like ring-stacks, form-boards and post-boxes could be graded in difficulty so that children could attain success more easily. Recently, this concept has been extended to mentally handicapped adolescents. Jeffree and Cheseldine (1982) selected five board games, such as bingo and snakes and ladders, and for each they prepared a graded series of simplified games. These were then used in school and at home by the young people's parents. Assessments carried out before and after the intervention showed increases in the quantity and quality of interactions with peers.

Adapting and designing toys is a particularly attractive way of intervening in children's play. It is unobtrusive; it need not require adult company, and it is certainly more ecologically valid than the alternatives considered in the previous section.

Modelling

Showing children how to play with toys is a time-honoured way of widening their repertoires. The case studies presented by Hewson *et al.* (1980) and by McConkey and Jeffree (1980) show that *sustained* modelling of pretend play by parents or teachers can result in more advanced play behaviours with mentally handicapped children.

Indeed, McConkey and Martin's (1984a) longitudinal study took this a stage further, albeit unintentionally. They observed that five mothers in their study, of their own accord, modelled more pretend play for the children than did the other five mothers. When the children's play patterns were compared, they found that the modellers' children showed an earlier onset and higher levels of pretend play than did the infants whose mothers mainly observed. These findings are all the more significant because they emerged from a natural experiment and are a reminder of the power for progress that is available in spontaneously occurring parent–child interactions (Crawley and Spiker, 1983).

The possibility of a more able child providing models or 'tutoring' for a less able child is an issue relevant to the mainstreaming or integration of handicapped children in ordinary settings. As yet, play skills rarely feature in these studies, but there are indications from a small investigation undertaken by Morris and Dolker (1974) that highly interactive children can elicit co-operative play responses from a socially withdrawn child, particularly when they are paired with reinforcement and shaping procedures. However, these had no effect when two low-interacting children were paired together. I predict that we shall see many more studies concerning peer tutoring in the future.

Finally, the results of the study by Berger and Cunningham (1983) are a reminder that there is a time for modelling and a time for non-modelling! Their aim was to increase the frequency of smiling and vocalising in the Down's infants, and to do this they advised mothers: (a) only to imitate the infant's behaviour; (b) to imagine the baby was having his photograph taken and to try to get him to smile as much as possible; and (c) to talk to the baby naturally. Only the first of these conditions elicited increased smiling and vocalisations. This they attributed to mothers giving their children more time to respond (see p. 294).

Telling others

Lastly, a more general way of facilitating play is by making parents and staff more informed about play. As part of our research in Dublin, my colleagues and I have been exploring a new method of doing this – videocourses (McConkey *et al.* 1982). Our *Let's Play* course consists of six videoprogrammes, five dealing with a different aspect of play (exploration, social, energetic, imaginative and skilful), with a final review programme. In each, we illustrate how the play of mentally handicapped children develops and pinpoint specific ways by which parents and staff can nurture that type of play. Observation charts are provided for each play area and suggested activities listed. During the course the parents are requested to select one or two 'new' play activities each week.

Our evaluation has shown that parents rate the course positively, although they preferred some aspects to others. However, 3 months after the course was completed we visited the families to see what changes, if any, there were in the children's play and in the mothers' reactions to play. Overall, mothers gave more instances of the child playing and they reported specific increases in pretend, fine-motor, and cognitive play activities and more examples of the child being included in the housework.

Moreover, the parents rated themselves more enthusiastic about their contacts with their children (see p. 293), not only during play but also when dressing and shopping with the children.

Beyond play

With non-handicapped children, it remains a contentious issue whether play tutoring/training results in gains in other aspects of development. Without going into the intricacies of the debate, the balance of evidence seems to suggest that this is certainly a possibility (Rubin *et al.*, 1983). Equally, then, there should be exciting days ahead in the realm of mental handicap research. As a flavour of this, let me recount the unexpected outcome of a study which I carried out with Heather Martin and Susan Martin (Martin *et al.*, 1984).

Our aim was to encourage mentally handicapped children to use two- or three-word sentences. We designed three play settings – a miniature playground, a kitchen scene made of felt figures, and a variety of picture games such as posting pictures of foodstuffs through the mouth of a cut-out face. As the children played, the teacher gave the appropriate sentence models describing what the children were doing. Our theory was that this should encourage the children to talk in sentences. To test it we used two groups of children, one receiving the teacher's models, the other a control group which merely played with the toys in the teacher's presence. To our surprise, both groups showed significant improvements on post-training assessments 3 weeks later, and these gains were maintained at re-testing after 4 weeks. Various control procedures ascertained that the games were not an artefact of measurement. Thus, the daily experience of representational play in the presence of an attentive adult had a more potent effect on the children's expressive language than did the teacher's models. Our explanation was that the play experiences gave the children sustained practice at creating relationships between familiar referents. Hence, they had become more adept at identifying and understanding relationships – a prerequisite for the use of sentence rules.

These results need to be replicated with other children in other settings before we can carol the efficacy of play-based interventions. What they at least do – and certainly what they did for me and my colleagues – is to open the possibility that under the right mix of circumstances (in this case regular exposure to play settings attuned to the children's mental abilities in the presence of an encouraging adult), mentally handicapped children can make their own discoveries about the world.

(In this section I have made no reference to the studies which have come to be known as 'play therapy'. In the main, their goal has been to use play as a means to an end, for example in dealing with emotional disturbance. Because of clinical demands, they are frequently lacking in experimental rigour or adequate controls. Readers wishing to pursue this topic in the context of mental handicap should consult the recent review by Leland (1983).)

THE VALUE OF PLAY

So where do we go from here? In the manner of the best television documentary, I have gathered reactions from some eminent experts to give us pointers. Their comments were framed in the context of play for all children, but I have taken the liberty of making further interpretations specifically for children who are likely to be considered mentally handicapped. Here is how they see the value of play and the implications it has for parents and professionals eager to nurture the growth of Down's infants.

Friedrich Froebel (1826): 'Play is the highest phase of child development ... for it is the self-active representation of the inner.'
Play can yield insights into children's understanding and thinking. To date, psychologists, teachers and therapists have had to rely mainly on 'tests' to obtain what they could of this information. This need be so no longer; research into play has shown us another way and one which offers many advantages (Newson, 1976; McConkey, 1984). Children are observed in natural and familiar settings, their capacity for self-initiated and self-maintained activities is sampled and their interactions with familiar adults, be it parent or teacher, can be easily incorporated into the assessment. Tests could become a relic of history.

I admit, though, that this new approach will only come to fruition when we have more information on the development of play in atypical children, obtained from longitudinal studies with large representative samples. Such data will tell us:

(a) the developmental sequences to expect and whether or not they differ markedly from those found with normal children – existing evidence, as we have seen, is somewhat contradictory;

(b) the correspondences that exist between play and other aspects of development, for example the relationship between pretending and aspects of language acquisition.

With these data we could also begin to trace further some of the reasons why children's play varies. How much do intra-child variables, such as muscle tone, attentiveness and emotionality, influence their play compared to 'environmental' variables such as home background and parental interactions. These data are just beginning to seep through for non-handicapped infants (e.g. Bee *et al.*, 1982), but we cannot assume that they will hold for infants with Down's Syndrome.

However, all this could prove to be wishful thinking. Longitudinal projects are costly and difficult to mount. We may have to be content with smaller scale projects in which approximately 20 infants are followed throughout the first 5–7 years of their lives. If such projects were replicated in several locations, the accumulating data would be an invaluable legacy for future generations. Could you play a part in this?

And, in case you think the concept of assessment through play is new, it is nearly 2000 years since Ovid wrote: 'In our play we reveal the kind of people we are.'

Jerome Bruner (1972): 'Play is ... a means of learning in a less risky situation.'
Research into mental handicap has barely begun to contemplate this possibility. The notion that mentally handicapped people have a 'spontaneous learning deficit' has had a pervasive influence on the design of intervention programmes. More often than not, these have sought to eliminate the need for spontaneous learning through explicit, step-by-step, structured teaching rather than by nurturing through training the individual's capacity for spontaneous learning. Yet, imposed rote knowledge runs certain risks – the main one being that the learning is confined to certain situations and tasks; it fails to generalise to novel contexts (Dearden, 1968).

With ordinary children, evidence is accumulating that play can aid problem solving (Cheyne and Rubin, 1983). With atypical children, we need to contrast the efficacy of structured interventions based around detailed teaching procedures, such as those used in the Portage Scheme, with those centred on developmentally appropriate play (see Chapter 17 for further discussion of this issue). Perhaps the time has come to give play a chance as a vehicle of learning. The risk of failure is small; the potential rewards are great.

David Elkind (1976): 'Play is ... an expression of having attained mastery and portrays an action, the joy of being in control.'
I wonder how often mentally handicapped people experience this joy? As we have seen, adults have few choices of leisure pursuits or even of friendships. Surely, these data must cause us to reflect on the priorities we have in the services we offer today's children so that we can avoid a repetition with tomorrow's adults. First, there must be a concerted drive by parents and professionals to facilitate friendships among handicapped children. Second, we need to further their competence in leisure pursuits with the same resources we are willing to expend on work skills and self-care training. But, foremost of all, we need to encourage mentally handicapped people to take more control of their lives by giving them choices and through respect for their preferences. This can begin from the earliest days and last a lifetime. Action-based research projects are needed to identify the critical elements in achieving these ambitions. If you have succeeded, tell others; if you are still trying, keep going.

Brenda Crowe (1983): 'Play is a feeling.'
We need this reminder. Psychological research into play has become fixated on ability rather than on the emotional dimension of play. We must learn more about parents' feelings – of the joys as well as the trials of parenthood and how to make

the former outweigh the latter. Existing evidence suggests that focusing on play will get us off to a head start.

We must also learn more about children's feelings and how they express them. Can we reduce ambiguities and misinterpretations either by changing the child's method of expression or by making the onlooker more perceptive?

And we must learn more about the feelings of adults who are mentally handicapped; their feelings not just of the present but also about the past. The play experiences we offer our children today are in part a reflection of our own desires and recollections of childhood. If we could but listen to mentally handicapped people reminiscing...

Brian Sutton-Smith (1979): 'Play is the fool that might become king.'
The values that our society holds are slow to change, but they are changeable. One need look no further than at the way mentally handicapped people are treated now compared to 100 years ago. But how will they be viewed in 100 years time? And what will historians make of today's services with their current priorities and values? What value might succeeding generations place on nurturing play and leisure? George Santayana's words of nearly a century ago might have more effect on them than they have had on our generation: 'To condemn spontaneous and delightful occupation because they are useless for self-preservation shows an uncritical prizing of life, irrespective of its content.'

APPENDIX: RESEARCH STUDIES ON PLAY AND LEISURE

This appendix lists research studies known to the author in April, 1984. Brief details are given of each to supplement the information presented in the text and to facilitate comparisons across studies. The tables will help readers to select articles on particular aspects of play and leisure.

The following criteria were used in the selection of articles.

1. The sample included Down's Syndrome or mentally handicapped children and adults and/or their families.

2. The topic was judged relevant to play and leisure.

3. The article presents objective data obtained from interviews, rating scales, observations or tests.

The studies are grouped into five tables, according to the primary aim of the investigation. In a few instances, studies are allocated to more than one table, but this was kept to a minimum. Within each table, the studies are listed alphabetically by authors.

Abbreviations used

CA	Chronological (actual) age.
DA	Developmental age (derived from developmental scale).
DS	Down's Syndrome.
ESN(S)	British term to denote moderately and severely handicapped children, namely 'educationally subnormal–severe'.
MA	Mental age (derived from intelligence tests or similar).
MH	Mental handicap – unspecified.
X̄	Mean or average.

Table 15.1 *Surveys of play/leisure activities of mentally handicapped children/adults*

Authors	Numbers (% DS)	Age range (years.months)	Sample	Information given
Cheseldine and Jeffree (1981)	214 (37% DS)	13.4–19.8	All teenagers attending ESN(S) schools in Greater Manchester, England	1) Survey of youth organisations accepting MH People 2) Teenagers' leisure pursuits and friendship patterns 3) Parents' attitudes
Katz and Yekutiel (1974)	128	17.0–50.0	All graduates of two sheltered workshops in Israel	1) Parents' perceptions of leisure-time problems 2) Types of leisure time activities 3) Activities with opposite sex and friendship patterns
McConkey and Jeffree (1975)	223 (38% DS)	1.7–5.0	All aged under 5 years classified as ESN(S) in Greater Manchester, England	1) Comparisons between play abilities of Down's and non-Down's children 2) Parents' concerns
McConkey *et al.* (1981)	207 (12% DS)	15.0–64.0	All mentally handicapped people living at home in one community care area of Dublin, Ireland	1) Leisure activities of adults 2) Reasons given for their non-participation in leisure pursuits
McEvoy and McConkey (1983)	67 (39% DS)	2.0–15.0	Sample drawn from day centre attenders, Dublin, Ireland	1) Play activities at home with different people 2) Mothers' perceptions of play
Reiter and Levi (1981)	44 (% DS not given)	17.0–35.0	Random sample of attenders at social club, sheltered workshops and open employment, Israel	Comparison between leisure pursuits of mentally handicapped and non-handicapped people
Richardson (1979)	76 (26% DS)	2.0–3.11	All children with moderate/severe developmental delays in West Central Scotland	1) Children's play abilities 2) Mothers' reactions to play
Walsh and McConkey (1983)	185 (54% DS)	0.7–5.0	All children under 5 years referred to a mental handicap service in 1982	People playing with the mentally handicapped child

Table 15.2 *Studies comparing the play activities of handicapped and non-handicapped groups of children*

Authors	Groups	Age ranges (years)	Matched	Observations	Play measures	Information
Bradley-Johnson et al. (1981)	10 DS 10 Ordinary	0.11–1.4 0.115–1.05	CA	Structured presentation of objects in university clinic	Duration of 3 types of play acts	1) Infants' mouthing, manipulation and visual exploration of objects 2) Response to novelty
Casby and Ruder (1983)	20 MR	2.5–2.8	Expressive language—MLU	Structured presentation of objects in individual sessions	Number of objects used symbolically	1) Relationship between language and symbolic play
	20 Normal	1.7–2.8				2) Characteristics of objects in eliciting symbolic acts
Horne and Philleo (1942)	25 MH 25 Ordinary	x̄ 11.0 x̄ 7.5	MA	Free play in familiar playroom	Time and incidence of play with toys	Toy/activities preference
Hulme and Lunzer (1966)	18 MH (10 DS) 18 Ordinary	3.5–11.5 2.0–4.5	MA	Free play at nursery/day centre	Ratings of play in terms of its organisation	1) Play ratings varied with MA 2) Language and reasoning abilities
Jeffree and McConkey (1976)	9 MH (6 DS) 10 Ordinary	4.9–9.7 1.6–3.5	DA	Free play with standard toy sets in part of classroom	Frequency and duration of pretend play acts	Correlations of pretend play and DA scores
Linford et al. (1971)	11 DS 32 Ordinary	4.8–8.0 3.0–5.0	MA	Free play with large-scale apparatus in experimental playroom	Frequency of movements and time spent on activities	1) Children's movements 2) Preferences for activities
Phemister et al. (1978)	76 MH 38 Ordinary	3.0–19.0 0.9–2.5	DA (approx)	One day in usual setting	Frequency of opportunities, activities and adult availability	1) Comparison between children's activities 2) Variations across home, day centre, hospital school, hospital ward
Riguet and Taylor (1981)	10 DS 10 Autistic 10 Normal	6.0–12.0 6.0–12.0 2.0–4.0	MA	Structured presentation of toy sets in experimental room	Rating on 5-point play scale	1) Play levels across groups 2) Effect of modelling

Study	Sample	Age	CA/MA	Procedure	Measures	Findings
Serafica and Cicchetti (1976)	12 DS 12 Ordinary	$\bar{X}$ 2.95 $\bar{X}$ 2.8	CA	Infants reaction to 8 episodes with mother/stranger present/absent	Frequency counts	Comparison of children's approaches to mother, fine and gross manipulation objects
Switzky *et al.* (1979)	12 MH 12 Ordinary	$\bar{X}$ 2.7 + $\bar{X}$ 3.8 $\bar{X}$ 2.4 + $\bar{X}$ 3.7	CA + MA	Structured presentation of stimuli in experimental room	Duration of exploration/play	Exploration time varies with age and complexity of objects
Tilton and Ottinger (1964) Data reanalysed Weiner *et al.* (1969)	12 MR 13 Autistic 18 Ordinary	3.3–6.4 3.7–6.7 3.7–5.11	CA	Free play with standard set of toys	Frequency counts of play actions	Play acts with toys – differences across groups
Weiner and Weiner (1974)	20 MR 20 Normal 20 Normal	$\bar{X}$ 6.5 $\bar{X}$ 6.0 $\bar{X}$ 3.0	CA + MA	Free play with standard set of toys in experimental room	Frequency counts at 20-second intervals of 10 play categories	Discriminating variables among the 3 groups of children

Table 15.3 *Studies of factors influencing the play of mentally handicapped children*

Authors	Numbers	Age ranges (years.months)	Variables	Observations	Play measures	Information
Cicchetti and Sroufe (1976)	14 DS	0.4–1.6 longitudinal	1) Age 2) Cognitive maturity 3) Type of stimuli	30 stimuli presented by mother in home	Incidence of smiling/laughing to item	Children's affective reactions
Crawley and Chan (1982)	20 MH (13 DS)	1) 2.8–3.6 2) 4.1–6.1	1) Age 2) Degree of handicap	Free play in outdoor playground	Frequency of social behaviours	Social interactions with teachers and peers
Cunningham et al. (1984)	50 DS	1.7–6.0	1) Age 2) MA 3) Language	Standardised tests administered in home	Symbolic Play Test (Lowe and Costello, 1976)	Relationship of symbolic play with MA and language development
Flavell and Cannon (1977)	11 MH	11.0–26.0	1) Range of toys	Free play with standard set of toys in classroom	Duration of enjoyment with each toy	Preferences for toys and relationship with cost and staff predictions
Hill and McCune-Nicolich (1981)	30 DS	1.8–4.5	1) Age 2) MA	Free play with standard set of toys	Frequency of pretend play acts	Correlations between ranking of symbolic play and CA and MA
Jeffree and McConkey (1976)	9 MH (6 DS)	4.9–9.7	1) DA 2) Modelling 3) Types of toys	Free play with standard sets of toys in part of classroom	Frequency and duration of pretend play acts	Changes in children's pretend play acts
van der Kooij (1978)	38 MH	7.0–11.0	1) Sex 2) Toy preferences 3) IQ	Free play with standard set of toys in university playroom	Frequency of play acts with toys	Toy preferences: sex differences Relationship with IQ
McConkey and Martin (1984)	10 DS	1.0–2.0 longitudinal	1) CA 2) Mother playing/ observing	Free play with standard set of toys in home	Frequency of play acts	Changes in play actions with age and more pretend with mothers playing
McConkey (1985)	10 DS	1.0–2.0 longitudinal	1) CA	Free play with ring-stacking toy	Frequency of exploratory and relational play acts	Changes in play actions and steps involved in learning to place rings on stack

Author (year)	N	Age	Variables	Measures	Setting	Focus
Motti *et al.* (1983)	31 DS	3.0–5.6	1) Mental Scale Scores 2) Affective	Rating scales for various dimensions of play	Free play with standard set of toys in experimental room	Correlations with DA and affective measures Interrelationships among play scale
Odom (1981)	21 MH	4.6–8.11	1) Age 2) MA	Rating scales	Free play in classroom	Correlations between play and CA and DA
Riguet and Taylor (1981)	10 DS	6.0–12.0	1) Modelling 2) Types of toys	Ratings on 5-point scale	Structured presentation of toy sets in experimental classroom	Effects of modelling and less realistic toys
Thomas *et al.* (1981)	1) 17 MH 2) 36 MH 3) 6 MH 4) 15 MH	6.4–16.2 3.6–16.6 3.6–16.0 5.8–16.4	Varying toy characteristics Number of toys	Latencies prior to contact No. of activities	Structural presentation of toys in experimental room	Toy play of severely handicapped children in long-stay hospital
Whittaker (1980)	34 MH (2 DS)	7.3–18.6	Developmental sequences	Symbolic Play Test (Lowe and Costello, 1976)	Individual administration of test	Developmental sequence with profoundly retarded children in long-stay hospitals
Wing *et al.* (1977)	108 MH + language delayed (21 DS)	5.0–14.0	1) MA 2) Language	3-point rating	Free play in home or classroom	Relationship between symbolic play and language development

Table 15.4 *Studies of parents' play with mentally handicapped children and their perceptions of play*

Authors	Parents		Age of child (years.months)	Type of study	Measures of parents	Information
Berger and Cunningham (1983)	1) 6 Mothers	DS	0.1–0.6 longitudinal	Observations of mothers in home	Frequencies of mothers' speech, imitations of baby, attempts to elicit smile	Early social interactions of mothers and the effects of changes in their style on DS infants
	6 Mothers	NH	0.5–0.6			
	2) 12 Mothers	DS	0.35–0.4			
	12 Mothers	NH				
Cook and Culp (1981)	8 Mothers	DS	x̄ 1.8	Observation of mothers playing in the home	Frequencies of toys presented	No differences between mothers with developmentally age-matched infants
	8 Mothers	NH	x̄ 1.0			
Crawley and Spiker (1983)	18 Mothers	DS	1.10–2.15	Observations of mothers at home	10 rating scales of mothers	Relationship between mother and child behaviours; Individual variations; Home stimulation
Jeffree and Cashdan (1971)	28 Mothers	NH	x̄ 12	Interviews with mothers at home	Play acts with ring-stacking and pretend play toys	Changes in mothers' play acts with toys and as child's play matures
	28 Mothers	NH	x̄ 4.5			
McConkey and Martin (1983)	10 Mothers	DS	1.0–2.0 longitudinal	Observations of mothers playing at home		
McEvoy and McConkey (1983)	67 Mothers	NH	2.0–15.0	Interviews with mothers at home		Attitudes to play/toys and reactions to interacting with child during play, dressing and shopping
Stoneman *et al.* (1983)	8 Mothers	DS	4.0–7.0	Observations of parents/child at home	Role parents adopted during interactions with mother/child; father/child; mother/father/child	Comparisons between two groups of parents and mothers and fathers
	8 Fathers	DS				
	8 Mothers	NH	4.0–7.0			
	8 Fathers	NH				
Wulbert *et al.* (1975)	20 Mothers	DS	Not given	Interview/observation	Ratings on Caldwell Inventory of Home Stimulation	Comparison between three groups on total and sub-test scores
	20 Mothers	LD	3.0–5.6			
	20 Mothers	NH	3.0–5.6			

NH = non-handicapped.
LD = language delay.

Table 15.5 *Studies evaluating ways of facilitating play and leisure activities*

Authors	Numbers	Age ranges (years.months)	Intervention	Setting	Measures	Information
Anderson *et al.* (1983)	60 MH	23.0–66.0	9-week activity programme	Residential centre – professional staff	Frequency and duration of social interactions	Activity programmes for adults in residential centres
Flavell (1973)	3 MH	8.0–14.0	Physical guidances and reinforcements	Experimental room	Frequency of appropriate play and self-stimulation	Increasing contact with toys
Hewson *et al.* (1980)	Case study multiply handicapped child	5.5 years	Special toys modelled play	Home	Frequency of appropriate play acts	Toy design Planned play programme
Jeffree and Cheseldine (1982) Knapczyk and Yoppi (1975)	23 ESN(S) pupils 5 MH	13.0–19.0 8.0–10.0	Simplified table-top games Social praise and tokens	School and home Developmental training centre	Type of activity chosen by skill levels Frequency of competitive + co-operative responses	Evaluation of 'programmed' games Reinforcement increasing social interactions
McConkey (1980)	65 MH (54% DS)	3.4–8.4	Graded toys	Schools	Percentage of children succeeding at each level of difficulty	Grading toys to children's abilities
McConkey and Jeffree (1980) McConkey *et al.* (1982)	2 Case studies DS 34 MH (40% DS)	2.5 + 3.5 2.0–15.0	Modelling pretend play Videocourse for parents on play	Home (playgroup) Home	Frequency of play actions Incidence of play activities	Pretend play increased by active modelling Changes in children's play and mothers' perceptions after parent training course
Martin *et al.* (1984)	23 MH (78% DS)	4.0–10.0	Specially designed representational toys	Experimental room in school	Frequency of sentence usage in expressive language	Improvements in language following play sessions

Morris and Dolker (1974)	6 Severely MH	4.0–12.0	Pairing high and low interacting children	Partitioned classroom	Frequency of 'co-operation cycles'	Increasing social interactions
Richardson et al. (1981)	16 Severely MH	7.0–16.0	Specially designed toys	Experimental room	Frequency of play acts with toys	Design features of toys and advantages over conventional toys
Schleien et al. (1981)	6 MH adults	27.0–52.0	Leisure skills programme	Group home	Frequency of 'quality' leisure acts	Components of programme – selection new activities, reinforcement, instruction, counselling
Strain (1975)	8 MH	4.0–5.0	Sociodramatic activities and social reinforcement	Special facility classroom	Percentage of intervals engaged in social play	Changes in social play patterns
Wehman et al. (1976)	3 Severely MH	29, 31, 32	Training in manipulating toys	Experimental room in residental centre	Percentage of time interacting with toys and peers	Increasing play with toys

REFERENCES

Anderson, S.C., Grossman, L.M. and Finch H.A. (1983). Effects of a recreation programme on the social interaction of mentally retarded adults. *J. Leisure Res.* (in press).

Baumeister, A.A. (1967). Problems in comparative studies of mental retardates and normals. *Am. J. Ment. Defic.* **71**, 869–75.

Bee, H.L., Barnard, K.E., Eyres, S.J., Gray, C.A., Hammond, M.A., Spietz, A.L., Snyder, C. and Clark B. (1982). Prediction of IQ and language skill from perinatal status, child performance, family characteristics, and mother–infant interaction. *Child Dev.* **53**, 1134–56.

Berger, J. and Cunningham, C. (1983). Early social interactions between infants with Down's Syndrome and their parents. *Health Visitor* **56**, 58–60.

Bradley, R.H. and Caldwell, B.M. (1977). Early environment and changes in mental test performance in children from 6 to 36 months. *Dev. Psychol.* **12**, 93–7.

Bradley-Johnson, Friedrich, D.D. and Wyrembelski, A.R. (1981). Exploratory behaviour in Down's Syndrome and normal infants. *Appl. Res. Ment. Retard.* **2**, 213–28.

Bruner, J. (1972). Nature and uses of immaturity. *Am. Psychol.* **12**, 687–708.

Casby, M.W. and Ruder, K.F. (1983). Symbolic play and early language development in normal and mentally retarded children. *J. Speech & Hearing Res.* **26**, 404–411.

Cheseldine, S.E. and Jeffree, D.M. (1981). Mentally handicapped adolescents: their use of leisure. *J. Ment. Def. Res.* **25**, 49–59.

Cheyne, J.A. and Rubin, K.H. (1983). Playful precursors of problem solving in preschoolers. *Dev. Psychol.* **19**, 577–84.

Cicchetti, D. and Sroufe, L.A. (1976). The relationship between affective and cognitive development in Down's Syndrome infants. *Child Dev.* **47**, 920–29.

Cook, A.S. and Culp, R.E. (1981). Mutual play of mothers with their Down's Syndrome and normal infants. *Int. J. Rehab. Res.* **4**(3) 542–4.

Crawley, S.B. and Chan, K.S. (1982). Developmental changes in free-play behaviour of mildly and moderately retarded preschool-aged children. *Ed. & Train. Ment. Retard.* **17**, 234–9.

Crawley, S.B. and Spiker, D. (1983). Mother–child interactions involving two-year olds with Down's Syndrome: A look at individual differences. *Child Dev.* **54**, 1312–23.

Crowe, B. (1983). *Play is a Feeling.* London: George Allen & Unwin.

Cunningham, C.C., Glenn, S.M., Wilkinson, P. and Sloper, P. (1984). Mental ability, symbolic play and receptive and expressive language of young children with Down's Syndrome. *J. Child Psychol. & Psych.* (in press).

Dearden, R.F. (1968). *The Philosophy of Primary Education.* London: Routledge and Kegan Paul.

Eheart, B.K. (1982). Mother–child interactions with nonretarded and mentally retarded preschoolers. *Am. J. Ment. Defic.* **87**, 20–25.

Elardo, R., Bradley, R. and Caldwell, B.M. (1975). The relation of infants' home environments to mental test performance from six to thirty-six months: A longitudinal analysis. *Child Dev.* **46**, 71–6.

Elkind, D. (1976). *Child Development and Education: A Piagetian Perspective.* New York: Oxford University Press.

Flavell, J.E. (1973). Reduction of stereotypes by reinforcement of toy play. *Ment. Retard.* **11**, 21–3.

Flavell, J.E. and Cannon, P.R. (1977). Evaluation of entertainment materials for severely retarded persons. *Am. J. Ment. Defic.* **81**(4), 357–61.

Froebel, F. (1826). *The Education of Man.*

Hewson, S., McConkey, R. and Jeffree, D.M. (1980). The relationship between structured and free play in the development of a mentally handicapped child: A case study. *Child: Care, Health and Development* **6**, 73–82.

Hill, P.M. and McCune-Nicolich, L. (1981). Pretend play and patterns of cognition in Down's Syndrome children. *Child Dev.* **52**, 611–17.

Horne, B.M. and Philleo, C.C. (1942). A comparative study of the spontaneous play activities of normal and mentally defective children. *J. Gen. Psychol.* **61**, 33–46.

Hulme, I. and Lunzer, E.A. (1966). Play, language and reasoning in subnormal children. *J. Child Psychol. & Psych.* **7**, 107–123.

Jeffree, D.M. and Cashdon, A. (1971). The home background of the severely subnormal child: A second study. *Brit. J. Med. Psych.* **44**, 27–33.

Jeffree, D.M. and Cheseldine, S.E. (1982). A new leisure class. The effect of training in leisure-time occupations on ESN(S) school leavers. *Child: Care, Health and Development* **8**, 283–94.

Jeffree, D.M. and McConkey, R. (1976). An observation scheme for recording children's imaginative doll play. *J. Child Psychol. & Psych.* **17**, 189–97.

Katz, S. and Yekutiel, E. (1974). Leisure time problems of mentally retarded graduates of training programs. *Ment. Retard.* **12**, 54–7.

Kellmer-Pringle, M. (1975). *The Needs of Children*. London: Hutchinson.

Knapczyk, D.R. and Yoppi, J.O. (1975). Development of cooperative and competitive play responses in developmentally disabled children. *Am. J. Ment. Defic.* **80**, 245–55.

Kooij, R., van der (1978). A study of the play behaviour of retarded children. *Int. J. Rehab. Res.* **1**, 329–41.

Leland, H. (1983). Play therapy for mentally retarded and developmentally disabled children. In Schaefer, C.E. and O'Connor, K.J. (eds), *Handbook of Play Therapy*. New York: Wiley–Interscience.

Linford, A.G., Jeanrenaud, C.Y., Karlsson, K., Witt, P. and Linford, M.D. (1971). A computerized analysis of characteristics of Down's Syndrome and normal children's free play patterns. *J. Leisure Res.* **3**, 44–52.

Lowe, M. and Costello, A. (1976). *Manual for the Symbolic Play Test (Experimental Edition)*. Windsor: NFER.

McConkey, R. (1980). Designing and evaluating toys for the mentally handicapped child. *J. Pract. App. Dev. Hand.* **3**(3), 10–15.

McConkey, R. (1984). The assessment of representational play: A springboard for language remediation. In Müller, D.J. (ed.), *Remediating Children's Language: Behavioural and Naturalistic Approaches*. London: Croom-Helm.

McConkey, R. (1985). Changing beliefs about play and handicapped children. *Early Child Develop. and Care* (in press).

McConkey, R. and Jeffree, D.M. (1975). Pre-school mentally handicapped children. *Brit. J. Educ. Psych.* **45**, 307–11.

McConkey, R. and Jeffree, D.M. (1980). Developing children's play. *Spec. Ed.: Forward Trends* **7**, 21–3.

McConkey, R. and Martin, H. (1983). Mothers' play with toys: a longitudinal study with Down's Syndrome infants. *Child: Care, Health and Development* **9**, 215–26.

McConkey, R. and Martin, H. (1985). The development of object and pretend play in Down's Syndrome infants: A longitudinal study involving mothers. *Trisomy 21* (in press).

McConkey, R., McEvoy, J. and Gallagher, F. (1982). Learning through play: the evaluation of a videocourse for parents of mentally handicapped children. *Child: Care, Health and Development* **8**, 345–59.

McConkey, R., Walsh, J. and Mulcahy, M. (1981). The recreational pursuits of mentally handicapped adults. *Int. J. Rehab. Res.* **4**(4), 493–9.

McCune-Nicolich, L. (1981). Towards symbolic functioning: structure of early pretend games and potential parallels with language. *Child Dev.* **52**, 785–97.

McEvoy, J. and McConkey, R. (1983). Play activities of mentally handicapped children at home and mothers' perceptions of play. *Int. J. Rehab. Res.* **6**(2), 143–51.

Martin, H., McConkey, R. and Martin, S. (1984). From acquisition theories to intervention strategies: An experiment with mentally handicapped children. *Br. J. Dis. Commun.* **19**, 3–14.

Mogford, K. (1977). The play of handicapped children. In Tizard, B. and Harvey, D. (eds), *Biology of Play*. London: Heinemann Medical.

Morris, R.J. and Dolker, M. (1974). Developing cooperative play in socially withdrawn retarded children. *Ment. Retard.* **12**, 24–7.

Motti, F., Cicchetti, D. and Sroufe, L.A. (1983). From infant affect expression to symbolic play: The coherence of development in Down Syndrome children. *Child Dev.* **54**, 1168–75.

Newson, E. (1976). Parents as a resource in diagnosis and assessments. In Oppé, T.E. and Woodford, F.P. (eds), *Early Management of Handicapping Disorders.* Amsterdam: Associated Scientific Publishers.

Nicolich, L. (1977). Beyond sensorimotor intelligence: Assessment of symbolic maturity through analysis of pretend play. *Merrill–Palmer Quart.* **23**, 89–101.

Odom, S.L. Jr. (1981). The relationship of play to developmental level in mentally retarded, preschool children. *Ed. & Train. Ment. Retard.* **16**, 136–41.

Phemister, M.R., Richardson, A.M. and Thomas, C.V. (1978). Observations of young normal and handicapped children. *Child: Care, Health and Development* **4**, 247–59.

Piper, M.C. and Ramsay, M.K. (1980). Effects of early home environment on the mental development of Down Syndrome infants. *Am. J. Ment. Defic.* **85**(1), 39–44.

Reiter, S. and Levi, A.M. (1981). Leisure activities of mentally retarded adults. *J. Ment. Defic.* **86**, 201–203.

Richardson, A.M., Reid, G. and Phemister, M.R. (1981). Play materials for mentally handicapped children. *Child: Care, Health and Development* **7**, 317–29.

Richardson, S.N. (1979). *Julie? She's a love.* Glasgow: Scottish Society for Mentally Handicapped Children.

Riguet, C.B. and Taylor, N.D. (1981). Symbolic play in autistic, Down's and normal children of equivalent mental age. *J. Autism & Dev. Dis.* **11**, 439–48.

Rosenblatt, D. (1977). Developmental trends in infant play. In Tizard, B. and Harvey, D. (eds), *The Biology of Play.* London: Heinemann Medical.

Rubin, K.H., Fenn, G.G. and Vandenberg, B. (1983). Play. In Hetherington, E.W. (ed.), *Carmichael's Manual of Child Psychology: Social Development.* New York: Wiley.

Schleien, S.J., Kiernan, J. and Wehman, P. (1981). Evaluation of an age-appropriate leisure skills program for moderately retarded adults. *Ed. & Train. Ment. Retard.* **16**, 13–19.

Serafica, F.C. and Cicchetti, D. (1976). Down's Syndrome children in a strange situation: Attachment and exploration behaviours. *Merrill–Palmer Quart.* **22**, 137–50.

Stoneman, Z., Broady, G.H. and Abbott, D. (1983). In-home observations of young Down's Syndrome children with their mothers and fathers. *Am. J. Ment. Defic.* **87**, 591–600.

Strain, P. (1975). Increasing social play of severely retarded pre-schoolers with socio-dramatic activities. *Ment. Retard.* **13**, 7–9.

Sutton-Smith, B. (1979). *Play and Learning.* New York: Gardiner Press.

Switzky, H.N., Ludwig, L. and Haywood, H.C. (1979). Exploration and play in retarded and nonretarded preschool children: Effects of object complexity and age. *Am. J. Ment. Defic.* **83**, 637–44.

Thomas, G.V., Phemister, M.R. and Richardson, A.M. (1981). Some conditions affecting manipulative play with objects in severely mentally handicapped children. *Child: Care, Health and Development* **7**, 1–20.

Tilton, J.R. and Ottinger, D.R. (1964). Comparison of the toy play behaviour of autistic, retarded and normal children. *Psychol. Rep.* **15**, 967–75.

Tizard, J. (1964). *Community Services for the Mentally Handicapped.* London: Oxford University Press.

Vandenberg, B. (1982). Play: a concept in need of a definition? *Hum. Dev.* **6**, 15–20.

Walsh, J. and McConkey, R. (1983). Home activities of young mentally handicapped children. Unpublished paper, St Michael's House, Dublin.

Wehman, P. (1978). Leisure skill programming for severely and profoundly handicapped persons: State of the art. *Br. J. Soc. & Clin. Psychol.* **17**, 303–53.

Wehman, P., Karan, O. and Rettie, C. (1976). Developing independent play in three severely retarded women. *Psychol. Rep.* **39**, 995–8.

Weiner, B.J., Ottinger, D.R. and Tilton, J.F. (1969). Comparisons of the toy-play behaviour of autistic, retarded and normal children: A re-analysis. *Psychol. Rep.* **25**, 223–7.

Weiner, E.A. and Weiner, B.J. (1974). Differentiation of retarded and normal children through toy-play analysis. *Multivar. Behav. Res.* **9**, 245–52.

Whittaker, C.A. (1980). A note on developmental trends in the symbolic play of hospitalised profoundly retarded children. *J. Child Psychol. & Psych.* **21**, 253–61.

Wing, L., Gould, J., Yeates, S.R. and Brierley, L.M. (1977). Symbolic play in severely mentally retarded and in autistic children. *J. Child Psychol. & Psych.* **18**, 167–78.

Wulbert, M., Inglis, S., Kriegsmann, E. and Mills, B. (1975). Language delay and associated mother–child interactions. *Dev. Psychol.* **11**, 61–70.

16 Attaining Basic Educational Skills: Reading, Writing and Number

Susan Buckley

INTRODUCTION

The literature on children with Down's Syndrome contains little information regarding their likely attainments in the area of academic skills. This state of affairs probably reflects two facts. Until recently, the care and training of individuals with Down's Syndrome were undertaken mainly in institutions, where the emphasis was on care (most were run on hospital lines) and any training that did take place concentrated on social skills. The right to education for children remaining in the community and being brought up by their parents is also a recent innovation. In the UK, education did not become mandatory for most Down's children until 1971. Prior to that date, some children were fortunate enough to attend junior training centres but, as in hospitals, the emphasis was on social training, and staff were neither trained as teachers nor expected to be competent in teaching academic skills.

Apart from the fact that the care and training facilities lacked an educational emphasis, the accepted view of medical experts and psychologists leaned heavily towards the importance of biological factors in determining and limiting intellectual capacity. Data from intelligence tests in the first half of this century suggested that the majority of Down's children functioned in the severely retarded range (Engler, 1949). It was assumed that this was an irremediable fact and no one expected academic success from people of such limited ability. The possible significance of early environmental experience in determining such IQ levels was largely ignored until very recently, and is reviewed elsewhere in this volume (see Chapter 10).

Gibson (1978), in his extensive review of the literature, states that:

> The orthodox position has been that Down's Syndrome individuals do not profit much from academic study, although a few are observed to develop reading and writing skills. Many Down's Syndrome children are exposed to traditional academic training simply because it has parent status value. The outcome is frequently an increase in stress levels for the child and a decline in self regard without any useful educational gain. Dedicated parents or teachers have had some success with the brighter Down's Syndrome child, probably because they have made intuitive adjustments in teaching to accommodate the disability profile of the syndrome and of the individual.

Is this position justifiable? Before this question can be answered it is necessary to review the evidence concerning the extent of academic achievements in Down's Syndrome, the methods used to teach such children, the possible significance of the data for future teaching, and the as yet unanswered questions.

READING

The published evidence on the extent of reading skills in Down's children is of two kinds, individual case studies and the results of early intervention programmes. Until 1969, the only accounts of reading skills were in the individual life histories of Down's individuals as described by their parents.

Since the pioneering work of Rhodes *et al.* (1969), at Sonoma State Hospital in the USA, demonstrated the effectiveness of educational intervention, there has been an increasing number of early intervention programmes for Down's children. Several of these programmes have included reading in the skills taught and provide some data on the progress of the children and methods used.

These two sources of evidence give some indication of the possible reading attainments but leave a number of issues unanswered.

Individual case studies

One of the earliest accounts of reading skills of a man with Down's Syndrome is provided by Butterfield (1961), in a paper entitled 'A provocative case of over-achievement by a mongoloid'. He describes the attainments of a 36-year-old man, recently admitted to an institution on the death of his mother. This man was assessed as having an IQ of 28 but had achieved reading and spelling standards at a 10-year-old level. He was able to play the piano, purchase items at a self-service store, complete housework, write legibly, execute errands for neighbours, make and sell pot holders, and care for all his personal needs. He had been excluded from school and his education and training had been provided by his mother.

Seagoe (1964) described the progress of his Down's son and included in the account is a sample of the child's typewritten diary. A similar level of achievement is found in Nigel Hunt's diary, *The World of Nigel Hunt*, published in 1966. Nigel typed his diary himself. The book contains no normative data on his level of reading and spelling, but the style of the narrative would suggest about a 10-year-old level of achievement. (Perhaps the most poignant aspect of Nigel's book is the foreword written by his father, describing the sceptical and unhelpful attitudes of the 'experts' they encountered.)

Two further examples of the achievements of Down's children taught by their parents are provided by Duffen (1976) and Smith (1976). Duffen describes the progress of his daughter, Sarah, who began to learn to read at 3½ years of age. At 7 years she had a Griffiths DQ of 83 and a reading age of 9 years. At 11 years, her father reports that she can read the following sentences with understanding: 'The soloist was not in a convenient position for seeing everyone in his audience.' 'Psychology is a science which seems to fascinate both the adult and the adolescent student.' She can also write such sentences, spelling all the words correctly. Sarah reads extensively for pleasure and has completed her education within the normal school system.

Smith (1976) describes the progress of his daughter, Judith. Judith began to learn to read at 3 years of age, and at 7 years could read over 1000 words, write reasonably well and could send messages to her father by reading from the page and transmitting words using deaf and dumb sign language.

These individual case studies probably illustrate the tip of the iceberg. Despite the lack of adequate survey data on the reading skills of Down's children, a small survey by Smith (1976) in response to a letter published in *Parents' Voice* (the journal of the Royal Society for the Mentally Handicapped) suggests that many Down's children do achieve useful reading skills. Smith reports that in a sample of 100 children, 17% were able to read and write well and to do so without help; 23% were able to read well without help and to write with some help; and a further 15% were able to read and write, but required help to do both; 14% were able to read with considerable help; 29% were not able to read or write at all. (The remaining 2% were in full-time hospital care and are not included in the analysis of data.)

While there may be undisclosed bias in Smith's sample, it certainly indicates that a large proportion of Down's children (40%) may be able to acquire a useful level of independent reading ability. Vignettes included in the Smith study and elsewhere indicate that many Down's adults achieve a level of reading that allows them to read for pleasure in addition to having acquired a useful social skill. Unfortunately, most of these descriptions contain no data on the child's developmental level or language skills at the outset of the teaching. The common factor which emerges from many of the accounts is that all the children received intensive structured teaching.

Early intervention programmes

The first intervention programme for Down's children which included the teaching of reading was that of Rhodes *et al.* (1969). In this project, an intensive language development programme was devised for a group of Down's children, resident in a hospital. The programme was highly structured throughout the children's day and the resulting progress of the children was quite dramatic.

What emerges from this report is a picture of severely retarded children who, in 2½ years, changed from essentially non-verbal youngsters, communicating only through bodily gestures and inarticulate sounds, to children with a relatively small but very usable expressive vocabulary, the ability to comprehend a number of basic concepts and to read and enjoy simple books.

Reading was not initially considered for inclusion in the teaching programme, but the observation that some of the children were able to recognise their printed names led to a reading programme being developed. At the time of the report, five of the nine children were reading sentences. All were reading some single words. The authors conclude: 'It has been shown not only that severely retarded mongoloids with measured IQs as low as 32 can be taught to read and comprehend what they are reading, but also that the amount of time, energy and expense required is not prohibitive.'

An interesting and important feature of the work of Rhodes *et al.* is that they recognised that teaching reading could be an integral part of a language programme. Children were taught to read words they did not necessarily understand, but comprehension exercises and games were included to teach meaning.

Two other major intervention programmes for Down's children reported similar findings. In 1971 a special service and demonstration programme was initiated by the Experimental Education Unit, Child Development and Mental Retardation Center, University of Washington in the USA (Haydn and Haring, 1977). This project provided an intensive early education programme for Down's pre-school infants from the age of 18 months. Reading was introduced into the programme in the advanced pre-school class, for the 4 to 5 year olds. All the nine children discussed in the report were able to learn to read 30 or more flashcards in a year. One child could match and select 103 words at the age of 5. In the next stage (the kindergarten class) the children continued their sight reading programme. Phonics was introduced once the child had a 'sight vocabulary of 75 to 100 words and sufficient attending skills'.

In 1975, a model early intervention pre-school for Down's children was established at Macquarie University, Australia. Two themes governed the educational philosophy and practice on the project – the application of operant learning techniques and the principle of normalisation. By 1981, 23 children had participated in the programme, 11 of these had moved on to school, 9 of whom were in normal schools (Pieterse and Treloar, 1981).

Reading, writing and number skills were introduced in the advanced pre-school group (3–5 years). Results are given for the 1981 class of 11 children ranging in age from 3 years 8 months to 5 years 11 months. The sight vocabularies of 10 of the children ranged from 10 to 100 or more words. The eleventh child was able to match and select family names but was not yet attaching a verbal label to the written words himself. Two younger children aged 3 years 4 months and 3 years 2 months are recorded as having sight vocabularies of 2 and 13 words respectively.

The Macquarie Programme is the only study which provides published data on the progress of older children and allows comparison of IQ, language and reading scores.

Table 16.1 shows the achievements of eight Down's children, now in normal schools, who were students in the early intervention project. The mean Stanford–Binet IQ for the group was 59 (range 48–67), yet their mean reading age (Schonell) was 7.2 years (range 6.0–9.4 years). Their chronological ages now range from 7.0 to 9.3 years (mean 8.0 years). Thus, their reading achievements are much nearer normal for their age than would be expected given their IQ scores.

The data presented also illustrate that the children's reading skills are, without exception, more advanced than their spoken language skills, either receptive or expressive.

Table 16.1 The reading and language skills of 8 Down's Syndrome children from the Macquarie programme (adapted from Pieterse and Treloar, 1981)

Child	Chronological age (years. months) 1981	Stanford–Binet IQ	Reading skills			Language skills				
			Schonell[1] Reading age (years. months)	Neale[2] Reading age (years. months)	Neale[2] Comprehension age (years. months)	Reynell[3] Verbal comprehension age (years. months)	Reynell[3] Expressive language age (years. months)	Zimmerman[4] Auditory comprehension age (years. months)	Zimmerman[4] Verbal ability age (years. months)	Language quotient
1	9.3	48	7.2	7.8	—	4.9	5.00	6.0	4.10	59
2	8.8	50	7.2	7.6	6.6	3.8	6.11	5.0	5.0	62
3	8.6	66	9.4	9.3	7.4	7.0	7.0	7.0	7.0	83
4	8.0	64	6.10	7.0	6.9	5.6	7.0	6.0	5.9	74
5	7.7	50	7.0	7.2	—	4.11	3.10	4.9	4.6	62
6	7.3	64	6.10	6.11	6.3	4.7	5.5	5.6	5.1	74
7	7.3	64	6.4	—	—	4.2	4.5	4.10	4.3	64
8	7.0	67	6.0	—	—	4.0	4.7	5.1	4.6	69

[1]Schonell Graded Word Reading Test. [2]Neale Analysis of Reading Ability. [3]Reynell Developmental Language Scale. [4]Zimmerman Preschool Language Scale.

In Britain, results similar to those being achieved at Macquarie were reported by Saunders and Collins (1972) in an account of the work of a private educational establishment, now closed. At Penny Gobby House School (named after a Down's child), the children were taught in the same intensive structured way as in the other intervention programmes cited. All the children described in this account were reading words by 4 years and being introduced to phonics.

Finally, Buckley and Wood (1983) have been teaching a representative sample of 14 Down's pre-school children in a home-based early intervention study (the Portsmouth Down's Syndrome project), using parents as teachers. Table 16.2 illustrates the progress of this group of children on the structured reading

Table 16.2 *The reading skills of children in the Portsmouth project, August 1983 (from Buckley and Wood, 1983): the relationship between age, IQ, language and reading skills*

Child	Chronological age (years–months)	Griffiths DQ	Age at which first words spoken (years–months)	Language development August 1983	Age at which first words read (years–months)	Reading progress August 1983
1	5-4	93.9	2-0	7–8-word sentences	2-7	700 words simple books
2	7-0	66.2	1-3	5–6-word sentences	4-0	70 words/sentences beginning books
3	5-6	81.9	2-1	7–8-word sentences	3-0	50 words
4	5-10	53.4	2-10	100+ single words	5-4	8 words
5	6-2	58.7	2-6	100+ single words; 2-word phrases	5-10	4 words
6	5-2	74.6	2-2	80+ single words; 2-word phrases	—	Matching 4 words
7	5-6	65.1	1-10	100+ single words; 2-word phrases	—	Matching 4 words
8	5-6	57.2	2-4	100+ single words; 2-word phrases	—	Matching 3 words
9	5-3	72.1	2-6	100+ single words; 2-word phrases	—	Matching 3 words
10	5-1	50.9	2-6	20 single words	—	Matching, selecting and naming pictures
11	5-11	37.8	—	3 Makaton signs	—	—
12	5-5	61.2*	3-2	Profoundly deaf child		
13	5-7	76.7*	2-1	Left study May 1981		
14	5-8	63.3*	3-1	Left study June 1981		

*DQ 1981.

Three children (12, 13, 14) were not included in the reading programme. The mother of the profoundly deaf child (12) did not wish to continue to participate in regular teaching, though kept in touch and received visits as requested. The remaining two children had to leave the study on starting school placements at the request of the school head teacher. Child 11 has not yet started the reading programme.

programme. This sample of children included all the Down's children between 2 and 4 years of age living at home in two local health districts. (An outline of the reading programme is given in the Appendix to this chapter.) Three of the children were reading single words before 5 years of age and a further 2 children by 6 years.

The extent of reading skills in Down's Syndrome

The literature reviewed so far illustrates that many Down's children are able to master the early stages of reading. In all the studies, most children have at least mastered some single words.

The evidence from the individual cases reported indicates that some Down's children will be able to progress to a level of reading that is both useful and pleasurable (Hunt, 1966; Duffen, 1976). However, it is not possible to determine from the evidence the extent to which the achievements of these exceptional Down's children reflect greater innate potential at the outset, or the intensive teaching they have received. Nor is it possible to extrapolate the findings from such individual cases to the Down's population as a whole.

The results being reported from pre-school nursery projects such as those at Washington and Macquarie certainly suggest that many Down's children can begin to learn to read, but it is not yet possible to predict the ceiling of their achievements. In both groups, there is a range of individual differences in reading performance reported. Only further long-term follow-up will determine the proportion of Down's children able to progress from the single-word reading stage to reading prose fluently and with comprehension. It is also not clear that the Down's children enrolled in these university-based projects are a representative sample of Down's children in general. Parents have to be willing to participate and to take their children to the programmes. This may lead to a bias in the samples; the parent with other young children and no transport is less likely to participate in such projects and, from the reports available, few severely affected Down's children feature in them.

The results of the Portsmouth project may be a more realistic indication of the extent of early reading skills across the Down's population as a whole. Of the 10 children started on the reading programme at the time of the report, with ages ranging from 5.1 to 7.0 years, the range of reading skills achieved varies greatly. Two children (1 and 3 in Table 16.2) were able to learn to read flashcards at a very early age (2 years 7 months and 3 years 0 months) and with great ease. Very few teaching trials were required to teach these two children new words. They seem to have a special aptitude for the task and to enjoy it. Gillham (1981) reports similar findings for two 4-year-old Down's children taking part in a language programme.

A further three children were reading some words by the age of 6 years, but the size of their sight vocabularies ranged from 4 to 70 words, and they all required more intensive structured teaching and practice to reach this level of achievement than the first two children. The remaining five children, all between 5 and 6 years of age, were mastering the first stage of the reading programme and were able to match words.

Only three of the children were able to read sentences and simple books, by 5–6 years of age. However, it is possible that the children in the Portsmouth group have received less intensive teaching overall (as it is a home-based project) than those children in the nursery school programmes.

The relationship between reading and language

In a number of the studies already mentioned, the authors commented on the possibility that the reading skills of young Down's children can be used to improve their understanding and use of spoken language. This point is clearly illustrated by Duffen (1976), who, when describing the progress of his daughter Sarah, stated:

> Sarah's reading ability has considerably helped the development of her speech. The critical discovery was that Sarah read, remembered and later used, in the correct context, sentences that she was quite incapable of remembering when she just *heard* them. This was quite an accidental discovery, made when I put together flashcard words that Sarah had learnt to read individually, into sentences. One of them was 'We went to Exeter'. A week after reading this sentence Sarah reproduced it in speech, voluntarily and in context, i.e. just after we had been to Exeter again. At that stage in Sarah's development, she was quite incapable of reproducing a sentence such as 'It is my turn' even after many spoken repetitions by me and even though she could repeat each individual word correctly and even though she clearly understood, from her actions, what 'It is my turn' meant. In the early days of her reading development, it was often possible to pick out items from her improving speech and relate them back in part or whole to sentences she had read.
>
> Sarah was still at the 'one word' speech stage when she was reading and understanding sentences several years ahead of that stage in the usual sequence of language development. Though the discrepancy between speech output level and reading comprehension level has now been much reduced, she can still read at levels well ahead of her speech output level (at 8½ years).

Support for the view that spoken language develops from reading for Down's children is also provided by Saunders and Collins (1972): 'It would be true to say that through our work we have taught some children to speak through teaching reading. We do not wait for children to speak before we start teaching language and reading. One can ask which card says "tree" and which says "house" and the children can look and find them'.

Several detailed case histories in this account illustrate developmental progress similar to that of Sarah.

These authors are actually suggesting that mastering a written language is in some way easier than mastering a spoken language for Down's children. Words that are *seen in the written form* are retained more readily than words *heard in the spoken form*. Since meanings (semantics) and grammar (syntax) are the same for both forms of the language, these central language processes can be learned from either the auditory or visual form of the language. Progress in one form should reinforce and aid progress in the other.

The research into cognitive deficits in Down's Syndrome may provide some explanations for the advantages of visual over auditory language for these children. Mastering spoken language is a complex process made up of many separate skills.

Unfortunately, research suggests that the Down's child may be hampered by deficits at all stages in the process.

First, to learn to understand words, the child must be able to hear them, and to hear quite small differences between similar-sounding words. A number of studies have reported significant hearing defects in Down's individuals. Rigrodsky *et al.* (1961) reported 60% of those in their study with deficits mainly in the slight to moderate range. Cunningham and McArthur (1981), in a study of 24 Down's infants, reported that 80–85% had moderate to severe hearing losses. Keiser *et al.* (1981) reported that, in a group of 51 Down's adults, 74% had some degree of hearing impairment.

These figures all indicate that hearing loss is likely to be of considerable significance in Down's Syndrome, and that many such children have losses which would certainly make hearing speech difficult. A child with minor hearing losses may be severely disadvantaged when discriminating between similar-sounding words such as 'cheese' and 'trees' or 'hat' and 'cat'.

In order to listen to, retain and understand speech, good short-term memory is required: the stimulus – the word or sentence – only exists for a short time. In the case of a sentence, a string of words must be retained in memory, before the meaning of the sentence can be worked out. Any deficiency in auditory short-term memory would be a considerable handicap when trying to comprehend spoken language. Written words, pictures or signs are all stimuli which can remain in view for as long as required, so do not place the same demand on short-term memory.

There is little research which has looked specifically at memory processes, but several of the studies support the view that Down's children do have a short-term memory deficit for auditory information, and that this is greater than any deficits they may have for visual information (Bilovsky and Share, 1965; Burr and Rohr, 1978; McDade and Adler, 1980; Marcell and Armstrong, 1982).

A number of studies suggest that Down's children understand more spoken language than they are able to produce spontaneously, i.e. they understand more advanced sentences than they can produce (Benda, 1960; Cornwell, 1974). So, even when the Down's child has learned to understand spoken language, further problems seem to hamper the progress of his own speech. In order to speak, the child has to be able to think of the words he needs and then to organise the motor patterns to produce the correct spoken words. The Down's child may have a variety of difficulties in organising speech, even if he knows what he wishes to say. Dodd (1975) has suggested that some of the articulatory problems may be primarily motor and due to 'an inability to use learned sequences of articulatory movements'. This, in turn, may reflect the difficulty that Down's children have in establishing 'learned motor programmes' for controlling skilled muscle movements (Frith and Frith, 1974).

The fact that Down's children can articulate words more clearly when repeating them (Dodd, 1976) than when speaking spontaneously, suggests that poor articulation is only part of the problem. Maybe they have difficulty retrieving a clear auditory memory (phonological code) for the words they wish to use. Recent studies demonstrating the ability of Down's children to use sign language (Kotkin and Simpson, 1978; Le Provost, 1983) suggest that they are able to master the underlying processes of a language, to comprehend symbols and to use them expressively, but have greater difficulty when trying to do this in the auditory/ spoken mode than in other visual or motor modes.

Data from individual cases in the Portsmouth Project group (Buckley and Wood, 1983) suggest that gesture or sign language is much easier for some Down's children to master, and this continues to be a system that is more accessible to the child, even when speaking and reading. Several of the children have been observed using Makaton signs spontaneously when reading; the sign is made by the child as a first response to the flashcard, while he is attempting to organise and produce the spoken word. The children seem to use this quite spontaneously, as though it were an easy, natural system for them. Evidence from the study of sign language in the deaf child (Kretschmer, 1976; Goldin-Meadow *et al.*, 1976) suggests that gesture is a natural, available form of language, appearing earlier than speech in the developmental sequence and obeying the same basic rules as any other language system.

Finally, several experimental studies reinforce the view that Down's children have particular difficulty when required to use auditory input/vocal output channels. Bilovsky and Share (1965), using the Illinois Test of Psycholinguistic Ability, looked at the spread of subtest scores for Down's children. The scores for motor encoding (the ability to express ideas in gesture rather than vocally) were on average 21.8 months above their own language age norm, and 14.6 months above on visual decoding (the ability to understand pictures with little or no vocal demands), while for the auditory–vocal automatic and sequential subtests, scores were on average 14 months below their own language age norm. (These findings have subsequently been confirmed by Rempel (1974), and Rohr and Burr (1978).)

Scheffelin (1968) compared the effectiveness of four stimulus–response channels for a paired-associate learning task. The children made *twice* as many errors in the auditory–vocal condition than in the visual–motor, visual–vocal or auditory–motor conditions. Scheffelin pointed out that at an early stage the learning of spoken language can be considered as a sequence of auditory–vocal tasks and that 'functionally the Down's Syndrome child may be similar to the hard of hearing child and may be amenable to similar types of instruction'.

To summarise, it would seem that there is considerable evidence to support the view that Down's children have a range of impairments which will make learning language from speech particularly difficult for them. The evidence emerging regarding their aptitude for sign language such as Makaton, and the evidence reviewed regarding the reading skills of some of the children, suggests that they may find these visual languages easier to learn, and that these can be used to build up language and subsequent speech for the Down's child.

Unique features of reading in Down's Syndrome

An island of ability?

The reader may well have already noted that some of the Down's children described earlier in the chapter were able to learn to read single words at very early ages. In the Macquarie programme (Pieterse and Treloar, 1981), three children read their first words between 3 and 4 years of age. In the individual case reports of Smith (1976) and Duffen (1976), both children were reading at 3 years. Orme *et al.* (1966) and Talbot (1981) report individual cases of Down's children reading at 4 years. The authors' contact with parents throughout the UK suggests that there are many more Down's children showing such skills, as yet unrecorded. Buckley and Wood (1983) report one Down's child reading at 2 years 7 months, another at 3 years, and all the published accounts reviewed report reading skills in 4- and 5-year-old Down's children.

These Down's children are showing reading skills as good as or more advanced than would be expected even for normal children. Although Clark (1976) and Durkin (1962) have described normal children reading fluently by the age of 5, and Lynn (1963) and Krippner (1963) described single-word reading skills in individual children of 33 months and 18 months respectively, such children tend to be regarded as exceptional and highly intelligent. In educational circles in both the UK and USA, it has been the accepted wisdom that children are not ready to read until 5 years old, or even later (Morphett and Washbourne, 1931; Downing and Thackray, 1972; Coltheart, 1979).

Some of the Down's children continue to show reading skills well ahead of those expected for normal children. For example, one Down's child in the Portsmouth Project was able to read some 700 single words, and was reading books for pleasure at 5 years of age. Her reading age was some 2 years ahead of her chronological age. Sarah Duffen (Duffen, 1974) had a reading age of 8–9 years when 7 years old. These children all have delayed development in other areas, especially speech, and most have IQs in the mildly retarded range.

The only study which reports normative data for reading, IQ and language is the Macquarie programme (see Table 16.1). One child, William, had a reading age in advance of his chronological age. These children *all* had reading ages in excess of those that might be predicted on the basis of their IQs, which ranged from 48 to 67 (suggesting they are fairly representative of the Down's Syndrome population; certainly not an exceptionally bright group). Their reading ages ranged from 6.0 to 9.4 years (chronological ages 7.0 to 9.3 years). An IQ test is a crude measure of ability and assumes the normal development of a range of cognitive skills, in a particular interrelated sequence. Certainly, for this group of children, the IQ scores are probably not helpful in indicating their present or future range of specific achievement.

It is also interesting to note that, for all these children, their scores on the language measures were consistently *below* their reading scores. For those four children for whom reading comprehension scores are reported, they were consistently ahead of spoken language comprehension scores. All these findings confirm the view expressed in the previous section, that for some Down's children written language is easier to master than spoken language.

A unique reading process?

In all the published studies, the Down's children who are reading are only at the single-word stage of speech development when beginning to read. This means that learning to read for the Down's child is a completely different process from that for the normal 5 year old. The normal child has mastered an enormous range of language skills by the age of 5 and is speaking in sentences of near adult complexity. When he learns to read, he is simply learning an alternative written code for the spoken language he has already mastered. The Down's child is learning to read as if it were a first language. He has to learn the *sound* and the *meaning* of each word as he progresses through the flashcard vocabulary. He is learning to speak and to read side by side. The authors of several of the studies clearly recognise this fact and have designed their reading programmes as if they were teaching a first language (Rhodes *et al.*, 1969; Cairns and Pieterse, 1979; Buckley and Wood, 1983).

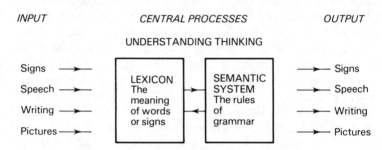

Fig. 16.1 A simple model of any language system

    Fig. 16.1 presents a simple model of a language system, which will suffice for signing, speaking or reading. In each case, to understand the language the child has to perceive a symbol (sign, spoken word or written word) and to attach meaning to that symbol (which may require using his knowledge of grammar, in the case of sentences). To produce the language himself, to convey his thoughts and wishes, the child has to decide what he wants to say and then organise the output in the form of signs, speech or writing.

    The central processes (in the lexicon, the semantic system and the child's thoughts) are common to all the forms of language. When a normal child learns to talk, he learns to associate the sound of the word with its meaning. He will already have some concepts or meanings in his lexicon for pictures and real objects, i.e. he will recognise his ball and a picture of a ball, then learn the spoken word 'ball'; he can either imagine it as a visual picture or name it. He has a whole range of stored meaning (or concepts) in his lexicon and two ways of representing them symbolically – speech or pictures. When the normal child then learns to read, he is simply adding another symbol form – a visual (orthographic) image of the printed word – to the sound (phonological) image and the picture that he already has attached to the meaning in his lexicon.

    The lexicon can be thought of as rather like a dictionary. Until recently, it was thought that the only codes for the dictionary were spoken (phonological) forms of words, so that the normal reader looked at print and his brain transferred that into the (phonological code) sound for the word, before the brain could find the meaning of the word. This is logical since most children do build most of their lexicons by listening to spoken language. However, recent studies suggest that is not the case, but that all readers can go straight to the meanings in the lexicon from either the print (orthographic) form or the spoken (phonological) form (Coltheart *et al.*, 1977; Jorm, 1983a). They can also convert print to silent speech and vice versa. This is important because it suggests that any one form of language can be totally independent of the other forms, and consequently that a child could learn to read without being able to understand or produce spoken language.

Evidence from two of the children in the Portsmouth Project suggests that Down's children are *not* translating print to speech in order to retrieve the meaning of the word, but are going straight from the visual form of the word to its meaning, because they make semantic errors. A semantic error occurs when the word the child produces for the flashcard is not correct but has the same meaning as the flashcard word. Some of the semantic errors recorded are, for example, closed for shut, ship for harbour, go to bed for sleep (Buckley and Wood, 1983). The child must look at the printed word, translate it directly into its meaning, and then find a spoken word to fit the meaning.

This type of error is not found in the early stages of reading in normal children, whose errors tend to be partly phonological, reflecting an effort to code the sounds of the letters in the words and then to construct a sensible word known to them, e.g. region for reign, increase for incense (Doctor, 1978). Marcel (1980) suggests that this is because normal beginner readers do not yet have many print (orthographic) codes for words in their lexicons – only speech (phonological) codes – so that they cannot go straight from print to meaning easily, but need to go from print to silent speech to meaning.

This kind of phonological error never occurs in the Down's children studied. They have no knowledge of the relationship between letters and sounds, so could not use this particular guessing strategy to work out how a word might sound and be pronounced from its spelling. Apart from semantic errors, the most common errors for the young Down's children are visual, confusing words which look alike, e.g. hair and rain, this and shoe, book and Mark (Buckley and Wood, 1983).

The young Down's child, being taught to read single whole words, is learning them as if they were an idiographic or picture language and had no print-to-sound relationships. It has been suggested by Jorm (1983a) and Coltheart (1980) that this is how skilled readers read anyway, recognising whole word patterns. Contrary to common beliefs that learning phonics is essential for successful reading, it seems that it is a useful trick, i.e. given that you know the rules for converting print to sounds, you can work out how to pronounce new unfamiliar words and, conversely, you can work out how to spell words, but that this coding system is not used for normal reading (and is only useful for regular words anyway).

The reading performance of these young Down's children shows that mastering phonics is not necessary for reading. That is not to say that it is not useful and important to children who can master the rules; indeed, the work of Frith (1978, 1979) and Bradley and Bryant (1979) demonstrates that the ability to recode phonologically is an important aid to good reading and spelling – but it is not essential. It is, in any case, only of any relevance in a language where there is sound-to-print correspondence between the written and spoken forms. It is an irrelevant skill if the written script is idiographic, as in one form of Japanese script (Kimura and Bryant, 1983).

These conclusions clearly have significance for groups such as deaf, dyslexic and aphasic children as well as for Down's children. Reading can be taught as if it were idiographic and it can stand alone, separate from speech, as a usable language system.

Is it right-hemisphere reading in Down's Syndrome?

Numerous studies indicate that in most people the two sides of the cerebral cortex in the brain (the right and left hemispheres) are specialised to control different processes (Springer and Deutsch, 1981). For most right-handed people, the main speech functions are in the left hemisphere, so that damage to that side of the brain leads to some type of speech loss (aphasia). Such people are described as left-dominant for language. Recently, several studies have suggested that the reverse may be the case for children with Down's Syndrome, that is, they may be right-dominant for language (Anderson and Barry, 1975; Reinhart, 1976; Sommers and Starkey, 1977; Hartley, 1981).

There are two possible explanations of this finding. It could suggest that the language processes normally in the left hemisphere have developed in the right: it is known that this is possible following brain damage in infancy, and occurs in some people simply as a consequence of unusual brain organisation, possibly related to genetic factors (Levy, 1978). In this case, speech and language development should be normal. Alternatively, it could mean that the important language processes in the left hemisphere are not functioning well in Down's children and they are forced to rely on those language processes usually found in the right hemisphere. In this case, speech and language development would not be normal. Some of the evidence suggests this may be a more plausible explanation than the first.

Until recently, it was thought that the right hemisphere, in people left-hemisphere dominant for language, played very little part in language processes. However, recent studies have shown that this is not the case and have begun to describe which processes seem to be in the right hemisphere (Moscovitch, 1976; Zaidel, 1978). In brief, the right hemisphere is normally mute and cannot produce speech, and only a limited amount of writing (though recovery after brain damage suggests the right hemisphere can develop speech in some circumstances (Hecaen, 1978)). However, the right hemisphere has a substantial lexicon for both written and spoken words, though it seems to use the whole patterns of the words (in either mode) to recognise them. It is not able to use sound-to-print (grapheme to phoneme) coding at all and has poor short-term memory for verbal material. The right hemisphere is poor at comprehending long, non-redundant sentences and seems to have only a rudimentary syntax system (grammar rules) (Levy, 1978). It is poor at invoking the sound image of a word (necessary for spontaneous speech), and seems more adept at processing visual–spatial information and is specialised for the perception of music.

People dependent on right-hemisphere language functions should be able to understand more language than they can easily produce. They will be able to understand single words and short sentences, either written or spoken. They will use speech that is limited in grammatical complexity, i.e. short, simple sentences, and will not be able to use phonic rules to work out sounds from spelling, or vice versa. Their lexicons (that is, the number of words they understand) will be built up on the basis of repeated exposure to the whole words – either written or spoken – associated with their meaning.

There would seem to be a striking similarity between the kind of language the right hemisphere is capable of producing and the characteristic speech and language of Down's children, with its limited use of simple syntax ('telegraphic speech') (Lenneberg *et al.*, 1962; Evans and Hampson, 1969; Evans, 1977; Rondal, 1980; Wiegel-Crump, 1981), as well as poor articulation in spontaneous speech (Dodd, 1976), perhaps partly due to poor sound images for words and the need for intensive, repetitive instruction (Haydn and Haring, 1977; Buckley and Wood, 1983).

A further piece of evidence in support of the right-hemisphere language hypothesis in Down's Syndrome comes from the observation of semantic errors in reading (Buckley and Wood, 1983). It has already been noted that semantic errors have not been reported for normal beginning readers when reading single words. They are, however, characteristic of the residual reading skills of patients with 'deep dyslexia' following brain damage (Coltheart, 1980). Deep dyslexia is the result of left-hemisphere damage, and the residual skills are thought to be based on right-hemisphere functions.

Finally, Zaidel (1978) reported an individual case study, suggesting that the right hemisphere has to translate print to meaning and then meaning to sound and is incapable of going directly from print to sound, though it may be able to do the reverse (sound to print). Here, sound refers to the whole-word sound pattern.

If this hypothesis is correct, it has implications for the choice of appropriate teaching methods for the Down's child. Rote repetition of whole words (spoken or written) in association with their meanings will be important. There will be no point in using methods which teach phonic (left-hemisphere) skills if these are difficult or impossible for the child to use. It will also be important to limit the complexity and length of sentences used.

Conclusions

In summary, then, reading for the Down's child may be unique in several ways.

1. Some Down's children seem to have a particular ability for reading at a very early age. This reading skill may be used to develop their language and speech.

2. Learning to read is not the same process for Down's children as it is for normal children. Down's children are learning to read as if it were a first language. Consequently, their range of language skills is built up in a different order and using different strategies from those of normal children. Reading and speaking (two forms of language code) are being learned together and are building up the internal lexicon and semantic systems together.

3. For some Down's children, reading is mastered as if it were an idiographic language, and had no sound-to-print correspondence.

4. It is suggested that the reading and language skills of Down's children may rely on right-hemisphere processes in the brain.

Effective methods for teaching Down's Syndrome children to read

All the research discussed so far, and the conclusions of the previous section, have implications for the design of reading programmes for Down's children. It is interesting to note that all the research reports which relate the successful teaching of reading to Down's children have used similar methods. The common features of the successful programmes are as follows.

1. A carefully structured behavioural approach, breaking the skill into its component parts and teaching them one step at a time. Such behavioural approaches also emphasise the importance of practice, extension and generalisation of skills and of errorless learning techniques.

2. The choice of vocabulary is based on the principles which would apply to any first language programme. First-sight words taught are selected on the criteria that they are likely to be among the first words in the child's spontaneous speech vocabulary and that they are likely to be meaningful and interesting to him. The child then moves on to two-word phrases of the type to be found in developing speech. This means that early reading schemes for normal children are not suitable for the Down's child: the syntax (grammar) is likely to be considerably more advanced than he is able to comprehend at this stage of language development.

Individual reading books need to be developed for each child and the level of syntax matched to his own stage of language development. The recognition that reading materials should match language development is important at whatever age a Down's child begins to learn to read.

3. Reading is taught by 'look and say' whole-word methods in all the published reports, and this continues even if phonic skills are introduced later. Even in studies which mention the teaching of phonic skills, there is no evidence concerning the extent to which the Down's children understand or use them. It should be noted that drawing attention to the letters in words and giving the letters names and sounds is as much a strategy for increasing the child's use of visual differences and similarities between words, as it is a means of teaching sound-to-print rules. Any visual cues to discrimination of visually similar words will be useful to the Down's child. Phonic skills will also be useful if the child can master them, but are not necessarily essential.

Contrary to common belief, there is no evidence to suggest that there is any limit to the number of whole words a child can learn by the 'look and say' method. Indeed, one child (No. 1 in Table 16.2) in the Portsmouth study mastered some 700 words in this way at the age of 5 years and had no difficulty with plurals or the derivatives (e.g. -ing, -ed endings).

These characteristics of successful reading programmes do, in fact, capitalise on the unique features of reading in Down's children already outlined. A detailed handbook of teaching methods suitable for the Down's child, giving all the information needed by parents or teachers wishing to teach their child to read and supplemented by a video tape showing Down's children reading, has been produced by the Portsmouth Down's Syndrome Project (Buckley and Wood, 1983), and may be obtained from the author.

Finally, a word of caution may be in order. It has already been pointed out that the evidence regarding the upper ceiling of the development of reading skills in Down's children has not been established, though single case studies give some evidence that reading can become a useful and pleasurable skill for them. The published studies at present report that many Down's children are able to master single words. However, reading single words and reading sentences fluently and with comprehension are two very different skills. It would be foolish to suggest that success at the first stage could in any way predict success at the second stage.

To read a sentence aloud, a sequence of words has to be reproduced rapidly in the right order. Down's children are hampered by the speed with which they can organise this process and by articulation problems. To understand a sentence, the words have to be held in a memory store because the order of the words may affect the meaning of the sentence. It has been suggested that to comprehend sentences, auditory short-term memory is important and uses the sound codes for the words. Therefore, this is likely to be quite difficult for Down's children. If, as is possible, visual short-term memory can be just as effective, even though it does not seem the strategy of choice for normal people (Baddeley, 1979; Jorm, 1983b), then this is a further reason why reading is easier than speaking and listening for Down's children.

In any event, it is important to realise that Down's children may have a series of problems to surmount and should be given extra time to process material and reproduce it. It is also likely that their reading will depend heavily on what are described as 'bottom-up' processes by reading experts. Normal readers read by a mixture of two processes, 'bottom-up' and 'top-down' strategies. 'Bottom-up' refers to the process of decoding the print, word by word and sentence by sentence, from the written text. 'Top-down' refers to the fact that skilled readers do not need to do this – they can skim through a sentence, only reading some key words but filling in the rest of the meaning from their stored knowledge in their memories.

It is reasonable to suggest that the Down's child will not be so quick to use his available knowledge and that his reading will be a slower, 'bottom-up' process. This does not matter provided he reads with comprehension – whichever strategies he can use.

NUMBER

The development of number skills and concepts in Down's Syndrome has hardly been studied systematically at all. A number of studies make passing reference to the range of skills some children have attained, but do not give details. As with the literature on reading, this evidence comes mainly from individual case studies and the early intervention programmes.

Individual case studies

Unfortunately, few studies report the extent of number skills in children, but the following examples may serve to illustrate the range of possible development. Penrose, in the foreword to Nigel Hunt's diary (Hunt, 1966), states of Nigel:

> With respect to the concept of numbers he seems definite about one, two, three and four but sometimes counts the same person twice. He speaks of thousands and millions to indicate magnitude. Indeed, his understanding of the ordinal significance of numbers is accurate. He does not, however, indicate that he can appreciate the abstract idea of cardinal numbers as used in addition and subtraction. On the other hand, he can recognise the equivalence of words with the same meaning in different languages.

Smith (1976), writing about his daughter, Judith (aged 7), says:

> A cheap pocket electronic calculator has helped her to add simple numbers, and she enjoys this game immensely. I am currently teaching her to deal with money. I am learning the techniques which really work, and she can give me almost any value from ½p to £1.00 from her pile of mixed coins. She is learning which 'group' of coins to give me. For example, I have taught her, when asked for 8p, to give me either 5+2+1, 5+1+1+1, 2+2+2+2 or eight 1p coins. She is enjoying the game of 'shops' each evening and is learning very rapidly.

Judith could, at this stage, count to 1,000 accurately.

Duffen (1979), describing the progress of his daughter, Sarah (aged 11), writes:

> She can multiply 78,657 by 59, add 98,211 to 64,599, take 74,122 from 83,271 and get the correct answers without the use of a calculator (though she can use one) or written tables. She can plot the points (1,3) (2,5) (3,1) (2,4) on a graph and label them. She can shade in the region x<3 and the region y>4.

These examples are the only ones which give any meaningful detail. Other accounts suggest Down's children are able to count or handle money but give no indication of the range of these skills. One consistently reported finding is that number skills seem to be relatively more difficult for the Down's child to master than other skills, such as reading. This comment occurs frequently in parents' own accounts of their children's progress (Smith, 1976).

Early intervention programmes

The only early intervention programmes which include data on the teaching of number skills are the Washington project (Haydn and Dmitriev, 1975) and the Maquarie programme (Thorley and Wood, 1979; Pieterse and Treloar, 1981). These are both pre-school projects and so include data on the early stages of number skills only, but again both report that number is more difficult than reading for the Down's child at this stage.

In the list of minimum developmental objectives, for the advanced pre-school group in the Washington project, is the following number item: 'Understand number concepts from one to three'. Haydn and Dmitriev (1975) reported that all ten children had mastered this objective by 5 years, but give no more detail.

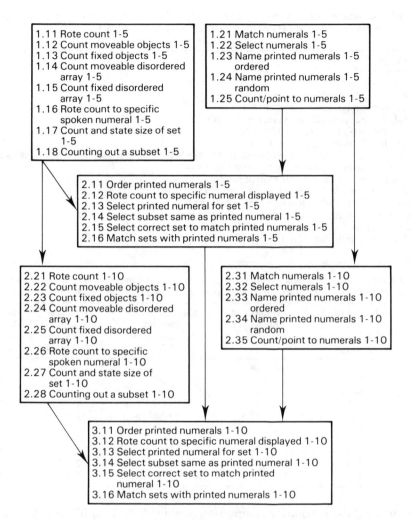

Fig. 16.2 The minimal objectives in number, Macquarie pre-school programme (Thorley and Wood, 1979). Reproduced with permission.

The Macquarie programme has developed a precise number curriculum based on the work of Gelman and Gallistel (1978). This is the only published account of any systematic attempt to teach number skills to Down's children, and some preliminary results are reported by Thorley and Wood (1979). Fig. 16.2 shows the teaching objectives.

At the time of the report, one 5 year old had mastered all 38 objectives and two further children in this age group had mastered 30 (79%) and 23 (61%) of the objectives by the time they were due to move on to regular schools. The remaining five children, aged from 3 years 5 months to 4 years, had mastered between 1 and 16 objectives. One child had exceeded the objectives and his additional skills at the age of 5 years are given in Table 16.3.

Table 16.3 *The number skills achieved by one 5-year-old Down's child in the Macquarie programme (from Thorley and Wood, 1979) (in addition to those objectives listed in Fig. 16.2). Reproduced with permission.*

1. Count backwards from 10
2. Write numerals (1 to 10)
3. Count to 39
4. Place numerals (1 to 20) in order
5. State what number comes next (1 to 20)
6. Supply missing numerals in a sequence (1 to 20)
7. State which is bigger, e.g. 5 or 3? 9 or 14?
8. State which is smaller, e.g. 7 or 11? 5 or 9?
9. Match perceptually on the basis of number (1 to 5) when the nature, size, colour and array patterns are varied – given a command of the form 'Put 4 on 4'
10. Estimate numbers 1 to 5 on the basis of pattern
11. Create sets numerically equivalent to a given set (1 to 10)
12. Create sets numerically 1 less than a given set (1 to 10)
13. Create sets numerically 1 more than a given set (1 to 10)
14. Correctly answer a set of 10 mixed addition examples,
    adding 1 or 2, in the form $7 + 1 = \square$
    $$2 + 6 = \square$$

Table 16.4 *Comparison of number skills with age, developmental quotient, language and and reading skills for 10 children on the Macquarie programme, 1981 (adapted from Pieterse and Treloar, 1981)*

Child	Chronological age (years–months)	Number of objectives (%)	Developmental quotient (average from DSI)	Language age (years–months)	Reading (number of sight words)
1	5–11	8	0.67	3–0.75	39
2	5–2	45	0.85	3–9	49
3	5–2	45	0.86	4–1.5	53
4	5–1	92	0.92	4–10.5	100+
5	5–1	37	0.78	2–8.5	41
6	4–4	—	0.76	2–3.75	10
7	4–0	3	0.86	2–6.75	17
8	3–8	6	0.92	2–10.5	19
9	3–4	—	0.78	2–1.5	2
10	3–2	3	1.09	3–0	13

The only data which allow a comparison of number skills with chronological age, developmental quotient, language and reading development are presented in Table 16.4. The data on ten children in the Macquarie programme are presented in the 1981 report (Pieterse and Treloar, 1981).

With such a small sample, and no normative data for the number programme objectives available, it is difficult to evaluate the significance of the data. Some of the 5 year olds attained a range of skills in counting, sets and recognising numerals, probably on a par with many normal children and certainly providing a basis for later work.

However, when reviewing the progress of an older group of children from the Macquarie programme (for whom reading data are presented in Table 16.1), Pieterse and Treloar (1981) reported that they were all bottom of the class for number work. Only three of these eight children were bottom of their class for reading, in fact four of them were in the top half of their class, one being sixth in a group of 27, another eighth in a group of 20.

The reason that number work is more difficult may be because of the need to begin to grasp the abstract nature of number fairly early on. Reading can be a skill applied to largely concrete material. Certainly, the narratives of Down's children in the accounts of Seagoe (1964) and Hunt (1966) illustrate that they do, perhaps, live in a world of a fairly concrete nature and that more complex, abstract concepts are difficult for them. On the other hand, the limitations may reflect the limits of the teaching they have received.

The vignettes and the scant data from intervention programmes do no more than illustrate the wide range of possible achievements of Down's children. All the children who have made exceptionally good progress have received intensive instruction based on carefully structured programmes. The progress of some of the Down's children would suggest that the conclusions of some earlier studies, such as those of Cornwell (1974) and Kostrewski (1965), may be unjustified. Cornwell reported 'a gross impairment in numerical skills which improved somewhat in age but in all cases remained low' on the basis of a study of 38 Down's children ranging in chronological age from 5 to 19 years and in mental age from 0.1 to 5.10 years on the Stanford Binet scale. The six number tasks in this study ranged from selecting items from 1 to 4 to counting from 1 to 7, and hardly seem to be a sufficiently adequate sample of number skills to warrant such a sweeping conclusion.

Kostrewski (1965) reported some Down's children able to add and subtract numbers up to 10, but found no recorded instance of successful multiplication or division, although Potolsky and Grigg (1942) had reported that, in a sample of home-reared Down's children they studied: '50% could perform simple additions; 30% could perform long additions of three place numbers; 35% knew their multiplication tables, but only 5% could perform long multiplication; 30% can perform subtraction of three place numbers.'

These early studies have been interpreted by authors such as Gibson (1978) as evidence of a clear cognitive ceiling for Down's Syndrome reflecting an inability to handle abstract symbols. None of the studies, however, provides any evidence regarding the extent of teaching received by the Down's children involved. It is quite possible that many of them had received no appropriate teaching of number at all and had therefore had no opportunity to develop an understanding of number or to develop and generalise the use of number skills in practical settings.

Conclusions

It is not possible to draw any general conclusions regarding the extent of number skills that may be achieved by the Down's child from the available evidence. Certainly, some of the evidence presented suggests that beliefs about the ceiling of possible achievements reflect the inadequacy of teaching as much as any limiting cognitive deficits. Clearly, further studies of the kind reported by Thorley and Wood (1979) are needed. Only the evaluation of such systematic, intensive structured programmes will lead to an understanding of the limits of the Down's child's ability to develop number skills and to the development of appropriate teaching programmes.

It should be emphasised, perhaps, that language is important for number. Many of the concepts which the child needs to learn to handle have language labels rather than numerical labels, e.g. bigger, smaller, more than, less than, many, few, big, little. A promising and productive approach to teaching number which integrates language and number development is that of Green and Laxon (1978), as described in their interesting and readable book, *Entering the World of Number*. This programme has been designed with the normal child in mind, but would warrant systematic evaluation with a sample of Down's children.

WRITING

Writing skills may be thought of in terms of two components – language and motor skill, i.e. knowing what to write and being able to write it down. Material reviewed elsewhere in this chapter and in the chapters on language and motor skills will therefore be relevant to this issue and will not be discussed extensively here.

The literature on Down's Syndrome makes almost no mention of writing skills; some of the case studies described make passing references. Smith (1976) and Duffen (1974) both report that their daughters 'write well' as the result of much practice from early ages. Hunt, in the foreword to his son's book (Hunt, 1966), points out that Nigel had difficulty with writing, but found typing much easier. The only example of a structured writing programme comes from the Macquarie programme (Pieterse and Treloar, 1981). The objectives for the drawing and pre-writing programme are set out in Table 16.5.

Table 16.5 *The drawing and pre-writing programme for the Macquarie programme: the advanced pre-school project (Pieterse and Treloar, 1981). Reproduced with permission.*

Objective	
1. Copy a circle	9. Trace lines
2. Copy +	10. Trace a circle
3. Copy V	11. Copy letters
4. Draw a face	12. Trace a name
5. Draw a square	13. Copy a name
6. Draw a man	14. Trace words
7. Copy a triangle	15. Copy words
8. Draw between lines	

The authors point out that these objectives need to be broken down into a set of sub-skills, and they apply, as in the other areas of their programme, behavioural techniques in the teaching programme. Table 16.6 illustrates the way in which sub-skills might be taught for Task 5 in Table 16.5. Objectives may be further broken down, or the number of interim objectives reduced, according to the child's rate of progress.

Table 16.7 illustrates the achievements of the children in the advanced pre-school class, on the drawing and pre-writing programme in 1981. The Macquarie staff noted that the children did not maintain drawing skills over time. It was necessary to provide regular practice of previously learned writing skills through the class

Table 16.6 *An example of sub-skills and teaching procedures for the drawing and pre-writing programme (Pieterse and Treloar, 1981). Reproduced with permission.*

Level	Sub-skill objective	Teaching procedures
2	The child will draw a square in imitation	Demonstrate the activity for the child. Say 'I go down, across, up, across. You do it.'
3	The child will draw a square when prompted verbally	Prompt the child verbally as he draws: say 'Go down, across, up, across.'
4	The child will draw a square when prompted physically	Prompt the child physically to draw a square, stopping at each corner before proceeding with the next line
5	The child will join four dots to make a square	Draw four dots on the paper. Say 'I'm going to join the dots, see – a square.' Draw more dots and prompt the child to join the dots

Task 5: The child will copy a square on the verbal cue 'Draw a square'. Note this is Level 1. If the child is unable to make progress on this objective, the teacher selects the appropriate entry levels and then progresses up to Level 1 as the child succeeds on the earlier sub-skills.

Table 16.7 *Progress on the pre-writing programme of children in advanced pre-school, Macquarie, 1981 (adapted from Pieterse and Treloar, 1981)*

Child	Chronological age (years–months)	Developmental quotient	Number of prewriting objectives achieved	
			Feb. 1981	Nov. 1981
1	5–11	0.67	3	9
2	5–2	0.85	7	9
3	5–2	0.86	5	7
4	5–1	0.92	7	14
5	5–1	0.78	3	6
6	4–4	0.76	1	4
7	4–1	0.67	0	1
8	4–0	0.86	0	3
9	3–8	0.92	0	1

activities. In some cases, the child found it difficult to discriminate different stimuli. Having learnt to copy +, the child would no longer do so when working on copying V, but would respond with a V to both stimuli. It was then necessary to alternate the stimuli in a random pattern to establish the necessary discrimination.

Frith and Frith (1974) and Henderson *et al.* (1981) advanced the view that some of the problems the Down's child has in executing skilled movements, such as those required for speaking and writing, are due to a deficit in building up 'motor programmes' in the brain for these movements. If, as is suggested, the Down's child does have this deficit, then the implication is that he will need much more repetitive practice to achieve acceptable levels of performance. He will need to copy shapes, letters and numerals over a template before attempting to produce them without aid. Errorless learning techniques will be important – plenty of correct practice at tracing and then copying.

If, as Anwar (1981) suggests, proprioceptive feedback – that is, feedback from the muscle movements to the brain – may be integrated with other information from vision, then practice at tracing may also help the child to remember shapes.

Use of multisensory methods, involving touch, movement and vision, has often been advocated as beneficial for slow-learning children. Recent work by Hulme (1981) provides some support for this hypothesis.

Anwar (1981) suggested a further novel strategy, copying blind-folded. She states: 'perhaps writing and copying skills could be improved in older Down's Syndrome subjects by incorporating a number of teaching trials where visual feedback from the hand would be prevented. Thus, the subject would be forced to attend to only one feedback system, i.e. proprioception.' Presumably, this might aid the establishment of motor programmes, though only if the child traced over an accurate template.

In the current state of knowledge, the only practical advice that can be suggested is that it would seem useful to build up practice of copying and tracing numbers, shapes, letters and words from an early age as they are being learned by the child. Tracing over the shapes, with a pencil or a finger, may help the child remember the shapes and will help to improve his motor skills for later independent writing. Considerable careful practice will be needed to develop reasonable handwriting, and it may be more sensible and useful for some children to learn to use a typewriter.

A FINAL OVERVIEW

It is now possible to return to the issues raised in the introduction to the chapter and evaluate Gibson's (1978) view of the value of teaching academic skills to Down's children. The reader will recall that, in Gibson's view: 'Many Down's Syndrome children are exposed to traditional academic training simply because it has parent status value. The outcome is frequently an increase in stress levels for the child and a decline in self-regard without any useful educational gain.'

The material reviewed in this chapter, despite the unanswered questions which have been highlighted, illustrates that there is little evidence to support Gibson's view. Indeed, so few Down's children have had the opportunity to benefit from intensive training programmes over a long period of time that the evidence to support Gibson's statement is simply not available.

In fact, the review of recent studies of reading suggests that the teaching of reading may be of considerable educational importance to the Down's child. The evidence suggests that:

1. many Down's children can begin to learn to read at the pre-school stage;
2. reading is an important 'way-in' to language and should be taught as part of a language programme;
3. the reading abilities of young Down's children may build upon the relative strengths of the cognitive skills in these children.

In the case of structured number teaching programmes, the evidence would suggest that a useful range of practical number skills can be acquired by many Down's children, provided that teaching begins early. For both reading and number skills, the long-term implications of intensive teaching remain to be evaluated, but the evidence available already demonstrates little correlation between achievements in these areas and IQ.

Writing is the least researched area. Obviously, useful writing skills depend on language and reading competence, but beyond that are hampered by motor skill problems. However, improvement with practice has been reported, and the use of a typewriter may be an ideal pragmatic solution.

Perhaps the main area for future research effort should be the evaluation of the effectiveness of alternative teaching strategies for these academic skills. A number of different approaches to reading have been advocated for the retarded, including Rebus systems, pictograms and DISTAR. None has been systematically evaluated for Down's children. Similarly, there is no clear agreement on the appropriate curriculum sequences or methods for teaching number to the retarded. It is the author's view that the strategy of evaluating carefully constructed remedial programmes is the most productive research strategy for uncovering the relative strengths and weaknesses of cognitive processes in Down's Syndrome. Such an analysis of the range of skills the Down's child is capable of acquiring, through the appropriate amount and style of teaching, may not only bring a new appreciation of the implications of the handicap, but may also contribute to our understanding of cognitive development in general.

APPENDIX: AN OUTLINE OF THE LANGUAGE AND READING PROGRAMME USED IN THE PORTSMOUTH PROJECT (BUCKLEY AND WOOD, 1983)

The chart illustrates the stages in the programme: each child works with pictures first, then single words on flashcards, and learns to match, select, name (as separate stages) for both pictures and words. Each child will work through the stages in the same order, but may spend time extending vocabulary and comprehension if not yet able to name.

Vocabulary is selected from the first words that children use, including family names and words the child can say. For first flashcards, words are chosen that clearly differ visually. Once a number of flashcards are mastered, phrases are built *as they would be spoken* by a child at this stage of language development, e.g. Daddy gone, baby sleep.

While the programme chart sets out the framework for teaching the reading of single words in careful stages, parents are also encouraged to use the vocabulary being taught at any stage during normal daily activities in order to expand the child's 'meaning' of the word and to encourage spontaneous use. Considerable emphasis is also placed on the importance of reading to the child, to extend his knowledge and to encourage him to enjoy books and reading.

(A video programme and handbook, giving more detail for parents and teachers, is available from the author.)

Portsmouth Down's Syndrome Project: the language and reading programme

	Pictures		Words	
Stage 1: Matching* (only visual recognition of similarity required of child)	*Sample activity* This is a '. . .'. Show me one the same. Start with 1 pair of identical pictures – then 2 – increasing to lotto games with 4 to 8 pictures	P.1	*Sample activity* This word says '. . .'. Show me one the same. Start with 1 pair of identical flashcards – increase to 2 pairs – and build 1 pair at a time to 8 pairs	W.1
Stage 2: Selecting (child must now learn to associate verbal label with picture or word)	*Sample activity* This is a '. . .'. Please give me the '. . .'. Start with 1 picture, increase 1 at a time to choice of 8. Use same picture as in Stage 1	P.2	*Sample activity* This word says '. . .'. Child repeats after teacher. Give me the word which says '. . .'. Start with 1 flashcard, increase as child learns, 1 word at a time to choice of 2/3/4/5/6	W.2
Stage 3: Naming (verbal response now required from the child)	*Sample activity* Show the child a picture – ask 'What is this called?' – working through with same picture sets as above, introducing new pictures/vocabulary as child is ready	P.3	*Sample activity* Show child the card. 'What does this word say – ". . ."? If correct response not given quickly, teacher names to ensure errorless learning and prevent guessing	W.3
Stage 4: Checking or teaching meaning (child must show verbal or written label has some meaning)	*Sample activity* Set out 8 objects on the table. For each picture, 'Can you find me the one that is like this?	P.4	*Sample activity* Set out pictures or objects. Give child flashcard: 'What does this say? Which picture does it go with? Can you show me what it means?' – gesture required	W.4

ŒStages 1–4 can be carried out with objects before pictures.
Errorless learning techniques are employed throughout – the child is directed to complete the correct response if he does not do so at every single step of teaching.

REFERENCES

Anderson, A. and Barry, W. (1975). The development of cerebral dominance in children attending regular school classes, special classes for the M.R. and special schools for the M.R. PhD thesis. Carlton University.

Anwar, F. (1981). Motor function in Down's Syndrome. *Int. Rev. Res. Ment. Retard.* **10**, 107–138.

Baddeley, A.D. (1979). Working, memory and reading. In Koters, P.A., Wrolstad, M.E. and Bouma, H. (eds), *Processing of Visible Language*, Vol. 1. New York: Plenum Press.

Benda, C.E. (1960). Mongolism: Clinical manifestations, pathology and etiology. In Bowman, P.E. (ed.), *Mental Retardation*. First International Medical Conference. New York: Grune & Stratton.

Bilovsky, D. and Share, J. (1965). The ITPA and Down's Syndrome. *Am. J. Ment. Defic.* **70**, 78–82.

Bradley, L. and Bryant, P.E. (1979). The independence of reading and spelling in backward and normal readers. *Dev. Med. & Child Neurol.* **21**, 504–14.

Buckley, S. and Wood, E. (1983). *The extent and significance of reading skills in pre-school children with Down's Syndrome.* Paper presented at conference of British Psychological Society, London.

Burr, D.B. and Rohr, A. (1978). Patterns of psycholinguistic development in the severely mentally retarded. *Soc. Biol.* **25**, 15–22.

Butterfield, E.C. (1961). A provocative case of overachievement by a mongoloid. *Am. J. Ment. Defic.* **66**, 444–8.

Cairns, S. and Pieterse, M. (1979). Down's Syndrome Project. Reading Programme. Macquarie University.

Clark, M.M. (1976). *Young Fluent Readers*. London. Heinemann.

Coltheart, M. (1978). Lexical access in simple reading tasks. In Underwood, G. (ed.), *Strategies of Information Processing*. London: Academic Press.

Coltheart, M. (1979). When can children learn to read – and when should they be taught? In Waller, T.G. and Mackinnon, G.E. (eds), *Reading Research*, Vol. 1. New York: Academic Press.

Coltheart, M. (1980). Reading, phonological recoding and deep dyslexia. In Coltheart, M., Patterson, K. and Marshall, J.C. (eds), *Deep Dyslexia*. London: Routledge & Kegan Paul.

Coltheart, M., Jonasson, J.T., Davelaar, E. and Besner, D. (1977). Access to the internal lexicon. In Dornic, S. (ed.) *Attention and Performance Vol. 1*. New York: Academic Press.

Cornwell, A.C. (1974). Development of language, abstraction and numerical concept formation in Down's Syndrome children. *Am. J. Ment. Defic.* 79, 179–90.

Cunningham, C. and McArthur, K. (1981). Hearing loss and treatment in young Down's Syndrome children. *Child: Health, Care and Development* 7, 357.

Doctor, E.A. (1978). Studies on reading comprehension in children and adults. Unpublished PhD thesis, Birkbeck College, University of London.

Dodd, B. (1975). Recognition and reproduction of words by Down's Syndrome & non-Down's Syndrome retarded children. *Am. J. Ment. Defic.* 80, 306–11.

Dodd, B. (1976). A comparison of the phonological systems of mental age matched, normal, severely subnormal and Down's Syndrome children. *Br. J. Dis. Commun.* 11, 27–42.

Downing, J. and Thackray, D. (1972). *Reading Readiness*. London: University of London Press.

Duffen, L. (1974). *Teaching Reading to Teach Talking*. Cheam: Down's Babies Association, South East Branch.

Duffen, L. (1976). Teaching reading to children with little or no language. *Remed. Ed.* 11, 139.

Duffen, L. (1979). For reading read listening. *Learning* 1, 61–3.

Durkin, D. (1962). Reading instruction and the five year old child. *Challenge and Experiment in Reading*. New York: Scholastic Magazines.

Engler, M. (1949). *Mongolism*. Bristol: John Wright.

Evans, D. (1977). The development of language abilities in mongols: a correlational study. *J. Ment. Defic. Res.* 21, 103.

Evans, D. and Hampson, M. (1969). The language of mongols. *Br. J. Dis. Comm.* 3, 171–81.

Frith, U. (1978). From print to meaning and from print to sound, or how to read without knowing how to spell. *Visible Lang.* 12, 43–54.

Frith, U. (1979). Reading by eye and writing by ear. In Kolers, P.A., Wrolstad, M.E. and Bouma, H. (eds), *Processing of Visible Language*, Vol. 1. New York: Plenum.

Frith, U. and Frith, C.D. (1974). Specific motor disabilities in Down's Syndrome. *J. Child Psychol. & Psych.* 15, 293–301.

Gelman, R. and Gallistel, C.R. (1978). *The Child's Understanding of Number*. Cambridge, Mass.: Harvard University Press.

Gibson, D. (1978). *Down's Syndrome. The Psychology of Mongolism*. Cambridge: Cambridge University Press.

Gillham, B. (1981). *Learning to Read to Learn to Talk*. Surrey: Early Childhood.

Gillham, B. (1983). *Two Words Together*. London: George Allen & Unwin.

Goldin-Meadow, S., Seligman, M. and Gelman, R. (1976). Language in the two-year-old. *Cognition* 4, 189–202.

Green, R.T. and Laxon, V.J. (1978). *Entering the World of Number*. London: Thames & Hudson.

Hartley, X.Y. (1981). Lateralisation of speech stimuli in young Down's Syndrome children. *Cortex* 17, 2.

Haydn, A.H. and Dmitriev, V. (1975). The Multidisciplinary Preschool Program for Down's Syndrome children at the University of Washington Model Preschool Center. In Friedlander, B.Z., Kirk, G.E. & Sterritt, G.M. *Exceptional Infant*, Vol III.

Haydn, A.H. and Haring, N.G. (1977). The acceleration and maintenance of gains in Down's Syndrome school age children. In Mittler, P. (ed.), *Research to Practise in Mental Retardation*, Vol. 1. Baltimore: University Park Press.

Hecaen, H. (1978). Right hemisphere contribution to language functions. In Buser, P. and Rongel-Bouser, A. (eds), *Cerebral Correlates of Conscious Experience*. Amsterdam: Elsevier.

Henderson, S.E., Morris, J. and Frith, U. (1981). The motor deficit in Down's Syndrome children. A problem of timing? *J. Child Psychol & Psych*. **22**, 233–45.

Hulme, C. (1981). *Reading Retardation and Multi-sensory Teaching*. London: Routledge and Kegan Paul.

Hunt, N. (1966). *The World of Nigel Hunt*. London: Darwen Finlayson.

Jorm, A.F. (1983a). *The Psychology of Reading and Spelling Difficulties*. London: Routledge & Kegan Paul.

Jorm, A.F. (1983b). Specific reading retardation and working memory: A review. *Br. J. Psychol*. **74**(3), 311–42.

Keiser, H., Montague, J., Wold, D., Maune, D. and Pattison, D. (1981). Hearing loss of Down's Syndrome adults. *Am. J. Ment. Defic*. **85**, 467–72.

Kimura, Y. and Bryant, P. (1983). Reading and writing in English and Japanese: a cross-cultural study of young children. *Br. J. Dev. Psychol*. **1**, 143–54.

Kostrewski, J. (1965). The dynamics of intellectual and social development in Down's Syndrome: Results of experimental investigation. *Roczniki: Filozoficzne* **13**, 5–32.

Kotkin, P.A. and Simpson, S. (1978). The effect of sign language on picture naming in two retarded girls possessing normal hearing. *J. Ment. Defic. Res*. **22**, 19.

Kretschmer, R.B. (1976). Language acquisition. *Volta Rev*. **78**, 60–67.

Krippner, S. (1963). The boy who read at 18 months. *Exceptional Children*. **30**, 105–109.

Lenneberg, E.H., Nichols, I.A. and Rosenberger, E.F. (1962). Primitive stages of language development in mongolism. *Proc. Assoc. Res. Nerv. & Ment. Dis*. **42**, 119–37.

Le Provost, P.A. (1983). Using the Makaton vocabulary in early language training. *Mental Handicap* **11**(1), 29–30.

Levy, J. (1978). Lateral differences in the human brain in cognition and behavioural control. In Buser, P. and Rongel-Bouser, A. (eds), *Cerebral Correlates of Conscious Experience*. Amsterdam: Elsevier.

Lynn, R. (1963). Reading readiness and the perceptual abilities of young children. *Ed. Res*. **6**, 10–15.

McDade, H.L. and Adler, S. (1980). Down Syndrome and short-term memory impairment: a storage or retrieval deficit? *Am. J. Ment. Defic*. **84**, 561–7.

Marcel, A. (1980). Surface dyslexia and beginning reading: a revised hypothesis of the pronunciation of print and its impairments. In Coltheart, M., Patterson, K. and Marshall, J.C. (eds), *Deep Dyslexia*. London: Routledge & Kegan Paul.

Marcel, M.M. and Armstrong, V. (1982). Auditory and visual sequential memory of Down syndrome and non-retarded children. *Am. J. Ment. Defic*. **87**(1), 86–95.

Morphett, M.V. and Washbourne, C. (1931). When should children begin to read? *Elem. Sch. J*. **31**, 496–503.

Moscovitch, M. (1976). On the representation of language in the right hemisphere of right handed people. *Brain & Lang*. **3**, 7–71.

Orme, J.E., Fisher, F.J.S. and Griggs, J.B. (1966). The big words. *New Ed*. **12**, 25–6.

Pieterse, M. and Treloar, R. (1981). *The Down's Syndrome Program*. Progress Report 1981. Macquarie University.

Potolsky, C. and Grigg, A.E. (1942). A revision of the prognosis in mongolism. *Am. J. Orthopsych*. **12**, 503.

Reinhart, C. (1976). *The Cerebral Lateralisation of Speech Processes in Down's Syndrome and Normal Individuals*. Canadian Psychological Association 37th Annual Meeting, Toronto.

Rempel, E.D. (1974). *Psycholinguistic Abilities of Down's Syndrome Children*. Proceedings of American Association of Mental Deficiency, Chicago.

Rhodes, L., Gooch, B., Siegelman, E.Y., Behrns, C. and Metzger, R. (1969). *A Language Stimulation and Reading Program for Severely Retarded Mongoloid Children*. California Mental Health Research Monograph, 11. State of California, Department of Mental Hygiene.

Rigrodsky, S., Prunty, F. and Glovsky, G. (1961). A study of the incidence, types and associated etiologies of hearing loss in an institutionalised mentally retarded population. *Trng. Sch. Bull.* **58**, 30–44.

Rohr, A. and Burr, D.B. (1978). Etiological differences in patterns of psycholinguistic development of children IQ 30 to 60. *Am. J. Ment. Defic.* **82**, 549–53.

Rondal, J.A. (1980). Verbal imitation by Down's Syndrome and non-retarded children. *Am. J. Ment. Defic.* **85**, 318–21.

Saunders, J. and Collins, J. (1972). *Teaching Mentally Handicapped Children*. Hove: Penny Gobby House School.

Scheffelin, M. (1968). A comparison of four stimulus–response channels in paired-associate learning. *Am. J. Ment. Defic.* **73**, 303–307.

Seagoe, M.V. (1964). *Yesterday was Tuesday, All Day and All Night: The Story of a Unique Education*. Toronto: Little, Brown.

Smith, W.W. (1976). *How Soon is Early?* East Grinstead & District Society for Mentally Handicapped Children.

Sommers, R.K. and Starkey, K.L. (1977). Dichotic verbal processing in Down's Syndrome children having qualitatively different speech and language skills. *Am. J. Ment. Defic.* **82**, 44–53.

Springer, S.P. and Deutsch, G. (1981). *Left Brain, Right Brain*. San Francisco: Freeman.

Talbot, J. (1981). Pre-school reading. *Parents Voice* **31**, 1.

Thorley, B.S. and Wood, V.M. (1979). Early number experiences for preschool Down's Syndrome children. *Austral. J. Early Childh.* **4**, 15–20.

Wiegel-Crump, C.A. (1981). The development of grammar in Down's Syndrome children. *Ed. & Trng Ment. Retard.* **16**, 24–30.

Zaidel, E. (1978). Lexical organisation in the right hemisphere. In Buser, P. and Rongel-Bouser, A. (eds), *Cerebral Correlates of Conscious Experience*. Amsterdam: Elsevier.

Life Chances

17 Parent Involvement and Early Intervention

C.C. Cunningham and S.M. Glenn

The first need of parents when they are told that they have a child with Down's Syndrome is to come to terms with the diagnosis. For some, the decision will be whether or not to take the baby home; for others whether to pursue active medical treatment for any life-threatening conditions. All, however, have to begin the process of constructing an understanding of what the diagnosis means for the child, themselves and the family. For many, their previous knowledge and experience of babies and parenting will not seem relevant for the baby with Down's Syndrome, and so they have a void – no framework to help them anticipate the immediate and long-term consequences of the diagnosis. This creates uncertainty about how they will cope, what they should do, and how to make sense of what is happening. And this uncertainty is likely to produce anxiety and stress. Their immediate need, therefore, is to begin the process of reconstructing new frameworks of understanding. There are several foci for these frameworks. (1) The child: 'What are Down's Syndrome children like?' 'What do they need?' (2) Themselves as parents of a handicapped child: 'Why did it happen to me?' 'What did I do?' 'How do I feel about it?' 'Why do I feel this way – what does it mean?' Most parents initially have very strong reactions and can be surprised at the strength of their feelings (MacKeith, 1973). Indeed, this may shock them as much as the diagnosis itself and lead to an examination of their self-concept, values, attitudes and aspirations. (3) Lastly, they will focus on their family, in terms both of the reactions of family and friends and the future they face: 'How do we tell Grandma or the other children?' 'Why does my husband not feel like I do?' 'What effect will it have on the other children?'

The process of reconstructing these new models obviously takes time. It requires information and experience, each part of which has to be examined, adjusted in relation to past experience, considered from different perspectives, and reformulated in respect of their changing models, current feelings and views of the future. In this process, well organised and knowledgeable counselling can help if it takes place within a context of regular support, which is seen by parents as both relevant and practical.

347

A MODEL OF ADJUSTMENT

Several models of parental reactions and the process of adjustment have been put forward to guide professional counselling (Blacher, 1984). Cunningham (1979a), for example, describes a four-phase model, beginning with an initial shock phase, manifested in emotional disorganisation and paralysis of action, which can last for a few minutes or several days and requires emotional support. This is followed by a reaction phase, often expressed in sorrow, grief, disappointment, anxiety, anger, denial, and is the start of a process of reintegration. Such reactions can be seen as coping strategies which enable the parents to explore possibilities and reconstrue their situation, and, seen in this way, reactions such as denial allow the parents to control the amount of uncertainty they can deal with at a given time. They also test out and learn about their own feelings through interaction and observation of others. Parents need someone who will listen and help them to explore their reactions by suggesting alternative explanations, providing accurate information and emphasising that such feelings are neither unusual nor pathological.

Parents then move toward an adaptation phase. They have developed sufficient reformulated frameworks of understanding to allow them to anticipate the future to some extent. Initially, this manifests itself in selecting a direction to pursue which will solve some problems and in formulating questions relevant to this end.

Finally, an orientation phase is reached, when parents begin to organise, seek help and plan for the future. They have established a working model to guide their behaviour and are in more control of their actions. They have achieved a 'functional acceptance', which allows them to get on with day-to-day living at a reasonably balanced level. Of course, reformulation is continual, and acceptance, whatever this means, is an ever-changing construct.

This stage model must be seen as a framework to guide interpretation, not as a prescribed set of behavioural outcomes that all parents must go through. Some will never experience certain aspects; others go through the phases in parallel not sequentially. Most parents oscillate between phases, and invariably there are overlaps.

The formulation of frameworks is how we all cope with new situations. Coping can be seen to consist of strategies aimed at avoiding or reducing stress, and stress as the imbalance between the demands placed on the parents by the situation and the resources available to meet these demands (Ray *et al.*, 1982). The coping resources will include: (a) their physical and emotional wellbeing during this period, which will be influenced by (b) individual ability and problem-solving experience; (c) support from family, friends and services, i.e. the social network; (d) utilitarian resources such as finance, mobility, etc.; and (e) their current framework of values, beliefs, and feelings of self-efficacy (Folkman and Lazarus, 1980).

To formulate a plan of action, joint parent–professional assessments have to be made of the family's coping resources, together with an understanding of their reactions, feelings and the process of adjustment. This will include an identification of: (a) possible sources of stress; (b) resources for coping; (c) needs, and short- and long-term goals; and (d) strategies aimed at achieving these goals. An overt statement of shared goals allows for the evaluation of progress by parents and professionals alike.

THE FORMATIVE PERIOD

The initial period after the diagnosis is formative and likely to have long-term implications. Parents are vulnerable and often in an aroused emotional state which makes them particularly sensitive to the actions and statements of others. They are trying to understand their own feelings and partly do so by detailed consideration of other people's reactions. Thus, when the diagnosis of Down's Syndrome is withheld for what is to them no good reason, they express considerable dissatisfaction (e.g. Carr, 1970; Pueschel and Murphy, 1976; Cunningham and Sloper, 1977). It may be seen as implying that they were unable to cope with the diagnosis or that there was something to hide – a stigma. They may anyway have felt both these things, and the behaviour of professionals reinforces these fears.

They may also be trying to understand their own feelings of rejection, or of not valuing this baby compared to the one that was wanted. Any suggestion by the professional of devaluing the infant, by ignoring him or her, appearing curt and uninterested, emphasising what the child will *not* do rather than giving a more balanced perspective, is likely to interact with parental feelings and produce reactions of anger toward or rejection of the professional. Further, parents are unlikely to perceive the service in the same way as professionals; for example, they do not differentiate professional roles and functions to the same degree. Thus, they are more likely to generalise from the negative reactions of one professional to others, thus endangering the development of future positive interactions.

Interactions can also be threatened when parents seek to understand their own reactions by testing them out on friends, relatives and professionals. Alternatively, they may deny their own feelings and project them on to others. Because parents are often under considerable stress and in emotional disarray, these normal methods of coping and learning can be forced to extremes by the urgency of the situation, and this can result in making hasty judgements and in problems in interrelationships. Hence, we must be aware that this period is a particularly sensitive one, which is formative and demands high quality support. Such support could: (a) reduce current stress and leave less painful experiences which will not then adversely influence any future crises; (b) show parents that professional support is useful and productive, thus encouraging parents to be aware of the potential of support and seek it out before any severe crisis is upon them; (c) help parents to understand the process through which they are going and the method of analysing what is happening (e.g. by developing goals and coping strategies). In this way it may help them to apply similar approaches in future.

That such a support service is not currently available is confirmed by the large number of studies reporting considerable parental dissatisfaction with services (e.g. Drillien and Wilkinson, 1964; Stone, 1973; Gayton and Walker, 1974; Spain and Wigley, 1975; Pueschel and Murphy, 1976; Cunningham and Sloper, 1977; Lucas and Lucas, 1980; Springer and Steele, 1980). There can also be few professionals who have not experienced the aggressive and anguished outpourings of parents about 'how they were told', 'unsympathetic professionals', 'lack of support' and 'lack of knowledge' of professionals.

Many professionals interpret this as an inevitable consequence of parental anger or guilt at having a child with Down's Syndrome. But to do so is to use a pathological framework to interpret parental behaviour in much the same way as it was years ago when the child's condition was used to explain lack of development or bizarre behaviour. In a recent study, Cunningham *et al.* (1984) reported a comparison of parents receiving a 'model service' of disclosure of the diagnosis of Down's Syndrome and early support based upon recommendations in the literature with retrospective studies and a contemporary control group. The seven families experiencing this 'model service' made no critical comments about the service to an independent researcher when the infant was 6 months old, compared with a 42% satisfaction rate for the retrospective control group and a 25% satisfaction rate for the contemporary control group. What was also striking was the spontaneously expressed confidence these parents had in the services, and the few apparent instances of severe problems of adjustment. Much more research is required on the effects of such early support programmes. Particularly, we need to examine the nature of parent–professional relationships and how early support influences future potential crisis periods such as entering and leaving school, and the nature of support and information that parents require at these times.

Parents' needs for emotional support and help in understanding feelings and family reactions may not be expressed as openly or explicitly as their need for information on methods of helping the child. Parents' perception of the role of the home visitor will influence the questions they ask. Thus, if the home visitor projects a role of being mainly interested in the child and suggesting activities to facilitate development, parents may fail to express a need for counselling in other areas. Also, parents who have not themselves experienced the positive benefits that such counselling can bring, may fail to seek it. Some parents may not want it: 'You know the psychologists and the social workers have this concept that every parent with a handicapped child wants to talk about it all the time. That's garbage.' (Turnbull and Turnbull, 1982).

How far, then, should the professional take such statements at their face value? This presents the counsellor with the dilemma of whether explicitly to introduce a topic, such as marital relationships. One approach (Cunningham, 1982) is to discuss a range of needs, reactions and possibilities that have been found, but stating that they do not apply to all parents and emphasising that this is not to suggest that all parents have similar experiences. The parent is then left with the decision as to whether to pursue the issue, privately or openly. Once again, this emphasises the need for negotiation, with the parents maintaining control and making their own decisions.

Finally, for most parents, information on practical activities which can be reasonably expected to help the baby's development can be very therapeutic. In the first days, explaining that, within the context of the wider issues noted above, various activities with the baby can facilitate development, gives parents positive ideas which can be immediately implemented. It is essential that the parent achieves success and is able to observe short-term, positive benefits. If they do not achieve this in their first attempts, they are likely to develop negative expectations about their own abilities, the baby and the future. In turn, they are likely to be less willing to try other ideas, seek out information or work with services. Belief in the value of such activities is reflected by the rapid expansion of early intervention programmes in recent years.

EARLY INTERVENTION

Early intervention programmes assume that the early years of life are particularly important for later development. This view has not gone unchallenged (e.g. Clarke and Clarke, 1976), but, as argued earlier, support for the family should start in the formative years when family interaction patterns are being established. Further, Gray and Wandersman (1980) maintain that any effect on these interaction patterns will continue beyond the intervention period, and that home-based programmes are more likely than centre-based ones to adapt to meet the needs and values of particular families.

Thus, there is considerable debate about how to conceptualise and help young children with Down's Syndrome. Currently, the most common approach has been to focus on the child's development using psychometric tests (or check-list derivatives) of sensorimotor and cognitive development. But such approaches are being increasingly recognised as limited, since (as noted above) they neglect variables related to the ecology of the family and may be based on restricted models of child development (for example, neglecting social and emotional factors). Thus, by focusing on psychometric definitions of mental deficiency (for example delayed development), and by directing our intervention procedures towards 'speeding up' progress, as assessed by developmental tests, we are in danger of restricting conceptualisation, implementation and evaluation alike. In discussing a different approach, we will focus on three issues.

1. Evaluation: how effective is early intervention?
2. Implementation: who, where, when and how often?
3. Conceptualisation: who is the focus of intervention and what models of development are used?

Evaluation

Head Start programmes in America gave some impetus to early intervention programmes for children with Down's Syndrome, but these studies are based on disadvantaged, rather than organically impaired, children. Thus, the samples are likely to vary on biological factors and between and within cultural effects. Care must be taken, therefore, in generalising results between the different populations. Reviews of Head Start (Bronfenbrenner, 1975; Stedman, 1977) have generally concluded that the greatest cognitive gains were made by children introduced into structured child–parent programmes at age 1–2 years. There is evidence that such gains largely disappear within 3 years of cessation of the programme. However, using a wider range of measures, Lazar and Darlington (1978) followed up children who had been in high-quality, well-designed programmes, and showed significant positive effects of early intervention on measures of scholastic attainment and both parent and child attitudes to schooling and vocational aspirations.

Looking at children who are at risk because of biological factors, Simeonsson *et al.* (1982) reviewed 27 studies describing early intervention. Twenty-five reported effectiveness on the basis of subjective clinical judgements; statistical procedures were used in 16 of the studies, and 13 of these reported effectiveness. Carr's review (see Chapter 10) also reports positive, if limited, outcomes, for infants with Down's Syndrome. However, both reviews note that many studies failed to meet common criteria for scientific acceptability, and Halpern (1984) concluded that the benefits of such intervention remain unmeasured and undefined.

As well as varying in methodological adequacy, these studies also varied along such dimensions as age of starting, focus on parents or child, length, intensity, place and type of intervention, intervener characteristics and outcome measures. This variability (and lack of specificity of aims and methods) leaves much uncertainty about which developmental aspects are influenced and what processes mediate developmental changes in the child. For example, because they made use of retrospective control groups and outcome measures restricted to cognitive development, many of the studies have been unable to ascertain whether the effects of intervention are limited to reducing 'hidden deprivation'. The slower development of earlier samples, for example, may have resulted from societal differences, such as changes in basic health and medical care, and/or low expectations derived from society's conception of Down's Syndrome, which is transmitted to the parents and then manifested in both the quality and quantity of parent–child interaction.

Thus, while there appears to be evidence for some limited effectiveness of intervention, a wider range of measures is necessary. Future research has to evaluate not only child measures, but also parent measures, such as attitudes to the child and child rearing, satisfaction with the intervention programme, interrelationship with the home visitor, ability to learn strategies, willingness to apply these, the relationship to existing family coping resources and, last but not least, the nature of parent–child interactions. In addition, measures of sociological change, including values, attitudes and aspects of service provision, are needed.

Implementation

Who?

In the studies reported, the main intervener was one of the following: physiotherapist, paediatric nurse, speech therapist, lecturer, psychologist, nursery nurse, health visitor, occupational therapist, volunteer parent, social worker (e.g. Rayner, 1978; Revill and Blunden, 1979; Pugh, 1981). Cunningham *et al.* (1982) compared the development of two groups of infants with Down's Syndrome: with one group the primary intervener was a psychologist, for the other a trained health visitor.

Essentially similar patterns of facilitated development and parental satisfaction were found in both groups. These studies indicate that the particular professional background of the intervener may be relatively unimportant, when specific training is given. The range of professionals involved, together with the need to develop skills which may be derived from many of the contributing professions, suggests the value of short multidisciplinary courses, with the parents contributing to, as well as participating in, the courses. Many of the currently available courses are organised for one group of professionals (for example doctors, teachers, psychologists, social workers, health visitors). This works against the development of transdisciplinary thinking focused on families with children with special needs. Instead, it encourages compartmentalisation of needs and prevents the support services from viewing the family as a whole. It also results in the involvement of a wide range of professionals, with the attendant danger of conflicting ideas and advice. Training should be given to multidisciplinary groups, including parents, since few new developments are so specific that they are relevant to only one profession (Mittler, 1983).

Where?

Usually, intervention has been either home based or clinic based. The setting up of child development units in the UK, in response to the 1976 Court Report, has meant that many more parents are now being given the opportunity to attend sessions at local centres.

Proponents of home visiting, however, have argued that this is more appropriate on several grounds. (a) Some parents are unable or unwilling to travel to reach a centre. (b) There may be a high drop-out rate for attendance at centres with only the highly motivated parents remaining, and the families most at risk may therefore receive least help. (c) Because infant stimulation is carried out in the home, often using the child's own toys and taking into account the mother's daily routine, it is more flexible to individual family needs. (d) Parents feel more in control of events in their own home and therefore there is a better chance of establishing a 'partnership' relationship. (e) There is increased likelihood of professionals meeting all family members, and ascertaining sociocultural factors.

On the other hand, many parents of children with Down's Syndrome often feel isolated, particularly in the early years, and parent groups run by parents or through child development units may help to provide peer group support. Parent workshops based on lectures, practical activities and group discussion invariably report that parents rate informal and formal discussion with other parents as a most important aspect (Cunningham and Jeffree, 1975; Firth, 1982).

Recent research has demonstrated that the nature of the social support received by parents is an important variable for optimal development of non-handicapped and socially 'at-risk' children (Lazar and Darlington, 1978; Bee *et al.*, 1982; Slaughter, 1983). It is a question for future research how far such variables are critical in the development of children with Down's Syndrome, and how far parent groups based in a centre can act in a supportive manner. Many families of Down's children have a supportive social network, but presumably the attitudes and knowledge base of the network may be the key variables. Home visiting will probably continue to be important in the early months, but, where desired, parent groups may be able to provide additional sources of support of a more continuous nature. It should be emphasised that not all parents of a child with Down's Syndrome will want to attend parents' groups; they may see this as part of the 'labelling' process. However, at least half of the mothers of Down's children express the desire to meet with other parents (Cunningham and Sloper, 1977) by the time the child is 6 months old.

When?

Most approaches have assumed that the sooner one starts active structured stimulation of the infant to compensate for learning difficulties, the better the long-term outcome. However, there have been few attempts to examine this question directly. In our cohort study (Cunningham, 1983), 181 families with Down's children were visited from the first weeks of life and provided with an intervention programme. We related age of starting (i.e. between the first week and ninth month of life) and developmental scores at 2 and 3 years. Children beginning the programme before 6 months of age attained higher scores than others until they reached 1 year of age, but after this no differences were found. *Thus, age of starting (in the first year) did not appear to be a critical variable for the child.*

Other studies have shown that children in programmes for some time are more advanced in attainment than those just commencing (e.g. Clunies-Ross, 1979), but generally fail to look at the 'catch-up' phenomenon over an extended period. No evidence is available as yet from which to determine if there *is* a critical starting period, after which permanent secondary handicap will ensue. The outcome measures normally used are concerned with the attainment of developmental milestones derived from standard tests, and it is possible that wider and more sensitive measures of such areas as initiative, exploration, creativity and social interaction would produce different results, especially if the key variables are related to parent–child interaction.

How often?

This question has two parts:

(a) how often does one need to visit the home?
(b) how often does one need to carry out the stimulation activities with the infant?

In our study we found that visiting rate to the home, whether at weekly, bi-weekly or 6-weekly intervals, had little effect on developmental outcomes, but parents did prefer bi-weekly visits. This is consistent with the results of Sandow *et al.* (1981), which showed no overall differences between bi- and 8-weekly visited groups of mentally handicapped pre-school children.

Few studies have attempted to compare the intensity of the programme with developmental gains. Within our cohort we have several sub-samples where parents have been asked to carry out activities very intensively (i.e. three to five times a day), repeating the activity several times, and have compared these to less intensive groups, where parents use their own discretion and apply the activities in a more flexible manner. The areas concentrated upon were sitting, reaching, walking, manipulation of objects, object permanence and imitation. The overall results indicate *some* advanced attainment for the intensive groups during the period of intervention *but no long-term benefits*. All groups attained similar levels within a few months of returning to a less intense programme. Also, the differences were generally small and usually specific to the task. There was some indication that the slower developing children benefited more by the intensive training, but again differences were small. It is possible that alternative approaches focused on different aspects of development may have different results, and research is needed to show where and when such efforts are likely to be most worthwhile.

For the present, it would appear that providing parents with a knowledge of child development and help in interpreting the child's behaviour, insights into observation, interaction and ideas on how to facilitate the child's development in a reasonably organised but flexible way are as beneficial in the first 2 years of life as more intensive approaches with set daily exercises and activities and detailed recording.

Conceptualisation

Since the majority of early intervention programmes aim to provide parents with advice on how to enhance their child's development, and are thus mainly infant focused, the nature of the curriculum is a vital, though somewhat neglected, issue.

The nature of the curriculum

The two main perspectives guiding intervention programmes have been behavioural and cognitive psychology, both of which deal with observable behaviour. However, for the behaviourist, elementary units of behaviour are seen as discrete and independent, shaped by reinforcement contingencies consequent upon a child's action on the environment. For cognitive psychologists, on the other hand, behaviour is analysed in terms of internal processes, with development being seen as the sequential formation of cognitive structures through which the child operates selectively on the environment. (This perspective includes Piaget's theory, as well as the skill theories of Connolly (1970) and Fischer (1980).)

The 'teaching' implication from the first viewpoint is to organise environmental events in order that the desired behaviour is elicited and reinforced immediately. This demands that the major control lies with the teacher. By contrast, the cognitive view stresses that imposing too rigid a structure, which restricts active selection on the part of the child, may not be conducive to development. Seibert and Hogan (1983), for example, argue that the objectives of intervention should not be specific behaviours but functions and concepts, and objectives should therefore be defined in terms of a range or class of behaviours that accomplish a similar function (for example, how to get someone else's help to achieve a desired object), or that represent a similar concept (for example, objects have names).

Early childhood education for non-handicapped children generally emphasises cognitive development and its role in describing the child's changing capacity to make sense of the environment. Thus, such things as play, problem solving and the capacity to use skills flexibly in different situations have been emphasised. In special education, however, we have children who learn more slowly, and may need help to learn things that other children learn spontaneously. And here the emphasis has been in general on how the developmentally delayed child is different or deficient in development, with the result that intervention strategies have often become based round the achievement of particular behaviours via behaviourist techniques. Thus, whereas for non-handicapped children the emphasis may be on the encouragement of spontaneous learning, for the delayed child a far more structured programme is developed. Furthermore, such programmes largely focus on the performance of the child on specific products of development, rather than on the processes of development.

We need to question whether an uncritical acceptance of this traditional view affects our teaching strategy with mentally handicapped children. Sigel (1979) commented: 'Traditionally, I would suspect infants at risk are viewed as less actively involved with their environment, and as relatively immobile receivers rather than initiators of interactions'; and 'If children are indeed outreaching organisms, and if children, even though at risk, are able to process information and seek out stimulation, then those who influence the nature of the child's environment should allow for these possibilities.' By emphasising how Down's children are different and deficient in learning, we may therefore be using highly structured procedures which precisely inhibit the development of initiation and exploration.

Often, extrinsic reinforcement is used to increase the frequency of desired behaviours. Yet there is increasing concern in the 'normal' literature on the possibly deleterious effects of using externally structured rewards to produce learning in children (e.g. Donaldson, 1978). Play, with its absence of externally imposed goals, has been emphasised as a crucial factor in the development of young children (e.g. Bruner *et al.*, 1976; see also Chapter 15). Donaldson (1978) argues: 'We enjoy best and engage most readily in activities which we *experience as freely chosen*. We do not like being controlled, we like controlling ourselves.' Papousek (1969) demonstrated that infants as young as 4 months old will interact with their environment in such a way as to control and master it. Recent studies of children with Down's Syndrome and of profoundly handicapped children (Glenn and Cunningham, 1984a; 1984b) with developmental levels of less than 1 year, indicated that the children responded enthusiastically and for long periods of time when they were presented with equipment which enabled them to interact with their environment in a freely chosen and predictable way. Thus, while not denying the advances that have been achieved by the use of operant frameworks, we should be aware of the dangers of being over-influenced by a deficit-training model of handicap and thereby underestimating the active part played by the children in influencing the course of their own development.

In fact, no one type of programme appears to be more effective than another, providing that planning, objectives and organisation of learning activities are used. As noted earlier, in our programme for Down's infants, children of parents receiving emphasis on behavioural principles and training of specific tasks were not significantly more advanced than those of parents receiving a programme emphasising developmental change and flexibility.

If one adopts a more cognitive process model, then traditional psychometric methods of assessment are inadequate since they do not specify the underlying processes which lead to success on particular test items. As an alternative, the Piagetian-based sensorimotor scales of Uzgiris and Hunt (1975) are increasingly being used to assess and guide intervention (e.g. Uzgiris and Hunt, 1983; Kahn, 1984). Similarly, Seibert and Hogan (1983) have developed a social communication scale based on concepts and skills that the research literature indicates the normally developing child has mastered by 24 months. They see these partly as a guide to intervention in the social domain for at-risk infants and partly as a research instrument designed to test hypotheses about prerequisites for the acquisition of language. Within frameworks such as these, some researchers have continued to look for process differences between non-handicapped children and those with Down's Syndrome (see Chapter 13). However, Brooks and Baumeister (1977) caution that such studies need to go on to show that any differences found do indeed affect children's functioning in the everyday environment. The implication is that intervention studies need to be directed in the light of these supposed differences.

The central issue is, therefore: should we apply highly structured teaching methods in order to compensate for 'spontaneous learning' disability (Clarke and Clarke, 1973) and, if so, will these neglect or prevent the development of such abilities? Clearly, children need a basic set of skills in order to interact with the environment. If, for example, the Down's child has motor difficulties which prevent reaching, manipulation and hence exploration of objects, or sitting up and walking, then this may result in failure to achieve his or her intended ends and lead to frustration.

A major emphasis of structured programmes is to plan for a high probability of success on the part of the child in order to reduce this continual failure. However, it must be noted that success is defined in terms of teacher/parent-selected goals rather than child goals, as would be the case in play activities. What we require is more objective information on the processes of development and on which aspects may be more appropriately facilitated by one technique, which by another. To some extent this will be governed by the type of difficulty the child manifests.

This can be exemplified from the area of mother–infant interactions. Studies of non-handicapped children indicate that the quality of early mother–infant interactions is positively related to later cognitive and social development (Yarrow *et al.*, 1972; Bradley and Caldwell, 1976; Bee *et al.*, 1982). Crawley and Spiker (1983) reported similar findings for 2-year-old children with Down's Syndrome, showing that individual differences in mother–child interactions may be related to mental development. Other studies with Down's children have indicated disturbances in mother–infant interaction during the second year of life – in particular, more intrusive and directive maternal behaviour when compared to non-handicapped mother–infant pairs (Jones, 1977; Buckhalt *et al.*, 1978).

For very young infants with Down's Syndrome, a number of studies have shown delay in the onset of and qualitative differences in eye-gaze (Berger and Cunningham, 1981), smiling, and later in laughter (Cytryn, 1975; Cicchetti and Sroufe, 1976), which may partially result in disturbed interaction patterns. Thus, Berger and Cunningham (1983) found that, by 6 months of age, there were increased vocal clashes, reduced reciprocal turn-taking, and higher levels of mother activity in mother–infant interactions for Down's children compared to non-handicapped dyads. Part of this may also result from the parent's conception of the child as being handicapped and needing more stimulation and effort. When mothers were asked to reduce their level of stimulation by only imitating infant behaviours, increased infant vocalisation was found. Studies have been carried out on the development of visually directed reaching (Cunningham, 1979b), eye-gaze (Berger and Cunningham, 1981), and differential responses to auditory stimuli (Glenn and Cunningham, 1984a). All found that the mean duration of response (i.e. the amount of time the infant spent looking at an object or face, or listening to an auditory stimulus before switching attention) was generally longer for Down's infants than for non-handicapped infants. This might indicate the need for longer time to react to or process the incoming information and respond to it. Thus, high levels of parent/teacher stimulation, with limited time to respond, may prevent the necessary processing being completed, and thus fail to facilitate development. If, as suggested above, interactions are crucial to the development process, then intervention in terms of helping parents explore methods of synchronised interaction may be essential and more critical in the long term than highly structured training on specific tasks.

Affleck *et al.* (1982) extended this notion when they argued that unless the interaction patterns between mother (and presumably all family members) and infant are pleasurable and satisfying, then it is unlikely that parents will be able to learn effective intervention skills. This argument is given some support by Ainsworth (1979), who found that infants who had mothers who were sensitive to their behavioural cues were more securely attached at 1 year of age, and, in later years, were more socially responsive, curious and outgoing, as well as having higher scores on cognitive and language ability tests than those who had mothers who were rated as insensitive. Mothers with Down's infants require information and guidance on differences which affect the child and on how to interpret the intentionality and function of the child's behaviour in order to enhance this sensitivity. This requires knowledge, not just of specific developmental tasks, but of the developmental process and how to use this to help the infant. Thus, if the mother finds she can interact successfully and interprets this as important for the child, she is likely to maintain this behaviour. Moxley-Haegert and Serbin (1983) demonstrated this by comparing the effectiveness of a developmental education programme with one based on child management for parents of developmentally delayed children. They found that the children in the developmental education group gained more skills, and the parents participated more in the treatment. They concluded that developmental education appears to enable parents to discriminate small developmental gains which facilitate intrinsic motivation when working with their children.

It is also reasonable to suggest that parents who have a knowledge of development and developmental processes are also more likely to capitalise on opportunities to facilitate the child's development than those restricting their activities to specific task training. This emphasis on the parent–child interaction as the main mediator of treatment programmes supports the argument that the focus of early intervention should be on the parent and the family ecology, and that we need to extend our current emphasis on training of developmental milestones toward this broader conception. Thus, we return to the argument of Bee *et al.* (1982) that, unless parents have an acceptable level of social support, it is unlikely they will be able to take much pleasure in their infant or be receptive to intervention suggestions. Families must function at a minimum level of healthy adjustment, cohesion and balance between resources and needs, if they are to profit from the home support programme.

CONCLUSIONS

We need to move away from the notion of parents as trainers of the child and as extensions of the therapist, towards a model of a consumer partnership in which parents are active participants exercising control over the nature of the partnership. Similarly, we need to move towards more cognitive models of early development which stress the infant as an active participant in the learning process rather than a passive or deficient recipient of externally controlled events. Within this framework, more emphasis is required on the early parent–infant interaction patterns and in particular on ways of facilitating parent sensitivity to infant cues. This is likely to be more difficult with Down's infants as a consequence of their specific difficulties. Parents require detailed information on the possible nature of such problems, the developmental process, and then about the interaction between the two.

Since such interactions are set up in the first months of life, this should be seen as a formative period requiring professional counselling and support. In the initial period after the diagnosis, parents are likely to be in a state of shock and disorganisation. Before they can enter into pleasurable interactions with the infant, they will need to come to terms with their feelings and reactions and consider the impact on their family. And, to do this, they will need counselling, to varying degrees, that provides them with a framework to understand their reactions and those of other family members. This in turn should facilitate family interaction patterns and reduce friction and stress consequent upon uncertainty and lack of information. Such a framework should also help maintain the necessary support system which forms a sound base from which to assist the infant.

Since this is a process of change which takes time, the intervention needs to be regular and continuous and relevant to the needs as expressed by the family. In order to ascertain these individual needs, the home visitor/intervener must establish a relationship based on mutual respect, which allows the parents to decide upon the role(s) they wish to take and the degree of involvement. To do this, the home visitor must be able to demonstrate competence in counselling, knowledge of the child, development and strategies to facilitate development.

Clearly, there are many uncertainties about the best ways to intervene. Earlier models based on behavioural paradigms and developmental milestones have met with limited success but are inadequate. We need to reconceptualise parent involvement and early intervention and develop broader evaluation methods. It would be a mistake to assume we already know how to intervene with families of Down's children and that this is no longer a priority for investigation. It would also be a mistake to dismiss too hastily the possible benefits of early intervention in the context of the family, based upon the current limited success indicated by the restricted evaluations derived from normative psychometric tests.

REFERENCES

Affleck, G., McGrade, B.J., McQueeney, M. and Allen, D. (1982). Promise of relationship-focused early intervention in developmental disabilities. *J. Spec. Ed.* **16**, 413–30.

Ainsworth, M. (1979). Infant–mother attachment. *Am. Psychol.* **34**, 932–7.

Bee, H.L., Barnard, K.E., Eyres, S.J., Gray, C.A., Hammond, M.A., Spietz, A.L., Synder, C. and Clark, B. (1982). Prediction of IQ and language skill from perinatal status, child performance, family characteristics and mother–infant interaction. *Child Dev.* **53**, 1134–56.

Berger, J. and Cunningham, C.C. (1981). The development of eye contact between mothers and normal and Down's Syndrome infants. *Dev. Psychol.* **17**(5), 678–89.

Berger, J. and Cunningham, C.C. (1983). Development of early vocal behaviours and interactions in Down's Syndrome and non-handicapped infant–mother pairs. *Dev. Psychol.* **19**(3), 322–31.

Blacher, J. (1984). Sequential stages of parental adjustment to the birth of a child with handicaps: fact or artefact. *Ment. Retard.* **22**, 55–69.

Bradley, R.H. and Caldwell, B.M. (1976). The relation of infants' home environment to mental test performance at fifty-four months: a follow-up study. *Child Dev.* **47**, 1172–4.

Bronfenbrenner, U. (1975). Is early intervention effective? In Bronfenbrenner, U. (ed.), *Influences on Human Development*. New York: Dryden.

Brooks, P.H. and Baumeister, A.A. (1977). A plea for consideration of ecological validity in the experimental psychology of mental retardation. *Am. J. Ment. Defic.* **81**, 407–16.

Bruner, J.S., Jolly, A. and Sylva, K. (1976). *Play – Its Role in Development and Evolution*. Harmondsworth: Penguin.

Buckhalt, J.A., Rutherford, J.B. and Goldberg, K.E. (1978). Verbal and nonverbal interaction of mothers with their Down's Syndrome and non-retarded infants. *Am. J. Ment. Defic.* **82**, 337–43.

Carr, J. (1970). Mongolism: telling the parents. *Dev. Med. & Child Neurol.* **12**, 213–21.

Cicchetti, D. and Sroufe, L.A. (1976). The relationship between affective and cognitive development in Down's Syndrome infants. *Child Dev.* **47**, 920–29.

Clarke, A.D.B. and Clarke, A.M. (1973). *Mental Retardation and Behavioural Research*. IRMR Study Group No. 4. Edinburgh and London: Churchill Livingstone.

Clarke, A.M. and Clarke, A.D.B. (1976). *Early Experience: Myth and Evidence*. London: Open Books.

Clunies-Ross, G.G. (1979). Accelerating the development of Down's Syndrome infants and young children. *J. Spec. Ed.* **13**(2), 170–77.

Connolly, K. (ed.) (1970). *Mechanisms of Motor Skill Development*. London: Academic Press.

Crawley, S.B. and Spiker, D. (1983). Mother–child interactions involving 2-year-olds with Down's Syndrome: a look at individual differences. *Child Dev.* **54**, 1312–23.

Cunningham, C.C. (1979a). Parent counselling. In Craft, M. (ed.), *Tredgold's Mental Retardation*. 12th edn. London: Baillière-Tindall.

Cunningham, C.C. (1979b). Aspects of early development in Down's Syndrome infants. PhD Thesis, University of Manchester.

Cunningham, C.C. (1982). *Down's Syndrome: An Introduction for Parents*. London: Souvenir Press.

Cunningham, C.C. (1983). *Early Development and its Facilitation in Infants with Down's Syndrome*. Final Report, Part 1, to DHSS. London: HMSO.

Cunningham, C.C. and Jeffree, D.M. (1975). The organisation and structure of workshops for parents of mentally handicapped children. *Bulletin of British Psychology* **28**, 405–11.

Cunningham, C.C., Aumonier, M.E. and Sloper, P. (1982). Health visitor support for families with Down's Syndrome infants. *Child: care, health and development* **8**, 1–19.

Cunningham, C.C., Morgan, P. and McGucken, R.B. (1984). Down's Syndrome: is dissatisfaction with disclosure of diagnosis inevitable? *Dev. Med. Child Neurol.* **26**, 33–9.

Cunningham, C.C. and Sloper, P. (1977). Parents of Down's Syndrome babies: their early needs. *Child: care, health and development* **3**, 325–47.

Cytryn, L. (1975). Studies of behavior in children with Down's Syndrome. In Anthony, E.J. (ed.), *Explorations in Child Psychiatry*. New York: Plenum Press.

Donaldson, M. (1978). *Children's Minds*. London: Fontana.

Drillien, C.H. and Wilkinson, E. (1964). Mongolism: when should the parents be told? *Br. Med. J.* **2**, 1306–1307.

Firth, H. (1982). The effectiveness of parent workshops in a mental handicap service. *Child: care, health and development* **8**, 77–91.

Fischer, K.W. (1980). A theory of cognitive development: the control and construction of hierarchies of skills. *Psychol. Rev.* **87**, 477–531.

Folkman, S. and Lazarus, R.S. (1980). An analysis of coping in a middle-aged community sample. *J. Health & Social Behav.* **21**, 219–39.

Gayton, W.F. and Walker, L. (1974). Down's Syndrome: informing the parents. *Am. J. Dis. Child.* **127**, 510–12.

Glenn, S.M. and Cunningham, C.C. (1984a). Selective preferences to different speech stimuli in infants with Down's Syndrome. In Berg, J.M. (ed.), *Perspectives and Progress in Mental Retardation*. Vol. 1, pp. 201–210. Baltimore: University Park Press.

Glenn, S.M. and Cunningham, C.C. (1984b). Selective auditory preferences and the use of automated equipment by severely, profoundly and multiply handicapped children. *J. Ment. Defic. Res.* **28**, 281–96.

Gray, S.W. and Wandersman, L.P. (1980). The methodology of home-based intervention studies: problems and promising strategies. *Child Dev.* **51**, 993–1009.

Halpern, R. (1984). Lack of effects for home-based early intervention? Some possible explanations. *Am. J. Orthopsych.* **54**, 33–42.

Jones, O.H.M. (1977). Mother–child communication with pre-linguistic Down's Syndrome and normal infants. In Schaffer, H.R. (ed.), *Studies in Mother–Infant Interaction*. London: Academic Press.

Kahn, J.V. (1984). Cognitive training and its relationship to the language of profoundly retarded children. In Berg, J.M. (ed.), *Perspectives and Progress in Mental Retardation*. Baltimore: University Park Press.

Lazar, I. and Darlington, R.B. (1978). *The Lasting Effects after Pre-School*. Washington, DC: WS Department of Health, Education and Welfare, Pub. No. (OHDS) 79-30178.

Lucas, P.J. and Lucas, A.M. (1980). Down's Syndrome: breaking the news to Irish parents. *J. Irish Med. Assoc.* **3**, 248–52.

MacKeith, R. (1973). The feelings and behaviours of parents of handicapped children. *Dev. Med. & Child Neurol.* **15**, 24–7.

Mittler, P.J. (1983). Planning for future developments. In Mittler, P.J. and McConachie, H.R. (eds), *Parents, Professionals and Mentally Handicapped People: Approaches to Partnership*. London: Croom Helm.

Moxley-Haegert, L. and Serbin, L.A. (1983). Developmental education for parents of delayed infants: effects on parental motivation and children's development. *Child Dev.* **54**, 1324–31.

Papousek, H. (1969). Individual variability in learned responses in human infants. In Robinson, R.J. (ed.), *Brain and Early Behaviour*. London: Academic Press.

Pueschel, S. and Murphy, A. (1976). Assessment of counselling practices at the birth of a child with Down's Syndrome. *Am. J. Ment. Defic.* **81**, 325–30.

Pugh, G. (1981). *Parents as Partners*. London: National Children's Bureau.

Ray, C., Lindsop, J. and Gibson, S. (1982). The concept of coping. *Psychol. Med.* **12**, 385–95.

Rayner, H. (1978). The Exeter home-visiting project: the psychologist as one of several therapists. *Child: care, health and development* **4**, 1–7.

Revill, S. and Blunden, R. (1979). A home training service for pre-school developmentally handicapped children. *Behav. Res. & Ther.* **17**, 207–214.

Sandow, S.A., Clarke, A.D.B., Cox, M.V. and Stewart, F.L. (1981). Home intervention with parents of severely subnormal pre-school children. *Child: care, health and development* **7**, 135–44.

Seibert, J.M. and Hogan, A.E. (1983). A model for assessing social and object skills and planning intervention. In McClowry, D. and Richardson, S. (eds), *Infant Communication: Development, Assessment and Intervention*. New York: Grune and Stratton.

Sigel, I.E. (1979). Application of research to psychoeducational treatment of infants at risk. In Kearsley, R.B. and Sigel, I.E. (eds), *Infants at Risk: Assessment of Cognitive Functioning*. New Jersey: Lawrence Erlbaum.

Simeonsson, R.J., Cooper, D.M. and Scheiner, A.P. (1982). A review and analysis of the effectiveness of early intervention programmes. *Pediatrics* **69**, 635–41.

Slaughter, D.T. (1983). Early intervention and its effects on maternal and child development. *Mono. Soc. Res. Child Dev.* No. 202, **48**(4).

Spain, B. and Wigley, J. (eds.) (1975). *Right from the Start: A Service for Families with a Young Handicapped Child*. London: NSMCH.

Springer, A. and Steele, M.W. (1980). Effects of physicians' early parental counselling on rearing of Down's Syndrome children. *Am. J. Ment. Defic.* **85**, 1–5.

Stedman, D.J. (1977). Important considerations in the review and evaluation of educational intervention programmes. In Mittler, P.J. (ed.), *Research to Practice in Mental Retardation, Vol. 1: Care and Intervention*. Baltimore: University Park Press.

Stone, H. (1973). The birth of a child with Down's syndrome: a medico-social study of thirty-one children and their families. *Scott. Med. J.* **18**, 182–7.

Turnbull, A.P. and Turnbull, H.R. (1982). Parent involvement in the education of handicapped children: a critique. *Ment. Retard.* **20**, 115–22.

Uzgiris, I.C. and Hunt, J.McV. (1975). *Assessment in Infancy: Ordinal Scales of Psychological Development*. Urbana, Illinois: University of Illinois Press.

Uzgiris, I.C. and Hunt, J.McV. (1983). *Research with Scales of Psychological Development in Infancy*. Urbana, Illinois: University of Illinois Press.

Yarrow, L.J., Rubenstein, J.L., Pedersen, F.A. and Jankowski, J.J. (1972). Dimensions of early stimulation and their differential effects on infant development. *Merrill Palmer Quart.* **18**, 205–19.

18 Agreeing Not to Intervene: Doctors and Parents of Down's Syndrome Children at a Paediatric Cardiology Clinic

David Silverman

The treatment of Down's children with multiple handicaps has received a great deal of publicity recently, arising from spectacular legal actions in both the UK and the USA. This chapter reports a small-scale study of out-patient consultations with such children at a paediatric cardiology unit. It describes the special form that such consultations take and considers some of the policy questions that arise.

TWO EXAMPLES OF DEVIANT CONSULTATIONS

In a research project on the careers of paediatric hospital patients and their families, a particular type of deviant out-patient consultation has proved to be of special interest. This occurs at one of the limited number of UK centres approved for paediatric cardiology medicine. The unit concerned is technically sophisticated and has a high national and international reputation. It offers forms of investigation, surgery and surgical follow-up that would have been unusual only a few years ago. The full battery of assessment techniques is available for all children and, subject to the balance of risks involved and to a relatively conservative policy of surgical intervention, which limits the amount of elective surgery, the unit has made a dramatic difference to the lives of many sick children and their families. Generally speaking, therefore, it would be right to assume that parents come to develop high expectations of what the unit can do to assess and, where possible, to correct their children's heart conditions.

Bearing this in mind, let us look at two curious, deviant cases. Both children concerned have a ventricular-septal defect ('hole in the heart') with pulmonary-vascular hypertension (complications associated with damage to the lungs – see Chapter 3).

A different version of this chapter – a paper prepared for a sociological audience – is listed in the reference list as Silverman (1981).

The first transcript is an extract from an out-patient consultation between a doctor at the unit and the mother of Anna, aged 4½. Anna was referred to the unit by another hospital because recent chest infections suggested that her heart condition needed reviewing. The doctor completed his examination, confirmed the diagnosis to Anna's mother and discussed a letter he was going to send to the referring hospital.

(Transcript 13:8)
1. D. Well, why don't, we know what's going on, why don't I write to Dr L. with what we think about her, and then you can discuss it further with /
2. M. / Yes, yes /
3. D. / him when you see...
4. M. I'd rather...um...um...I don't really want anything done about her, I just wanna, you know...her left alone really...
5. D. Sure, sure.
6. M. You know and just...just...you know.
7. D. Well I think that's absolutely right. Um and it's what...that's what I think as well. But I don't think her heart abnormality is seriously interfering with her enjoyment of life.

(/ indicates overlapping utterances)

A proper analysis of this extract would depend on a discussion of the stages through which a 'normal-form' consultation unfolds. This we will postpone for the moment. Nonetheless, two striking features of the transcript stand out. First, although the initial disposal decision (reference back to Dr L.) is made by the doctor, the mother volunteers, at utterance 4, a preference against medical intervention. This appears to be rather curious, given both the seriousness of the child's diagnosis just presented and the high expectations of treatment that parents at the unit usually come to have. Furthermore, it is relatively unusual for parents to volunteer, without first being asked by the doctor, their disposal preferences and then to do so in a way which is so assertive of parental rather than medical claims over the child.

Second, at utterance 5, the doctor concurs with what the mother says and, at utterance 7, expresses his complete agreement with it ('I think that's absolutely right'). One implication of this is that not only is no surgical intervention envisaged but that further diagnostic tests are being ruled out. One such test, which is a very common means of assessment, is cardiac catheterisation. It involves passing a small flexible tube into the heart under x-ray control. Pressures are measured, blood samples are taken and, finally, fluid is injected to outline the inside of the heart in order to take a cine x-ray. Where a serious heart abnormality is suspected, cardiac catheterisation is commonly used. Indeed, some out-patient consultations often resemble a (justified) attempt to 'sell' parents on such an invasive diagnostic technique, especially where the child is asymptomatic and consequently not readily defined by parents as 'sick'.

However, here the doctor adopts a passive response. Instead of emphasising the need for further assessment, he accepts the mother's desire to withdraw her child from the prospect of medical interventions. Consequently, the claims of the social world (parents' rights and parents' special knowledge) seem to fall into place with the claims of the medical world (clinical definitions and decisions). Perhaps it is even possible (as we shall discuss later) that the parents' and doctor's shared desire for inaction has, partly, a common *social* root and that, in this case at least, the practice of high-technology medicine ultimately defers to socially grounded criteria. Certainly, the presence of social criteria in the doctor's desired disposal is suggested by his juxtaposition of the child's clinically diagnosed condition and 'her enjoyment of life' (utterance 7).

It is important, however, not to exaggerate the claimed unusual character of this interaction before a sounder analytic basis can be established for that claim. Elsewhere, as here, parents are involved in decisions about disposals. It is the varying character of that involvement which will need further investigation. Again, especially where the risks of surgery are relatively high, a child's current asymptomatic status and, by implication, 'enjoyment of life', do enter into the stated grounds of medically proposed disposal decisions. It is once more a question of the degree to which such socially grounded criteria as 'enjoyment of life' play a *central* part in a parent–doctor discourse.

Finally, it should be emphasised that nothing said here is intended to evaluate the clinical appropriateness of any of the assessment or treatment measures employed. The author possesses no competence for such an evaluation and, in any event, the concern in this chapter is not with disposal decisions *per se* but with the social organisation of the discourses in which decisions are announced, disputed or confirmed.

Let us turn to a second illustrative example of the kind of 'deviance' to be more fully discussed later. The transcript concerns Bill, a child aged 6. Like Anna, Bill was referred from another hospital. Before the fragment below, Bill was examined and the parents told the diagnosis. This is similar to Anna's, except that Bill may have an additional atrial septal defect (a second 'hole').

(Transcript 57:4–6)

1. D. Um, if we er, if we were to want to do more, or you wanted us to do more about him, then we would do some special heart tests on him.
2. M. Well, we're quite happy with him as he is now, aren't we?
3. D. Yes.
4. M. You know, I mean it's not affected 'im really at all. Has it altered at all since he was, since he was first diagnosed?
5. D. Well the x-rays haven't, except that he's got a chest infection now. (Discussion between doctor and parents about Bill's appetite and weight.) But um no, no not appreciably. I mean I'm inclined to agree with you because nothing's happened very much and that we should not interfere in a little boy when he's OK.
6. D. His heart may slow him up a very little bit, but not significantly at this stage and he can go on like this for many, many years.
7. M. Oh that's great.
8. D. On the other hand, if you felt that, um, he was very breathless and

couldn't play with other children and were worried about him, then we'd go ahead and investigate him and close the hole.

9. F.   At the moment, he seems to cope quite well.

10. M. I don't want him messed about with sort of unnecessary, this is the thing we both feel.

Immediate parallels suggest themselves with the earlier transcript. Once again, the parents express a desire to let things stand. Although both children have a congenital heart condition, their parents seem prepared to accept their imperfections and want to avoid an operation and even further tests. Anna's mother just wants 'her left alone really'; Bill's parents are 'quite happy with him as he is now' and 'don't want him messed about with'. Again, the doctor concurs in the decision against further investigation.

Two special features of this latter encounter stand out. First, the decision about catheterisation is presented by the doctor as largely dependent on parental choice. At utterance 1, he links together clinical and family decision-making: 'If we were to want to do more, or you wanted us to do more about him, then we would do some special heart tests on him'. By utterance 8, he is presenting the catheter decision as *entirely* a matter of parental choice: 'if you...were worried about him, then we'd go ahead and investigate him...'. This kind of reference to consumer choice is relatively rare at the pre-catheter stage. What generally seems to happen is that the clinical decision about disposal is made and presented in such a way that it encourages parents to assent, despite whatever doubts they may have. Yet, here the ball is placed very firmly in the parents' court. Second, the salience accorded to the social world in the former transcript is here enlarged upon. At utterance 5, the doctor's reference to 'a little boy' who is 'O.K.' accords with the parents' earlier socially grounded observation that 'it's not affected 'im really at all'. By utterance 8, the doctor is giving a central role to the parents' observations both of Bill's physical symptoms (breathlessness) and his social behaviour (playing with other children). At this point, the doctor is quite prepared to let the parents make the disposal decisions and to do so in terms of their everyday parental competence (i.e. being 'worried about him'). In many other cases, the fact that a child is relatively asymptomatic may make the clinical decision that catheterisation is required that much harder to sell to the parents. Here, the fact that Bill's parents do not observe many symptoms is used as a means to justify a passive disposal.

If the reader is by now prepared to accept, for the moment, the claim that these encounters take relatively deviant forms, questions arise about *why* this deviancy should arise and *how* deviant consultations can nonetheless come to exhibit, to participants and observers alike, an orderly character. The 'why' question will be dealt with first since its answer seems relatively straightforward and, although no doubt relevant to discussions of clinical and social policy, goes beyond the confines of a database, limited, as in this chapter, to transcripts of out-patient consultations.

Central to the answer is that in both out-patients already considered and in the ten other consultations discussed in this chapter, all the children have Down's Syndrome. A common physical disability in such children is some form of congenital heart disease. In turn, a relatively more frequent form of that disease in

Down's children is an atrial-ventricular canal defect. This means that one of the two valves between the ventricles and the atria is missing. In the present sample of 12, taken at random over 1 year from the out-patients at the unit concerned, the distribution of conditions is as follows, in approximate order of severity.

Ventricular-septal defect (VSD)	1
Tetralogy of Fallot	1
VSD and/or atrial-septal defect (ASD) plus pulmonary hypertension	6
AV canal	3
Univentricular heart	1

From the doctor's point of view, it is clear that the existence of Down's Syndrome, in addition to congenital heart disease, is central to assessment. Letters to referral agencies invariably begin with a reference to the condition (e.g. 'Thank you for sending me this little boy with Down's Syndrome'). The clinical significance of the combination of Down's Syndrome and heart disease is complex, but involves factors which very often point in the direction of passivity or inaction. Among these can be noted the following.

1. Down's children have a relatively high mortality rate at surgery.

2. The lung damage that is often associated with their heart condition is, for a while, self-compensating, so that they become relatively asymptomatic.

3. Corrective operations may increase the flow of blood to damaged lungs which can no longer cope. Where there is such damage and the resistance in the lungs is high, studies show that life expectancy is longer *with* a hole than without it.

4. The cardiac catheterisation test has a very small risk of fatality. Why undertake it, when surgery (for the above reasons) is so unlikely?

Against this, doctors recognise and point out to parents that the prognosis with, for example, AV canal and pulmonary hypertension is not good. Although self-compensating processes can mean a perfectly normal childhood, such children often die very suddenly in their late teens. However, Down's children have, in any event, a life expectancy which may be limited to 40 years. This generates a complicated calculus of (possible) years added on versus the risks of surgery. Hovering in the background is a comparison with the efficiency of surgery on 'normal' children, which, if successful, can lead to a far longer life expectancy. Bearing in mind the trauma of surgery for child and family and its opportunity cost for Down's children relative to other children, doctors often make a decision not to intervene. Only where there is a clearly correctable condition involving a relatively low-risk operation are catheterisation and surgery usually contemplated. The case of tetralogy of Fallot in the sample is, for instance, one of few cases to have been catheterised and operated on by the unit – but even here, at the consultation recorded, the parents are dissuaded from thought of further surgery and are told that the child's continuing chest infections are a product of Down's Syndrome and not directly linked to the heart. Elsewhere, the calculus usually produces non-intervention. For instance, after a most open and sympathetic consultation with the elderly parents of a Down's child with an AV-canal defect, the doctor told a researcher that an identical case but without Down's Syndrome would have been recommended for immediate catheterisation and surgery.

Enough has been said to indicate the clinical factors which are contraindications to surgery from the doctors' point of view. Down's children present a limiting case for the unit's general commitment to assessment using the full range of procedures, including cardiac catheterisation, and to the appropriate surgical response, before school age, where life is threatened or likely to be significantly shortened. The argument that the risks and trauma of surgery need to be balanced against its likely results is technically correct and morally powerful.

From the doctor's point of view, then, the best outcome of a typical Down's consultation is if the parents can be convinced that intervention, while possible, is not likely to be useful. In terms of this premise, fortunately, hardly any parents need convincing. Anna's mother, as we have already seen, wants her child 'left alone', while Bill's parents are 'quite happy with him as he is now'. Overall, in 11 out of 12 consultations examined, the parents indicated similar views to these.

At first glance, it appears relatively easy to explain a general parental lack of enthusiasm for the use of invasive tests or operations on their children. However, this fails to pay attention to the anxieties and troubles created by the symptoms of congenital heart disease, or to the publicity given by the media to 'miracle cures', especially in the area of heart surgery. Consequently, parents of children with severe symptoms often come to the unit with high expectations of what can be done for their child. In non-Down's cases, then, it is usually only the parents of asymptomatic children who may display much initial wariness about surgical interventions. How do we account for the *general* unwillingness of Down's parents to contemplate surgery?

The first thing to bear in mind is that such parents may well have made a prior adjustment to their child's limited future, with or without a heart condition. In the maternity hospital or immediately afterwards, it can be expected that parents will be encouraged to think realistically and to limit their expectations for such children. By the time they attend the paediatric cardiology unit, most will have got used to the idea that they cannot expect their child to live to a ripe old age (for an exception, see Eric's mother below). Hence, it is not such a great shock to be told that his life expectancy may be still shorter, or that he is a little more 'imperfect' than they had imagined.

Seen from their point of view, they have experienced the vast familial trauma of having produced an 'imperfect' child. They have then been told that medicine can only, at best, handle any symptoms that arise but cannot put to rights the genetic defects. They may also have been encouraged to concentrate upon the usually happy personality of such children and upon what they can contribute to family life. Consequently, with the assistance of the medical profession itself, faced with an irremediable defect, they will usually have developed a *demedicalised* version of their child well before they set foot in the out-patients' clinic.

Inextricably mixed up in these world views are elements of simple medical fact and vast moral evaluations. Doctors are usually conscientious employers and sympathetic transmitters of medical fact. Yet both doctors and parents exist in a moral universe full of assumptions about 'normality', 'perfection' and 'handicap', which are difficult to extricate from rational decision-making. All parties have to make decisions about an issue which is clouded from every side. To what extent is it possible or desirable to spend resources on perfecting the imperfectible? To what extent is there any worthwhile medical, social or moral return in intervening where there is such a multiplicity of intractable and ultimately fatal problems? Both doctors and parents find themselves on unexpectedly tricky ground. Armed with modern techniques, doctors expect to set out to render the body whole and free from illness; but what happens when that body can never be made whole? Parents want to have everything possible done to help their sick children; but is it fair to subject them to the trauma of surgery for such little potential gain? Faced with these dilemmas, it is understandable that there should develop a consensus against subjecting the child or family to further trauma through invasive treatments.

These considerations go some way towards answering the question about why this apparently deviant behaviour should arise. However, as already pointed out, the answer is speculative, since it depends on ascribing motivations to both parents and doctors where the only hard evidence is what doctors write in letters to referral agencies. In the well-worn phrase, 'further research is needed', and such research would doubtless have an application to the general debate about social attitudes towards and practices regarding the handicapped.

THE SOCIAL ORGANISATION OF THE CONSULTATION

The rest of this chapter is addressed to the *how* question: how are these encounters socially organised? Given their location in a highly specialised unit devoted to sophisticated means of assessment and treatment, how do the parties discursively manage to justify inaction? And, to the extent that this involves a degree of demedicalisation of everyone's concerns, how too is this accomplished?

The elicitation sequence

Prior to the examination of the child, the doctor will seek information from the parents about symptoms such as breathlessness or blueness, which are associated with congenital heart disease. This part of the consultation is referred to here as the elicitation sequence. I am not concerned here with the content of the doctor's questions but with the *form* of his initial question.

In order to establish some picture of the normal form of this question, I examined 22 out-patient consultations selected at random from those carried out by one doctor at this unit during the course of 1 year, but excluded Down's cases. The results are set out in Table 18.1.

Notice that in this table reference to the child's 'wellness' is made, in two different forms, in a majority of cases (13 out of 22). Now look at the questions asked of Down's children (Table 18.2). (Of the 12 cases discussed in this chapter, I have used here only the 10 who were seen by the same doctor as in Table 18.1.)

Table 18.1 *Initial elicitation question (random sample)*

Is he/she well?	11
From your point of view, a well baby?	2
Do you notice anything wrong with her?	1
From the heart point of view, she's active?	1
How is he/she?	4
Not asked	3
Total	22

Table 18.2 *Initial elicitation question (Down's Syndrome cases)*

Is he/she well?	0
From your point of view, a well baby?	1
Do you notice anything wrong with her/him?	0
As far as his heart is concerned, does he get breathless?	1
She gets a few chest infections?	1
How is he/she (this little boy or girl in himself/herself)?	6
None	1
Total	10

Given the small sample with which we are dealing, one clearly would not want to generalise too much from Table 18.2. Nonetheless, it is interesting to note that the most favoured question to Down's families is no longer 'Is he/she well?', but some form of 'How is he/she?'. This latter question is asked in 60% of all such cases and 'Is he/she well?' is asked only in a variant form and then in just 1 case out of 10. The comparable figures for the random sample (Table 18.1) are reversed: 22% for 'How is he/she?' and 60% for 'Is he/she well?'.

At this point, the reader may, understandably, feel this to be a trivial finding. However, I hope to show that the initial form of the elicitation question turns out to be important in establishing a framework for viewing the Down's child which is maintained and embellished at subsequent stages of the consultation. The point about the distribution in Table 18.2 is that *none* of the questions asked carries any implication that the doctor himself might think that he was dealing with a well child. The variant form of 'From your point of view, a well baby?', used in one case, clearly only enquires about the parents' views, while not implying that the concept of 'wellness' is the doctor's own. The other two minority questions that are asked go further and imply that 'illness' rather than 'wellness' is the appropriate frame of reference for thinking about the child (as evidenced in breathlessness and chest infections).

What might be the significance of the preference for the 'How is he/she?' form when questioning Down's families? It could be argued, speculatively, that the significance of this form is its very neutrality. 'How is he?' could, after all, be asked about anyone from a healthy child with a runny nose to a dying, elderly person. However, unlike the question 'Is he well?', it carries no implication that a concept of 'wellness' would even be appropriate to such a person. More precisely, the question 'How is he?' *can* be asked of an acutely sick or chronically handicapped person (or, indeed, in the neuter form, of an object). To enquire whether such a person is 'well' looks wrong in most circumstances (the ordinary-language philosopher J.L. Austin calls such linguistic errors 'infelicities'). So one significant feature of the use of this form may be that, unlike 'Is he well?', it leaves open the possibility that the person being discussed could not reasonably be thought to be 'well'.

From this, two implications follow. First, by excluding issues of 'wellness', a space is created for other criteria to be used in assessing the child. As we have already seen, social criteria such as 'enjoyment' may play an important part in parent–doctor discourse about Down's children. Second, in medical encounters, like meetings with the Inland Revenue, assessments lead to particular disposals of cases. To assess a child in terms of 'wellness' implies a medical obligation to try to restore the unwell child to a state of health. By avoiding the use of the parameter well/unwell, the doctor helps to prepare the way for an eventual decision not to intervene. An 'unwell' child has to be restored to its normal state of 'wellness'. Handicapped children, like these, cannot be said to have any such normal state. Born imperfect, they are imperfectible. Self-evidently, therefore, the restorative role of medical intervention becomes problematic.

Some of the 'deviant' character of these encounters is becoming clearer. However, we must strengthen the case with more evidence and also attempt to show the *co-operative* character of the practices to which we are referring. To do so, let us follow the consultations through their ordered stages.

The elicitation stage is completed by a reply from a parent or other adult accompanying the patient. We have already noticed how the form of the doctor's question precludes the issue of wellness or unwellness which arises in the cases of 'normal' children with episodes of illness. Interestingly enough, Down's parents generally respond to the doctor's question by deepening the sense of the possibly problematic health status of their child implied by the form of the question. Their responses make clear their own uncertainty about the present state of their child's health and their limited expectations about his or her future. Two examples illustrate the point.

(64:1) M. Well, she's all right today.
(61:1) M. Well, he's plodding along steadily, you know, he's er (stops).

In transcript 64, the mother qualifies her favourable response by indicating that good health has not been a stable feature of her child's life. Development rather than present health seems to be the concern of the other mother in transcript 61; viewed in the former terms, her child is only 'plodding along steadily'.

These developmental concerns are taken up in another consultation with different parents and doctors. Their conversation, about 4-year-old Cathy, takes a still more depressing turn.

(Transcript 65:1–2)
1. D2   So how are you managing with her at home?
2. M.   Well she's not much different from last year.
3. D2   Does she have much vocabulary?
4.   (Child making lots of noise.)
5. M.   You stop it. She started school recently but she's not changed that much, has she really?

   6. F.   No, not really.
   7. M.   Not really, no. She's just the same. She's got two 'ands, but apart from that I mean/
   8. D.   Yes/
   9. M.   She's the same. She's still in nappies.

Here, the consultation seems to have moved altogether out of issues of 'wellness' into the developmental concerns which normally dominate clinics for handicapped children. Once again, we see the family co-operating with the doctor in moving the talk towards specifically social relevances.

There are only two exceptions to this pattern of family responses at the elicitation stage. The first, concerning Donald, aged 2, is very easily cleared up. An initially highly optimistic response speedily gives way to the same uncertainties that we found earlier.

(Transcript 56:1)

   1. M.   He's very, very well/
   2. D.   Good/
   3. M.   Er, he's teething at the moment/
   4. D.   Yes/
   5. M.   But um other than that he's, well he can be on a good day/
   6. D.   Mm/

Being well 'on a good day' seems to imply the same doubts as being 'all right today' (64:1 above). The second apparently atypical case concerns Eric, another boy just 2 years old. Here, Eric's mother persists in offering an optimistic response, implying Eric's apparent normality.

(Transcript 62:1–2)

   1. D.   How is he?
   2. M.   Oh fine (laughs).
   3. D.   Good.
   4. M.   More energy than what I've got.
         (Pause)
   5. D.   Do you notice any change in his colour?
   6. M.   No, none at all. I was told, you know, they kept saying to me, does he change colour, does he go blue? I said no. Does he go blue when he's ill? *No*, you know.
   7. D.   That's lovely, excellent.
         (Pause)
   8. M.   I think he's more healthy than what I am.

At this stage, this reads like a routine out-patient consultation about an asymptomatic child without Down's Syndrome or other handicap. We have to look beyond the examination stage to realise that Eric's mother is, rather poignantly, maintaining a front of 'normality' in the face of her child's poor outlook. She is able to do so because Eric's cardiac condition, an atrial-ventricular canal defect, is, in the short term, self-compensating and so produces few symptoms. The long-term outlook, as the doctor implies below, is poor for a Down's child with an AV canal condition. This portion of the transcript comes after a 2-year appointment has been made.

(Transcript 62:3–4)

1. D.   I doubt very much if it will change anything, but it's very nice to see how well he is.
2. M.   Yes, seeing as he wasn't expected to live when they first sent him to you.
3. D.   Well, we also, do you remember, we also said at the start that it was the sort of abnormality that very often compensates extremely well so that the children grow up and live a...
4. M.   ...normal life.
5. D.   ...perfectly normal sort of childhood.
6. M.   He seems to be quite normal, you know, he, er, he's got plenty of energy, he's got more energy than I, he wears me out.

In a very touching manner, Eric's mother seeks to maintain her own version of Eric's present and future 'normality' against all the evidence which she is offered. At utterance 2 she uses the doctor's statement of 'wellness' in order to denigrate the mistaken pessimism that coloured the picture she was apparently given by her referring agency. When the doctor rightly introduces fresh doubts about the future, she bravely intervenes, hoping that he is going to say that Eric can still have 'a normal life'. But the reality is otherwise. Eric can only be expected to have 'a perfectly normal sort of *childhood*' (utterance 5). Yet, still his mother insists on his apparent 'normality', returning, at the end, to her earlier theme of his 'energy'.

It has already been mentioned that one implication of the tacit recognition by doctor and parents alike of a child's genetic imperfection was that it prepared the way for a demedicalised form of disposal which recognises the child's limited prospects, with or without surgery. This case is rather different. Eric's mother does maintain a picture of Eric's essential normality. But, given his currently asymptomatic state, this does not serve here as a basis for surgical intervention. Eric is constructed not as an ill child who can be made well, but simply as a well child. His mother has managed to live with Eric's double handicap by remaining firmly in the present and, despite what she is told by the doctor, trusting in the wonders that the hospital is supposedly working (see utterance 2 above). In fact, the sole medical intervention has been a drug which the doctor decided to withdraw at this consultation. Consequently, but only for the moment, Eric's mother is able to live in a world of 'wellness' which can exist side by side with clinical realities.

Notwithstanding this sad case, the data suggest that the elicitation stage typically serves to establish Down's children as *outside* the continuum of wellness – unwellness normally applied to ordinary people. Given a shared recognition of the present handicap and limited future of such children, doctors and parents alike can establish for each other the good sense of avoiding invasive forms of medical intervention and of concentrating upon the social functioning of the child.

The diagnosis stage

The elicitation stage is followed by the physical examination of the child and, sometimes, by a discussion between the doctors present. The family members are usually non-participant observers of these stages of the consultation. Since there seems to be no noticeable difference here between consultations with Down's and those with other children, I will move on to the next stage where the doctor explains the likely diagnosis to the family.

Wherever possible, the diagnosis-statement is preceded by some reassurance from the doctor – usually some version of: 'The first thing to say is that he's very well.' Such reassurance establishes a secure backdrop for setting out the reasons behind a proposed disposal. For instance, parents of a child with an innocent murmur are, thereby, set on the path towards a forthcoming discharge. At the other extreme, parents with an asymptomatic child who, nonetheless, has congenital heart disease can be reassured about his present state but then told later in the consultation that the probable diagnosis is potentially serious and needs investigating by means of a catheter.

Using the random sample of 22 cases as earlier, three forms of post-examination explanation were found.

1. An immediate reference to the 'wellness' of the child.
2. Some other form of 'reassurance' (e.g. 'the hole is closed').
3. Bold statements of diagnosis without reference to 'wellness' or reassurance.

The distribution is presented in Table 18.3.

When examining Table 18.3, it should be borne in mind that the statement of diagnosis is always constrained by the clinical facts about the condition concerned. The parents of a seriously ill, blue or breathless baby can hardly be given much reassurance about the diagnosis. Therefore, this distribution may be limited by the range of conditions involved; only a stratified random sample would reveal the full picture. Nevertheless, it is interesting to note that reassurance, in one form or another, occurs in two-thirds of the cases (15 out of 22).

Let us now look at what happens in consultations with Down's Syndrome families. (In Table 18.4, all 12 such consultations have been used because, in the

Table 18.3 *Statement of diagnosis (random sample)*

Well/doing splendidly	9
Reassurance	6
Straight diagnosis	7
Total	22

Table 18.4 *Statement of diagnosis (Down's Syndrome cases)*

Well/doing splendidly	1
Reassurance	2
Straight diagnosis	9
Total	12

two consultations excluded earlier, the second doctor withdrew before the examination of the child took place.) Once again, it must be conceded that the range of conditions involved here may skew the distribution. However, we should remember that, within limits, it is open to the doctor to put a reassuring gloss on a wide range of diagnoses. Many of the children here have few symptoms reported by their parents. Nevertheless, the doctor generally refrains from reassurance and usually offers a blunt statement of the diagnosis. For instance:

D. Our feeling about her was, as you know, she has a hole between the two pumping chambers.

D. He does have a hole in the heart.

D. She does have a heart abnormality.

D. She obviously does have a heart abnormality.

Yet, in no case does the statement elicit stated doubt or dissent from the parents. Only with Eric's mother does the doctor offer any obvious reassurance. Presumably in the light of her unrealistic version of Eric's present condition and future prospects, the doctor plays for time and offers an initially favourable gloss on his examination: 'I think he's doing splendidly.'

Overall, less than one-third of the random sample are offered a straight diagnosis compared to three-quarters of the Down's cases. This treatment of the diagnosis-statement, with its studious avoidance of any reference to the 'wellness' of the child, fits neatly with the picture presented at the elicitation stage. As noted earlier, the role of medical intervention becomes very unclear and limited for a child that is discursively constituted outside of the continuum 'well–unwell'. An unwell child can be restored to health. A child that seems well at the moment may, nonetheless, have an underlying disease which needs to be treated if his apparent wellness is to be preserved. But a child who is not altogether whole or is imperfect may turn out to be imperfectible.

There is a curious irony here. At first glance, the bold statement of the existence of congenital heart disease might seem to be an obvious preface to the kind of remedial action which, nonetheless, is not recommended. The problem, for the moment, is not the lack of action, or its clinical or moral grounds, but the discursive organisation which allows non-intervention to follow smoothly from the statement of the diagnosis.

We can understand this organisation best by returning to the dynamics of the normal out-patient consultation. The form in which the diagnosis-statement is couched is designed to secure parental consent to the doctor's preferred disposal. However, it is the *immediate* disposal that is at issue here, not the long-term treatment that may be required. Thus, unless the parents specifically ask for more, the doctor will usually only provide sufficient information and reassurance to move the child on to the next stage of treatment. The question of long-term prognosis, for instance, is very rarely raised by a doctor at a first out-patient consultation leading to a catheter. Not only do questions of genuine clinical uncertainty arise but also, unless parents specifically ask for more, the doctor may want to avoid too many complicated issues coming to the fore at one short meeting.

The medical framework for the normal out-patient consultation is, then, 'step by step'. Such a developmental frame of reference fully accords with the medical understanding, supported by this research, that parents' adjustment to their child's health status is a slow, sometimes painful process (see Baruch, 1981). At the same time, it neatly fits into the paediatrician's developmental version of health.

With Down's cases, this symmetry between social and clinical realities seems to work in an opposite direction. The developmental frame of reference is only of limited appropriateness here. A Down's child, as doctors and parents know, has a limited future. For the normal child, all things being equal, it may make sense to plan medical interventions in a step-by-step manner, over many years, related to the child's development (a very good example of this is the work of the Cleft Palate Clinic reported in Silverman, 1983). In turn, the parents can gradually adjust to the stresses involved in having a sick child. But parents of Down's children can be assumed already to have made that adjustment before they come to the paediatric cardiology unit.

This foreshortening of the future means that a 'step-by-step' framework would look odd to the latter parents. A brutal frankness is required for parents who, presumably, already know the worst. There is no point in waiting for the situation to unfold gradually as the 'site' of the consultation changes. The situation for them has *already* unfolded.

So a reference to 'wellness' is doubly inappropriate here. First, it implies a diagnostic scheme which is inappropriate in many situations to children with considerable handicaps. Second, it suggests a state of normality to which unwell children can be returned by means of medical interventions which, in this case, are powerless or counterproductive.

The disposal stage

The co-operative production of a child who is neither 'well' nor 'unwell' lays the basis for the discussion at the disposal stage of the consultation. By removing the child from the normal continuum of illness, a non-interventionist disposal decision has been prepared which can then be justified by appealing to a non-medicalised version of the child.

The clinical contraindications to catheterisation and surgery were noted earlier in the chapter. As before, we shall look at the disposal stage of the consultation in terms of its discursive organisation. How does the doctor present a preferred disposal involving neither catheterisation nor surgery? Upon examining the data, non-intervention is defended on six grounds.

1. The self-compensating character of the present cardiac abnormality and, hence, the possible dangers of correction.

2. The limited life expectancy of a Down's child.

3. The technical feasibility of corrective surgery but its doubtful effects, given (1) and (2).

4. The right of the parents actively to decide.

5. The possibility of postponing parental confirmation of a decision for non-intervention.

6. The good sense of intervening medically in other, more minor, complaints.

We can pass speedily over item 1, noting merely that the doctor's account to parents is usually both detailed and clear. The second point, limited life-expectancy, is more interesting. It has already been suggested that, without parental questioning, doctors in the unit engage in very little discussion of long-term prognosis, especially at the early stages of a child's long medical career. With Down's families, however, the long-term future of the child plays a frequent part in the discussion of the disposal decision.

We have already seen how, in Eric's case, the doctor resisted the implication that he could expect a normal life. Despite an atypical, optimistic mother, he insisted that what was at stake was a normal *childhood*. Elsewhere, he talks very easily in terms of a limited life expectancy. For instance:

(Transcript 60:3)

D. Now, her life-expectancy without doing anything could well be many, many years. All right? I mean certainly childhood and the rest of it.

M. Yes.

Here, the limited expectations *implied* by the mutual avoidance of reference to 'wellness' earlier in the consultation are openly recognised. This recognition carries the further implication that the disposal decision is centrally related to the limited life expectancy of the Down's child. Donald, whom we last met at the elicitation stage, is discussed in very much these terms. His mother has just heard the diagnosis of an ASD, leaky mitral valve and possible VSD:

(Transcript 56:3)

D. I think, quite honestly, that I would not be keen long-term on surgery into his heart because if we're correct in our diagnosis, I think it's correct but to be absolutely certain we'd need to do more tests...but then it is the sort of condition that if the leak through the valve does not get worse he may be stable for the first 30 to 40 years of life, and under the circumstances there would be absolutely no indication to do anything because, um, he might well have, more likely to have other problems before he's 50 than the theoretical possibility...(Pause). OK?

M. Right, yes.

Notice how the word 'stable' is used about Donald's likely outlook. Once again, as earlier, the word 'well' is avoided. The bleak long-term future is expressed in the phrase 'other problems'. Despite its vagueness, Donald's mother seems to follow the rationale behind the disposal and to concur immediately with it.

Now, an unwillingness to engage in tests or complicated surgery might strike parents as reflecting badly upon the technical skills of the hospital. A third basis for defending non-intervention is, then, to stress that it is not the lack of technical skills but the doubtful consequence of intervention which is the problem. For instance, discussing Fiona, with VSD and pulmonary hypertension:

(Transcript 60:4)

D. I want to make it absolutely clear it isn't because we can't do the operation, it's because, as a result of the lung factor, to do it, if she comes through, it might decrease not increase her life expectancy. In fact, one or two children that you see in the papers who go off to other countries for heart operations, they go with this sort of problem because people raise a lot of money for them to go and when they get there, of course, the operation isn't done or nothing can be done. It isn't that we can't do the operation, it is that it is not in her interests because of the lung problem.

Elsewhere, the purely technical feasibility of the operation is stressed in two other consultations involving Down's children. One of these is Gloria, aged 2¾, with the same diagnosis as Fiona. While Fiona's parents are offered a more or less clear-cut disposal recommendation, the doctor appeals much more to Gloria's mother's right of choice. On three separate occasions, interspersed with a presentation of the risks of surgery, he states that medical intervention ultimately depends on the family:

(Transcript 64:3–4)
D. Um, I think what we do now depends a little bit on parents' feelings...
D. Now it depends, it depends a little bit on what you think...
D. It depends very much I think on your own personal views as to whether we should proceed.

As we saw with Anna's and Bill's parents, the decision about catheterisation is clearly referred to the parents. Yet this reference to consumer choice is atypical across the run of consultations at the pre-catheter stage. What generally seems to happen is that a clinical decision to catheterise is taken and then justified to the parents, depending upon the patency of the condition. Parental consent still arises, but usually only in a formal sense. For example, the doctor may say: 'What we would like to do, if you agree (with your consent), is a small test...'

The insistence upon the parents' right to choose in these cases seems to serve three functions. First, it re-emphasises the availability of surgery at the hospital. If the parents take the decision not to intervene, then this can clearly constitute no threat to the status of the unit's surgical skills. Second, in an area where clinical and moral considerations shade so easily into one another, an emphasis on parental decision-making, backed up with strongly worded advice against intervention, serves to free doctors from the role of playing God, while making it very likely that the eventual decision will go in the direction which they favour. The third function of parental decision-making relates to the political character of this kind of encounter. Most medical encounters work on the assumption that the doctor can offer some worthwhile service by diagnosing illness and, more importantly, curing it. With Down's children the relevance of this service is limited, first by the prior existence of an all-powerful diagnosis and, second, by the inability of the doctor either to cure the condition or, in most cases, to correct its side-effects. Consequently, the political role of the doctor is weakened.

Given the detailed statement of the balance sheet and the frequent appeal to parental decision-making, the disposal stage tends to be much longer with Down's children than with others. Even after the decision is taken, both parents and doctor continue to discuss the child, but the frame of reference is no longer clinical. While, at earlier stages of the consultation, the ground is prepared for non-intervention, the framework is largely clinical. Now, the child suddenly ceases to be a source of clinical data and is constituted as a social subject. Clinically speaking, parents and doctors seem to have no choice but to view the Down's child as irreparably damaged. Yet, because the child is clinically not whole, both parties have a common interest in reconstituting him as socially whole and located within a social whole (the family).

From the parents' side, the social constitution of the child is achieved by stressing his ability to cope with physical symptoms and thus to play a full part in family life. An earlier example of this arose when Bill's mother asserted: 'I mean it's not affected 'im really at all' (57:4–6). For her, Bill's unfavourable clinical outlook is balanced by his ability to cope. Clinically speaking, Bill may be a lost cause; to her, he is a worthwhile member of the family. It is almost as if, in not being affected by his heart condition, Bill is deliberately trying to do his best to make life easier for his family. 'He seems to cope quite well', his father says (57:6).

A similar theme of social worth is taken up by Fiona's parents. They tell how her 'resistance to colds' seems to be better. Like Bill, it seems that Fiona is doing her bit and, in doing so, is paying a tribute to what the hospital has done for her:

(Transcript 60:5)

1. F.   Well, I must admit since we saw you…She's been markedly improved.
2. M.   ( )
3. F.   Oh yes, much more lively, much more alert. It's a marvellous improvement…
4. F.   And she paces herself, you see. If she gets out of breath, she stops whatever she's doing till she thinks she can do it again.

In more routine cases, where parents offer such social formulations of symptoms which may indicate congenital heart disease, they are persuaded by doctors that things like breathlessness, in conjunction with other clinical evidence, must be taken more seriously. Yet in Down's cases, such social formulations are usually unchallenged and are sometimes, as we shall see in a moment, offered by the doctor himself. The social constitution of such children allows doctors to find immediately understandable grounds for their preferred disposals and permits parents to build a less damaging picture of their child's present and future.

Faced with a patient with a poor outlook, with or without surgery, the doctor too joins in the demedicalisation of the child via an emphasis on a social conception of a normal, happy childhood. At the beginning of this chapter, it was seen how the doctor lessened the salience of Anna's heart abnormality by maintaining that it was not 'seriously interfering with her enjoyment of life' (13:8). The theme of 'enjoyment' and 'happiness' is also central to this depiction of Gloria, in the context of medical non-intervention:

(Transcript 64:6–7)

1. D.   I mean, do you think a happy child of four, playing and growing up with other children and then, perhaps, you know, either late teens or twenties just very peacefully passing away might be…

(Compare this to his statement to Fiona's parents):

D.   You should enjoy a happy little girl who plays and does everything normally and could have many happy years ahead of her without doing anything (60:5)

SUMMARY

We have seen how consultations with Down's children at this unit take an unusual, deviant form that I have called 'demedicalised'. Progressively, through the orderly stages of the consultation, a picture is built up of a child who can never be fully 'well', with or without medical interventions, but may nonetheless be viewed within a social framework of happy family life. Consequently, we usually find an attempt to limit the saliency of medical actions and to relate symptoms of illness to their impact on family life. Faced with an irreparably damaged child, parents and doctor retreat into manageable stereotypes of the essentially 'wonderful' nature of childhood. In this way, doctors ultimately withdraw their clinical gaze and co-operate with parents in producing a demedicalised, social vision of a tolerable future.

Using a sample of 12 cases, I have sought to support the argument with conversational material drawn from different stages of the consultation and with quantitative comparisons with a random sample of 22 non-Down's cases. However, it is easy to see that, to some extent, each consultation is a self-contained unit and has its own particular course of development. Therefore, although considerations of space do not allow me to provide a full transcript of a single consultation, I have nonetheless included, in the Appendix, extracts from all the stages of a consultation which has not so far been used. It is hoped that this will illustrate the argument on the basis of the internal workings of a single consultation. A problem which I cannot overcome, given the present database, is the unrepresentativeness of using the work of just one doctor in a single unit. Clearly, any firm conclusions, about both the medical experiences of Down's children and the significance of the demedicalised form, must depend on adequate comparative material.

Within these constraints, what tentative conclusions may be drawn from the kind of co-operative practices observed here? The first thing to remark is that, curiously, we have discovered what is, in some respects at least, a fair approximation of the kind of medical encounter favoured by many liberal reformers. Instead of dwelling in a largely unintelligible, clinical realm, we have seen the doctor move into and encourage social formulations of the child's present and future status. The consequence has been a consultation which is usually longer than most and which seems to allow the family to air their anxieties and hopes. More than most medical encounters, we observe here something close to a family decision-making format, where the consumer is offered considerable information and is allowed to make an informal choice.

However, we should not exaggerate the extent of the 'consumerism' noticed both here and in a cleft-palate clinic offering cosmetic surgery to teenagers (Silverman, 1983). In the latter clinic, consumerism seemed to be a specific product of a cultural norm, demanding that only the subject himself could decide whether his appearance should be altered. It was limited by the observed inability of many children to formulate their concerns and desires. Here, a consumerist form arises because of the limited capacities of medical science to 'cure' a genetically damaged child and because a complex number of social and moral issues are involved which doctors realise should properly be left to the family to decide. Once again, consumerism is limited both by the moral weight of the doctor's (probably welcome) advice and by the family's prior adjustments to the birth of a Down's child.

Nonetheless, it would be wrong to infer that these consultations are simply a reflection of medical domination, albeit in slightly modified forms. First, parental decision-making does have an independent role to play. For instance, we have noticed two cases where parents have demanded and obtained catheterisation and surgery for their children, although the balance of risks and gains seemed just as problematic as elsewhere. Second, it should be recognised that the problems which doctors face with these children partly reflect real moral dilemmas which we have not been prepared to face or to solve. Presumably, for instance, the issue of a handicapped child outliving his or her parents, raised with Gloria's mother, could only arise because society has not been able to offer sufficient care for the handicapped.

PRACTICAL IMPLICATIONS

A fascinating American study indicated that medical judgements about the significance of the mental damage sustained by Down's children make doctors predisposed not to intervene on congenital heart disease unless parents are actively in favour. In a study of a number of paediatric cardiology units, Crane (1975) revealed that surgeons presented with case histories said they were much more likely to operate upon a given heart condition where the child had a urogenital anomaly than when it had Down's Syndrome (Table 18.5). Moreover, Crane went on to point out that what the doctors *said* probably *overestimated* the actual intervention rate with Down's children. Using a complete 5-year listing of all Down's children catheterised at one teaching hospital, and controlling for *type* of heart condition, 39% of Down's cases received surgery, compared to 65% of non-Down's. In A-V canal cases, 29% of Down's children received surgery,

Table 18.5 *Percentage of surgeons prepared to operate according to patient's type of damage (adapted from Crane, 1975)*

Severity of cardiac condition	Non-cardiac conditions		
	Urogenital	Down's Syndrome (parents in favour of surgery)	Down's Syndrome (parents not in favour of surgery)
Mild (PDA)	93	56	‡
Moderate (tetralogy)	90	59	18
Severe (A-V canal)	82	50	12

‡Figure not available.

compared to 100% of non-Down's. Furthermore, social variables such as being an only child or first-born played a significant part in the extent of surgical intervention with Down's children.

This study has supported Crane's findings within consultations themselves. The practical reality often seems to be the enactment of a clinic's policy which is hidden from parents and rarely discussed even between medical staff. Variations in clinic policy between hospitals and regions have caused public controversy in both neonatal and renal units (*Lancet*, 1981) and illustrate that here factors such as geography can have an undesirable effect on the extent and nature of treatment.

One sort of response that I have recently encountered in Brisbane, Australia, is for parents' groups to contact families of Down's neonates to offer advice on which local hospitals are prepared to intervene on associated congenital anomalies (such as congenital heart disease). Although this has merits as a short-term response, consumerism, with all its inherent limits, can hardly serve as a continuing basis for social policy. Moreover, it is possible that parents' groups may serve to press intervention upon some parents who may have reasons for not wanting to intervene. An alternative, more general response has been made in the debate within medical ethics, particularly in relation to 'passive euthanasia' (Robertson and Fost, 1976; Waldman, 1976; Campbell and Duff, 1979).

One school of thought (represented by Campbell and Duff) argues that life and death decisions should be left to doctors and parents alone. Crane suggests that 'ethical guidelines' should be erected. Both positions are rejected by Robertson and Fost: ethical guidelines related to the net social utility of a person's future, they say, would set us on to a 'slippery slope', while the joint doctor–parent decision-making solution fails to examine the impact of emotional trauma upon parents' capacities for rational choice. So, instead, Robertson and Fost suggest a committee-based decision-making process relying on an appeal to 'disinterested' persons (see also Waldman, 1976).

This debate has the merit of emphasising that the real issue is *not* the final decision itself, since there are no satisfactory *a priori* grounds for arguing that surgical intervention is always right or always wrong for these children. However, because the family concerned will have to live with the consequences of any decision, there is a strong argument that the process of decision-making should not involve reference to external standards or to Olympian bodies of 'disinterested' persons.

However, even if decisions are left to doctors and parents, as Campbell and Duff suggest, there remains the strong possibility that parents will continue to be persuaded according to a predetermined clinical policy. What seems to be required is an encounter between doctor and parents where *all* the various options and their consequences are discussed. The child is not simply a social object, but equally a clinical, moral, political and legal *subject*. Yet what we have observed here is a formulation of the child which merely *reverses* the interpretation normally found in the clinic, i.e. by making social formulations prior to clinical formulations.

What, then, can be done? Three things seem clear. First, doctors have no *special* competence in the ethics of decision-making. When it comes to making ethical decisions, no group in society is more competent than any other. But where somebody has to be prepared to talk about delicate and unpleasant issues, doctors are put in a position where they speak as the voice of authority and are listened to accordingly. Second, a hasty out-patient consultation is probably not the best situation in which to decide life and death issues. Indeed, this has been partly recognised in our unit where the opportunity is sometimes given to parents to 'go away and think about it'. Third, the evidence of variability in Down's children's abilities and family support suggests that any uniform hospital policy may do an injustice to a particular child.

One possible direction of change would be to *lengthen* the decision-making process and to *enlarge* the decision-making team. It would help if there were facilities for parents of Down's children to discuss the issues involved with a whole range of relevant parties, including other parents and appropriate professionals such as social workers. The final decision about intervention should only be made after the family has had the opportunity to think about a range of possible responses.

As a very tentative suggestion, it might be possible to establish a *three-stage* decision-making process. Initially, an out-patients' clinic could be used to explain the diagnosis and the purely clinical risks and gains of intervention. This should be followed by a wide range of encounters between the parents and other relevant parties; other parents and professionals should visit the parent's own home where possible. Finally, a second clinic should be held where the parents could discuss their final decision with the doctor concerned.

The aim of this process would be to allow the full range of social and clinical possibilities to be discussed with as few preconceptions as possible on either side. It would succeed to the extent that it replaced stereotyping with a response to proven individual needs. Here, as elsewhere, the 'messiness' of unique and variable decisions may be preferable to the neatness of ethical theories and hospital policies.

APPENDIX: EXTRACTS FROM ONE OUT-PATIENT CONSULTATION
(Transcript 55)

The patient, Helen, is a 1-year-old Down's baby with an AV canal defect and pulmonary hypertension. She is accompanied by her mother (M) and father. The extracts are organised using the stages of the consultation discussed in the chapter.

Elicitation stage: avoidance of 'wellness'

1. D. Well, how is she? Dr X has written to me and has also sent the catheter films that were done in – . Um, can I ask you a few questions? How is she in herself?
2. M. Well, I've been pleasantly surprised to be quite honest. (Mother continues with details of colds, chest infections and breathlessness.)

Elicitation stage: social definition of symptoms

3. D.   Do you think her breathlessness interferes with her enjoying doing things, or not?
4. M.   Well not, not up to the present.

Diagnosis stage: avoidance of reassurance

1. D.   We know from the, er, catheter that Dr X sent us, that she has a complicated heart abnormality. It's the sort of abnormality that, um, is always difficult to correct. (Doctor reviews the risks of surgery.)

Disposal stage: the 'enjoyment' theme
(Follows discussion of risks of surgery.)

1. D.   That could be counterbalanced with what is her life going to be without an operation? The answer to that is, probably very good. She may well have a relatively normal / childhood.
2. M.   /Yes.
3. D   (Continues to review the possibilities without surgery.) However, doing nothing, she may have a virtually normal childhood...but not that much and perhaps not enough to interfere with her pleasure in play and walking and doing things. Because of Down's Syndrome, even with surgery, er, life-expectancy is not quite the / same.
4. M.   / No.
5. D.   ...as it would be with a normal child.

Disposal stage: consumer choice

6. D.   So I think these are the issues, though at that point having tried to say that the technical side from our point of view, I mean she's your child / (laughter).
7. M.   / Well thank you very much...appreciate because, um, we felt that, um, first of all, we didn't really understand what was possible from the technical point of view and secondly we weren't quite...What you have told us has been very helpful.

Question time: redefining physical conditions in terms of 'enjoyment'

1. M.   Um, she is likely, I suppose, to suffer some degree of physical disability, um, when she gets short of breath and things?
2. D.   When you say *physical* disability, she may be a bit on the small side and

she may get a little bit more puffed than some children. Whether you call that, you know, disability, in inverted commas, but I think disabilities are abnormalities, if you like, that interfere with her pleasure and progress and enjoyment of childhood and to that extent, no I don't think she will be disabled so that she can't take part.

Ending: postponing the decision

1. D. Um, do you wanna let me know when you and your husband have talked things over?
2. M. Yes.
3. D. You can either telephone or drop a line or come up again.
4. M. Thank you very much. Bye.
5. D. Bye bye.

REFERENCES

Baruch, G. (1981). Moral tales: parents' stories of encounters with health professionals. *Soc. Health & Illness* **3**(3).

Campbell, A.G.M. and Duff, R.S. (1979). Deciding the care of severely malformed or dying infants. *J. Med. Ethics* **5**, 65–7.

Crane, D. (1975). *The Sanctity of Social Life: Physicians' Treatment of Critically Ill Patients.* New York: Russell Sage.

Lancet (1981). Ethics and the nephrologist. *Lancet* 14 March, 594–6.

Robertson, J.A. and Fost, N. (1976). Passive euthanasia of defective newborn infants: legal considerations. *J. Paed.* **88**(5), 883–9.

Silverman, D. (1981). The child as a social object: Down's Syndrome children in a paediatric cardiology clinic. *Soc. Health & Illness* **3**(3), 254–74.

Silverman, D. (1983). The clinical subject: adolescents in a cleft-palate clinic. *Soc. Health & Illness* **5**(3), 253–74.

Waldman, A.M. (1976). Medical ethics and the hopelessly ill child. *J. Paed.* **88**(5), 890–92.

19 After School: Work and Employment for Adults with Down's Syndrome?

David Lane

The raising of expectations and the level of achievements of people with Down's Syndrome have brought in their train many new problems. Not only does educational practice now assume that Down's children should be educated, but their enhanced performance in social skills and educational attainment poses acutely the problem of whether or not they are capable of 'independent living' and what is entailed by this phrase. In the past, the institutionalisation of mentally handicapped people either in hospitals or colonies solved this problem. Since the 1970s, there has been greater emphasis placed on 'community care'; the Jay Report (1979) advocated that 'mentally handicapped people should lead a life which is as normal as possible'. This is the latest in a long line of policy reports calling for the care of the handicapped 'in the community' (*Better Services*, 1971; DHSS, 1976). But community care in part depends on the performance and acceptance of the handicapped as participatory members of the community. Most people's lives revolve around their work and occupation. It is therefore of vital importance to develop a philosophy and strategy for the mentally handicapped Down's adult.

In seeking solutions to the problem of a lifestyle for the Down's adult, we need to clarify first whether employment should be an objective and, second, to appraise the extent to which, and under what conditions, a Down's adult is employable. Finally, we should also consider what alternatives there are to going to work and having an occupation.

Modern industrial societies place a premium on employment. Employment is not just work: many people work but are not employed – housewives, mothers and students are examples. Employment means selling one's labour for a wage. Employment entails work and much more besides. There are four main functions of going out to work. First, employment provides an income, which in turn enables a person to improve his or her standard of living. Despite the provision of welfare by the government, monetary rewards are one of the greatest incentives for a person to seek work. Second, employment gives a structure to the day. It occupies

The research on which this chapter is based was financed by a grant from the British Social Science Research Council. Research assistance was provided by Teresa Goodenough.

time in a regularised fashion; the day is meaningfully punctuated with travel, activity and breaks. Third, employment brings the employee into social contact with other people with whom he or she may have an affinity; the work setting can be a place of conviviality. Fourth, being employed, or having a job, gives a person a recognised place in the world, a social status and a sense of self-respect. It is this constellation of roles, and psychological and economic rewards, that makes employment such a crucial activity to people's lives and, conversely, explains why unemployment may often have such devastating social consequences.

Professionals who support the line of thinking which advocates 'normalisation' of the handicapped in the community, also favour a higher participation rate in employment (see, for example, International Labour Organisation, 1968). The National Development Group for the Mentally Handicapped (1977) recognises that 'The need for meaningful employment is a fundamental one for mentally handicapped people...' The group anticipates an increase in the proportion of mentally handicapped people who, 'given suitable training and help, are capable of working in open or sheltered employment...We are confident that the number of people discharged to open employment could be considerably increased'.

In practice, however, and as we shall see below, employment for the adult with Down's Syndrome is the exception rather than the rule. Our knowledge of the activity of Down's adults is limited and fragmentary. Studies of adult mentally handicapped usually do not specify the position of people with Down's Syndrome but describe larger groups. Alan Walker's (1982) seminal study of handicapped young people and the labour market included a wide range of young people: 43 were ESN(S), 36 were physically handicapped, 152 were ESN(M), 34 maladjusted. (My own examination of the files in the National Children's Bureau revealed that only 9 Down's individuals were in the sample, and of these many were untraceable in their last school years.) Generalisations made in such researches about the life chances of the handicapped may not apply to Down's subjects. My own research has been based on questionnaires administered to careers officers, a detailed empirical study of one local authority area, interviews and correspondence with numerous professionals concerning the work activity of Down's people, and finally, interviews of the Down's adults and their parents (for details see, Lane, 1980, pp. 45–7).

The typical transitionary period from school to the outside world of a young person with Down's Syndrome is shown in Table 19.1. Until the 1981 Education Act, three main types of schools were designated: ESN(S), for the severely subnormal (to cater for children with IQs of under 50 and including the profoundly intensive-care handicapped); ESN(M) schools, which encompass children in the 'mild' range of IQ 50–70; and hospital schools, which were intended for the most profoundly multihandicapped. In practice, behaviour and labelling of different kinds of children lead to many children outside of these IQ bands being allocated to the respective schools (Tomlinson, 1982). A small but growing number of Down's children attend 'special units' in ordinary schools, with varying degrees of integration into the school. The actual formal type of education, however, may not vary very much from that of the ESN(S) or ESN(M) school. Small numbers of Down's children also attend schools in the private sector: these are the 'special unit'

Table 19.1 *Placements of Down's young people, post 16 years*

	Designated ESN(S)		Designated ESN(M)	
	16–18 years average take-up (%)	Post 18 years (%)	16–18 years (%)	18-post years (%)
Stay at school	45	0	50	0
Further education college: life skills or job preparation courses, Manpower Services courses	5	5	15	10
Voluntary sector training schemes (e.g. Lufton Manor, Rathbone), residential care (village-type communities)	5	5	10	10
Adult training centre (ATC), sheltered workshop	25	65–75	20	55–65
Hospital	5	10	0	0
Stay at home, day care	15	10–20	5	14–24
Employment	0	0	0	1

type or are private schools catering for slow learners. Since 1981, the designation of these schools in the public sector has been changed, all are now called schools for children with severe or moderate learning difficulties. In practice, the organisation of the curriculum and recruitment of pupils to these schools have not changed significantly. By far the greatest proportion of children with Down's Syndrome attend ESN(S) schools. (Parents' associations allege that improper stigmatisation allocates Down's children to the 'S' schools, irrespective of ability; see Report of Down's Children's Association on the Warnock Report, 1979. Practice varies greatly: in one LEA, all Down's children are in schools for those with severe learning difficulties; in another, of the total school population only 2 were in schools for children with moderate learning difficulties; in yet a third authority, as many as 15% are said to be in the latter type of school.)

The destinations of children from the ESN(S) and ESN(M) types of schools are shown in the second and fourth columns of Table 19.1. It must be emphasised that there are great regional variations. Many local authorities provide very little in the form of post-16 education; others allow young Down's people to stay on at school to 19 or to transfer to courses at institutions of further education. While the exact proportions may vary from one LEA to another, some generalisations may be made concerning the destinations of school leavers.

The vast majority of young Down's adults are to be found at adult training centres (ATCs). A negligible number from schools for severely handicapped children and very few from the schools for children with moderate learning difficulties either enter employment, or stay in employment for long. In the study by Innes *et al.* (1978) of 'mental subnormality' in north-east Scotland, not one Down's adult in this study was employed. In interviews with disablement resettlement officers, not one placement of a person with Down's Syndrome could be remembered. In fact, at the local Job Centre, no Down's adult had been registered in living memory (i.e. the rather short one of four years). Careers' officers for special schools in the south and east of England rarely if ever place a

Down's child in employment. As one careers' officer put it: 'If a child in an ESN(S) school is considered a product (*sic*) for employment in open industry, then he would be taken out of the ESN(S) system before the age of 14.' The overwhelming majority of specialist careers' officers surveyed (21 out of 29) did *not* even 'deal regularly' with cases of people with Down's Syndrome; only 7 did so (one did not answer). The careers' officers replied that their role was mainly to place such clients with an adult training centre; a few had direct contact when cases arose of 'out-county' training courses in such places as Lufton Manor. There is considerable evidence to suggest that it is assumed that all Down's leavers will progress to the ATC. The careers' officers only intervene when they are contacted by headteachers or parents.

Adult training centres vary greatly in their objectives. Some provide work taken in from industry. Pay for such work rarely exceeds £2 per week for the trainees. Other centres (often called social education centres) emphasise educational work (literary, number) training in social skills (using buses, shopping). The aims of such centres are to encourage community participation, including preparation for employment. Study of the record of ATCs in placing trainees in jobs showed a very low level of success. In all the ATCs visited by the author, placement was an unusual event, and it was usually unknown for a Down's trainee to be placed. At an employment preparation unit, whose trainees are drawn from the most employable young persons in ATCs in a large West Midland county borough, only 1 out of 146 trainees had Down's Syndrome. (This trainee was admitted in 1983; in the previous 2 years no Down's people were admitted – telephone interview with manager.) A study by Stocks (1983) of 4302 trainees at ATCs in six English counties found that only 5 had been placed in open employment during a 1-year period. ATCs are therefore seen as places which provide day care for the mentally handicapped.

As to the 'out-county' training courses run by voluntary bodies, such as the Royal Society for Mentally Handicapped Children and Adults, Down's young people are in a small minority among their trainees. At the Advanced Social Training Unit of the RSMHC, only five Down's trainees had been recruited in a 5-year period. This unit caters for those of IQ levels between 45 and 85 and, while the average IQ of trainees (67) is higher than that of the Down's population, I was told that one of the reasons for the low number of Down's trainees is that there are relatively few referrals. Information provided by the National Society's Pathway Scheme showed that, out of 104 job placements, only 2 were people with Down's Syndrome. The National Officer advised that placement occurs only rarely because of a very low rate of referrals (four only). (Data here refer to the late 1970s, early 1980s.)

In the local authority studied in some depth, only one Down's adult was located in normal full-time employment. (This was on the basis of interviews with professionals in health, social services and education, and extensive knowledge of the local area by the research assistant, who was also a part-time employee of the local society for mentally handicapped children and adults.) Another young adult was in effect a voluntary worker in a religious order. This gave her independence and work, but she was not strictly speaking employed. These two positions had been found by the parents of the Down's adults.

In Birmingham, observation of courses organised by MSC and the voluntary society, Elfrida Rathbone, revealed no Down's young people in attendance. At a college of further education with a special education section, one Down's person was on a social skills course; none was placed on any vocational course (telephone interview). In a neighbouring borough, after much parental pressure, one Down's school leaver secured a place on a job preparation unit at a college of further education. At another large college in the West Midlands conurbation, only one Down's trainee was on the MSC work preparation course on horticulture organised by the college for 'low ability groups' (written communication). A check on the employment of Down's leavers at a Birmingham secondary school for the mentally retarded with a positive employment record revealed that of some 25 Down's school leavers over the past 8 years, 4 had entered employment but none had been able to sustain a job.

Although the data are patchy, they all point conclusively to the fact that very few Down's young people enter employment. In practice, the school leaver has three possibilities: attendance (sooner or later) at an adult training centre, staying at home, or, for relatively few, a place in a residential community.

The reality of the situation falls far short of the objectives of normalisation adumbrated at the beginning of this chapter. How, then, can one explain this discrepancy between ideal and practice? Are we to question the validity of the ideals or the practice?

Part of the reason why Down's young people do not enter the labour market is that many people think that work and employment are to be shunned. Such negative attitudes towards employment are compounded with respect to paid labour for the handicapped. The arguments one encounters are as follows. Rather than work providing satisfaction to the recipient in terms of monetary reward, personal gratification and social esteem, labour is regarded as something intrinsically obnoxious. It is stultifying to the development of the individual's personality. Such views are also deeply embedded in various philosophies which deal with people's attitude to work. A strain in Christian theology before the Reformation regarded work as punishment for sin, and Marxists view wage labour under conditions of capitalism as alienative. Such attitudes are echoed in various ways by professionals and field workers dealing with the transition from school to work of young people with Down's Syndrome.

Work as alienation has a long history in the social sciences. Alan Walker is one of the more radically inclined commentators who has singled out the handicapped as being particularly prone to exploitation and alienation. Walker (1982, pp. 8–9) points out that handicapped persons are located in unskilled 'dead-end jobs' which are not unionised, are lowly paid, offer little security, have poor physical conditions and irregular hours. In such conditions, the handicapped are liable to even greater exploitation than 'normal' workers, and therefore employment should be discouraged, if not completely banned.

Ten instructors at an ATC were questioned about their attitudes to the goals of the centre. All ten ranked first its task of 'social training'; education came second. Whelan and Speake's national survey of ATCs found that only 4.2% 'stress training for employment or for production and work training' (Whelan and Speake, 1976, Table 23). In a survey of instructors in Sheffield ATCs, Armstrong *et al.* (1977) found that instructors saw the first aim of the centres as being to 'help trainees to develop abilities to the full', and the lowest ranking (of 8) was accorded to the aim of accustoming 'the trainees to work towards a high level of productivity'.

In discussions with ATC staff, it became clear that many had rejected industrial employment as a means to satisfy their own ambitions. Training for life in the community revolves around creating a community for themselves and the trainees in the centre. Instructors often point out that 'doing a job of work' under modern factory conditions is not a satisfactory activity for anyone, least of all for the mentally handicapped.

The instructors were asked about their preferences for the Down's trainees at the centre. There was almost unanimous agreement that *sheltered* employment was 'desirable' (only 1 out of 10 instructors thought this was not the most appropriate activity). Not one Down's trainee was thought to be ready for employment. In view of the instructors' attitudes towards employment in general, these conclusions may not be at all surprising.

The views of the instructors at this centre are probably typical of ATCs as a whole. Stocks (1983) found a lack of interest and attitudes of general defeatism by staff in his study of the placement of trainees in employment. However, it must be emphasised that by no means all ATC managers and staff have such a negative approach to open employment and to the capabilities of Down's young people. In an interview with another manager in the same area, quite a different policy unfolded. He thought that anyone with an IQ over 45 should be able to hold down a job. This manager saw Down's trainees at the top end of the ATC ability range – they could be gainfully occupied in unskilled jobs such as packing, assembly, etc. Another manager (questioned by post), with 20 years experience with mentally handicapped adults, wrote: 'I find that for many years (Down's adults) have been grossly under-rated and, up to about five years ago, there has been the tendency to develop them (*sic*) into what I call "trained handicapped persons". In other words, trained to become handicapped...I believe that too many in the mildly retarded range are not assisted early enough because of their Down's Syndrome label at birth.' Mark Gold, an American psychologist and entrepreneur employing mentally handicapped adults, estimates that 95% of Down's adults, under the right conditions and with proper training, are employable (interview).

The attitudes of parents may be crucial in determining the placement of Down's young people when they leave school. We interviewed all the parents (17) of Down's trainees at the centre plus the parents of the two Down's adults with jobs. Six of the parents thought that their offspring would 'like to get a job outside the centre' if it were possible. They were then asked what form of activity they thought 'most appropriate' for their children. Three thought 'open employment' most appropriate, two a sheltered workshop, one a residential community (i.e. such as Home Farm Trust), 12 the training centre; one answered that the trainee 'needed constant supervision'. (These figures add up to 18 as one respondent gave two answers.) As to the kind of work which could be done, two said farm work, two opted for domestic work and three thought that repetitive or unskilled (manual) work was appropriate. When asked whether they thought that their offspring 'would ever have a chance to do a job of work outside the centre', 12 said no; not one said yes; the remainder did not know.

We may now turn for comparison to the parents of the two Down's people at work. Like the parents of the ones at the ATC (16 out of 17 thought that their offspring liked going there), those with Down's children at work thought that they 'loved it'. The type of work done included kitchen work, washing up, gardening, sweeping and washing floors and making beds. Both of these Down's adults had had a few jobs; they thought that even if the present job terminated, the parents would be able to find an alternative.

A final but major piece to our picture must be the attitude of adults with Down's Syndrome themselves. The Down's trainees were asked about their attitudes to the centre. Eleven 'liked coming to the centre' and six did not. It should be noted that this was a rather more negative response than anticipated by the instructors and the parents; by the former, it was thought that 15 out of the 17 liked coming, one not, and about one there was uncertainty. Of the parents, only one thought that their offspring viewed attendance at the centre unfavourably. The response of the trainees was also rather less positive than the findings of the Wandsworth study (Wandsworth Social Services, 1976), in which 88% of those questioned gave a positive response. The difference is probably due to the fact that the interviewer was not a member of the staff and our question also contained a negative evaluation ('Do you like coming to the centre *or not*?'). The Wandsworth question had a built-in tendency for the answer to be yes.

The trainees were then asked whether, if it were possible, they would 'like to get a job outside the centre'. Thirteen said yes, 2 said no, and 2 others were uncertain. These data again confirm the findings of the Wandsworth survey, where 76% of trainees expressed a desire for a job outside the centre. We asked this question later in a rather different way: 'If you had a choice tomorrow when you get up, would you prefer to go to work or would you prefer to come as usual to the centre?'. Twelve said that they would prefer to go to work, 4 to go to the centre, and 1 did not give a definite answer. These answers were highly correlated with the previous responses. When asked whether they thought they would 'get a chance to do a job outside the centre' or would 'have to stay in the centre', only 6 thought that they would get a job; 7 thought that they would, in fact, stay in the centre; 4 did not answer.

There is here, then, a definite area of conflict between the aspirations of the Down's trainees for work and the present activity of the centre for social and educational development, and it is possible that this creates a feeling of 'containment' on the part of some of the trainees. It should also be noted that the aspirations of some of the trainees were tempered by a realistic sense of accommodation to their situation.

The views of the two Down's adults in employment were similar. The two liked their work and place of work very much. They could not really conceive of being employed anywhere else. One had been to an ATC and, though he liked it there, he preferred a job: he wanted to 'go higher up and to have better pay'. His earnings were on the basic scale giving a take-home pay of £32.70 per week (1979). The only thing he did not like about the job were the inconvenient hours. The other young person had not been to an ATC, though she had views about it: 'It wasn't proper work there'. She had no comment as to what she did not like about her present job. Payment was not received for labour performed, though pocket-money was given from the social security payment. As to independence, one thought that he was able to cope with living alone, and the preference was for living in a place of his own. The other adult in employment was also confident that she could live independently and again preferred to live alone rather than in a group. We found that the majority of the ATC Down's trainees also, if given the chance, would prefer a 'place of their own' rather than communal living. (We seem to take for granted that 'normal' human beings should live in nuclear groups, whereas anyone in need of care should 'naturally' be placed in communal living.)

While it is apparent that there may be ambiguity about some of the answers, a number of fairly clear conclusions may be drawn from the data collected. First, there is a clear preference on the part of the trainees to do a job of work outside the centre. This is a conclusion of some importance, as the ATC studied was not concerned with work activity and emphasised the development of social and educational skills. The trainees were more pragmatic when it came to the possibility of work. Two could be ruled out as impossible ('bus driver' and 'filling in forms') – the nearest jobs known to be done by Down's adults are tractor driving (Texas, USA) and filing (Birmingham office). The remaining six were more realistic – they wanted jobs like woodwork, digging, gardening, helping in a cafe or shop, and 'rolling up posters'. These responses are in agreement with those of the study of Ramot *et al.* (1979). In a survey of 38 severely retarded employees (IQ 30–56) in a sheltered workshop, they found that 76% were not prepared 'not to work at all' and that only 21% 'enjoyed missing days off work'.

Second, there is a clear difference between the trainees' aspirations and those of the staff and parents, who see the activity of the ATC as an end in itself. Here we confirm the findings of the Wandsworth study where it was found that there were 'important differences between the views of the mentally handicapped...and the perception of these views by parents and staff...' (Wandsworth Social Services, 1976).

Third, the two Down's people working in the community would seem to be models which many of the trainees would like to follow.

In the various surveys and interviews reported above, many conflicting attitudes are noted towards whether mentally handicapped adults can and should be employed. These attitudes stem from many sources at different levels: from an implicit and usually not thought-out philosophy about the role of the handicapped person in society; from estimates of the ability of the handicapped, and appraisals of this ability; and from lack of knowledge about the potentialities of employment. The first thing that many of the handicapped and those responsible for them want is a care situation. Hence, the positive response of the parents interviewed to the ATC (to its teachers and instructors and its work) is a reflection of the fact that the ATC provides relief for the family and a safe, fairly happy, care situation for the mentally handicapped adult. These views are extended to the concern for residential care and are foremost in the thoughts of the protagonists of residential communities, hostels and supervised group homes. The emphasis here is on care and containment. This philosophy is a positive one in many ways: it provides assurance for parents, and a good, often high-quality caring environment for the handicapped person. Many advocates of such provision stress the risks which the handicapped person may face in a less structured and segregated setting. In our survey, these views have been put most strongly by parents and have been echoed in the practice of the teachers and instructors at the one ATC.

The other views we have encountered (though in a minority) regard work to be desirable in itself. Again, this position is underpinned by an ideology which is usually only partially developed by its exponents. The underlying philosophy is grounded in the idea that the handicapped person should live and participate in the community on equal terms with others. Being gainfully employed is a major component of this philosophy. (This viewpoint is discussed by Tizard and Anderson, 1979.) As noted above, to become 'part of the community', a person needs to be employed; with employment goes 'normal living', a structured day, and income. Data from interviews with mentally handicapped adults show a preference for 'real' work. Despite an immediate environment which does not encourage or prepare for the world of work, the adults with Down's Syndrome in our survey aspired to a work role. (Whether they knew exactly what it entailed is irrelevant at this point.)

One might also take issue with the objection that, as all work is dull and boring, it should be denied to the handicapped. The fallacy of this argument is that the dullness of work resides in the work. Whether a task is dull and boring is a matter of perception of the observer. People bring their own perceptions to work. Of the adult population as a whole, it has been found that 73% of skilled workers said that they 'enjoyed work a lot', and the comparative figure was 66% for unskilled workers. In the same survey, it was found that a majority would not give up work even if they had the opportunity to do so without loss of pay (Barter, 1978; Fraser, 1980; Jahoda, 1982). There is much testimony to the fact that many handicapped persons do not regard routine work as boring. A study by Ramot *et al.* of motivation to work by mentally handicapped adults (mentioned above) found that 88% of respondents (N=34) regarded their work as repetitive, but that 65% felt that this was 'very good', and another 29% considered this to be 'all right'; only 3% regarded repetition as being 'very bad' (Ramot *et al.*, 1979). This does not mean, of course, that the handicapped should be given all the jobs that others do not want to do, and neither does it mean that all mentally handicapped persons are suitable for all routine jobs.

One factor which must be taken into account is that a complex network of social relationships is to be found in the work place, and these social relationships are part of the work situation. To deprive the handicapped person of work is to deprive him of contact with all the people whom he may meet at work. A final reason why work cannot be reduced to the 'intrinsic character of a task' is to be found in the earning power which employment gives to the employed person. The work potential of the handicapped cannot realistically be considered independently of financial incentives. Hence, motivation and effort extended by Down's adults in artificially created work situations (i.e. where there are no financial rewards) cannot be taken as indicative of their potential.

Their 'potential' has been seriously underestimated by the labelling of the group under consideration as 'mongols' and a legacy of a destructive medical typology (see Chapter 1). Early twentieth-century writers shared a 'consensus that Down's Syndrome is usually of mid-trainable to custodial-level intelligence at maturity and shows a decreasing variability of degree of mental retardation as age increases. The condition appeared not only to regress intellectually with age, but the range of performance diminished into adult years. These two conclusions were used to justify group disposal practices and essentially custodial management' (Gibson, 1978). More recent studies of IQ have questioned these assumptions. Social psychologists and sociologists view genetic anomaly as conditioning but not determining behaviour, and thus have stressed educational and social influences on the behaviour of the Down's person. Empirical study of Down's people living at home, rather than in hospitals or institutions, has 'identified a less custodial level and comparatively more educable level...' (Gibson, 1978). However greatly opinion is divided, it is generally agreed, by both field workers and psychologists, that the intellectual level of persons with Down's Syndrome is improving and that various forms of stimulation and educational training are placing many in the 'educable class'. Just how many is a bone of contention.

There is often an implicit ideological conflict between a 'medical model' of analysis, which sees the chromosomal disorder determining and effectively limiting behaviour, and a more behavioural one adopted by some social psychologists emphasising the trainability and educability even of persons with low levels of intelligence. Also, capability, or 'social competence', is not a static state. Not only do custodial care and institutionalisation reinforce low levels of capacity, but also expectations of competence and type of training are determinants of competence levels.

Social skills and the ability to collaborate with people are of supreme importance in work situations. The legacy of segregated education in special establishments for 'handicapped' children undoubtedly lessens opportunities for social learning from other 'normal' children. Whatever the advantages which may accrue from the specialist teaching skills, it denies the child the opportunity of forming relationships with 'normal' children (even if this is sometimes unpleasant). It does not develop self-awareness. In the provision of special door-to-door transport to and from school, it completely reduces the level of danger to which the child is exposed and prevents him or her from learning how to cope with the environment. Segregation of children in school also tends to channel the Down's school leaver automatically to the ATC where his or her role of being handicapped is reinforced, which this research would suggest is likely to produce a better trained and more educated but still a handicapped person. This is because the emphasis is on the individual's level of competence, rather than on overcoming the implications of that disability.

If the mentally handicapped are to be integrated into the community, then the activity of institutions attended by Down's people must be consistently and systematically linked to, and be part of, life in the community. It follows from this that segregation of mentally retarded persons in separate institutions (playgroups for the handicapped, special schools) should not be the norm, but only the exception. An emphasis should be placed on normalising relations between the mentally retarded and 'ordinary' people. Mentally handicapped persons must learn how to adopt acceptable roles in their relations with peers and people in authority. They should be put into situations (often involving risk) where they might learn by making mistakes. If people with Down's Syndrome are likely to experience negative responses because of their stigmata, then they should be exposed to this kind of behaviour earlier rather than later. Mentally retarded adults are different from 'normal' adults in some ways – their levels of speech and measured intelligence are below average – but in many other respects (e.g. social behaviour) there is a considerable range of competence. Much of the 'bad behaviour' of the mentally handicapped has been copied from the behaviour of other often disturbed individuals. *Behaviour* is learned and not determined by a chromosomal abnormality. If the appearance of Down's Syndrome leads to stereotyped behaviour on the part of normal people, then the sooner the handicapped learn that they are different, the sooner they are put in a position where they may learn a form of behaviour that will enable them to cope.

Once the structural barriers which divide the mentally retarded from 'normal' persons are overcome, expectations of what the retarded adult can do should rise, and more will become 'employable'. A problem here is the inertia and conservatism of present institutions. Field workers (teachers, ATC instructors, paediatricians) will sometimes concede the 'desirability' of work or of the 'potential' of the handicapped. When they consider the 'reality' of actual cases, differences of judgement begin to appear and reliance on essentially custodial practices continues. The 'reality of the situation' is invariably a description of what the person does under existing 'training strategies, instruction capabilities and expectancies of staff' (Gold, 1975).

Given the opportunity and right conditions, what kind of jobs may be successfully performed by young adults with Down's Syndrome and what can parents do to facilitate the employability of their offspring? There is no single and simple answer to this question. The capabilities of individual young people vary. Opportunities for employment differ. The education and training provided in schools and further education also vary greatly. Positive attitudes of those in positions to facilitate employment and the drive necessary to help Down's school leavers are invariably lacking. There are limits to what parents can do when faced with prejudiced and ignorant professionals. One can, however, indicate some of the possibilities and how attempts might be made to overcome some of the obstacles.

Jobs which are suitable for school leavers from schools for children with moderate learning difficulties should be suitable for most Down's young people. In my own study of young Down's adults, I discovered 9 Down's in sheltered employment (8 at a residential community for handicapped and 1 at another residential community); 3 were working in horticulture and gardening, and the others in printing (press operators), woodcutting (cutting wood under supervision), housework and making soft toys; one in open employment was a kitchen porter, carrying implements (plates, etc.), washing up and doing odd jobs. A response to a written enquiry to another residential community catering especially for adults with Down's Syndrome informed me that they help with the housework and domestic jobs, including gardening. In the USA, adults with Down's Syndrome are engaged in tractor driving, housework (including ironing), soldering electric components and car driving (oral data from Mark Gold). A manager of an Australian sheltered workshop wrote to say that 'two Down's Syndrome persons occupy roles of leading hand in each section. They do not have any lack of ability to perform or to plan and develop the day's work.' Of the two Down's people found work in the Pathway Scheme of the RNSMHC, one was employed as a council labourer and another as a 'general assistant' by a book company. In the ATCs study, Down's trainees were engaged with other trainees in packing activities, assembly, gardening and lowly skilled woodworking jobs. These, however, were performed in an environment not requiring speed or great effort on the part of the trainees. We may generalise by saying that a wide range of unskilled and semi-skilled jobs are within the *intellectual* competence of most Down's school leavers.

Access to a job, as noted above, is a rare occurrence for school leavers with Down's Syndrome. In addition to the structural changes discussed above, we may also consider more specific impediments to employment which may be ameliorated within the present arrangements. The 29 specialist careers' officers were asked to describe from their experience the 'major impediments' to the employment of Down's school leavers. Their answers may be classified into four different groups.

1. The appearance, slowness, lack of skills, and inflexibility of Down's people.
2. The lack of sympathy of employers and other employees.
3. Structural problems of the economy, particularly unemployment levels.
4. Institutional inhibition: 'lack of imaginative initiatives, such as enclaves' (i.e. units of handicapped people in work places).

These attitudes were shared to a greater or lesser extent by the other groups surveyed (except the Down's persons themselves). The instructors in the training centre and the headteachers added 'over-protective parents'. One other major practical problem encountered is the inability of adults with Down's Syndrome to use public transport independently. Even if the other constraints do not exist, lack of mobility appears a major obstacle.

The first set of problems are to do with the constitution and training of people with Down's Syndrome. There is no reason why appearance should be a liability. Many people are employed whose physical appearance is worse than that of Down's persons. Parents might pay extra attention to clothes, cleanliness and smartness. Slovenliness is learned behaviour, and not caused by trisomy 21. Poor muscle tone may be improved by exercise. In extreme cases, the unsightly protrusion of the tongue with its associated dribbling may be cured by surgery. 'Lack of skills' calls for a change in emphasis in schools and at home. Few special schools have workshops and many lack gymnasiums. Schools should alter their curricula to give more training in practical skills. (The lack of such facilities in special schools, especially the very small ones, is also a good reason for further comprehensivisation in the state sector.) 'Inflexibility' has to do with the lack of experience of Down's children: they are often shielded from any form of decision-making, and their responses are mechanical. A greater exposure of Down's children to uncertainties – in the street, at school and in preparation for life – is essential. Otherwise, Down's young people will not be able to cope with any, even minor, problem that confronts them.

The other sets of impediments to employment all have to do with the labour market. The most important is that of structural unemployment. It is obvious that if the total number of school leavers is in excess of the total number of vacancies, then some leavers must remain unemployed. However, it does not follow that the mentally handicapped should carry the brunt of unemployment. Unemployment affects all types of labour, skilled and unskilled. The mentally handicapped seek jobs among the unskilled and low-paid categories of labour. It is here that they may have an advantage over better qualified workers. They will be prepared to accept such jobs on a permanent, rather than temporary or fleeting, basis. The wages paid in such jobs are such that people with mortgages and dependants are often better off on social security. They will not consider such jobs. This is not the case for the Down's unemployed person, who will undoubtedly be better off with the wages offered than on social security and the small earnings received from an ATC. (Stocks (1983) has demonstrated empirically that ATC trainees would receive from 25% to 33% more money by taking the unskilled work on offer.) It is not only the money in employment that makes it preferred to unemployment: 'Work is psychologically supportive even when conditions are bad and by the same token unemployment is psychologically destructive' (Jahoda, 1978); it defines aspects of 'personal status and identity' (Fraser, 1980).

In some sectors of the economy, it is difficult to obtain labour in the early 1980s. This is particularly the case in the hotel and catering businesses. To take one example, Tony Stocks set out to place a number of trainees from an ATC in employment. In an 8-day search (in 1981), he found 16 vacancies which he and the employer considered suitable for ATC trainees. (These were: assistant gardener, shelf-filler, kitchen assistant, waiters, cleaners, dishwashers, and refuse collectors.)

It is also not always true that employers are not prepared to try to take *suitable* mentally handicapped trainees. In my own study of employers who had taken on a total of 16 mentally handicapped employees (including one with Down's Syndrome), it was found that the latter compared favourably with other (non-handicapped) employees doing similar jobs.

The employers were asked in what ways their mentally handicapped personnel were 'satisfactory employees'. They listed the following attributes: clean, tidy, good appearance, reliable, 'fantastic loyalty', 'very willing', have 'less time off', are regular good time-keepers, they 'do as they are told', they 'don't query instructions'.

Employers were also asked about the 'unsatisfactory' aspects of their work. Here, the 'lack of flexibility' for multi-skilled work was mentioned. Lack of basic skills (money sense, literacy) was seen to hinder job prospects, but was not a problem insofar as work was concerned, because the required tasks did not require reading or money skills. The employers pointed out that the mentally handicapped people had their social problems (disagreements with other workers, 'bad temper'), but in this they were not unlike other employees.

Stocks also found that many employers had an altruistic sympathy for handicapped and impaired persons. The general tone of his findings is that insufficient effort is made by the statutory bodies to seek out such employers. As one employer put it in the survey I conducted, 'There are still many hurdles to break down. Firms should accept responsibility for mentally handicapped people – we have a worker here who has a mentally handicapped child...I can see your point about such people possibly being in factories and approaches by [the interviewer] are good because it reminds us of the problem. What we need is a pilot scheme in this area to demonstrate the potential...and then more may come as a result. We must break down attitudes...there is a lack of knowledge on such things...' Adult training centres could promote work teams which go out to industry, to work as 'enclaves'. A change of attitude is clearly called for, with a greater emphasis on entrepreneurial activities.

The great danger about accepting unemployment and institutional care for Down's adults is that it becomes defined as a way of life, with its own advantages. This seems to me to be an erroneous and highly damaging policy which will effectively condemn disabled groups of the population to an inferior standard of life.

Present facilities are geared to institutional care of adult persons with Down's Syndrome. Potentialities are not being realised. This chapter has indicated three reasons for this. First, expectations in the past have been very low: our survey showed that the guardians (parents, teachers, instructors, doctors) of mentally handicapped adults seek a caring rather than an independent environment. Second, intermediaries – careers' officers and DROs – often tend to label people with Down's Syndrome as a homogeneous group requiring care and being incapable of employment. Third, though the policy of the DHSS and social services departments endorses the normalisation of the handicapped person in the community, this policy is not effectively put into practice. (The same may also be said for DES policy of encouraging the handicapped to be educated in ordinary schools.) Adult training centres, even when formally set up as institutions for social and educational training, can easily slip into activities which become an end in themselves. Such conditions will not change overnight. The parent is often confronted with an institutional care situation which may be the only facility available. The ATC is undoubtedly a most necessary facility at present and should be supported and strengthened in its activity. It is hoped that this chapter will provide some guidelines as to how this can be done.

At the beginning of the chapter, four principal roles provided by employment were defined. They provide a basis for appraising the activities of the adult training centre. First, the trainee ought to have an adequate personal income; training strategies in the ATCs should be linked in some way to reward work and effort. Second, the centre should aim to give a similar structure to the day as that in a work environment. Down's adults like to think of themselves going out to work like the rest of the family. Hours of labour should resemble the world of work, not that of school. Third, the great positive advantage of the ATC is that the Down's person may find there other people with whom he or she can have friendships. The ATC should be seen not only as a training centre but also as a social one. It is the fourth function of employment – giving status and self-respect – that ATCs find difficult to achieve. Here, a greater outward-going practice, the development of enclave work schemes, and the provision of contract labour will not only give the Down's adults a sense of earning money, but may also give them the satisfaction that they are in the real world of work.

REFERENCES

Armstrong, G.A., Heron, A. and Race, D. (1977). Staff attitudes and activities in adult training centres, *ERG Reports*, No. 2, p.7. Sheffield: Department of Psychology, Sheffield University.

Barter, J. (1978). *Computers and Employment*. London: National Opinion Polls.

Better Services for the Mentally Handicapped (1971). Cmnd 4689. London: HMSO.

DHSS (1976). *Priorities for Health and Personal Services in England*. London: HMSO.

Fraser, C. (1980). The psychology of unemployment. In Jeaves, M. (ed.), *Psychological Survey*, No. 3. London: George Allen & Unwin.

Gibson, D. (1978). *Down's Syndrome*. Oxford: Oxford University Press.

Gold, M.C. (1975). Vocational training. In Wortis, J. (ed.), *Mental Retardation and Development Disabilities: An Annual Review*, Vol. 7.

Innes, G., Johnson, A.W. and Miller, M.W. (1978). *Mental-Subnormality in N.E. Scotland*. Scottish Home and Health Department.

International Labour Organisation (1968). *Organisation of Services for the Mentally Retarded*, p.20. Geneva: International Labour Office.

Jahoda, M. (1978). The impact of unemployment in the 1930s and 1970s. Paper to the British Psychological Society (Annual Conference, 1978).

Jahoda, M. (1982). *Employment and Unemployment: A Social–Psychological Analysis*. Cambridge: Cambridge University Press.

Jay Report (1979). *Report of the Committee of Enquiry into Mental Handicap Nursing and Care* (Chairperson, Mrs Peggy Jay), Vol. 1, p. 45. Cmnd 7268-1. London: HMSO.

Lane, D. (1980). *The Work Needs of Mentally Handicapped Adults*. London: Disability Alliance.

National Development Group for the Mentally Handicapped (1977). *Day Services for Mentally Handicapped Adults*. London: NDGMH.

Ramot, A., Harpak and Cna'an (1979). *Work Motivation of Residents in a Home for the Mentally Retarded*. Jerusalem: Ministry of Labour and Social Affairs.

Stocks, A. (1983). Adult training centres and open employment, MSc thesis, Cranfield.

Tizard, J. and Anderson, E. (1979). *The Education of the Handicapped Adolescent: Alternatives to Work for Severely Handicapped People*. Paris: OECD.

Tomlinson, S. (1982). *A Sociology of Special Education*, Chapters 4 and 7. London: Routledge and Kegan Paul.

Walker, A. (1982). *Unqualified and Underemployed*, p. 19. London: Macmillan.

Wandsworth Social Services (1976). *Survey of Mentally Handicapped in Adult Training Centres* ii. London: Wandsworth Social Services.

Whelan, E. and Speake, B. (1976). *The National Survey of Adult Training Centres in England and Wales*. Manchester: Manchester University.

20 Recent Developments in the Law and Down's Syndrome

Michael Gunn

This chapter considers recent developments in English law that affect the mentally handicapped and, hence, people with Down's Syndrome, who are not recognised as a separate legal group. Where possible international comparisons are drawn, particularly between England and the USA.

There have been two significant pieces of legislation in England and Wales: the Education Act 1981, concerning special education; and the Mental Health Act 1983, concerning compulsory hospitalisation and guardianship. In addition, the courts have decided two important cases – *Re B (a minor)* (1981)[1] and *R* v. *Arthur* (1981)[2] – which consider the right to life of the Down's baby.

THE EDUCATION ACT 1981[3]

Integration

The United Nations Declaration on the Rights of Mentally Retarded Persons (1971) establishes the mentally retarded person's right to education to enable him to 'develop his ability and maximum potential'. It is generally thought that educating a mentally retarded child with other children will fulfil this vague provison (Stratford, 1981; Mitchell, 1983). However, general education legislation and common-law provisions are insufficient to ensure this.

In England, the principle of integration provides the basis for the 1981 Education Act (Warnock Report, 1978; Hannon, 1982). Children with 'special educational needs' are to be educated in ordinary schools, a reference not only to the school environs, but also to all activities as far as possible. Where this is not possible, the child can be placed in a special or independent school. However, there are conditions which qualify somewhat the mandate for integration. Integration is subject to parents' views, to the ability of the school to meet the child's needs, to the provision of efficient education for the other children, and to *the efficient use of resources*. The final condition requires a firm commitment on the part of local education authorities.

Resources are also an obstacle in the USA,[4] where integration (or mainstreaming) is required by the Education of All Handicapped Children Act, 1975, as a precondition for federal funding. The state must assure 'all handicapped children the right to a free appropriate public education' (Herr, 1976),[5] which requires mainstreaming unless there are particularly good reasons for exclusion. If the legislative requirements are not fulfilled, the child is entitled to claim damages. This has led to considerable litigation giving rise to doubts about the efficacy of the legislation (Rebell, 1981). Two recent cases consider what constitutes an appropriate education.[6] The decisions differ because an individualised response is required, although there are some irreducible demands, for example that special education provisions must not be limited to a maximum of 180 days per year.[7]

The demands of the 1975 Act are supported by other federal legislation, especially the anti-discrimination provision in Section 504 of the Rehabilitation Act, 1973.[8] To deny mainstreaming without compelling educational justification constitutes discrimination.[9] The Developmentally Disabled Assistance and Bill of Rights Act provides support,[10] since the Education Act only concerns children between the ages of 3 and 21. These demands are also underpinned by the argument that mainstreaming is a constitutional right,[11] although this argument has never been tested in the courts.

Classification

The English Education Act 1981 makes a major break from the past in not laying down specific categories as prerequisites of special education.[12] More children are thus covered by the legislation – some 20% as opposed to 2% under the previous legislation (DHSS, 1981).

The Act applies to children with 'special educational needs', that is, with a 'learning difficulty which calls for special educational provision'. This is further defined to include children, even those under 5 years, having greater difficulty in learning than children of the same age or having a disability depriving them of the ability to make use of educational facilities. It would appear, then, that most, if not all, Down's children would be covered.

This approach – similar to the US one in that it refers to 'handicapped children', especially those with specific learning disabilities – means that the dangers of rigid classification are avoided, in particular the social stigma attached to medically based labels in educational provision (Sorgen, 1976; Hayes and Hayes, 1982). In Australia, it has been argued that classification is contrary to Article 7 of the UN Declaration since it is potentially prejudicial and discriminatory (Hayes and Hayes 1982). This is avoided in England and the USA, where an individualised decision takes all the relevant factors into account.

Identification and assessment of children with special educational needs

Most children with special educational needs can be accommodated in ordinary schools. A few, perhaps 2%, will require the local education authority to go further and 'identify' them. If a child is identified as requiring special educational provision from the authority, an assessment of the child's needs must be made. The authority must seek educational, medical, psychological and any other desirable advice, and it must take into account parental representations and any information from health or social service authorities.[13] This reflects an international call for multidisciplinary assessments (Mitchell, 1983).

After the assessment, the authority must make a statement, if appropriate, of the child's educational needs, which should specify the educational and non-educational provision necessary for the child. This individualised report compares closely with the 'individualised educational programme' (IEP) in the USA. The IEP, however, identifies the abilities of the child and the annual goal to be achieved, and this gives rise to claims that an agency has been negligent if the child fails to fulfil the goals – a possibility for litigious parents that is not open in England.

In the USA 'education' has a wide meaning, including basic self-help and social skills, which might include toilet training, dressing and feeding.[14] It could also include hospital care as a 'related service' if it is part of an educational placement.[15] It would be surprising if a significantly different approach is adopted in England.

Parental involvement

The Education Act 1981 recognises the important role parents play in the educational provision for their children. Parents have a duty to secure appropriate education for their child,[16] and the fulfilment of this duty in the child's best interests, is usually, but not always, unchallenged. Not everybody, however, is happy with parental involvement, and some believe that decisions should only be taken by appropriately qualified professionals. The author, while recognising that some parents might be awkward or unreasonable, dismisses this objection.

The Act requires parents to be involved at all stages.[17] Parental views must be considered when deciding whether the child should be in an ordinary school or in a school at all. If a parent is dissatisfied with the school placement, he or she can appeal (Bull, 1980). If the authority is not making any special arrangements for the child, the parent can request an assessment, which the authority must carry out unless it believes the request to be unreasonable. The authority is never bound by the parents' views.

If the authority is to take action, parental involvement is greater. If the authority intends to assess the child, a notice must be served upon the parent(s), informing them that the authority proposes to make an assessment, of the procedure to be followed, of the named officer who can be contacted, and of the parents' right to make representations and submit written evidence. In the USA such information must be provided in the parents' native language, if possible. Good practice requires this in England. If the authority receives representations, it must consider them. If it decides not to assess the needs of the child, it must inform the parent, who cannot appeal but may request an assessment at a later date. If the authority decides to assess the needs of the child, the parent must be informed.

If, on assessing the child, the authority decides not to make any special educational provision, the parent can appeal to the Secretary of State, who cannot overrule the authority's decision but may ask it to reconsider. If the authority is to make special educational provision, it must make a statement of the provision proposed.

Before the statement is made, the authority must give the parent a copy of the draft and an explanation of his or her rights. Often, the parent will agree, but if not, there is a carefully laid down procedure, which can be lengthy and appears to be rife with litigation possibilities.[18] The parent may make representations about the draft statement, and require a meeting with a named officer. If the former, the authority must consider them and then may make a statement in the original form, a modified form, or not at all. Either way, it must inform the parent. If the latter, this will lengthen the procedure, since the parent can require further specialised meetings if dissatisfied initially. The authority has considerable discretion in the later meetings, since it decides what information is necessary, what the relevant advice is and who the appropriate people are. If the opinion of the authority is unreasonable, that could be a ground for litigation. (In the USA, by contrast, parents are entitled to see all relevant records.)

This later meeting gives rise to some professional concern as it requires full and frank discussion, thereby raising the problem of confidentiality which may worsen the position in special education (Sowell, 1983). Professionals cannot be forced to reveal what is conceived to be confidential information at the meeting but might have to do so in the course of litigation.

After the meeting(s) the authority can make a statement, which the parent cannot prevent, although the parent is entitled to a copy, a notice of the right to appeal, and notice of the named officer. The appeal goes to an appeal committee, which can consider the special educational provision in the statement. The authority is not bound by the decision of the committee, which can only remit the case to the authority for reconsideration. Then the authority must inform the parent. The committee can, of course, confirm the statement.

Should the parent still be dissatisfied, he or she may appeal to the Secretary of State, who can amend the statement, confirm it or direct the authority to cease to maintain it. The Secretary of State at this stage does have the power to overrule the decision of the authority.

Thus, parents have considerable involvement in the special educational provision for their child at all stages which, in the main, is well received (Hannon, 1982; Russell, 1983) and reflects an international trend (Mitchell, 1983).

THE MENTAL HEALTH ACT 1983[19]

The Mental Health Act 1983 is not all new, but an update for the 1980s and 1990s. It is essentially designed for people suffering from mental illness. Many of its provisions seem singularly inappropriate to mentally handicapped people in general and Down's individuals in particular. Similar problems occur elsewhere,[20] although in other countries/states a distinction is drawn between mental illness and mental handicap. For example, New York's Mental Hygiene Law (Herr, 1983) deals with mental retardation and mental illness separately.

Hospitalisation

Compulsory admission procedures

Should it be possible to admit a mentally handicapped person to hospital? The international preference is for community-based care and treatment. However, Parliament recognised instances when mentally handicapped people might have to be hospitalised, either because of mental illness or because of the handicap itself. However, in attempting to ensure that fewer mentally handicapped people could be admitted to hospital, the relevant definitions have been changed. There is now a central concept of 'mental impairment', which mirrors 'mental retardation' in New York. Both require: the impairment to originate at an early developmental stage (in England the phrase being 'arrested or incomplete development of mind'); impairment of intelligence (so the US court warnings surrounding IQ tests are appropriate) (Sorgen, 1976; Neuberger, 1981); and abnormal behavioural characteristics. Mental impairment can be either simple or severe, the distinction being a matter of degree; it also requires impairment of social functioning. A Down's individual is covered by these definitions, since the chromosomal defect is present at birth. However, not all Down's people are either abnormally aggressive or seriously irresponsible. Thus, many of them cannot be compulsorily admitted to or detained in hospital, unless for a short, non-renewable period (maximum 28 days), when the applicable definition is 'mental disorder'. This includes a 'state of arrested or incomplete development of mind', *simpliciter*, thus covering all Down's people. These changes under the 1981 Act should reduce the number of people who can be compulsorily admitted to hospital.

Basic admission procedures in England and the USA are strikingly similar. In England, the patient must be mentally impaired such that hospital care and treatment are appropriate. It must be impossible to provide this care and treatment elsewhere, and hospitalisation must be for the patient's health or safety or for the protection of other people, which is akin to, though not the same as, the 'dangerousness' requirement. If the patient is suffering from simple impairment, the treatment received in hospital must be such as 'to alleviate or prevent a serious deterioration of the patient's condition' – the 'treatability' requirement. Either the patient's nearest relative or an approved social worker (an expert) can apply for the patient's admission, the application being based upon two medical recommendations. If the hospital accepts the patient, the detention lasts for up to 6 months, when it is renewable. This is admission for treatment.[21]

In New York, the patient must be mentally retarded such that he or she is in 'need of involuntary care and treatment'. The patient must not be capable of understanding the need for such care and treatment. In England, if the patient has such understanding, it argues in favour of voluntary admission. This also indicates that the patient has the right to refuse treatment and hospitalisation, which is not implied by the English conditions.

In New York, it is implied that hospitalisation be the least restrictive alternative, a constitutional requirement in the USA.[22] This requirement appears in England and other legislation.[23] The English admission requirements are phrased in *parens patriae* terms not requiring dangerousness, whereas the trend in the USA is towards a need for an overt dangerous act on the part of the patient before admission is permissible (Ennis and Emery, 1978).[24] However, there are notorious difficulties in predicting dangerousness.[25] The application for hospitalisation in New York can be made by a number of people, including the patient's nearest available relative and welfare officials. (The width of the English definition of 'nearest relative' means that there is little practical difference.) The application must be supported by two medical recommendations. If the hospital accepts the patient, the initial detention lasts for up to 60 days.

In England, the doctor can renew the detention, initially for 6 months, and thereafter annually. He or she must establish that the same conditions as for initial admission still apply, except where the patient is severely mentally impaired, when, if not treatable, it must be established that he or she would be incapable of caring for him/herself if not in hospital. At first sight, there is greater protection in New York, since if the director of the hospital wants to continue the detention of the patient, he or she must apply to the court. The difference between the two systems is, however, illusory, since an actual hearing is not automatic. In England, the patient has the option of applying to a Mental Health Review Tribunal, which can order discharge if not satisfied that the conditions are fulfilled. The difficulty in both jurisdictions is the dependence upon patient initiative. This is partly overcome in England: if a patient does not apply to a tribunal for 3 years, the case is automatically referred by the hospital managers. Also, patients must be provided with information of their position under the Mental Health Act on admission and continued detention. In New York, the information is not supplied to the patient but to the nearest relative and the Mental Health Information Service.

Discharge usually occurs with the lapse of time or a decision by the doctor or managers of the institution. In England, the patient can apply at regular intervals to a tribunal, which is an independent body made up of lawyers, doctors and laymen, having powers of discharge which the hospital cannot obstruct. Its efficacy, however, is open to question, particularly the independence of its decision-making (Peay, 1982). There is no equivalent body in New York, although the patient may apply to the court for a writ of *habeas corpus* – a non-specific means of redress.

This brief comparison of admission and detention procedures indicates a similarity, which suggests a relatively healthy state of affairs. The drawback is that in England very few people are admitted or detained under this provision. If compulsory admission is undertaken, it will usually be by one of the two short-term powers, where the protections for the patient are fewer. The first of these is admission for assessment, lasting for up to 28 days, where the patient must be suffering from mental disorder. The conditions for admission are not as stringent as those already considered. However, the patient now has the right to appeal to a tribunal within the first 14 days of detention. The second is admission for assessment in an emergency, when basically the same conditions apply, except that only one doctor is involved and admission lasts for a maximum of 72 hours. Under the 1959 Act this was the most widely used power. It remains to be seen whether practice will change. It is difficult to conceive of instances where these powers would be necessary with Down's individuals, although the former might perhaps be used to assess the person's behavioural characteristics.

Informal admission procedures

Overall, it is unlikely that a patient will find him/herself in hospital under compulsory powers. Most admissions and detentions are through the informal admission procedure.[26] This does not require the signing of any forms, unlike its precursor – voluntary admission under the Mental Treatment Act 1930. But how many informal patients have actually consented to be in hospital? The answer is few, particularly for Down's people. Doubts about the informal admission procedure abound. There are no statutory means of protecting patients' rights, but a presumption that they can withdraw their consent or leave the hospital, as a last resort. Greater exercise of compulsory powers would be inappropriate.

A lesson can be learnt from New York, where there are two alternatives to involuntary admission. Herr (1983) categorises these as 'voluntary' and 'non-objecting' admission. The former requires the patient to make a written application indicating willingness to enter hospital, the patient being able to understand and be suitable for voluntary admission. This, in theory, ensures that the admission is truly voluntary. The latter creates a middle ground between voluntary and involuntary admission. Admission is limited to patients with a severe degree of impairment. It is similar to, but not the same as, involuntary admission. It attempts to achieve a means whereby severely mentally impaired people can be admitted to institutions, without the full rigours of compulsory admission, but providing minimal appropriate safeguards through the overview of the Mental Health Information Service.

Something similar could be considered in England. The position in practice in New York is not perfect, no system will be which involves the compromise of so many different interests, but the solution might lie in the direction of non-objecting admission.

The New York Mental Health Information Service has an overview function of patients in hospital. A similar body, and one which it is hoped will be more successful, has been established in England: the Mental Health Act Commission. This is designed to protect the position of individual detained patients, and may also take on board informal patients. However, it is not concerned with service provision, dealt with by the Health Advisory Service. The Commission will ensure that the forms of admission are properly filled in, that patients are provided with information, that nothing illegal is being done (for example, the improper provision of treatment), and that patients and staff have no complaints. This is an attempt to prevent the inquiries that bedevilled the service in the late 1960s and early 1970s.

Consent to treatment

For the first time, consent to treatment has been addressed by statute in England. However, the provisions of the 1983 Act seem particularly inappropriate to Down's individuals. Any form of treatment, except psychosurgery, surgical implantation of hormones to reduce male sexual drive, electroconvulsive therapy, and chemotherapy after the first 3 months, can be given without the patient's consent, provided it is for mental disorder. Therefore most forms of treatment for Down's people, such as behaviour modification, can be given without the patient's consent (Wexler, 1981). The exception is chemotherapy, but even here the patient's lack of consent can be overridden. If the patient cannot or will not consent to drugs 3 months after they were first given, an independent doctor can say that the treatment should be given, provided he or she has consulted with two non-medical professionals involved with the patient. Their advice does not have to be followed, but this consultation provides the first recognition of the multidisciplinary approach.

The position in the USA varies. Eighty-eight per cent of states recognise a qualified right to refuse psychotropic medication, whereas the other 12% recognise no right to refuse (Callahan and Longmire, 1983). In New South Wales, Australia, a superintendent can consent to treatment upon an involuntary patient, if he or she is satisfied that the treatment is necessary or desirable for the safety or welfare of the patient.[27]

If the patient is in the hospital informally, he or she may refuse any treatment. What if the patient cannot consent? Technically, the treatment cannot be given, unless it is a necessary emergency operation.[28] It is often assumed that lack of dissent is consent, or that patients can be put under pressure to consent when faced with discharge or staff displeasure – an unsatisfactory solution for patients and staff. The possibility of third party consent, for example by a parent,[29] which seems to be effective in the USA (Friedman, 1976), and which enables the guardian to consent on behalf of the incompetent patient, must be considered (Hayes and Hayes, 1982).

Rights to treatment

Treatment concerns not only the right to refuse, but also the right to receive appropriate treatment. In the USA there have been moves towards recognising this right. In *Wyatt* v. *Stickney*, the court required that there be an individualised treatment or habilitation programme for patients, that the hospital provide a humane psychological and physical environment, that there be adequate qualified staff, and that programmes be provided in the least restrictive manner possible (Burt, 1976; Friedman, 1976; Halpern, 1976). Later, the court had to appoint a monitor, and an effort is being made to require the diversion of more revenue to the Alabama Department of Mental Health (Marchetti, 1983). The right to treatment has been considered also by the Supreme Court in *Youngberg* v. *Romeo*.[30] This underlines the mentally retarded patient's right to the basic necessities of life, reasonably safe living conditions, freedom from undue restraints, and minimally adequate training to at least retain exercise of other Constitutional rights, if not to enhance such exercise. This decision is limited, but other courts have seized upon it and seem to be expanding it.[31] These cases are underlined by federal legislation. The Civil Rights of Institutionalised Persons Act 1980[32] seeks to prevent '... egregious or flagrant conditions which deprive such persons of any rights, privileges or immunities secured or protected by the Constitution or laws of the United States...' This will be successful if the Attorney-General adopts an enlightened attitude, but doubts exist that such an attitude will prevail (*Mental Disability Law Review*, 1983).

There is no such legislation in England and no prospect of similar court action as there is no written statement of rights which can be interpreted for the benefit of mentally handicapped people. The courts can be of some importance in securing the discharge of patients and in ensuring that health and social service authorities fulfil their functions. But the 1983 Act provides a defence to civil or criminal proceedings for a member of staff who purports 'to act in accordance with the Act' and does not act in 'bad faith or without reasonable care'.[33] This does not apply to informal patients. Perhaps this defence is acceptable; it certainly has a long history.[34] The Act also provides a considerable barrier to the patient's access to the courts. The consent of the Director of Public Prosecutions is required in criminal cases and the leave of the High Court in civil cases. Yet there is no evidence that mental patients are necessarily vexatious litigants. The lack of such a provision has caused no problem in Scotland.[35] In any case, vexatious civil litigants can be stopped by the Attorney-General applying to the High Court.[36]

None of these provisions applies to health authorities, but there is an important barrier to suing social service authorities. If the authority fails to fulfil its responsibilities, the Secretary of State becomes involved through the default power and may call an inquiry. This prevents court action.[37]

Community care

It is widely accepted that community care is most appropriate for mentally handicapped people. This was recognised in England by the Government Paper (Cmnd. 4683), *Better Services for the Mentally Handicapped* (1971), and has been strikingly reaffirmed in Italy (Hicks, 1984). The Mental Health Act 1983 has little to say about community care: it is not concerned with service provision, nor is it particularly creative. The Act, though, does consider guardianship and after care.

In the past guardianship[38] was intended to ensure that people could be treated in the community with some sort of overview, but the results were depressingly poor and guardianship was virtually never used.[39] This was possibly because the guardian had too many powers, but these have since been reduced. It is now often argued that the guardian has too little power: the guardian can only require the patient to live in a particular place, to attend somewhere for education, training, occupation or medical treatment (but not to undergo it), and to grant access to a doctor or social worker. Perhaps, however, the real reason for the failure of guardianship was the pressure on the resources of local authorities (finances and manpower) which are either the guardian or the body to which the guardian is responsible. The new regulations should reduce the burden on local authorities, since they no longer imply a virtual parental role over the patient (Gunn, 1984). The 1983 Act has suceeded in bringing the guardianship option into professional debate, with the result that it may be used more frequently in future. It would seem an effective way of ensuring that many Down's individuals live in a reasonable fashion in the community without too many restrictions upon their freedom, and it also avoids institutionalisation.

After care[40] was introduced despite Government opposition, which pointed out the existing duty to provide this under health legislation.[41] The new provision, though, places a duty upon both health and social service authorities to provide after care to *individual* patients. But it is difficult to see how a patient could litigate for failure to supply after care, partly because of the default power (see p.409). More importantly, there is no definition of after care. It is a matter for the authorities, and, provided the decision is taken reasonably and at a policy level, it is not challengeable in court. Finally, the duty only applies to patients who have been compulsorily detained for a relatively long period, thus covering very few patients in hospital. Nevertheless, along with the closure programmes of the large mental hospitals, it should result in extra pressure to provide community facilities.

In the USA, the courts are decrying the practice of leaving mentally handicapped people in hospital and are beginning to examine community placement as a required alternative to hospitalisation. The move is backed by court decision (Herr, 1983), some state legislation[42] and federal legislation such as s. 504 of the Rehabilitation Act 1973. However, the same obstacle exists as in England – that of resources. The federal funding by Medicaid is only for institutional authorities, and yet it is vital to health service provision. Nevertheless, there is more scope for direct pressure, and this is being brought to bear on the Medicaid funding (Herr, 1983, pp. 168–70).

THE RIGHT TO LIFE

The English courts have recently decided two cases involving the right to life of babies suffering from Down's Syndrome: *Re B (a minor)*[43] and *R. v. Arthur*.[44] They apply also to babies suffering from any form of mental handicap, and perhaps also physical handicap.

Re B (a minor)

This case concerned a Down's baby girl whose parents refused to consent to a life-saving operation to clear an intestinal blockage. The parents were motivated by the expectation of an unpleasant life for their child. The local authority made the child a ward of court and sought the court's support for the operation. The judge authorised the operation, until he discovered that the doctors were unwilling because of parental objections. The authority appealed to the Court of Appeal, which decided what were the paramount interests of the child and demanded, *on the facts of the case*, that the operation be carried out. Lord Justice Templeman indicated that different circumstances could have led to a different result. He said: 'There may be cases...of severe *proved* damage where the future is *so* uncertain and where the life of the child is *so bound* to be *full* of pain and suffering that the court *might* be driven to a different conclusion...' (emphasis added). How extraordinary the medical treatment was would be a contributory factor. Happily, the baby eventually went home to her parents.

Mental handicap, *simpliciter*, thus, is not sufficient to deprive a Down's baby of the basic protection provided by English law of the right to life through medical treatment. The details of this case might be difficult to apply, but it provides readily understandable general guidance.

R. v. Arthur

The same cannot be said of *R. v. Arthur*, the trial of a paediatric consultant charged with the murder of a Down's baby boy. Four hours after the birth, the defendant saw the parents, who had rejected the baby, and then prescribed nursing care only and a drug, dihydrocodeine, to be given in 5 mg doses at the nurses' discretion. At that time, the child was known to be suffering from Down's Syndrome; it was not known that the child had potentially fatal defects.

The charge of murder was replaced by attempted murder on direction by the judge, because of the incomplete and inaccurate forensic evidence. The jury found the defendant not guilty after hearing the evidence and the judge's full direction. This decision has no legal significance and is not open to question. However, it may influence prosecution policy, since it suggests a reluctance on the part of juries to convict doctors in such circumstances. The Director of Public Prosecutions has recognised this.[45]

It must be assumed that the jury followed the direction of the judge, Farquharson J. Occasionally trial directions assume great legal as well as practical importance, such as that of Mcnaghten J. in *R. v. Bourne*,[46] which regulated legal abortions until the Abortion Act 1967. It is unlikely that the direction in *R. v. Arthur* will achieve such status, since it was deficient in its consideration of the legal issues involved.

The judge's direction

The judge appears to have assumed that a doctor is not liable for murder if he allows a baby to die, particularly when its parents have rejected it. The judge indicated that these facts might be described as failing to act. This is debatable for three reasons.

First, it is not necessarily the case that a doctor would not be liable for failure to act. There is usually no liability for omissions (Smith and Hogan, 1983, pp. 43–7), but there is if the person who failed to act owed a duty of care to the victim, such as in *R. v. Instan*,[47] where the girl did have a duty to provide her aunt with the necessities of life. Since she did not, she was guilty of manslaughter. If the failure is deliberate, there is no reason why the crime should not be murder, which is accepted in *R. v. Gibbins & Proctor*.[48] It is axiomatic that doctors owe a duty of care to their patients. The baby in this instance would appear to have been a patient. The duty would impose, at least, an obligation to make reasonable efforts to keep the patient alive. But doctors are not obliged to do everything in their power to fulfil their duty. This is accepted by Templeman L.J. in *Re B (a minor)*. However no such analysis on these lines is to be found in the judge's direction in *R. v. Arthur*.

Secondly, the judge appears to have laid great weight upon the parents' rejection of the child. This cannot in itself be sufficient, as can be seen from *Re B*. Parental decisions can be wrong. If this child had been normal there would have been no argument about liability if the parents had rejected the child, say because it was a boy and not a girl.

Thirdly, it is questionable whether the events were accurately described as 'allowing the child to die'. A drug was prescribed and given. That seems to be an act. The effect and purpose of the drug may be to lower the child's demand for sustenance and hence accelerate death. It is clearly arguable that there was a 'positive act'. No consideration is given to this at all.

Another weakness of the direction is that the judge recited the evidence of eminent doctors as to medical practice without comment. This gives the impression that what was done was in accordance with medical ethics and, therefore, legal. Doctors do not make law; the courts do, and individual ethical considerations may be wrong. Moreover, the expert witnesses also commented on the motives of the defendant, although motive is generally irrelevant to liability. However, it can be argued (Smith and Hogan, 1983, p. 277) that good motive is the basis of the direction of Devlin J. in *R. v. Adams*,[49] where it is indicated that doctors are not guilty of murder when they provide painkilling drugs which they know will accelerate the death of the patient. This could have been of some assistance to the defendant in this case, but no analysis of this sort is to be found in the direction.

Thus, the direction is open to major criticisms.[50] It fails to give much-needed guidance to the medical and other professions involved in the care of young babies. However, a different direction would not necessarily have led to a different result.

The US experience

The position is not much clearer in the USA, since the answer depends upon the facts of the case. In *Maine Medical Center* v. *Houle*,[51] the court ordered that surgery be performed on a child although the parents had refused consent before and the child had severe physical handicaps at birth. The court declared that 'the most basic right enjoyed by every human being is the right to life itself'. This appears to be supported by *Re Baby Girl Obenauer*,[52] where parental refusal to authorise a life-saving operation was a ground for making the child a ward of court.

Different facts can produce different results, as in the Phillip Becker case. In 1979, a Californian juvenile probation department alleged that Phillip, a 12-year-old Down's boy, was not provided with the 'necessities of life' and should be declared a ward of court, which would ensure that he received surgery for a congenital heart defect – an unexceptional form of medical treatment for which Phillip's parents had refused their consent. The juvenile courts refused to make the declaration and appeals by the probation department to the Court of Appeals and the Supreme Court failed.[53] The Court of Appeals[54] stressed the importance of parental autonomy as a Constitutional provision, which has to be balanced with the sanctity of life. Ordinarily, the wishes of the parents would prevail. Should the state wish to act contrary to them, a serious burden falls upon the state before a court could substitute its judgement for that of the parents. The burden had not been fulfilled, so the appeal failed. This decision was received with much scorn, some of it over-harsh (Will, 1980).

Later, friends of Phillip applied to become his guardians. The Californian Civil Code permits guardianship of a child being given to someone other than the parents when that is in the child's best interests. The Court of Appeals was convinced that this was the case, since retention of custody by the parents had 'caused and will continue to cause serious detriment to Phillip' (Herr, 1984). The different result was achieved, because the court was required to give paramountcy to the interests of the child.

Parental autonomy is nevertheless recognised by the courts in America as being of fundamental importance. It was on that basis that the District Court in Columbia struck down the 'Baby Doe Regulations' of the Department of Health and Human Services, which were intended to prevent hospitals from withholding food or medical care from handicapped infants (Strain, 1983). Further, a parental decision to refuse surgery, though accepting conservative medical treatment, on an infant born with spina bifida and serious complicating disorders was upheld by the New York Court of Appeals on the ground that the person claiming to interfere did not have sufficient ground to do so[56]. Sufficient public disquiet was caused by these instances for the federal government to put forward the Child Abuse Amendments Act of 1984. This aims to secure its objectives by making compliance a condition of federal funding. This legislation makes for an interesting comparison with the English proposals and shows how similar the problems are on both sides of the Atlantic. It makes it clear that in no circumstances should a child be deprived of food, drink or medication. Further, it indicates that the child should receive 'medically indicated treatment' except in three circumstances: (a) the infant is chronically and irreversibly comatose; (b) where the provision of such treatment would (i) merely prolong dying, (ii) not be effective in ameliorating or correcting all of the infant's life-threatening conditions, or (iii) otherwise be futile in terms of the survival of the infant; or (c)where the provision of such treatment would be virtually futile in terms of the survival of the infant and the treatment itself under such circumstances would be inhumane. If treatment is not given, that will amount to child neglect and bring into play the child protection agencies (*Mental and Physical Disability Law Reporter*, 1985).[57]

Summary

What appears to be accepted by the courts, then, is that in some instances it is appropriate to permit handicapped babies to die, because their prognosis is so bad. This is only so, however, in extreme cases.

Recently, suggestions have been made to provide a limited defence to murder for doctors[58] when dealing with neonates. One is a single-clause Bill designed to give confidence to both the public and the medical profession (Mason and McCall Smith, 1983, pp. 88–90). The other is longer and more detailed, making the same points and designed to regulate the 'widely accepted medical practice in relation to seriously and irreversibly handicapped babies' (Brahams and Brahams, 1983, p. 146). These suggestions concentrate on the baby whose prognosis is very bad, either in terms of severe physical or mental disability which cannot reasonably be dealt with by medical treatment. This would mean that, if two doctors (one a consultant paediatrician) agree, have the consent of the parents and act in good faith, they would not be liable to legal action if they allowed the child to die (Brahams) or arranged for the termination of life (Mason and McCall Smith). According to the author, the latter might be going too far if it permitted active interference. In fact, the argument in principle needs to be addressed, without depending upon prosecution policy (Howard, 1983). An answer has not so far been provided, and the question must be considered morally, ethically and practically.

CONCLUDING REMARKS

The US courts have an innovative facility in securing the rights of Down's people, whereas in England rights must arise from statute. Prior to the Education Act, 'the constitutional position (was) not ... conducive to the formulation of rights-based claims in education' (Hannon, 1982, p. 278). The situation is similar where the existing legal mechanisms 'provide an inadequate means of protection for the retarded ... child in the school system' (Hayes and Hayes, 1982, p. 132). However, the Education Act remedies this in England.

The federal/state legislature split in the USA is significant, since it enables the federal legislature to take a broader view uncluttered by detailed administrative considerations, resulting in the mainsteaming policy and the underpinning of the institutionalised person's rights. The single legislature does not have this freedom nor, more importantly, the time.[59] In addition, there has been no thorough review of the needs of intellectually handicapped people – as has taken place in Queensland, Australia, for example.[60]

This grim survey ignores the European Convention on Human Rights, which permits the detention of mentally disordered people within limits. There must be an independent discharge body.[61] This was considered by the European Court in *X. v. United Kingdom*,[62] the result of which led to the work of the Mental Health Review Tribunals being extended, particularly in relation to criminally detained patients. The Convention may have an important role in the future with regard to the right to personal relationships (Hoggett 1984) and voting. The Council of Europe has recently propounded a recommendation concerning the legal protection of persons suffering from mental disorder placed in hospitals as involuntary patients.[63] This can only have an indirect effect, but Paragraph 5(1) is particularly interesting:

> A patient...has a right to be treated under the same ethical and scientific conditions as any other sick person and under comparable environmental conditions. In particular, *he has the right to receive appropriate treatment and care* (emphasis added).

Finally, attention should be drawn to the persuasive influence of the Declaration on the Rights of Mentally Retarded Persons, which was adopted by the General Assembly of the United Nations on 20 December 1971. It has been considered above in the context of the Education Act.

NOTES

1. [1981] 1 WLR 1421.
2. Transcript of Judge's Direction on 3, 4 and 5 November 1981: Martin, Meredith and Co. Ltd.
3. See Advisory Centre for Education, Summary of the Education Act 1981. For US comparison, see Hurst, A. (1984). Legislating for special education. *Special Education: Forward Trends* **11**, 6–9.
4. See Hannon (1982) p. 282 and *Pinkerton* v. *Moye* 509 F. Supp. 107 (1981).
5. 20 USCA ss. 1401–1461 at 1412(1).
6. *Murphy* v. *Pennsylvania Department of Education* and *Cothern* v. *Mallory* both (1983) 7 Mental Disability Law Review 477.
7. *Battle* v. *Pennsylvania* 629 F. 2d. 269 (1980).
8. 29 USCA ss. 700–794.
9. *Hairston* v. *Drosick* 423 F. Supp. 180 (1976) at p. 184; see Forsyth, T.L. (1981). Protections for the handicapped in federally financed programs and Southeastern Community College v. Davis. *Southern California Law Review* **54**, 1053–75, 1063; and Burgdorf, R.L. and Bell, C.G. (1981). Eliminating discrimination. *Mental Disability Law Review* **8**, 64–71.
10. 42 USCA ss. 6000–6081.
11. See *Brown* v. *Board of Education* 347 US 483 (1954); *Pennsylvania Association for Retarded Children* v. *Pennsylvania* 334 F. Supp. 1257. There is no constitutional right to public education itself: *Plyler* v. *Doe* 72 L. Ed. 2d 786 (1982).
12. Compare Sweden as indicated in Mitchell (1983).
13. Education (Special Educational Needs) Regulations 1983, SI 1983 No. 29, regulations 4–9.
14. *Battle* v. *Pennsylvania* supra n. at p. 275.
15. See, for example, *McKenzie* v. *Jefferson* (1983) 7 MDLR 454 cp. *Papacodo* v. *Connecticut* 328 F. Supp. 68 (1981).
16. Section 17, Education Act 1981.
17. The position in the USA is similar, see 20 USCA s. 1415.
18. See Annotations to the Education Act 1981 in Current Law Statutes.
19. There are a number of useful guides.
    Bluglass, R. (1983). *A Guide to the Mental Health Act 1983*. London: Churchill Livingstone.
    Carson, D. (1983). Mental processes: the Mental Health Act 1983. *Journal of Social Welfare Law* 195–211.
    Gostin, L.O. (1983). *A Practical Approach to Mental Health Law*. London: MIND.
    Gostin, L.O. (1983). Perspectives on mental health reform. *Journal of Law and Society* **10**, 47–70.
    Gostin, L.O., Meacher, M. and Olsen, M.R. (1983). *The Mental Health Act 1983: A Guide for Social Workers*. Birmingham: BASW.
    Gunn, M.J. (1983). The Mental Health (Amendment) Act 1982. *Modern Law Review* **46**, 318–29.
    Gunn, M.J. (1983) How law is determined. *Mental Handicap* **11**, 147–9.
    Gunn, M.J. (1984). The Mental Health Act 1983 – guardianship and hospitalisation. *Mental Handicap* **12**, 8–9.

Hoggett, B.M. (1983). The Mental Health Act 1983. *Public Law* 172–90.

Hoggett, B.M. (1984). *Mental Health Law* 2nd edn. London: Sweet and Maxwell.

Jones, R.M. (1983). *The Mental Health Act 1983*. London: Sweet and Maxwell.

The present position and proposals for reform are remarkably similar to those in Queensland; see Campbell, I.G. (1983). Proposed changes to the mental health and criminal justice systems in Queensland. *Criminal Law Journal* **7**, 179–206.

20. See, for example, New South Wales, Minnesota and North Carolina.

21. Section 3, Mental Health Act 1983, and related sections.

22. See, for example, *Wyatt* v. *Stickney* 334 F. Supp. 1341 (1971) and 344 F. Supp. 387 (1972).

23. For example in Bavaria, from *International Digest of Health Legislation* **33**, 724–5 (1982).

24. See *O'Connor* v. *Donaldson* 422 US 563 (1975).

25. See, for example:

    Blackburn, R. (1984). The person and dangerousness. In Miller, D.J., Blackman, D.E. and Chapman, D.J. (eds), *Psychology and Law*. Chichester: John Wiley.

    Cocozza, J.J. and Steadman, H.J. (1976). The failure of psychiatric predictions of dangerousness: clear and convincing evidence. *Rutgers Law Review* **29**, 1084.

    Prins, H. (1983). Dangerous behaviour: some implications for mental health professionals. In Bean, P. (ed.), *Mental Illness: Changes and Trends*, pp. 55–74. Chichester: John Wiley.

    Sepejak, D.S., Webster, C.D. and Menzies, R.J. (1984). The clinical prediction of dangerousness: getting beyond the basic question. In Miller, D.J., Blackman, D.E. and Chapman, D.J. (eds), *Psychology and Law*. Chichester: John Wiley.

26. In 1979, 14 739 out of 15 911 admissions. Appendix to White Paper: *Reform of Mental Health Legislation* (1981) Cmnd 8045, London: HMSO.

27. See Hayes and Hayes (1982) pp. 160 and 51; Mental Health Act (NSW) 1958 s.109A.

28. See Skegg, P.D.G. (1974). A justification for medical procedures performed without consent. *Law Quarterly Review* **90**, 512–30. Skegg justifies a doctor 'in proceeding, without consent, with any procedure, which it would be unreasonable, as opposed to merely inconvenient to postpone until consent could be sought'. He also states that '... if a patient is likely to be permanently incapable of consenting, and no one is authorised to consent on his behalf, a doctor should be justified in doing whatever good medical practice dictates should be done in the patient's interests.'

29. See *Gillick* v. *West Norfolk and Wisbech Area Health Authority* [1983] 1 WLR 859 and per Sir Norman Bryan in Hayes and Hayes (1982) p.56.

30. 73 L.Ed. 2d 28 (1982).

31. See, for example, *Association of Retarded Citizens of North Dakota* v. *Olsen* 713 F 2d. 1384 (1983); and *Woe* v. *Cuomo* (1985) 9 MDLR 280.

32. 21 USCA s. 1997.

33. Section 139, MHA 1983.

34. See, for example, s. 330, Lunacy Act 1890.

35. Section 107, Mental Health (Scotland) Act 1960.

36. Section 42, Supreme Court Act 1981.

37. Section 124, MHA 1983.

38. Sections 7–9, MHA 1983.

39. 138 times in 1979, see Appendix to White Paper: *Reform of Mental Health Legislation* (1981). Cmnd 8045. London: HMSO.

40. Section 117, MHA 1983.

41. See para. 2(1) of Sch. 8 and s. 22(1) National Health Service Act 1977 and Jones, supra. n. 19 at pp. 142–143.

42. See, for example, California.

43. See Note 1 above.

44. See Note 2 above.

45. The *Daily Telegraph*, 15 February 1982, p.6.
46. [1939] 1 KB 687.
47. [1893] 1 QB 450.
48. (1918) 13 Crim. App. Rep. 134.
49. [1957] Crim. L.R. 265.
50. See Brahams and Brahams (1983) and Mason and McCall Smith (1983) and *Mental and Physical Disability Law Reporter* (1985).
51. Action no. 74–145, Cumberland, Maine, Superior Court, Feb. 14 1974, reported in the President's Committee on Mental Retardation (1974), *Compendium of Law Suits Establishing the Legal Rights of Mentally Retarded Citizens*, Washington, p.66.
52. Decision of the Juvenile and Domestic Court, Morris County, New Jersey, on Dec. 2nd 1970 reported in *Compendium of Law Suits* p. 67.
53. 63 L.Ed. 2d 784 (1980).
54. 156 Cal. Rep. 48 (1979).
55. *American Pediatrics Association* v. *Heckler* (1983) 7 MDLR 231. See also *United States* v. *University Hospital* 729 F. 2d, 144 (1984), 8 MPDLR 284.
56. *Weber* v. *Stony Brook Hospital* 456 N.E. 2d 1186 (1983), 8 MPDLR 23.
57. P.L. 98–457 and 45 C.F.R. Part 1340.
58. Also suggested by D.P.P., see *Daily Telegraph*, 15 February 1982, p.6.
59. It is unlikely that mental health legislation will be reconsidered in the next 20 years.
60. Parliamentary White Paper on Services for Intellectually Handicapped People in Queensland, 1982.
61. Article 5(1) and (4).
62. European Court of Human Rights, Series A, Judgment of 5 November 1981.
63. No R (83)2, 22 February 1983, Council of Europe: Committee of Ministers.

REFERENCES

Brahams, D. and Brahams, M. (1983). The Arthur case – proposal for legislation. *Journal of Medical Ethics* **9**, 12–15.

Bull, D. (1980). School admissions: a new appeals procedure. *J. Social Welfare Law* 209–233.

Burt, R.A. (1976). Beyond the right to habilitation. In The President's Committee on Mental Retardation, *The Mentally Retarded Citizen and the Law*. New York: Free Press.

Callahan, L.A. and Longmire, D.R. (1983). Psychiatric patients' right to refuse psychotropic medication: a national survey. *Ment. Disability Law Rev.* **7**, 494–9.

DHSS (1981). *Education Act 1981*. Circular 8/81. London: HMSO.

Ennis, B.J. and Emery, R.D. (1978). *The Rights of Mental Patients*, pp. 35–52. New York: Avon Books.

Friedman, P.R. (1976). *The Rights of Mentally Retarded People*, pp. 97–105. New York: Avon Books.

Gunn, M.J. (1984). The Mental Health Act 1983 – guardianship and hospitalisation. *Mental Handicap* **12**, 8–9.

Halpern, C.R. (1976). The right to habilitation. In The President's Committee on Mental Retardation, *The Mentally Retarded Citizen and the Law*. New York: Free Press.

Hannon, V. (1982). The Education Act 1981: new rights and duties in special education. *J. Social Welfare Law* 275–84.

Hayes, S.C. and Hayes, R. (1982). *Mental Retardation: Law Policy and Administration*, pp. 107–110. Sydney: Law Book Co.

Herr, S.S. (1976). *The Right to an Appropriate Free Public Education*. In The President's Committee on Mental Retardation, *The Mentally Retarded Citizen and the Law*. New York: Free Press.

Herr, S.S. (1983). *Rights and Advocacy for Retarded People*. Lexington: D.C. Heath.

Herr, S.S. (1984). The Phillip Becker case resolved: a change for habilitation. *Ment. Retard.* February, 30–35.

Hicks, C. (1984). The Italian experience. *Nursing Times* 21 March, 16–18.

Hoggett, B.M. (1984). *Mental Health Law* 2nd ed. London: Sweet and Maxwell.

Howard, J. (1983). Legislation is likely to create more difficulties than it resolves. *J. Med. Ethics* **9**, 18–20.

Marchetti, A.G. (1983). Wyatt v. Stickney: a historical perspective. *Appl. Res. Ment. Retard.* **4**, 189–206.

Mason, J.K. and McCall Smith, R.A. (1983). *Law and Medical Ethics*, Ch. 7. London: Butterworth.

Mental Disability Law Reporter (1983). **7**, 5. Editorial comment.

Mental and Physical Disability Law Reporter (1985). **9**, 71–2, Editorial.

Mitchell, D.R. (1983). International trends in special education. *Ment. Retard.* **33**, 6–13.

Neuberger, E.K. (1981). Intelligence tests: to be or not to be under the Education for All Handicapped Children Act of 1975. *Northwestern University Law Rev.* **76**, 640–68.

Peay, J. (1982). Mental Health Review Tribunals and the Mental Health (Amendment) Act. *Criminal Law Rev.* 794.

Rebell, M.A. (1981). Implementation of court mandates concerning special education: the problems and the potential. *J. Law and Ed.* **10**, 335–6.

Reform of Mental Health Legislation (1981). Cmnd. 8045, London: HMSO.

Russell, P. (1983). The Education Act 1981. *Concern* **49**, 6–13.

Smith, J.C. and Hogan, B. (1983). *Criminal Law*, 5th edn, pp. 43–7. London: Butterworth.

Sorgen, M.S. (1976). Labelling and classification. In The President's Committee on Mental Retardation, *The Mentally Retarded Citizen and the Law*. New York: Free Press.

Sowell, D. (1983). Special education and the 1981 Education Act. *Contact* Summer, 39–43.

Strain, J.E. (1983). 'Baby Doe II' Regulations. *New Engl. J. Med.* **309**, 443–4.

Stratford, B. (1981). *Children with Special Educational Needs*. Nottingham: University of Nottingham.

The President's Committee on Mental Retardation (1976). *The Mentally Retarded Citizen and the Law*. New York: Free Press.

Warnock Report (1978). *Report of the Committee of Enquiry into the Education of Handicapped Children and Young People (1978)*. Cmnd. 7212. London: HMSO.

Wexler, D.B. (ed.) (1981). Behavior modification: legal restrictions on token economies. In *Mental Health Law*, pp. 213–42. New York: Hennum.

Will, G.F. (1980). The case of Phillip Becker. *Newsweek* 14 April.

21 Possibilities and Achievements

Rex Brinkworth

In 1982, the *Sun* newspaper dubbed as 'The Most Heartwarming Achievement of the Year' the publication in Britain of the first book by a Down's Syndrome person. It was Nigel Hunt's celebrated journal of visits to London and abroad (Hunt, 1982). An Early Day Motion was put down in the House of Commons congratulating Mr Hunt, and the publishers had to rush out a quick reprint to meet the heavy demand. All this despite the fact the book had first been printed 16 years earlier by an American publishing house and was freely available in British libraries at the time of its 're-launch' (Hunt, 1967). So, what caught the popular imagination in 1982 which only drew academic interest in 1966? The cynic may point to skilful publicity by the Down's Children's Association, but the finest PR is to no avail in an unresponsive climate.

There is no doubt that society's view had begun to change since government policy altered and parents were encouraged to look after their handicapped children at home rather than confine them to institutions. Down's children have been cutting a higher profile ever since, and for many that profile has been a sharp contrast to the traditional image of the institutional 'mongol'. Many parents have been surprised that their worst fears have not been realised. They have brought up children who have given them problems and heartaches, but also a great deal of joy and satisfaction. Parents of abler children have proudly paraded their skills so that Nigel Hunt's big headlines and warm editorials have been repeated many times since – the boy in the Scouts with an arm full of badges, the girl who can type, the lad who speaks two languages and is near the top of his class in an ordinary school, or the champion swimmer or musician. The media seems to have opened its heart to the mentally handicapped in a manner which may well mirror society's general ignorance of the potential of Down's children.

There is a danger, of course, in pursuing such publicity too far, but many parents feel that Down's Syndrome has had such a bad press for so long that it will do no harm if the pendulum swings too far the other way occasionally. A close study of many of these articles indicates that realism is rarely left out: an acknowledgement is usually present of the wide range of ability in Down's children stretching right back to the profoundly handicapped, and of the physical and medical problems that can beset them. But positivism is common to them all – an almost evangelical zeal

419

to spread the word that it really isn't as bad as all that. (One or two have gone right over the top into the realms of 'every home should have one'.) Much of this zeal to speak out can be traced to the trial in 1981 of the late Dr Leonard Arthur, the Derby paediatrician found not guilty of attempting to murder a Down's baby. Parents were stung by the defence's assertions that Down's children were 'walking timebombs of disease and defects' and by the failure of the prosecution to counter these efforts to 'rubbish' their potential.

These views emerge through the work of the Down's Children's Association, the charity founded as the Down's Babies Association in Birmingham in 1970. It was parental pressure which had made the association seek to challenge the traditional charitable approach to raising money by exploiting the pathetic. For some it would be a resigning matter if the DCA advertised using the helpless tear-jerker – the image designed to trigger a donation without triggering a change in traditional prejudices. Thus the Down's Children's Association threw down the gauntlet to a leading advertising agency to come up with posters which would educate without exaggeration and encourage people to give not only money but also goodwill, understanding and willingness not to pass by on the other side.

While one can detect signs of change in society's attitudes, there is a long way still to go. Down's Syndrome has not had an auspicious history. Early attitudes can be seen in the common practice in the Classical world of leaving weaklings to die on the open hillsides. For the Spartans to have played a more active role in seeing these children's demise would have risked bringing down the wrath of the gods. A glimpse of a more benevolent atmosphere comes in fifteenth-century Mantua through the painting of a Madonna and Child by Andrea Mantegna. The features of the child are generally accepted by medical opinion as indicating the sitter was Down's, a daring suggestion to make about Our Lord (Stratford, 1982). Needless to say, later generations had the picture banned, not least the Victorians whose values about handicap cast a heavy shadow over present-day attitudes. They developed the institution to a fine art and it does not help that many of them still stand and, worse, are still occupied. The Victorians destroyed a pattern of life for the mentally handicapped which had reached its most benign in the age of the village idiot. In pre-industrial Britain the few mentally handicapped who survived at least had a role to play in their community, even if it was at their own expense. Some saw their simplicity as a virtue, others as a legitimate subject for the arts – the squire's son in the eighteenth-century ballet, *La Fille mal Gardée*, is testimony to that. The Victorians ended those days of pastoral integration with an efficient and often well-meaning segregation which finds expression today in such areas as education, housing and employment. These are three areas where the Down's Children's Association is encouraging change and good practice.

EDUCATION

Society may have learned to see parents bring up their Down's children at home, but finds it harder to envisage those children being educated in an ordinary school alongside unhandicapped children, as suggested in the 1981 Education Act. Down's children are beginning to compete for scarce nursery places, and when they reach the age of statutory full-time education, some parents of normal children are finding it hard to cope with the fact that a Down's child might actually do better than their own child, although this is a problem confined only to the most able Down's children. The 1981 Education Act applies equally to all children with special needs, however severe their handicap, but in practice it is only the abler ones who áre finding mainstream placements and, indeed, mainly the parents of abler children who are seeking them. For the moment in Britain the special school is still usually the destination of Down's children. The main struggle in special education is ESN(M) versus ESN(S). There are still education authorities which refuse to place Down's children in ESN(M) schools, whatever their capacity, as a matter of principle. The children are placed in ESN(S) schools where they can sometimes decline in the company of children of much lower capacity and often little or no speech. It is not a satisfactory situation where headteachers can say: 'We don't take mongols here – the other parents won't like it'. And it becomes even less so when abler Down's children are holding their own in the mainstream.

HOUSING

A recent seminar in London on the question of integrating adult mentally handicapped people into the community was called *The Return of the Village Idiot*. It acknowledged that the mentally handicapped were not going to return to the community from which they were ousted by the Victorians without problems, but some initial ridicule and intolerance was probably worth it if the end-result was a more understanding society. Integration of this kind has recently got a bad name through media coverage of long-institutionalised individuals finding a grim life alone in the outside world. For some parents of Down's children, the ideal future lies in a village for the mentally handicapped where money or charity can secure peace of mind in pastoral tranquillity. Others see this as disguised Victorian institutionalism, and vow that the future of their children lies in the community in which they grew up, in a hostel or other sheltered accommodation if not at home.

More and more parents are vowing that their Down's children will not live with them until their dying day but, if able enough, will somehow find semi-independence. The sight of an ageing Down's person shuffling alongside even more aged parents whose yoke as carers has never been lifted has spurred some parents into becoming more determined than ever that their children will leave home sooner or later. The parents then get the retirement they deserve and the child is allowed to develop an existence which can carry on uninterrupted when its parents are gone – particularly important now that many Down's adults can be expected to live out their three score years and ten. An enormous amount of work needs to be done in preparing this future: cajoling local authorities into building sheltered accommodation, making it easier for parents to bequeath their own homes, to become hostels, and persuading the property market that a house of Down's adults next door is not going to cause a dramatic loss of value. Small hostels in residential streets seem to bring out the worst prejudices. Viewers of the television programme

Crossroads saw an example when the sub-plot surrounding the commendable presence in the case of Nina Weill, a 6-year-old Down's girl, turned to this issue. But the fictional prejudice was nothing compared to reality a few months later in a village in the north-east of England. Residents protesting at a proposal for a group home for Down's adults issued a statement to the local planning committee declaring that 'all grades of mongols have committed murder and acts of violence' and that the house and grounds would have to be 'secure' in order that the residents' children could run free with safety. And that was 1984.

EMPLOYMENT

Employment of any kind is a big bonus for the mentally handicapped and demands an imaginative and enlightened employer if it is to be dignified and successful. For abler Down's children, the chances are increased if they avail themselves of their right to full-time education up to the age of 19, something not all education authorities are prepared to provide, but which is of vital benefit to 'slow learners'. The Down's Children's Association has first-hand experience of being an employer of a Down's person. The office junior at the head office of DCA in London's Oxford Street is one (see Fig 21.1). Extra demands are made on the other staff, but the problems are outweighed by the richness of having a working relationship with one of the very people one is seeking to help. For the casual telephone caller to be answered quietly and efficiently by a Down's person is an experience which no leaflet or poster about the DCA could convey.

Fig. 21.1 The Down's Syndrome girl employed as the office junior at the Oxford Street offices of the Down's Children's Association receives instruction on the office microcomputer from the director, Maggie Emslie. Anja Souza is 20 and doing a sandwich course in word-processing. (Photo: Gerry Mason)

Thus, we have considered social issues which by and large pass by the less able Down's child. The choices are limited for the minority of very severely handicapped Down's children, but the rewards of progress are no less great. The thrill of a 5 year old uttering his first decipherable word is as intense as that of another 5 year old reciting word-perfect the Lord's Prayer or getting a recognisable tune out of a violin. Relatively speaking, the Down's child's task may have been much more difficult. The Down's Children's Association seeks to give these children as much support and encouragement as the others, and is backing a 3-year research programme at Nottingham University into the needs and treatment of profoundly mentally handicapped.

What is encouraging to parents of all Down's children, whatever their inherited abilities, is the effect of early stimulation programmes. Over the 14 years that the DCA has been in existence, and for some years before that, evidence collected by the author has consistently shown a greater improvement in children who have followed early intervention compared with those who have not. One of the first programmes was pioneered through the association (Brinkworth, 1972). Over the years thousands of schedules have been supplied to parents in 40 different countries providing detailed help for children from birth.

Early intervention programmes have been criticised for placing too onerous a burden on families who may plunge themselves into the depths of guilt when they find that they cannot keep up. It is certainly true that it is hard to find parents who feel they are doing what they regard as enough. But the association would argue that the state of mind is the important thing; to be aware that in any odd spare moment or while doing other things, there are things to be said and done which can help the child along; to be aware of likely problems and to be able to spot them as soon as they arise. There is also value to new, bewildered parents of having *something* to do – clear guidelines for action at a time when so much seems in doubt. It gives a sense of direction and purpose and, since no one can tell the final degree of mental handicap, optimism is excusable. A prophecy of doom can be dangerously self-fulfilling. Parents who expect nothing, do nothing and attain nothing for their child. If the initial view does turn out to be slightly overoptimistic, the results are not so damaging as over-pessimism. Parents generally learn to adjust their sights gradually over a long period and come to terms with achievements not being as great as might be expected, just as a normal parent survives the realisation that his normal child is not going to be a top footballer or virtuoso musician. But the child for whom no hope at all is given is automatically condemned to a level of development which may be far below his potential at birth, and this is much more serious.

The association's records show that some 60% of children who followed the early intervention programme can be classified as only mildly mentally handicapped (see Fig 21.2). The whole range of ability has been pushed up, and even those who in the past would have been classified as severely subnormal are not, in general, at such a low level as children who have not followed such a programme. At present the association's early intervention programme is in written form, but a project is well underway at the DCA's National Centre for Down's Syndrome, run in conjunction with Birmingham Polytechnic, for the production of high quality

Fig. 21.2 A Down's child who is realising every inch of his potential—Marc Riche, aged 15, with his mother after winning his gold medal in ballroom dancing. (Photo: *Solihull News*)

audiovisual material. This is not only for parents, but also for doctors and other health workers concerned with Down's Syndrome. The association already runs an extensive information service for professionals, organising conferences and courses for them and providing lecturers for meetings.

In her first year as the association's first Director, Maggie Emslie has presided over the transformation of an essentially parent-led volunteer organisation into a major professional body held in respect by the medical profession and accumulating an expertise in heavy demand. These links with the medical profession are important in view of the uneasy relations which many parents have spoken of in their dealings with doctors, particularly paediatricians. These complaints, less frequent now than they used to be, centred on a feeling that too pessimistic a picture had been painted at the bedside: 'Take home your broken doll' and 'He'll never be more than a vegetable' are just two of the quotations from paediatricians which individual parents have recalled with bitterness. There have also been complaints that paediatricians, who usually break the news, appear ill-equipped and untrained in counselling for such a delicate and critical task. It is often this interview which decides parents whether or not to reject their child, and there are a number of parents who initially rejected but later took their child back after hearing other views presented differently.

Whether or not a particular couple accept or reject their Down's child is not a concern of the Down's Children's Association; help is available equally for natural or foster parents. What it is concerned to see is that parents take their decisions in the light of accurate, up-to-date knowledge. Doctors with only a passing knowledge of Down's Syndrome cannot be criticised too much when it is realised that some of their textbooks, such as that of Illingworth (1975), contain baldly inaccurate statements that, for instance, Down's children can never learn to read and write. Not only is it commonplace for many to do so, but the new reading scheme pioneered at Portsmouth (see Chapter 16) with DCA backing has Down's children reading at the age of 3.

The medical profession has traditionally been wary of using help from the voluntary sector, expressing fears that bringing parents of Down's children into hospitals to talk to new parents could do more harm than good. To meet these fears the DCA is running training courses for parents to learn how to be counsellors. Applicants are carefully vetted by professionals in the field of counselling, and only those with potential undergo the training. There has been a general welcome from the medical profession, whose members are now assured that if they decide to call a trained parent counsellor to the bedside, it will be a professional job without histrionics but with accurate information disseminated by a person the patient can directly identify with. The 1981 Education Act has put an obligation on health authorities to 'consider' putting parents in touch with appropriate voluntary organisations. Many do, but others do not, and 3 years after the Act came into force parents could still be found in the community up to 8 months after having a Down's child without ever having been put in touch with another parent. The result is that many voluntary organisations resort to stealth to find out when new handicapped children are born because the authorities cannot be relied on to pass on information about them.

The Down's Children's Association is proud of its numerous self-help groups up and down the country, groups where new parents can meet freely with others in a similar predicament and talk about a subject with which friends and neighbours have long got bored. The activities of these groups vary from occasional drinking sessions at the local pub to elaborate fund-raising events. But they exist mainly to welcome the new member to a corner of the community where there need be no embarrassment. A recent incident at a London group serves to illustrate one of the wider aspirations of the Down's Children's Association. A mother arrived at the group carrying a newborn Down's child. The baby was admired and cuddled as any new baby would be and the mother accepted the warmth of her reception with a beaming smile as if there was nothing wrong with her baby at all. The truth of the matter was that she had known for many years another member of the group and had watched with detached interest the progress of her now 3-year-old daughter. So when she gave birth to her own Down's baby, she felt she had nothing to fear. If someone can find a way of preventing Down's Syndrome, all well and good, but as long as it is with us let us hope society can grow to react like that mother.

REFERENCES

Brinkworth, R. (1972). *Advice to Parents*. London: DCA.
Hunt, N. (1967). *The World of Nigel Hunt – The Diary of a Mongoloid Youth*. Beaconsfield: Darwen Finlayson.
Hunt, N. (1982). *The World of Nigel Hunt*. Aset Recycling.
Stratford, B. (1982). Down's Syndrome at the Court of Mantua. *Maternal & Child Health: J. Family Med.* June, 7(6).

Index